P9-CDW-046

OPVS GENTILIS DE FABRIANO

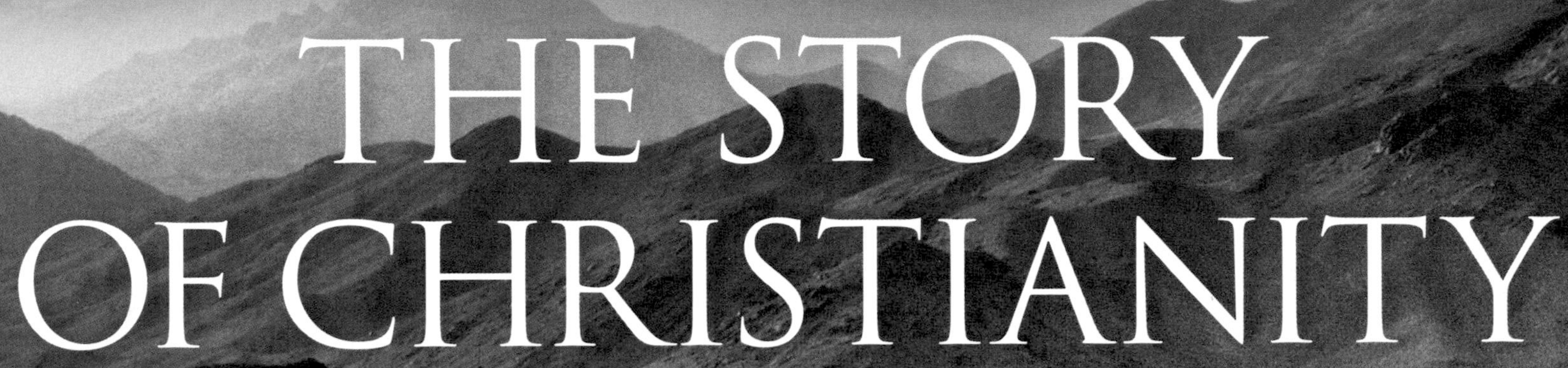

THE STORY OF CHRISTIANITY

A Chronicle of Christian Civilization From Ancient Rome to Today

JEAN-PIERRE ISBOUTS

NATIONAL GEOGRAPHIC
WASHINGTON, D.C.

REGNI CAELORVM TV ES PETRVS ET SVPER
DILIGO TE
O PETRE
NC VNA FIDES
MVNDO REFVLG

CONTENTS

PAGE 1: *"The Adoration of the Magi" was painted by Italian artist Gentile da Fabriano (1370–1427) in 1423.* **PAGES 2–3:** *Pilgrims worship near Mount Sinai—the site, according to the Bible, where God spoke to Moses.* **PAGE 4:** *The central crossing of St. Peter's Basilica in Rome is surmounted by a dome designed by Michelangelo Buonarroti (1475–1564).*

Introduction

CHRISTIANITY'S IMPRINT ON HUMAN CIVILIZATION

The winged lion on the Basilica of San Marco in Venice, Italy, is the symbol of the Evangelist Mark.

OPPOSITE: *This photo of Prague in winter reveals the diversity of churches built throughout the city's rich history.*

How did Christianity develop from a small community of Galilean fishermen to a movement that would conquer the Roman Empire, and ultimately the world? How did the idea of a compassionate, benevolent God race through the Roman realm like wildfire, without the means of mass communication that we take for granted today? How did the Christian movement, once established, sink roots in almost every region it touched, there to prosper for centuries, blending with native cultures to produce truly indigenous traditions? How pervasive was the impact of Christianity on Western civilization—and what role does it continue to play in our modern world?

These are the questions that inspired the writing of this book. It reflects the fact that for a third of all people around the globe—78.4 percent of Americans alone—Christian values continue to be relevant in our modern times. Even though in Europe, Christian worship has suffered attrition as a result of the growing secularization of that continent, Christian churches in Africa, Asia, and Latin America continue to enjoy vibrant growth. So what is it that has made the Christian idea so irresistible through the two millennia of its history? Why are the questions raised by Jesus of Nazareth in Antiquity still relevant in modern times?

One answer may lie in the indelible footprint that Christianity has pressed in the human condition—in our ethics, in our culture, and in our sense of self. Throughout the great upheavals of human history, the Christian ideal continued to serve as a moral compass, even though in practice, its precepts were often abandoned. As several critics have pointed out, more wars have been fought under the banner of Christendom than any other single cause. But by the same token, the Christian faith has always been a cornerstone for the development of human civilization. This is true not only for the great cathedrals of Europe or magnificent works of art and music, but also for the development of laws, ethics, schools, universities, libraries, and hospitals with which Europe slowly emerged from its Dark Ages. Even as late as the 20th century, Jesus' emphasis on social justice and compassion would inspire people across the Christian spectrum, including a Baptist minister from Montgomery, Alabama, to fight for the rights of men and women regardless of the color of their skin.

There are many ways to approach the evolution of Christianity from ancient Rome to the present day. One is to follow the institutional history of Christianity through its long and fragmented history up through the growth of the many denominations of

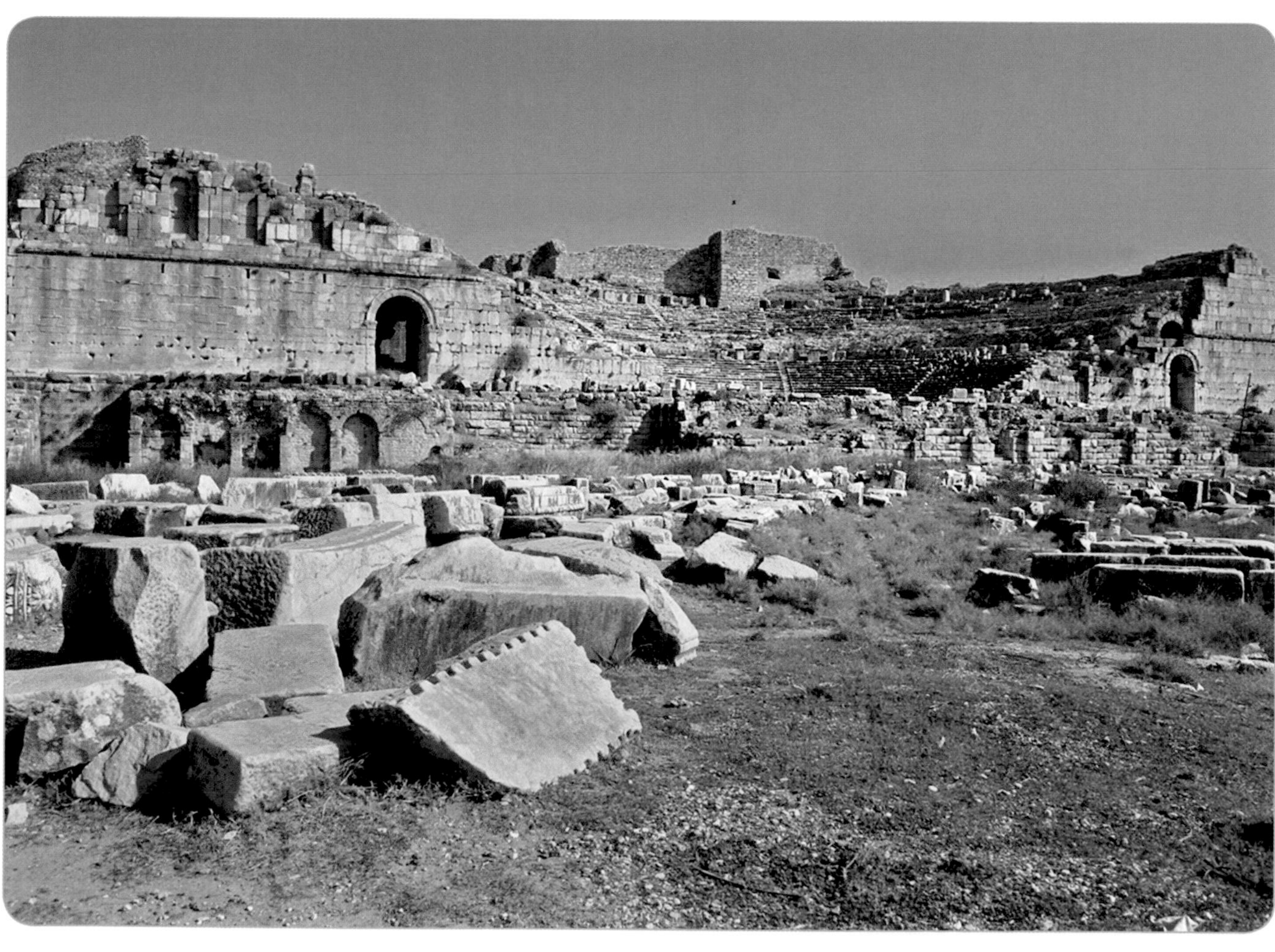

This theater in Miletus, a city in Asia Minor visited by Paul during his third journey, was built in the second century C.E.

today. In recent years, several outstanding books have been published about this aspect of historical Christianity, including the writings of Diarmaid MacCulloch, David Bentley Hart, and Robert Bruce Mullin, who graciously served as a consulting reader on this book. By contrast, what *The Story of Christianity* attempts to do is to explore the *human* element—the social, cultural, and political fabric of Christendom through the ages. In doing so, we will try to understand why the ideas of a Jewish reformer from Galilee would resonate so strongly with the aspirations of the Greco-Roman world, ultimately creating a new civilization, a *Western* civilization, in the process.

For example, modern research has shown that the astonishing growth of Christianity was to some extent due to a highly unusual convergence of events. One was the birth of the Roman Empire, which fused the disparate overseas possessions of the Roman Republic into a unified political and economic commonwealth. Another factor was the ruthless 33-year rule of King Herod, which devastated the rural society of Lower Galilee. A third development was the corrosion of Rome's state religion into a propaganda cult, which produced a deep yearning for a new religion, a genuine *spirituality,* throughout the Greco-Roman world. This led to all sorts of experiments with various Asian religions—not only pagan cults such as those of Isis and Serapis, but also monotheistic traditions such as Zoroastrianism and the Mithraic Mysteries in the decades before and after the birth of Christ. Most of these religions, however, insisted on some form of exclusivity: Only a certain class, group, or demographic was qualified to join the ranks of the faithful.

Christianity's idea of God was different. Jesus' vision was a Kingdom of God that was open to all, regardless of class, race, or gender. It promised eternal salvation to the wealthy and the poor, to senators and slaves, in equal measure. It is this idea that would take the Greco-Roman world by storm and ultimately conquer the Roman Empire itself, despite discrimination from without and often crippling theological disputes from within.

Another important insight is that the growth of Christianity was greatly facilitated by Rome's huge investments in the infrastructure of the Mediterranean basin. At its peak, the Roman road system covered some 250,000 miles, of which about 50,000 miles were paved—an astonishing achievement by the standards of Antiquity. Under Trajan, no fewer than 29 major highways connected the Roman capital to its Empire. In this newly unified "market," the Roman coins, the *sesterce* and *denarius,* became the de facto currency of the realm. This in turn fostered a growing prosperity that was largely concentrated in the cities—the beginning of European urbanization—which in turn attracted vast numbers of people from surrounding rural territories. This magnified the impact of Christian proselytizing efforts in those cities.

Lastly, without the critical role played by Paul of Tarsus, the Greco-Roman world—and by extension, we ourselves—might never have heard about the charismatic rabbi from Nazareth. It was Paul who in Jerusalem argued strongly for a mission to Asia Minor, gateway to the Roman Empire, and for baptizing souls regardless of whether they were Jewish or Gentile. Furthermore, it was Paul who articulated Jesus' "Kingdom of God" message into an idea that the largely Gentile population could understand. Thus, the teachings of a Jewish Messiah who had come to redeem

FOLLOWING PAGES: *"The Miraculous Draught of Fishes" was painted by Jacopo Bassano (1510–1592) in 1545.*

his people, his "sheep of Israel," were translated into a redemptive program that could embrace the world.

What modern research—including the works of Bart Ehrman, a consultant for this book—has also shown is that Paul and the Apostles were not alone in carrying Jesus' message of salvation to the world of their time. Scores of other early Christians—soldiers, merchants, sailors, officials, anyone with a motive and the means to travel—were critical in disseminating the seeds of Christianity, using the superb means of communication that the Romans were thoughtfully building at the time.

This, however, also accounts for the fact that throughout the first and second centuries, a number of "Christianities" would emerge without the involvement or guidance of either Paul or the other Apostles. Many of these movements would arrive at a different interpretation of what Jesus was about, based on oral traditions that were circulating at the time. Some of these emphasized his Jewishness and developed a form of Christianity that remained largely faithful to Jewish customs. Others ignored the Jewish context of Jesus' ministry altogether, and concluded that he had been a divine being in the Platonic mold, who showed his followers how to discover the secret knowledge of God within themselves. Bereft of a canon, an authorized scripture of Christian thought (the Gospels would not be written until the latter part of the first century), these diverging communities would produce the intense theological debates that would vex Christianity from the second century onward. In some way, those debates are still continuing, as reflected in the fragmentation of Christendom today.

Indeed, the Christian community of the 21st century is perhaps more diverse than at any time in its history. Having reigned as the dominant force of European civilization for nearly two millennia, Christianity has moved from its ancient cradle to seek new growth in the Americas as well as the emerging nations of Africa. Brazil, Mexico, and Colombia alone account for a quarter of all Catholics in the world. Of these, Brazil is the largest Catholic country, with 123 million adherents; but the fastest growing religious movement in Brazil is evangelical churches, now followed by 25 percent of all Brazilians.

Between the fields of Galilee and the *favelas* of Brazil spans a 2,000-year arc of human experiment, guided by the words of a preacher who came to this Earth to teach humankind about faith in a compassionate God and compassion for one another. Trying to reconstruct this arc in an illustrated book such as this, covering two millennia across multiple continents, is a near-impossible task that demands choices. Therefore, while this book aims to be as comprehensive as possible, its primary focus will be on the Latin, Orthodox, and Protestant Churches of Europe, since Europe was the primary arena of Christian thought and development through the 18th century. From that point on, however, our attention will increasingly shift to the New World, which today is one of the leading energy centers of Christianity.

Throughout, our story will aim to celebrate the fruits of Christian civilization—in art and architecture, in music and literature, in philosophy and science, and simply in the advancement of human dignity—that serve to remind us of the true legacy of Jesus, the Christ.

JEAN-PIERRE ISBOUTS

OPPOSITE: *This richly adorned 14th-century Byzantine panel depicts St. Michael, an archangel in Jewish, Christian, and Islamic teachings.*

ΟΜΕΓΑϹ
ΜΙΧΑ

1
CHAPTER

THE LIFE OF JESUS

4 B.C.E.–30 C.E.

Jesus came to Galilee, proclaiming the good news of God.

GOSPEL OF MARK 1:14

How did Christianity begin? The answer is obvious: with the life and ministry of Jesus of Nazareth. Regardless of how Jesus has been interpreted through the ages—as a Jewish rabbi and reformer, as the Messiah foretold in Hebrew Scripture, or as the Son of God—few would dispute that Jesus was the catalyst for a religious movement that would sweep across the Roman Empire and eventually encompass the world.

Jesus was born in Lower Galilee, a region where he spent much of his youth and adult life. Galilee was culturally very different from the heartland of Judea to the south, principally because it had always been surrounded by foreign territory: the Phoenician region of Sidon and Tyre to the northwest, Roman Syria (originally Aram-Damascus) to the northeast, and Roman Nabatea (the Bible's Ammon and Moab, today's Jordan) to the east. It was a mostly landlocked enclave, though blessed with plentiful water springs and access to the Sea of Galilee.

Galilee, a largely agricultural region because of the great fecundity of its valleys, was deeply affected by the arrival of the Herodian dynasty. Ironically, King Herod, who ca 39 B.C.E. was declared "King of the Jews" by the Roman Senate, was not of

ABOVE: *This Byzantine mosaic of Jesus was created for the Hagia Sophia in Constantinople, which is now Istanbul, Turkey.*

OPPOSITE: *The shore of the Sea of Galilee, between Capernaum and Chorazin, is the setting for many of the scenes described in the Gospels.*

PRECEDING PAGES: *"The Adoration of the Magi" by Florentine artist Sandro Botticelli (1445–1510) was painted around 1478.*

Jewish origin. His family hailed from Idumea, a territory referred to in the Hebrew Scriptures as Edom, which is the equivalent of today's Negev desert and southern Jordan. With the active support of Roman forces, Herod was able to recapture Judea from the usurper-king Antigonus, heir to the Hasmonean throne, in 37 B.C.E. He began an iron-fisted, 33-year rule that would forever change the face of Judea—and, consequently, Galilee as well.

Herodian Rule

First, Herod created a defensive bulwark around his kingdom, anchored by a number of fortresses such as Masada in the Judean Desert, the Herodion just south of Jerusalem, and the Machareus fortress in the Transjordan, where John the Baptist was eventually put to death. This was followed by a number of monumental building projects in the Hellenistic style that sought to elevate Judea's prestige to a par with its neighbors: Roman Egypt, Syria, and Phoenicia. The most spectacular of these was the construction of a state-of-the-art harbor on the Mediterranean coast. Herod named the city Caesarea (in honor of Octavian Caesar—named Emperor Augustus in 27 B.C.E.—and Octavian's

50 B.C.E.
Caesar and Pompey compete for control of Rome

49 B.C.E.
Caesar crosses the Rubicon and takes his legion onto native Roman soil

48 B.C.E.
Caesar defeats Pompey at Pharsalia

47 B.C.E.
Antipater's son Herod is appointed governor of Galilee

adoptive father, Julius), and called the port complex Sebastos ("August" in Greek), likewise dedicated to the Roman Emperor.

In Jerusalem, the King built a palace, a theater, a hippodrome, and an amphitheater for gladiatorial fights, which, as Jewish historian Josephus tells us, "greatly offended the Jews." As a conciliatory gesture to his Jewish subjects, Herod vastly expanded the Jerusalem Temple, which, though demolished by Neo-Babylonian King Nebuchadnezzar in 586 B.C.E., had been rebuilt 70 years later with the support of Persian King Cyrus the Great.

The Temple had been the center of Jewish worship throughout Judea and beyond for centuries. The first Book of Kings credits King Solomon with building the Temple sometime in the second half of the tenth century B.C.E. By Jesus' time a priestly community, including chief priests described in the Gospels, had long supervised the sacrificial cult on a large altar in front of the Temple, assisted by scores of Levites, officials, and laymen. Overall control of the Temple cult was in the hands of the Sadducees, a quasi-aristocratic elite of priests who occupied the finest mansions in the Upper City. Much of their wealth derived from the Temple treasury, which received tithes from Jewish communities throughout the Roman Empire and also served as Judea's central bank. Since the collection of the Temple tax was protected and facilitated by the Romans, the Temple treasury grew exponentially, bolstering the power of the Sadducees.

King Herod, however, retained the ancient Hasmonean right to appoint the high priest himself. These he recruited from priestly families from Babylonia, whose loyalty to the King was beyond question. After his death, the Romans continued the practice of appointing politically reliable high priests. One such priestly family, the house of Annas (or Ananus), would produce no fewer than seven high priests, including Annas himself (in office 6–15 C.E.) as well as a son-in-law, Joseph ben Caiaphas (in office 18–37 C.E.), who would sit in judgment of Jesus.

How did Herod finance this vast construction program? Judea—later known as Roman Palestine—was a poor region, devoid of copper or gold mines, timber, or export-quality agricultural surplus, all commodities that sustained the economies of Roman possessions elsewhere. The only potential source of wealth that Roman Palestine did have was the highly fertile agricultural region in Galilee. For much of Israel's history, almost every Galilean was involved with agriculture,

OPPOSITE TOP: *This bust of Augustus was probably completed after his death in 14 C.E. Augustus was the founder of the Roman Empire and its first emperor.*

OPPOSITE BOTTOM: *The Roman amphitheater of Caesarea was built in the first century C.E. and expanded during the second century.*

LIFE AND TIMES

The Land of Galilee

According to Josephus, Lower Galilee was a region anchored between Ptolemais (today's Acco) in the west and the Sea of Galilee in the east. The Sea of Galilee, shaped in the form of a harp (*kinor* in Hebrew) is referred to in Hebrew Scripture as Lake Kinneret (Numbers 34:11). Because of its location, Galilee had always been surrounded by foreign territory: Galilee, a shortening of the Hebrew *galil ha-goyim,* means "circle of the peoples." The key to Lower Galilee's fertility is its abundant supply of water. In the region around the Nazareth Ridge, springs such as the Nahal Sippori provide a stable source of water all year round. These springs are fed by subterranean aquifers, which made the region so uniquely suited for agriculture in Jesus' time. In a 1992 study, Israeli archaeologist Zvi Gal identified no fewer than 25 springs between the Nazareth Ridge and Geba'ot Allonim, some of which may date as far back as the Early Bronze Age.

Even today, Lower Galilee still boasts several lush olive orchards.

47 B.C.E. **The Library of Alexandria is destroyed by fire**

46 B.C.E. **Herod suppresses a rebellion led by Hezekiah the Galilean**

46 B.C.E. **Northern Africa is added to the Roman Empire**

46 B.C.E. **Julius Caesar introduces the Julian calendar of 365 days**

says Jewish historian Josephus, who claims there were no fewer than 204 agrarian villages and hamlets across the region.

Herod had discovered Galilee's natural wealth while serving as Galilee's governor under Hyrcanus, the puppet ruler installed by Pompey the Great after the latter's conquest of Judea in 63 B.C.E. Upon his return as the region's new King, Herod decided to exploit Galilee's agricultural bounty to finance his construction boom in Judea. He faced a problem, however. Most of Galilee's fields were cultivated by subsistence farmers, whose land had been held by their clans for generations. Subsistence farming is inherently inefficient, for its primary purpose is to sustain a farmer's family with small quantities of broad-spectrum crops. This would typically include grains for bread and animal fodder; vitamin-rich vegetables such as onions, cabbage, squash, and beets; and occasionally grapes, olives, or figs. Much of Jesus' parable literature refers to this type of farming.

Herod had other ideas. He wanted Galilee's farming industry consolidated into large estates that could produce high-yield, single-purpose crops, destined for export to nearby cities and foreign markets. That was the reason why Herod had built a large port in Caesarea to begin with: to sell his surplus produce.

The conversion of Galilee's ancient subsistence community into single-purpose estates, each run by a professional "steward" (*phronimos* or *oikonomos* in the Gospels), was accomplished through wholesale land confiscation, following the imposition of heavy taxes that were guaranteed to plunge farmers into deep debt. Farmers were not the

Here is a reconstruction of **HEROD'S MAGNIFICENT SANCTUARY PLATFORM,** *built around the Second Temple between 20 B.C.E. and 62 C.E., as seen from the southwest.*

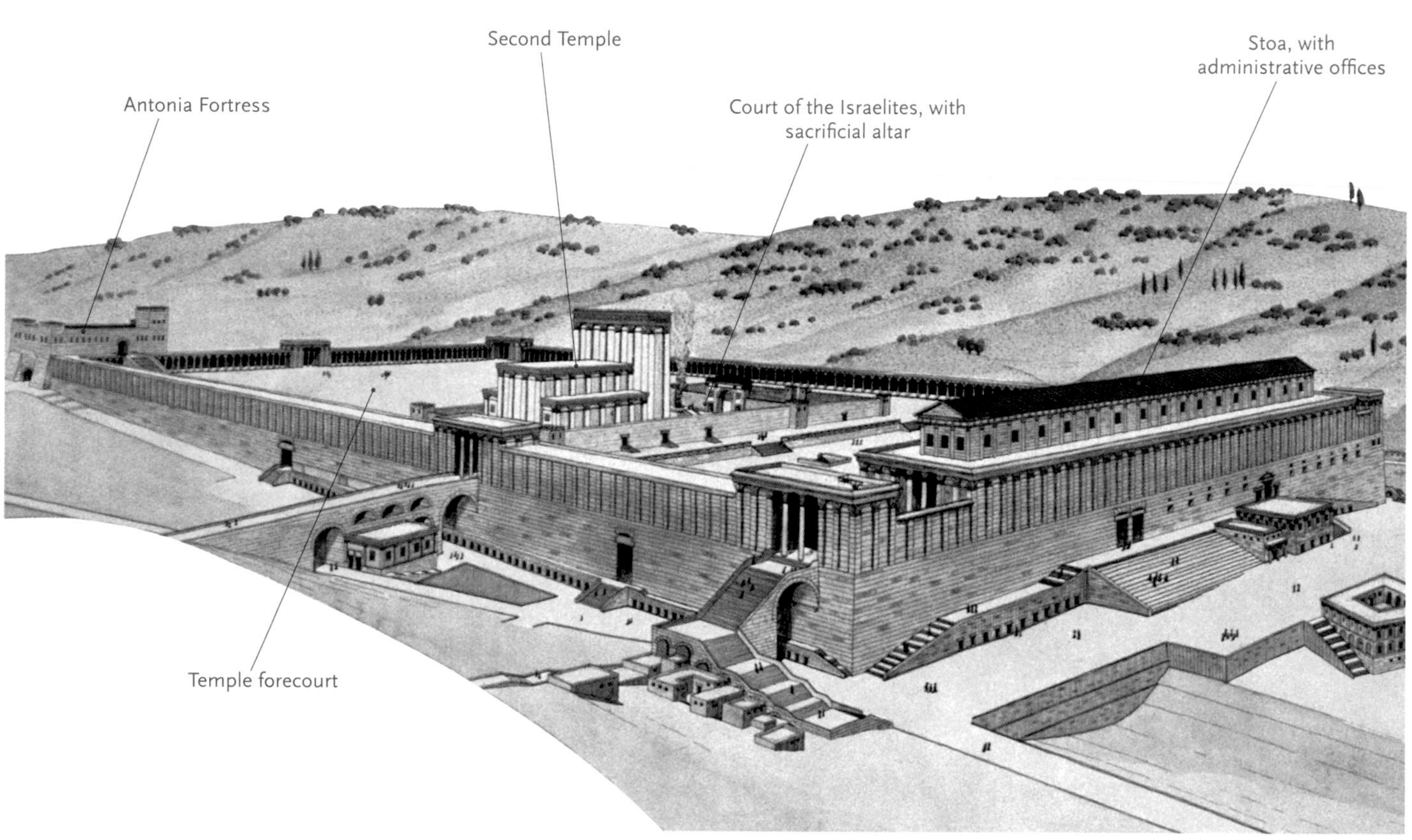

45 B.C.E.
Roman Tower of the Winds, a water and solar clock, is built in Athens

44 B.C.E.
Julius Caesar is assassinated by conspirators Brutus and Cassius

44 B.C.E.
Herod imposes massive taxes on Galileans to raise funds for Cassius

44 B.C.E.
Mount Etna on Sicily erupts

When his mother Mary had been engaged to Joseph, but before they lived together, she was found to be with child from the Holy Spirit.

GOSPEL OF MATTHEW 1:18

only ones taxed; Herod imposed new taxes on virtually every other element of the Galilean economy, including a salt tax, fishing polls, custom duties for the transfer of produce from one region to the other, and taxes on "manufacturing" such as the production of salted fish. This explains the loathing for "publicans," or tax collectors, in the Gospels. Thus, by the time Jesus was born, many of Galilee's agricultural families were being uprooted and deprived of their land, which in the decades to come would produce the multitudes of poor, malnourished people who followed Jesus wherever he went.

Jesus' Childhood

According to the Nativity narratives in the Gospels of Matthew and Luke, Jesus was born to a maid named Mary (or *Miriam* in Aramaic), who lived in the village of Nazareth and was betrothed to a man named Joseph (or *Josef*). In Luke's Gospel, an angel appeared to Mary and told her she would conceive before her wedding day by the power of the Holy Spirit. She was to call her son Jesus, or *Yeshua* in Aramaic, which is a contraction of *Yehoshuah,* meaning "YHWH is salvation." Upon hearing the news, her fiancé Joseph "planned to dismiss her quietly," since a premarital pregnancy brought disgrace on the young woman and her family. But according to the Gospel of Matthew, an angel appeared to Joseph, urging him not to hesitate "to take Mary as your wife, for the child conceived in her is from the Holy Spirit" (Matthew 1:19, 21).

The exact date of these events is uncertain. Tradition has fastened Jesus' birth in the first year of our calendar, but this conflicts with Luke's Gospel, which sets the story "in the days of King Herod of Judea." Matthew also refers to "the time of King Herod, after Jesus was born." King Herod died in March or April of 4 B.C.E., so Jesus' birth must have occurred before that date.

According to the Gospel accounts, Jesus' parents were poor. Thirty-three days after the birth, as prescribed by Leviticus, Mary traveled to the Temple to make an offering and restore her state of purity. Luke states that they offered a sacrifice of "a pair of turtledoves or two young pigeons," instead of a first-year lamb, in accordance with the provision in Leviticus that such was permitted if the parents were poor (Leviticus 12:6-8; Luke 2:22-24).

Jesus grew up in his parents' home in Nazareth. His father, Joseph, is described as a carpenter, but it is more likely that he was a farmer who supplemented his income with woodworking jobs. Recent research suggests that because of his woodworking skills Joseph and his son Jesus might have been involved in the construction of Sepphoris, the new capital built by Herod Antipas (Herod the Great's son), located just six miles north of their hamlet of Nazareth. While growing up, Jesus must have observed his father as he toiled on his land: sowing seeds, pruning the orchard, and reaping the harvest. This would explain why so many of Jesus' parables use the vernacular of Galilean agriculture, rather than carpentry. Similarly, the morning

Period Artifacts

FIRST CENTURY C.E.

Combs dating to the Roman occupation have been found in Masada and other Judean sites.

A hairpin with gold ornamentation betrays the Hellenistic style popular in Judea during the Roman occupation.

Greek-style gold bracelets were favored by the upper classes in Judea.

43 B.C.E.
First compilation of the Ayurveda, a Hindu medical treatise

43 B.C.E.
Octavian, Mark Antony, and Lepidus form a triumvirate in Rome

43 B.C.E.
Roman poet Ovid is born

42 B.C.E.
Caesar's assassins Brutus and Cassius are defeated at the Battle of Philippi

"Christ in the House of His Parents" was painted by English pre-Raphaelite artist John Everett Millais (1829–1896) in 1849. The painting depicts Mary consoling the young Jesus, who has cut his hand on a nail—a foreshadowing of his future Passion.

This earthenware vessel is typical of the type of pottery used in first-century Palestine.

ritual of baking bread would have made an impression on him. Most Galilean farmers lived with their families and relatives in multifamily dwellings, grouped around a courtyard that usually featured a clay oven. The remains of many such multifamily dwellings have been excavated throughout Galilee.

Mary and the other women in the community would begin each morning by baking fresh bread. They first ground kernels of grain into flour using a stone mill, then mixed the flour with water, oil, and yeast before rolling the dough into round flat cakes. These dough patties would be baked in a clay oven until the bread rose and was ready to eat. References to this ritual would return in the Our Father prayer that Jesus taught his disciples—"Give us this day our daily bread"—and also in the Gospel of John, where Jesus declares, "I am the bread of life" (Matthew 6:11; John 6:35).

The Missing Years of Jesus' Youth

Unfortunately, the Gospels are largely silent on the "missing years" of Jesus' youth. Modern developmental psychology has taught us that adolescence is a critical period when a person's cognitive and emotional abilities are shaped,

42 B.C.E.
The Roman Empire is divided between Octavian, Mark Antony, and Lepidus

40 B.C.E.
Parthians invade Palestine in support of Antigonus, a pretender to the throne

40 B.C.E.
Herod flees to Rome and persuades the Senate to declare him King of all Palestine

40 B.C.E.
Mark Antony donates 200,000 scrolls from Pergamon to the Library of Alexandria

but there is little information available that can help us understand the factors that influenced Jesus' early years. Some of these gaps, however, can be filled in from other sources, notably the writings of Josephus and a Jewish collection of legislative debates known as the Mishnah. Though the Mishnah texts were only organized and combined in the early third century, several scholars believe that some of these disputes reflect conditions in Judea and Galilee during the first century, before the destruction of the Temple.

From the Mishnah, for example, we learn that Lower Galilee was a culturally diverse territory, in which small villages such as Nazareth were populated by devoutly observant Jews, whereas larger towns and cities tended to reflect the influence of Greco-Roman, or Hellenistic, culture. Jesus was aware of this cultural dichotomy, for in the Gospel of Matthew he urges his disciples to avoid the larger cities and townships of Galilee, and to "go nowhere among the Gentiles." Instead, his ministry was focused on Jewish communities, "the lost sheep of the house of Israel" (Matthew 10:5-6).

And Jesus increased in wisdom and in years, and in divine and human favor.

GOSPEL OF LUKE 2:52

An important issue related to Jesus' childhood is the question of whether he was formally educated. The Gospel accounts suggest that Jesus had a thorough knowledge of Hebrew Scripture. According to Luke, he could read from the scrolls. Rabbinic sources from the late second and third century C.E. suggest that larger townships often maintained a synagogue school where young boys received education in Scripture, starting at age six. The principal purpose of these schools was not to teach young boys to write, but to give them a rudimentary understanding of the Jewish Law. The idea for such schools arose during the Hasmonean era, when Pharisee scholar Simeon ben Shetah (or Shatach, ca 120–40 B.C.E.) decreed that every

LIFE AND TIMES

Mary and Joseph

The Nativity accounts state that Mary and Joseph were betrothed; that Joseph descended from the House of King David; and that Mary, while a virgin and not yet wed, conceived a child by the Holy Spirit. They also tell us that Mary lived in a hamlet called Nazareth, but the residence of Joseph is uncertain; Matthew implies that Joseph lived in Bethlehem, while John's Gospel suggests that Joseph was "from Nazareth." What is clear is that Mary and Joseph were poor, and probably sustained their family by cultivating an ancestral plot of land In addition to Joseph's woodworking skills. This explains why many of Jesus' parables are inspired by Galilean agriculture, rather than carpentry. Modern studies suggest that the average peasant family in Lower Galilee owned around four acres. Each acre yielded around 1,320 pounds or some 22 bushels, enough to feed two people. Allowing for crop rotation and taxes, this means that the average farmer needed to plant at least 0.625 acres per person in his household. Mark wrote that Mary and Joseph's family eventually numbered four boys, "James and Joses and Judas and Simon," as well as at least two daughters (Mark 6:3). It is unclear, however, whether these are Mary's children, or Joseph's children from an earlier marriage (which would validate the Catholic doctrine of Mary's perpetual virginity). To feed so many mouths, Joseph would have to cultivate at least 5.5 acres, underscoring the assumption that most rural families in Galilee labored below subsistence levels.

A Galilean farmer's house has been reconstructed in Qasrin, Upper Galilee. The scene provides a glimpse of first-century daily life in early Jewish communities in Galilee.

39–37 B.C.E. Herod lands in Palestine and battles Antigonus for control of Judea

38 B.C.E. Mark Antony returns to Egypt

37 B.C.E. Herod conquers Jerusalem; Antigonus is executed

36 B.C.E. Herod appoints his brother-in-law Aristobulus III as high priest

large town should have a *Bet ha-Sefer,* or House of the Book, but it is unlikely that this program was actually implemented before the destruction of the Temple in 70 C.E. Nevertheless, such Scripture schools or *yeshivot* did exist, notably in Judea and perhaps even in Sepphoris. Recent excavations have uncovered a number of stone vessels, prized for their ritual purity (stone vessels could not become ritually impure), which would suggest that notwithstanding its Hellenistic flavor, the Galilean capital may have included a large Pharisaic community. Whatever the case may be, Jesus must have acquired some expertise in Scripture and Torah exegesis in order to be called by the honorific *rabbi,* or teacher, as the Gospels attest.

The writings of Josephus, moreover, show us that the years of Jesus' adolescence were marred by political tension throughout Roman Palestine. At the time of King Herod's death in 4 B.C.E., his kingdom was divided among his sons (and one sister) into four separate territories. Judea was to be ruled by his son Archelaus, while Galilee and Perea (the Transjordan) was given to his other son Antipas (later known as Herod Antipas). The territory to the northeast of the Sea of Galilee, including the Gaulanitis (today's Golan region), was allotted to Herod's son Philip, whereas the King's sister, Salome, received the leftovers: the coastal enclave around Azotus, today's Ashdod, and the region around Phaesalis.

Archelaus's ascension prompted a revolt; many Judeans were fed up with Herod's crushing taxes. One of the resistance groups was led by "Judas the Galilean," the son of

OPPOSITE: *"Christ Among the Doctors" was painted by the Master of the Catholic Kings (active around 1485–1500) in 1495.*

This cardo, or main thoroughfare, was excavated in the ancient city of Sepphoris, the capital of Galilee.

35 B.C.E.
Aristobulus III is drowned on orders of Herod

34 B.C.E.
Dalmatia is added to the Roman Empire

32 B.C.E.
Herod launches war against Nabatea

32 B.C.E.
Octavian and the Roman Senate declare war on Cleopatra and Mark Antony

But when [Joseph] heard that Archelaus was ruling over Judea in place of his father Herod, he was afraid to go there.

GOSPEL OF MATTHEW 2:22

another rebel leader, Hezekiah, who had led a revolt at the beginning of Herod's rule. The Roman governor in Syria, Varus, suppressed the revolt with great bloodshed. "All places were full of fire and slaughter," says Josephus. The region around Sepphoris, a rebel stronghold, came in for particular punishment. Since Nazareth was located only six miles away from Sepphoris, it is likely that Mary, Joseph, and Jesus, then a toddler, were affected by these reprisals as well.

Ten years later, in 6 C.E., Archelaus's misrule in Judea had become intolerable. A delegation of Jewish and Samaritan noblemen traveled to Rome to request Archelaus's removal. Augustus acceded to the request, but rather than giving the territory to another Herodian heir—such as Philip or Antipas—the Emperor chose to turn Judea into a Roman province. It would therefore be governed by a Roman prefect, reporting to his superior, the Roman governor of Syria. Since this position was a vacancy, two new Roman diplomats soon set sail for the east: Coponius, the new prefect of Judea, and Quirinius, the new governor of Syria. Since neither knew what Judea could yield in annual tribute (a major concern for the treasury in Rome), they agreed to conduct a tax census. This is the same census that Luke cites as the reason why Joseph and Mary

A second-century fresco depicting the Eucharist was found in the Catacombs of Priscilla in Rome. The catacombs were dug into the tuff, a soft volcanic rock used to make bricks and lime.

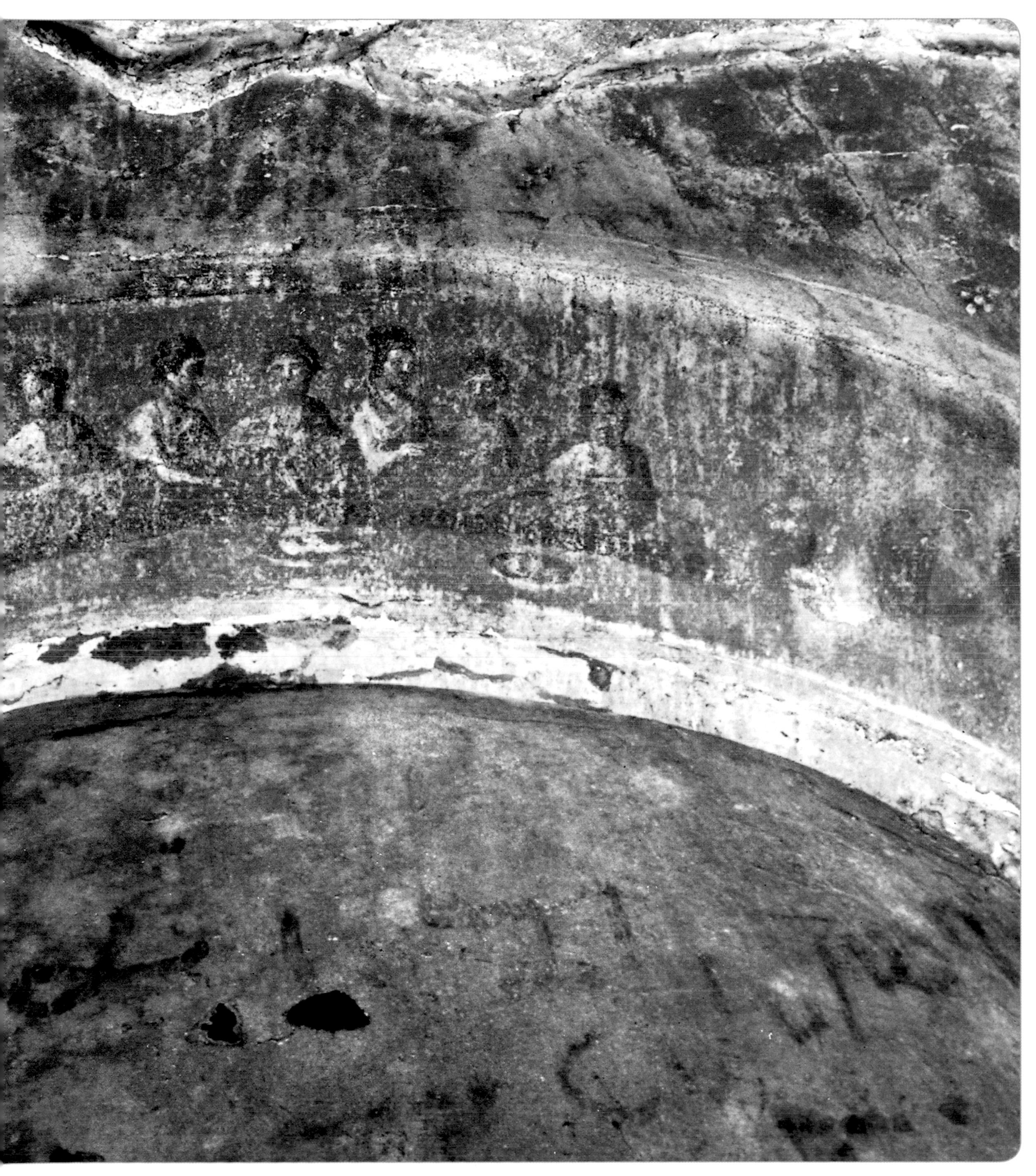

had to travel to Bethlehem to be counted (although his dating is probably inaccurate: The Quirinius census took place in 6 C.E., not 5 or 4 B.C.E.).

This census launched another uprising, for many farmers believed that the Roman registration was simply an overture for even more punishing taxes, continuing the suppression of subsistence farming begun by Herod. One resistance movement was led by a Pharisee named Zaddok, who urged his followers to practice noncompliance with any decree issued by the Romans. In Zaddok's eyes, the Roman census was unlawful because it meant to assess land that belonged to God, not to Rome. Quite possibly, this is the resistance movement that ultimately coalesced into the party of the Zealots—the group that launched the disastrous Jewish War some 60 years later. A book by Reza Aslan suggests that Jesus was a follower of the Zealot doctrine, and that this was the reason he was crucified, though this suggestion has not found broad scholarly support.

SCRIPTURE AND FAITH

The Dead Sea Scrolls

The Dead Sea Scrolls are a collection of biblical texts and secular documents found in caves near the Dead Sea in 1947. In close proximity to these caves, archaeologists uncovered the ruins of a monastic settlement near Khirbet Qumran, on the northwestern shore of the Dead Sea. This elaborate complex, guarded by a tower, contained what archaeologists believe were a library, a dining hall, a potter's workshop, kilns, ovens, and a system of cisterns for ritual ablutions. This has led some scholars to identify the Qumran community with a group known as the Essenes, described by Josephus. The buildings also featured a large room tentatively identified as a scriptorium, where scribes may have compiled the Dead Sea Scrolls, in the expectation of the coming of a Messianic Israel. Several scholars have pondered a possible association between the Qumran community and John the Baptist. For example, the Qumranite community texts require that members hand over their property and possessions "to the hand of the man who is the examiner over the possessions of the many." Similarly, John the Baptist told his listeners, "Whoever has two coats must share with anyone who has none; and whoever has food must do likewise" (Luke 3:10-11). Both the Qumranites and John the Baptist lived in the desert, in search of an ascetic lifestyle, subsisting on a Spartan diet. What's more, the Qumran concept of a Teacher/Prophet who urges repentance has parallels in the portrayals of both John the Baptist and Jesus, who are also referred to as Teachers (Luke 3:12; John 3:26).

These remains of the first-century Qumran settlement are believed to have been inhabited by a sect that produced the Dead Sea Scrolls.

Jesus and John the Baptist

What we do know from the New Testament is that when Jesus was about 32 or 33 years old, he decided to join the movement of John the Baptist, a dissident preacher who lived on the other side of the River Jordan, in the region of Perea, ruled by Herod Antipas. With his keen eye for historical context, Luke sets the stage of John's ministry in the "fifteenth year of the reign of Emperor Tiberius, when Pontius Pilate was governor of Judea, and Herod was ruler of Galilee" (Luke 3:1). The most plausible date is therefore the year 28 C.E.

John was a prophet who wore a garment of camel's hair and ate a Spartan diet of locusts, just like the prophet Elijah, who is also described as "a hairy man, with a leather belt around his waist" (Matthew 3:4; II Kings 8). Matthew's comparison of John to Elijah is deliberate, for it reminded his audience of Malachi's vision that "I will send you the prophet Elijah before the great and terrible day of the Lord comes" (Malachi 4:5).

Like many other religious movements at the time—such as those of the Zealots and the Essenes—John the Baptist rejected the sacrificial cult and corruption of the Temple priesthood and clamored for a return to a society wholly ruled by the precepts of the

31 B.C.E. A large earthquake occurs in Judea

31 B.C.E. Mark Antony is defeated at the Battle of Actium; he and Cleopatra commit suicide

31 B.C.E. Herod pledges his allegiance to Octavian

30 B.C.E. Augustus confirms Herod as King of Judea

Roland de Vaux, a French Dominican priest, found potsherds and other artifacts, dated between 150 B.C.E. and 70 C.E., in this area near the Dead Sea—among the remains of the first-century Qumran settlement.

Torah, the Jewish Law. John injected urgency into his campaign by warning that the nation's lawlessness—primarily its neglect of the Jewish Law—was bound to invite the wrath of the Lord, who would send a fearsome, divinely appointed commander—the Messiah—to eject the foreign occupiers and install a true reign of God.

The idea of a violent intervention that would "cleanse" the Jewish nation was not new. Much of the eschatological literature in the two centuries preceding Jesus speaks of a return of God's "Anointed One" (*Mashiach,* or Messiah; in Greek, *Christos*), who by virtue of a great cataclysmic event would restore an Israel beholden to the word of God. The identity of this Messiah was not entirely clear. While the Book of Daniel speaks of an angel, "one like a son of man," the authors of the Dead Sea Scrolls in Qumran envisioned *two* messiahs: one a military commander from the "Branch of David," and the other a priest known as the "Messiah of Aaron."

John's sermons reflect the militant tenor of this literature. He depicts his Messiah as a ruthless conqueror: "His winnowing fork is in

Period Artifacts

FIRST CENTURY C.E.

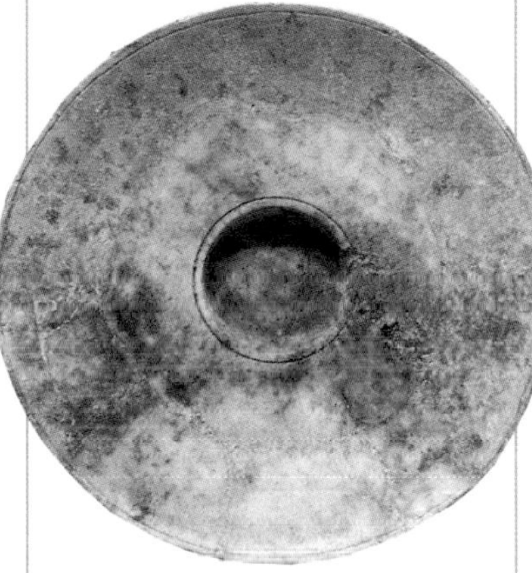

A Greek plate features a depression for fish sauce, a popular condiment.

Delicate Roman flasks such as this one were used for perfumed oils.

30 B.C.E.
Egypt is annexed as a Roman province, ending its 3,000-year independence

29 B.C.E.
Herod places his beloved wife, Mariamne I, on trial

28 B.C.E.
Herod's theater in Jerusalem is inaugurated

28 B.C.E.
Chinese imperial astronomers create first record of sunspots

SCRIPTURE AND FAITH

The Pharisees

James Jacques Joseph Tissot (1836–1902) painted "The Pharisees Question Jesus."

The Pharisees (derived from the Hebrew *perushim,* or separated ones) were a group of priests and pious laymen committed to the practice of Jewish Law in every aspect of life, rather than merely within the Temple precinct. Thus, the Pharisaic concern for purity, often maligned in the Gospels, was actually an attempt to transfer the priestly rules governing purity from the Temple to the home. In doing so, the Pharisees rejected the Sadducee emphasis on the sacrificial cult as the principal redemptive activity, for they felt that pious Jews should please God in everything they did. Similarly, whereas the Sadducees considered the Torah a closed book, the Pharisees continued to debate the application of Scripture to everyday life—a corpus that became known as the Oral Law. The Pharisees also accepted the idea of the immortality of the soul and the resurrection after Judgment Day—two concepts that would return in the teachings of Jesus.

his hand, to clear his threshing floor and to gather the wheat into his granary." All those who resisted would be burned like chaff "with unquenchable fire" (Luke 3:17). John reserved special scorn for the rampant corruption among the region's elites, such as tax collectors and the military. In the Gospel of Luke, John orders the "publicans" to "collect no more than the amount prescribed to you"—the target amount set by the Roman census for each property—while soldiers were warned not to "extort money from anyone by threats or false accusation" (Luke 3:12-14).

"The Spirit of the Lord is upon me, because he has anointed me to bring good news to the poor."

GOSPEL OF LUKE 4:18

Shocked by his words, many listeners agreed to repent and accept John's ritual of purification: immersion and baptism in the water of the River Jordan. Jesus, too, agreed to be baptized. This seems a bit odd, for it would signal that Jesus, too, had to atone for sinful behavior. Matthew is aware of this incongruity, for in his version John resists Jesus' request to be baptized, saying, "I need to be baptized by *you,* and [yet] you come to me?" Jesus replied that it had to be, so as to fulfill "all righteousness" (Matthew 3:14-15).

As Jesus emerged from the water, says Mark, "he saw the heavens torn apart and the Spirit descending like a dove on him." A voice spoke from heaven, "You are my Son, the beloved; with you I am well pleased" (Mark 1:10-11). This is one of very few passages that appears, almost verbatim, in all four Gospels. The scene also clarifies the true meaning of Jesus' baptism, for the dove symbolizes the Holy Spirit that anoints Jesus as the Messiah. It was the moment of Jesus' calling to service. Like the prophets in Hebrew Scripture, he had been chosen by God to go and do God's work.

Jesus' Ministry

This calling is confirmed in a subsequent scene, as Jesus prepares to launch his ministry in the synagogue of Capernaum. Choosing a verse from the Book of Isaiah, he reads, "The Spirit of the Lord is upon me, because he has anointed me to bring good news to the poor. He has sent me to proclaim release to the captives and recovery of sight to the blind, to let the oppressed go free, to proclaim the year of the Lord's favor" (Luke 4:18; Isaiah 61:1). These two sentences accurately capture the type of ministry that Jesus intended to bring to Galilee.

Initially, his following was composed of some of the Baptist's disciples who gravitated to Jesus. In the Gospel of John, these disciples refer to Jesus as "Rabbi" and "Messiah" while they are still in the Baptist's camp (John 1:38-41). They included two brothers, both fishermen, known as Andrew and Simon Peter, and a man named Philip. All three hailed from Bethsaida, on the northern shore of the Sea of Galilee. The three followed Jesus to Galilee, where Jesus began to recruit other disciples from among the region's fishing community, using Capernaum as his base. Eventually, Jesus created an entourage of 12 principal disciples—

OPPOSITE: *"The Baptism of Christ" by Andrea del Verrocchio (1436–1488) includes an angel at far left that was painted by a young Leonardo da Vinci (1452–1519).*

27 B.C.E.
Octavian is named Augustus by the Roman Senate; beginning of the Principate

27 B.C.E.
Herod builds an acropolis in Samaria and names it Sebaste, in Augustus' honor

25 B.C.E.
A major drought forces Herod to import large quantities of grain from Egypt

25 B.C.E.
Galatia, future region of Paul's ministry, is added to the Roman Empire

ECCE AGNIVS

a number that is possibly inspired by the 12 tribes of Israel. In addition to the original three, he enlisted James and John, the sons of Zebedee, as well as "Bartholomew, and Matthew, and Thomas, and James son of Alphaeus, and Thaddaeus, and Simon the Cananaean, and Judas Iscariot, who betrayed him" (Mark 3:18-19). Jesus groomed these followers as "apostles" (*shaliach* in Aramaic, *apostolos* in Greek). They were not to behave as disciples in the traditional sense, but as active "delegates," charged with propagating Jesus' ministry and helping him arrange for transport, food, shelter, and security.

According to Mark, Capernaum was the hometown of Peter's wife. Her parental home became the headquarters of the budding movement. It was an inspired choice, for Capernaum was centrally located on the Sea of Galilee, connected by constant maritime traffic to the eastern shore and the territory of the so-called Decapolis, or Ten Greek Cities, and via the western shore to the hinterland of Lower Galilee.

The Miracle Stories

In the initial phase, Jesus focused much of his activity on the area confined by Bethsaida,

"Jesus Cures the Bleeding Woman" is a sixth-century Byzantine mosaic in the Basilica of S. Apollinare Nuovo, in Ravenna, Italy.

23 B.C.E.
Herod's palace in Jerusalem and the Herodion fortress in the Judean Desert are built

22 B.C.E.
Construction begins on the harbor of Caesarea Maritima on the Mediterranean coast

21 B.C.E.
Work begins on the expansion of the Second Temple in Jerusalem

19 B.C.E.
Construction of the Pont du Gard begins, as part of the aqueduct of Nîmes

Chorazin, and Capernaum, all within a day's walking distance. His preaching drew large crowds, not least because Jesus sometimes engaged in miraculous feats, such as exorcisms (the healing of an individual possessed by an "unclean spirit"). As Josephus attests, in ancient times a man, or a woman, could only be recognized as divinely inspired if he or she possessed magical or supernatural powers. Exceptional men and women, possessed by the Spirit of God, were expected to do extraordinary things. Mark says that after Jesus performed his first exorcism following his presentation in the Capernaum synagogue, "his fame began to spread at once throughout the surrounding region of Galilee" (Mark 1:27-28).

It soon became apparent that Jesus' ability to heal was not limited to mental illness, but could be used for physical afflictions as well. He cured Peter's mother-in-law of a severe fever and healed a paralytic man who had been lowered into the house through the roof (Matthew 8:14; Mark 2:1-4). As soon as word of these miraculous healings spread, Jesus was overwhelmed by a stream of people hoping to be cured. "They brought to him all the sick," says Matthew, "those who were afflicted with various diseases and pains, demoniacs, epileptics, and paralytics" (Matthew 4:24). The pressure became so great that Jesus told his disciples "to have a boat ready for him because of the crowd, so that they would not crush him" (Mark 3:9).

The reports of Jesus' miracles are still actively debated by modern scholars. While the nature miracles are difficult to assess with modern methods, some medical experts believe that the afflictions described in the healing miracles betray symptoms of chronic malnutrition. This is not surprising, given that thousands of farmer families had lost their land to Herodian confiscation. But as is the case of most biblical stories, we should also consider the allegorical power of the miracle accounts. The core tenet of Jesus' ministry, the "good news" (*good-spell* in Old English, or "gospel") that he wished to bring to the Jews of Galilee, was that of a Kingdom of God, but not in the same manner as John the Baptist and other eschatological preachers had envisioned it.

SCRIPTURE AND FAITH

The Miracle Stories

Among the miracle accounts, the stories of healing occupy a special place. There is a consistent pattern to Jesus' diagnostic approach. He observes the patient, touches him, and says, "Your sins are forgiven" (Mark 2:5). In Jesus' day, birth defects and chronic diseases were believed to be God's punishment for sins—either by the patient or by his parents. When, in the Gospel of John, the disciples encounter a man who has been blind from birth, they ask Jesus, "Rabbi, who sinned, this man or his parents, that he was born blind?" (John 9:1-2). Jesus rejected this belief. "Neither this man nor his parents sinned," Jesus replied; "He was *born* blind so that God's works might be revealed in him" (John 9:3).

Jesus' healing technique thus began with eliminating the idea that one suffered *because one deserved to*. This is the meaning of the words "your sins are forgiven." The second part of Jesus' healing formula involved the question of faith. "Do you have faith?" he invariably asks. Faith in God's power lies at the core of Jesus' teachings. When we place our trust in God, he asserts, everything is possible, though few disciples follow his example (Matthew 6:30). Without faith, therefore, one cannot heal—a concept shared by Asian mind-body medicine. Indeed, as Jesus tells the woman healed from her blood flow, "Daughter, your faith has made you well" (Mark 5:34). Healing the sick illustrated Jesus' vision that faith, love, and compassion would realize the Kingdom of God.

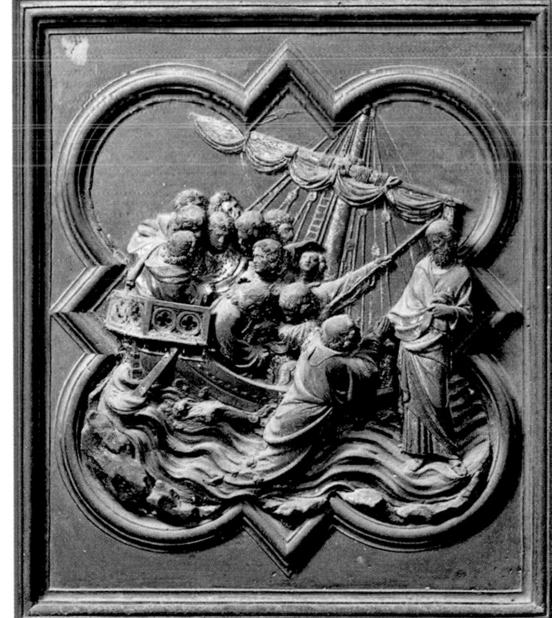

"Jesus Walks on Water and Saves Peter" is one of the panels cast by Lorenzo Ghiberti (1378–1455) for the North Doors of the Florence Baptistery.

13 B.C.E. **Herod designates Antipater II, his son by his wife Doris, as his heir**

12 B.C.E. **Alexander and Aristobulus, Herod's sons by Mariamne I, are added to the succession**

9 B.C.E. **The harbor of Caesarea Maritima is inaugurated**

9 B.C.E. **Augustus chastises Herod for waging war against Nabatea**

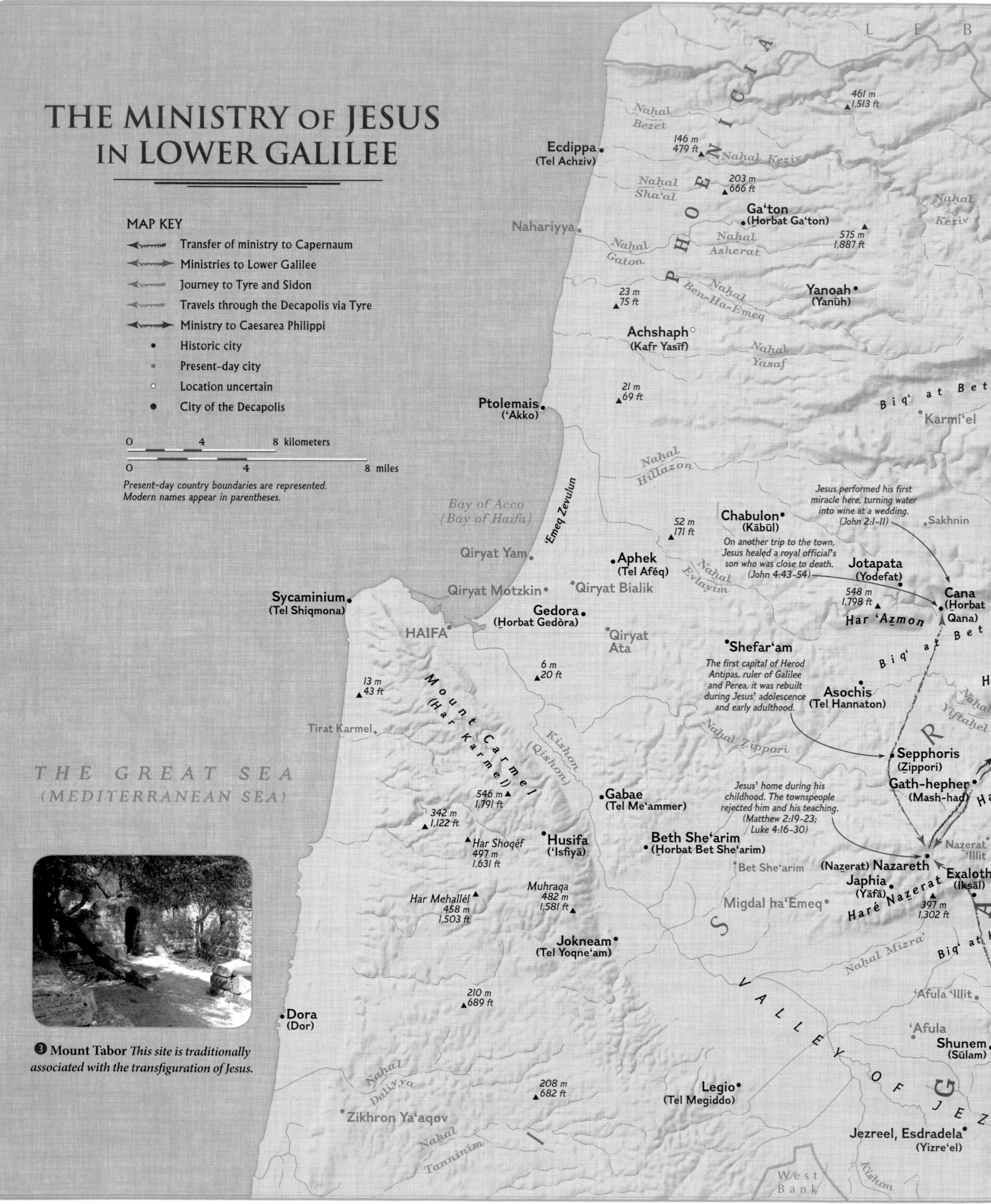
THE MINISTRY OF JESUS IN LOWER GALILEE
MAP KEY
Transfer of ministry to Capernaum
Ministries to Lower Galilee
Journey to Tyre and Sidon
Travels through the Decapolis via Tyre
Ministry to Caesarea Philippi
Historic city
Present-day city
Location uncertain
City of the Decapolis
0 4 8 kilometers
0 4 8 miles
Present-day country boundaries are represented.
Modern names appear in parentheses.
PHOENICIA
Ecdippa (Tel Achziv)
Nahariyya
Ga'ton (Horbat Ga'ton)
Yanoah (Yanūh)
Achshaph (Kafr Yasīf)
Ptolemais ('Akko)
Bay of Acco (Bay of Haifa)
'Emeq Zevulun
Qiryat Yam
Qiryat Motzkin
Qiryat Bialik
Aphek (Tel Aféq)
Chabulon (Kābūl)
Jesus performed his first miracle here, turning water into wine at a wedding. (John 2:1-11)
On another trip to the town, Jesus healed a royal official's son who was close to death. (John 4:43-54)
Jotapata (Yodefat)
Cana (Horbat Qana)
Har 'Azmon
Sakhnin
Karmi'el
Sycaminium (Tel Shiqmona)
HAIFA
Gedora (Horbat Gedòra)
Qiryat Ata
Shefar'am
The first capital of Herod Antipas, ruler of Galilee and Perea, it was rebuilt during Jesus' adolescence and early adulthood.
Asochis (Tel Hannaton)
Sepphoris (Zippori)
Gath-hepher (Mash-had)
Tirat Karmel
Mount Carmel (Har Karmel)
Kishon (Qishon)
THE GREAT SEA (MEDITERRANEAN SEA)
Gabae (Tel Me'ammer)
Jesus' home during his childhood. The townspeople rejected him and his teaching. (Matthew 2:19-23; Luke 4:16-30)
Husifa ('Isfiyā)
Beth She'arim (Horbat Bet She'arim)
Bet She'arim
Nazareth (Nazerat)
Nazerat 'Illit
Japhia (Yāfā)
Exaloth (Iksāl)
Haré Nazerat
Migdal ha'Emeq
Har Shoqéf
Har Mehallél
Muhraqa
Jokneam (Tel Yoqne'am)
VALLEY OF JEZ
'Afula 'Illit
'Afula
Shunem (Sūlam)
Dora (Dor)
Legio (Tel Megiddo)
Jezreel, Esdradela (Yizre'el)
Zikhron Ya'aqov
West Bank

❸ **Mount Tabor** *This site is traditionally associated with the transfiguration of Jesus.*

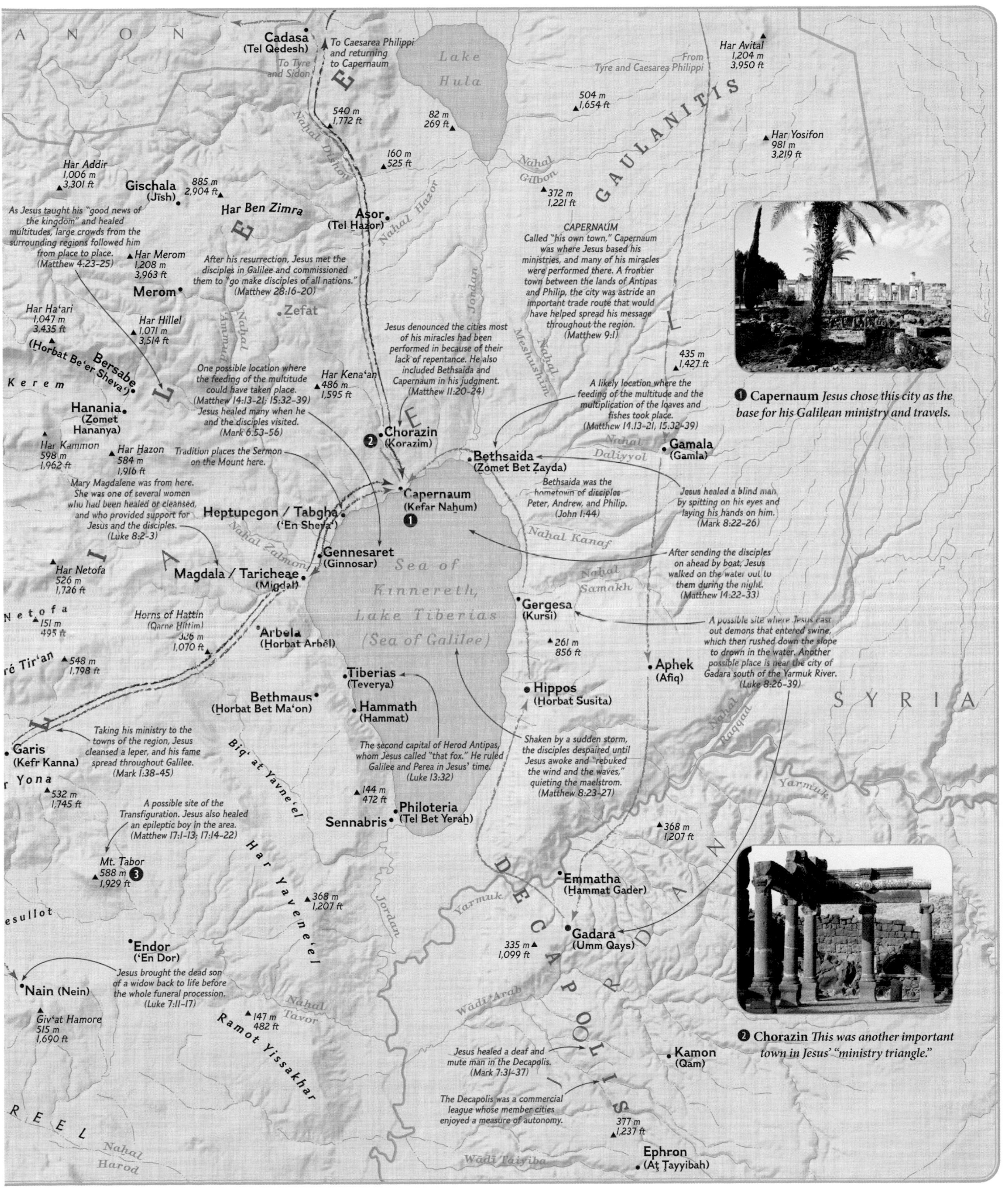

A N O N
Cadasa
(Tel Qedesh)
To Tyre and Sidon
To Caesarea Philippi and returning to Capernaum
Lake Hula
From Tyre and Caesarea Philippi
Har Avital
1,204 m
3,950 ft
504 m
1,654 ft
540 m
1,772 ft
82 m
269 ft
Nahal Dishon
GAULANITIS
Har Yosifon
981 m
3,219 ft
160 m
525 ft
Nahal Gilbon
Har Addir
1,006 m
3,301 ft
Gischala
(Jīsh)
885 m
2,904 ft
Har Ben Zimra
372 m
1,221 ft
Asor
(Tel Hazor)
Nahal Hazor
As Jesus taught his "good news of the kingdom" and healed multitudes, large crowds from the surrounding regions followed him from place to place. (Matthew 4:23-25)
Har Merom
1,208 m
3,963 ft
After his resurrection, Jesus met the disciples in Galilee and commissioned them to "go make disciples of all nations." (Matthew 28:16-20)
CAPERNAUM
Called "his own town," Capernaum was where Jesus based his ministries, and many of his miracles were performed there. A frontier town between the lands of Antipas and Philip, the city was astride an important trade route that would have helped spread his message throughout the region. (Matthew 9:1)
Merom
Zefat
Jordan
Har Ha'ari
1,047 m
3,435 ft
Har Hillel
1,071 m
3,514 ft
Nahal Ammud
Nahal Meshushim
Jesus denounced the cities most of his miracles had been performed in because of their lack of repentance. He also included Bethsaida and Capernaum in his judgment. (Matthew 11:20-24)
435 m
1,427 ft
Bersabe
(Horbat Be'er Sheva')
Kerem
One possible location where the feeding of the multitude could have taken place. (Matthew 14:13-21; 15:32-39)
Jesus healed many when he and the disciples visited. (Mark 6:53-56)
Har Kena'an
486 m
1,595 ft
A likely location where the feeding of the multitude and the multiplication of the loaves and fishes took place. (Matthew 14.13-21, 15:32-39)
Hanania
(Zomet Hananya)
Chorazin
(Korazim)
Gamala
(Gamla)
Nahal Daliyyot
Har Kammon
598 m
1,962 ft
Har Hazon
584 m
1,916 ft
Tradition places the Sermon on the Mount here.
Bethsaida
(Zomet Bet Zayda)
Mary Magdalene was from here. She was one of several women who had been healed or cleansed, and who provided support for Jesus and the disciples. (Luke 8:2-3)
Capernaum
(Kefar Nahum)
Bethsaida was the hometown of disciples Peter, Andrew, and Philip. (John 1:44)
Jesus healed a blind man by spitting on his eyes and laying his hands on him. (Mark 8:22-26)
Heptupegon / Tabgha
('En Sheva')
Nahal Kanaf
Nahal Zalmon
Gennesaret
(Ginnosar)
After sending the disciples on ahead by boat, Jesus walked on the water out to them during the night. (Matthew 14:22-33)
Har Netofa
526 m
1,726 ft
Magdala / Taricheae
(Migdal)
Sea of Kinnereth, Lake Tiberias (Sea of Galilee)
Nahal Samakh
Netofa
151 m
495 ft
Horns of Hattin
(Qarne Hittim)
326 m
1,070 ft
Gergesa
(Kursi)
Arbela
(Horbat Arbel)
A possible site where Jesus cast out demons that entered swine, which then rushed down the slope to drown in the water. Another possible place is near the city of Gadara south of the Yarmuk River. (Luke 8:26-39)
261 m
856 ft
548 m
1,798 ft
Aphek
(Afiq)
Tiberias
(Teverya)
Hippos
(Horbat Susita)
Bethmaus
(Horbat Bet Ma'on)
Hammath
(Hammat)
SYRIA
Nahal Raqqad
Garis
(Kefr Kanna)
Taking his ministry to the towns of the region, Jesus cleansed a leper, and his fame spread throughout Galilee. (Mark 1:38-45)
The second capital of Herod Antipas, whom Jesus called "that fox." He ruled Galilee and Perea in Jesus' time. (Luke 13:32)
Shaken by a sudden storm, the disciples despaired until Jesus awoke and "rebuked the wind and the waves," quieting the maelstrom. (Matthew 8:23-27)
Biq'at Yavne'el
Yarmuk
532 m
1,745 ft
144 m
472 ft
Philoteria
(Tel Bet Yerah)
Sennabris
A possible site of the Transfiguration. Jesus also healed an epileptic boy in the area. (Matthew 17:1-13; 17:14-22)
368 m
1,207 ft
Har Yavne'el
Mt. Tabor
588 m
1,929 ft
DECAPOLIS
Emmatha
(Hammat Gader)
368 m
1,207 ft
Jordan
Gadara
(Umm Qays)
335 m
1,099 ft
Endor
('En Dor)
Jesus brought the dead son of a widow back to life before the whole funeral procession. (Luke 7:11-17)
Nain (Nein)
Wadi 'Arab
Giv'at Hamore
515 m
1,690 ft
147 m
482 ft
Nahal Tavor
Ramot Yissakhar
Jesus healed a deaf and mute man in the Decapolis. (Mark 7:31-37)
Kamon
(Qam)
The Decapolis was a commercial league whose member cities enjoyed a measure of autonomy.
377 m
1,237 ft
REEL
Nahal Harod
Wadi Taiyiba
Ephron
(At Tayyibah)

❶ **Capernaum** *Jesus chose this city as the base for his Galilean ministry and travels.*

❷ **Chorazin** *This was another important town in Jesus' "ministry triangle."*

The Kingdom of God

Traditionally, the "Kingdom" concept envisioned a nation governed by Jewish Law and ruled by a true Davidic king, rather than a Herodian tyrant or a Roman despot. But to Jesus, "Kingdom of God"—or "Kingdom of Heaven," a term that piously avoids using the name of "God"—apparently meant something different: not a political entity, but a new compact for the social and spiritual renewal of Jewish society. Jesus' "Kingdom" doctrine envisioned a return to the Judaism espoused

ABOVE: *"Christ Healing the Possessed Man," an 11th-century fresco by an anonymous artist, depicts a miracle story related in the Book of Matthew.*

LEFT: *The Sermon on the Mount is depicted on this rare fourth-century relief from the Vigna Maccarani in Rome.*

8 B.C.E.
Herod reconciles with Augustus

7 B.C.E.
Alexander and Aristobulus are tried by their father, Herod, and executed

6 B.C.E.
Herod moves to curb the influence of the Pharisees

5 B.C.E.
Antipater II, Herod's heir, is charged with treason. Antipas is named heir instead

by prophets like Amos, Micah, and Hosea, who urged their followers to focus not on the sacrificial cult but on the core pillars of the Torah: compassion, social responsibility, and faith in God. This idea may be encapsulated in Jesus' emphatic statement, "Do not think that I have come to abolish the Law or the Prophets . . . I have come not to abolish, but to fulfill," suggesting a deep sense of continuity with the Torah's commitment to social justice (Matthew 5:17).

What's more, some of Jesus' statements suggest that the Kingdom of God society would not come about as a result of a violent military overthrow or some great cataclysmic disaster, but as a grassroots movement. "The kingdom of God is not coming with things that can be observed," Jesus says in the Gospel of Luke, "for in fact, the kingdom of God is *among you*" (Luke 17:20-21). His many sayings on the topic, however, are not consistent. At times it appears as if the Kingdom of God is imminent; elsewhere, Jesus implies that it still lies well into the future. Some sayings indicate the Kingdom is of earthly origin; others again suggest that the Kingdom will be realized in heaven.

Perhaps the most vivid illustration of the Kingdom as a socioreligious utopia is provided by Jesus' famous Sermon on the Mount:

Blessed are the poor in spirit,
for theirs is the kingdom of heaven.
Blessed are those who mourn,
for they will be comforted.
Blessed are the meek,
for they will inherit the earth.
Blessed are those who hunger and thirst
for righteousness, for they will be filled.

MATTHEW 5:3-6

Seen in this context, the miracle stories could be seen as a realization of the Heavenly Kingdom on Earth. Hunger, a major issue among the uprooted population of Galilee, would be banished forever, as vividly shown by the miraculous multiplication of loaves and fishes to feed the 5,000 (Matthew 14:13-21; Mark 6:31-44; Luke 9:10-17; John 6:5-15). Those afflicted with disease would be healed, just as Jesus had healed the man with leprosy (Mark 1:41). And those who died would find new life, just as the daughter of Jairus had been resurrected from the dead (Mark 5:41).

The Itinerant Preacher

Encouraged by the response to his teachings, Jesus began to travel beyond the immediate orbit of Capernaum. From Bethsaida, he sailed to "the other side of the sea," which Mark calls the "country of the Gerasenes." Here, he performed an exorcism that compelled the evil spirits to flee to a herd of swine feeding nearby (Mark 5:1-13). Though lost to us, the allegorical meaning of this miracle would have been obvious to Jesus' contemporaries, because demons were considered the acolytes of Satan. Thus, Jesus proved that his power could trump Satan and all his works.

Then, says Mark, Jesus used a boat to cross to the other side. Eventually he reached the town that Matthew refers to as Magadan, which probably means Magdala. Magdala, located on the western shore of the lake, was a major processing center of the Galilean fishing industry. One of Jesus' followers came from this town. Her name was Mary, "the Magdalene," but the Gospels tell us little about her background. Unlike other women named Mary in the Gospels, who were related to either Jesus or to his Apostles, Mary Magdalene appears to be unattached, which was unusual. It is possible that Mary Magdalene hailed from an affluent family, and thus enjoyed a greater level of

Healing Miracles

CA 30 C.E.

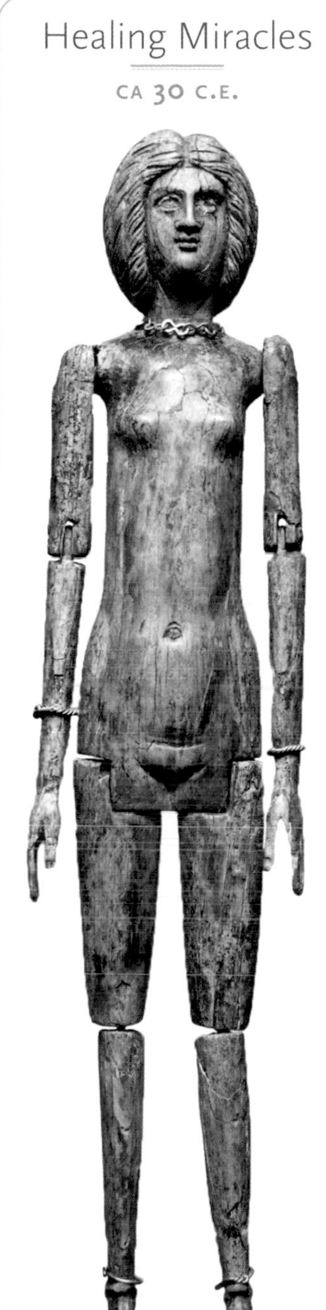

The healing miracles form part of the oldest oral traditions about Jesus. The knowledge of human anatomy and health was still limited, as evidenced in this doll from the late first century C.E.

4 B.C.E. **Young demonstrators remove the golden eagle from the Temple as a Roman symbol**

4 B.C.E. **Putative date of birth of Jesus**

4 B.C.E. **Antipater II is executed**

4 B.C.E. **Herod dies; Augustus confirms Herod's will dividing his kingdom among his sons and sister**

independence. Luke says that she belonged to a group of women who "provided for them out of their own resources" (Luke 8:2-3). Near the end of Jesus' ministry, Mary Magdalene would emerge as one of his bravest and most devoted followers.

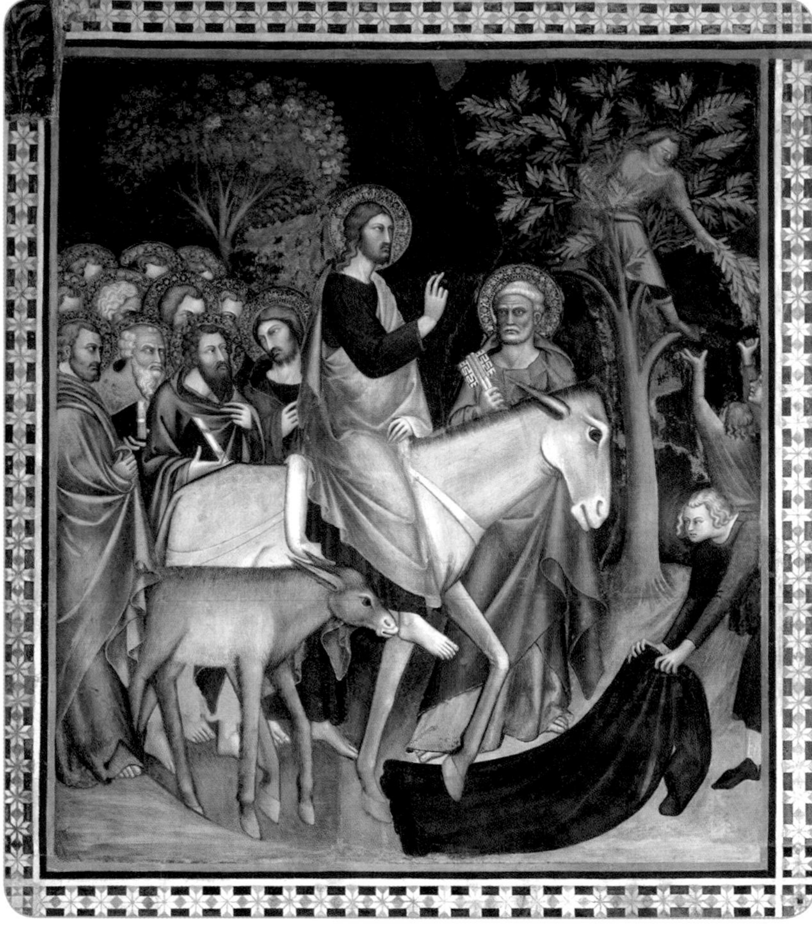

"The Entry of Christ Into Jerusalem" was painted by Italian artist Barna da Siena around 1350. Jesus' entry in Jerusalem is one of the few events described in all four Gospels.

Jesus' journeys gradually moved beyond Galilean territory. Encouraged by the presence of foreigners in the crowds, Jesus traveled north, to Tyre in Phoenicia, which was a Hellenized and thoroughly Gentile region. From here he went to Sidon, another Phoenician coastal city some 35 miles north, before turning south for a visit to the Decapolis, the Gentile territory east of the Jordan (Mark 7:31). Here was Caesarea Philippi, which would soon become a major Greco-Roman city. While there, on the threshold of returning to his native land, Jesus felt the need to reflect on his ministry to date. Had he been successful? Were his words and actions having an impact? Were the people prepared to abandon their selfish ways and embrace the principles of the Kingdom of God? He turned to his disciples and asked, "Who do people say that I am?"

The disciples pondered the question. Some said, "John the Baptist." Others replied, "Elijah." Still others hedged their bets and said, "One of the prophets." Then Jesus asked them, "But who

After sending away the crowds, he got into the boat and went to the region of Magadan.

GOSPEL OF MATTHEW 15:39

do *you* say that I am?" Simon Peter stood up and proclaimed, "You are the Messiah." In the Gospel of Matthew, this is when Jesus embraces Simon Peter, saying, "on this rock I will build my Church" (Matthew 16:18). Though lost in English, Jesus actually uses a pun on Peter's name, for *Petros* in Greek means "rock."

Alas, upon his return to the heartland of his ministry, Jesus saw that little had changed. "Woe to you, Chorazin!" he cries in the Gospels of Luke and Matthew; "Woe to you, Bethsaida! If the powerful deeds performed among you had been done in Tyre and Sidon, they would have changed their ways long ago, sitting in sackcloth and ashes!" (Matthew 11:21; Luke 10:13).

4 B.C.E.
Herod's son Antipas assumes title of tetrarch of Galilee and Perea

4 B.C.E.
While Archelaus, new ruler of Judea, is in Rome, a rebellion erupts

4 B.C.E.
Judas, son of Hezekiah of Galilee, leads a revolt in Galilee

4–3 B.C.E.
The Jewish revolts are suppressed by Roman forces; Sepphoris is burned

Soon thereafter, as Luke tells us, Jesus set his face to go south, to Jerusalem (Luke 9:51). Like the prophet Jeremiah before him, he would appeal to his fellow Jews in Judaism's most sacred sanctuary, the Temple. The Apostles followed him with apprehension. "Jesus was walking ahead of them," says Mark, "and those who followed were afraid" (Mark 10:32). Their fear was well founded. Roman forces in Jerusalem were known to be on high alert during Passover, since the feast celebrated Israel's liberation from another foreign despot: Pharaoh of Egypt. Even worse, it had only been a few years since the Roman prefect, Pontius Pilate, had bloodily suppressed a protest inside the Temple forecourt, prompted by rumors that Pilate was planning to seize funds from the Temple treasury in order to build a Roman aqueduct. The Apostles must have known that even the slightest disturbance would be met with immediate force.

Jesus' Arrest

Mark relates how Jesus made a triumphant entry into Jerusalem, seated on a donkey—the event celebrated to this day on Palm Sunday. "Many people spread their cloaks on the road," says Mark, "and others spread leafy branches that they had cut in the fields" (Mark 11:7). Jesus' destination was the forecourt of the Temple; but because "it was already late, he went out to Bethany with the twelve" (Mark 11:11). In Bethany lived his relatives Mary and Martha; here the group found shelter for the night.

When Jesus did finally reach the Temple during his next visit, he was shocked to find that Herod's massive forecourt was filled with money changers, doing brisk business

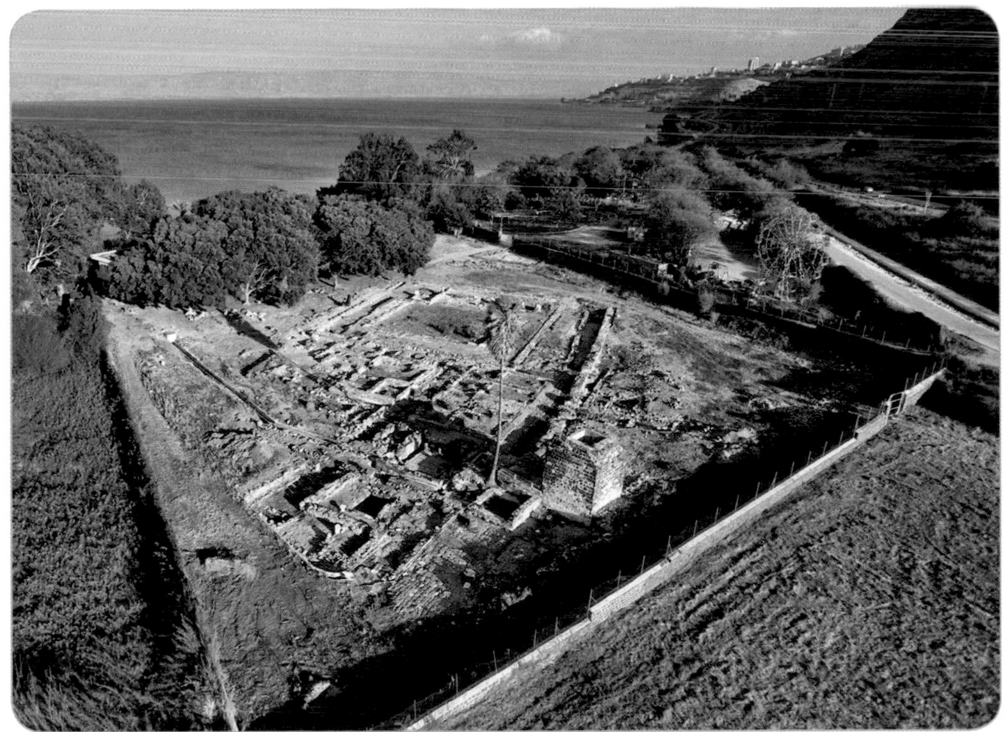

An aerial view shows the stunning site of ancient Magdala, near the Sea of Galilee, now undergoing a new excavation campaign.

LIFE AND TIMES

Tithes and Taxes

Farming in the Euphrates valley of Syria, the birthplace of agriculture some 10,000 years ago

Traditionally, a Galilean farmer was expected to pay taxes (in kind) to two constituencies: the Temple and the secular government. The Book of Numbers states that a tenth of the harvest was to be given to the Levites, including "the grain of the threshing floor and the fullness of the wine press" (Numbers 18:27). Once every seven years, during the so-called Sabbatical year, farmers were exempt from paying the tithe, since the land was supposed to lie fallow (Leviticus 25:4). But the secular government demanded payment as well. During periods of foreign occupation, farmers rendered their tribute to the foreign potentate, while during the Hasmonean era, taxes were paid to the royal house in Jerusalem. This changed under King Herod. Although Herod cultivated a large court, he was still a vassal king expected to pay a tribute to Rome. As a consequence, the secular tax layer on his subjects was doubled: Tribute was due to *both* a foreign ruler *and* a Jewish king, in addition to the Temple tithes. This pushed may Galilean farmers into a spiral of debt, usually ending in the foreclosure of their lands.

2 C.E. **Augustus' grandson and heir Lucius dies**

4 C.E. **Augustus' other grandson Gaius is killed; Augustus adopts Tiberius**

5 C.E. **First use of the adjustable caliper in China**

6 C.E. **Archelaus is removed from office and banished to Vienne, Roman Gaul**

The Tyrian silver shekel, such as this one dated around 68 C.E. and inscribed with "Jerusalem the Holy," was the only type of currency permitted within the Temple.

RIGHT: *A view of the traditional location of Gethsemane on the Mount of Olives*

converting Roman currency into Temple shekels. All pilgrims who wished to purchase a sacrificial lamb or dove inside the Temple could only do so with Tyrian shekels, since Roman (and many other) coins bore a portrait of a living person (such as the Emperor), which was forbidden in ancient Judaism. Some scholars have suggested that this commerce usually took place on the Mount of Olives, far from the Temple complex, which would explain why Jesus was so deeply aggrieved by this unseemly trade. He "began to drive out those who were selling and those who were buying in the temple, and he overturned the tables of the money changers and the seats of those who sold doves." Raising his voice, Jesus said, "Is it not written, 'My house shall be called a house of prayer for all the nations'? But," he added, paraphrasing Jeremiah's Temple sermon, "you have made it a den of robbers" (Jeremiah 7:11; Mark 11:15-17). It is quite possible that this violent demonstration, and Jesus' angry outburst, led to the warrant for his arrest. Mark writes that as soon as "the chief priests and the scribes heard it, they kept looking for a way to kill him" (Mark 11:18).

The Synoptic Gospels suggest that it was now the 14th of Nisan, the eve of Passover, when Jerusalem was filled to overflowing with Passover pilgrims. Determined to stay in the city, rather than returning to Bethany, Jesus sent two of his disciples to find a place for them. They should follow a man with a jar, and when he reached his house, they were to ask where the Teacher could celebrate Passover with his disciples (Mark 14:14). The followers did as they were told, and found a large upper room. This is possibly the same place where, according to the Book of Acts, the disciples met during Pentecost, after the crucifixion (Acts 12:12-13).

Once they were seated for their evening meal (possibly the *seder,* or Passover meal), Jesus announced, "One of you will betray me, one who is eating with me" (Mark 14:18). That man was Judas Iscariot. Judas had secretly promised the chief priests that he would lead them to Jesus in exchange for 30 pieces of silver (Mark 14:11; Matthew 26:15).

Now, as they were reclining at the table, Jesus broke bread—the unleavened kind, since it was Passover—blessed it, and gave it to the disciples, saying, "Take, eat; this is my body." Then Jesus took a cup and said, "Drink from it, all of you; for this is my blood of the

covenant, which is poured out for many for the forgiveness of sins" (Mark 14:23-24). With this, Jesus instituted the Eucharist, a Greek word which means "thanksgiving," which would be reenacted in many Early Christian communities until it became the quintessential liturgical sacrament of Mass.

After the supper had ended, Jesus led his followers to the Mount of Olives, to a

OPPOSITE: *In this detail of "The Taking of Christ" (ca 1602) by Michelangelo Caravaggio (1571–1610), Judas kisses Jesus as a soldier arrests him and the disciple John cries out for help.*

6 C.E.
Augustus annexes Judea as a Roman province; first procurator is Coponius

6 C.E.
Quirinius, the new governor of Syria, initiates a census in Judea

6 C.E.
Annas (Ananus ben Seth) is appointed high priest by Quirinius

6 C.E.
The Roman census provokes a new revolt; party of the Zealots is formed

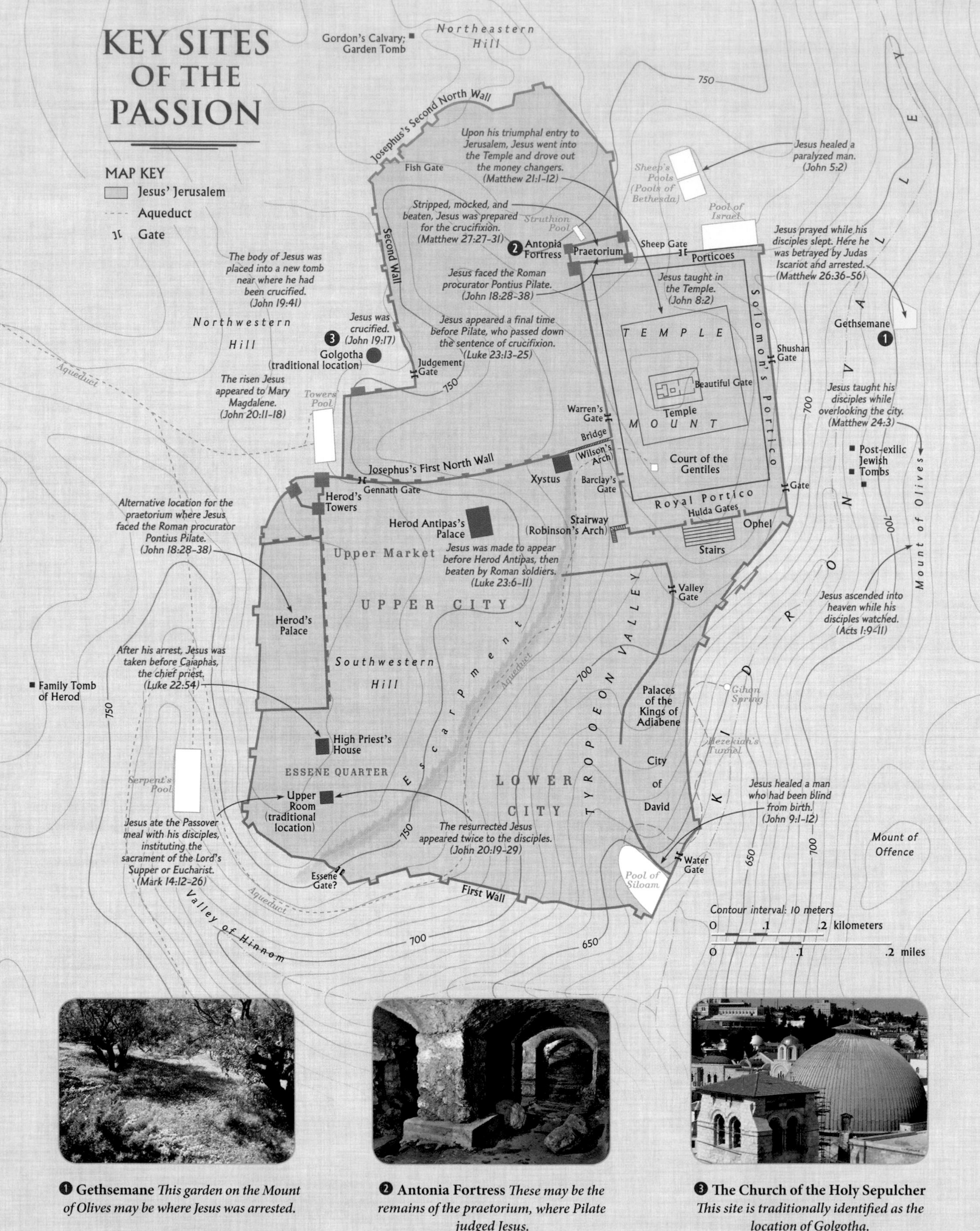

KEY SITES OF THE PASSION
MAP KEY
Jesus' Jerusalem
Aqueduct
Gate
Gordon's Calvary; Garden Tomb
Northeastern Hill
750
Josephus's Second North Wall
Upon his triumphal entry to Jerusalem, Jesus went into the Temple and drove out the money changers. (Matthew 21:1-12)
Jesus healed a paralyzed man. (John 5:2)
Sheep's Pools (Pools of Bethesda)
Fish Gate
Stripped, mocked, and beaten, Jesus was prepared for the crucifixion. (Matthew 27:27-31)
Struthion Pool
Pool of Israel
Second Wall
Antonia Fortress
Praetorium
Sheep Gate
Porticoes
Jesus prayed while his disciples slept. Here he was betrayed by Judas Iscariot and arrested. (Matthew 26:36-56)
The body of Jesus was placed into a new tomb near where he had been crucified. (John 19:41)
Jesus faced the Roman procurator Pontius Pilate. (John 18:28-38)
Jesus taught in the Temple. (John 8:2)
Solomon's Portico
Gethsemane
Northwestern Hill
Jesus was crucified. (John 19:17)
Jesus appeared a final time before Pilate, who passed down the sentence of crucifixion. (Luke 23:13-25)
TEMPLE MOUNT
Shushan Gate
Golgotha (traditional location)
Judgement Gate
Aqueduct
Beautiful Gate
The risen Jesus appeared to Mary Magdalene. (John 20:11-18)
Towers Pool
Temple
Jesus taught his disciples while overlooking the city. (Matthew 24:3)
Warren's Gate
Bridge
(Wilson's Arch)
Court of the Gentiles
Post-exilic Jewish Tombs
Josephus's First North Wall
Xystus
Barclay's Gate
Gate
Gennath Gate
Herod's Towers
Royal Portico
Hulda Gates
Alternative location for the praetorium where Jesus faced the Roman procurator Pontius Pilate. (John 18:28-38)
Herod Antipas's Palace
Stairway (Robinson's Arch)
Ophel
Stairs
Upper Market
Jesus was made to appear before Herod Antipas, then beaten by Roman soldiers. (Luke 23:6-11)
Mount of Olives
UPPER CITY
Valley Gate
Jesus ascended into heaven while his disciples watched. (Acts 1:9-11)
Herod's Palace
KIDRON VALLEY
After his arrest, Jesus was taken before Caiaphas, the chief priest. (Luke 22:54)
Southwestern Hill
Escarpment
Family Tomb of Herod
TYROPOEON VALLEY
Palaces of the Kings of Adiabene
Gihon Spring
High Priest's House
Hezekiah's Tunnel
ESSENE QUARTER
City of David
Serpent's Pool
LOWER CITY
Jesus healed a man who had been blind from birth. (John 9:1-12)
Upper Room (traditional location)
Jesus ate the Passover meal with his disciples, instituting the sacrament of the Lord's Supper or Eucharist. (Mark 14:12-26)
The resurrected Jesus appeared twice to the disciples. (John 20:19-29)
Mount of Offence
Water Gate
Pool of Siloam
Essene Gate?
First Wall
Valley of Hinnom
700
650
Contour interval: 10 meters
0 .1 .2 kilometers
0 .1 .2 miles

❶ **Gethsemane** *This garden on the Mount of Olives may be where Jesus was arrested.*

❷ **Antonia Fortress** *These may be the remains of the praetorium, where Pilate judged Jesus.*

❸ **The Church of the Holy Sepulcher** *This site is traditionally identified as the location of Golgotha.*

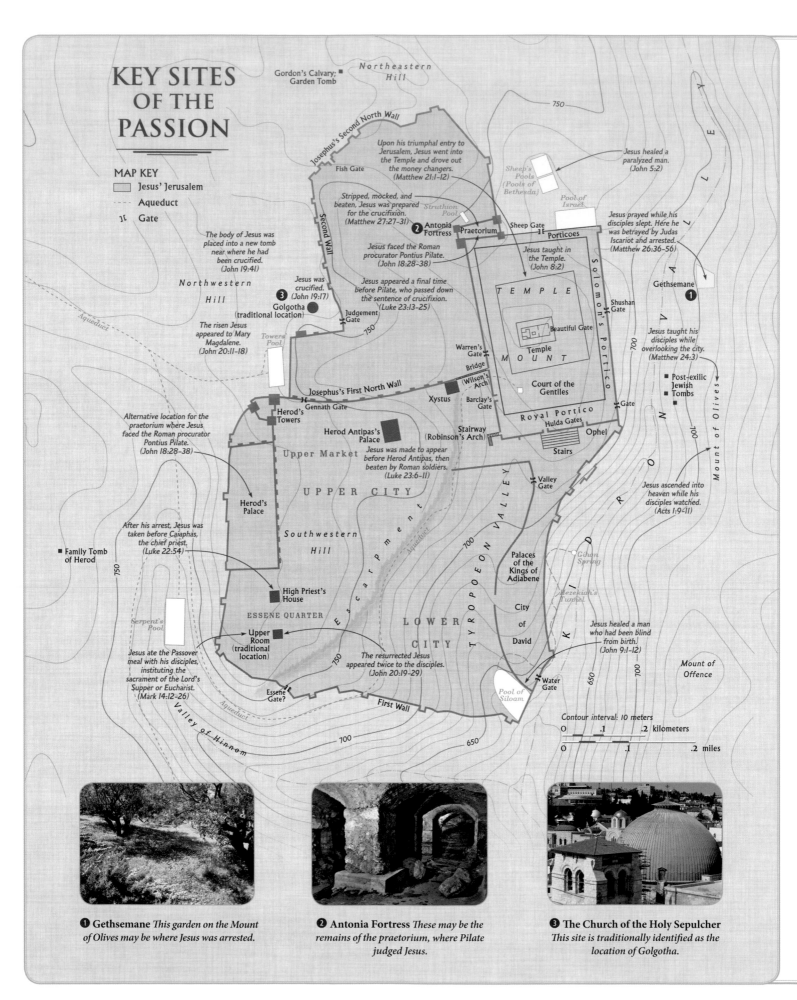

place called Gethsemane (Mark 14:36). This is where the Temple guards, led by Judas, caught up with him. Jesus was arrested and led away. Under normal circumstances, he would have been held in the Temple prison until such time that the full Sanhedrin could be convened to hear his case. This is what happened to Peter, John, and other Apostles upon their arrest (Acts 4:3; 5:17). But instead, Jesus was taken directly to the Jerusalem residence of the high priest, Caiaphas. This hastily organized indictment, first described by Mark (and reiterated in the three other Gospels), suggests that Caiaphas was eager to dispense with Jesus as soon as possible, without a full quorum of the Sanhedrin.

All of them asked,- "Are you, then, the Son of God?" He said to them, "You say that I am."

GOSPEL OF LUKE 22:70

But the high priest faced two problems. For one, without the full backing of the Sanhedrin, a high priest could not summarily order a man's death. His only alternative was to refer the matter to the Roman government in Judea. This raised a second issue. Jesus faced charges of disturbing the peace, and perhaps of blasphemy, in the Temple forecourt; neither of these was a capital offense. According to Mark, Caiaphas asked Jesus, "Are you the Messiah?" Jesus replied, "I am." Citing from the Book of Daniel and the Psalms, Jesus added, " 'You will see the Son of Man seated at the right hand of the Power,' and 'coming with the clouds of heaven'" (Mark 14:62, citing Psalms 110:1; Daniel 7:13-14). Caiaphas seized on these words, for they implied that Jesus was a Messiah determined to establish a new kingdom through power. This made him a political suspect. Such cases could only be heard by Roman officials.

As dawn broke on the next day, a hearing was held at the praetorium, where the Roman prefect, Pontius Pilate, had taken residence for the duration of Passover (Mark 15:15-16; Matthew 27:27). According to Mark, Jesus remained largely silent during the short proceedings. Since Jesus was not a Roman citizen but a colonial subject, Pilate did not need to observe the legal precepts of a Roman trial. Under the terms of the *ius gentium,* the law governing subject people, Roman officials had wide latitude in dispensing justice. This is why Paul, who did have Roman citizenship, was able to insist on a proper legal proceeding in Rome following his own arrest around 63 C.E. But Jesus enjoyed no such protection. What's more, the charge of political sedition invariably called for a sentence of death by public crucifixion, so that the prisoner could serve as an object lesson for all others contemplating political upheaval.

Jesus' Crucifixion

Jesus was scourged, as was common with prisoners condemned to death, for the blood loss would hasten his death on the cross. In Judea this was important, for under Jewish Law every condemned prisoner had to be taken down and buried before sundown (Deuteronomy 21:22-23). Jesus was led out of the praetorium and taken to the place of execution. This was a killing field named Golgotha, or "place of the skull" in Aramaic, located outside the city walls, as was customary. The execution detail reached Golgotha "on the third hour," roughly nine o'clock in the morning,

SCRIPTURE AND FAITH

The Second Temple

A model of the Second Temple, now located in the Israel Museum in Jerusalem

Under Herod's direction, the Second Temple in Jerusalem became briefly one of the largest sanctuaries in the Roman world. By filling in the hill on which the Temple was built, Herod created a vast outdoor enclosure, an esplanade large enough to hold thousands of worshippers with the Temple at its center. This large court, which would feature prominently in the Gospels, was surrounded by a large covered *peristyle* or colonnade, surmounted by Corinthian capitals and moldings. Around this enclosure rose a number of subsidiary buildings, including a basilica-type structure known as the Royal Stoa, which served as the seat of the Sanhedrin, the supreme Jewish Council. Herod's Temple complex was completed in 62 C.E., as corroborated by coins found during recent excavations, and destroyed during the First Jewish Revolt of 66–70 C.E. All that remains today is the outer wall, built by Herod to support the large esplanade around the Temple. A portion of this outer wall, known as the Western Wall, is the holiest site in modern Judaism.

6 C.E.
Antipas, now known as Herod Antipas, begins the rebuilding of Sepphoris

9 C.E.
The Roman legions led by Varus are destroyed by the Cherusci in the Teutoburg Forest

9 C.E.
Marcus Ambivulus succeeds Coponius as procurator of Judea

12 C.E.
Annius Rufus succeeds Marcus Ambivulus as procurator of Judea

whereupon a group of Roman specialists, known as immunes, nailed Jesus to the cross. A sign was posted above his head, which mockingly proclaimed the charge: claiming to be "The King of the Jews." Two other men, condemned as bandits, were crucified and set up on his right and left (Mark 15:26-27).

The Apostles were nowhere in evidence. They had fled and were most likely in hiding lest they be arrested as well. Only a small group remained, including "Mary Magdalene and Mary the mother of James the Younger," who might have been Jesus' mother (Mark 15:40).

When the sun began to set, the Romans went around to break the legs of the prisoners. Without the use of their legs, being suspended on a cross, the victims could not raise themselves up to force air into their lungs, and thus slowly suffocated to death. One of the soldiers raised his hammer to also smash Jesus' legs, but Jesus was no longer breathing. According to the Gospel of John, the soldier used his lance to pierce Jesus' side and see if there was a reaction (John 19:34). There was none.

According to an inscription, this elaborate ossuary contained the bones of Caiaphas ("Yosef bar Caifa"), quite possibly the high priest who arraigned Jesus, as well as the remains of Caiaphas's family.

Custom dictated that Jesus' body should be thrown into a burial ground reserved for executed criminals, but a member of the Sanhedrin named Joseph of Arimathea intervened. Mark implies that Joseph was sympathetic to Jesus' cause, since he "himself [was] waiting expectantly for the kingdom of God" (Mark 15:43). He persuaded Pilate to release Jesus' body into his custody. Joseph "wrapped it in the linen cloth, and laid it in a tomb that had been hewn out of the rock." (Mark 15:46). It was Friday afternoon, "the day before the Sabbath" by Jewish reckoning; no burial rites would be permitted after sundown. That is why the burial was done in haste, and why the proper anointing of the body could not be completed. Mary Magdalene and the women therefore resolved to return to the tomb after the Sabbath to complete this task (Mark 15:46).

> *Then Jesus, crying with a loud voice, said, "Father, into your hands I commend my spirit."*
>
> LUKE 23:46

When, by Jewish reckoning, three days had passed since Friday afternoon, Mary Magdalene, Mary "the mother of James," and a woman named Salome duly retraced their steps, bringing "spices, so that they might go and anoint him" (Mark 16:1). But when they arrived at the tomb, they were shocked to see that the stone covering the tomb, "which was very large," had been rolled back. Inside was a young man, dressed in a white robe, who told them that "Jesus of Nazareth, who was crucified . . . has been raised; he is not here" (Mark 16:6).

The other Gospels tell us that in the days that followed, Jesus appeared to his disciples in different locations. Sometimes he presented himself as a man of flesh and blood; he even bid Thomas to probe his wounds. At other times he appeared as an ephemeral being passing through a door (John 20:26-27).

The news of Jesus' resurrection galvanized the Apostles. They came out of their places of hiding and returned to Jerusalem. There, they resolved to continue Jesus' work and propagate the good news of the Kingdom in Judea and beyond. ■

OPPOSITE: *This detail of the Virgin Mary and the dead Christ is taken from "The Deposition from the Cross" by Fra Angelico (ca 1387–1455), painted in 1436.*

14 C.E.
Augustus dies and is succeeded by Tiberius

18 C.E.
Joseph Caiaphas, son-in-law of Annas, is appointed high priest in Jerusalem

26 C.E.
Pontius Pilate is appointed to succeed Valerius Gratus as procurator of Judea

30 C.E.
Jesus is tried and crucified on orders of Pilate during the Passover festival

2
CHAPTER

THE EARLY CHRISTIANS

ca 30–313 C.E.

And suddenly from heaven there came a sound like the rush of a violent wind, and it filled the entire house where they were sitting.

ACTS OF THE APOSTLES 2:2

Fifty days, or seven weeks, after Passover, Jewish pilgrims from all over the Roman world would travel to Jerusalem once again for another festival, the feast of *Shavuot* ("Weeks" in Hebrew, or "Pentecost" in Greek, meaning "fiftieth"). This feast celebrated God's presentation of the Jewish Law to Moses on Mount Sinai. According to the Book of Acts of the Apostles, this was also the day that the disciples of Jesus received divine inspiration to continue to proclaim his good news of the Kingdom. The Book of Acts, which documents the growth of early Christianity, describes how the "safe house" where the Apostles were staying was suddenly filled with "a sound like the rush of a violent wind," while "divided tongues, as of fire, appeared among them" (Acts 2:2-3). This inspiration galvanized the group to go out and address the thousands of pilgrims then passing through Jerusalem. Many of these Jews were from foreign lands, but this did not matter, as the Apostles found themselves able to speak "in other languages, as the Spirit gave them ability" (Acts 2:4).

The question was, however, how were the Apostles expected to continue a mission so closely associated with Jesus' highly individual vision? How could the movement be sustained

ABOVE: *A fresco of fishermen reveals the skill of Roman artists in the first century* C.E.

OPPOSITE: *This view shows Jerusalem's Western Wall at dusk, the holiest site in modern Judaism.*

PRECEDING PAGES: *"The Disciples Peter and John Running to the Sepulcher on the Morning of the Resurrection" was painted by Swiss artist Eugène Burnand (1850–1921) in 1898.*

Period Artifacts

90–350 C.E.

A bust of Julia Titus, sculpted ca 90 C.E., shows Roman sculpture at its apogee.

A delicate silver spoon features the Chi-Rho symbol, incorporating the first two letters of "Christos."

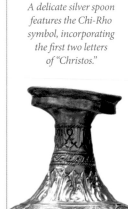

A lavishly decorated silver jug from the fourth century includes Christian motifs.

A well-preserved Roman road remains near Idlib, in northwestern Syria. These roads were vital to the maintenance and development of the Roman state, providing an efficient means of overland travel.

without his charismatic presence, his soaring oratory, and his wondrous works? The Book of Acts resolves this dilemma in the form of a sermon delivered by Peter, which articulates the new doctrine that the apostolic mission would henceforth espouse. First, it states that Jesus of Nazareth had been a man "with deeds of power, wonders and signs," who though condemned to the cross, had now risen from the dead. Second, it claims that his resurrection is evidence that Jesus had indeed been the Messiah, the Anointed One (or *Christos* in Greek), as foretold in Hebrew Scripture. And third, that all those who were prepared to repent their sins and be baptized in the name of Jesus (the) Christ, would receive the gift of the Holy Spirit (Acts 2:22-39). These three tenets still firmly anchored the apostolic movement within Second Temple Judaism; it was not, as yet, a separate religion that sought to distance itself from the Jewish Law. Indeed, in every respect these early disciples continued to live as practicing Jews. They prayed in the Temple, observed the Sabbath, and followed the precepts of the Torah (Acts 2:45, 15:5).

Acts states that as many as 3,000 men and women responded to Peter's call. These new followers were warmly welcomed and invited to share in the group's table fellowship, including "the breaking of bread and the prayers."

37 C.E.
Tiberius dies; is succeeded by Gaius Caligula

37 C.E.
Pontius Pilate is recalled to Rome

CA 38 C.E.
Jews are persecuted in Alexandria

CA 40 C.E.
One of the earliest Christian communities is founded in Corinth

These new believers were also called upon to "sell their possessions and goods and distribute the proceeds to all, as any had needed," just as John the Baptist had done before (Acts 2:42-45; Luke 3:11). What's more, the power to perform miracles, so crucial to establish a prophet's authority and credibility, was now passed from Jesus to Peter. In the weeks and months to come, says Acts, Peter performed several miraculous feats, such as healing the lame man at the "Beautiful Gate" of the Temple. Peter and the Apostle John also preached in Solomon's Portico, the large colonnade to the east of the Temple esplanade, and were able to baptize many.

The Sadducees observed the growth of the "Jesus following" with considerable alarm. They had believed that by crucifying Jesus, his Messianic movement had been suppressed. The idea that Jesus had been resurrected from the dead was a further provocation, because the Sadducees (unlike the Pharisees) firmly rejected the immortality of the soul, let alone the possibility of physical resurrection.

In due course, Peter and John were arrested and interrogated by Caiaphas and his father-in-law, Annas, which indicates the extraordinary interest that the Annas family took in the destruction of Jesus and his movement (Acts 4:5-6). No proof of any seditious activity could be found, however, so both Apostles were released, though this reprieve was temporary. Soon thereafter, as Peter and the Apostles were preaching in Solomon's Portico in the Temple, they were once again arrested and brought before the Sanhedrin. This time, it was a Pharisee named Gamaliel, "a teacher of the law," who intervened on their behalf (Acts 5:34-39). By way of a warning, the Apostles were flogged before being set free. Caiaphas, however, remained determined to destroy the movement as soon as the next opportunity presented itself.

The Murder of Stephen

As the apostolic movement grew, the followers began to meet in each other's homes to talk about Jesus' teachings and share in table fellowship. This idea of private assembly is the root meaning of the Greek word *ekklesia,* or

PERIOD ART

Roman Art and Architecture

In the late first and early second centuries, Roman art achieved its apogee in styles and forms that would determine the emergence of Christian art in the centuries to come. The hallmark of imperial art was a new form of naturalism of such illusive quality that it would not be matched until the Italian Renaissance of the 15th century. Roman painters excelled at creating realistic and sometimes startlingly "impressionistic" panoramas of landscapes or intimate gardens, often using an intuitive perspective, giving the interiors of urban villas a pleasingly bucolic air. Using Greek statuary as their model, Roman sculptors produced statues of Roman gods, emperors, and prominent Romans with an equally startling realism, aided by such technical innovations as the marble drill. But Rome's greatest achievement, and one in which it superseded its Greek models, was unquestionably its architecture, governed by a delicate system of proportions documented by Roman architect Vitruvius and referred to as the Golden Ratio. Whereas the Greeks primarily used traditional post-and-beam construction, the Romans developed arches and vaults as their principal support technology. Unlike the Roman temple and theater, which drew heavily on Greek models, Roman architects also developed some quintessentially Roman archetypes, such as the large public baths complex and the central forum, found in virtually all major cities throughout the Empire. Another invention was the aqueduct, an engineering marvel that could convey fresh water from faraway mountains over many miles.

The realism of this garden scene, which dates to the first century C.E.*, is startling. The fresco was uncovered in the House of Livia.*

41 C.E.
Agrippa I, grandson of Herod the Great, is appointed King of Roman Judea

41 C.E.
Emperor Caligula is assassinated and succeeded by Claudius

41 C.E.
Claudius affirms the right of Jews to observe their religious practices in the Roman Empire

CA 43 C.E.
Romans invade Britain

SCRIPTURE AND FAITH

The Christian Old Testament

"Moses and the Tablets of the Law" was painted by French artist Laurent de la Hyre (1606–1656).

Hebrew Scripture—the Old Testament, in Christian parlance—was written mostly in Hebrew (with segments in Aramaic), which most Christians in the Roman Empire were no longer able to read. Instead, they availed themselves of a Greek translation of Hebrew Scripture, known as the Septuagint. One legend claims that this translation was commissioned by King Ptolemy II, a bibliophile who wanted to equip the Library of Alexandria with the scriptures of every people in the world. By the time the Septuagint was compiled, a number of other Jewish texts were in circulation, including wisdom sayings, poetry, prayers, and histories such as the books of the Maccabees, Tobit, and Ecclesiasticus. Though not included in the Hebrew canon, they were accepted into the Septuagint, which is why these so-called "apocrypha" (or "hidden books") do appear in Roman Catholic and Orthodox Bibles, but not in Hebrew Bibles. Protestant editions followed the rabbinical decision not to include these apocrypha.

"gathering," which later would be translated as "Church." Among these new disciples was a group whom the Book of Acts describes as "Hellenists" and probably included Greek-speaking Jews from Egypt and other foreign territories. Tensions between the "Hellenist" and "Hebrew" factions, always present in the Diaspora, rose to the surface when some claimed that the Greek widows in the group did not receive their fair share of food (Acts 6:1). Other Greek followers, led by a man named Stephen, began to distance themselves from the obedience shown by Hebrew followers toward the Temple. By this time, many followers in the Diaspora had long since built their liturgical life around the synagogue, rather than the Temple. This threatened to split the budding apostolic community just when it was coming under pressure from the Sadducee priesthood as well. These tensions also began to erode the idea that the apostolic mission was simply a reform movement within traditional Judaism.

Stephen was denounced to Caiaphas and the Sanhedrin for "speaking blasphemous words against Moses and God." Delighted with this opportunity, Caiaphas had Stephen arrested and arraigned in front of the Sanhedrin. Stephen was allowed to defend himself, but his claim that "the Most High does not dwell in houses made with human hands" enraged the crowd. He was dragged off and stoned to death—the first Christian martyr. A young man named Saul witnessed the mob scene with satisfaction, accepting the cloaks of those involved in the stoning (Acts 7:48-58).

The murder of Stephen had its intended effect. Many followers fled from Jerusalem to find sanctuary elsewhere, in places like Cyprus, Phoenicia, Damascus, and Antioch. The deacon Philip moved to Samaria, a territory that many Jews avoided, and was successful in forming a Christian community. Peter left as well, and performed healing miracles in Lydda and Joppa. Only a core group remained in Jerusalem, soon to be led by a man named James, Jesus' brother.

Paul of Tarsus

This is when a man named Paul makes his appearance. Originally known as Saul, Paul would play a pivotal role in the growth of the apostolic mission. Paul was born in the city

ABOVE: *"Saints Peter and Paul" is the work of Italian artist Carlo Crivelli (ca 1435–1493).*

OPPOSITE: *This rare 11th-century Byzantine fresco depicts the Pentecost, the moment when the Holy Spirit descended on the Apostles in the form of fiery tongues.*

CA 44 C.E.
King Agrippa I dies; Judea reverts back to a Roman province

CA 44 C.E.
Cuspius Fadus is appointed Roman procurator of Judea

CA 46 C.E.
Tiberius Alexander replaces Cuspius Fadus as Roman procurator of Judea

CA 47 C.E.
Greek historian Plutarch is born

صورت حلول الروح القدس على تلاميذه الاطهار يوم

of Tarsus in Cilicia (today's southern Turkey), and trained as a Pharisee. According to the Book of Acts, he was a pupil of the distinguished rabbi Gamaliel, who may be the same Gamaliel who intervened on the Apostles' behalf in front of the Sanhedrin. At that time, Saul was actively involved in the persecution of Jewish Christians. In his Letter to the Galatians, he confessed that because of his zeal in oppressing the apostolic movement, he was able to advance "beyond many among my people of the same age" (Galatians 1:14). This is borne out by his prominent presence at the execution of Stephen, despite his youth. The Book of Acts specifically states that "Saul approved of their killing him" (Acts 8:1).

In the wake of Stephen's death, Saul soon discovered that many early Christians had fled to Damascus, and he asked for permission to continue his pursuit. Damascus was located in Syria, beyond the jurisdiction of both the Roman prefect and the Jewish high priest, but Saul was determined to root them out and "bring them bound to Jerusalem" (Acts 9:2). Then, on his way north, a divine intervention took place. A light from heaven flashed around him. Saul fell to the ground and heard a voice saying, "Saul, why do you persecute me?" (Acts 9:4). This was the turning point; from this time forward, Saul—later called Paul—devoted himself wholeheartedly to advancing the apostolic mission. He even assumed the authority of an Apostle, though

> *That day a severe persecution began against the church in Jerusalem, and all except the apostles were scattered throughout the countryside of Judea and Samaria.*
>
> ACTS OF THE APOSTLES 8:1

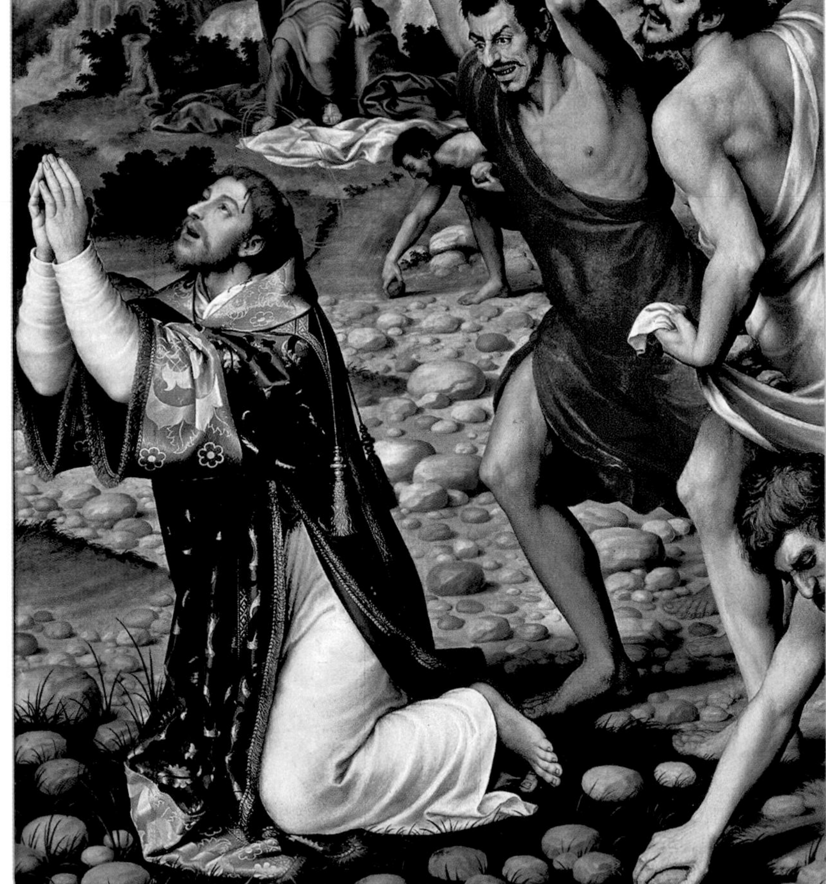

"The Martyrdom of Saint Stephen" was painted by Spanish artist Juan de Juanes. Stephen is traditionally considered the first martyr of Christianity.

CA 48 C.E.
Ventidius Cumanus replaces Tiberius Alexander as Roman procurator of Judea

CA 52 C.E.
Antonius Felix replaces Ventidius Cumanus as Roman procurator of Judea

CA 54 C.E.
Claudius dies and is succeeded by Nero, son of his wife, Agrippina

CA 57 C.E.
Paul writes his Letter to the Romans

"The Conversion of St. Paul" is the work of Italian artist Michelangelo Caravaggio (1571–1610). According to the New Testament, this event led Paul to become a follower of Jesus.

the original Apostles had all been handpicked by Jesus. Paul believed that since he was chosen by Jesus in heaven, his words carried the same power as the original 12.

Naturally, Paul's sudden conversion was received with much skepticism and suspicion. Many disciples believed he was a fifth columnist, with orders to infiltrate the movement so as to denounce the followers. This may explain why the relations between Paul and the Jerusalem group would be strained—with significant consequences for the growth of early Christianity, as we will see.

Together with a disciple named Barnabas, Paul began to define an apostolic mission of his own. He was struck by the way he and Barnabas were able to establish a Christian community in Antioch, capital of Roman Syria; in fact it was here that the term "Christians" (or *Christianos* in Greek) was coined to identify Christ's disciples (Acts 11:21). Together with Barnabas and a disciple named John Mark, Paul set out on what would become a journey in Asia Minor, today's Turkey.

This first campaign met with mixed results. Paul baptized the Roman consul, Sergius Paulus, in Cyprus, but met stiff opposition from Jewish communities in Antioch-in-Pisidia, Lystra, and Derbe. Along the way he made an astonishing discovery. While many Jewish communities were opposed to the message of Christ as the Messiah, many Gentiles were quite receptive.

This was not without precedent. Though most Apostles—like other observant Jews—

HISTORY AND POLITICS

The Appeal of Early Christianity

A fourth-century fresco depicts a beardless Jesus as a Roman orator, dressed in a toga.

Why were Gentiles so attracted to Jesus' message? How to explain the rapid growth of the Christian movement despite the lack of a cohesive message, or the presence (at least before 66 C.E.) of a foundational text? The simplest answer is that Christian spirituality was populist and egalitarian. It offered redemption to everyone, regardless of social class or race. This may also be the reason why Christianity was often shunned by elites, including the Roman aristocracy. For Gentiles who were attracted to the monotheism of Judaism, Christianity offered a faith in one God devoid of the more onerous precepts of Covenant Law, including the dietary laws and circumcision. Moreover, the stories of Jesus' healings and exorcisms resonated in a world where mystery and magic were ingredients of everyday life. Paul's argument that Jesus was the "Son of God" (Acts 9:20) was eminently plausible for Gentiles raised in the polytheistic Roman world.

CA 58 C.E.
Putative date of Paul's arrest in Jerusalem and transfer to Caesarea

CA 58 C.E.
Roman poet Juvenal is born

CA 58 C.E.
Emperor Ming-Ti introduces Buddhism to China

CA 60 C.E.
Porcius Festus replaces Antonius Felix as Roman procurator of Judea

SCRIPTURE AND FAITH

The Apologiae

A painting by Giuseppe Franchi (1565–1628) is believed to depict Ignatius of Antioch.

A number of Christian intellectuals sought to address Roman prejudice against Christianity, arguing that the Christian faith was a law-abiding religion founded on love, compassion, and devotion. Quadratus of Athens (writing around 125 C.E.); Justin Martyr (ca 100–165); and Tertullian of Carthage (ca 160–220) all wrote such *apologiae* in defense of their faith, though many of these works have been lost. They emphasized Christian charity, such as caring for the sick and the poor, or burying the dead, as evidence that Christian values strengthened Roman society. Some even tried to harmonize Christology with Greek philosophy. The theologian Origen (ca 185–254), for example, compared the creative word of God (*Logos*) with the quintessential Platonic "reason" that permeates all living things, just as the Jewish philosopher Philo had argued before him. The works had little impact. Bishop Ignatius, a prominent leader of the early Church, suffered a martyr's death in the arena around 108 C.E.

refrained from contact with Gentiles because they did not honor the Jewish purity laws, Peter had received a vision in Joppa that suggested that the prohibition against the conversion of Gentiles was lifted. Shortly thereafter, Peter baptized a centurion named Cornelius and his family (Acts 10:28). There was a difference, however. Peter and the Jerusalem community accepted those Gentiles who were known as "God-fearing" followers, men and women who embraced *both* Judaism and Christian baptism. Paul, on the other hand, found that while many Gentiles were attracted to Christian spirituality, they weren't interested in adopting Jewish customs as well. Certain precepts of the Torah, such as the need to be circumcised and observe the kosher dietary laws, were a strong deterrent for many Gentiles. This raised a question: Should a convert to Christ also be expected to become Jewish?

For the Jerusalem Apostles, the answer was affirmative. They had traveled with Jesus and had seen firsthand how Jesus had shunned most Gentile towns. For them, faith was inseparable from Jesus' own example as a Jewish rabbi. But Paul disagreed. He believed that the Jewish rite of circumcision—and indeed, much of the Torah—had been replaced by baptism and faith in Christ. "Real circumcision is a matter of the heart," he wrote in his Letter to the Romans; "it is spiritual, not literal" (Romans 2:29). By so preaching, Paul consciously released the early Christian movement from its Jewish roots, knowing that the Gentile population of Asia Minor was far more numerous than its Jewish population.

Paul's Second Journey

Paul embarked on a second and even more ambitious mission. While Barnabas went

back to Cyprus, Paul left for Asia Minor to visit the Christian communities he had founded on his first visit, accompanied by a disciple known as Silas (or "Silvanus"). In Lystra, Paul was joined by a follower named Timothy, who shortly thereafter became Paul's assistant, and eventually his confidant and protégé. A vision prompted Paul to leave Asia Minor and travel across the Aegean Sea to Greece. Here, the narrative in the Book of Acts changes from the third to the first person ("we immediately tried to cross over to Macedonia"), which, some authors believe, suggests that Luke, the presumed author of Luke's Gospel as well as the Book of Acts, had now joined Paul's entourage (Acts 16:10).

The group was successful in establishing Christian communities in Philippi and Thessalonica, but in the cosmopolitan city of Athens Paul encountered a mostly skeptical audience. He preached on a hill known as the Areopagus, which still exists today, and told his listeners that he had found an altar in the city dedicated "to an unknown God." "What therefore you worship as unknown," Paul said, "this I proclaim to you now" (Acts 17:23). Paul traveled to Corinth, then a

CA 60 C.E.
Putative date of Paul's embarkation for Rome

CA 62 C.E.
Heron of Alexandria designs a steam engine, water clock, water fountain, and odometer

CA 62 C.E.
Lucceius Albinus replaces Porcius Festus as Roman procurator of Judea

CA 62 C.E.
James, head of the Jerusalem Church, is killed on orders of High Priest Ananus

rapidly growing urban center, where he lived for a while and nurtured an active Christian community among Gentiles, as his Letters to the Corinthians (I and II) attest.

Sometime after 54 C.E., Paul left on a third missionary journey, this time using the city of Ephesus as his base. His experience of these lengthy travels, during which he often had to cope with rising tensions in communities like Corinth, was poured into his Letter to the Romans, which summarizes his view of the Christian faith. The ideas contained in this letter, one of seven epistles that are unquestionably attributed to Paul, would become the bedrock of the future Catholic Church. The letter postulates that faith in Christ had superseded Jewish Law; that each Christian community was part of the "body of Christ" and should therefore be governed by love, rather than internal strife; and that faith in the Christian God held the promise of eternal life. "Just as Christ was raised from the dead by the glory of the Father," Paul wrote, "so we too might walk in newness of life" (Romans 6:4).

New Developments in Judea

While Paul traveled through the eastern Mediterranean, important changes were taking place in Judea. For a brief period, between 41 and 44 C.E., Judea was ruled by a grandson of King Herod named Herod Agrippa, a friend of Emperor Gaius, better known as Caligula (r. 37–41 C.E.). According to the Book of Acts, King Agrippa ordered one of the Jerusalem Apostles, James the son of Zebedee, to be put to death in order to curry favor with the local population (Acts 12:1-3). Caligula's successor, Emperor Claudius, was more favorably disposed to Judaism, but was

OPPOSITE: A 15th-century fresco of the Italian School features St. Peter and St. Paul.

The PANTHEON IN ROME, one of the best preserved Roman monuments in the world, was built by Emperor Hadrian in 126 C.E. as a temple to all the gods of Rome.

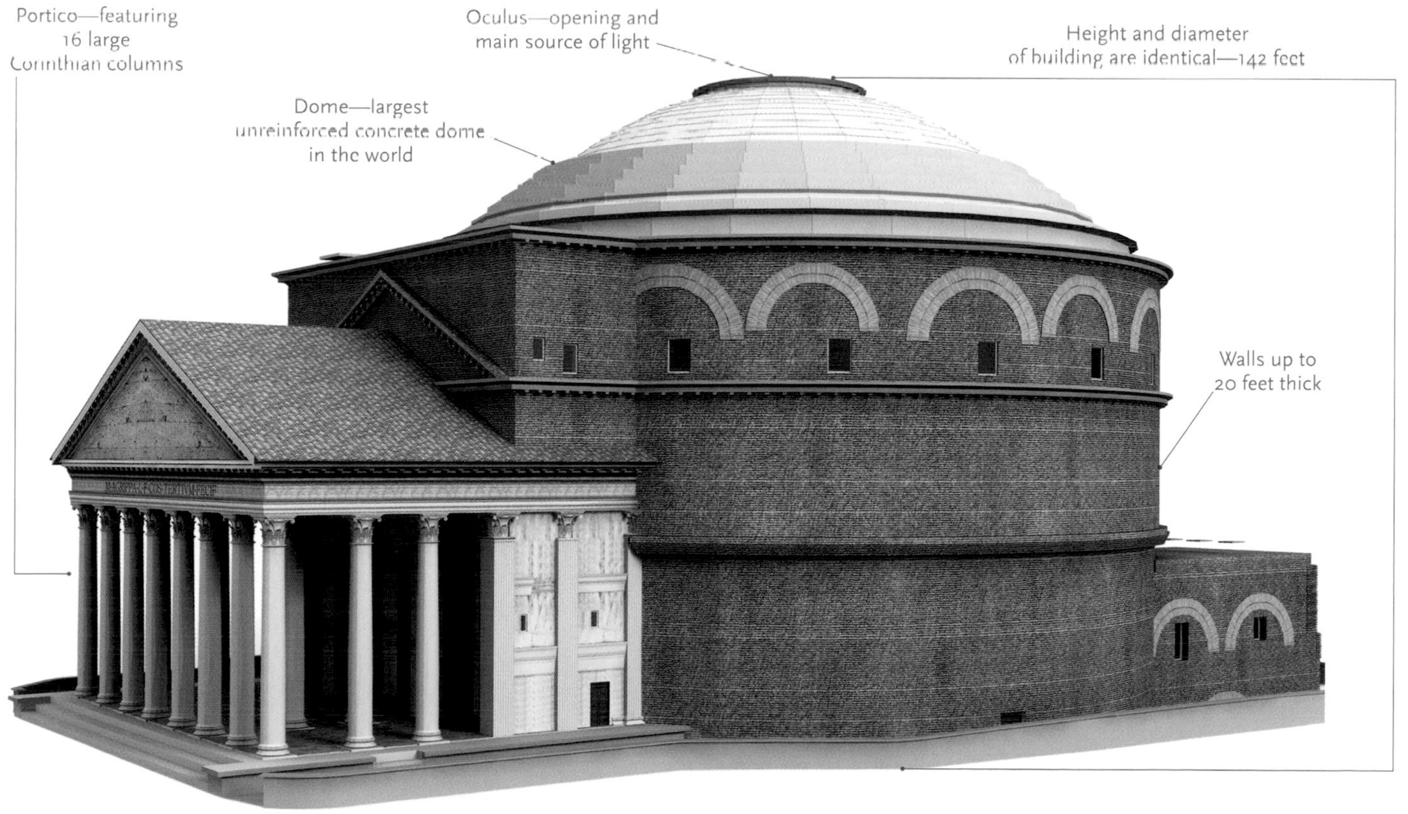

64 C.E. Nero blames the Christians in Rome for a fire that ravaged the city

CA 64 C.E. Traditional date for the deaths of Peter and Paul in Rome

64 C.E. Gessius Florus replaces Lucceius Albinus as Roman procurator of Judea

65 C.E. Seneca is ordered by Nero to commit suicide

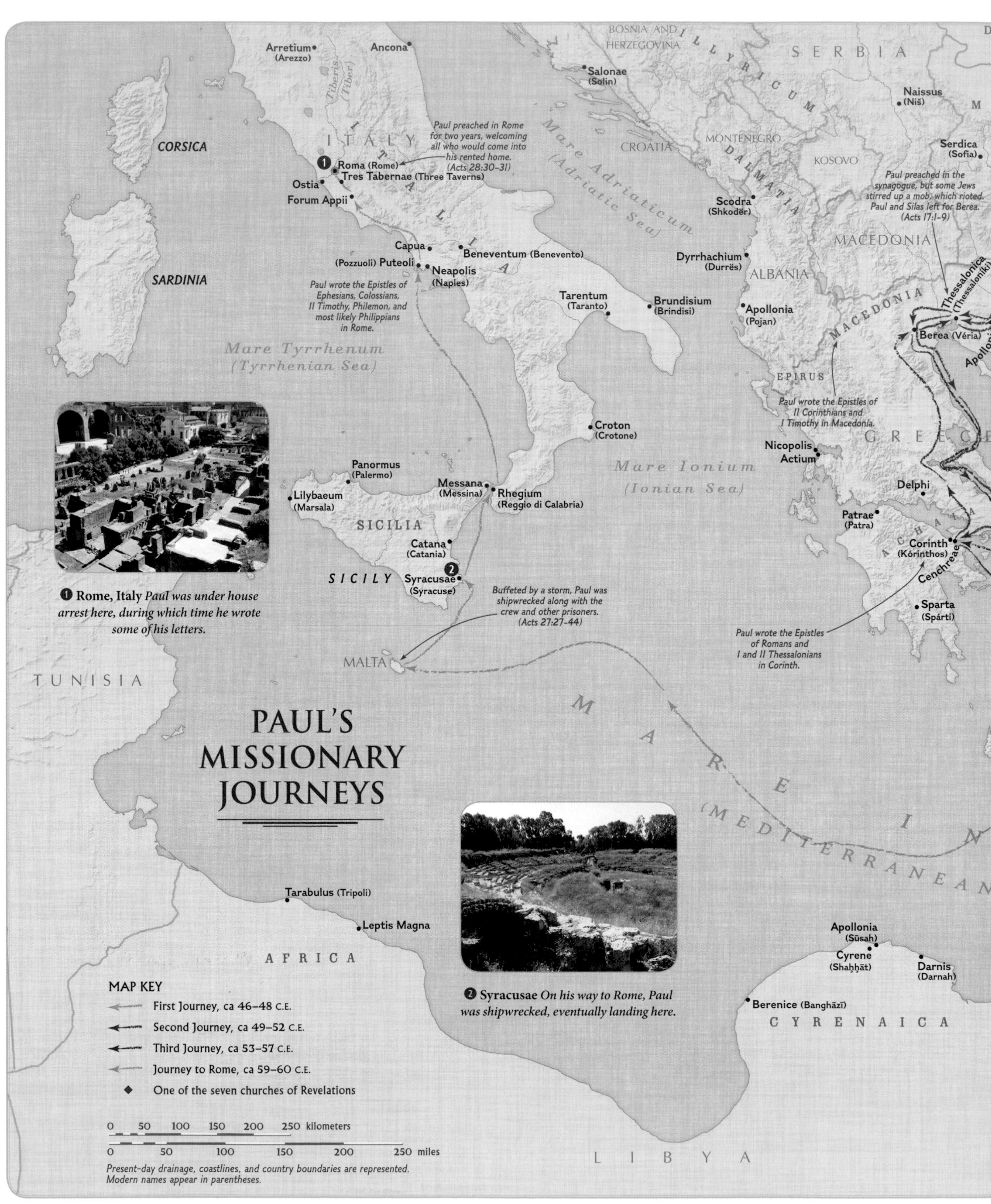

PAUL'S MISSIONARY JOURNEYS
Arretium (Arezzo)
Ancona
Tiberis (Tiber)
Salonae (Solin)
BOSNIA AND HERZEGOVINA
ILLYRICUM
SERBIA
Naissus (Niš)
CORSICA
ITALY
ITALIA
Paul preached in Rome for two years, welcoming all who would come into his rented home. (Acts 28:30-31)
Roma (Rome)
Tres Tabernae (Three Taverns)
Ostia
Forum Appii
Mare Adriaticum (Adriatic Sea)
CROATIA
MONTENEGRO
DALMATIA
KOSOVO
Serdica (Sofia)
Scodra (Shkodër)
Paul preached in the synagogue, but some Jews stirred up a mob, which rioted. Paul and Silas left for Berea. (Acts 17:1-9)
MACEDONIA
SARDINIA
Capua
Beneventum (Benevento)
(Pozzuoli) Puteoli
Neapolis (Naples)
Dyrrhachium (Durrës)
ALBANIA
Paul wrote the Epistles of Ephesians, Colossians, II Timothy, Philemon, and most likely Philippians in Rome.
Tarentum (Taranto)
Brundisium (Brindisi)
Apollonia (Pojan)
Thessalonica (Thessaloniki)
Berea (Véria)
Apollonia
Mare Tyrrhenum (Tyrrhenian Sea)
EPIRUS
Paul wrote the Epistles of II Corinthians and I Timothy in Macedonia.
Croton (Crotone)
GREECE
Nicopolis
Actium
Mare Ionium (Ionian Sea)
Panormus (Palermo)
Messana (Messina)
Rhegium (Reggio di Calabria)
Lilybaeum (Marsala)
Delphi
SICILIA
Patrae (Patra)
ACHAIA
Corinth (Kórinthos)
Cenchreae
Catana (Catania)
SICILY
Syracusae (Syracuse)
Buffeted by a storm, Paul was shipwrecked along with the crew and other prisoners. (Acts 27:27-44)
Sparta (Spárti)
Paul wrote the Epistles of Romans and I and II Thessalonians in Corinth.
MALTA
TUNISIA
MARE INTERNUM (MEDITERRANEAN SEA)
Tarabulus (Tripoli)
Leptis Magna
AFRICA
Apollonia (Sūsah)
Cyrene (Shaḩḩāt)
Darnis (Darnah)
Berenice (Banghāzī)
CYRENAICA
LIBYA
MAP KEY
First Journey, ca 46–48 C.E.
Second Journey, ca 49–52 C.E.
Third Journey, ca 53–57 C.E.
Journey to Rome, ca 59–60 C.E.
One of the seven churches of Revelations
0 50 100 150 200 250 kilometers
0 50 100 150 200 250 miles
Present-day drainage, coastlines, and country boundaries are represented. Modern names appear in parentheses.

❶ **Rome, Italy** *Paul was under house arrest here, during which time he wrote some of his letters.*

❷ **Syracusae** *On his way to Rome, Paul was shipwrecked, eventually landing here.*

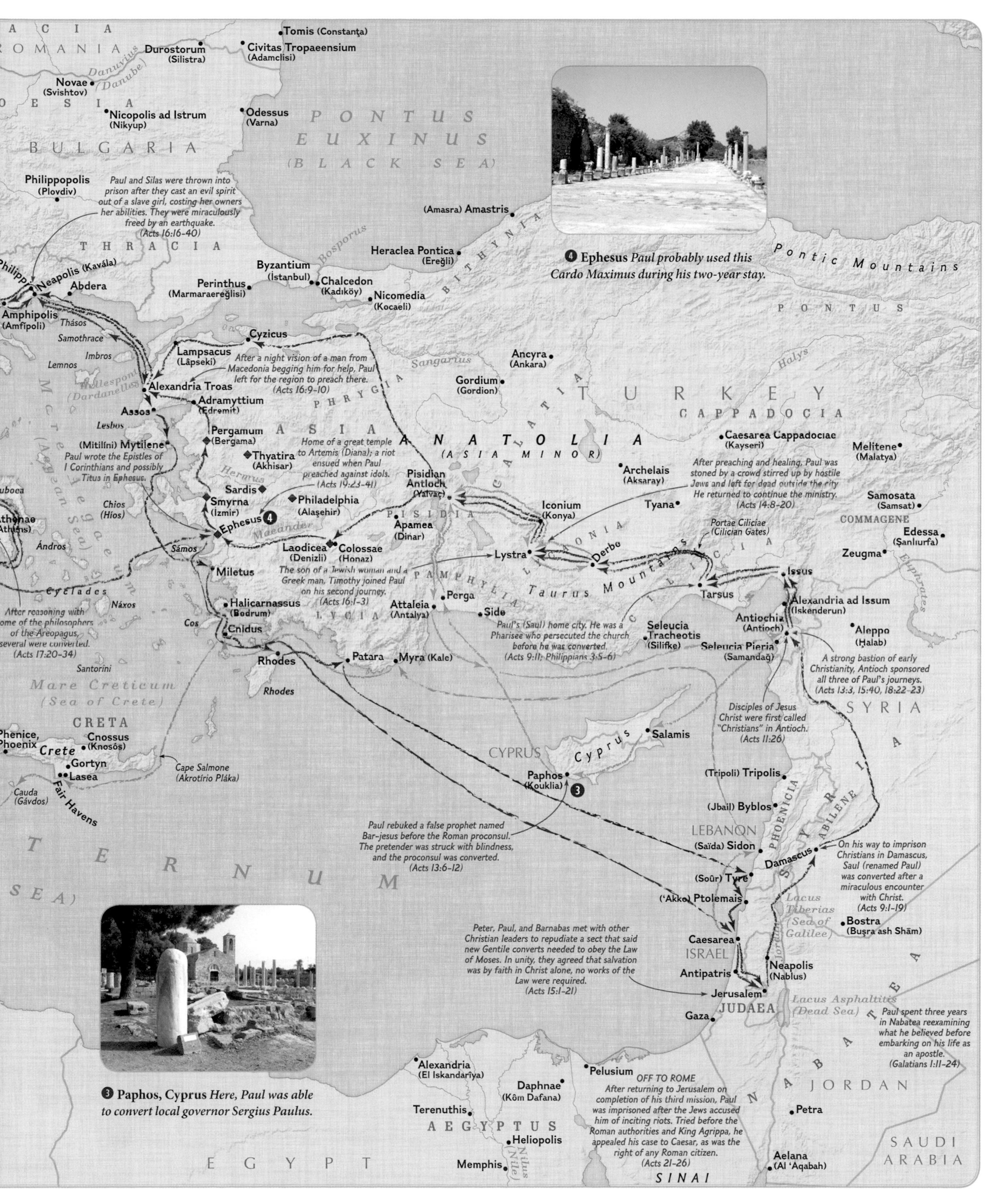

ACIA
ROMANIA
Durostorum (Silistra)
Tomis (Constanța)
Civitas Tropaeensium (Adamclisi)
Danuvius (Danube)
Novae (Svishtov)
OESIA
Nicopolis ad Istrum (Nikyup)
Odessus (Varna)
PONTUS EUXINUS (BLACK SEA)
BULGARIA
Philippopolis (Plovdiv)
Paul and Silas were thrown into prison after they cast an evil spirit out of a slave girl, costing her owners her abilities. They were miraculously freed by an earthquake. (Acts 16:16-40)
THRACIA
Bosporus
(Amasra) Amastris
BITHYNIA
Heraclea Pontica (Ereğli)
Byzantium (İstanbul)
Chalcedon (Kadıköy)
Nicomedia (Kocaeli)
Perinthus (Marmaraereğlisi)
Philippi
Neapolis (Kavála)
Abdera
Amphipolis (Amfípoli)
Thásos
Samothrace
Imbros
Lemnos
Cyzicus
Lampsacus (Lâpseki)
After a night vision of a man from Macedonia begging him for help, Paul left for the region to preach there. (Acts 16:9-10)
Hellespont (Dardanelles)
Alexandria Troas
Adramyttium (Edremit)
Assos
Lesbos
PHRYGIA
Sangarius
Ancyra (Ankara)
Gordium (Gordion)
GALATIA
Halys
TURKEY
CAPPADOCIA
Pontic Mountains
PONTUS
Pergamum (Bergama)
ASIA
(Mitilíni) Mytilene
Paul wrote the Epistles of I Corinthians and possibly Titus in Ephesus.
Thyatira (Akhisar)
Home of a great temple to Artemis (Diana); a riot ensued when Paul preached against idols. (Acts 19:23-41)
ANATOLIA (ASIA MINOR)
Caesarea Cappadociae (Kayseri)
Melitene (Malatya)
Archelais (Aksaray)
After preaching and healing, Paul was stoned by a crowd stirred up by hostile Jews and left for dead outside the city. He returned to continue the ministry. (Acts 14:8-20)
Hermus
Sardis
Pisidian Antioch (Yalvaç)
Euboea
Smyrna (İzmir)
Philadelphia (Alaşehir)
Chios (Hios)
PISIDIA
Iconium (Konya)
Tyana
Samosata (Samsat)
COMMAGENE
Athenae (Athens)
Ephesus
Maeander
Apamea (Dinar)
Portae Ciliciae (Cilician Gates)
Edessa (Şanlıurfa)
Mare Aegeum (Aegean Sea)
Ándros
Sámos
Laodicea (Denizli)
Colossae (Honaz)
LYCAONIA
Lystra
Derbe
CILICIA
Zeugma
Euphrates
Miletus
The son of a Jewish woman and a Greek man, Timothy joined Paul on his second journey. (Acts 16:1-3)
Taurus Mountains
Issus
Cyclades
PAMPHYLIA
Tarsus
Náxos
After reasoning with some of the philosophers of the Areopagus, several were converted. (Acts 17:20-34)
Halicarnassus (Bodrum)
Attaleia (Antalya)
Perga
Side
Alexandria ad Issum (Iskenderun)
Cos
LYCIA
Paul's (Saul) home city. He was a Pharisee who persecuted the church before he was converted. (Acts 9:11; Philippians 3:5-6)
Seleucia Tracheotis (Silifke)
Antiochia (Antioch)
Aleppo (Halab)
Cnidus
Seleucia Pieria (Samandağ)
Rhodes
Patara
Myra (Kale)
A strong bastion of early Christianity, Antioch sponsored all three of Paul's journeys. (Acts 13:3, 15:40, 18:22-23)
Santorini
Rhodes
Mare Creticum (Sea of Crete)
SYRIA
Disciples of Jesus Christ were first called "Christians" in Antioch. (Acts 11:26)
CRETA
Phenice, Phoenix
Crete
Cnossus (Knosós)
Gortyn
Lasea
Fair Havens
Cauda (Gávdos)
Cape Salmone (Akrotírio Pláka)
Salamis
CYPRUS
Cyprus
Paphos (Kouklia)
(Tripoli) Tripolis
(Jbaïl) Byblos
PHOENICIA
ABILENE
LEBANON
Paul rebuked a false prophet named Bar-jesus before the Roman proconsul. The pretender was struck with blindness, and the proconsul was converted. (Acts 13:6-12)
(Saïda) Sidon
Damascus
On his way to imprison Christians in Damascus, Saul (renamed Paul) was converted after a miraculous encounter with Christ. (Acts 9:1-19)
MARE INTERNUM (SEA)
(Soûr) Tyre
('Akko) Ptolemais
Lacus Tiberias (Sea of Galilee)
Jordan
Bostra (Buşra ash Shām)
Peter, Paul, and Barnabas met with other Christian leaders to repudiate a sect that said new Gentile converts needed to obey the Law of Moses. In unity, they agreed that salvation was by faith in Christ alone, no works of the Law were required. (Acts 15:1-21)
Caesarea
ISRAEL
Neapolis (Nablus)
Antipatris
Jerusalem
JUDAEA
Lacus Asphaltitis (Dead Sea)
Gaza
Paul spent three years in Nabatea reexamining what he believed before embarking on his life as an apostle. (Galatians 1:11-24)
NABATAEA
Alexandria (El Iskandarîya)
Pelusium
OFF TO ROME
After returning to Jerusalem on completion of his third mission, Paul was imprisoned after the Jews accused him of inciting riots. Tried before the Roman authorities and King Agrippa, he appealed his case to Caesar, as was the right of any Roman citizen. (Acts 21-26)
Daphnae (Kôm Dafana)
JORDAN
Terenuthis
AEGYPTUS
Petra
Heliopolis
Nilus (Nile)
EGYPT
Memphis
SINAI
Aelana (Al 'Aqabah)
SAUDI ARABIA

❹ **Ephesus** *Paul probably used this Cardo Maximus during his two-year stay.*

❸ **Paphos, Cyprus** *Here, Paul was able to convert local governor Sergius Paulus.*

nevertheless persuaded to evict all Jews from Rome in 49 C.E., because, as Roman historian Suetonius wrote, "the Jews were constantly causing *disturbances* at the instigation of *Christ" (Chrestus)*.

Herod Agrippa died suddenly in 44 C.E. Claudius had no choice but to turn Judea back into a Roman province, to be ruled by a Roman procurator, the first of whom was Cuspius Fadus (r. 44–46 C.E.). These Roman officials failed to stabilize the restless Jewish province; in the span of 16 years, Judea would be ruled by no less than five different procurators, most of whom were either inept or corrupt. To complicate matters, Agrippa's son, Agrippa II (r. 48–70 C.E.), was allowed to take control of smaller territories around Judea.

It was during this volatile period that Paul returned to Jerusalem to meet with James and the apostolic community in Jerusalem. But word of his active proselytizing in Asia Minor and Greece had preceded him. Shortly after his arrival, he was denounced for teaching "all the Jews living among the Gentiles to forsake Moses" (Acts 21:21). Falsely accused of taking a Gentile past the *soreg*, the sacred enclosure surrounding the Temple precinct, Paul was arrested and imprisoned in the Antonia Fortress of Jerusalem. In 60 C.E., after the arrival of a new procurator called Porcius Festus, Paul successfully appealed to the imperial authorities for a proper Roman trial, given that he was a Roman citizen. Festus, who had little grasp of the Jewish laws, referred the matter to Agrippa II. The Jewish King listened to what Paul had to say, then told Festus, "This man could have been set free if he had not appealed to the emperor" (Acts 26:28–29). Paul was placed on a vessel bound for Rome with other prisoners, though the journey was delayed when his ship foundered during a heavy storm. Upon his arrival in Rome, Paul was placed under house arrest for two years, which he spent writing letters to the faithful and receiving visitors.

The high-priestly Annas family had followed these developments with interest. When Festus suddenly died in 62 C.E.,

OPPOSITE: *"Saint Paul Writing" was painted by Dutch artist Jacob Adriaenszoon Backer (1608–1651).*

SCRIPTURE AND FAITH

Paul's Epistles

Our information about Paul is derived from two sources: the Book of Acts of the Apostles, and the Epistles written by Paul himself, or written on his behalf (or under his name) by his disciples. These Epistles are actually the oldest Christian documents still in existence today. The Epistles to the Thessalonians are commonly believed to be among Paul's first letters, whereas those to the Romans and (if authentic) Colossians should be dated near the end of Paul's ministry, between 57 and 58 C.E. Much about Paul's journeys is uncertain, but a discovery in the early 20th century allows us to pinpoint his stay in Corinth. According to the Book of Acts, Paul was accused by the Jews of Corinth of "persuading people to worship God in ways that are contrary to the law." The presiding judge, a man named Gallio, who was "proconsul of Achaia," dismissed the charge, given that it was not pertinent to Roman law (Acts 18:12-17). While excavating in the Temple of Apollo in Delphi, archaeologists discovered an inscription that refers to a governor named "L. Iunius Gallio" from 52 C.E. Some two years later, Paul embarked on a third missionary journey, this time using Ephesus as his base. During this journey, Paul wrote his famous Letter to the Romans, in which he conveys the greetings of several of his followers, including a man named "Erastus, the city treasurer" (Romans 16:23). In 1929, excavators found a first-century limestone fragment in Corinth inscribed with the words "Erastus, in return for his aedileship, laid [this pavement] at his own expense."

This limestone fragment from Corinth may refer to "Erastus, the city treasurer" described in Paul's Letter to the Romans.

66 C.E.
The Jewish Rebellion in Palestine against the Romans breaks out

CA 66–70 C.E.
Mark writes his Gospel, the oldest of the four canonical Gospels

67 C.E.
General Vespasian arrives in Galilee to suppress the Jewish Rebellion

68 C.E.
Emperor Nero commits suicide and is succeeded by Galba

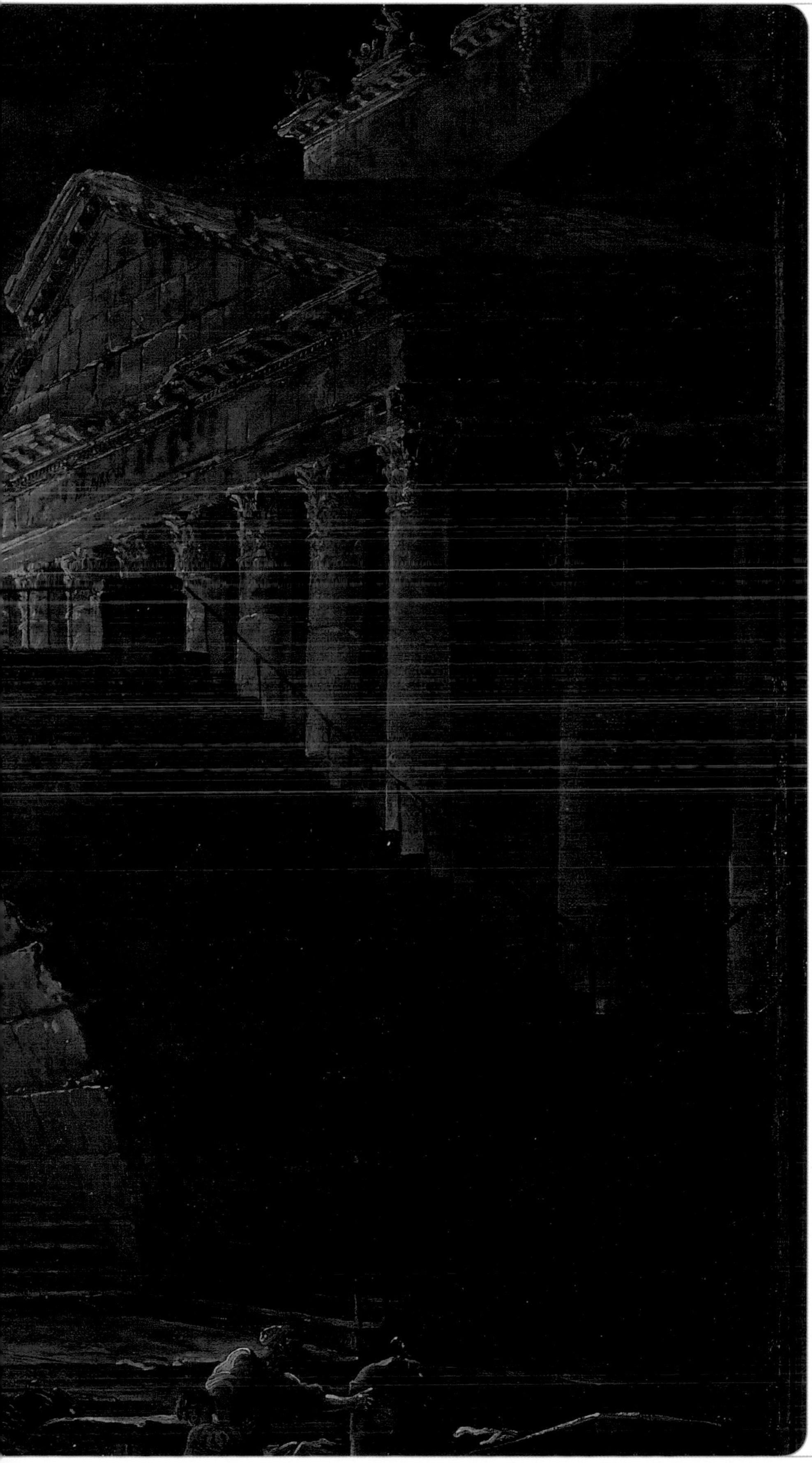

Mad with rage, pretending not to hear the orders of their general, the soldiers rushed on, hurling their torches into the sanctuary.

JOSEPHUS, *THE JEWISH WAR*

the new high priest Ananus, son of Annas, chose the moment to destroy the apostolic mission in Jerusalem once and for all. He arranged for the indictment of James, the brother of Jesus, in front of the Sanhedrin. This time, there were no Pharisees willing to spring to the Apostles' defense. James was thrown off the Temple parapet and stoned to death.

Two years later, in 64 C.E., a great fire devastated Rome. Many Romans believed that Emperor Nero (r. 54–68 C.E.) had set the fire in order to build a new planned city. Aware of these rumors, Nero passed the blame on to Rome's Christian communities. Scores of Christians were arrested and executed. Tradition suggests that Peter was swept up in the persecution. How Peter would have made his way from Judea to Rome is not clear. The Book of Acts only describes Peter's missionary work in Roman Palestine, although Paul's Letter to the Galatians, written around 53 C.E., describes an encounter with Peter in Antioch (Galatians 2:11). According to the apocryphal Acts of Peter, when Peter was condemned to be crucified he insisted on being crucified upside down. The prominent Christian theologian Tertullian of Carthage (ca 160–220 C.E.) claims that Paul was also

"The Fire of Rome, 18 July 64 A.D." was painted by French artist Hubert Robert (1733–1808). The fire, which spread rapidly, destroyed nearly two-thirds of the city.

put to death at this time. The other Apostles are believed to have died martyrs' deaths in Palestine and Asia Minor, with the exception of John, son of Zebedee.

Other Christian Movements

Despite Roman opposition, the Book of Acts depicts the early Christian Church as a rapidly growing movement throughout the Empire. Modern research by scholars such as Bart Ehrman and Elaine Pagels, however, has shown that there were actually multiple Christian movements circulating around the Mediterranean, many of which disagreed with Paul's interpretation of Jesus and his teachings. Paul was very much aware of this opposition. According to the first Letter to Timothy (ostensibly sent by Paul to his assistant, but probably written much later), Paul told Timothy to remain in Ephesus to prevent "heresy" from affecting the church there (I Timothy 3-5).

The fragmented nature of Christianity's growth was caused by several factors. First, there was no authoritative scripture that explained the tenets of Jesus' Kingdom of God doctrine. Instead, many of the budding Christian communities had to rely on oral traditions about Jesus, which often differed in scope and emphasis. This is why each of the Gospels features passages that don't appear in the others.

Second, as we saw, Paul and the Apostles were not the only ones who were propagating the new faith. There were other individuals, fired by faith in Christ, who introduced their families and friends to Jesus throughout the Empire without apostolic guidance. Many of these were Jewish Christians. The Christian community in Rome, for example, existed well before Paul's arrival on the scene.

Biblical scholarship has offered the confusing term "Gnosticism" for many of these other Christian movements. Some of these sects adhered to the belief that deep

OPPOSITE: This fine Byzantine ivory plaque depicts the Evangelist Matthew, one of the four Evangelists whose Gospels were included in the New Testament canon.

SCRIPTURE AND FAITH

The New Testament Emerges

As Christianity grew, a great number of Christian texts began to circulate, often claiming Apostolic authority. Some of these texts rejected Paul's resurrection theology and instead emphasized the individual revelation of the divine within oneself. Prompted by this confusing proliferation, several Christian theologians sought to develop an official "canon" of Christian scripture. Justin Martyr (ca 100–165 C.E.) had already recognized the preeminence of the Gospels of Matthew, Mark, and Luke. Bishop Irenaeus of Lyons (140–ca 203 C.E.) added the Gospel of John. Irenaeus also specifically included the letters of Paul in his collection, believing that these Epistles were also divinely inspired. The theologian Tertullian accepted Irenaeus's suggestion and coined the phrase "New Testament," for in his view Christian scripture had replaced or "fulfilled" the "Old" Testament enshrined in the Hebrew Bible. Other popular texts, such as the Gospel of Thomas, the Gospel of Peter, the Gospel of Mary, and the Gospel of Philip, were emphatically excluded as "heretical" writings. Eventually, the Book of the Acts of the Apostles, the Epistles of Peter, and the "Apocalypse of John," known today as Revelation, were added. Still, many disputes ensued: Orthodox Christianity, for example, would not recognize this canon until 692. A page from a second-century text known as the Muratorian fragment, discovered in 1740, is the oldest known list of the New Testament canon.

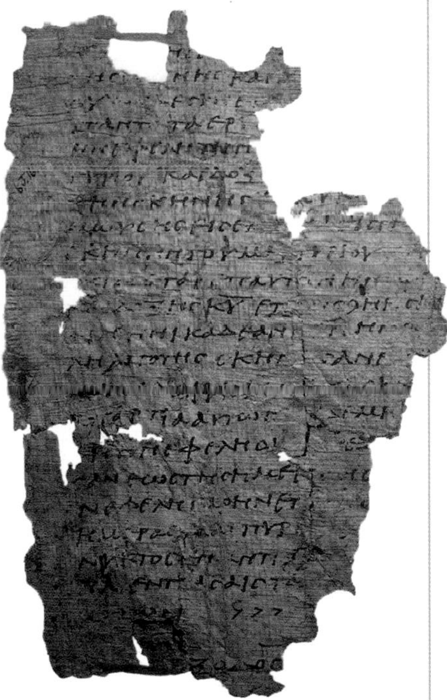

The oldest known fragment of the Book of Revelation is the so-called Oxyrhynchus scroll.

CA 69 C.E.
Rome is ruled by three emperors in succession: Galba, Otho, and Vitellius

CA 69 C.E.
Vespasian is proclaimed Roman Emperor

CA 70 C.E.
Titus captures Jerusalem and destroys the Second Temple

CA 73 C.E.
Besieged by the Roman Tenth Legion, Jewish zealots on Masada commit mass suicide

meditation and immersion in the divine would ultimately lead to a secret knowledge (or *gnosis* in Greek) of God. This idea was popular, for it agreed with the premise in Greek philosophy that each human being carried inside himself a spark of the divine. For the Gnostic Christians, this also explained the reason why Jesus often spoke in parables. True knowledge of God was a precious and potentially dangerous secret, which could only be revealed to those who proved themselves worthy of that knowledge.

Other Christians, such as the Docetists, believed that Jesus' physical presence had been an illusion and that, by contrast, he had always been a divine being. Yet another sect, led by a wealthy individual named Marcion (ca 85–160 C.E.), son of the Bishop of Sinope (today's Sinop in Turkey), believed that Christianity should be fully uncoupled from Hebrew Scripture and the Jewish Law. By contrast, the Ebionites—a group that may have originated in the Jerusalem community—held true to their Jewish roots, and believed that Jesus had always been a mere mortal.

Many aspects of nontraditional Christianity would have appealed to modern Christians. The discovery of 13 bound books near the Egyptian city of Nag Hammadi in

The painting titled "The Destruction of the Temple of Jerusalem" is the work of Italian classicist artist Francesco Hayez (1791–1881).

CA 73 C.E
Yohanan ben Zakkai establishes a new Jewish religious academy in Yabneh

CA 75 C.E.
Putative date of the book *The Jewish War* by Josephus

CA 75 C.E.
Vespasian begins construction of the Colosseum

CA 75–85 C.E.
Putative date of the Gospel of Matthew

1945 opened a fascinating window on the world of these Christians. Some Gnostic sects even claimed their apostolic authority from Mary Magdalene, based on the so-called Gospel of Mary, discovered in Cairo in 1896. Furthermore, these nontraditional Christians stressed the validity of individual revelation: of becoming, in a sense, an apostle in one's own right, anticipating Protestantism by some 1,500 years. These Christians believed that what Jesus had shown was a deeply intimate way for any individual to communicate with God, without intervention by priesthood. Some scholars have argued that these ideas threatened the hierarchical model of authority, delegated via bishops and presbyters, that the traditional or "catholic" (literally "universal") church was trying to build.

The Aftermath of the Jewish War

In 66 C.E., the long-dormant tensions between Jews and their Roman overlords in Judea finally erupted in an all-out war of rebellion. After vacillating for several months, Nero finally dispatched an expeditionary force to Judea, led by General Vespasian and his son Titus. Midway in the campaign, Vespasian returned to Rome to be proclaimed Emperor, leaving Titus to prosecute the war with typical Roman ruthlessness. In 70 C.E., Titus captured Jerusalem following a brutal and protracted siege. Herod's Second Temple complex, completed only a decade earlier, was destroyed. The priestly apparatus, including the Sadducees, faded away and ceased to exist. With them died the rites of Temple worship and animal sacrifice, a key feature of Judaism since the earliest days of Israel.

This sestertius (a Roman coin) with the legend "Judea Capta" ("Judea Captured") was struck after the defeat of the Jewish Rebellion in 70 C.E.

ABOVE: *"The Triumph of Faith, or Christian Martyrs in the Time of Nero" was painted by French artist Eugene Romain Thirion (1839–1910).*

CA 79 C.E.
Titus succeeds his father, Vespasian, as Emperor

CA 79 C.E.
Pompeii and Herculaneum are destroyed by the eruption of Vesuvius

CA 80–90 C.E.
Putative date of the Gospel of Luke

CA 81 C.E.
Titus dies, is succeeded by his brother Domitian

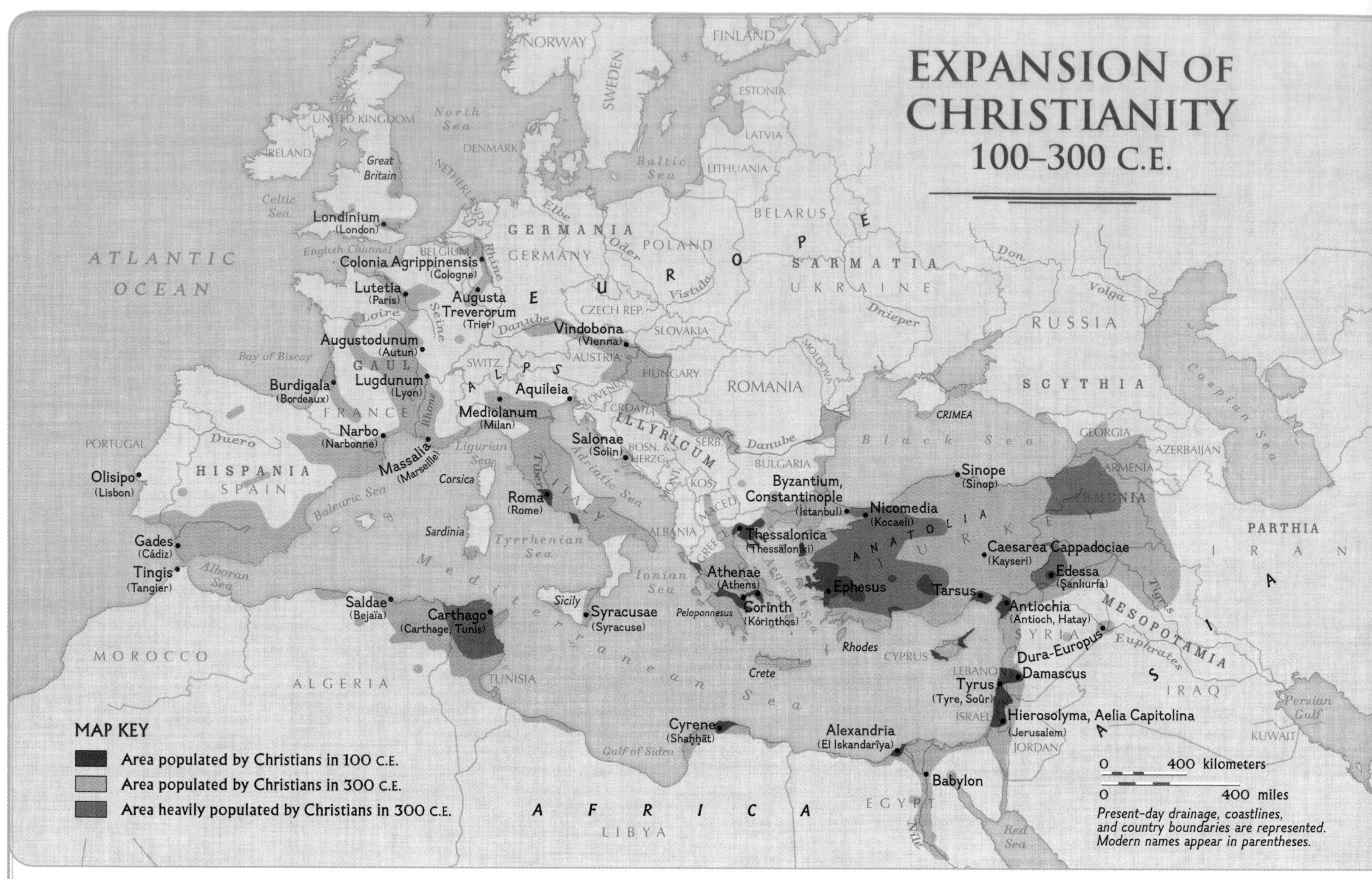

OPPOSITE: A detail of the sixth-century Madaba mosaic map shows a schematic representation of Jerusalem during the Byzantine period.

But the Jewish faith survived. A group of rabbinical sages led by Yohanan ben Zakkai (ca 30–90 C.E.) developed a new form of Jewish spirituality, focused on scriptural commentary and synagogue worship. Several scholars have suggested that this group included many Pharisees, who for more than a century had compiled a corpus of debates, known as the Oral Law, on the subject of how to apply the Torah precepts to everyday life. In doing so, they had unwittingly prepared themselves for a time when the Temple would no longer exist, aided by the experience of Diaspora Jews, who had long since built a community life around the synagogue rather than the Temple in Jerusalem.

The Jewish War was equally traumatic for early Christian communities, many of which had continued to observe the Jewish Law while professing loyalty to the Roman state. It is therefore not surprising that the first attempt to collect the sayings of Jesus into a theological treatise—a *Gospel*—was undertaken in this period, particularly in Rome, where Jewish Christians must have been under grave suspicion while Roman forces were fighting the Jewish rebels in Judea. According to most scholars, it was Mark who wrote the first canonical Gospel in 66 C.E., while living in Rome. It is also believed that both Matthew and Luke then used Mark's Gospel as a major source. Matthew arguably composed his Gospel in Antioch between

CA 85–90 C.E.
Putative date of the Book of Acts of the Apostles

CA 85–100 C.E.
Putative date of the Gospel of John

CA 95 C.E.
Putative date of the book *Antiquities of the Jews* by Josephus

96 C.E.
Domitian is assassinated and succeeded by Nerva

75 and 85 C.E., whereas Luke may have written his between 80 and 90 C.E., although the exact dating continues to be a matter of debate, and the location of Luke is uncertain. The Gospel of John is usually believed to be the youngest Gospel, probably written near the end of the first century C.E.

Roman Persecution

Scholars do not agree, however, on the extent to which the Roman prohibition of Christianity was enforced between the first and second centuries. Bishop Eusebius of Caesarea (263–339 C.E.), for example, claimed that Emperor Domitian (r. 81–96 C.E.) launched a severe persecution of both Jews and Christians, though this is not reflected in Roman documents of the period. There were doubtless episodes of violent conflict, often instigated by local communities who harbored suspicions about Christian worship and its practice of eating "Christ's body" and drinking "Christ's blood." Modern research suggests that some of this hostility was the result of tensions between Jewish and Christian groups themselves.

At the same time, the negative attitude toward Christians stemmed to some extent from the fact that Christian values and worship were very different from pagan ritual. The Christian emphasis on love (*agapè* in Greek, meaning charitable love), regardless of class boundaries, was often ridiculed in a society where classes were rigorously separated and love in a religious context was often associated with Dionysian rites. Based on Jesus' sayings, Christians also rejected divorce and infidelity, which were widely practiced in the Roman Empire, mostly by men but also by women. The most damning aspect of Christianity in the eyes of Roman officialdom, however, was the refusal by

LIFE AND TIMES

Aelia Capitolina

This citadel underneath the Damascus Gate in Jerusalem formed part of the triumphal gate built by the Romans.

The layout of today's Old City of Jerusalem has changed considerably from the Jerusalem that Jesus and the Apostles knew. After suppressing the second Jewish Revolt (132–135 C.E.), Roman Emperor Hadrian ordered that the ancient city of Jerusalem should be destroyed, and a pagan city be built in its place. This Roman city was named Aelia Capitolina: Aelius was Hadrian's *gens* or tribe, and Capitolinus referred to the god Jupiter Capitolinus. A temple to Jupiter was built on top of the ruins of the Second Temple. Like most Roman cities, Roman Jerusalem was designed using a grid pattern anchored on a main north-to-south avenue, the *cardo*, bisected by a *decumanus* running east to west. Both the primary and secondary *cardo* streets are preserved in the course of the Suq Khan-ez-Zeit and Al-Wad streets, which converge at the Damascus Gate. Some elements from the original Roman city gate have recently been excavated.

98 C.E.
Nerva dies and is succeeded by Trajan

CA 110 C.E.
Oldest known use of paper for writing in China

116 C.E.
Trajan extends Roman Empire into Parthia

CA 117 C.E.
Putative date of Tacitus' *Histories*

Christians to offer sacrifices to the Roman gods, and particularly the reigning Emperor. This reinforced the impression of Christianity as a foreign cult profoundly at odds with Roman interests. Augustus had always emphasized the role of the Roman state religion as the one element that fused the disparate peoples and cultures within the Empire together. It was this "faith of our fathers" that gave Roman civilization its moral foundation. Little wonder, then, that the Roman historian Tacitus referred to Christianity as a "deadly superstition," whereas Pliny the Younger called it "a superstition taken to extravagant lengths."

Nevertheless, the extent to which Christian persecution became a matter of state policy continues to be debated. Domitian's animus was apparently not directed at Christianity exclusively, but against any cult that refused to recognize him as *dominus et deus* (Lord and God), or sacrifice to his patron gods, Jupiter and Minerva. Domitian's successors, Trajan (r. 98–117 C.E.) and Hadrian (r. 117–138 C.E.), were too busy expanding and consolidating the Roman Empire to concern themselves with such foolish notions. When the younger Pliny asked Trajan for instructions with regard to Christians in Bithynia, the Emperor counseled moderation and stressed that suspected Christians should be given the opportunity to recant.

Another factor was the fact that many Christians avidly sought martyrdom in an effort to imitate Christ's suffering. Tertullian, for example, tells the story of a group of Christian faithful who appeared before Arrius Antoninus, the Roman governor

Though various elements are taught in the several books of the Gospels, it makes no difference to the faith of believers, since all things are declared by one guiding Spirit.

MURATORIAN FRAGMENT OF THE NEW TESTAMENT CANON

LIFE AND TIMES

The Catacombs

Early Christians did not generally follow the Roman practice of cremation, perhaps because they believed that the body of the faithful would rise again on the Day of Judgment. Burial therefore became an important part of Christian ritual; many Christians would help those in their community who were too poor to pay for it. The problem for Christians in Rome and other major cities was *where* to bury the dead, given that Christianity was not an officially sanctioned religion, and burial within the city limits was strictly forbidden for hygienic reasons. Many turned to a practice that was already common among the poor—going underground to create subterranean burial chambers known as *catacumbae,* or catacombs. In Rome proper, most of these catacombs were dug in the soft volcanic rock along the main roads leading to Rome, such as the Via Appia, the Via Ostiensis, and the Via Tiburtina. The dead were wrapped in linen and placed in *loculi,* or burial niches; wealthier families would commission large subterranean tombs. In Rome alone, excavators have identified more than 60 catacomb networks, some equipped with galleries across multiple levels up to a depth of 60 feet. One example is the catacomb network of Domitilla, the legendary niece of Emperor Domitian, spread over some nine miles of underground caves. One of Rome's oldest catacombs, it is also among the best preserved. One crypt contains a vivid fresco depicting the martyr Veneranda (or Venera) being accompanied to heaven by the legendary martyr St. Petronilla.

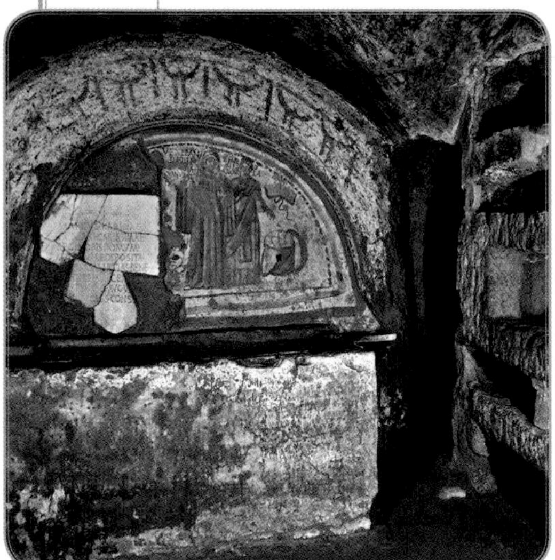

A room in the Catacombs of Domitilla with "oculi" for burial depicts the Christian martyrs Veneranda and Petronilla.

117 C.E.
Trajan is succeeded by Emperor Hadrian

122 C.E.
Hadrian's Wall is built in Britain

132 C.E.
Outbreak of Second Jewish Rebellion, known as the Bar Kokhba Revolt

CA 132 C.E.
Chinese astronomer Zhang Heng develops a planetarium

of Asia, demanding to be put to death. Antoninus demurred, telling them to go and "jump off a cliff" if they so fervently desired death. When Ignatius, the bishop of Antioch (ca 35-108 C.E.) was condemned to the arena, he eagerly looked forward to his death, and wrote how he longed to be "ground by the teeth of the wild beasts, [so] that I may be found to be the pure bread of Christ."

As tensions between different Christian movements intensified, martyrdom became for some Christians a badge of honor, a sign that they alone were the spiritual heirs of Christ. Some Gnostic Christians scoffed at this idea, arguing that the God of Jesus Christ could never desire such pointless human sacrifice. Nevertheless, the lure of martyrdom was strong, and many legends of heroic men and women who gladly went to their deaths would continue to circulate in the coming centuries. Some of these martyrs would find pride of place in Rome's extensive Christian catacombs.

Meanwhile, Christianity continued to expand. As archaeological excavations have shown, Christian chapels sprang up in unexpected corners of the Empire, founded by unknown missionaries well beyond the original orbit of James, Peter, Paul, Thomas, or John. At one point, Pliny the Younger complained that there were so many Christians in Bithynia and Pontus (the Black Sea coastal region of today's Turkey) that pagan demand for sacrificial animals had dropped precipitously. Christianity was also introduced into Egypt via Alexandria, which had a large Jewish community, and from there spread rapidly among both Greek and Coptic-speaking communities. One of these groups would later bury the collection of Gnostic texts found at Nag Hammadi.

The Christian faith also spread northward, using the ancient trade routes of Mesopotamia along the Tigris and Euphrates Rivers. By the middle of the second century, Edessa had become an important center of Christian activity. The availability of the Gospels in the local language, Old Syriac, was a major factor in this conversion activity—a situation that would soon be repeated in Europe. Even the diatessaron, an attempt by theologian Tatian the Assyrian (120–180 C.E.) to "harmonize"

A Roman bas-relief shows Emperor Marcus Aurelius (r. 161–180 C.E.) and his family offering a sacrifice in gratitude for the Emperor's victory over Germanic tribes.

135 C.E.
Second Jewish Rebellion is suppressed

135 C.E.
Emperor Hadrian razes Jerusalem and builds a new city, Aelia Capitolina, in its place

138 C.E.
Emperor Hadrian dies and is succeeded by Antoninus Pius

CA 140 C.E.
Simeon ben Gamaliel II moves the Yabneh Academy to Galilee and forms a new Sanhedrin

An aureus, or gold coin, depicts Emperor Diocletian (r. 284–305).

OPPOSITE: *"The First Council of Nicaea," the work of an anonymous 16th-century artist, depicts the gathering of Christian bishops who convened in Nicaea in 325.*

the four Gospels into one Gospel, was written in Syriac. Church tradition claims that the Apostle Thomas carried the Gospel to India, although scholars believe that it was actually the work of Syriac missionaries who revered Thomas as their patron saint. By the time the church theologian Pantaenus of Alexandria traveled to India around 180 C.E., he found many flourishing Christian communities.

The Organization of the Church

As Christianity grew, the question of how to manage this far-flung movement became urgent, not only because of the pressure of occasional persecutions, but also because of the constant challenge of dissident Christian sects. Many early Christians, including Paul, believed that Christ would return in their lifetime; therefore, the need for organization was irrelevant, for Jesus himself would lead his church. This belief was perpetuated into the next generation, for whom destruction of the Temple in Jerusalem was a clear sign that the End Times were imminent. The same collective expectation gained currency after the destruction of Jerusalem under Hadrian in 135, when many church leaders preached that the Second Coming was upon them. But for others, the organization of the church could no longer be postponed. These Christians remembered the hierarchical system that Paul himself had articulated in his first Letter to the Corinthians: "God has given the first place to apostles, second to prophets, and third to teachers" (I Corinthians 12:28). The term "apostle" in Paul's parlance referred not only to the original 12, but also to anyone to whom the risen Christ had revealed himself, including Paul. Already, Christian communities had begun to appoint priestly leaders or *presbyters,* chosen on the basis of their ability and faith. Many of these presbyters were still laymen, often married and involved in a trade or profession, rather than being full-time ordained priests.

Eventually the position of bishop emerged as certain prelates claimed an authority as lawful descendant or appointee of an Apostle—what later generations would call the "apostolic succession." By the end of the first century, the bishop exercised authority over all Christian activity in his allotted territory, usually from his seat in one of the Roman Empire's main cities. After the upheaval of the Jewish War, which all but obliterated the position of Jerusalem in the hierarchy, the bishoprics of Rome, Alexandria, and Antioch became the dominant centers of Christian guidance. This structure of delegated authority coalesced as an increasing number of dissident sects challenged the prevailing Church theology in the second century. By creating an apostolic "forum" in the form of a *synod,* the bishops were in a better position to develop a unified defense against the constant challenge of dissident theologies, as well as Roman persecution.

Do not pronounce judgment
before the time,
before the Lord comes,
who will bring to light
the things now hidden
in darkness.

LETTER (OF PAUL) TO THE CORINTHIANS 4:5

161 C.E.
Antoninus Pius dies and is succeeded by Lucius Verus and Marcus Aurelius as co-Emperors

169 C.E.
Lucius Verus dies; Marcus Aurelius reigns as sole Emperor

177 C.E.
Commodus, son of Marcus Aurelius, becomes co-Emperor

180 C.E.
Marcus Aurelius dies; Commodus reigns as sole Emperor

ПЕРВЫИ СОБОРЪ СТЫХЪ ОЦЕ

Period Artifacts

100–200 C.E.

Suspended oil lamps such as this one were used to light Roman homes in the second century.

A remarkable funerary portrait of ca 100 C.E. depicts a boy named Eutyches.

Christianity in the Third Century

As Rome's power went into decline and the Empire became increasingly prone to barbarian invasions, Roman persecution of Christians became more widespread. Under pressure of the invaders, many Romans were swept by nationalistic fervor and rallied to Roman gods in the hope of salvation. By contrast, many Christians refused military service in Rome's legions, which was considered unpatriotic. Thus, Christian communities often found themselves targeted as scapegoats in times of national crisis. Church documents state that in 202, Emperor Septimius Severus (r. 193–211) prohibited Christians from any conversion activity in the Empire, which set off a new wave of oppression. The situation became even more difficult after Emperor Decius (r. 249–251) ordered that all citizens obtain a *libellus,* certified proof of faithful sacrifice to Roman gods, on pain of death. Scores of Christians submitted, while others refused to comply and were executed; one of these victims was Pope Fabian (r. 236–250), the 20th pope since Peter.

Decius' successor, Valerian (r. 253–260) maintained the law of *libellus,* but his son Gallienus, who ruled as co-Emperor (or "Caesar"), abrogated the law after his father was captured by the Persian King Shapur I. Gallienus went even further by restoring all confiscated property to its Christian owners. All throughout the Empire, Christians rejoiced and poured their efforts into rebuilding their shattered communities, restoring houses of worship, baptizing new converts, and appointing new bishops, so that by the end of the third century there were a hundred bishops on the Italian peninsula alone.

Unfortunately, the period of religious liberty was brief. In 284, the constant pressure of barbarian invasions led to a vast overhaul of the imperial organization originally established by Augustus. In Rome, a tetrarchy, or *Dominate,* was established, whereby the executive power of emperor was divided between four rulers: two principal emperors and two subordinate Caesars, each tasked to defend one of four territories of the Empire. These four regions were called prefectures, further divided into 12 "dioceses"; the term was later adopted by the Church to denote the dominion of a bishop. In order to be closer to the front, the two principal Emperors, Diocletian (r. 284–305) and Maximian (r. 286–305), also established forward headquarters: one in Milan and one in Nicomedia, just a few miles from a city called Byzantium.

But the barbarian invaders were relentless. At the dawn of the fourth century, they cut many ancient trade routes, causing the collapse of markets throughout the Empire. Thousands roamed the streets, hungry and out of work. Romans cast about for someone to blame, and once again Christian communities proved a convenient target. A popular

CA 185 C.E.
Bishop Irenaeus proposes an anthology of the Gospels of Matthew, Mark, Luke, and John

CA 185 C.E.
Chinese astronomers observe a supernova in the constellation Centaurus

192 C.E.
Emperor Commodus is murdered; Septimius Severus succeeds him

193 C.E.
Emperor Septimius Severus permits the persecution of Christians by local Roman officials

polemic of 303, written by Greco-Roman philosopher Porphyrius (or Porphyry, 232–304), fanned the flames by denouncing the "baseness of the Jewish Scriptures" and argued that "though Christ is supposed to have been most pious, the Christians are a confused and vicious sect."

When in 299 the *Pontifex Maximus*—chief priest of the Roman cult—declared the omens of a sacrifice invalid because of the presence nearby of Christians, a new wave of persecutions began in earnest. Bishop Eusebius, an early historian of the Church, argues that the new oppression was instigated by one of the Caesars, Galerius, but modern historians believe that Diocletian was the senior man in charge, and that no organized purge could have been undertaken without his approval. They cite as evidence that Diocletian was also energetically involved in the suppression of another religion named Manichaeism. Inspired by the work of the Persian prophet Mani, this cult developed a rapid following which in many parts of the Empire rivaled the growth of Christianity.

All Christian worship was now outlawed. Many church leaders were arrested, tortured, and put to death, while new churches built during the Gallienus restoration were razed to the ground. Diocletian, the ablest emperor

OPPOSITE: A triumphal arch was erected in the city of Jerash on the occasion of the visit of Emperor Hadrian to the city.

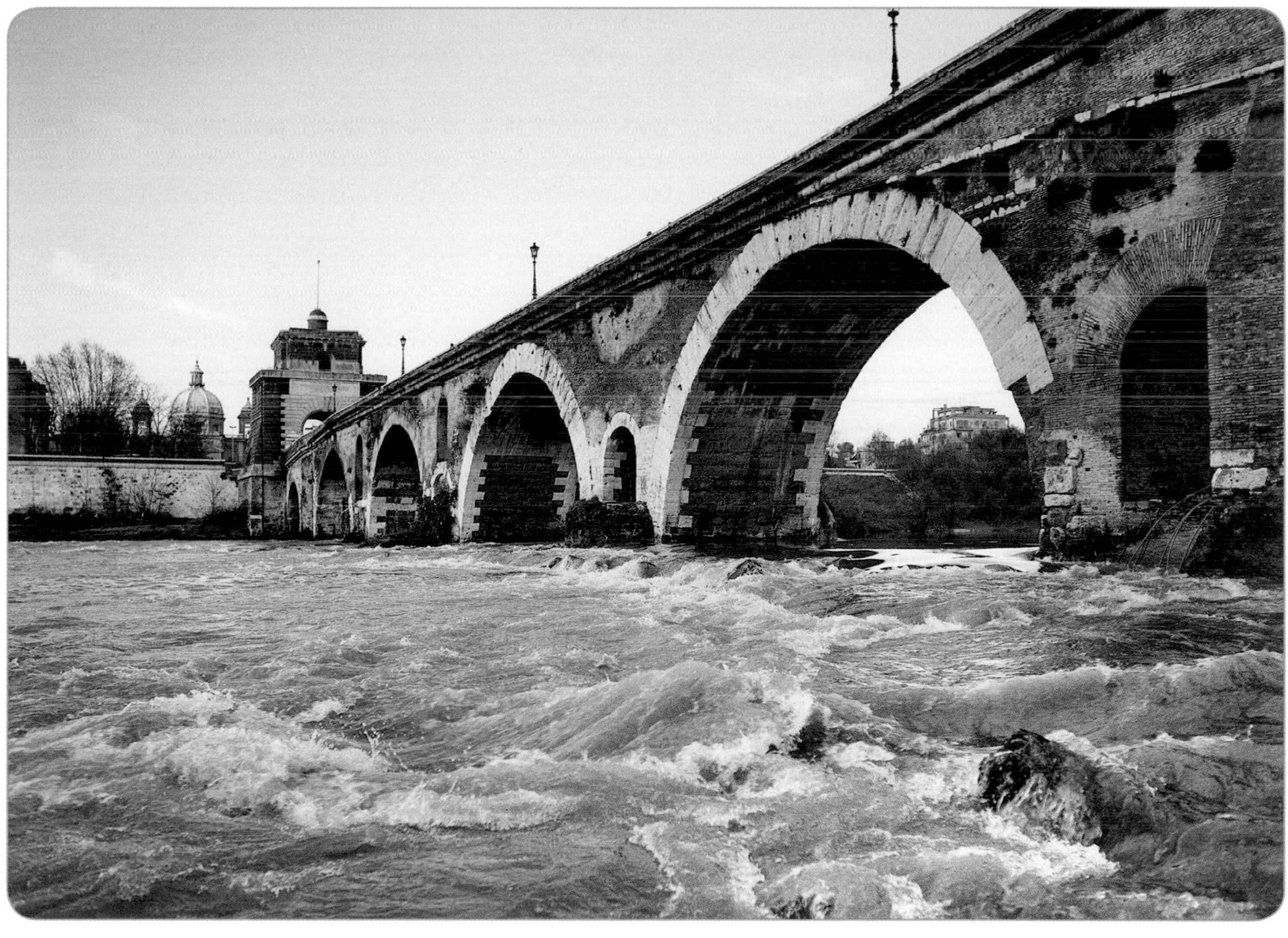

The Milvian Bridge over the Tiber River was the location of a climactic battle for control of the Roman Empire.

CA 200 C.E.
The Huns invade Afghanistan

CA 215 C.E.
Baths of Caracalla are built in Rome

CA 220 C.E.
End of the Han Dynasty in China

CA 220 C.E.
First Goth invasions of the Roman Empire

since Hadrian, may be credited with preserving the Roman Empire for another hundred years, but he also very nearly succeeded in destroying the Christian world.

Constantine the Great

In 305, Diocletian made an astonishing decision: He decided to abdicate, forcing his co-ruler Maximian to do the same. Diocletian was in poor health, and looked forward to spending his final years in the sumptuous palace he had built in Spoleto (now Split, Croatia). This automatically elevated their Caesars, or vice-regents, Galerius (r. 305–311) in the East and Constantius I Chlorus (r. 305–306) in the West, to the position of co-Emperors. Both then appointed their own Caesars.

Galerius distinguished himself by officially abrogating Diocletian's persecutions, reaffirming Gallienus's policy of tolerance—a fact largely forgotten by history, which tends to give the credit to Constantine. When Constantius suddenly died in 306 in Eburacum (present-day York, England) and his troops pronounced his son, Constantine, the new Emperor, the Praetorian Guard in Rome promptly elevated Maxentius, son of Maximian, to Emperor status as well. Confusion reigned as Rome was once again convulsed in civil war. Six years later Constantine faced the army of his last opponent, Maxentius, near a crossing over the Tiber River known as the Milvian Bridge.

The events that followed are shrouded in legend. Christian writer Lactantius (ca 240–320) wrote that on the eve of battle, Constantine had a dream in which he was told to decorate the shields of his soldiers of "the heavenly sign of God," the monogram of Christ (the Greek letters chi and rho, the first two letters of the Greek word *Christos*).

> *About noon, when the day was already beginning to decline, he saw with his own eyes the trophy of a cross of light in the heavens, above the sun.*
>
> EUSEBIUS OF CAESAREA, *LIFE OF CONSTANTINE*

Eusebius, on the other hand, describes Constantine's vision of a luminescent cross in the sky just above the sun, blazing with the Greek words *en toutoi nika* ("by this [sign] conquer"). Whatever the case may be, Constantine was able to defeat the army of Maxentius on the morrow, and credited his victory to the God of the Christians.

The Battle of the Milvian Bridge was a turning point in the history of Christianity. In 313, Constantine issued the Edict of Milan, declaring a policy of religious toleration throughout his domain, pertaining to *all* cults, including Christianity. Constantine himself was not baptized until he lay on his deathbed; the triumphal arch that was erected in his honor—the Arch of Constantine at the eastern end of the Roman Forum—contains pagan motifs rather than Christian symbols. But in many other respects, Constantine honored his debt to the Christian God. He promised a full restitution of all Christian holdings seized by the state, while Christian citizens who had been exiled were invited back. In 324, Constantine secured his power by defeating his last remaining rival, Licinius, at Chrysopolis in Asia Minor, and Christianity in the Roman Empire was secure at last. ■

OPPOSITE: *The fresco "The Battle of the Milvian Bridge" was painted by Giulio Romano (1492–1546) in the Raphael Stanze of the Vatican.*

"The Dream of Constantine" was painted by Italian artist Piero della Francesca (ca 1415–1492).

CA 221 C.E.
Roman citizenship is conferred on every person in the Empire

249 C.E.
Emperor Decius initiates a persecution of individuals who refuse to worship Roman gods

261 C.E.
Emperor Gallienus ends persecution of Christians

CA 300 C.E.
Bishop Eusebius codifies first canon of the New Testament

3
CHAPTER

THE BYZANTINE EMPIRE

313-600 C.E.

Thus the pious emperor, glorifying in the confession of the victorious cross, proclaimed the Son of God to the Romans.

EUSEBIUS, *LIFE OF CONSTANTINE*

Few periods would witness such transformative changes in the growth of Christianity as the fourth century. In the year 300, Christians still represented an underclass in the Roman Empire. Though the fervor of official persecution had abated, the prejudice against Christian practices had not. Worship continued, but mostly in private homes rather than in church halls built for this purpose. Career advancement within the imperial administration was reserved for pagans, rather than Christians. As before, Christian life persisted on the periphery of the Roman state.

This would change in the span of less than 75 years, by the end of which Christianity emerged as the sole state religion of the Empire, with the Emperor exercising equal authority in both temporal and spiritual matters. Whereas membership of a Christian congregation was previously an impediment to state employment, it now became a requirement, a sine qua non.

None of this would have happened if Constantine had not used the power of his imperial office to sweep away the remaining vestiges of discrimination and actively promote the Christian

ABOVE: *This reliquary for a piece of the True Cross of ca 955 is one of the few Byzantine treasures to have survived the sack of Constantinople in 1204.*

OPPOSITE: *The Basilica of Maxentius, later renamed after Constantine, shows the virtuoso building technique using cement of early fourth-century Rome.*

PRECEDING PAGES: *"Moses with the Tablets of the Law" is a sixth-century fresco from St. Catherine's Monastery in the Sinai, Egypt.*

Church throughout his realm. The turning point, as tradition has it, was the Battle of the Milvian Bridge, but in truth Constantine had always looked favorably on Christianity, influenced by his mother, Helena, who was a deeply pious Christian. Although Constantine himself was not baptized until he was near death, the Emperor actively encouraged the growth of the Church, promising full restitution of all Christian property that had been confiscated in the preceding decades of official persecution. Those who had been exiled for their belief were invited back, while Christians were once again offered key positions in the imperial administration.

But Constantine soon ran into opposition from his co-Emperor, Licinius, who had cosigned the Edict of Milan in 313. Licinius was alarmed by Constantine's massive purge of officials appointed by the former emperor, Maxentius, and his allies. The Praetorian Guard, the elite force that had backed Maxentius's claims, was disbanded, while the vast basilica that Maxentius had started building near the Roman Forum, one aisle of which still stands today, was now renamed the Basilica of Constantine. At the same time, Constantine ordered a vast church to be built on the traditional site of Peter's grave, the Mons Vaticanus, or Vatican Hill.

These initiatives convinced Licinius, a dedicated pagan, that Constantine was plotting to oust him, take sole control of the Roman Empire, and turn it into a Christian realm. In response, Licinius rescinded the toleration promised in the Edict of Milan and renewed the oppression of Christian communities in his jurisdiction. Christian properties were once again confiscated, while known Christians were ousted from office.

Fatefully, a group of barbarian tribes chose this moment to invade Thrace (an area roughly equivalent to today's Bulgaria and European Turkey), located in Licinius's half of the Empire. This gave Constantine a perfect pretext to invade his rival's territory. In 324, he defeated his co-Emperor in a battle at Chrysopolis (today's Üsküdar, on the Anatolian shore of the Bosporus). Rather than

PERIOD ARCHITECTURE

The Christian Basilica

What should a Christian temple look like? The archetype of the pagan temple was not suitable for mass assemblies. Pagan worship was often conducted by individuals, in private, whereas the Christian celebration of the Eucharist was usually attended by hundreds of believers. Moreover, few Christians would be comfortable praying in a pagan temple. In response, Constantine's architects turned to a building type previously used as a civic center and courthouse. This was the basilica, based on a Greek building known as a *stoa basileios,* or "hall of the king." The *stoa* was essentially a covered gallery where business could be transacted and assemblies could be held. Some of these *stoai* eventually featured double or even triple galleries. When the Romans adopted the design, they raised the center gallery into a nave so that light from the clerestory windows could illuminate the hall below. As a secular structure, the basilica form had no prior religious connotations, and was therefore perfectly suited for Christian use. What's more, a Roman basilica often featured a semicircular apse at either end for statues of the reigning emperor or deities. In the Christian version, only one apse was retained; this is where the altar was placed.

This remarkably well-preserved Roman basilica, built in the mid-first century C.E., is located near the entrance of Pompeii.

ABOVE: *This bust of Constantine I (ca 280–337 C.E.) from a colossal statue of the Roman Emperor, is now at the Capitoline Museum in Rome. He was the first emperor to adhere to Christianity.*

OPPOSITE: *Ancient lanterns adorn the side aisles of the Basilica of the Nativity in Bethlehem. Built during the Justinian era, it is one of the oldest Roman churches still in use.*

313
Constantine I and Licinius sign the Edict of Milan

318
Construction begins on St. Peter's Basilica on Vatican Hill

320
Chandra Gupta founds the Gupta Dynasty in India

324
Constantine I defeats his co-Emperor Licinius at the Battle of Chrysopolis

SAINTS AND CLERICS

Empress Helena

"Saint Helena with the True Cross" is the work of Lucas Cranach the Elder (1472–1553).

Empress Helena (ca 248–330) was the mother of Constantine the Great and consort to Emperor Constantius. To this day, her name is indelibly linked to the birth of the Holy Land as a pilgrimage destination for Christians throughout the realm. Though Emperor Constantius divorced her at some time before 289 to marry a lady of higher birth, her son Constantine brought her back to court after his own elevation to Emperor. Constantine charged her to travel to Roman Palestine in an effort to identify and restore the holy sites associated with the life of Jesus. She complied, and traveled throughout Palestine so that, as her biographer Eusebius wrote, she could "worship at the place whereon his feet have stood." Helena built churches in Bethlehem, Nazareth, and the Mount of Olives, while also supervising the construction of the first Church of the Holy Sepulcher at the reputed location of Christ's burial and resurrection.

appointing a new co-emperor, he assumed sole control of the Roman realm, just as Licinius had feared.

The New Christian Liturgy

Now, it seemed, there were no longer any obstacles to Rome's wholehearted embrace of the Christian Church. Constantine established a new seven-day calendar, starting with Sunday as the *Dies Domini,* or Day of the Lord (a name that lives on in the Italian *Domenica* and the French *Dimanche*). A "liturgical year" was adopted, regulating the various Christian festivals and feast days in an annual calendar and culminating in Holy Week, which led to the most important day of all, Easter. Church services, which at home chapels still had an informal character, were formalized into an elaborate liturgy filled with litanies, hymns, and prayers, perfumed with incense and illuminated by prodigious quantities of candles. Many of these early rites still survive in Eastern Orthodox liturgy. Since many copies of the Christian Bible had been lost in the fires of official persecution, the imperial administration also financed the copying of new Bibles on a large scale.

The development of an indigenous Christian liturgy, to be attended by the growing congregations of Christian faithful, also demanded the conception of a new form of a temple, a *Christian* temple, which could

325 Empress Helena commissions the Church of the Nativity in Bethlehem

325 Opening of the Council of Nicaea

331 Capital of the Roman Empire is formally moved to Constantinople

333 The pilgrim from Bordeaux visits Judea

house hundreds or even thousands of worshippers at one time. This was a radical departure from pagan practice, in which sacrifice and worship were often performed by individuals in private. The typical Roman temple was therefore ill suited to the mass-assembly needs of Christian liturgy. What's more, most Christians would have been offended to worship in a building so redolent of polytheism.

In response, Constantine's architects developed a new archetype of a house of worship, exemplified by the vast Christian sanctuary that the Emperor ordered built over the traditional site of the tomb of Peter in Rome. This new church, known as St. Peter's, used the basilica form, which up to that point had been used throughout the Roman Empire as a civic center for local administration and the courts. St. Peter's Basilica took 25 years to construct and stood for more than a millennium—vivid testimony to the excellence of Roman architectural technology. It was in this church that Charlemagne would be crowned Emperor of the Holy Roman Empire in 800. Then, in the early 16th century, during the heyday of the Renaissance, the need to replace the aging building became manifest. It was finally torn down in 1506 and replaced with the current St. Peter's Basilica, which itself took 120 years to build.

OPPOSITE: This impression of the original St. Peter's Basilica in Rome, built by Constantine the Great, was drawn by Domenico Tasselli before the church was demolished in the 16th century.

Until the Edict of Milan, Christian worship often took place in private homes. This reconstruction shows a typical WORKING-CLASS RESIDENTIAL AREA *in a major Roman city around the third century* C.E.

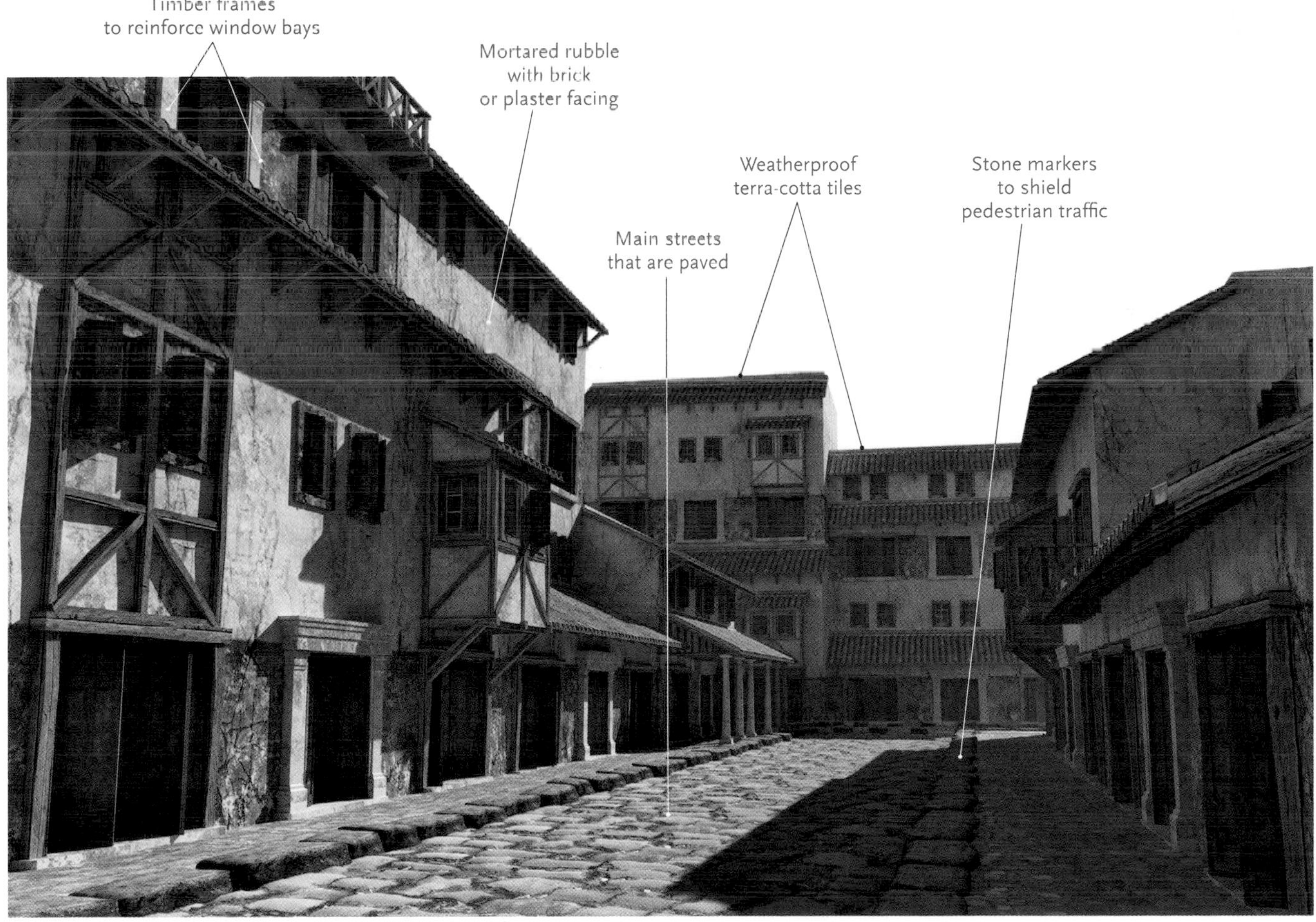

337
Constantine I is baptized on his deathbed

337
Constantine is succeeded by his son, Emperor Constantine II

337
Struggle for the throne among Constantine's sons leads to a temporary division of the Empire

340
Emperor Constantine II is killed

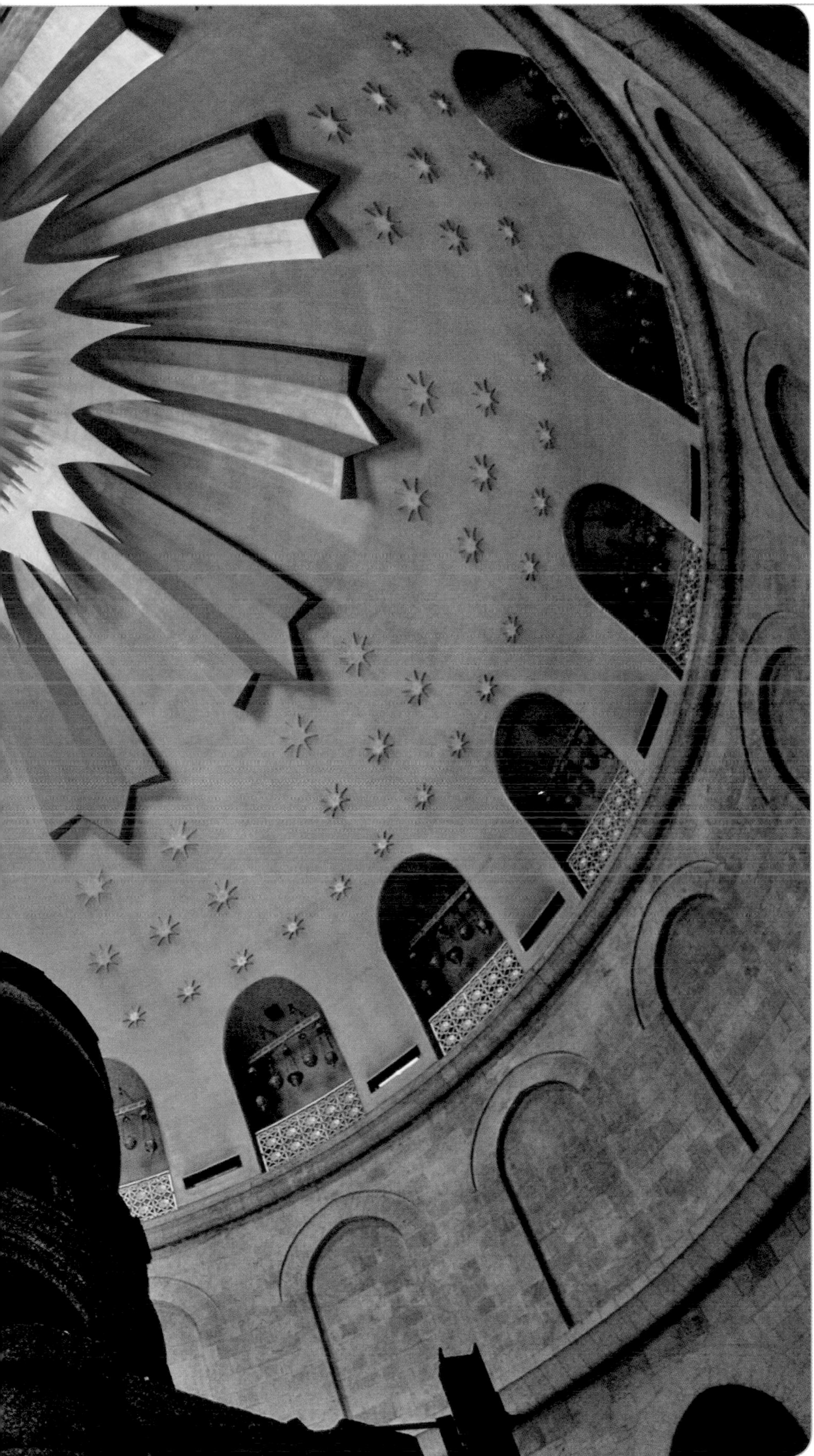

Ironically, Constantine himself refused to be baptized, and continued to serve as Pontifex Maximus, supreme priest, of the official Roman cult. This did not prevent him from appointing scores of new bishops, who now held a status equivalent to that of a Roman senator. Given that high-ranking Christian clergy were exempt from taxes, the competition for these positions was often fierce.

The Building of the "Holy Land"

Constantine's building zeal was not limited to the heartland of Rome. In the mid-320s, the Emperor sent his mother, Empress Helena, to Roman Palestine to try to identify and preserve the holy sites associated with Jesus' life, backed by the full resources of the Roman treasury. Helena first focused her efforts on locating the scene of Jesus' crucifixion and entombment in Jerusalem. Tradition held that during the construction of the Roman city of Aelia Capitolina, Emperor Hadrian ordered a temple of Venus to be erected on the site of Golgotha, perhaps in an effort to erase any vestiges of Christian worship. If this is true, then his decision actually had the opposite effect. In the years to follow, Christians would flock to the place as a site of pilgrimage, so that by the time of Helena's arrival, everyone—including the local bishop, Macarius—knew exactly where Christ's tomb was located. Empress Helena immediately ordered the Venus temple razed and commissioned the construction of a church dedicated to the "Holy Sepulcher"—the first of several churches by that name to be built in the centuries to come.

The sudden transformation of Christianity from an illicit cult to the most-favored religion in the Roman realm took the Jewish communities of Judea by surprise. Since the second century, the Romans had given the Jewish patriarchate in Tiberias considerable autonomy

The Rotunda in the Church of the Holy Sepulcher marks the presumed location of the tomb of Christ. The site of the Jerusalem basilica is also venerated as Golgotha, where Jesus was crucified.

in governing the land. Roman procurators had long since recognized that the Jewish rabbinate could act as a stabilizing force, governing the territory at little risk, and thus sustain the impression of home rule and preempt political agitation. But now, almost overnight, that same region found itself transformed from a Roman province into a Christian "Holy Land." The Roman city of Aelia Capitolina was solemnly renamed Jerusalem—but in a thoroughly Christian mold. The power of the Jewish patriarchate was curtailed, and finally disbanded. Intermarriage between Jews and Christians was forbidden. The bishop in Jerusalem was elevated to the status of patriarch, placing Jerusalem on a par with Rome and Alexandria.

Meanwhile, Helena's architects, having torn down Hadrian's temple of Venus, had excavated the summit of Golgotha hill so as to create a level surface, which only left the place of the crucifixion and the presumed tomb exposed. Over these, two structures were being built: a massive, five-aisled basilica—similar to the church of St. Peter then rising on

A Bedouin prays near the summit of Jebel Musa in the Sinai desert, the presumed location of Mount Sinai, where according to the Bible God spoke to Moses.

350
Co-Emperor Constans is murdered; Constantius II is the sole ruler of the Roman Empire

350
The Persians recapture Armenia from the Byzantine Empire

350
The Schola Cantorum for church singing is founded in Rome

352
A special tax levy on non-Christians prompts a revolt by Jews and Samaritans

Vatican Hill in Rome—and a rotunda (known as the *Anastasis* or "resurrection") over the location of Christ's resurrection. In between lay the rocky outcropping of Golgotha itself. Interestingly, fourth-century records make no mention of the "True Cross," which as tradition tells us, Empress Helena had uncovered as well. This would suggest that the cross was identified much later, for it would soon become the centerpiece of veneration at the Church of the Holy Sepulcher.

Around the late fourth century, a pilgrim traveled to the emerging Holy Land. This was a wealthy noblewoman by the name of Egeria, from the Rhône Valley or Aquitaine in France, who recorded her experience in a long letter called *Itinerarium Egeriae*. Egeria first spent time visiting holy sites in Egypt, which was being incorporated into the principal Christian pilgrimage itinerary. Near Jebel Musa, the Mountain of Moses, she visited "the place where it rained manna and quails upon them," and the bush "out of which the Lord spoke in the fire to Moses"—the first reference to Jebel Musa as "Mount Sinai," the place where Moses received the Ten Commandments. Here, too, Empress Helena had ordered a small church to be built. In the sixth century, Emperor Justinian would expand this church into a fortified enclosure that later became known as St. Catherine's Monastery, which continues to function as a monastic community to this day.

Egeria also visited some of the monastic settlements that had been founded in Egypt,

The light is brought forth from within the cave, where a lamp is always burning day and night, while vesper psalms and antiphons are sung for a considerable time.

THE PILGRIM EGERIA ON JERUSALEM LITURGY, CA 370

SCRIPTURE AND FAITH

The Monastic Movement

Though there were other hermits before him, Anthony of Egypt (251–356) is typical of the so-called anchorite ascetics who sought the solitude of the desert to devote themselves wholeheartedly to prayer. According to his biography, written by Bishop Athanasius, Anthony was tempted in the desert by the devil, which he overcame through the power of prayer. Later, the theme of "The Temptations of St. Anthony" would become a popular motif in Western art. Anthony eventually found his long-sought solitude in an abandoned Roman fort, where he refused to see visitors and only accepted small quantities of food through a crevice in the wall. But when the throng of disciples wishing to join him became too great, he finally relented and organized a monastic settlement in the eastern desert under the motto "pray and work," anticipating the Benedictines by some 200 years.

The idea of a monastic community, known as *cenobitism*, was taken up by Pachomius (290–346), an early follower of Anthony. Between 318 and 325, he established his first monastery in Tabennisi, Egypt, which welcomed men and women. It is estimated that by the time of Pachomius's death, there were some eight monasteries in Egypt with several hundred monks and nuns. In the years to come, cenobitic communities would become a particularly welcome refuge for widows and unmarried women, who under Roman rule enjoyed no special protections until the advent of Constantine's reforms. Athanasius' biography of Anthony was widely copied in Latin, thus sowing the seeds of the great monastic movement in Western Europe.

"The Temptation of St. Anthony" was painted by a young Michelangelo (1475–1564).

354
St. Augustine of Hippo is born

360
Scrolls begin to be replaced by codices (books)

360
The Huns invade Europe

361
Constantius is succeeded by Emperor Julian

PERIOD ARCHITECTURE

The Arch of Constantine

The Arch of Constantine in Rome was built between 313 and 315.

Constantine's achievements were recognized by the Roman Senate, which voted to build a triumphal arch in his honor. This Arch of Constantine still stands at the eastern end of the Roman Forum, in the shadow of the Colosseum, and is one of the best preserved of all Roman monuments. The perfect proportions of the arch, with a large central *fornix* for the main traffic and two smaller *fornices* for pedestrians, were much admired in the Renaissance and have been imitated many times. What is remarkable, however, is that the arch does not include any Christian symbols, but instead features themes of military campaigns and pagan sacrifice. The reason is simple: The arch was built in such a rush that its designers simply pilfered much of its sculptural ornamentation from older monuments.

On the principal facade of the monument, for example, perched over the lateral arches, are roundels taken from a monument to Hadrian, dedicated to hunting and sacrifice. The lateral sides of the arch are decorated with panels from Trajan's times. The sculpted features of these emperors were carefully modified so as to better resemble Constantine himself.

usually far removed from the towns and hamlets along the Nile. "The monks who dwelt there received us very warmly," she wrote, "showing us every kindness." The idea of seeking solitude in the desert so as to be closer to God was not new; many other religions, then and now, advocated the blessings of meditation in remote places. This was the reason John the Baptist, as well as the Qumran community, had chosen to live in the Judean wilderness, and why Moses received the tablets from God in the heart of the Sinai desert. What was new in Christian practice, however, was the idea of *cenobitic* monasticism: the idea of creating settlements where pious men and women could pray and meditate together while pooling their needs for water, food, and security.

As the scholar Robert Bruce Mullin has noted, in some ways the figure of the saintly hermit was the successor to the martyr, now that persecutions had ceased. Whereas previously a martyr was glorified by his imitation of Christ's suffering on the cross, that role was now taken over by the ascetic in his deliberate negation of physical needs. Several of these hermits, such as Anthony of Egypt, became holy men in their own right, sometimes endowed with the reputed power to perform miracles.

The True Cross

Egeria also traveled to Jerusalem, where she described the services held at the Church of the Holy Sepulcher. Her detailed account gives us a fascinating glimpse of the development of Christian liturgy in the latter part of the fourth century. "As soon as the doors of the *Anastatis* are opened before cockcrow," she wrote, referring to the rotunda of the church, "hymns are said, and palms and antiphons are sung in response," followed by Matin hymns at daybreak. In the evening at Vespers, she reported, "all the people assemble at the *Anastatis* in the same manner, and all the candles and tapers are lit, making a very great light."

Egeria is the first known witness to describe the presence of a cross in the church. This, she wrote, was believed to be the cross on which Jesus was crucified, known in the years to come as the True Cross. Egeria's account suggests that its discovery was not, as yet, attributed to Empress Helena. Kept in a "silver-gilt casket," as she wrote, the "holy wood" was only taken from its container and exhibited once a year, on Good Friday. On that day, all the faithful were invited to step forward to kiss the sacred wood, though under heavy guard, since at one point, some pious soul was said to "have bitten off and stolen a portion of the sacred wood."

The Church of the Holy Sepulcher was only one of a number of churches sprouting up all over the Holy Land. Another fourth-century pilgrim, a woman named Paula who features prominently in the writings of Jerome, describes

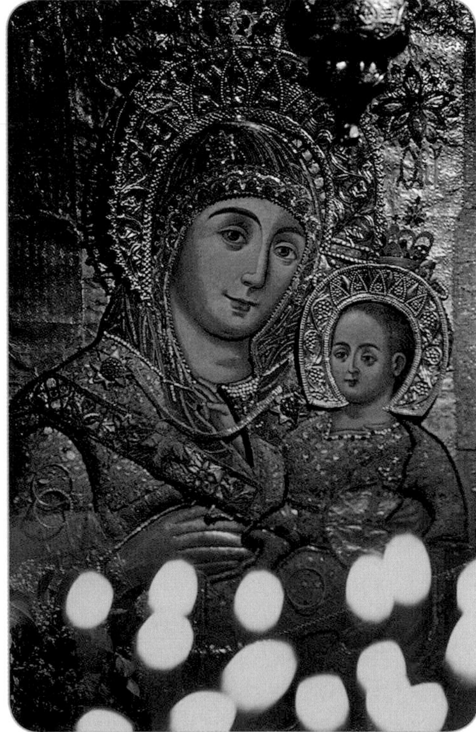

361 **Julian "The Apostate" attempts to restore Rome's pagan cult**

363 **Julian dies after the Battle of Samarra**

364 **The Empire is divided between Valens and Valentinian I**

376 **Visigoths and Alans invade the Byzantine Empire**

This wall of the Bucoleon Palace is all that remains of the Great Palace complex of the Byzantine emperors in Constantinople, now Istanbul, Turkey.

OPPOSITE: *A modern icon depicts the Virgin Mary and Jesus in the Church of the Nativity in Bethlehem.*

a church that was built over the "Grotto of the Savior" in Bethlehem. Originally commissioned by Empress Helena in 325 in the form of a five-aisled basilica, the church culminated in an octagon, a favored Christian motif of Roman architects, over the presumed site of Jesus' birth.

The Founding of Constantinople

Notwithstanding his devotion to nurturing the growth of Christianity, Constantine was well aware of the troubled state of the Roman Empire, which continued to suffer the threat of foreign invasions, particularly in the West. In response, the Emperor enacted a number of major reforms. The civil and military administrations, traditionally closely entwined, were separated so as to foster a more professional officer corps. The aureus, the standard gold currency in Rome's imperial heyday, was replaced by the solidus, which was only 72 percent gold, to combat the growing inflation in the Empire. The solidus would remain in circulation throughout the thousand-year history of the Byzantine Empire and medieval Europe until the Renaissance.

But Constantine also decided that the future of the Empire lay in the East, rather than the West. While much of Gaul and Spain were under pressure from barbarian hordes, and countless agricultural estates in Italy were either decaying or abandoned, the population centers of Asia Minor were enjoying robust growth. Trade in the East was flourishing, in part due to the relatively peaceful relations with the surrounding territory, such as Persia and

380
Emperor Theodosius orders all subjects to become Christian; pagan sacrifice is prohibited

380
Reign of Chandra Gupta II in India ushers in a time of great stability and prosperity

381
First Council of Constantinople orders every Christian to pledge the Nicene Creed

382
Gothic invaders of Illyricum are made honorary citizens of Rome

Period Artifacts

300–600 C.E.

A simple pilgrim's amulet from the fourth century is stamped with the Greek cross.

This Byzantine ivory, dating from the fourth century, is one of the earliest depictions of the crucifixion of Christ.

This liturgical vessel, or pyxis, with Christ and the Virgin dates from the seventh century.

dominions beyond. As a result, Constantine decided to build a new Roman capital, Roma Nova, near the town of Byzantium, originally founded by Greek settlers in 657 B.C.E. Located on the mouth of the Bosporus, the strategic waterway between the European and Asian continents, the site was well chosen. If properly fortified, the new Roman capital could dominate all trade and military traffic between East and West, as well as all naval shipping between the Mediterranean and the Black Sea. Better yet, it was blessed by a natural harbor known as the Golden Horn.

The new city was designed and built virtually from scratch, using the best innovations that Roman architects had to offer. Fortunately, whereas Roman sculpture and art had entered a steep decline, Roman architecture was still in its ascendancy, powered by new inventions such as the perpendicular vault and cement. The new capital—eventually renamed Constantinopolis, or "city of Constantine" in Greek—rose in less than 20 years, a stupendous achievement, but with an important difference from any previous newly built city. The Emperor decreed that Constantinople would be a *Christian* city, endowed with churches and chapels, rather than pagan temples.

The Duality of Christ

But all was not well. Relieved from the scourge of persecutions, the nascent Church was now tormented by internal disputes over the nature of Christ's divinity. What exactly did it mean that Christ was both human and divine? The restless Greek mind, which had struggled with the paradox of divinity and mortality since the days of Plato, could not resist debating the issue. A prominent presbyter from Alexandria named Arius (256–336) sought to resolve the matter by claiming that since Christ was "begotten by the Father," he could therefore not be of the same divine *substance* as the Father. After all, based on the Gospel accounts, God was in existence well before he begot Christ; therefore the two could not be *consubstantial*. Ergo, since Christ was not as "everlasting as the Father," Arius wrote, he should be considered as *subordinate* to the Father.

> *There is one and the same Person, that of the Father, from whom the Son is begotten and the Holy Spirit proceeds.*
>
> GREGORY OF NYSSA, BISHOP OF NYSSA

The simple logic of this solution appealed to many believers. Arius's ideas spread like wildfire and became a movement; even Bishop Eusebius, a man of great authority at Constantine's court, professed his support for the concept, known as Arianism. But the bishop of Antioch, traditionally a more conservative see (bishop's jurisdiction) than the more free-thinking see of Alexandria, vehemently denounced it and even threatened to excommunicate Eusebius if he persisted in his support for this heresy.

At first, Constantine did not grasp the significance of this theological debate and simply ordered the bishops to settle the matter. But when Arianism continued to grow in popularity and orthodox bishops clamored for action, Constantine realized that an intervention was necessary. In 325, the Emperor summoned some 220 bishops to a synod in Nicaea, located

OPPOSITE: *The interior of Abuna Yemata church, chiseled out of the side of a cliff in northern Ethiopia, is covered with frescoes of saints.*

383 — **Roman forces begin to evacuate Britain**

383 — **Emperor Magnus Maximus conquers Gaul and Spain**

389 — **Theodosius issues decree criminalizing worship of any religion other than Christianity**

390 — **The Mouseion complex, including the Library of Alexandria, is plundered and destroyed**

PERIOD ART

The Byzantine Mosaic

The fifth-century Oratory of Galla Placidia is located near San Vitale Church in Ravenna, Italy.

Whereas Greek artists had excelled in painting, and Roman sculptors achieved a realism not surpassed until the Baroque era, Byzantine artists developed an entirely different style, using the medium of the mosaic. The ephemeral quality of mosaics was perfectly suited to evoke a sacred, otherworldly air, unlike the anthropomorphic art of ancient Rome. In the mosaics of the San Vitale in Ravenna, built by the great Emperor Justinian (r. 527–565), there are no suggestive perspectives or landscapes that denote an earthly presence, for the Byzantine artist was not concerned with mortal life. His attention was focused on the eternal life, shown in the highly stylized, two-dimensional outlines of saintly figures set against the impenetrable gold of heaven. This uniquely Byzantine style would spread throughout the Empire, adorning churches and monasteries from Ukraine to the Sinai, and from Antioch to Egypt.

near today's city of Iznik in Turkey, and presided over the meeting himself. That a major theological issue would be decided under auspices of a Roman emperor was unprecedented. In fact, here lay the seed of a question that would vex medieval Christianity in the centuries to come. Who exercised the greatest authority over the Christian Church: the temporal power of the Byzantine (and later, Holy Roman) Emperor, or the sacred authority of the papal see in Rome?

The synod at Nicaea debated at length the issue of whether Christ's relationship to God was of *similar* substance but subordinate, as Arius advocated, or of the *same* substance ("consubstantial"), as the traditional faction led by Athanasius, the bishop of Alexandria, believed. In Greek, the two terms were so similar (*homoiousion,* "of similar substance" versus *homoousion,* "of the same substance") that the fate of the Church literally hinged on a single letter, one *iota.*

Virtually all bishops felt that if Arius succeeded in "demoting" the divinity of Jesus, a whole new wave of theological heresies would follow. When a final vote was called, the consubstantiality clause as articulated by Athanasius was adopted. The resulting "Nicene Creed" is still recited during the Roman Catholic Mass to this day: "We believe . . . in Jesus Christ, the only Son of God . . . *consubstantial* with the Father" (previously phrased as "*one in Being* with the Father" before the recent revisions by Pope Benedict XVI). Two bishops, however, did not accept the Nicene doctrine, and they continued to propagate the Arian view under pain of excommunication and death. And the fear of the Catholic bishops was realized when two other "heretical" movements, the Nestorian church and the Monophysite church, broke with mainstream Christianity and began to make many converts, particularly in the Middle East. Indeed, the nature of Christ's divinity would continue to fester until the Council of Trent (1545–1563), though some believe it was never fully resolved.

Julian the Apostate

Near the end of his reign, Constantine's behavior became erratic. He ordered the death of his eldest son Crispus (by his first wife, Minervina) as well as his second wife, the Empress Fausta, in 326, on the pretext that they had an "immoral" relationship. Modern historians suspect that a power struggle for the succession was taking place behind the scenes. As it happened, Constantine fell ill in 337 and on his deathbed asked to be baptized.

Constantine was succeeded by his son Constantine II (r. 337–340), who had served as his father's subordinate since 317, but he was expected to rule jointly with his brothers Constantius II and Constans as co-Emperors. This unfortunate arrangement promptly led to a bloody contest for control of the throne, resulting in a temporary division of the Empire. The

390
After the Massacre of Thessalonica, Theodosius is forced to make a pilgrimage of penance

399
John Cassian, also known as John the Eremite, arrives in Constantinople

403
John Chrysostom, Archbishop of Constantinople, is deposed

410
Rome is sacked by the Visigoths

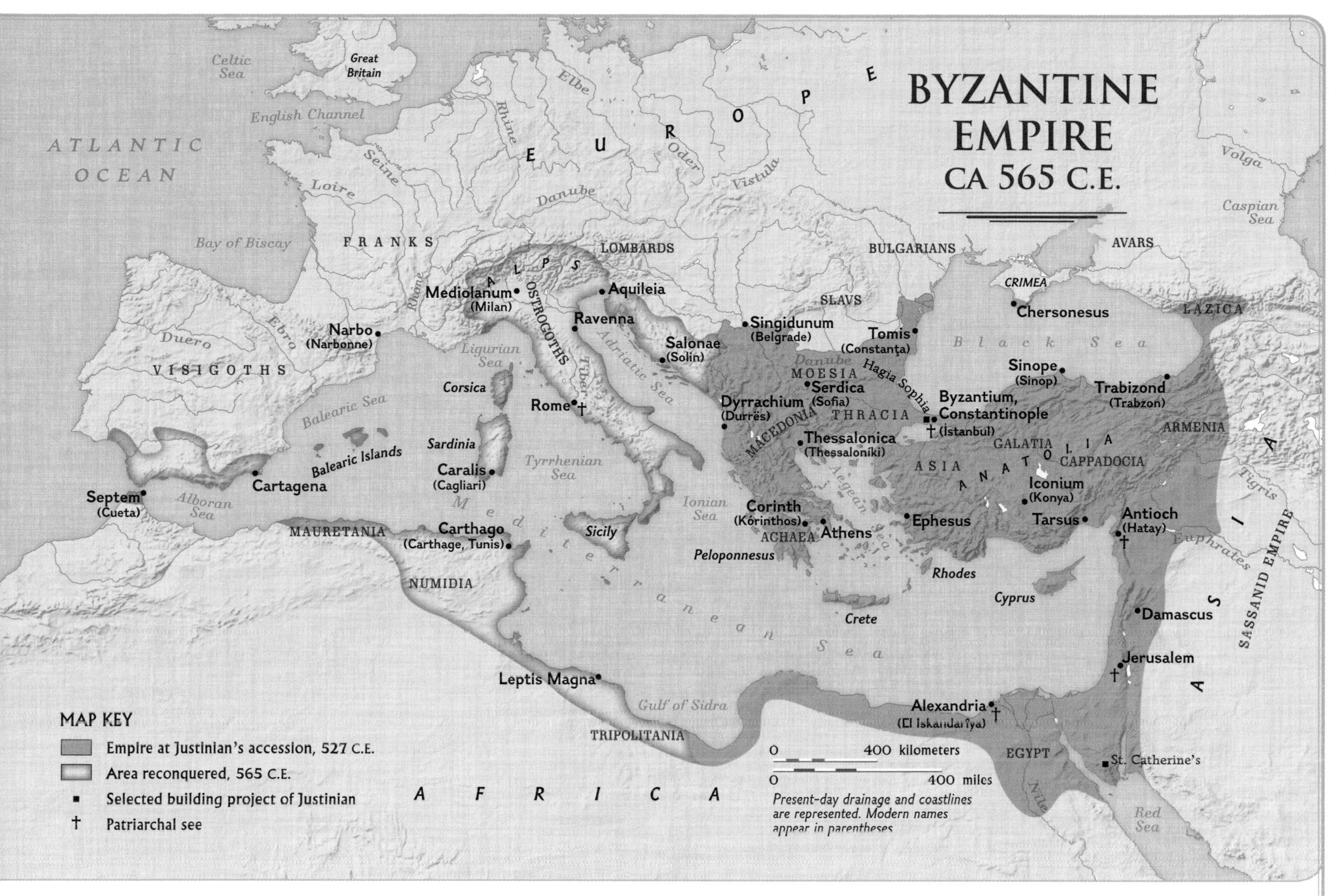

contest had religious dimensions as well. Constantine II, in charge of the West, was devoted to the Nicene Creed, whereas Constantius favored Arianism. The tensions between the three co-Emperors did not end until Constantine II was killed in 340, followed by the murder of Constans in 350. This left Constantius II (r. 337–361) as the sole ruler of the Roman Empire, now unified once more.

Constantius distinguished himself by successfully fending off invasions in the Germanic north and the Balkans. In religious matters, however, he violated the principles of the Edict of Milan—full religious tolerance for all cults—by marginalizing those who refused to be baptized into the Christian faith. Much of the urban population had already done so, knowing that being baptized was crucial to soliciting any form of imperial patronage, but things were different in the countryside. Here, the resistance to Christian worship was particularly strong among the rural population, the *paganos,* who were beholden to polytheistic rites closely associated with agriculture. The term "pagan" is derived from them.

In Judea, Constantius went as far as to impose a special tax on non-Christians in 352, which led local Jews and Samaritans to rise in revolt. This uprising was so brutally suppressed that it prompted a Second Diaspora. Many of the fleeing Jews chose to settle in the Talmudic centers of Persia (then the

OPPOSITE: A modern icon depicts Arius, the founder of the Arian movement. Arius asserted that since Christ was "begotten by the Father," his divinity was subordinate to the divine being of God the Father.

412
Cyril becomes patriarch of Alexandria

413
Augustine writes *The City of God*

428
Nestorius becomes patriarch of Constantinople

431
During the Council of Ephesus, Nestorius is deposed as patriarch of Constantinople

Sassanid Empire), or along the Red Sea, outside the reach of the Emperor. As a result, by the beginning of the sixth century a large part of Mediterranean maritime commerce was in Jewish hands. Other Jewish communities chose to stay in Roman Palestine, however, as evidenced by the beautiful mosaics of the sixth-century Beth Alpha synagogue, which among other images depict the wheel of the zodiac and the sacrifice of Isaac.

This magnificent mosaic of a zodiac was discovered in the remains of the fourth-century synagogue of Beth Alpha.

OPPOSITE: *This votive platter showing Byzantine Emperor Theodosius on his throne was made to commemorate the tenth anniversary of the Emperor's reign.*

Constantius's successor, Emperor Julian (r. 361–363), engineered a radical about-face. Raised as a Christian but appalled by the massacre of his older male relatives in the bloody purges after Constantine's death, Julian believed that only a return to Rome's ancient gods could save the Empire. While he did not outlaw Christianity, he certainly sought to stem the rapid growth of the Church by withholding state funds, by purging his court of Christian officials, and by actively promoting Rome's pagan cult. The construction of churches was suspended. Some bishops who rose in protest, such as Gemellus of Ancyra (today's Ankara), were executed. To justify his new policy, Julian personally drafted a polemic, "Against the Galileans," which attacked Christianity as immoral. For this, he is often referred to as "Julian the Apostate" by Christian authors.

In Judea, on the other hand, Julian caused great excitement not only by eliminating the punishing taxes against non-Christians, but also by announcing his intention to rebuild the Second Temple in Jerusalem. Jews in Judea were overjoyed and hailed Julian as a new Cyrus the Great (the Persian king who had allowed the Jews to rebuild the First Temple in 515 B.C.E.). Perhaps Julian hoped that by resurrecting Temple Judaism, the growing influence of Christianity in Palestine could be curbed. Before these plans could come to fruition, however, the Emperor was struck by a spear during the Battle of Samarra against Sassanid forces in 363. A few days later, he succumbed to his wounds.

Though brief, Julian's rule had shocked the Christian population in the Roman Empire to the core. His regime had exposed the deep resentment against Christianity among Rome's conservative class, particularly the nobility. Thus, when Theodosius I (r. 379–395), a pious Christian, rose to the throne, this Emperor was determined to eradicate any further challenges to the Christian faith. One year after his ascension, he issued an imperial decree that ordered *all* of his subjects to embrace Christianity and to "profess the faith which we believe has been communicated by the Apostle Peter to the Romans." Blood sac-

448
Synod of Constantinople rejects Monophysitism

450
The White Huns invade India

451
The Council of Chalcedon leads to a break in the Church

455
Rome is sacked by the Vandals

rifice to pagan gods was prohibited. Thus, in the closing years of the fourth century, Christianity had triumphed at last. Some 350 years after the crucifixion, it had become the sole religion of the Roman Empire. From this time forward, historians refer to the Roman realm as the *Byzantine* Empire.

One Realm, One Faith

Theodosius, too, faced conflict along the borders as well as from within. Unable to stem an invasion by Goths in Illyricum, a province roughly analogous to today's Croatia and northern Albania, the Emperor decided to simply accept the invaders by making them honorary Roman citizens. A treaty signed in 382 specified that as long as the Gothic tribes pledged allegiance to the Byzantine Emperor and agreed to have their militias absorbed in the Roman legions, they were effectively granted autonomous rule in the Balkans. It was an ominous development, born from expediency, which further accelerated the crumbling of the Empire.

A devout Christian, Theodosius turned toward the still-festering conflict between Nicene Christianity and Arianism. Prodded by Ambrose, the highly influential bishop of Milan, the Emperor convened the First Council of Constantinople in 381. One of its "canons," or doctrinal resolutions, specified that every Christian should pledge the Nicene Creed. Bishops who continued to support the Arian movement, such as Demophilus of Constantinople, were deposed, while all churches suspected of Arian sympathies were brought under control of Catholic priests.

The same synod also established the canonical definition of the Catholic Trinity, a concept first explored by the Nicene Council, based on theological arguments advanced by the so-called Cappadocian Fathers—bishop Basil of Caesarea; his brother Gregory, bishop of Nyssa; and Gregory of Nazianzus, patriarch of Constantinople. The question was whether, in addition to the Father and the Son, the Holy Spirit was likewise divine or not. The Council of Constantinople found that whereas the Son was "begotten" from the Father, the Holy Spirit "proceeded" from Him—language that continues in the Catholic and other denominational liturgy to this day.

Although in the early years of his reign Theodosius had been relatively tolerant of pagan practices, between 389 and 391 he moved to firmly establish Christianity as the sole religion of the realm. His decree *Nemo se hostiis polluat* made the worship of other cults and religions a criminal offense, resulting in forfeiture of one's property. All Roman holidays not yet converted to Christian purpose were abolished, and on the Forum in Rome the last vestige of Roman piety, the Temple of the Vestal Virgins, was closed.

Nevertheless, large tracts of the Empire, notably in Spain, Gaul, and rural enclaves in Italy, still remained stubbornly pagan. Large-scale

Period Artifacts

335–600 C.E.

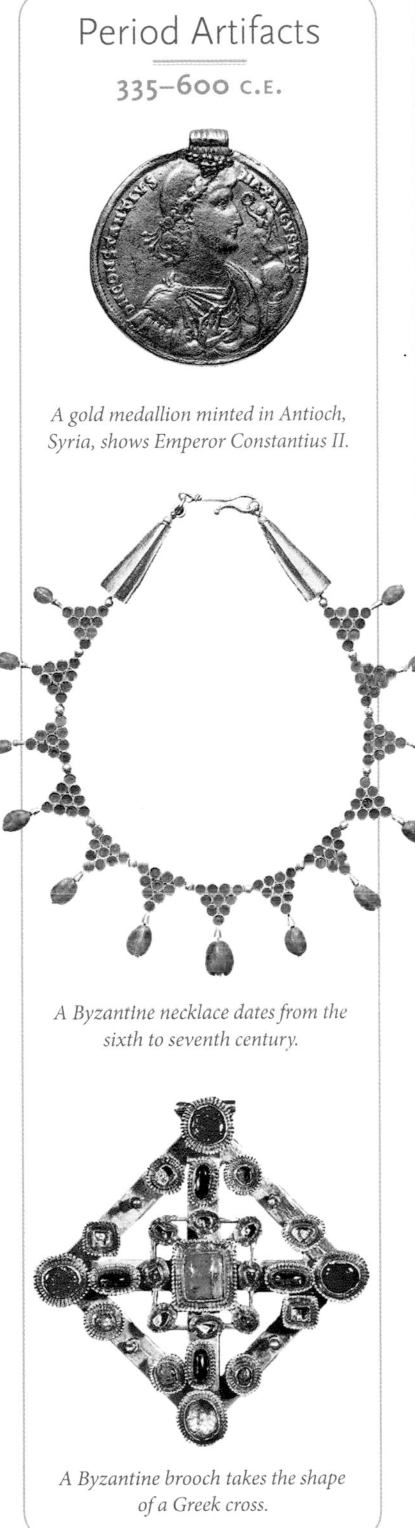

A gold medallion minted in Antioch, Syria, shows Emperor Constantius II.

A Byzantine necklace dates from the sixth to seventh century.

A Byzantine brooch takes the shape of a Greek cross.

476
The last Roman co-Emperor in the West, Romulus Augustulus, is deposed

493
Ostrogoth King Theodoric the Great establishes a kingdom on the Italian peninsula

518
Riots in Constantinople prompt Justin to depose Anastasius and proclaim himself Emperor

525
Justin appoints Justinian as "Caesar" of the East

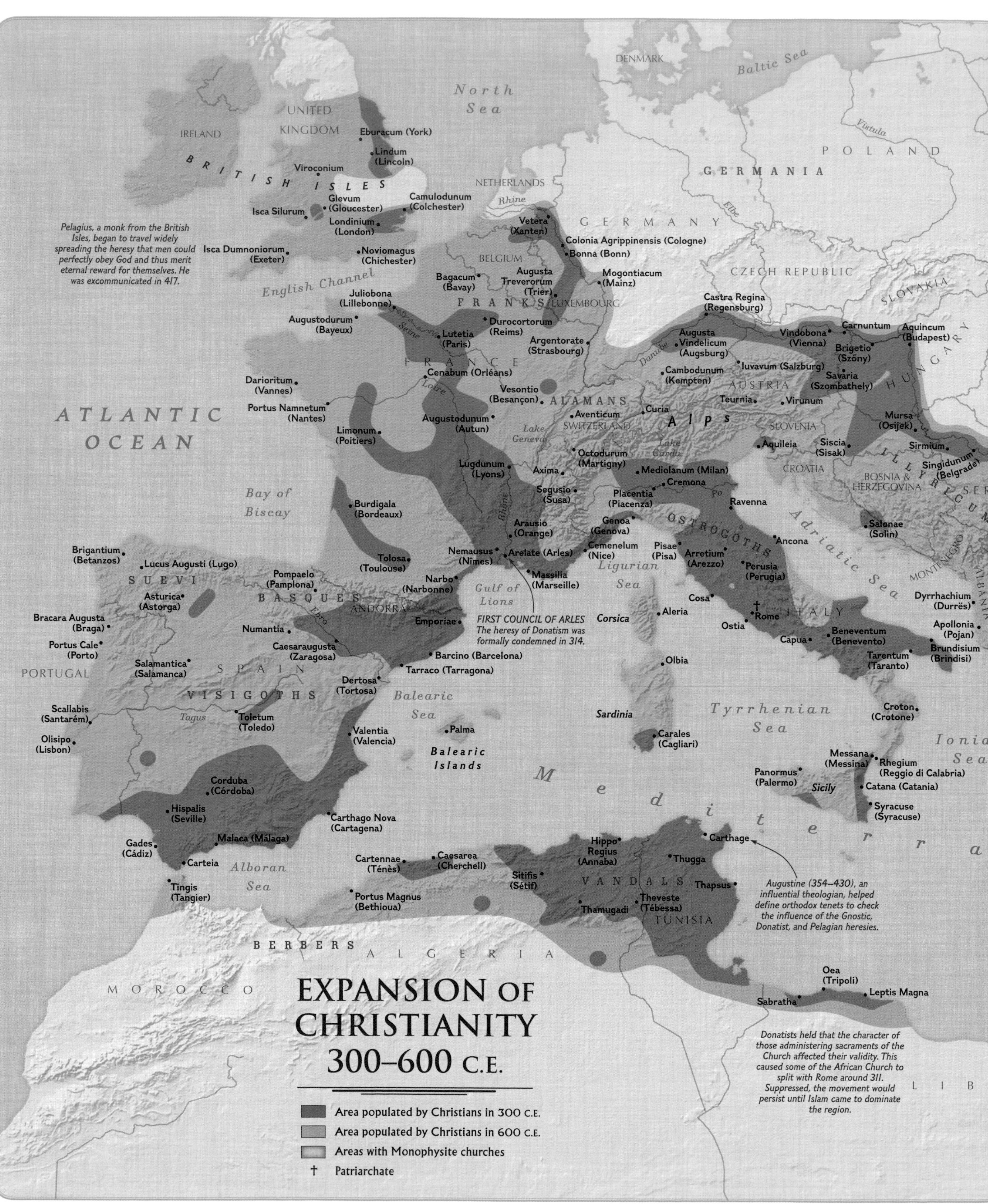
EXPANSION OF CHRISTIANITY 300–600 C.E.
Area populated by Christians in 300 C.E.
Area populated by Christians in 600 C.E.
Areas with Monophysite churches
† Patriarchate
Pelagius, a monk from the British Isles, began to travel widely spreading the heresy that men could perfectly obey God and thus merit eternal reward for themselves. He was excommunicated in 417.
FIRST COUNCIL OF ARLES
The heresy of Donatism was formally condemned in 314.
Augustine (354–430), an influential theologian, helped define orthodox tenets to check the influence of the Gnostic, Donatist, and Pelagian heresies.
Donatists held that the character of those administering sacraments of the Church affected their validity. This caused some of the African Church to split with Rome around 311. Suppressed, the movement would persist until Islam came to dominate the region.
ATLANTIC OCEAN
North Sea
Baltic Sea
English Channel
Bay of Biscay
Gulf of Lions
Ligurian Sea
Balearic Sea
Alboran Sea
Tyrrhenian Sea
Adriatic Sea
Ionia Sea
Mediterra
IRELAND
UNITED KINGDOM
BRITISH ISLES
DENMARK
NETHERLANDS
BELGIUM
LUXEMBOURG
GERMANY
GERMANIA
POLAND
CZECH REPUBLIC
SLOVAKIA
HUNGARY
AUSTRIA
SWITZERLAND
SLOVENIA
CROATIA
BOSNIA & HERZEGOVINA
MONTENEGRO
ILLYRICUM
FRANCE
FRANKS
ALAMANS
ANDORRA
BASQUES
SUEVI
SPAIN
VISIGOTHS
PORTUGAL
ITALY
OSTROGOTHS
VANDALS
TUNISIA
ALGERIA
MOROCCO
BERBERS
LIB
Alps
Rhine
Elbe
Vistula
Danube
Seine
Loire
Rhône
Ebro
Tagus
Po
Lake Geneva
Lake Garda
Corsica
Sardinia
Sicily
Balearic Islands
Eburacum (York)
Lindum (Lincoln)
Viroconium
Glevum (Gloucester)
Camulodunum (Colchester)
Isca Silurum
Londinium (London)
Isca Dumnoniorum (Exeter)
Noviomagus (Chichester)
Vetera (Xanten)
Colonia Agrippinensis (Cologne)
Bonna (Bonn)
Mogontiacum (Mainz)
Augusta Treverorum (Trier)
Bagacum (Bavay)
Juliobona (Lillebonne)
Augustodurum (Bayeux)
Durocortorum (Reims)
Lutetia (Paris)
Argentorate (Strasbourg)
Castra Regina (Regensburg)
Augusta Vindelicum (Augsburg)
Cambodunum (Kempten)
Iuvavum (Salzburg)
Vindobona (Vienna)
Carnuntum
Brigetio (Szőny)
Aquincum (Budapest)
Savaria (Szombathely)
Teurnia
Virunum
Curia
Aventicum
Octodurum (Martigny)
Vesontio (Besançon)
Cenabum (Orléans)
Darioritum (Vannes)
Portus Namnetum (Nantes)
Limonum (Poitiers)
Augustodunum (Autun)
Lugdunum (Lyons)
Axima
Segusio (Susa)
Mediolanum (Milan)
Cremona
Placentia (Piacenza)
Aquileia
Siscia (Sisak)
Mursa (Osijek)
Sirmium
Singidunum (Belgrade)
Burdigala (Bordeaux)
Arausio (Orange)
Genoa (Genova)
Ravenna
Salonae (Solin)
Ancona
Tolosa (Toulouse)
Nemausus (Nîmes)
Arelate (Arles)
Massilia (Marseille)
Cemenelum (Nice)
Pisae (Pisa)
Arretium (Arezzo)
Perusia (Perugia)
Narbo (Narbonne)
Brigantium (Betanzos)
Lucus Augusti (Lugo)
Pompaelo (Pamplona)
Asturica (Astorga)
Bracara Augusta (Braga)
Portus Cale (Porto)
Numantia
Caesaraugusta (Zaragosa)
Emporiae
Barcino (Barcelona)
Tarraco (Tarragona)
Salamantica (Salamanca)
Dertosa (Tortosa)
Scallabis (Santarém)
Toletum (Toledo)
Olisipo (Lisbon)
Valentia (Valencia)
Palma
Aleria
Cosa
Rome
Ostia
Capua
Beneventum (Benevento)
Dyrrhachium (Durrës)
Apollonia (Pojan)
Brundisium (Brindisi)
Tarentum (Taranto)
Olbia
Croton (Crotone)
Carales (Cagliari)
Corduba (Córdoba)
Hispalis (Seville)
Carthago Nova (Cartagena)
Malaca (Málaga)
Gades (Cádiz)
Carteia
Tingis (Tangier)
Messana (Messina)
Rhegium (Reggio di Calabria)
Panormus (Palermo)
Catana (Catania)
Syracuse (Syracuse)
Carthage
Hippo Regius (Annaba)
Thugga
Thapsus
Cartennae (Ténès)
Caesarea (Cherchell)
Sitifis (Sétif)
Portus Magnus (Bethioua)
Thamugadi
Theveste (Tébessa)
Oea (Tripoli)
Sabratha
Leptis Magna

FIRST COUNCIL OF CONSTANTINOPLE
Convened in 381 to address Apollinarian teaching, this gathering affirmed the doctrine that Jesus is fully human.
Nestorius, the Patriarch of Constantinople, was a proponent of the idea that Christ was two distinct persons, human and divine. He was deposed and died in 450 as an exile.
COUNCIL OF CHALCEDON
Answering the heresy of Eutyches, this council upheld the doctrine that Jesus is both human and God in one person in 451.
FIRST COUNCIL OF NICAEA
Called in 325 to answer the heresy of Arius and others threatening the Church. The full divinity of Christ was upheld.
COUNCIL OF EPHESUS
Countering Nestorius, the Church declared in 431 that Christ is a unified person with two natures, divine and human.
Nestorian Church created in 433 by Eastern clergy after the edict of the Council of Ephesus.
Eutyches (378–452), a monastic leader, espoused teaching that denied the orthodox position that Christ is fully human and God in one person. Monophysite churches in the East broke with Rome and Constantinople.
Apollinaris (ca 310–390), the Bishop of Laodicea, taught that Jesus' human nature was limited to his body; his mind and spirit divine. The heresy was condemned.
Athanasius (ca 296–373) was the Bishop of Alexandria and the principal opponent of Arianism.
Arius (250–336), an ascetic preacher, split the Church with his teaching that Christ was a lesser being than the eternal creator. He would be excommunicated and his teaching declared false.
Long association with Judaism made Ethiopia a fertile target for evangelism. Frumentius (ca 300–380) brought Christianity to the kingdom. The Ethiopian Church doctrine is similar to Coptic beliefs.
ARMENIAN CHURCH
JACOBITE CHURCH
COPTIC CHURCH
SARMATIA
UKRAINE
RUSSIA
SCYTHIA
KAZAKHSTAN
TURKMENISTAN
Caspian Sea
Caucasus Mts.
GEORGIA
AZERBAIJAN
ARMENIA
Azerb.
Lake Sevan
Lake Van
Lake Urmia
IRAN
Parthia
ROMANIA
BULGARIA
KOSOVO
MACED.
GREECE
Black Sea
Aegean Sea
Asia Minor
TURKEY
SYRIA
IRAQ
KUWAIT
LEBANON
CYPRUS
ISRAEL
West Bank
Dead Sea
JORDAN
Gaza Strip
SAUDI ARABIA
EGYPT
Red Sea
Mediterranean Sea
Volga
Don
Dnieper
Dniester
Danube
Tigris
Euphrates
Nile
Panticapaeum
Chersonesus
Pityus (Pitsunda)
Troesmis
Tomis (Constanța)
Durostorum (Silistra)
Civitas Tropaeensium (Adamclisi)
Viminacium
Oescus
Serdica (Sofia)
Philippopolis (Plovdiv)
Nicopolis (Nikopol)
Stobi
Heraclea
Thessalonica (Thessaloníki)
Perinthus (Marmaraereğlisi)
Constantinople (İstanbul)
Chalcedon (Kadıköy)
Nicomedia (Kocaeli)
Nicaea (İznik)
Prusa (Bursa)
Dorylaeum
Sinope (Sinop)
Amisus (Samsun)
Pompeiopolis
Trapezus (Trabzon)
Satala
Zela (Zile)
Megalopolis
Tigranocerta
Ancyra (Ankara)
Caesarea Cappadociae (Kayseri)
Melitene (Malatya)
Amida (Diyarbakır)
Edessa (Şanlıurfa)
Samosata (Samsat)
Cyrrhus
Pisidian Antioch (Yalvaç)
Iconium (Konya)
Tarsus
Pergamum (Bergama)
Smyrna (İzmir)
Ephesus
Miletus
Laodicea
Attalia (Antalya)
Myra (Kale)
Cnidus
Rhodes
Ambracia
Nicopolis
Delphi
Athens
Corinth (Kórinthos)
Sparta (Spárti)
Crete
Gortyn
Salamis
Paphos (Kouklia)
Antiochia (Antioch)
Seleucia Pieria (Samandağ)
Dura Europos
Ctesiphon
Palmyra
Emesa (Homs)
Tripolis (Tripoli)
Heliopolis (Baalbek)
Damascus
Tyre (Soûr)
Bostra (Buşra ash Shām)
Caparcotna
Caesarea
Jerusalem
Gaza
Petra
Pelusium
Alexandria (El Iskandarîya)
Ptolemais
Cyrene (Shaḥḥāt)
Memphis
Oxyrhynchus
Hermopolis
Ptolemais
Coptus
Thebae
0 50 100 150 200 250 kilometers
0 50 100 150 200 250 miles
Present-day drainage and coastlines are represented.
Modern names appear in parentheses.

conversion to Christianity, notably by local elites, would not begin until the sixth century—and by virtue of the charisma of missionaries, rather than by the force of law.

The End of the Western Empire

Encouraged by the criminalization of paganism, clergy throughout the realm began to ransack pagan temples, destroying thousands of statues of Roman deities while making off with a vast haul of silver, gold, and other treasure. When challenged by outraged pagan worshippers, one monk declared, "There is no such thing as robbery for those who truly possess Christ." In Alexandria, Bishop Theophilus personally supervised the wholesale destruction of the Mouseion complex, including the still-functioning Alexandrian Library. The culture of Roman Antiquity had effectively come to an end.

No one is to go
to the sanctuaries,
walk through the temples,
or raise his eyes to statues created
by the labor of man.

EMPEROR THEODOSIUS, 391

An even more alarming development took place in Callinicum (today's Ar-Raqqah in Syria), where a group of monks turned their wrath on a local Jewish synagogue. Until now, Jews had not been affected by the criminal prohibition of non-Christian worship. When news of the incident reached Theodosius, he promptly ordered the local bishop to finance a full restoration of the synagogue. Incensed, Bishop Ambrose demanded that Theodosius

525
Justinian marries Theodora

527
Justinian I ascends the throne of Byzantium

529
Justinian adopts a series of legal reforms known as the Justinian Codex

532
Justinian signs the "Treaty of Eternal Peace" with Persian King Khosrow I

rescind the order and that the synagogue be left in ruins. Theodosius complied.

In 390, public sentiment turned against the Emperor. The people of Thessalonica, fed up with having a garrison of unruly Goths in their midst as a result of the Emperor's decision to absorb these tribes, staged a riot. In the melee, the local Goth commander was killed. Determined to suppress the discontent, Theodosius allowed some 7,000 inhabitants of the city to be herded into the local hippodrome, where they were slaughtered by the Goth militias. This bloodbath caused such a backlash that even Theodosius' close ally Bishop Ambrose was forced to denounce this infamy, going as far as to threaten the Emperor with excommunication unless he publicly repented. Duly humbled, the Emperor made a pilgrimage of penance, dressed in the garb of a commoner. All of Constantinople was shocked by this public humiliation of a Roman Emperor by a Christian bishop.

In the second century, when the Roman Empire was at its zenith, a citizen could travel from the misty moors of Britain to the deserts of Mesopotamia without ever crossing a border. By the fifth century, however, the Western part of the realm had shrunk to a shadow of its

An Ethiopian Orthodox priest in Lalibela displays the processional cross of his church, Bieta Masqal, or House of the Cross.

OPPOSITE: *This Byzantine icon depicts the Three Cappadocian Fathers: St. Gregory, St. John Chrysostom, and St. Basil the Great. The Cappadocia region, in today's Turkey, was an early site of Christian activity.*

532
The Nika Riots lead to the destruction of the old Hagia Sophia

534
General Belisarius defeats the Vandal forces in North Africa

537
The new church of the Hagia Sophia is consecrated

537
The Ostrogoth siege of Rome is rebuffed

The sixth-century Basilica of San Vitale in Ravenna, one of the oldest Byzantine churches in Italy, contains some of the best-preserved mosaics from the period of Emperor Justinian I.

former self. In 405, a mass migration of Germanic tribes, possibly fleeing from Huns invading from farther east, plunged into Gaul, causing havoc on a vast scale. In 410, Roman control of Britain evaporated. That same year, Rome was sacked by the Visigoths, followed by Vandals in 455. Spain was carved up between Vandals and other tribes. Byzantine forces, beset by strife and distracted by competing rivals for the throne, were powerless to intervene. The last Roman co-ruler in the west, Romulus Augustulus, was deposed in 476, although Julius Nepos, hanging on to a rump state in Dalmatia, claimed the title of Western Roman Emperor until his assassination in 480. By the end of the fifth century, the Italian peninsula had become a kingdom ruled by Theoderic the Great, King of the Ostrogoths (454–526).

The Justinian Renaissance

The Empire in the East, however, would continue for another thousand years, and soon enjoy a renaissance under the leadership of one of Byzantium's greatest emperors, Justinian I (r. 527–565). He was originally named Petrus Sabbatius, the son of a family of low birth.

540
King Khosrow I invades Syria and Asia Minor

540
Ravenna, the last major Byzantine outpost on the Italian peninsula, falls

550s
Byzantine silk production begins after missionaries bring back silkworms from China

550
The crucifix emerges as a church ornament

Following the holy fathers we teach with one voice that the Son [of God] and our Lord Jesus Christ is to be confessed as one and the same.

COUNCIL OF CHALCEDON, *DEFINITION OF FAITH*

During his childhood, his intellect caught the attention of his uncle, a consul named Justin, who served as adviser to the court of Emperor Anastasius I (r. 491–518). During Anastasius' rule, extensive fortifications had been built along the eastern frontier, which played a major role in deterring the barbarian invasions that had destroyed in the Empire in the west. Anastasius had been raised in an Arian household, however, and as Emperor had become enchanted with another "heresy," the Monophysite doctrine. Monophysitism, as the name implies, solved the continuing question of Christ's duality by declaring that Jesus was of a *single* nature, divine through and through. To those around him, he had merely *seemed* to take on human form.

The Catholic Church attacked this latest challenge to its spiritual authority with the same vehemence with which it had fought the Arian heresy. But Monophysitism spread throughout the East with alarming speed. In 451, at the Council of Chalcedon, the matter would result in a permanent break between the Catholic Church and the so-called Oriental Orthodox churches, which all supported the Monophysite doctrine. This group includes, among others, the Coptic, Ethiopian, Syriac, Armenian, and Indian Orthodox churches.

The conflict between supporters of the Chalcedon doctrine—the "Chalcedonians"—and their opposition, the "non-Chalcedonians," continued to destabilize the church. When Anastasius tried to appoint dissident clergy to positions in Constantinople and Antioch, the cities erupted in revolt. The growing tensions culminated in a carefully staged riot in front of Anastasius' palace in 518, when the Emperor was 80 years old, with protestors loudly clamoring for his abdication. Who orchestrated this event has never been established with certainty, but Justin was able to exploit the turmoil by staging a coup and proclaiming himself Emperor. Petrus, duly renamed "Justinian" in his patron's honor, joined his court and eventually became Justin's closest adviser. When his patron died in 527, Justinian succeed him as sole Emperor of the Byzantine Empire.

Perhaps in an effort to hide his humble origins, Justinian clothed his reign with the greatest pomp Byzantium had ever seen, as evidenced by the beautiful mosaics in the San Vitale in Ravenna, the principal Byzantine outpost in Italy. In one panel, Justinian is depicted with his entourage of officers, advisers, and clergy in shimmering finery, while opposite him is a separate mosaic of his Empress, Theodora, and her ladies-in-waiting.

Much of this wealth derived from trade in luxuries from eastern Asia, notably silk, gems, and exotic spices. To carry these into Byzantium, traders had to navigate the treacherous Silk Road, through the territory of Rome's ancient foe, Persia. Anxious to protect this vital lifeline, Justinian negotiated a peace treaty with the Persian King, Khosrow I Anoushirvan, in 532, which was optimistically termed the "Treaty of Eternal Peace." In truth, the Byzantine treasury was compelled to pay Khosrow a ransom of 11,000 pounds of gold, in keeping with Byzantium's custom of buying off an

LIFE AND TIMES

The Great Plague

A third-century fresco from Ostia depicts men unloading a grain ship.

In 541, the Byzantine Empire was afflicted by an outbreak of bubonic plague that is believed to have been unprecedented in scale. Some scholars speculate the disease was introduced by rats on grain ships arriving from Egypt, which continued to serve as the Empire's main food supply. The Byzantine author Procopius first reported the outbreak in the harbor of Pelusium, then one of Egypt's main ports. The plague rapidly spread to all corners of the Byzantine realm, from Asia Minor and Roman Arabia in the east to Denmark and Roman Britain in the west. Procopius wrote that the daily toll rose to more than 10,000 people in Constantinople (though modern historians place the figure at 5,000). Justinian remorselessly insisted on levying taxes as usual, even on estates devastated by the plague, in order to continue to fund his wars in the West. Some historians believe the plague accelerated the decline of the Byzantine Empire and invited the renewed incursion of barbarian tribes.

552
Byzantine general Narses defeats the Ostrogoths in Italy

552
Totila, King of the Ostrogoths, is killed in battle

552
Emperor Shotoko Taishi introduces Buddhism in Japan

553
General Narses captures Rome and Naples for Byzantium

enemy it could not defeat. Tensions between Byzantine and Persian spheres of influence continued unabated, channeled through various proxy wars in the region.

Justinian is chiefly remembered for the magnificent churches he built during his reign, which in many ways constitute the last great achievement of Roman architecture. "As soon as he took over the rule from his uncle, his measure was to spend the public money without restraint," says Procopius, a secretary of one of Justinian's generals. Indeed, the Emperor ordered the construction of the beautiful church of San Vitale in Ravenna, and rebuilt Empress Helena's basilica in Bethlehem, known as the Church of the Nativity, after it had been destroyed by rebellious Samaritans. Though damaged in clashes between Palestinian militants and the Israeli army in 2002, this basilica can still be admired to this day.

But Justinian's greatest work is undoubtedly the church dedicated to God as the source of Holy Wisdom, or Hagia Sophia, which has stood for 15 centuries and today, following a recent restoration, still welcomes visitors in Istanbul (notwithstanding the addition of four minarets from the 15th century onward, as a result of which the Hagia Sophia incongruously became a model for mosques throughout the Ottoman world).

Encouraged by the great prosperity of his Empire, and in the mistaken belief that his eastern borders were now secure, Justinian embarked on a grand quest to recapture western Europe and thus restore the Roman Empire once more. The initial campaign, led by his general Belisarius, met with considerable success. In 534, Belisarius's forces took North Africa from the Vandals. With the Mediterranean Sea under Byzantine control, Belisarius launched an invasion of the Italian peninsula, beginning with Sicily. The Byzantine army steadily made its way to Rome, which was captured in 536. At the same time another Byzantine general, Liberius, took control of the south of Spain.

The illusory glory of these victories, however, hid the fact that the Byzantine treasury was unable to maintain a protracted war on various fronts, particularly when the Ostrogoths mounted a stiff resistance. With Justinian's armies stretched to the limit in the West, Persian King Khosrow I saw his chance. In 540, Persian forces launched a surprise attack into Syria and Asia Minor, pushing as far as the

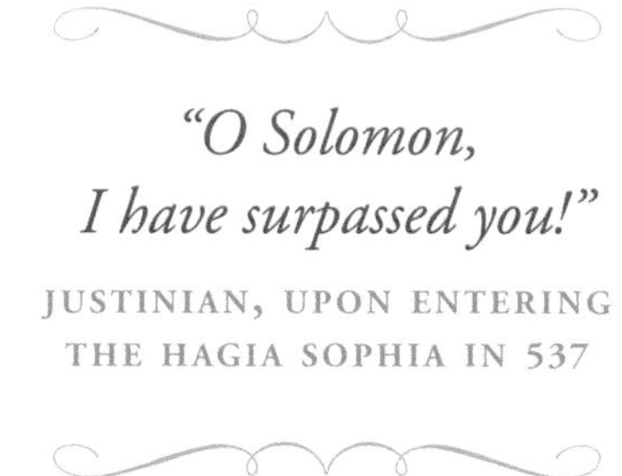

"O Solomon, I have surpassed you!"

JUSTINIAN, UPON ENTERING THE HAGIA SOPHIA IN 537

Black Sea. Belisarius, rushing reinforcements from the western front to the eastern, succeeded in halting the Persian King's advance, but he could not evict him from captured territory. The war dragged on for another 20 years, until in 562 a peace treaty was concluded. The peace came at a heavy cost: an annual tribute of 500 pounds of gold to the Persian King.

By then, the Justinian renaissance had run its course. In 565, Justinian died, leaving his successors, Justin II (r. 565–578) and Tiberius II (r. 574–582), with a depleted treasury and a population decimated by poverty and the plague. Meanwhile, the focus of the Christian Church had begun to shift: to the undiscovered pagan countries outside the Byzantine realm. ■

OPPOSITE: *A mosaic from San Vitale in Ravenna depicts Emperor Justinian I with his retinue of officials, guards, and deacons. Justinian's position at center emphasizes that he is the leader of both church and state.*

PERIOD ARCHITECTURE

The Hagia Sofia

The Hagia Sophia in Istanbul, built by Justinian I between 532 and 537, is the last great triumph of Roman engineering.

The original church dedicated to God as the source of Holy Wisdom, or Hagia Sophia, was destroyed during riots in 532. Justinian charged two of his finest architects, Anthemius of Tralles and Isidorus of Miletus, to build a new church that would surpass anything built in Christendom to date. To accomplish this, the architects had more than 10,000 workers at their disposal; cost was of no consequence. They designed a church that was based on an ambiguous plan: Though conceived as a basilica, the central nave is shaped as an elliptical hall, anchored by four semicircular chapels. It is crowned by a large dome, a stupendous creation that emphasizes the illusion of a circular church. Some 180 feet high and 100 feet wide, this vast sphere seems to float—an impression that is reinforced by the string of windows at the very base of the dome.

553
Fifth Council of Constantinople is held

559
General Belisarius repels a siege by Huns near Constantinople

562
A peace treaty is signed between Byzantium and Persia

565
Emperor Justinian dies and is succeeded by Justin II

MAXIMIA

4
CHAPTER

EXPANSION INTO EUROPE

300-650

Hitherto I have served you as a soldier: allow me now to become a soldier to God.

MARTIN OF TOURS
TO EMPEROR JULIAN

Soon after the emancipation of Christianity in the Roman Empire, missionaries bravely ventured into the dark corners of the European continent to spread the Gospel among the barbarian tribes, from the dark forests of northern Germany to the green pastures of Ireland.

As the former Roman Empire began to shrink to the southern territories around the Mediterranean—Italy, Greece, Asia Minor, Syria, and North Africa—Christian missionaries moved into regions now controlled by barbarian tribes, in search of souls to convert.

One of the first and most pivotal missions was undertaken by a man named Ulfilas or Wulfila ("little wolf," 313–383), who fearlessly moved among the Gothic tribes living in what today is modern Germany. Though some of these tribes may have originated in Scandinavia, by the third century they were occupying large tracts of Europe north of the Danube. From here, they steadily staged a number of violent incursions into the Roman Empire, pushing through the Balkans to plunder their way to Athens, moving as far as Cyprus. A century later, after the Goths had split into the Thervingi and the Greuthungi,

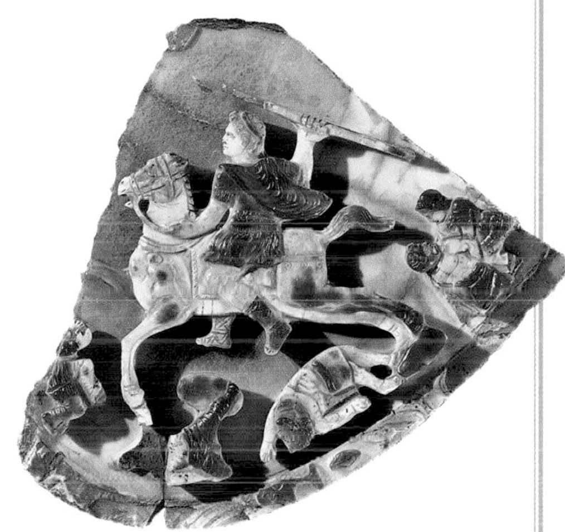

ABOVE: *A fourth-century cameo depicts a triumphant Roman emperor trampling barbarians.*

OPPOSITE: *According to local legend, the Rock of Cashel was the place where fifth-century Irish missionary Patrick converted the King of Munster.*

PRECEDING PAGES: *Michael Pacher (1434–1498) painted this portrait of Augustine in his "Altarpiece of the Fathers of the Church" of 1480. Pacher created the altarpiece for the Neustift Monastery, high in the mountains of northern Italy.*

Period Artifacts

550–1100

An Ostrogothic belt buckle dates from the sixth century.

Two eagle-shaped fibulae originated from sixth-century Spain.

The "Shrine of St. Patrick's Bell" dates from 1100.

separated by the Dniester River in today's Romania, they in turn were routed by invaders. These were the Huns, a warlike people from east of the Volga River in Russia, who pushed the Goths farther into former Roman territory.

It was during this volatile period that Ulfilas began his evangelizing efforts. His origins are uncertain. One source claims he had a Gothic father and a Roman mother, whereas another suggests that Ulfilas was born to Anatolian parents who were enslaved by Gothic tribes. Either scenario would explain why Ulfilas spoke the Gothic language fluently. While being educated for the priesthood, he also became proficient in both Greek and Latin, at a time when much of the Byzantine Empire continued to be preoccupied with Arianism. Dispatched by Bishop Eusebius of Nicomedia (no relation to Constantine's biographer Eusebius) to baptize the Goths, Ulfilas plunged into his mission, only to find his efforts rebuffed by the Thervingi, whose leader, Athanaric, feared that Christianity would subvert their ancient culture. Undaunted, Ulfilas retreated to Nicopolis (today's Nikyup in modern Bulgaria). Here, he realized that in order to develop a truly indigenous Gothic Christianity, he needed a Bible in the Gothic language. Thus, for the next few years, Ulfilas painstakingly translated the Bible from Greek into Gothic script, using many characters that he himself devised. This rare translation was partially preserved in the sixth-century *Codex Argenteus,* only discovered in the 16th century. On the strength of this Gothic Bible, Ulfilas renewed his efforts and was able to make large-scale conversions among the Gothic tribes.

Eventually, the Goths split into Visigoths, nominal allies of Rome, and the fearsome Ostrogoths, who considered Rome their sworn enemy. Both, however, were Christians in the Arian mold, largely as a result of Ulfilas's efforts. Indeed, while the Italian kingdom that the Ostrogoth King Theodoric the Great established was Christian in spirit, its Arian outlook created much tension with Catholic Christians on the peninsula.

While Ulfilas targeted the Goths of northeastern Europe, another missionary, Martin (316–397) set his sights on Gaul, which is roughly analogous to today's France. Unlike the northern territories, southern Gaul had been thoroughly Romanized in preceding centuries and still had a flourishing Greco-Roman culture, exemplified by such cosmopolitan cities as Vienne and Lyons. Born in Pannonia, today's Hungary, Martin originally joined the Imperial Horse Guard as a cavalry officer and was stationed in a garrison near Samarobriva (today's Amiens) during the reign of Emperor Julian the Apostate. According to a popular legend, told by his biographer Sulpicius (363–425), one day Martin approached the Amiens city gates and spotted a beggar sitting nearby. On impulse he took his sword, cut his Roman cloak, and gave one half to the beggar. That night, he had a dream in which Jesus wore the cloak he had cut, saying, "Martin, who

A bronze coin depicts Constans, Roman Emperor from 337 to 350. The reverse side depicts the resettlement of Christian Goths in 348.

313
Ulfilas, missionary to the Gothic tribes, is born

316
Martin of Tours is born

360
Martin of Tours founds a monastery in Ligugé

360
John Cassian, a pupil of John Chrysostom, is born

is still not baptized, clothed me with this robe." Martin renounced his military career, was baptized, and became a protégé of Hilary, Bishop of Poitiers.

In 360, under influence of the monastic movement in the East, Martin founded a monastery in Ligugé, one of the first abbeys established in France. Modern excavations indicate that the settlement was built on the remains of a Gallo-Roman villa, though most of the monks lived in nearby huts (or *locaciaci,* possibly the root of the word Ligugé). This monastery rapidly became the center of a radiating evangelizing effort as Martin traveled throughout southern France to convert the local pagans to Christianity. After being ordained the bishop of Tours, he founded a second monastery, the Abbey of Marmoutier, in 372. Unlike Ulfilas, however, Martin was a devoted Nicaenean (or "Catholic," a term coined by Emperor Theodosius I in 380) and fiercely opposed to the Arian movement then percolating into northern Europe. This would bind Christian Gaul more closely to Rome than to the Byzantine court of Constantinople—a relationship that would endure in the centuries to come.

[The Irish] cried out, as with one voice: "We appeal to you, holy servant boy, to come and walk among us."

PATRICK OF IRELAND

On the heels of Martin came a monk named Cassian (360–435), a pupil of the Christian sage John Chrysostom in Constantinople, who was ordained into the priesthood by Pope Innocent I in 405. Filled with fervor for Egyptian-style cenobitic monasticism, Cassian built a monastery near Marseille in 415, known as the Abbey of St. Victor. A prolific writer, Cassian also wrote several theological tracts including *De Institutis Coenobiorum* (*Institutes of Monastic Life*). This book formulates a set of rules for the contemplative life that would be a great influence on the

A remnant reveals a page from the Ulfilas Bible, a translation of Scripture from Greek into Gothic script. To complete this task, Ulfilas, an ordained bishop, devised the Gothic alphabet.

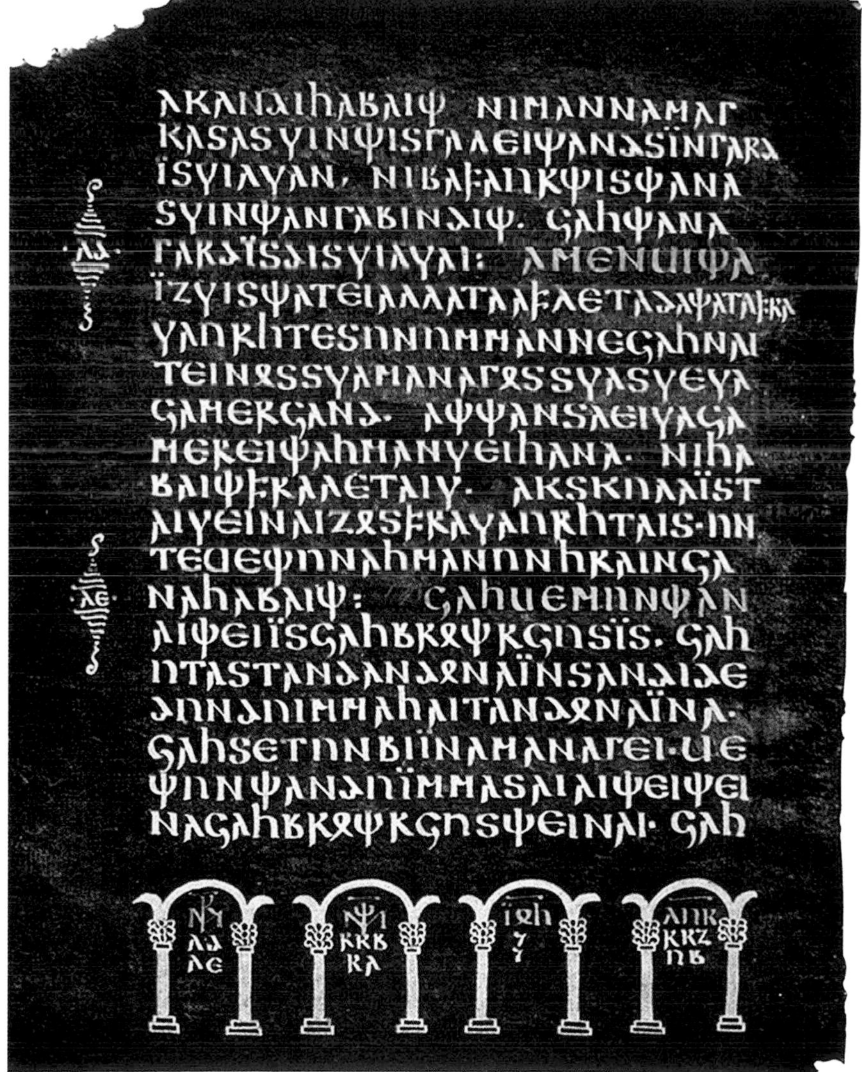

372
Martin of Tours founds a second monastery, the Abbey of Marmoutier

390
Patrick, missionary to the Irish, is born

400
Norse traders begin to spread throughout Europe

405
Cassian is ordained into the priesthood by Pope Innocent I

most important figure of early monasticism, Benedict of Nursia.

Patrick of Ireland

While Ulfilas evangelized among the Goths and Martin spread the Gospel in southern Gaul, another important mission was undertaken by Patrick (390–460) in today's Ireland. Unlike Gaul, Ireland had never been conquered by the Romans; therefore it had been touched by neither Roman polytheism nor Byzantine Christianity. According to one of his letters, Patrick was the son of a Roman deacon in Britain, born at a time when Roman control in that territory was crumbling. At age 16, Patrick was captured by pirates and sold into slavery in Ireland, where he remained for six years. This period in captivity opened his mind to Christ, he later wrote; as soon as he was able to escape, he returned to Britain and resolved to become a missionary.

Contrary to popular belief, Patrick was not the first missionary to spread the Gospel on the Emerald Isle. Among others, a priest named Palladius had been sent by Pope Celestine I as early as 431 to serve as bishop of Ireland, which suggests that there were already a number of Christian communities at the time, primarily in urban centers like Tara, which were ruled by knights or "High Kings." Modern research suggests that Patrick was sent in the 430s to replace Palladius, and that in subsequent lore the two figures were combined to produce the legend of St. Patrick. Regardless of these precedents, the evangelizing effort in Ireland was still a hazardous undertaking. Patrick and his acolytes were harassed and repeatedly imprisoned by the lords of local clans, while suffering fierce opposition from the local druids and magicians. Struggling against great odds, Patrick nevertheless succeeded in converting many thousands of men and women, among not only the peasantry but also the local nobility. This would later give rise to countless legends about this remarkable man.

OPPOSITE: A 17th-century Byzantine icon depicts St. John Chrysostom, an important early Church father and archbishop of Constantinople.

SAINTS AND CLERICS

Benedict

The most important figure in the development of a uniquely Western form of monasticism was Benedict (ca 480–ca 543). Son of a Roman nobleman in Umbria, Benedict moved away at age 20 to live the life of a hermit, repelled—as tradition tells us—by the licentious living of his fellow youths. He lived in a cave in the Simbruini Mountains with such extreme abstemiousness and devotion to prayer that he soon attracted a following. When the abbot in the nearby community of Subiaco died, Benedict was prevailed upon to take over the convent. But the monks soon bridled under his rule. According to a legend, they even tried to poison his wine, but fortunately the cup shattered as soon as Benedict prayed over it. A similar miracle prevented Benedict from eating poisoned bread. Eventually he moved away to establish 12 other monastic settlements, followed by the foundation of the large monastery at Monte Cassino in 529. Despite its near destruction during World War II, this monastery continues to function to this day. Benedict's greatest accomplishment, however, is the development of a set of rules that sought to reconcile the ascetic emphasis of Eastern cenobitism with a more humane communal lifestyle focused on prayer and service to others. Candidate monks were required to take the Benedictine Vow, promising obedience, chastity, and *conversatio morum*, a wholehearted devotion to sanctity. The Benedictine Rules would inspire the establishment of countless monasteries throughout Europe and lead to the foundation of the Benedict Order.

This fresco portrait of Benedict was painted by Gherardo Starnina (ca 1354–1409).

406 **Germanic tribes cross the Rhine**

410 **Visigoth King Alaric sacks Rome**

415 **Cassian founds the Abbey of St. Victor in Marseille, France**

429 **The Vandals establish a state in North Africa**

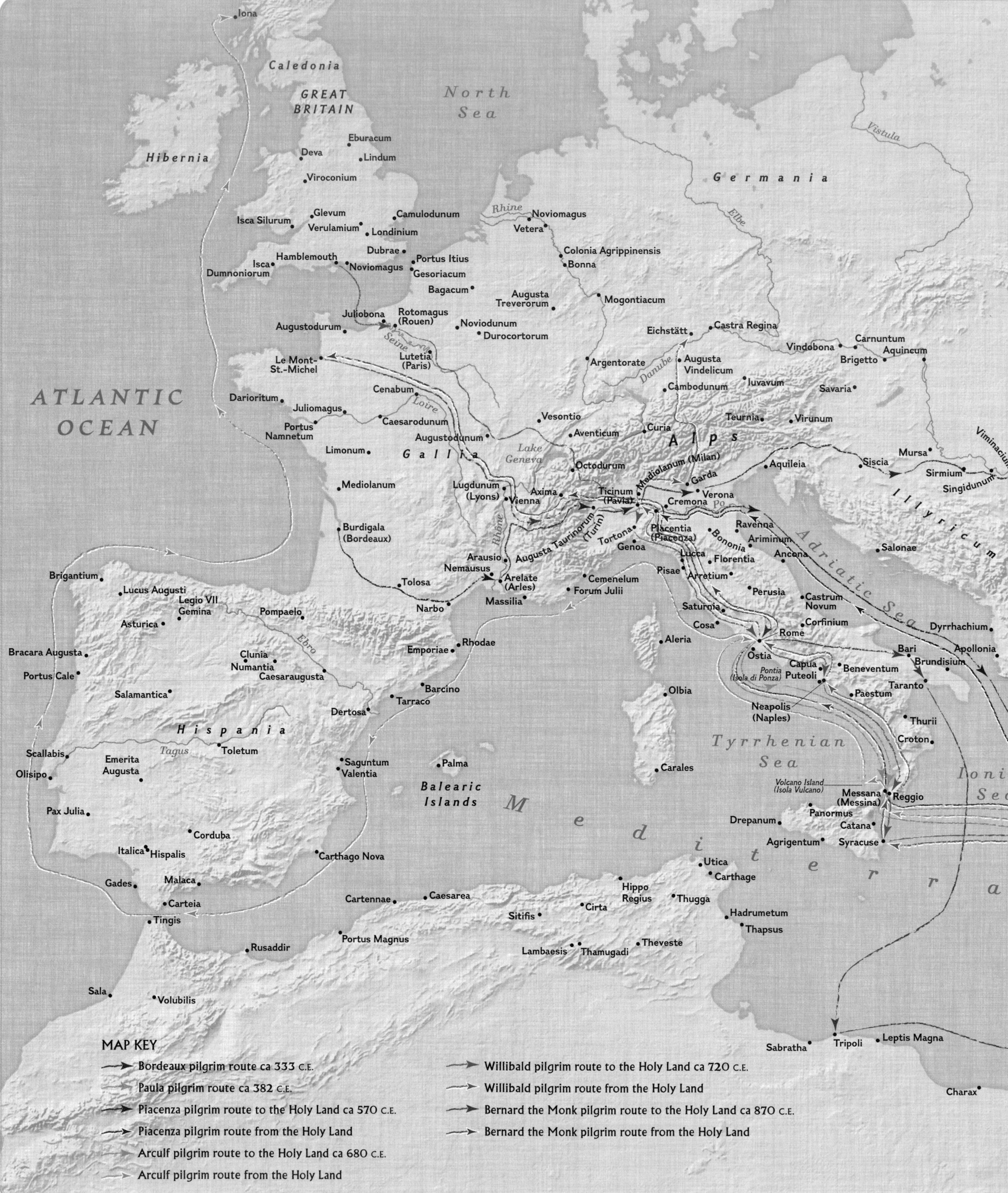

Iona
Caledonia
GREAT BRITAIN
North Sea
Hibernia
Eburacum
Deva
Lindum
Viroconium
Glevum
Camulodunum
Isca Silurum
Verulamium
Londinium
Dubrae
Isca Dumnoniorum
Hamblemouth
Noviomagus
Portus Itius
Gesoriacum
Bagacum
Rhine
Noviomagus
Vetera
Colonia Agrippinensis
Bonna
Augusta Treverorum
Mogontiacum
Germania
Elbe
Vistula
Juliobona
Rotomagus (Rouen)
Augustodurum
Noviodunum
Durocortorum
Seine
Lutetia (Paris)
Le Mont-St.-Michel
Eichstätt
Castra Regina
Carnuntum
Vindobona
Aquincum
Brigetto
Argentorate
Danube
Augusta Vindelicum
Cambodunum
Iuvavum
Savaria
ATLANTIC OCEAN
Darioritum
Cenabum
Loire
Juliomagus
Portus Namnetum
Caesarodunum
Vesontio
Teurnia
Virunum
Augustodunum
Aventicum
Curia
Alps
Viminacium
Limonum
Gallia
Lake Geneva
Octodurum
Mediolanum (Milan)
Aquileia
Siscia
Mursa
Sirmium
Singidunum
Mediolanum
Lugdunum (Lyons)
Axima
Vienna
Ticinum (Pavia)
Garda
Verona
Cremona
Po
Illyricum
Burdigala (Bordeaux)
Rhône
Augusta Taurinorum (Turin)
Tortona
Placentia (Piacenza)
Ravenna
Bononia
Ariminum
Genoa
Salonae
Arausio
Nemausus
Arelate (Arles)
Tolosa
Lucca
Florentia
Ancona
Adriatic Sea
Pisae
Arretium
Cemenelum
Forum Julii
Brigantium
Lucus Augusti
Legio VII Gemina
Massilia
Narbo
Perusia
Castrum Novum
Pompaelo
Asturica
Saturnia
Corfinium
Cosa
Dyrrhachium
Rome
Ebro
Rhodae
Emporiae
Aleria
Bari
Apollonia
Bracara Augusta
Ostia
Brundisium
Clunia
Numantia
Capua
Beneventum
Portus Cale
Caesaraugusta
Pontia (Isola di Ponza)
Puteoli
Taranto
Barcino
Paestum
Salamantica
Tarraco
Olbia
Dertosa
Neapolis (Naples)
Hispania
Thurii
Tyrrhenian Sea
Croton
Scallabis
Toletum
Tagus
Emerita Augusta
Saguntum
Valentia
Palma
Carales
Olisipo
Ionian Sea
Volcano Island (Isola Vulcano)
Balearic Islands
Messana (Messina)
Reggio
Mediterranean
Pax Julia
Panormus
Drepanum
Catana
Corduba
Agrigentum
Syracuse
Italica
Hispalis
Carthago Nova
Utica
Carthage
Gades
Malaca
Hippo Regius
Cartennae
Caesarea
Thugga
Carteia
Cirta
Sitifis
Hadrumetum
Tingis
Thapsus
Portus Magnus
Rusaddir
Theveste
Lambaesis
Thamugadi
Sala
Volubilis
Sabratha
Tripoli
Leptis Magna
Charax
MAP KEY
Bordeaux pilgrim route ca 333 C.E.
Paula pilgrim route ca 382 C.E.
Piacenza pilgrim route to the Holy Land ca 570 C.E.
Piacenza pilgrim route from the Holy Land
Arculf pilgrim route to the Holy Land ca 680 C.E.
Arculf pilgrim route from the Holy Land
Willibald pilgrim route to the Holy Land ca 720 C.E.
Willibald pilgrim route from the Holy Land
Bernard the Monk pilgrim route to the Holy Land ca 870 C.E.
Bernard the Monk pilgrim route from the Holy Land

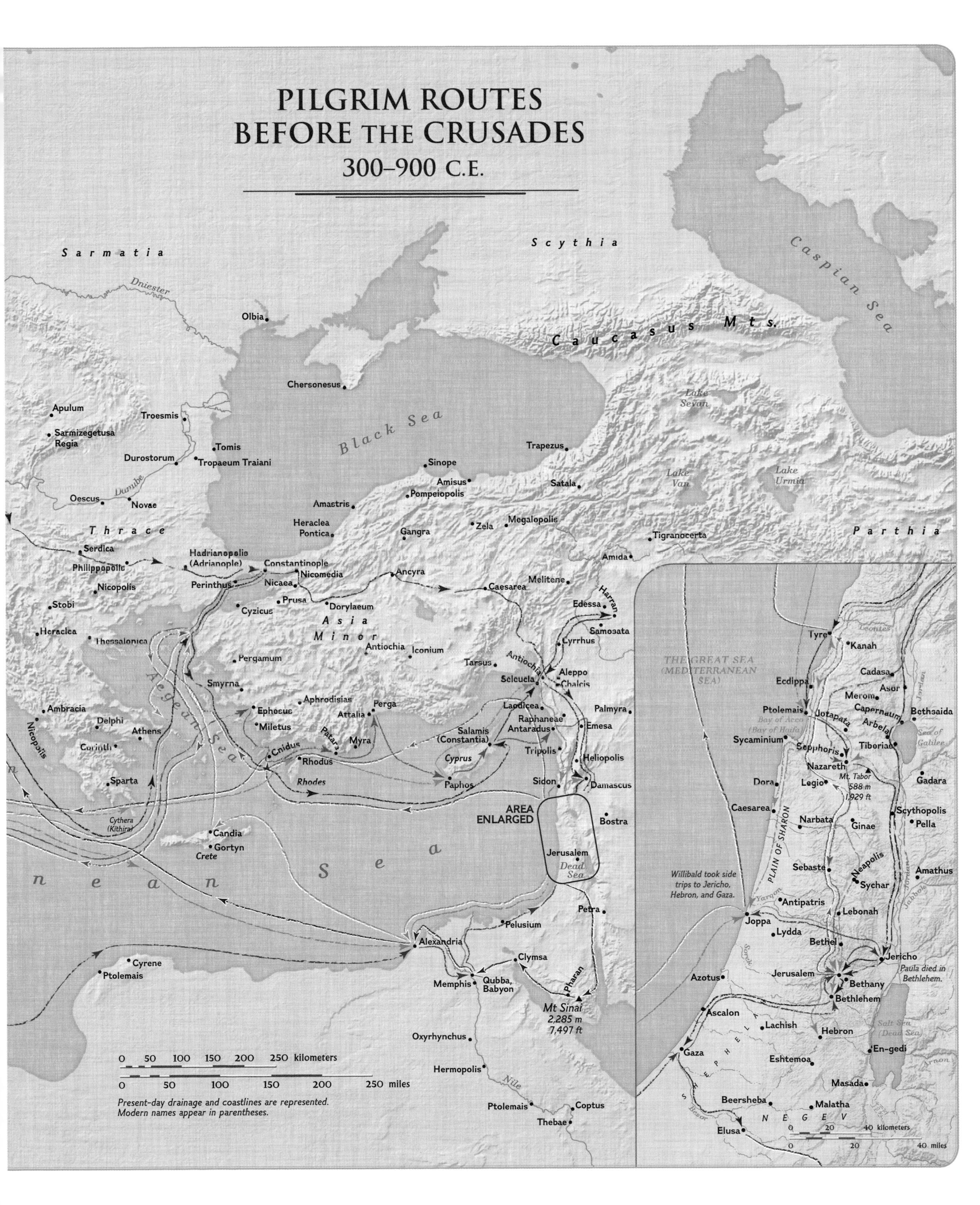

PILGRIM ROUTES
BEFORE THE CRUSADES
300–900 C.E.
Sarmatia
Scythia
Caspian Sea
Caucasus Mts.
Black Sea
Thrace
Asia Minor
Parthia
Aegean Sea
Cyprus
Rhodes
Crete
AREA ENLARGED
Constantinople
Jerusalem
Alexandria
Antioch
Damascus
Mt Sinai 2,285 m 7,497 ft
THE GREAT SEA (MEDITERRANEAN SEA)
Willibald took side trips to Jericho, Hebron, and Gaza.
Paula died in Bethlehem.
Mt. Tabor 588 m 1,929 ft
0 50 100 150 200 250 kilometers
0 50 100 150 200 250 miles
Present-day drainage and coastlines are represented.
Modern names appear in parentheses.
0 20 40 kilometers
0 20 40 miles

Fortunately, Ireland was largely spared the mass movement of barbarian tribes that caused such havoc in Western Europe. When Roman control of Britain collapsed under pressure of barbarian invasions and many Christian churches were suppressed, the Celtic Christians in Ireland kept the flame of Christianity alive. A legendary figure named Brigit (ca 451–525) is credited with founding the first monastery in Ireland near Kildare, welcoming both men and women. This monastery and others served to nurture and preserve the classical texts left by Roman civilization. Not without some justification has scholar Thomas Cahill claimed, "The Irish saved civilization."

SAINTS AND CLERICS

Augustine of Hippo

Augustine of Hippo, one of the most influential theologians of the early Catholic Church, was born in 354 in Thagaste (today's Souk Ahras, Algeria). He was raised by his mother, Monica, a devout Catholic, but after Augustine went to Carthage to study rhetoric, he flirted with other cults, notably Manichaeism. The young Augustine also indulged in much drinking and carousing, and had a long-term affair that produced a son, named Adeodatus. In 384, he was appointed to teach rhetoric at the imperial court in Milan. Here, Bishop Ambrose persuaded him to return to Catholicism. In 391, Augustine was ordained a priest in Hippo Regius (today's city of Annaba, Algeria), later rising to the position of bishop. Augustine turned his formidable intellect to the urgent questions of his day. This included the relationship between the body and the soul in Christian doctrine, and the nature of the Church as both a physical institution and a spiritual community of souls. He rejected the literal interpretation of certain notions in Scripture, such as the idea of Christ's reign as a thousand-year kingdom (a view known as *amillennialism*), which would resonate with some Protestant thinkers in centuries to come. The unhappy outcome of Augustine's love affairs may have influenced his later abhorrence of sexuality, and his attitude toward women in some of his writings. Nevertheless, his brilliant argumentation reveals him as truly a man on the threshold between Antiquity and the Christian era—as Thomas Cahill wrote, both the last classical and the first medieval man.

Giovacchino Assereto (1600–1649) painted Augustine and his mother, Monica.

The Barbarian Invasions

Nevertheless, large areas in fifth-century Europe still remained untouched by Christianity. As the vestiges of Roman law and order slowly dissipated, so did the social fabric of society—a process that was accelerated by the great popular upheavals of barbarian peoples throughout this period. What we should not forget, however, is that several of these tribes were Christians, having been converted by missionary pioneers such as Ulfilas. As Justo González has written, Christianity had gained a foothold among the Germanic "barbarians" long before these tribes broke into Roman territory. Most embraced a rather informal version of Arianism, however, rather than the Nicene Christianity enforced as orthodoxy within the Byzantine Empire. Other than the theological differences, this had political

431
Palladius is appointed bishop of Ireland

430s
Patrick replaces Palladius as bishop of Ireland

451
Brigit, founder of the first monastery in Ireland, is born

452
Pope Leo I persuades Attila the Hun not to sack Rome

ramifications as well, for regions touched by Arian Christianity would largely develop independently from the imperial and religious authority of Constantinople.

Visigoth King Alaric (370–410), for example, besieged and sacked Rome in 410, but being an Arian Christian, he made sure that churches were not harmed. In 428, the Vandals, likewise Arian Christians, invaded northern Africa and swept away Roman control of the Mediterranean. As they battled to invest the city of Hippo in 430, the theologian Augustine (354–430), a fervent advocate of Catholic doctrine and author of several highly influential works, lay dying. According to tradition, the Vandals burned the city but left Augustine's church and library untouched.

Then Attila the Hun (r. 434–453) swept into western Europe, and his followers had no such compunction about Christianity. Pushing pagan and Christian tribes alike into Gaul and beyond, they crossed the Alps and threatened the Italian peninsula itself. An unusual alliance of Visigoths and Germanic Alemanni, a ferocious tribe renowned for their military prowess, joined with Roman forces to try to stop the Huns, but to no avail. In 452, Attila was approaching Rome when the reigning pope, Leo I (r. 440–461) rode on

OPPOSITE: *The Rock of Cashel is closely associated with the legend of the fifth-century Irish missionary Patrick, a Christian missionary and bishop in Ireland.*

A French engraving shows the sack of Rome by the Visigoths in 410, led by Alaric I. This battle was a decisive event in the decline of the Roman Empire.

481
Clovis I, son of the Merovingian King Childeric I, begins his reign

486
King Clovis I of the Franks triumphs at the Battle of Soissons

496
Prodded by wife Clotilde, Clovis I converts to Catholicism

500
The iron-tipped moldboard plow is invented, greatly increasing agricultural yields

> *Let no one presume to attempt any illicit act contrary to the authority of the Apostolic See.*
>
> POPE LEO I

horseback to meet him, accompanied by two representatives from Emperor Valentinian III. What transpired next is uncertain, but Attila was persuaded to turn back—his wagon trains already overloaded with booty from northern Italy. For this, Pope Leo is often called "Leo the Great," though he himself adopted the title used previously by the chief priest of Rome's pagan cult: *Pontifex Maximus*. This title is still used by popes to this day.

Leo's dramatic intervention also boosted the prestige of the Roman papacy, which since the reign of Theodosius had been in danger of being overshadowed by imperial authority. During the Council of Chalcedon, the Catholic bishops solemnly agreed that the Apostolic See of Rome should be considered supreme, followed by the authority of Constantinople in second place.

The Kingdom of France

Throughout the fifth century, the mass movement of large tribal groups continued, accelerating the disintegration of Roman Europe. The Alemanni (the root of *Allemagne*, the French word for "Germany") established

French artist Jules Delaunay (1828–1891) painted this fresco of "Attila and His Army Marching on Paris." Attila was ruler of the Huns; during his reign, he was one of the most feared enemies of the Eastern and Western Roman Empires.

523 — **Yusuf As'ar Yath'ar, King of the Himyarites in Yemen, converts to Judaism**

523 — **War breaks out between Jewish Yemen and Christian Ethiopia**

529 — **Benedict of Nursia founds the monastery of Monte Cassino**

530 — **King Gelimer begins his reign over the Vandal kingdom in North Africa**

themselves in Alsace and northern Switzerland, which is why these regions are still German-speaking to this day. Another Germanic branch, the Visigoths, settled farther southwest, along the Loire River and in Aquitaine, from where they made their way to Spain. For the next three centuries, Spain would be ruled as a Visigoth kingdom, though often beset by dynastic strife as various factions fought for control of the throne.

"The Baptism of Clovis I" is a mural by French artist Joseph Paul Blanc (1846–1904). Clovis was the first king of the Franks, who united all the Frankish tribes.

Though Visigoths had always been Arian, in time the Catholic strand of Christianity began to prevail in Spain. In 589, at the Third Council of Toledo, Visigoth King Reccared I (r. 586–601) formally converted from Arian to Catholic Christianity. Meanwhile, several Catholic clerics such as Isidore of Seville (560–636), "the last scholar of the ancient world," in historian Montalembert's words, worked hard to preserve classical texts from Plato to Aristotle that the Roman era had bequeathed them. Thus, they laid the groundwork for the proto-Renaissance of the Iberian Convivencia in the eighth century.

The Franks were another prominent tribe. The meaning of the word "Frank" is uncertain, though eventually all of France (or *Frankreich* in German, literally "Frankish realm") would be named after them. Evicted from their native territory in the Rhineland by the Hun invasions, they originally settled in southern Gaul. Here, they assimilated with the local culture and ultimately produced linguistic adaptations of Latin that would evolve into the Romance languages of today. Like the Vandals and Visigoths, the Franks were keen to consolidate their gains into dynastic kingdoms. The fall of the last Roman Emperor in 476 merely facilitated their ambitions. As more and more Frankish fiefdoms were settled near such Roman centers as Tournai, Cambrai, and Le Mans, it was left to a strong leader to forcefully combine these into a sole Frankish kingdom. That man was Clovis I (r. 481–511), a son of the Merovingian King Childeric I and a former commander in one of the last serving Roman legions.

Beginning with the Battle of Soissons in 486, Clovis steadily brought virtually all of Roman Gaul under his sway, which is why French historians consider him the first true

HISTORY AND POLITICS

King Clovis

A funerary monument in the Church of St. Denis in Paris is dedicated to French King Clovis I.

Clovis (r. 481–511) is often considered the first king of a unified France. Trained as a commander in Rome's legions, Clovis turned against Syagrius, the Roman prefect in charge of Gaul, and defeated him at the Battle of Soissons. By 509, he ruled over much of what is today modern France. A committed pagan, he refused to be baptized, although his consort, princess Clotilde of Burgundy, was a Catholic. Clotilde gave birth to two sons and had each baptized in secret, but the first son died, and the second very nearly perished from an illness. This only hardened Clovis's opposition to Christianity. But eventually he realized that the world had changed, with France surrounded by Christian kingdoms. He may also have seen an opportunity to unify the people of France under a Catholic banner. On Christmas 496, he was baptized near Reims. Almost all of France's subsequent kings were anointed in Reims Cathedral.

531
The Franks occupy Thuringia

531
King Childebert I defeats the Visigoths in Spain

534
The Kingdom of Burgundy is annexed by the Franks

535
Benedict of Nursia writes the Rule governing the Benedictine Order

king of a united France. The name Clovis would eventually become "Louis" in French and be proudly adopted by 18 French kings.

Unlike the other tribes of Gothic origin, the Franks were committed pagans. But the splendor of Christian Roman civilization eventually worked its magic. Largely under the influence of his wife Clotilde, a Burgundian princess and a devout Catholic, Clovis agreed to be baptized in 496. He also decided that all of the people under his sway should be baptized forthwith. "All those who do not appear at the river tomorrow for baptism," he is reported to have said to his court, "will incur my deepest displeasure." Thus, France became a Catholic country.

PERIOD MUSIC

Gregorian Music

Pope Gregory the Great (r. 590–604) reinvigorated the papacy after years of political decline, in part due to his close familiarity with the imperial court in Constantinople, where he served as ambassador on behalf of Pope Pelagius II. Upon becoming pope in 590, he launched several missions to pagan territories in Europe, most famously east Britain, as well as the Low Countries and parts of Germany. He also contributed to the development of an authentic Western liturgy distinct from Eastern rites, including a *Kyrie* and *Pater Noster* (Our Father) placed right after the canon in Mass. The beautiful Gregorian plainsong tradition is named after him, even though Gregorian chants originated much later, as a fusion of Roman and Frankish song traditions dating to the time of Charlemagne. Gregorian music is monophonic, which means that all voices in the choir sing in unison, in the same serene pitch and rhythm, without any form of accompaniment. These liturgical songs were notated on often beautifully illuminated sheet music, which uses simple rhythmic symbols to identify either *longs* or *breves* (short notes).

Gregorian music had its greatest flowering in the ninth and tenth centuries. Some composers then began to experiment with organum, an early polyphonic style whereby voices move in parallel motion, separated by perfect fourths, fifths, or octaves. Organum would lay the foundation for the ars antiqua, or early polyphony, which liberated composers to explore a variety of harmonic textures across variable rhythmic patterns. This produced the tradition of the motet, a sacred work set to words meant to inspire piety and devotion among its listeners.

An illuminated Gregorian music manuscript from the 13th century depicts Pope Gregory the Great.

A Western Monasticism

As we saw, monasticism was born in Egypt from a desire for solitude and prayer, far removed from the hubbub of everyday life. In the West, by contrast, monasticism developed differently, in an effort to reconcile the contemplative life with works of charity for the surrounding community. As their role grew, abbeys and convents became important urban centers of knowledge, not only as guardians of ancient and Christian literature but also as medical centers, renowned for their cultivation of herbal gardens and other remedies. One of these early monastic "pharmacies," located in the old town of Dubrovnik, Croatia, continues to function to this day. Many monasteries also developed hospitals to care for the sick and destitute—all in imitation of Jesus' call for social compassion.

> *By losing the tranquility of the monastery, I learned how closely it should be treasured.*
>
> POPE GREGORY, *COMMENTARY ON JOB*

Thus, while the power and the influence of the former Roman Empire receded,

535 — The of the Indian Gupta Dynasty collapses

537 — King Arthur of the Britons is killed in the Battle of Camlan

540 — The Bible is translated into Ethiopian

542 — Beginning of a series of plagues, which decimate the European population

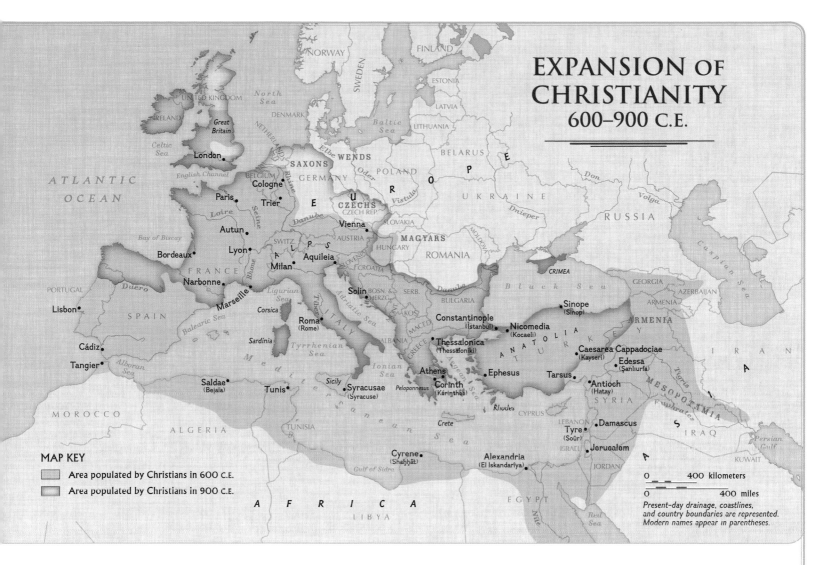

EXPANSION OF CHRISTIANITY 600–900 C.E.

MAP KEY

Area populated by Christians in 600 C.E.

Area populated by Christians in 900 C.E.

0 400 kilometers

0 400 miles

Present-day drainage, coastlines, and country boundaries are represented. Modern names appear in parentheses.

leaving the people in the West in a largely lawless society, Christian centers rushed to fill the vacuum. Whereas previously a Roman city or fort had served as the focal point of everyday life, that role was now assumed by the sometimes haphazardly constructed church or monastery, around which houses were built in a tight huddle, as if reaching out for protection. Dioceses were formed, which soon became the region's only source of education, medical care, and housing for the poor. Education under the Byzantine system had been in Greek, but in the West, public schooling (such as it was) was increasingly provided in Church Latin.

Meanwhile, dauntless missionaries continued to probe into the far corners of Europe. A popular legend relates how an abbot named Gregory (the future Pope Gregory the Great, r. 590–604) came across some fair-haired slave boys in the Roman Forum. He asked who they were, and they replied, *"Angli"*—"English." "No," said Gregory, *"non Angli sed angeli"*—"not English but angels." Upon his acceptance of the miter of St. Peter, this encounter may have inspired him to dispatch a monk named Augustine to east Britain, to evangelize among the pagan

This 19th-century print depicts the Irish nun Brigit of Kildare, one of Ireland's patron saints.

543
The Church of Saint-Germain-des-Prés is founded in Paris

544
Berbers revolt in North Africa

545
Cassiodorus founds a monastery at Squillace, in the south of Italy

550
Augustine converts the kingdom of Kent to Christianity

SAINTS AND CLERICS

Jerome's Bible

"Saint Jerome in His Study" was painted by Antonio da Fabriano around 1451.

The scholar Jerome (ca 347–420) was one of the principal Church theologians of the fourth century. Born in Stridon (which some believe is today's Ljubljana), Jerome studied rhetoric and philosophy in Rome, where he was impressed with the shrines of martyrdom. Following his baptism, he traveled widely but fell seriously ill in Antioch, and pledged to devote himself entirely to theological study. In the 380s, he was serving as secretary to Pope Damasus I when he accepted the pope's commission to create a new Latin translation of the Bible. After the pope's death, Jerome left for the Holy Land to spend the remainder of his life near Bethlehem. Here, he continued working on his translation, using the original Hebrew text of the Old Testament, while enjoying the financial support of a prominent Roman noblewoman named Paula. By the 13th century, Jerome's translation had gained such a following that it was known as the *versio vulgata*, the "commonly used translation."

Anglo-Saxons. Augustine's mission was remarkably successful. He even succeeded in baptizing the leading ruler of the region, King Aethelbert of Kent, who was married to the daughter of Christian King Charibert of the Franks. Soon, the first churches began to rise in the region, including the first Canterbury Cathedral.

The Benedictine Willibrord (ca 658–739) is credited with bringing the faith to the Low Countries. He became the first bishop of Utrecht and built a convent near Echternach in today's Luxembourg. Another Benedictine, Boniface (ca 675–754), entered the uncharted regions of northern Germany and became known as the Apostle of the Germans, converting many regions until his violent death in 754. His murder served to remind his mentor, Pope Gregory II, that large parts of Europe remained pagan and firmly opposed to Christianity.

The same sense of pagan lawlessness pervaded Scandinavia, long considered a dangerous hinterland that had rebuffed Christian overtures time and again. Willibrord tried to spread the Gospel in Denmark in the early eighth century, but with little success. A hundred years later, a monk named Anskar (801–865), the later bishop of Hamburg who became known as the Apostle to the North, was permitted to build a church in Birka, Sweden, but few Swedes felt compelled to convert. Not until the 11th century, under the reign of legendary King Canute (ca 985–1035) would Denmark, Norway, and parts of Sweden adopt Christianity, given that all those regions were under Canute's sway at that time. But many regions in Scandinavia would continue to resist the encroachment of the Christian faith and continue to cling to their ancient pagan customs.

They shot from their ballistas with such violence that on the twenty-first day they broke down the city wall.

ANTIOCHUS STRATEGOS ON THE PERSIAN CONQUEST OF JERUSALEM

The Persian-Byzantine Wars

A series of cataclysmic changes then gripped the East, which would have a profound impact on the growth of Christianity in the West. By the fourth century, Egypt had become largely Christian, in a tradition known as Coptic Christianity (the word "Copt" is rooted in the Greek word for Egypt, *Aigyptos*). At the same time, the Byzantine intolerance toward other faiths had forced many Jews to settle along the Red Sea as far as Yemen, spurring local trade. In 523, the King of the Himyarites in Yemen, Yusuf As'ar Yath'ar (r. 517–525) took the extraordinary step of converting to Judaism. The Himyarite Dynasty had always practiced an ancient form of monotheism known as Rahmanism, but Yath'ar's conversion effectively created the first sovereign Jewish state since the fall of the Hasmoneans in Judea.

Byzantium was not pleased, not in the least because Yath'ar (also known as Dhu Nuwas) proceeded to oppress the Christians in his kingdom. The growing Jewish presence along the Red Sea, along the sensitive Byzantine trade routes, was therefore a

OPPOSITE: *This 16th-century Turkish print depicts the Prophet Muhammad and the archangel Gabriel. According to Islam, in Muhammad's first revelation he was visited by Gabriel, who revealed to him a verse from the Quran.*

550 The St. Servatius Church in Maastricht, Netherlands, is begun

560 Scholar Isidore of Seville is born

570 Prophet Muhammad is born in Mecca

580 Pope Gregory the Great writes his book *Dialogues* on the life of Benedict

direct challenge to Byzantium's influence in the region. Constantinople had one strong ally: Ethiopia, located just across the Red Sea. Ethiopia had been converted by Coptic missionaries from Egypt as early as the fourth century, but despite the Ethiopians' Coptic Christianity they were solidly in the Byzantine camp. Ethiopia was also Yemen's principal rival in the Red Sea trade.

PERIOD ARCHITECTURE

The Dome of the Rock

Legend tells us that when Patriarch Sophronius surrendered the city of Jerusalem to Umar after a seven-month siege, he beseeched the Islamic conqueror to spare the people in the city. Remarkably, Umar agreed. A man of simple tastes who wore a threadbare tunic and subsisted on an ascetic diet of barley bread and dates, Umar was a far cry from the ostentatious Umayyad caliphs to follow. Once inside the city, Umar asked to be taken to Temple Mount, site of the former Jewish Temple and the reputed location of Muhammad's ascension into Heaven. Under Christian rule it had been turned into a garbage dump. According to a Muslim historian, Umar unfurled his cloak, filled it with debris, and began to clear the site.

The 35 acres of the Temple Mount became the Muslim al-Haram al-Sharif, the Noble Sanctuary of Muhammad's heavenly visit, as well as the traditional location of Abraham's sacrifice. Umar ordered that a wooden mosque be built on the sacred spot, which reportedly could hold 3,000 worshippers. This ultimately led to the greatest monument of early Islamic architecture, the seventh-century Dome of the Rock. Built by Umayyad Caliph Abd el-Malik (685–705), the Dome of the Rock's design combines circular and octagonal motifs to symbolize the transition from the earth to the divine. Below the Dome is a cave called the Well of Souls, where Muslims believe the souls of the dead will gather in anticipation of the Last Judgment.

The seventh-century Dome of the Rock is believed to mark the spot where the Prophet Muhammad briefly ascended into heaven.

The Prophet Muhammad is shown in an 18th-century portrait. Muhammad, born in Mecca in 570, was the founder of the religion of Islam.

In 523, after Yath'ar destroyed several Christian communities at Zafar and Najran, tensions between Yemen and Ethiopia sparked an all-out war. The Ethiopian general Abreha crossed the Red Sea, invaded southern Arabia, and proclaimed himself King. In response, local Arabian chieftains rallied to the other superpower in the region, Persia. The Persian troops easily vanquished the Ethiopian forces and occupied Yemen in the process, thus expanding Persia's sphere of influence at the expense of the Byzantine Empire. It was here, in the southern Arabian region of the Hijaz, that history's next chapter would be written.

The two most prominent townships in the Hijaz were Yathrib (later known as Medina) and the holy city of Mecca (or Makkah), home of the cubelike structure called the Kaaba, where several pagan deities

581
The Sui Dynasty achieves a reunification of China

589
King Reccared of Spain converts to Catholic Christianity

590
Pope Gregory the Great begins his papacy

604
Second Sui Emperor Yang Ti assumes the throne in China

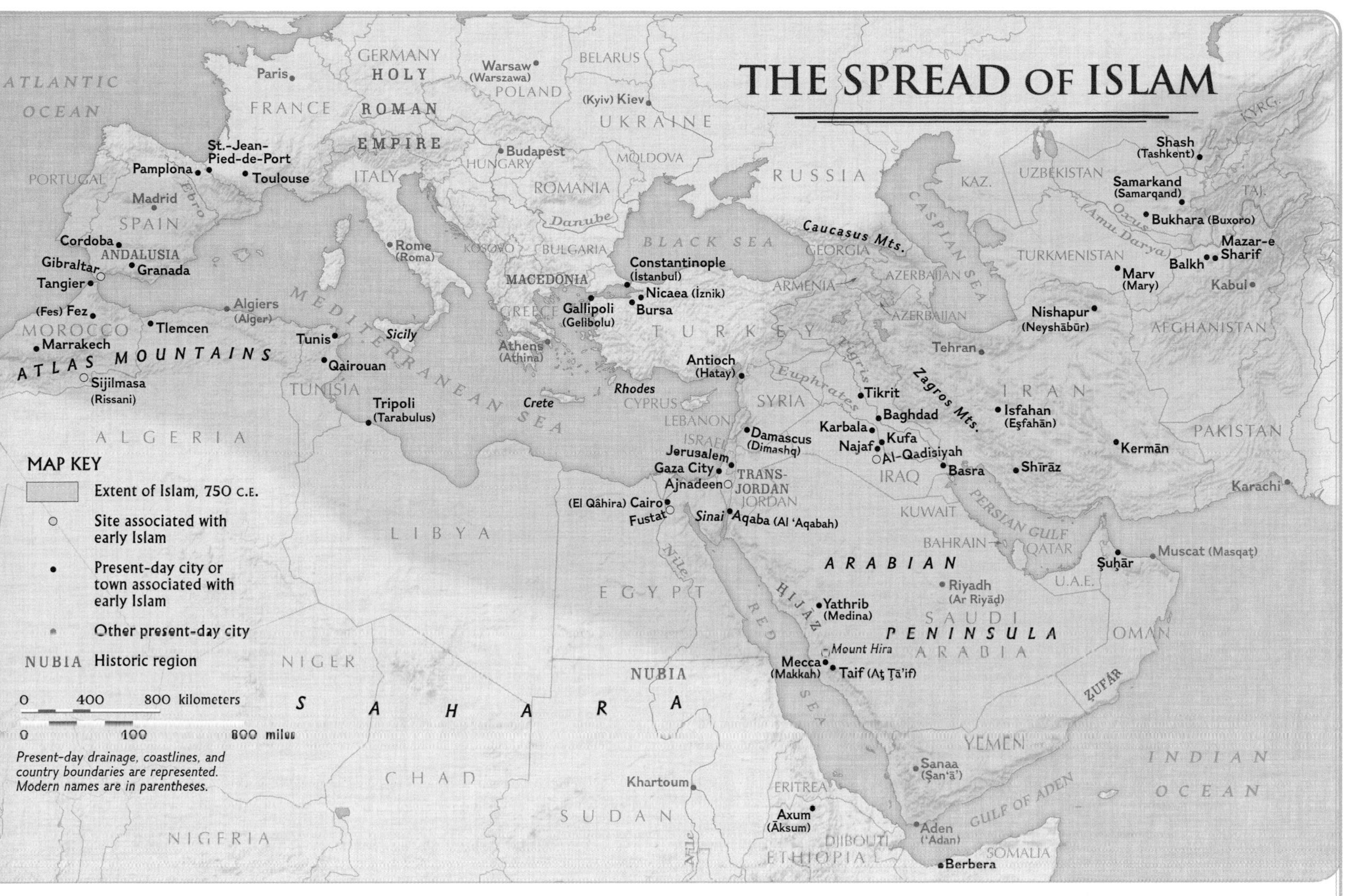

were venerated. In 570, a young woman from Mecca named Amina gave birth to a baby boy and named him Muhammad. Tragically, her husband Abdullah, a Hashemite, had died a few months earlier while visiting Yathrib. When Amina herself died soon thereafter, the orphan boy was raised by a succession of relatives within the Hashemite clan, and eventually became a trader like many others in Mecca. Thus, he traveled widely along the principal trade routes to Petra, Bostra, and other caravan markets. Along the way he must have come into contact with Jewish communities, which were heavily involved in the regional trade, as well as dissident Christian monasteries—such as Monophysites, Arians, and Nestorites, which we'll discuss in the next chapter—who had settled in Arabia, beyond the reach of Byzantine orthodoxy, to cater to the needs of passing travelers. Thus, we may presume that Muhammad became familiar with both the Jewish and Christian faiths, and possibly their Scriptures as well.

Muhammad married a wealthy widow named Khadija and soon enjoyed a life of affluence. But as tradition tells us, he became uncomfortable with the primitive idolatry and rituals of his tribe. He remembered that his grandfather had often retreated to a lonely cave in the hills of Jebel-an-Nur to meditate, and he began

610
Muhammad experiences his spiritual conversion through the angel Gabriel

611
Antioch is captured by the Persians

614
Persian general Shahrbaraz invades Byzantine Palestine

614
More than 65,000 Christians are killed in the Persian conquest of Jerusalem

> *Go and declare the goodness of your Lord; declare what has come to you from God and declare His bounty and grace in your mission.*
>
> MUHAMMAD IBN ISHAQ, *THE LIFE OF THE MESSENGER OF GOD*

to do the same. In 610, this is where he had his first revelation from God, communicated through the angel Gabriel. This and other revelations are recorded in the Holy Qur'an, the Scripture of Islam.

Thus, Muhammad received his calling to become a Prophet and to spread the faith of Islam throughout Arabia. Faced with fierce opposition from pagan tribes, he led his followers out of Mecca to create an Islamic community in Yathrib, which was soon renamed Medina. The date of this journey, the Hijrah, in 622 is reckoned as Year 1 A.H. (or *Anno Hegirae*) in the Muslim calendar. Using Medina as his base, Muhammad expanded his reach, often following pitched battles, until in 630 all of Arabia was unified under the banner of Islam.

The Persian Destruction of the Holy Land

While Arabia was slowly being transformed into a Muslim nation, another war had broken out between the Byzantine and Persian Empires. In 610, the year of Muhammad's first revelation, the Persian armies marched into Asia Minor. Antioch was conquered in 611, followed by much of Armenia, Syria, and the Caucasus kingdom of Lazica. In 614, the Persian general

Piero della Francesca (ca 1415–1492) painted the fresco "The Victory of Heraclius." Heraclius was Byzantine Emperor from 610 to 641.

Period Artifacts

FIFTH AND SIXTH CENTURIES

A fifth-century Visigoth buckle depicts a horse on a pedestal.

This gold votive cross is a good example of fifth-century Visigoth art.

A sixth-century shield from Umbria, Italy, depicts various battle scenes.

"Charlemagne Receiving the Submission of Witikind in 785" is the work of French artist Ary Scheffer (1795–1858). Witikind, a Germanic leader of the Saxons, was a chief opponent of Charlemagne during the Saxon Wars from 777 to 785.

Shahrbaraz entered Palestine, looting and burning his way toward Jerusalem. At that time, the Christian transformation of the holy city was still in full swing, with a majestic Church of the Holy Sepulcher rising on Golgotha. Streets that had once been filled with Jewish worshippers during holy festivals were now crammed with monks, prelates, and pilgrims from all parts of the Byzantine Empire.

The patriarch of Jerusalem, Zacharias, was wholly unprepared for the Persian invasion. The city's stout walls, painstakingly built by Emperor Valentinian and Empress Eudoxia (widow of Theodosius II), were breached by the Persian catapults in less than three weeks. More than 65,000 Christians were killed in the massacre that followed. Those who survived were rounded up and, in a replay of the Babylonian captivity, dispatched into exile. Most churches were burned to the ground, including the Church of the Holy Sepulcher. The True Cross was carried back to Persia as ordinary loot.

It took Byzantine Emperor Heraclius (r. 610–641) 12 years to plot a counteroffensive, but once it got under way the Byzantine armies were unstoppable. In short order they rolled up the Persian forces and dealt King Khosrow II a stinging defeat at the Battle of Nineveh in 627. The triumph was complete when, in 629, Heraclius

614
The Church of the Holy Sepulcher is destroyed

618
The Tang Dynasty initiates one of China's most important epochs

622
Muhammad and his followers move to Yathrib in a journey known as the Hijrah

626
Tang Emperor T'ai Tsung assumes the throne in China

solemnly returned the True Cross to Jerusalem. Christian control of the Holy Land was restored—or so it seemed.

The following year, 631, Muhammad made a last pilgrimage from Medina to the Kaaba in Mecca (now solely devoted to Allah), tracing the route of the *hajj* that millions of Muslims follow to this day. But the Prophet was already ailing. He died in June 632, without designating a clear line of succession.

The result was a power struggle between two groups: the original Meccans who had fled with Muhammad to Medina during the Hijrah of 622, led by Muhammad's father-in-law, Abu Bakr; and the Medina faction—the *ansar* or "helpers"—led by Muhammad's cousin and son-in-law, Ali. Much later, the Mecca faction would become known as *al-sunnah wa-l-jamaa*, followers of the traditions (*sunnah*) of the Prophet, while the Medina group would be identified as supporters of Ali or *shi'at Ali*. Here lay the seeds of the great schism in Islam, between Sunnis and Shiites, which continues to this day.

In 632, however, the Mecca faction won and established a dynastic line of *khalifa*, or "representatives," beginning with Abu Bakr (r. 632–634) and continuing with Umar

The **HAGIA SOPHIA** *in Istanbul, built by Emperor Justinian I between 532 and 537, has been remarkably preserved despite multiple earthquakes and centuries of neglect. After the Ottoman conquest of Constantinople, the church became a mosque.*

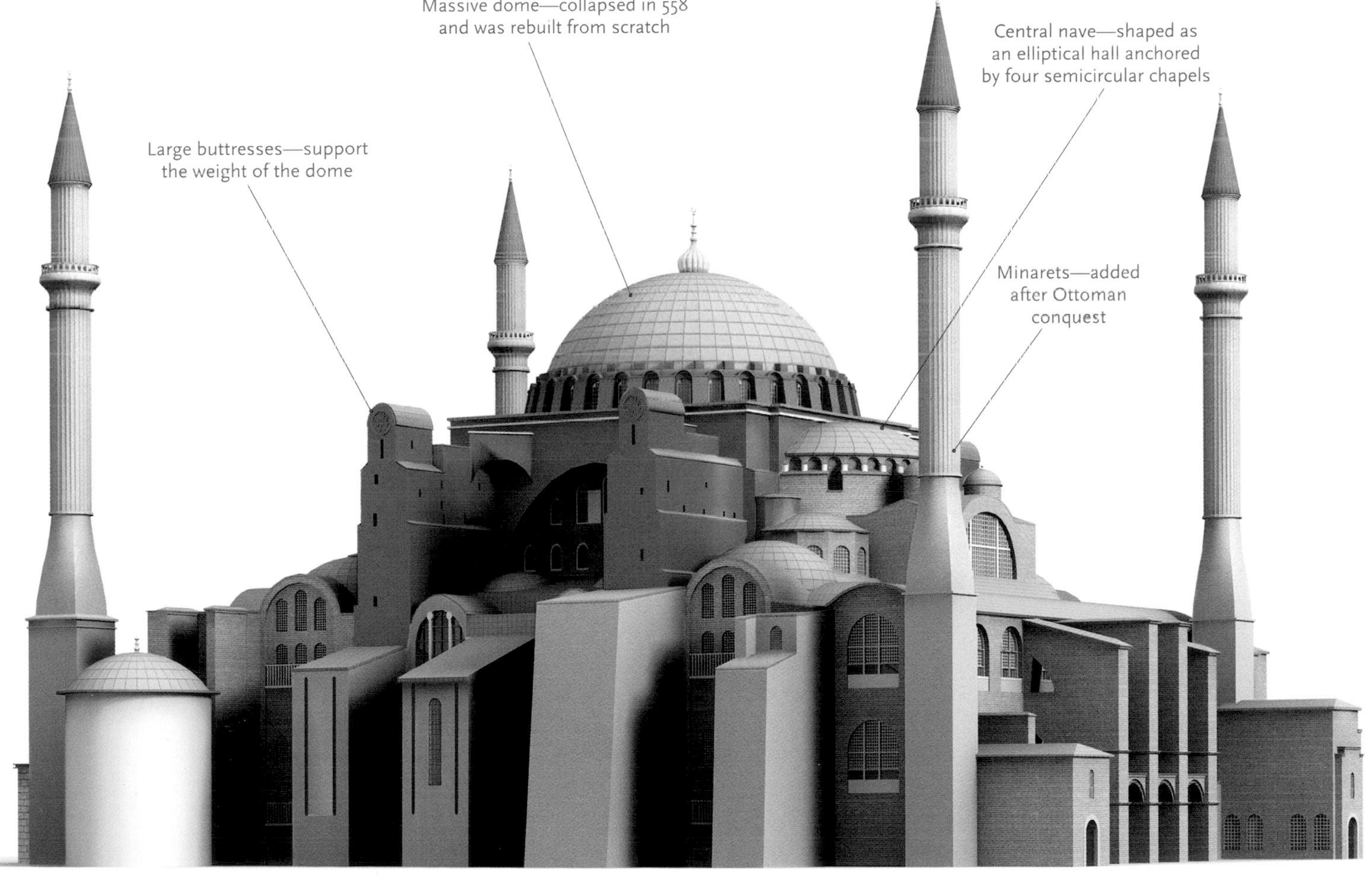

627 Emperor Heraclius defeats Persian King Khosrow II at the Battle of Nineveh

630 All of Arabia is unified under the banner of Islam

631 Muhammad makes a pilgrimage from Medina to Mecca, establishing the hajj

632 Muhammad's death prompts a power struggle between Medina and Mecca factions

HISTORY AND POLITICS

The Carolingian Renaissance

The most powerful figure in early medieval Europe is unquestionably Charles the Great, or Charlemagne (r. 800–814), who succeeded his father, Pepin the Short, as King of France. Charles gradually expanded his territory until he became de facto ruler of much of western Europe. A supporter of the papacy in Rome, Charles was crowned by Pope Leo III with the title of Holy Roman Emperor in an attempt to revive the splendor of the Western Roman Empire, albeit in a Christian mold. Charles actively supported the flowering of arts and architecture in what is often called the Carolingian Renaissance. Architects harked back to Roman models, such as the splendid Palatine Chapel in Aachen, inspired by the Basilica of San Vitale in Ravenna. Carolingian scholars freely copied texts by Roman and Greek authors, while artists developed a manuscript illumination inspired by classical sculpture.

This precious reliquary of Emperor Charlemagne was cast in 1349.

bin al-Khattab (r. 634–644). It was Umar who decided to move beyond the natural borders of the Arabian peninsula and take the Islamic conquest into the Byzantine and Persian realms. In 634, he plunged into Syria and Palestine and dealt a stunning defeat to the forces of the aging Emperor Heraclius at the Battle of Yarmuk in 636. In February 638, as legend tells us, Umar got off his white camel and walked into the city of Jerusalem. Not a single person was harmed, and Jerusalem became a Muslim city.

Umar then defeated the Sassanid army of Persia at the battle of Qadisiyya, after which his generals invaded Egypt and conquered Alexandria in 642. Thus, a scant 20 years after Muhammad's death, the Islamic Empire spanned from northern Africa to Iran. From what is today Morocco, the Muslim armies poured into Visigoth Spain, defeating its king and pushing north into the Frankish territory of Gaul.

Charlemagne

Terrified by the seemingly unstoppable Muslim steamroller, communities throughout Gaul coalesced around their Christian centers, whether village church or monastery. Suddenly, Christianity not only represented faith and charity, but also security—restoring a sense of regional identity where, in the aftermath of the Western Empire's fall, there was none. As a result, the Islamic conquest had the unintended effect of shaping Christian centers with an indigenous, truly "European" character.

At long last, the King of the Franks, Charles Martel (r. 718–741) drew a line in the sand over which the Muslims would not be allowed to pass. The Islamic armies were checked at the Battle of Poitiers in France. But it was left up to the greatest ruler of this era, King Charles the Great (or Charlemagne, r. 800–814), to finally drive the Muslims back into Spain. There, the Umayyad caliphs initiated a period of great cultural prosperity and interfaith collaboration, known as Il Convivencia.

From the lands
where the sun rises to western shores,
people are crying and wailing
. . . all lament the loss
of their Caesar
. . . the world laments
the death of Charles.

ANONYMOUS MONK
ON THE DEATH OF CHARLEMAGNE

Charlemagne, meanwhile, extended his reach across all of France and parts of Germany. In 800, he was crowned Holy Roman Emperor by Pope Leo III—a hereditary title that would be much coveted by Europe's kings in the centuries to come. Charlemagne used his unprecedented authority to harmonize Latin liturgy across most of western Europe, and to foster a new flowering of the arts, known as the Carolingian Renaissance.

Unfortunately, Europe's growing prosperity came at a cost, for it soon invited a new wave of invaders, principally the Vikings from the north, the Slavs from the east, and the Saracens from the south, who threatened to destroy Europe's fragile Christian identity. ■

OPPOSITE: *A 19th-century painting depicts the crowning of Charlemagne as King of the Lombards in 774. In 800, Pope Leo III crowned Charlemagne the Emperor of the Holy Roman Empire, a title he retained until his death in 814.*

642
Umar bin al-Khattab captures Alexandria

650s
The first canon of the Quran is compiled

658
Benedictine Willibrord, missionary to the Low Countries, is born

673
The Venerable Bede, a Benedictine chronicler of England, is born

5
CHAPTER

CHRISTIANITY IN THE EAST

650-1100

Many Christians have arrived in our midst... and they have spoken to us in their different ways.

KING ROSTISLAV OF MORAVIA, 862

From the ninth century onward, missionaries from both the European (or "Latin") Church and the Byzantine ("Greek" or "Eastern Orthodox") Church moved into the north and east of the European continent, making many converts. Meanwhile, another dissenting movement, known as Nestorian Christianity, used Sassanid Persia as its base to build a "Church of the East" in Asia, absorbing the early Christian settlements of India and reaching as far as China during the Tang Dynasty.

ABOVE: *The famous "Vladimir Madonna and Child" was painted by Russian artist Andrey Rublyov (1370–1430).*

OPPOSITE: *The interior frescoes of the Trinity Cathedral at the Monastery of Saint Ipatiev, near Kostroma, Russia, are outstanding examples of Orthodox art from the 17th century.*

PRECEDING PAGES: *This illustration of "The Baptism of Duke Borivoj by St. Methodius" was painted by a member of the Czech School in the early 20th century. Borivoj was the first duke baptized by Methodius, the venerable bishop of Moravia.*

From the tenth century onward, tensions between the Western and Eastern realms of the former Roman Empire began to escalate, driven not only by theological disputes but also by attempts of both the Greek and Latin domains to extend their spheres of influence. Much of this conflict would spill over in as yet unconverted lands in eastern Europe. Indeed, although the Byzantine Empire was located toward the eastern end of the Mediterranean, geographically it did not extend beyond the Black Sea. Farther north lay the Balkans and the vast realm of the Slavs, fertile territory for Christian conversion.

The sheer splendor of Byzantine (or Eastern Orthodox) Christianity had not gone unnoticed in these lands, even during

OPPOSITE: This depiction of "Czar Simeon I of Bulgaria Defeating the Byzantine Army" appears in a 12th-century Byzantine manuscript, known as the Codex Skylitzes Matritensis.

This spectacular panorama shows the southern coast of Crimea near Cape Meganom, where, according to tradition, the Apostle Andrew landed in the first century.

the brief period of the Iconoclastic Era, when the Byzantine Emperor forbade the display of all icons and other depictions of Christ and saints. This is perhaps the reason why several Slav rulers tolerated the intrusion of missionary probes by both European and Byzantine clerics as the Slavs sought to exploit the power play between East and West. At this time, religious and political power was still closely intertwined; hence, the adoption of either the Western (Latin) or Eastern (Greek) rites by people of the East also implied a de facto political alliance with either Rome or Constantinople.

One of the first eastern territories beyond Byzantium's borders to be converted was Armenia. According to tradition, the Apostle Thaddeus had been sent to Armenia from nearby Edessa to preach and baptize. Thaddeus was able to convert the daughter of King Sanatrook, but in doing so incurred the wrath of the King and was executed. Church fathers such as Eusebius and Tertullian confirm the existence of Christian communities in Armenia as early as the second and third centuries, when they suffered from severe persecution. In 301, however, King Tiridates III agreed to be baptized by a missionary named Gregory the Illuminator, thus making Armenia the first nation to adopt Christianity as its state religion.

The Danube Kingdoms

A typical example of the Christianization of eastern Europe is Moravia, today located in

625
Emperor Heraclius defeats a double attack by Avars and Persians at Constantinople

625
Pope Boniface V is succeeded by Pope Honorius I

627
Emperor Heraclius defeats the Persians at the Battle of Nineveh

628
Persian King Khosrow II dies

the east of the Czech Republic. In the ninth century, Moravian King Mojmir (r. 830–846) had begun to gravitate to the Western model of Christianity propagated by the bishop of Passau when he found himself deposed by Rostislav (r. 846–870). Rostislav feared that the missionary activity from the West would pave the way for political control, if not outright conquest, by the Frankish kings. Well aware of the growing tensions between the Latin and Byzantine Churches, he adroitly wrote a letter to the Byzantine Empire, deploring the "different ways" of Christianity that had confused his people, adding that "we Slavs are a simple people." "Therefore," Rostislav suggested, "we pray you send us someone capable of teaching us the whole truth."

The request did not fall on deaf ears. Two brothers, Cyril (ca 827–869) and Methodius (ca 815–885), who were both clerics, were promptly dispatched to Moravia to try to bring the region under the sway of Byzantium. Both spoke Slavonic fluently and were working on a Slavonic translation of the Bible as well as the Byzantine liturgy (a book known as a "missal"). In doing so, they created a Cyrillic alphabet, in much the same way that Ulfilas had developed a Gothic script to translate the Bible for the Goths. Soon a veritable Slavic Church began to emerge, which attracted many worshippers from neighboring territories such as Bohemia. Methodius eventually became archbishop of a bishopric that comprised

HISTORY AND POLITICS

Cyril and Methodius

The success of the evangelizing by the Byzantine clerics Cyril and Methodius in Moravia provoked the ire of Pope Nicholas I (r. 858–867) in Rome. Nicholas, a vigorous proponent of Roman primacy over all Christians, saw his European sphere of influence threatened by the rapid growth of Byzantine Christianity in Moravia. In 867, both missionaries were summoned to Rome to explain themselves. By the time they actually made it to the pontifical palace, however, Pope Nicholas had died and been succeeded by Pope Adrian II (r. 867–872), who was far more amenable to their proselytizing. Instead of the pontifical ire that Cyril and Methodius fully expected to suffer, they were received with open arms. Adrian urged them to continue their evangelizing efforts with the full power of papal authority. Cyril died before he could return, but Methodius made his way back and ultimately became the archbishop of Moravia, Serbia, and Bohemia.

This double portrait of Cyril and Methodius is a Romanesque work in tin from the 12th century.

629
Emperor Heraclius recaptures Jerusalem and restores the True Cross

630
Cotton is introduced in Arabia

635
The missionary Alopen enters China during the Tang Dynasty

637
The Persian capital of Ctesiphon falls to Muslim invaders

not only Moravia, but Serbia and Bohemia as well.

In the early 11th century, after Moravia and Bohemia were combined into one polity by Bretislaus I (r. 1035–1055), the King also changed his territory to the Latin rites. Only Serbia remained a predominantly Eastern Orthodox nation, and still is to this day.

In the Balkans, the warlord Asparukh had led a number of Bulgar tribes across the Danube in 680 to found the Bulgarian kingdom. Two centuries later, after attempts by both Western and Eastern missionaries to convert the country, King Boris I (r. 852–889)

We did not know whether we were in heaven or on earth. For on earth there is no such splendor, nor such beauty, that we are at a loss to describe.

VLADIMIR'S EMISSARIES ON THE HAGIA SOPHIA

succumbed to Byzantine pressure and agreed to be baptized according to the Eastern rite, but on one condition: that the Bulgarian Church would be fully autonomous, governed by an archbishop. When Photius, the patriarch of Constantinople, refused to accede to his request, Boris promptly turned to Pope Nicholas in Rome. Appraised of this fact, Photius hastily dispatched an archbishop and two bishops to Bulgaria to establish the Bulgarian Orthodox Church. Boris's son Simeon I (r. 893–927) took the next step in 917, when he declared the Bulgarian Church

In the midst of a snowy landscape, a priest meditates on the Gospels at Svyato-Kazansky hermitage, one of many Russian Orthodox communities.

to be fully independent from Constantinople, giving the archbishop the title of "patriarch." Simeon was also the first ruler to take the title of Tsar—meaning "Caesar"—to further distance himself from the Byzantine Empire.

Russia

Beyond these newly converted lands lay the vast steppes of Russia. The land of the Rus had not been impervious to early Christianity. According to one legend, the Apostle Andrew visited the Black Sea shores in the first century and erected a cross on a spot that later would become the city of Kiev. That place is today marked by the beautiful St. Andrew's Church.

Various other Byzantine missionaries had made their way into Russia over the years, though with limited success given the extreme challenges they faced. One was the language barrier; another, the stubborn adherence to indigenous pagan customs among Russian peasants; and third, the sheer vastness of the land. Only when the Cyril-Methodius translation of the Bible into Old Slavonic began to circulate among the nobility, particularly in the south of Russia, did Christianity begin to make some headway. In 950, Queen Olga, ruler of Kiev, allowed herself to be baptized by German missionaries, but proselytizing efforts were limited. It was her grandson Vladimir I

OPPOSITE: *The lovely St. Andrew's Church in Kiev was built in the 18th century, based on designs by Italian architect Bartolomeo Rastrelli (1700–1771).*

The Assumption Cathedral in Moscow's Kremlin is one of the oldest Russian Orthodox churches. The interior of the church is dominated by fresco paintings.

642
The Amr Mosque is built in Cairo

644
Umar bin al-Khattab is killed and is succeeded by Uthman ibn Affan

654
Islamic armies under General Muawiyah capture Cyprus

656
During riots in Medina, Caliph Uthman is assassinated

OPPOSITE: This illustration by Russian artist Andrey Rublyov (1370–1430) shows St. Sergius overseeing the construction of a church in Zagorsk.

The SAN MARCO BASILICA in Venice is one of the best known examples of Byzantine architecture. Constructed in the ninth century, it was built to house the relics of the Evangelist Mark.

(956–1015), a committed pagan, who in 987 decided that Russia should embrace monotheism as well. Unable to choose between Islam, Byzantine Christianity, and Latin Christianity, as legend tells us, Vladimir sent emissaries on a fact-finding mission to each of his neighboring territories.

The envoys to Muslim lands reported that these nations were devoid of pleasure, for the people could neither drink alcohol nor eat pork (one of Kiev's great culinary specialties). Those sent to the European north also came back with disappointing news, reporting the rather dry and joyless nature of German liturgy. But the emissaries to Byzantium brought back enthusiastic reports of the splendor of the Byzantine court and the breathtaking beauty of the Hagia Sophia. Impressed, Vladimir agreed to embrace Byzantine Christianity. The year 988 is still celebrated as the founding year of the Russian Orthodox Church. The first "metropolitan," the equivalent of a bishop in the West or a patriarch in the East, was established in Kiev under the auspices of the Byzantine patriarchate. Next, the population of Kiev was converted en masse, though whether this baptism was always voluntary is not clear. Vladimir, henceforth known as

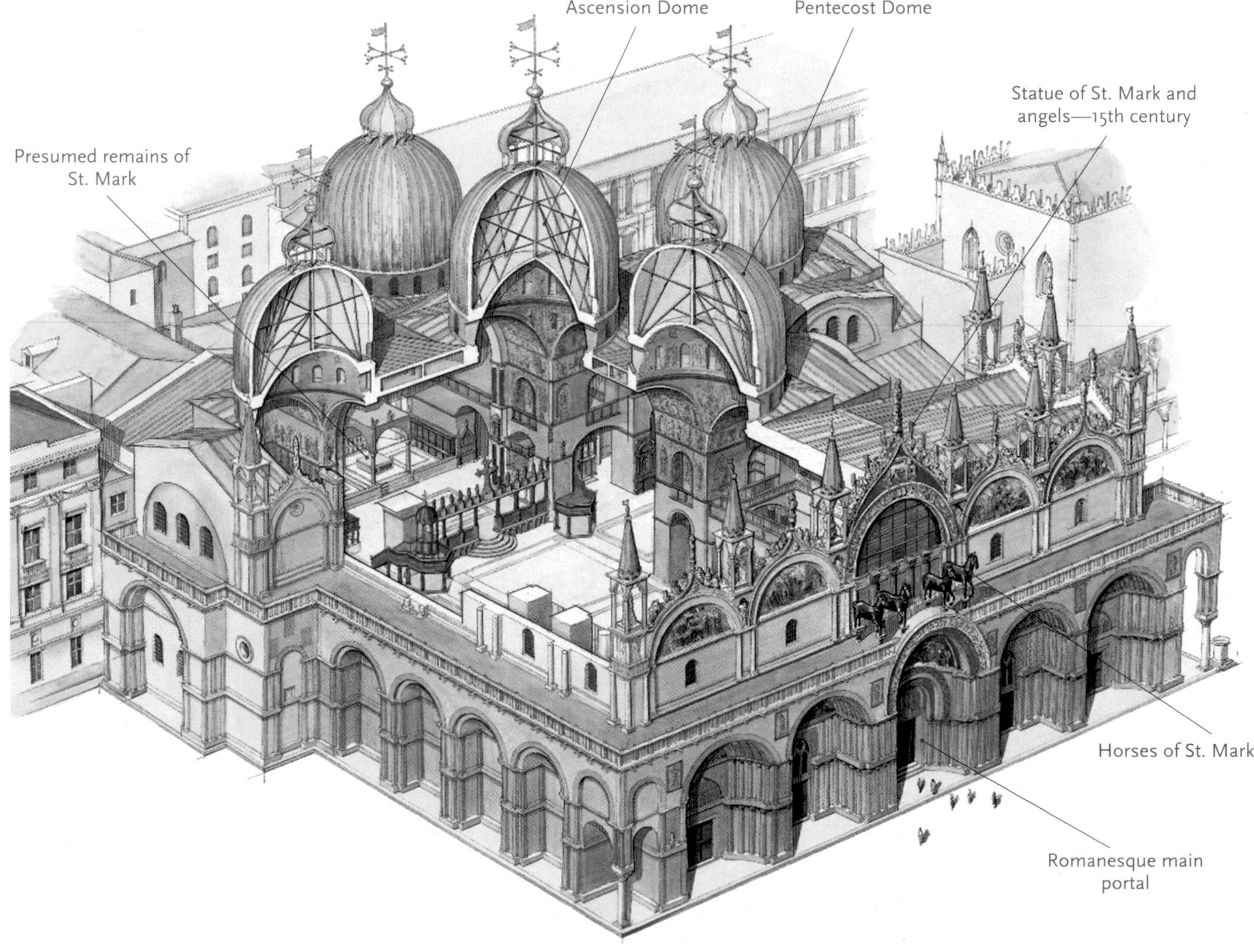

657
Followers of Ali and Uthman clash at the Battle of Siffin, the first intra-Muslim civil war

661
Caliph Ali is assassinated

661
Rise of the Umayyad Dynasty, a period of great Islamic flowering

673
Byzantine forces use "Greek fire" against Arab attackers

"the Great" in Christian literature, steadily expanded his territory, bringing the Eastern rite with him, until his borders pushed against the realms of Boleslav I of Poland and King Stephen I of Hungary.

The Golden Age of Kiev

What followed was what some historians have called the Golden Age of Kiev, when the city ranked as the first major center of Christian civilization in eastern Europe. Countless beautiful churches were built on the Byzantine model, which attracted a large number of talented artists and artisans. Many of these churches were the first tokens of monumental architecture ever built in the Ukraine, if not in Russia altogether. Most were conceived as wooden centralized structures topped by a series of domes painted in robin's-egg blue or covered with gold. Some of this architecture and decoration is still preserved in the Holy Sophia Cathedral in Kiev and the Church of the Savior in Berestove. Kiev's newfound pride also found expression in the imposing Golden Gates of Kiev, built by Yaroslav the Wise in 1017 and rebuilt (with considerable alterations) in 1982. Literature flourished as well, exemplified by such novellas as *Boris and Gleb*, the story of King Vladimir's heirs.

This golden era came to an end when Kiev was conquered by the Mongols in the early 13th century. The leaders of the Russian Church fled north, to Moscow, where they tried hard to restore the erstwhile glory of Kiev. Part of this effort was the development of an indigenous monastic movement, initiated by Sergius of Radonezh (1314–1392). More than 400 convents were built by Sergius and his followers, beginning with the great monastery of Trinity-St. Sergius Lavra near Moscow. Many abbeys were adorned by Russia's first great artist, Andrey Rublyov.

As a result, Moscow became the undisputed center of the Russian Orthodox Church from the 15th century forward. Indeed, after the fall of Constantinople in 1453, the Russian rulers declared themselves to be the legitimate heirs of the Byzantine Empire. Moscow became the "Third Rome." Byzantium's emblem of the double headed eagle, representing the fusion of Church and State, was incorporated in the Russian imperial standard.

Hungary and Poland

Long before the tenth century there were small but flourishing Christian communities in the Hungarian realm, formerly the Roman province of Pannonia, despite invasions by Huns and Avars. These early communities largely followed the Byzantine rite until the new Hungarian ruler Géza (r. 972–997) resolutely decided in favor of the Latin liturgy introduced by Western missionaries; today he is known by his Christian name—Istvan,

Karavas Treasure

CA 650

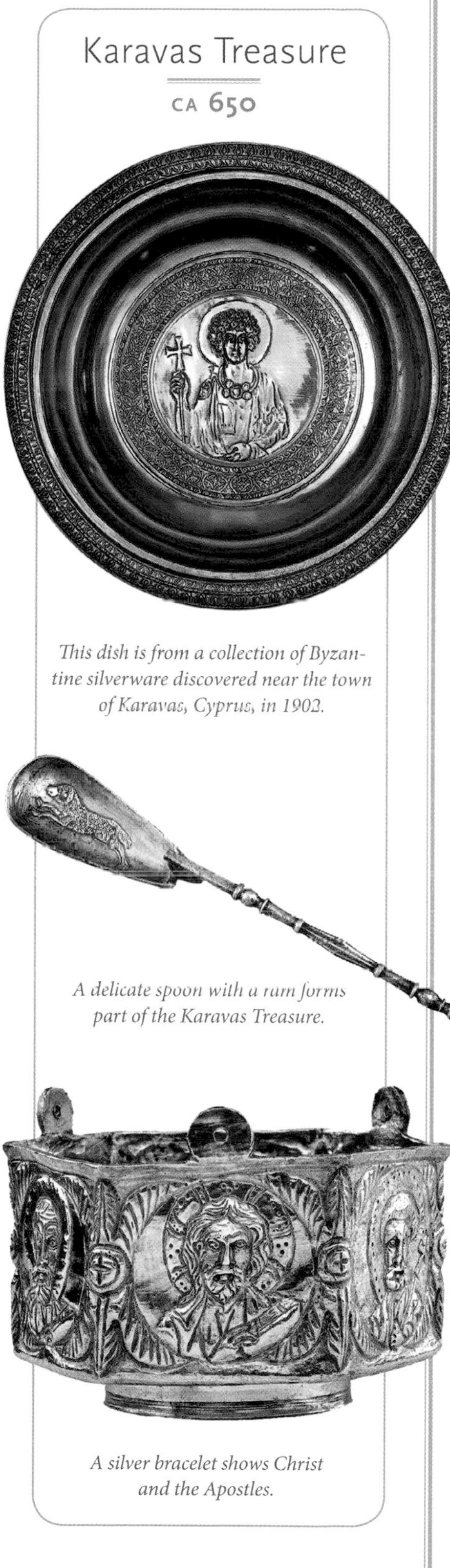

This dish is from a collection of Byzantine silverware discovered near the town of Karavas, Cyprus, in 1902.

A delicate spoon with a ram forms part of the Karavas Treasure.

A silver bracelet shows Christ and the Apostles.

675
Benedictine Boniface, the "Apostle to the Germans," is born

680
Warlord Asparukh founds the Bulgarian kingdom in the Balkans

717
Byzantine Emperor Leo III forbids all icons, initiating the period of Byzantine iconoclasm

718
Charles Martel rules over the Franks

or Stephen. Still, the growth of Christianity in Hungary was hampered by the lack of a Bible in the Magyar language. The Old Slavonic version was used, with some reluctance, until a true Hungarian translation of the Bible was finally completed in the 1430s.

In that same time frame, Poland was unified as a nation by a Polish duke named Mieszko I (930–992), who established the Piast Dynasty. In 966, Mieszko agreed to be baptized, opting for the Latin liturgy. In 1025, his son Boleslaw I Chrobry established an independent Polish Church with a metropolitan see in Gniezno. But in the years to follow, the unified monarchy was torn apart by competing noblemen, some of whom even invited the Germanic Teutonic knights to fight at their side. Not until the reign of the Piast King Casimir III (1333–1370) was the Polish kingdom restored, but at the cost of losing the regions of Silesia and Pomerania to the growing power on Poland's western flank—namely, Teutonic Prussia.

The Nestorian "Church of the East"

Meanwhile, several "dissident" churches continued to prosper both within and outside the borders of the Byzantine Empire. As we saw, the Coptic Church, which had split from the Eastern Orthodox Church after the Council of Chalcedon of 451, became the dominant Christian movement in Egypt. When the Christian kingdom of Armenia was overrun by Persia and Byzantium refused to come to its aid, Armenian bishops likewise abandoned the Chalcedon principles and opted for Monophysitism. Monophysists were also particularly strong in Syria.

Meanwhile, the ongoing controversy about the dual nature of Christ entered a new phase when Patriarch of Constantinople Nestorius (r. 428–431) proposed that Jesus was a mortal man until he was touched by the *logos* and became divine. Nestorius thus found himself opposed

OPPOSITE: "The Holy Trinity" is the most famous icon by Russian artist Andrey Rublyov (1370–1430). The icon depicts the three angels who visited Abraham at the oak of Mamre.

PERIOD ARCHITECTURE

The Holy Sophia Cathedral of Kiev

No building so captures the Golden Age of Kiev as the Holy Sophia Cathedral. Begun in 1037, just 50 years after Vladimir I decided to adopt Byzantine Christianity as the nation's faith, the cathedral was inspired by the Hagia Sophia in Constantinople, dedicated to Holy Wisdom. Some Russian historians believe the foundation of the church goes back even further, to 1011, during the reign of Vladimir himself. Its design would serve as the model for countless Russian Orthodox churches in the centuries to come, featuring a central nave flanked by two aisles and topped by no less than 13 domes. Five apses modulate the linearity of the basilica plan, giving it the same central emphasis so notable in the floor plan of the Hagia Sophia.

The church suffered during the invasion of the Mongols in 1240 and fell into disuse during the 16th century. In 1633, the metropolitan Mohyla ordered the cathedral restored, although much of the rebuilding by architect Octaviano Mancini involved the addition of Italian Baroque features, a style that was then becoming popular in Russia. After the Russian Revolution of 1917, the cathedral was earmarked for demolition, and only a concerted effort by the local population saved it from destruction (although the St. Mikhail monastery nearby was indeed torn down). Today, the church is once again used for liturgical services, although different factions within the Orthodox Church have laid claim to it. Consequently, it is currently governed by the Ukrainian Ministry of Culture.

Begun in 1037, the Holy Sophia Cathedral in Kiev, Ukraine, is one of the finest examples of Russian Orthodox architecture.

718
Leo's successor, Constantine V, continues to suppress the use of icons in worship

727
A revolt in Greece is brutally suppressed by Byzantine forces

732
Charles Martel stops the Muslim armies at Poitiers

751
Martel's son Pepin founds the Carolingian Dynasty

SCRIPTURE AND FAITH

The *Filioque* Controversy

This detail of a Russian icon depicts the Council of Nicaea of 325 C.E.

Among the many theological disputes between the Byzantine Church and the Latin Church in the West was an argument over the addition of the Latin word *filioque* ("and the Son") in the recitation of the Nicene Creed in European churches. The Latin version of the Nicene Creed, current since the eighth century, reads: *"Et in Spiritum Sanctum . . . qui ex Patre Filioque procedit"* ("And in the Holy Spirit, which proceeds from the Father and the Son"). The Eastern Orthodox Church charged that the Holy Spirit proceeds only from the Father, not from the Son. This issue remained a key source of contention at various councils. Eastern theologians charged not only that the addition was false, but also that the Latin Church did not have the authority to change the Nicene Creed, first formulated in 325, in any way. The controversy ultimately contributed to the Great Schism between the Eastern Orthodox Church and the Roman Catholic Church.

by both the Byzantine Nicene orthodoxy, which claimed that God and Jesus were of the same substance, and by the still powerful Monophysite movement, which argued that Jesus had been a divine being from the beginning. Nestorius vigorously objected to the Byzantine practice of referring to the Virgin Mary as *Theotokos* (God-bearer). Mary, Nestorius argued, should be exalted as the mother of Jesus, as *Christotokos* (Christ-bearer).

Fiercely opposed by Nestorius's opposite number in Alexandria, Bishop Cyril, the Nestorian theology was condemned by the Council of Ephesus in 431, and Nestorius was removed from his see. That did not stop his theological vision from catching on like wildfire. Just as Arianism had captured the imagination of the faithful in the third century, so too did Nestorianism grow by leaps and bounds throughout the Byzantine Empire. When the movement was condemned as heresy by the Council of Chalcedon in 451, its adherents fled to Sassanid Persia, eventually forming what became known as the "Church of the East." The Persian city of Nisibis became its intellectual center, attracting many scholars from the school of Edessa, one of the earliest centers of Christian exegesis in the East.

Palm Sunday services bring together Russian Orthodox worshippers in the All Saints Church in Yekaterinburg, Russia. The church commemorates the Romanov sainthood.

754 — **Benedictine missionary Boniface is murdered**

755 — **The start of the An Lushan Rebellion throws the Chinese Empire into turmoil**

757 — **King Offa of Mercia assumes the throne**

768 — **Pepin's son Charles, later called Charlemagne, assumes the throne**

A print from the 14th-century Persian School shows Genghis Khan in battle. Founder and Emperor of the Mongol Empire, Genghis Khan led the Mongol invasions that resulted in the conquest of most of Eurasia. Khan was favorably disposed toward Christianity, largely due to the influence of a daughter-in-law.

Prior to this period, Christian communities in Persia had suffered from heavy persecution because of their perceived role as agents of the Sassanids' sworn enemy, the Byzantine Empire. The arrival of large numbers of Nestorian refugees, however, convinced the Zoroastrian majority in Persia that these Christian dissidents had suffered grievously from Byzantine orthodoxy and would hardly promote Byzantine interests. Persian Christianity soon gravitated toward Nestorianism as its guiding theology, until Patriarch Mar Babai I (r. 497–502) formally declared the Persian Church to be Nestorian in character.

Because it could not expand into the hostile Byzantine territories, this Church of the East sought to move eastward, particularly when the outbreak of hostilities between the Persian King Khosrow I and Byzantine Emperor Justinian once again led to the persecution of Christians in the Persian realm. By the early seventh century, Persian missionaries were working in India, where they absorbed many of the Christian settlements that, as tradition has it, were

This rare mural painting of ninth-century Nestorian Christian services was found in the Qoco Temple of Xinjiang, China. It may depict a Palm Sunday service.

774 Charlemagne is crowned King of the Lombards

787 Empress Irene, consort of the deceased Emperor Leo IV, ends the iconoclasm period

790s The first wave of Viking invasions in Ireland, Scotland, and England

794 Charlemagne establishes his court at Aachen

HISTORY AND POLITICS

The Conquest of Hulegu Khan

A Persian manuscript shows Chinese warrior Hulegu Khan on his throne.

Hulegu Khan was a legendary Chinese warrior who came close to restoring Christianity in Persia, Syria, and the Holy Land. Born in 1218 as the grandson of Genghis Khan and brother of Kublai Khan, Hulegu was tasked to conquer the Muslim-controlled territories in southern Asia. Having conquered Baghdad in 1258 after a bloody siege, Hulegu's forces, led by Mongol general Kitbuqa, entered into an alliance with local Christian rulers, including Hetoum I of Armenia and the Frankish King Bohemond VI of Antioch, to take Syria and Palestine from Islamic rule. This unlikely alliance was surprisingly successful; in 1260, their armies captured Aleppo, followed by Damascus. Hulegu thereupon marched on Palestine, but upon the death of his brother he was forced to return to China. A much smaller force met the defending Muslim armies at the Battle of Ain Jalut in 1260 and was defeated, ending the hopes for a Christian restoration with the aid of Mongol forces.

originally established by the Apostle Thomas. The growth of the Nestorian Church in India was augmented when numerous Syriac Christians migrated to the Indian Coast near Malabar (today's Kerala province) in the ninth century.

Christianity in China

According to the so-called Nestorian Stele, a monument combining the Christian cross with Buddhist and Taoist symbols, the first Christian communities in China were established as early as the mid-seventh century. Scholars believe that the Christian faith must have been carried along the principal caravan routes of the Sassanid Empire by Christian traders and missionaries, following the Jazartes and Tarim Rivers into the Chinese heartland. The Nestorian Stele states that it was a missionary named Alopen who first crossed into China in 635, during the reign of Emperor Tang Taizong of the Tang Dynasty (618–907), and was able to establish a number of communities dedicated to the "Radiant Religion."

By the ninth century, the Church of the East (or the East Syriac Church, as it is sometimes called) had, in geographical terms, become the largest Christian movement of its time, stretching from Mesopotamia and Persia to India and China. Even the Islamic conquest of the Persian Empire could not temper its vibrancy.

The growth of Christianity in China came to a halt when Emperor Wuzong (r. 840–846), a devout Taoist, banned all religions other than Taoism in his reign. Christianity as well as Buddhism were severely curtailed. Some Christian communities persevered, though the collapse of the Tang Dynasty in the tenth century and the chaos of the subsequent Ten Kingdoms period made it difficult for these dioceses to remain in touch with one another.

Three hundred years later, after Mongol tribes had taken control of much of the Chinese heartland, it appeared that Christianity was poised for a renaissance. The great Genghis Khan (r. 1206–1227), who unified the Mongol tribes into one large empire, was favorably disposed to the Christian faith. This was chiefly due to the presence of Christians at

> *When the pure, bright Illustrious Religion was introduced to our Tang Dynasty, the Scriptures were translated, and churches built.*
>
> THE NESTORIAN STELE, CA 781

his court, notably the wife of one of his sons, a Keriat princess named Sorkaktani-beki. She bore several sons, including a prince named Hulegu ("warrior" in Mongolian), who recognized the role Christianity could play in creating a buffer against the ever-looming threat of Islamic Persia. In his travel records, the Italian explorer Marco Polo (ca 1254–1324) describes several visits to Nestorian settlements in both China and Mongolia.

In the mid-1250s, Hulegu Khan invaded Persia with an army that included scores of Christian soldiers and officers, many of whom hoped to restore Nestorian Christianity in the Persian Empire. Their hopes

The Arch of Ctesiphon, also known as Taq-I Kisra or the Arch of Khosrow, is the only remaining monument from the great capital city of the Persian Sassanid Empire.

800 — Pope Leo III crowns Charlemagne Holy Roman Emperor

801 — The monk Anskar, the "Apostle to the North," is born

812 — Byzantium recognizes Charlemagne as Holy Roman Emperor in the West

814 — Charlemagne dies

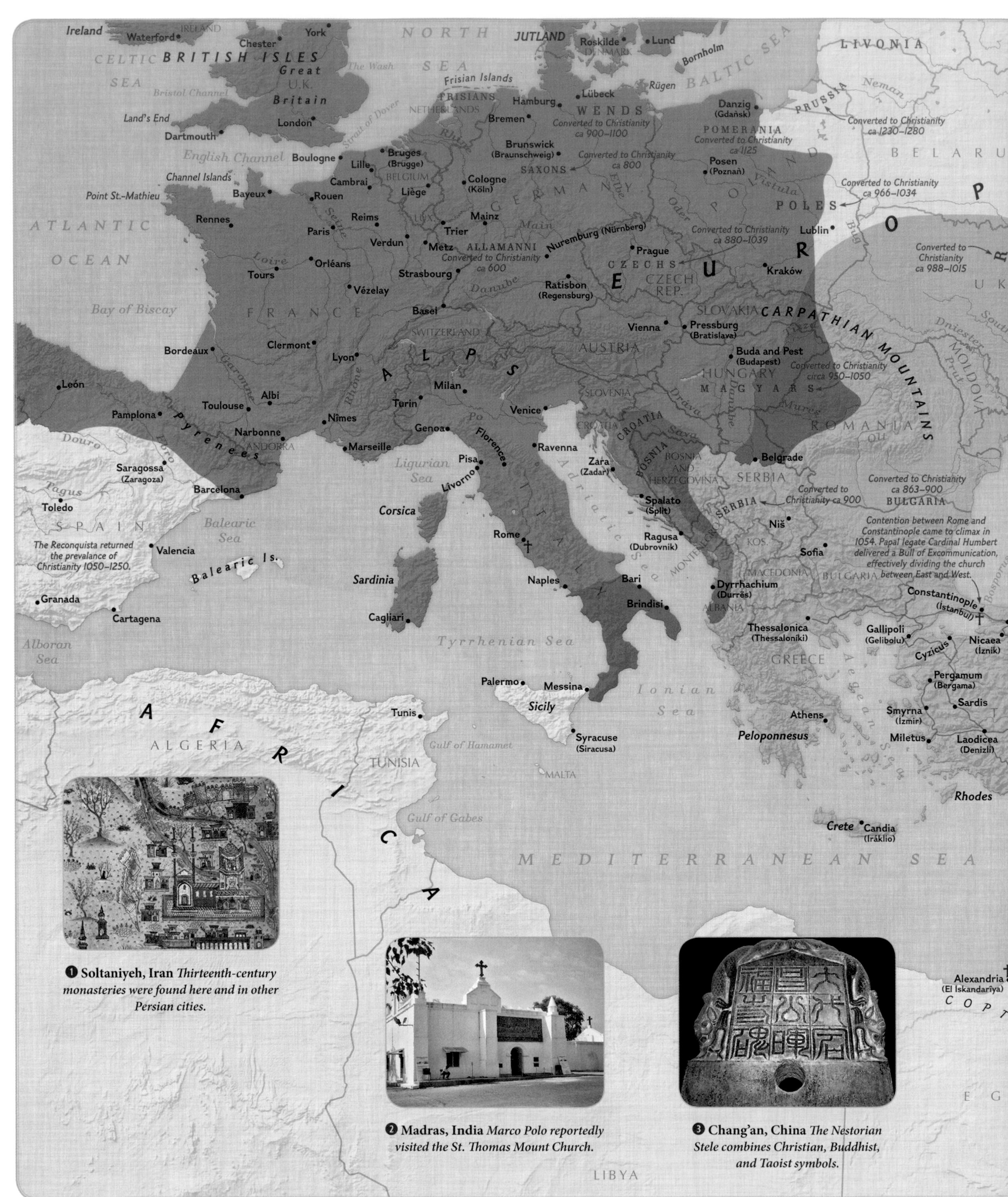

❶ **Soltaniyeh, Iran** *Thirteenth-century monasteries were found here and in other Persian cities.*

❷ **Madras, India** *Marco Polo reportedly visited the St. Thomas Mount Church.*

❸ **Chang'an, China** *The Nestorian Stele combines Christian, Buddhist, and Taoist symbols.*

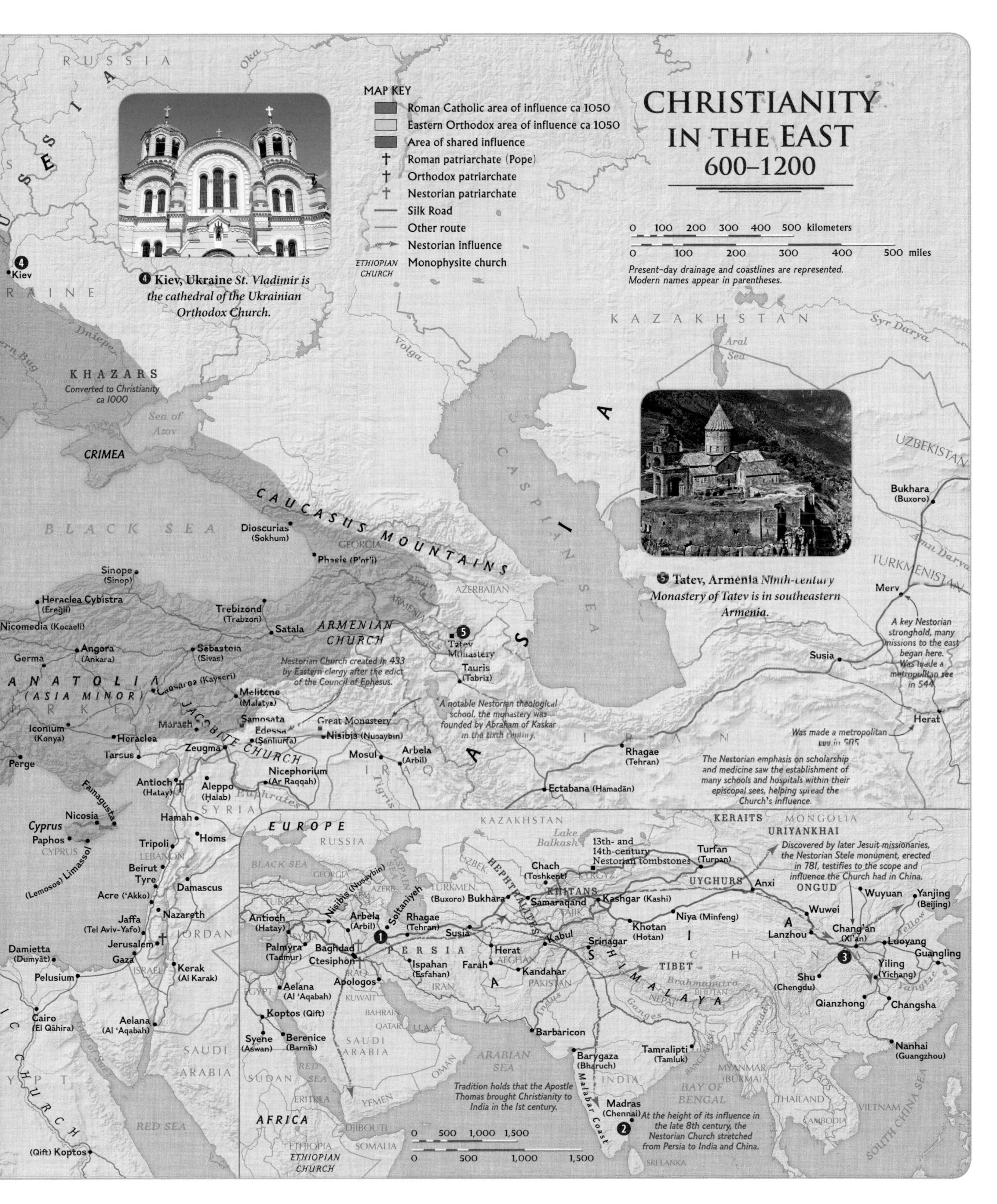
CHRISTIANITY IN THE EAST 600–1200
MAP KEY
Roman Catholic area of influence ca 1050
Eastern Orthodox area of influence ca 1050
Area of shared influence
Roman patriarchate (Pope)
Orthodox patriarchate
Nestorian patriarchate
Silk Road
Other route
Nestorian influence
ETHIOPIAN CHURCH Monophysite church
Present-day drainage and coastlines are represented. Modern names appear in parentheses.
KHAZARS
Converted to Christianity ca 1000
CRIMEA
BLACK SEA
CAUCASUS MOUNTAINS
ARMENIAN CHURCH
JACOBITE CHURCH
ANATOLIA (ASIA MINOR)
CASPIAN SEA
KAZAKHSTAN
Nestorian Church created in 433 by Eastern clergy after the edict of the Council of Ephesus.
A notable Nestorian theological school, the monastery was founded by Abraham of Kaskar in the sixth century.
A key Nestorian stronghold, many missions to the east began here. Was made a metropolitan see in 544
Was made a metropolitan see in 585
The Nestorian emphasis on scholarship and medicine saw the establishment of many schools and hospitals within their episcopal sees, helping spread the Church's influence.
Discovered by later Jesuit missionaries, the Nestorian Stele monument, erected in 781, testifies to the scope and influence the Church had in China.
13th- and 14th-century Nestorian tombstones
Tradition holds that the Apostle Thomas brought Christianity to India in the 1st century.
At the height of its influence in the late 8th century, the Nestorian Church stretched from Persia to India and China.

❹ **Kiev, Ukraine** *St. Vladimir is the cathedral of the Ukrainian Orthodox Church.*

❺ **Tatev, Armenia** *Ninth-century Monastery of Tatev is in southeastern Armenia.*

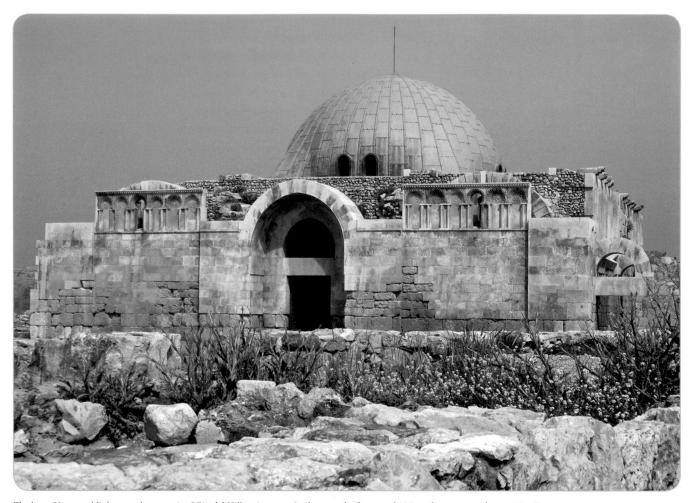

The large Umayyad Palace on the summit of Citadel Hill in Amman, Jordan, was built around 730 on the remains of preexisting Roman structures.

This Umayyad gold coin dates from 698. Coins such as this were the first to carry Arabic inscriptions.

were stymied when the death of Hulegu's brother, the Great Khan, forced Hulegu to return to China, leaving a much smaller force to continue the Mongolian conquest into Syria and Palestine. This army, led by a Christian general named Ked-Buka, was soundly defeated by vastly superior Islamic forces at the Battle of Ain Jalut in 1260. Ironically, Ain Jalut was located in the Jezreel Valley, a short distance from Jesus' hometown of Nazareth.

In the last decades of Mongol rule, several Christians in China still held out the hope for an alliance with the Church in the West, so as to create a common front against the Islamic Empire, but these initiatives did not bear fruit. As Robert Bruce Mullin has observed, one reason may be that European Christians feared the Mongol hordes more than the Islamic armies, even if some of these Mongols were baptized.

After the Mongol ruler Mahmud Ghazan (r. 1295–1304) formally converted to Islam in 1295, Christianity in China went once again into a steep decline, and disappeared

840 Emperor Wuzong bans all religions other than Taoism in China

843 Use of icons in Orthodox liturgy is officially sanctioned

845 A Viking force attacks Paris

846 Moravian King Mojmir is deposed by Rostislav

altogether under the xenophobic Ming Dynasty, which came to power in 1368. Political pressure may not have been the only reason; the difficulty of sustaining Christian communities across the far-flung steppes and mountain ranges of China, bereft of the type of strong government support that Christians enjoyed elsewhere, was probably an important factor as well. Archaeologists have not uncovered any Christian tombstones erected after the 1350s. As a result, Christianity in China would not return in any significant measure until the 19th century.

Christianity Under Islam

After the conquest of the Holy Land, Caliph Umar had continued his military campaign into the Sassanid Persian Empire, defeating the Persian forces at the Battle of Qadisiyya. In 637, the capital of Ctesiphon fell to the Muslim invaders. Today, the magnificent brick arch of the Sassanid palace of Ctesiphon, located near Baghdad, still bears the marks of the palace's destruction by Umar's forces. Five years later, the Islamic host plunged into Egypt and conquered Alexandria, followed by a series of assaults on Cyprus beginning in 649. A Roman possession since 58 B.C.E., Cyprus had adopted Christianity with the rest of the Roman Empire in the fourth century C.E. and had remained in the Byzantine orbit ever since. So prominent became its Church that its archbishop was made *autocephalous* (i.e., not subject to any higher patriarch or other ecclesiastical authority) by the First Council of Ephesus of 431, presided over by Emperor Theodosius II.

The Islamic attack on Cyprus was not led by Umar but by one of his generals, a former secretary of Muhammad named Muawiyah (602–680), who would later rule as the second Umayyad caliph. Muawiyah had long recognized that Islam could never safeguard the maritime routes to its new Mediterranean possessions without a navy that was the equal of, if not superior to, the vast Byzantine fleet. In 649, he began to organize a naval force, using dockyards in Egypt and Syria. Ironically, many of the new ships were crewed by experienced sailors from Christian

HISTORY AND POLITICS

The Convivencia in Spain

The three Abrahamic faiths—Judaism, Christianity, and Islam—enjoyed a rare period of peaceful coexistence in the Islamic-ruled region of Al-Andalus (today's Andalusia) in southern Spain. During the struggle between the Umayyads and the Abbasids for control of the Islamic Empire, the Umayyad nobleman Abd-al-Rahman III (r. 912–961), grandson of Caliph Hisham, fled to Al-Andalus and took control of the region. He initiated a Golden Age, welcoming an array of artists and scientists from all over Europe, regardless of their faith. The city of Córdoba became an unprecedented center of learning following the establishment of the University of Córdoba by Rahman's son, al-Hakam II (r. 961–976). One of Al-Hakam's ministers was a Jewish physician named Hasdai ibn Shaprut, who encouraged numerous Jewish scholars to come to Moorish Spain and participate in its great scientific revival. Al-Hakam's agents, meanwhile, scoured the bookshops of Alexandria, Damascus, and Baghdad in search of valuable books for the growing Library of Córdoba, which ultimately grew to 400,000 books, including works by Plato, Aristotle, Archimedes, and other Greek scholars that otherwise would have been lost to civilization. The library's catalog alone numbered 44 volumes. More than 5,000 calligraphists were employed in copying the works. In the Judería, the Jewish quarter of Córdoba, Muslim artisans built a synagogue for the city's Jewish population, decorated with their trademark Mudéjar stucco ornamentation. This synagogue is the only Jewish house of worship that survived the forced expulsion of the Jews after the Christian reconquest of Spain in 1492.

Moorish arcades line the interior of the Mezquita of Córdoba, Spain.

851
Vikings penetrate deep into England

860
A Viking fleet raids Constantinople

863
Cyril and Methodius begin translating the Bible in the Slavonic language

864
King Boris I of Bulgaria agrees to be baptized in the Byzantine rites

Sassanid Art

500–650

This Sassanid head was hammered from a single sheet of silver.

A seventh-century Sassanid dish shows King Yazdegerd III hunting.

A seventh-century plaque features a legendary bird with the head of a dog.

dissident sects—Copts, Monophysites, and Nestorians—who had suffered from Byzantine persecution. In 655, this massive fleet met the Byzantine navy at the Battle of the Masts, just off the coast of today's Antalya, and dealt the ships of Emperor Constans II a crushing defeat.

Prior to the battle, Muawiyah returned to Cyprus to take full possession of the island. As many Christians fled from the advancing Muslim armies, one Cypriot family decided to bury its treasure of silver dishes depicting scenes from the Old Testament. This treasure was uncovered by chance in 1902 near Karavas, a town near the Cyprus port of Lapithos, and is now known as the Karavas Treasure.

Thus, a mere 30 years after the death of the Prophet Muhammad, the Empire of Islam stretched from today's Libya to Persia, from the Black and Caspian Seas to the Persian Gulf. The stupendous success of this conquest was due, in no small measure, to the unique condition of the Middle East in the mid-seventh century. The two superpowers of the time, Byzantium and Persia, had exhausted themselves in a long series of battles that left both nations weary of war. Although Byzantine Emperor Heraclius had emerged triumphant from the Persian Wars, his state coffers were depleted. At the beginning of the Islamic Conquest, his standing army was dispersed throughout the northern Empire in the incessant struggle against barbarian invasions, and poorly positioned to check the Islamic advance.

But equally important, perhaps, was the fact that much of the population in the Byzantine and Persian realms welcomed Muslim forces as liberators from either Orthodox or Sassanid oppression, including Jews and dissident Christians. Islamic governors did not disappoint them. With the exception of Persia, where the Muslim conquerors initiated a brief persecution of Zoroastrians, the inhabitants of the new Islamic Empire were largely left to live, work, and worship as they saw fit. The Islamic rulers of the Rashidun Caliphate (also known as the "Four Righteous Caliphs") genuinely respected both Jews and Christians as "People of the Book," heirs to revelations from the same God who had spoken to Muhammad—although in the Muslim view, the Jewish and Christian interpretation of these revelations was not as pure as the Muslim interpretation of the Quran. Thus Jews and Christians were permitted to go about their business as *dhimmis,* as a protected religious minority.

There were some limitations, of course. All subject peoples were charged with an

"Khosrow II Stealing the True Cross" is a fresco by Italian artist Cenni di Francesco (1369–1415), from his series "Stories of the Cross" (1410).

871
Alfred the Great assumes the throne of the kingdom of Wessex

911
King Charles III is forced to cede a coastal area, later named Normandy, to the Norse

912
Umayyad nobleman Abd-al-Rahman III initiates the period of the Convivencia in Muslim Spain

917
King Simeon I of Bulgaria declares the Bulgarian Church's independence from Byzantium

occupation tax, the *jizya,* to support the new Islamic government and its armies, but Jews and Christians were taxed at a higher rate than that levied on Muslims. Furthermore, employment in the Islamic government and advancement through its ranks were limited to Muslims. This was sufficient reason for many to convert to Islam, particularly given the many shared tenets of faith between Judaism, Christianity, and early Islam—including the great reverence shown to Musa (Moses) and Isa (Jesus) in the Quran and the Hadith, the sayings of the Prophet.

The Arab armies were overwhelmed by their military successes. Stretched thin all over the Middle East, Umar and his successors had little choice but to govern by proxy, leaving much of the social and political infrastructure in place. All this would change in the centuries to come; but for the time being, Arab rule was remarkably tolerant toward both Jews and Christians.

After Umar was killed in 644 (by a Persian slave in his retinue), six prominent sheikhs in Mecca selected a new caliph named Uthman ibn Affan (r. 644–656). Unlike Abu Bakr and Umar, who like Muhammad were members of Mecca's Hashemite class, Uthman belonged to the aristocratic Umayyad clan. His selection infuriated the faction from Medina, who remained steadfast in their support of Muhammad's young cousin (and son-in-law) Ali. Imperious in bearing and autocratic in rule, Uthman continued Umar's conquests but favored members of his own clan in key positions of the army and administration. Even as he pushed the conquest into northwestern Africa, riots broke out in 656 in Medina. In the ensuing melee, Uthman was assassinated, although it is not clear which faction was responsible for his murder. A majority in Mecca demanded that a caliph be selected from the ranks of Muhammad's companions, like Abu Bakr and Umar, rather than from the nobility. The population of Medina insisted on the

This six-pointed star formed part of the Umayyad Palace of Khirbat al-Mafjar near Jericho in the Jordan valley. The structure was built during the reign of Caliph Hisham Ibn Abdelmalik between 724 and 743.

PERIOD ART

The Karavas Treasure

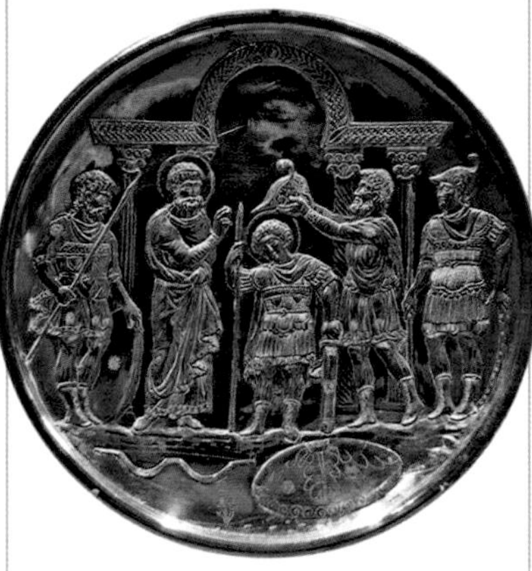

"The Anointment of David" forms part of a collection of Byzantine silverware discovered near Karavas, Cyprus, in 1902.

In 654, as Arab armies swept across Cyprus, a wealthy Christian family hastily buried its treasure, which consisted of 11 silver dishes with scenes from the Old Testament. This hoard was discovered in 1902, near Karavas, a port on the island's northern shore near Lambousa (ancient Lapithos). The silver works are true masterpieces of seventh-century Byzantine art, depicting scenes of the Old Testament; nine dishes are focused on the life of King David. One silver plate depicts the story of David and Goliath, including a scene in which David is outfitted in Hellenistic armor, and another in which the young warrior defeats the Philistine giant. The figures are beautifully raised from the silver and reveal the strong influence of Greek and Roman models. The dishes attest to the key role that Cyprus played in the Mediterranean trade between Constantinople's various possessions during the early Byzantine era.

919
King Henry I, "the Fowler," founds the German Ottonian Dynasty

927
Peter I becomes Tsar of Bulgaria

928
King Henry I conquers the Slav province of Brandenburg and Bohemia

936
King Henry I is succeeded by his son Otto I

Surely those who believe,
the Jews and the Christians,
whoever believes in God;
they shall have no fear,
nor shall they grieve.

QURAN 5:69

elevation of Ali. The latter prevailed. Thus, Ali was chosen as the fourth caliph since the death of Muhammad. But when Ali refused to bring Uthman's assassins to justice, a Muslim civil war—the first *fitna*—was brewing. In 657, the two sides came to blows at the Battle of Siffin, on the banks of the Euphrates, but the outcome was inconclusive. Four years later, Ali was assassinated. The Umayyads emerged triumphant and moved the capital of the new Islamic Empire from Mecca to the city of Damascus, where their power was unchallenged.

The Umayyad Dynasty introduced a great flowering of Arab culture, inspired by Greek, Roman, and Christian art and literature. Islam was, at the time, a worldly religion that encouraged the pursuit of science as the study of God's magnificent creation. Islamic scholars engaged in almost every field of science, from medicine to astronomy, from architecture to algebra. But in one important aspect of human endeavor, Islam was different. It did not permit the representation of living creatures, either in art or sculpture. Such a proscription is

The Battle of Siffin, in 657, is depicted in this 19th-century illustration from Kashmir. The battle was part of the first Muslim civil war, which lasted from 656 to 661.

950
Queen Olga, ruler of Kiev, is baptized by German missionaries

950
Europe lapses into the Dark Ages

955
King Otto I defeats the Magyars at the Battle of Lechfeld

960
Tai Tsoo of the Sung Dynasty defeats the Tatars

not found in the Quran, but rather in the Hadith, in which Allah is quoted as saying, "And who is more unjust than those who try to create the likeness of My creation?"

Islamic scholars interpreted this saying to mean that any human attempt to imitate God's creation was "weak" and meaningless. Since only God can create life, they argued, the artistic depiction of animals or people interferes with God's design—a position that has much in common with the abhorrence of "graven images" in ancient Judaism. Consequently, Islamic artists were forbidden to paint animals or human beings, although in several regions of the Empire, notably Persia, this proscription was roundly ignored.

The Period of Iconoclasm

The proscription of figurative art had major consequences beyond the Islamic Empire. In 717, Byzantine Emperor Leo III Isauros (r. 717–741), named after the Isaurian region in Asia Minor (today's Konya province in Turkey), declared that all use of religious icons (from the Greek word *eikoon*, "image") and any other representations of Christ or saints were henceforth forbidden. With this decree, the Emperor introduced the brief period of iconoclasm (literally "icon-breaking") in Byzantine Christianity. Leo's motives are unclear. One group of historians has pointed to the success of Islam as perhaps a more enlightened version of monotheism, whereas others see a desire to honor the second Mosaic commandment in Hebrew Scripture that "you shall not make for yourself an idol." Before long, icons were removed from churches throughout Constantinople and beyond; only the Chi-Rho (for *Christos*) and Alpha and Omega symbols were permitted.

The decree was greatly mourned by the faithful, who were accustomed to icons as pious objects in prayer, as well as monks who derived much of their livelihood from the production of sacred images. In 727, a revolt broke out in Greece, a major center of icon production, which was brutally suppressed.

The Latin Church in the West was stupefied by this sudden aversion to sacred art.

HISTORY AND POLITICS

The Great Schism

Ever since the ninth century, tensions had been growing between the Byzantine Church, governed by the patriarch of Constantinople, and the European Church, governed by the pope in Rome. Culturally, Byzantium still clung to Greek, whereas the dominant liturgical language in Europe was Latin. Several conflicts escalated these tensions. The West disparaged the Eastern Church for its struggle with heresies, while Constantinople looked down on the European Church as primitive and unsophisticated. In addition, both Churches laid claim to contested territories such as the Italian peninsula; when Norman hordes invaded the Italian south in 999, the pope refused to come to the aid of the hard-pressed Byzantine armies. Fifty years later, matters came to a head when Pope Leo IX appointed an archbishop in Sicily, which Byzantium claimed as its own jurisdiction. In retaliation, Patriarch Michael Cerularius of Constantinople ordered the closing of all Latin churches in the Byzantine capital. In essence, these and other disputes centered on a simple question: Who was the ultimate spiritual authority in Christendom, the pontiff in Rome or the patriarch in Constantinople? When, in 1054, a papal legate threatened Patriarch Michael with excommunication unless he accepted the primacy of Rome as "mother of all churches," the split between the two churches became final. The Crusaders' appropriation of former Byzantine territory in the Holy Land and the sack of Constantinople by Crusader mercenaries in 1204 eliminated any hope for reconciliation. Henceforth, Byzantine Christianity would become known as the Eastern Orthodox Church and Latin Christianity as the Roman Catholic Church.

This painting by Eugène Delacroix shows the sack of Orthodox Constantinople by Catholic forces during the Fourth Crusade.

962
King Otto I is crowned Holy Roman Emperor

966
Mieszko I of Poland agrees to be baptized in the Latin rites

973
King Géza of Hungary accepts Latin Christianity in his realm

987
King Vladimir I of Russia agrees to adopt Byzantine Christianity

Popes Gregory II and Gregory III strongly opposed the measure, and even went as far as to excommunicate all those who adhered to iconoclast principles, further inflaming the tense relations between East and West. Nevertheless, the iconoclast policy was enforced with great severity by Leo's son, Emperor Constantine V (718–775). Monasteries that continued to produce icons were confiscated, and artist-monks were tortured or killed.

An icon depicting Christ was painted by Russian artist Andrey Rublyov (1370–1430). Rublyov was a medieval painter of Orthodox icons and frescoes.

In some ways, the iconoclast controversy brought the centuries-old dispute over the true nature of Christ to a tipping point. If, as some theologians argued, Christ had always been divine, then the Mosaic proscription against idolatry should indeed be upheld. If, on the other hand, God had caused his Son to be made incarnate, and dwell among mankind as a human being, then surely God would not prohibit the depiction of Jesus in that capacity—as a man of flesh and blood. Theologian John of Damascus (ca 675–749) effectively captured the debate in arguing that matter, infused by the divine *logos,* is essential to our understanding of creation. Therefore, icons are as fundamental in the veneration of Christ as the written word of the Gospels, or the wood of the True Cross.

The iconoclast period came to an end during the reign of Empress Irene (a rare instance of a female ruler in Byzantine annals). Irene seized the levers of power upon the death of her husband, Emperor Leo IV, in 780 and continued as regent of her son Constantine VI until 802. Deeply devoted to the power of sacred images, she vowed to revoke the iconoclast decree, but a first attempt to do so during the Council of Constantinople in 786 was thwarted. One year later, she convened another council in Nicaea, and persuaded the clergy to agree to a distinction between "veneration" of images, which should be permitted, versus "worship" of images, which smacked of idolatry and should be prohibited. The compromise satisfied the bishops, and the Empire heaved a sigh of relief. The production of icons was restored, and once again the *iconostasis* in Orthodox Churches—the symbolic separation between the nave and sanctuary, between the congregation and the priest—shimmered with the gold of countless religious paintings. Subsequent emperors tried to reintroduce iconoclast policies, but in 843, the use of icons was officially and definitively established as a core feature of Orthodox liturgy and worship. This produced an explosion of new iconography in order to satisfy the long-suppressed demand for devotional paintings. When Constantinople fell in 1453, much of the production of icons shifted to Greece, already a major supplier, and to Moscow, the new heir to Eastern Orthodox Christianity. ■

It is obvious that when you contemplate God becoming man, then you may depict Him clothed in human form.

JOHN OF DAMASCUS,
ON THE DIVINE IMAGES

OPPOSITE: *"The Iconoclasts" is the work of Italian painter Domenico Morelli (1826–1901). The oil-on-canvas painting was widely praised when it was displayed at the Florentine Exposition in 1855.*

1017
Yaroslav the Wise builds the Golden Gates of Kiev

1018
King Canute of Denmark ascends the throne, uniting the crowns of England and Denmark

1025
Boleslaw I Chrobry establishes an independent Polish metropolitanate in Gniezno

1035
Moravia and Bohemia are combined by Bretislaus I as a Latin Christian kingdom

6
CHAPTER

THE AGE OF CONFLICT

900-1200

Think of the pilgrims who travel the Mediterranean; to what tributes, to what violence they are subjected!

GUIBERT OF NOGENT
ON THE CALL FOR THE FIRST CRUSADE

From the early 11th century onward, European Christendom became embroiled in a series of military expeditions against Muslim control of Palestine that are commonly referred to as the Crusades. Though these expeditions led to only a brief restoration of Christian rule in Palestine and Syria, the impact of the Crusades in Europe would be far more pervasive.

The Crusades were a unique series of military expeditions that found broad support among both the rulers and populations of Western Christendom. That these massive campaigns could be mustered at all, in a relatively short time, is vivid testimony to the extent to which much of Europe had recovered from the Dark Ages after the collapse of the Roman Empire. Most people of Europe were once again living in nation-states governed by secular and religious hierarchies, under the banner of Christendom. They once again enjoyed the nominal protection of laws, and the barbarian invasions that had tormented the continent in preceding centuries were now much less frequent. Commerce resumed, trade routes were reestablished, and Roman townships that had slowly disintegrated in the centuries past once again began to grow.

ABOVE: *A stained-glass window of 1248 from the Sainte-Chapelle in Paris depicts the resurrection of the dead on Judgment Day.*

OPPOSITE: *During the Second Crusade of 1147, the citadel of Aleppo, Syria, changed hands many times between Crusader and Muslim forces.*

PRECEDING PAGES: *"The Battle of Montgisard," by French artist Charles-Philippe Larivière (1798–1876), depicts the victory of Crusader King Baldwin of Jerusalem over the much larger Muslim forces led by Salah-ad-Din.*

The Crusader Era

1100–1300

A vessel displays the emblem of the Order of the Hospitallers, Knights of Malta.

This elegant ivory plaque depicts scenes from the New Testament.

The dagger and sleeve of the Grand Master of the Knights of Malta

Nevertheless, the Crusades inaugurated a period of intense and unprecedented violence that targeted not only Muslims in the Middle East but also any groups or individuals who did not submit to the Latin Christian Church. This is why modern historians continue to debate the social and political motives for the Crusades and the impact these expeditions ultimately had on Christianity and world history.

Certainly, one powerful source of friction was the deteriorating attitude of Muslim rulers toward Christians in their territories, particularly Western pilgrims to the Holy Land. The early caliphates, including the Umayyads, had respected the importance of pilgrimage, given that the Muslim hajj to Mecca is one of the five pillars of Islam. Thus, when a French prelate named Arculf arrived in Egypt in 679, during Umayyad rule, he was able to roam freely, visiting several Coptic monasteries in Egypt before continuing to Bethlehem and Jerusalem. Along the way, he recorded his impressions in a notebook known as *Historia Ecclesiae.* Published after his return, the book became a sensation and prompted a new wave of eager pilgrims to visit the Holy Land. The growing tension between the Byzantine and Islamic Empires did not deter these pious travelers, though many were forced to travel by sea via Alexandria, rather than using the overland route through Asia Minor and Syria. Conditions

The entry of King Louis VII of France and King Conrad III of Germany into Constantinople during the Crusades is depicted in this illustration by French artist Jean Fouquet (1420–1480).

954
Upon the death of Erik Bloodaxe, King of Northumbria, all English kingdoms are united

955
King Otto I defeats the Magyars, ending Hungarian invasions of Europe

962
King Otto I is crowned Holy Roman Emperor by Pope John XII

969
Fatimid Gawhar al-Siqilli conquers the Islamic Empire

for pilgrims improved further during the reign of the caliph Harun-al-Rashid (786–809), who corresponded regularly with his counterpart in Europe, Charlemagne. Prodded by the French King, Rashid even agreed to build a number of pilgrim hospices in Jerusalem and to ensure that Christian pilgrims were given full access to holy sites.

But this benevolent attitude disappeared when Rashid's enlightened rule came to an end. One French pilgrim, a nobleman named Frotmond, was so savagely robbed and beaten that he was left for dead on the road, naked and bleeding. Matters went from bad to worse in the wake of the Fatimid conquest of the Islamic Empire by Gawhar al-Siqilli in 969. His Shia rule, bent on enforcing Islamic orthodoxy, showed little tolerance toward Christians, particularly Christians from Islam's sworn enemy, Byzantium. One energetic Byzantine Emperor, John I Tzimiskes (r. 969–976), launched an invasion to free the Holy Land from Muslim rule. A skillful strategist, Tzimiskes captured many cities in Syria and Mesopotamia, and even succeeded in taking Nazareth and Caesarea, but was unable to move any farther.

Perhaps in retaliation, the sixth Fatimid caliph, Al-Hakim (r. 996–1021), launched a vast persecution campaign throughout his realm, including the destruction of Christian churches as well as Jewish synagogues. The Church of the Holy Sepulcher, painstakingly rebuilt after the Persian sack of 614, was once again torn down in 1008. The demolition was so thorough that even the foundations were destroyed, down to the bedrock. Other churches in Palestine were converted into mosques or changed into stables or depots. For this, Al-Hakim is sometimes referred to in Christian literature as "the Mad Caliph."

Christian pilgrims who, against all odds, still made it into the Holy Land came back with hair-raising stories of abuse, robbery, and beatings. One of these was a prelate named Gerbert, who in time would become Pope Sylvester II. Upon his return in 986, Gerbert issued an open letter calling upon the Christian world to liberate the beleaguered Christian communities in Palestine.

Thus, Europe slowly embarked on a path to war. Al-Hakim's son Ali az-Zahir and

PERIOD ARCHITECTURE

The Crusader Church of the Holy Sepulcher

Most scholars accept that the Church of the Holy Sepulcher, today located in the western part of Jerusalem's Old City, is the place of Jesus' crucifixion and burial. Twice destroyed, first by the Persians in 614 and then by the Fatimid caliph Al-Hakim in 1008, some restoration was undertaken during the reign of Al-Hakim's son and grandson. But for the most part, the church was still in ruins when the city was taken by Frankish Crusaders in 1099. A major effort was then undertaken to rebuild the church, using the Romanesque style, which had just begun to make its appearance in Europe. The new church was inaugurated in 1149, during the reign of Queen Melisende of Jerusalem. Among the new features added by the Crusaders was a slab known as the Stone of Unction, based on the legend that Christ's body was prepared for anointing on this spot. (The present stone, however, was installed in 1808 after a fire.) Above the main altar, over the spot believed to be the *omphalos*, or center of the world, the Crusaders built a domed structure known as the *Katholikon*. Today, the church is uneasily divided between Catholic Franciscans and Eastern, Coptic, Georgian, Syriac, and Armenian Christians. The interdenominational rivalry is not without tension. Protestant and Anglican Christians, meanwhile, sometimes prefer to gather at the Garden Tomb site discovered by General Gordon in 1882, located outside the current city walls.

The Church of the Holy Sepulcher was rebuilt by Crusaders in 1147, following its destruction by the caliph Al-Hakim in 1008.

973
Emperor John I Tzimiskes launches an unsuccessful invasion of the Holy Land

986
Prelate Gerbert, the future Pope Sylvester II, calls for the liberation of Palestine

996
Fatimid caliph Al-Hakim initiates a persecution of Jews and Christians

1008
The rebuilt Church of the Holy Sepulcher is once again destroyed

GRANET,

We have mingled with flowing tears, and there is no room left in us for pity.

IBN AL-ATHIR,
ON THE FALL OF JERUSALEM, 1099

his successor, Caliph Ma'ad al-Mustansir Billah (who ruled longer than any other caliph, from 1036 to 1094), recognized the danger and belatedly tried to make amends. In exchange for hefty sums pledged by the Byzantine Emperor Constantine IX, these caliphs authorized the reconstruction of the Church of the Holy Sepulcher, though little actual building was done. One source claims that the church at that point was little more than "a court open to the sky, with five small chapels attached to it." Nevertheless, for a moment it seemed that the momentum for holy war had stalled.

One reason was that Europe itself was distracted by two crises: the Great Schism of 1054, which made the split between the Eastern Orthodox and Roman Catholic Churches permanent, and the Investiture Conflict between the Holy Roman Empire and the Holy See in Rome. But when the ruling Fatimid Dynasty was ousted by the even more violent Turkish Seljuqs, led by Malik Shah (r. 1072–1092), the call for war rose again in Europe, particularly after a revolt among the population of Jerusalem was bloodily suppressed. In 1095, during the Council of Clermont, Pope Urban II formally called for a Crusade—literally meaning "taking up the cross" in French—to deliver the Christians in the Holy Land from Muslim rule.

French artist François-Marius Granet (1775–1849) painted this scene of Godfrey of Bouillon depositing the trophies of Askalon in the Church of the Holy Sepulcher.

The Crusader Campaigns

The papal call succeeded beyond all expectations. The tension between emperor and pope was set aside as scores of knights, and even greater numbers of foot soldiers, rose to the occasion. Urban tried to excuse women, monks, and men of poor health from service, but to no avail. Their enthusiasm may have been motivated by the papal pledge of "plenary indulgence," which essentially allowed the Crusaders to plunder to their heart's content.

The Battle of Hattin, which took place in 1187, is depicted in this 15th-century French manuscript. The battle took place between the Crusader kingdom of Jerusalem and the armies of the Ayyubid Dynasty.

OPPOSITE: *A bird's-eye view shows the Rotunda of the Church of the Holy Sepulcher with the Aedicule containing the tomb of Christ.*

In all, seven major Crusades and a number of lesser ones would be launched between 1096 and 1291, mostly with limited success. Only the First Crusade (officially termed an "armed pilgrimage"), led by illustrious figures such as Duke Godfrey of Bouillon, King Philip I of France, and the brother of King William II of England, Robert Curthose, was able to make substantial gains against Muslim forces. In 1099, Jerusalem was taken by Frankish Crusaders after both Jewish and Muslim inhabitants of the city united in a desperate defense of the city. Most of these defenders were massacred in the orgy of violence that followed.

Thus began a brief period of Christian rule, from 1099 to 1187, in the Holy Land. Four separate Crusader states were established. With Christian control of the holy city restored for the first time in 460 years, a "kingdom" of Jerusalem was formed, ruled by Godfrey of Bouillon. Godfrey, however, refused to assume the title of king and was addressed instead as Advocatus Sancti Sepulchri, "Defender of the Holy Sepulcher." Indeed, the first priority for the Crusaders was to rebuild the original Church of the Holy Sepulcher virtually from scratch. The new design restored the idea of combining two separate buildings—a basilica commemorating Golgotha with a rotunda surmounting Christ's tomb—into one structure, though two domes still mark these two functions from the outside. Furthermore, a bell tower was added. Allowing for various additions and restorations, this is the church that visitors to Jerusalem's Old City see today.

While rebuilding the foundations, the architects discovered the remains of Hadrian's original temple dedicated to Venus. This was converted into a chapel dedicated to Empress Helena, Constantine's mother, while a separate crypt was hewn for the tombs of Crusader knights, including Godfrey. Other basilicas were also built throughout the city to replace those that had been destroyed during the persecution of Al-Hakim, although only St. Anne's Church, near Stephen's Gate, remains as an original example of Crusader architecture in Jerusalem.

1010 — **Bishop Bernward builds St. Michael's Church in Hildesheim, Germany**

1023 — **The Knights Hospitaller order is formed to cater to pilgrims in the Holy Land**

1036 — **Caliph Ma'ad al-Mustansir Billah assumes power**

1036 — **Ma'ad al-Mustansir Billah permits reconstruction of the Church of the Holy Sepulcher**

The Muslim response soon followed. From 1100 onward, Crusader forces began to clash with Seljuk Turkish armies. In 1110, the sultan of Baghdad, Muhammad I, launched a series of attacks that led to considerable loss of life. This was followed by a concerted Muslim campaign to recapture Syria, commanded by Imad ad-Din Zengi (r. 1127–1146), the governor of Mosul and Aleppo. After a string of victories, Zengi invaded Edessa in 1144, conquering one of the Crusader states for the first time. This news so alarmed the West that Pope Eugene III, joined by prominent clerics such as Bernard of Clairvaux, called for a Second Crusade. This campaign, led by French King Louis VII and Bavarian monarch Conrad III, made it as far as Jerusalem but contributed little to the maintenance of Crusader power in the region, other than prompting Muslim rulers in the Middle East to declare a *jihad* against all Crusader states.

Zengi was assassinated in 1146, but one of his lieutenants, Salah-ad-Din (known to the West as Saladin) took over and soon confronted the Crusaders with the greatest Muslim army yet assembled. Though beset by attacks from Islamic rivals, Saladin was deeply angered by ambushes of unarmed Muslim pilgrimage and trading caravans by the militant Crusader knight Raynald of Châtillon. In 1187, he crushed the Crusader forces at the Battle of Hattin, leaving the knights with fewer than 15,000 men. Saladin then laid siege to Jerusalem with a force of nearly 80,000 Saracen warriors. The defenders had little choice but to capitulate, and on October 2, Saladin entered the city.

The fall of Jerusalem inevitably led to a call for a Third Crusade, this time led by Richard "The Lionheart" of England, but despite several attempts, Richard was unable to retake Jerusalem. Nevertheless, all was not lost. Given that both Richard and Saladin had a reputation for chivalry, an uneasy truce was declared, which granted Christian pilgrims unimpeded access to holy sites in Jerusalem—the principal war aim of the Crusades to begin with.

From there on, the Crusader states were gradually rolled back until the knights clung only to their stronghold in Caesarea, near

HISTORY AND POLITICS

Richard I

Richard I, known as the Lionheart (r. 1189–1199), is one of the most iconic characters to emerge from the Crusader era. The son of Henry II of England, Richard distinguished himself as a commander during the suppression of various revolts against his father's rule, only to lead a rebellion against the King himself. After Henry II died in 1189, Richard was crowned King in Westminster Abbey. The event led to much violence against Jewish families in England, based on the rumor that the King had ordered all Jews to be killed. Shocked by this rampage, Richard agreed to join Emperor Frederick Barbarossa in a Third Crusade as an act of penance. In 1191, Richard conquered Cyprus, then the port city of Acre on Palestine's Mediterranean coast, although his victory was marred by a quarrel with Austrian King Leopold V. Richard defeated Saladin's Muslim warriors at the Battle of Arsuf to the acclaim of all of Christendom. He then captured Jaffa, but failed to take Jerusalem. Tense negotiations between Saladin and Richard produced a three-year truce and a pledge to allow all Christians unimpeded access to sites in Jerusalem. After Richard returned to Europe, he was imprisoned by a vengeful Leopold V, but was released two years later. He then fought many battles to regain control of his kingdom, particularly in Normandy. While inspecting one of his forts in 1199, he was struck by a crossbow arrow shot by one of his own soldiers, and died soon thereafter. His reputation for chivalry inspired many songs and legends, particularly in connection with Robin Hood.

Merry Joseph Blondel (1781–1853) painted this portrait of Richard I "The Lionheart."

1049
Pope Leo IX initiates a program of reform in the papacy

1054
The Great Schism splits Christianity into the Eastern Orthodox and Roman Catholic Churches

1063
Pope Alexander II grants indulgences to all soldiers fighting to evict Muslim rule from Spain

1063
Construction begins on the Cathedral of Pisa

"The Massacre of the Jews by the People's Crusade" is a painting by French artist Auguste Migette (1802–1884). It depicts the massacre of Jewish people in Metz in 1095, during the First Crusade.

the place of Herod's great harbor. They were evicted at last by the Mamluk Sultan Baibars in 1275. From that moment on, the Mamluks remained in control of the Holy Land until Jerusalem fell to another Islamic invader, the Ottoman Turks, in 1517. These Muslim rulers would remain in place for the next 400 years.

The Legacy of the Crusades

It has been argued, with some justification, that the impact of the Crusades was more keenly felt in Europe itself than on the battlefields in the Islamic Middle East. In Spain, for example, the call for a Holy War against Islam reignited the efforts by Christian knights in the Spanish north to evict the Muslim rulers of Al-Andalus and other states in the south. This conflict had been growing since the tenth century, but Pope Alexander II's declaration of 1063 that granted indulgences to all Spanish soldiers, followed by the subsequent launch of the First Crusade, gave the campaign new impetus. Though the Second Crusade of 1147 accomplished little in the Holy Land proper, an offshoot of these armies joined with King Alfonso I of Portugal to successfully evict the Muslims from Lisbon. This was followed by the liberation of the Spanish city of Tortosa the following year. The full *Reconquista* of the peninsula

Early Romanesque Art

1150–1250

A Romanesque reliquary from 1200 is inset with precious gems.

This ciborium, used for holding hosts, belonged to the Knights of Malta.

"The Conversion of St. Paul" was produced in England around 1180.

1065
The Benedictine basilica of Cluny is completed

1066
Norman forces led by William the Conqueror defeat the Saxon rulers at the Battle of Hastings

1072
Turkish Seljuqs led by Malik Shah oust the Fatimid Dynasty

1079
Construction begins on Winchester Cathedral

would not be completed, however, until much later, during the reign of King Ferdinand and Queen Isabella of Aragon, when the last Emir of Granada was ousted in 1492. Many of the local Muslims, who considered themselves as Spanish as their Christian counterparts, decided to convert to Christianity, but these Moriscos would later suffer persecution during the heyday of the Spanish Inquisition. By 1610, all remaining Moriscos had been expelled from Castile and Aragon.

Another consequence of the Crusades was that western Europe was gripped by a wave of righteous passion, as well as a hatred of anything non-Christian, including Judaism. Thus, under the cry *"Deus vult"* ("God wills it"), countless Jewish communities were sacked and destroyed along the routes leading from northern Europe to embarkation points on the Mediterranean Sea. The Jewish population of the Rhineland, particularly in Speyer, Worms, and Mainz, was nearly wiped out by Crusader knights. Some of these massacres were motivated by animosity against the "murderers of Christ," while others were simply motivated by the desire to rob the wealth of these Jewish families.

The aversion to any beliefs that did not conform to Latin Christianity also befell members of Orthodox churches in the East. Some authors have cited the decision of Byzantine emperors to seek an alliance with Saladin as a motive for the growing European animus against Byzantium, though envy of Constantinople's famed culture and a desire for loot were key factors as well. Thus, when

"The Entrance of Pope Alexander III and Emperor Frederick I in Rome" is the subject of this 1407 fresco by Italian artist Spinello Aretino (ca 1350–1410).

1083
Construction begins on Ely Cathedral

1084
Bruno of Cologne founds the Carthusian order

1088
The University of Bologna is founded, one of the first academic institutions in Europe

1093
Construction begins on Durham Cathedral

Pope Innocent III called for a Fourth Crusade in 1198, the Crusader army instead diverted to Constantinople, where in 1204 they helped return a toppled Byzantine emperor, Alexius IV, to the throne. Unfortunately, Alexius found himself unable to pay the mercenaries for their services. The militias then went on a rampage, sacking the great Eastern Orthodox capital. Already weakened by Muslim conquest of its territory in Asia Minor, Constantinople never recovered from this calamity. Many in Europe, including the pope and Bernard of Clairvaux, strongly denounced the sack, which would poison relations between East and West for centuries to come. Some modern critics believe it still colors the relationship between Istanbul and the European Union to this day.

When I saw my standard upon the tower I dismounted, and kissing the ground, wept for the great mercy done to me.

JAMES I OF ARAGON, CONQUEROR OF VALENCIA, 1238

The excesses of the Fourth Crusade led to a call for a new campaign: a pure and spontaneous *levée* that was to be entirely devoid of greed and wanton slaughter. A Crusade led by children, in other words, whose hearts were pure, untouched by the evils of the world, and whose innocence would assuredly invite the blessing of God. Though opposed by most bishops and the pope, the call spread quickly and eventually rallied many thousands of eager adolescents, mostly between 16 and 21 years old. One group of youths traveled across the Alps to the port of Genoa, and another moved across France to Marseille.

What happened next is shrouded in the mists of time, but what is clear is that most of these young warriors were peasants with little understanding of military strategy or the use of arms. According to some sources, scores of them were sold as slaves in Marseille, while others claim that the teenage soldiers were robbed of their funds and scattered across Europe. Only a third of the 20,000-odd youths eventually made their way back home, though modern researchers have questioned this estimate. Several more Crusades would be launched in the centuries to come, but all failed to have any significant impact on Muslim control of the Middle East.

The Knightly Orders

Another by-product of the Crusader era was the creation of several military religious orders, some of which continue to this day. The most famous of these orders, the Knights Templar, was formed in 1119 when Baldwin II, King of Jerusalem (r. 1118–1131), charged a group of knights to protect Christian pilgrims to the Holy Land. Known for their white robes marked with a red cross, the Templars developed a particular expertise in finance and soon became one of the most powerful knightly organizations, with separate wings devoted to the military, finance, and charity. The loss of the Holy Land, however, left the order in search of a new mission. King Philip IV of France, who was deeply in debt to the order, exploited its disarray by arresting most of the Templar leadership in France. Several Knights Templar were burned at the stake

SAINTS AND CLERICS

Bernard of Clairvaux

Bernard of Clairvaux is shown in this anonymous missal from 1460.

Young Bernard joined the Cistercian order, and at age 25 he founded a new Cistercian abbey in a valley known as Val d'Absinthe, which he called *la claire vallée* ("the clear valley"). Later, the name became Clairvaux. Though a humble abbot, Bernard was soon the most respected moral voice of Christendom, never hesitating to criticize either bishops or kings for their failings. In 1130, during the Council of Étampes, he was called upon to choose between two rivals for the papacy, Anacletus II and Innocent II. He supported the latter. After the loss of the Crusader state of Edessa to Muslim armies, Bernard joined Pope Innocent in calling for a Second Crusade, but was deeply disappointed when the expedition failed to achieve its objectives. So persuasive were his manner and speech that mothers were said to hide their sons whenever Bernard came to town, for fear that they would want to become Cistercian monks.

1095 During the Council of Clermont, Pope Urban II formally calls for a Crusade

1096 First Crusade to liberate the Holy Land from Muslim rule begins

1096 The University of Oxford is founded

1098 The Cistercian order is established

ATLANTIC OCEAN
NORTH SEA
SCOTLAND
NORWAY
SWEDEN
DENMARK
JUTLAND
BRITISH ISLES
Irish
Ireland
Great Britain
ENGLAND
CELTIC SEA
Edinburgh
Newcastle
Dublin (England)
Waterford
York
Chester
Welsh
London
Dartmouth
Land's End
Oslo
Drammen
Uppsala
Lindesnes
Skagerrak
Kattegat
Vänern
Vättern
Gotland
Öland
Roskilde
Lund
Bornholm
BALTIC
Rügen
Danzig (Gdańsk)
Frisian Islands
Hamburg
Lübeck
WENDS
POMERANIA
Bremen
In 1147, Pope Eugene III encouraged a Crusade against the pagan Wendish slavs.
Brunswick (Braunschweig)
Magdeburg
BRANDENBURG
Posen (Poznań)
POL
Moray Firth
Firth of Forth
The Wash
St. Georges Channel
Bristol Channel
Strait of Dover
English Channel
Channel Islands
Point St.-Mathieu
Bruges (Brugge)
HOLLAND
Ghent (Gent)
Boulogne
Lille
Cambrai
Liège
Cologne (Köln)
HOLY ROMAN EMPIRE
SAXONY
Oder
SILESIA
Bayeux
Rouen
NORMANDY (England)
MAINE
Rennes
Paris
Reims
Verdun
Metz
Trier
Mainz
Nuremburg (Nürnberg)
Prague
MORAVIA
Orléans
Tours
Loire
Strasbourg
Ratisbon (Regensburg)
Danube
Pressburg (Bratislava)
Vienna
Vézelay
Basel
Council of Clermont
Answering a request from Byzantine Emperor Alexius Comnenus for aid to reclaim lands lost and in response to abuse of pilgrims to the Holy Land, Pope Urban II urged Christian rulers in 1095 to take up an armed pilgrimage aimed at taking Jerusalem back from Muslim forces.
First to answer the popular call in 1096, some 20,000 peasants and lesser nobility marched for the Holy Land. This "People's Crusade" fared poorly, and only 3,000 remained to join the bulk of the forces fighting to take Jerusalem.
FRANCE
ALPS
Bay of Biscay
Clermont
Lyon
Bordeaux
Cape Finisterre
Milan
Drava
Venice
Turin
Venetians
CROATIA
Sava
LEON AND CASTILLE
León
Oporto (Porto)
Sheltering from storms, a fleet carrying British forces bound for the Second Crusade stopped in Portugal. While in port the force aided King Alfonso in taking Lisbon in 1147 from Moorish forces.
NAVARRE
Pamplona
Toulouse
Albi
LANGUEDOC
Nîmes
Genoa
Ravenna
Zara (Zadar)
BOSNIA
Valladolid
PORTUGAL
Douro
Pyrenees
Narbonne
Marseille
Pisa
Florence
Lands of the Church
Spalato (Split)
Salamanca
Ligurian Sea
Livorno
Adriatic Sea
Saragossa (Zaragoza)
ARAGON
Venetians
Lisbon
Tagus
Barcelona
Corsica
Ragusa (Dubrovnik)
Toledo
Guadiana
Rome
SICILY
Balearic Sea
Bari
Cape St. Vincent
Cordova (Córdoba)
Valencia
Balearic Is.
Naples
Brindisi
Seville
Sardinia
DOMINION OF THE ALMORAVIDS
From 1209–1229 a Crusade was waged to root out the Cathar (Albigensian) heretical sect. They had revived the old dualist Gnostic ideas answered centuries before.
Pope Innocent III called for a Crusade in 1199 against nobility in Italy who posed a threat to the Papal States and disobeyed Church authority.
Cadiz
Granada
Cartagena
Cagliari
Strait of Gibraltar
Tangier
Alboran Sea
Tyrrhenian Sea
Palermo
Messina
Sicily
DOMINION OF THE HAMMADITES
Tunis
Syracuse (Siracusa)
King Louis IX of France died in 1270 of dysentery outside Tunis, causing his second Crusade to falter.
Gulf of Hammamet
ATLAS MOUNTAINS
MEDIT
Gulf of Gabes
0 200 400 kilometers
0 200 400 miles
Boundaries circa 1139 are represented. Modern names appear in parentheses.
AFRI
DOMINION OF THE ALMOHADS
Gulf of S

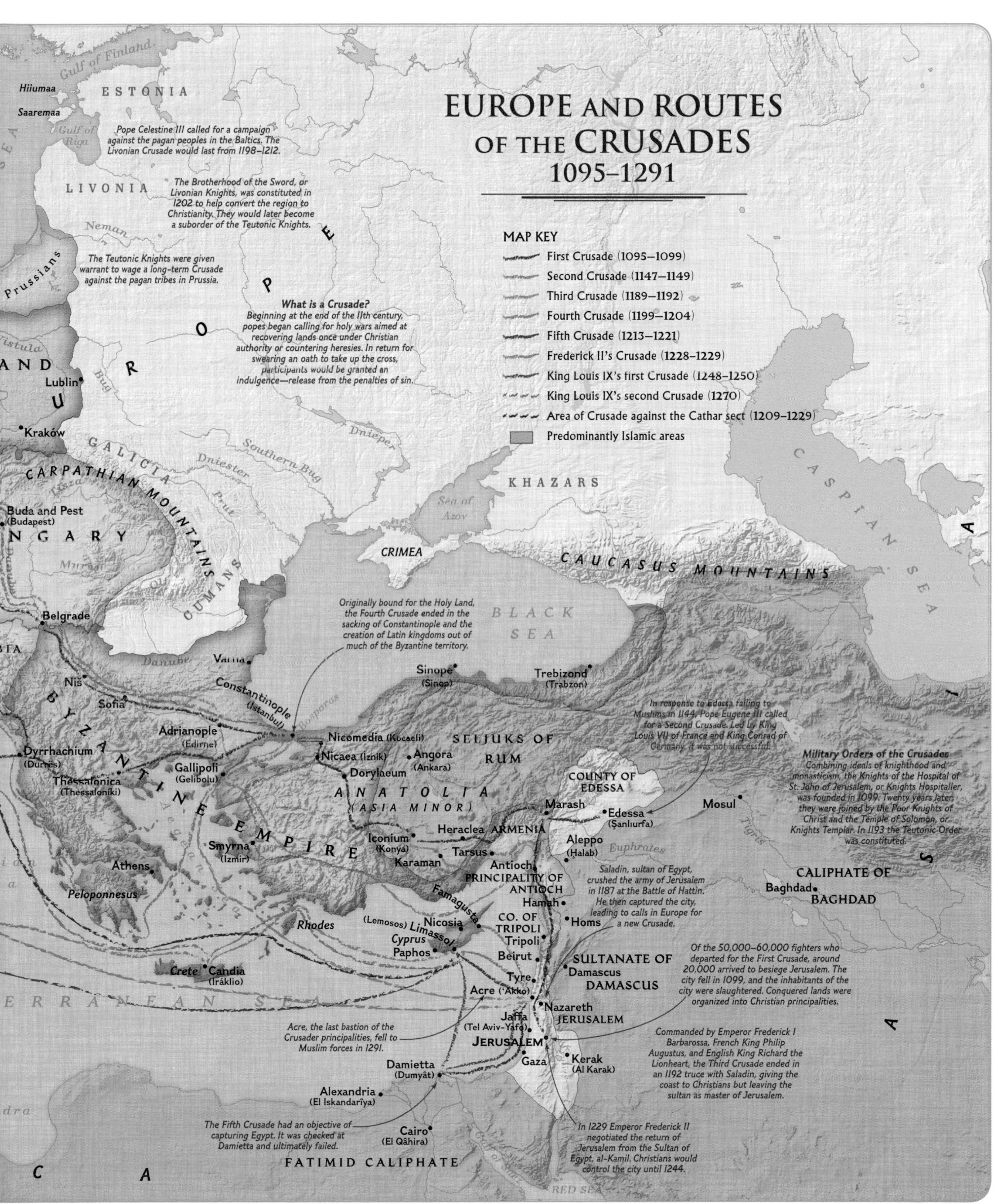

EUROPE AND ROUTES OF THE CRUSADES
1095–1291
MAP KEY
First Crusade (1095–1099)
Second Crusade (1147–1149)
Third Crusade (1189–1192)
Fourth Crusade (1199–1204)
Fifth Crusade (1213–1221)
Frederick II's Crusade (1228–1229)
King Louis IX's first Crusade (1248–1250)
King Louis IX's second Crusade (1270)
Area of Crusade against the Cathar sect (1209–1229)
Predominantly Islamic areas
Pope Celestine III called for a campaign against the pagan peoples in the Baltics. The Livonian Crusade would last from 1198–1212.
The Brotherhood of the Sword, or Livonian Knights, was constituted in 1202 to help convert the region to Christianity. They would later become a suborder of the Teutonic Knights.
The Teutonic Knights were given warrant to wage a long-term Crusade against the pagan tribes in Prussia.
What is a Crusade?
Beginning at the end of the 11th century, popes began calling for holy wars aimed at recovering lands once under Christian authority or countering heresies. In return for swearing an oath to take up the cross, participants would be granted an indulgence—release from the penalties of sin.
Originally bound for the Holy Land, the Fourth Crusade ended in the sacking of Constantinople and the creation of Latin kingdoms out of much of the Byzantine territory.
In response to Edessa falling to Muslims in 1144, Pope Eugene III called for a Second Crusade. Led by King Louis VII of France and King Conrad of Germany, it was not successful.
Military Orders of the Crusades
Combining ideals of knighthood and monasticism, the Knights of the Hospital of St. John of Jerusalem, or Knights Hospitaller, was founded in 1099. Twenty years later, they were joined by the Poor Knights of Christ and the Temple of Solomon, or Knights Templar. In 1193 the Teutonic Order was constituted.
Saladin, sultan of Egypt, crushed the army of Jerusalem in 1187 at the Battle of Hattin. He then captured the city, leading to calls in Europe for a new Crusade.
Of the 50,000–60,000 fighters who departed for the First Crusade, around 20,000 arrived to besiege Jerusalem. The city fell in 1099, and the inhabitants of the city were slaughtered. Conquered lands were organized into Christian principalities.
Commanded by Emperor Frederick I Barbarossa, French King Philip Augustus, and English King Richard the Lionheart, the Third Crusade ended in an 1192 truce with Saladin, giving the coast to Christians but leaving the sultan as master of Jerusalem.
Acre, the last bastion of the Crusader principalities, fell to Muslim forces in 1291.
The Fifth Crusade had an objective of capturing Egypt. It was checked at Damietta and ultimately failed.
In 1229 Emperor Frederick II negotiated the return of Jerusalem from the Sultan of Egypt, al-Kamil. Christians would control the city until 1244.
Hiiumaa
Saaremaa
ESTONIA
Gulf of Finland
Gulf of Riga
LIVONIA
Neman
Prussians
Vistula
Lublin
Kraków
Bug
E U R O P E
GALICIA
CARPATHIAN MOUNTAINS
Dniester
Southern Bug
Dnieper
Prut
Buda and Pest
(Budapest)
CUMANS
Belgrade
Danube
Varna
Niš
Sofia
Constantinople
(Istanbul)
Bosporus
Adrianople
(Edirne)
Dyrrhachium
(Durrës)
Thessalonica
(Thessaloníki)
Gallipoli
(Gelibolu)
BYZANTINE EMPIRE
Athens
Peloponnesus
Smyrna
(Izmir)
Rhodes
Crete
Candia
(Iráklio)
CRIMEA
Sea of Azov
KHAZARS
CAUCASUS MOUNTAINS
CASPIAN SEA
BLACK SEA
Sinope
(Sinop)
Trebizond
(Trabzon)
Nicomedia (Kocaeli)
Nicaea (Iznik)
Angora
(Ankara)
Dorylaeum
SELJUKS OF RUM
ANATOLIA
(ASIA MINOR)
COUNTY OF EDESSA
Marash
Edessa
(Şanlıurfa)
Mosul
Tigris
Euphrates
Heraclea
ARMENIA
Iconium
(Konya)
Karaman
Tarsus
Aleppo
(Halab)
Antioch
PRINCIPALITY OF ANTIOCH
Famagusta
Hamah
Homs
Nicosia
(Lemosos) Limassol
Cyprus
Paphos
CO. OF TRIPOLI
Tripoli
Beirut
SULTANATE OF DAMASCUS
Damascus
Tyre
Acre ('Akko)
Nazareth
JERUSALEM
Jaffa
(Tel Aviv-Yafo)
JERUSALEM
Gaza
Kerak
(Al Karak)
CALIPHATE OF BAGHDAD
Baghdad
Damietta
(Dumyât)
Alexandria
(El Iskandarîya)
Cairo
(El Qâhira)
FATIMID CALIPHATE
RED SEA

on trumped-up charges. This only served to increase the order's mystique, and though it was officially disbanded in 1307, the legend of the Templars still lives on—at least in the imagination of modern writers of fiction.

A second order, the Knights Hospitaller (or Order of St. John) was formed in 1023 and focused on the care of the poor and sick by building pilgrim hospitals throughout the Holy Land. The organization then became militarized as the threat of Muslim counterattacks grew. After the ouster of Crusader forces from Palestine, the Hospitallers retreated to Rhodes, where they built a large stronghold, and to Halicarnassus (now Bodrum), where they used the remains of the Mausoleum to erect an even more formidable fortress. After a massive naval attack by Suleiman the Magnificent in 1522, the knights withdrew to Malta, which they continued to govern until the Napoleonic conquest of 1798. The order still endures in various humanitarian organizations, including the Sovereign Military Order of Malta in Rome, which today has around 13,500 members.

A Templar Knight is truly a fearless knight, and secure on every side, for his soul is protected by the armor of faith.

BERNARD OF CLAIRVAUX, *IN PRAISE OF THE NEW KNIGHTHOOD*

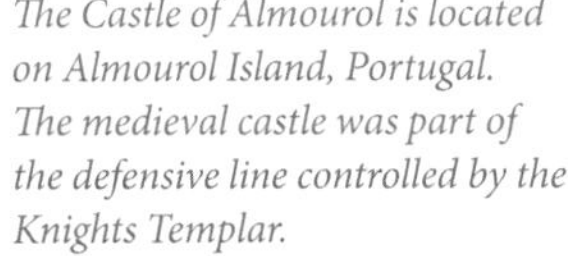

The Castle of Almourol is located on Almourol Island, Portugal. The medieval castle was part of the defensive line controlled by the Knights Templar.

1099
Frankish Crusaders capture Jerusalem

1099
Beginning of the 88-year Crusader rule of the Holy Land

1099
The Church of the Holy Sepulcher is rebuilt from the ground up

1100
Turkish Seljuqs battle Crusaders for control of the Holy Land

Another group, the Knights of the Teutonic Order, was formed in the dying days of Crusader-held Acre during the Third Crusade. Distinguished by their white mantles and black cross (which eventually became the symbol of the German armed forces), the knights withdrew to Hungary and launched a series of invasions of Latvia, Estonia, and Belarus in a campaign known as the Livonian Crusade. In time, they established control over much of the Baltic coast, forcefully converting rural communities—many of which still clung to their ancient ways—to Latin Christianity. In 1410 came a turning point, when the Teutonic army was defeated by Polish and Lithuanian forces at the Battle of Tannenberg, but their influence remained and would lay the seeds for Prussian militarism in centuries to come.

The most important result of the Crusader era, however, is that it reshaped both the culture and the political structure of western Europe. The marshaling of large-scale armies would produce the first emergence of national identities imbued with a sense of destiny, such as in France, England, Spain, and Portugal. The need for large-scale armament and increased firepower also prompted a small revolution in military technology, including the creation of the fortified castle, the improved crossbow, and eventually the handborne musket.

Finally, the wholesale departure of menfolk across all social classes encouraged a growing role for women—from Eleanor of Aquitaine, the Queen of France who proudly rode with her husband at the head of his army, to scores of peasant women who now assumed responsibility for work on their farms. Many educated women began corresponding with their husbands serving abroad, which would lay the foundation for the prominent role of women in poetry and letters in the centuries to come. There are even reports (mostly from Muslim sources) of women participating in combat against Islamic forces, but modern historians are inclined to question these accounts.

The Birth of the Romanesque Style

Perhaps the most profound and lasting legacy of the Crusades was a renewed desire to exalt the glory of Christianity itself, not

SCRIPTURE AND FAITH

The Veneration of Relics

Given that Christ, the Virgin Mary, and the saints of Christianity had lived in a distant time (Antiquity) and in a very different culture (that of the Middle East), a desire arose to "Europeanize" the faith and make its figures more tangible to the illiterate masses of the Continent. One way to accomplish this was by the veneration of their mortal remains. From the ninth century onward, this led to great rivalry among European cities in the procurement of relics, whose presence was guaranteed to attract thousands of pilgrims, thus boosting a city's prestige and prosperity. In 828, for example, Venetian raiders stole the reputed remains of Mark the Evangelist in Alexandria, which prompted the Venetian doge to commission the large Basilica of San Marco to house the saint's sarcophagus.

Similarly, the construction of the cathedral of Cologne was motivated by the arrival of the reputed relics of the Three Kings who had visited Jesus in the stable in Bethlehem, following their capture by Emperor Frederick Barbarossa during his invasion in Italy in 1154. The Romanesque church of Sainte-Marie-Madeleine in Vézelay, moreover, was begun in order to house the relics of Mary Magdalene, whose remains, according to a local legend, had been transferred to France in the ninth century.

By the 11th century, the competition became so fierce that a wide variety of relics were in circulation. To emphasize their rare and sacred nature, relics were usually placed in containers, or reliquaries, made of precious metals such as gold or silver and adorned with precious stones.

This Romanesque reliquary with angels is typical of Limoges art of the early 13th century.

1104
The abbey church of Vézelay is built

1115
Florence becomes a free republic

1119
Baldwin II, King of Jerusalem, creates the Knights Templar order

1122
The Concordat of Worms is held

O God, grant that we may be aflame with the spirit of love and discipline, and may ever walk before thee as children of light.

THE CLUNIAC PRAYER

only in painting and sculpture but also in a new form of church architecture. As we saw, throughout Europe's long period of recovery after the fall of the Western Roman Empire, attempts had been made to revive the great achievements of Late Antiquity. The Carolingian Palatine Chapel in Aachen, for example, was a conscious attempt to transfer the ephemeral beauty of the Basilica of San Vitale to German soil. But the upsurge of Christian piety in the wake of the Crusades spread the desire for larger, more monumental churches throughout Europe, far beyond the orbit of intellectual court circles in Aachen and Paris. The result was a movement that historians refer to as Romanesque, which was far less homogenous than we might assume. Rising standards of living and the growth of urban centers at the nexus of European trade produced a demand for church buildings that would express both Europeans' civic pride and their deep-felt Christian piety. Europe, in the words of an 11th-century monk named Raoul Glaber, wished to cover itself with "a white mantle of churches."

OPPOSITE: *The Basilica of Paray-le-Monial, in Burgundy, France, is a small-scale version of the famous abbey of Cluny, now largely destroyed.*

Inevitably, the designers of these churches sought to imitate the principal features of the only monumental architecture still extant: the remains of Roman temples, city gates, aqueducts, and baths that still dotted the European landscape. Unfortunately, the delicate system of mathematical proportions that sustained these Roman structures was long lost. Therefore, the medieval architects proceeded on the basis of empirical observation and trial and error, rather than on any scientific basis. The Roman arch was readily imitated, both in windows and in barrel vaults, but the engineering system behind it was not. A number of these churches, built in the "Roman-like" *(Roman-esque)* style, collapsed before they were even finished. The medieval architect learned from these mistakes by building more conservatively. Walls were thickened, window space was reduced, and barrel vaults were provided with supporting arches, in turn buttressed by heavy piers.

The successful ones—notably the massive Benedictine Basilica of Cluny, completed in 1065, and the beautiful abbey church of Vézelay of 1104, both in Burgundy—were studied and adapted to local building traditions and materials throughout Europe, particularly along the pilgrimage route to Santiago de Compostela in northern Spain. The most striking features of these early Romanesque churches were a fortresslike portico complex, usually flanked by two bell towers, followed by a long three-aisled nave and culminating in an elaborate architectural apex at the crossing point between nave and transept, surmounted by a tower. This Latin-cross configuration ended in a semicircular apse, surrounded by a string of radiating side chapels.

HISTORY AND POLITICS

Guelphs and Ghibellines

The conflict between the Holy Roman Emperor and the pope is reflected in the rivalry between the Ghibellines and the Guelphs in Italy. Frederick Barbarossa, Holy Roman Emperor between 1155 and 1190, wanted to extend his German realm into Italy. In 1154, his armies invaded Milan and Pavia, then forced their way through Tuscany to Rome, where the British-born Pope Adrian IV (r. 1154–1159) was struggling to stem a republican challenge to his rule. Frederick suppressed the republicans, whereupon Adrian crowned him Holy Roman Emperor. In later years, as relations between Frederick and Adrian's successors soured, many Italian city-states declared themselves as either supporting the pope (Guelph) or the emperor (Ghibelline). The latter reflected the interests of wealthy traders, whereas agricultural communities were traditionally on the side of the pope. Some authors believe that this rivalry is the background for the story of Romeo and Juliet.

A gold coin from Genoa depicts the emblem of the Ghibelline party.

1125
Troubadour music and culture emerge at Europe's courts

1130
Bernard of Clairvaux selects Pope Innocent II at the Council of Étampes

1137
The Cathedral of Mainz, Germany, is completed

1142
Imad ad-Din Zengi invades Crusader-held Syria

By the time it was finished, Cluny was the largest building complex of Europe until the construction of St. Peter's in Rome in the 16th century. Sadly, this grandest of all French Romanesque churches was destroyed after the French Revolution of 1789, although its main features can still be admired in a smaller-scale sister church, located in nearby Paray-le-Monial. In time, as security in Europe improved and the threat of Muslim invasions diminished, these Romanesque churches lost their fortresslike character. Elaborate reliefs and sculpture groups, designed to educate the Christian masses, were added to exterior facades. As the confidence of these builders grew, so too did the size of the windows. Whereas early Romanesque churches are notable for their dark interiors, a century later basilicas would enjoy additional shafts of sunlight through clerestory windows in the upper nave, as well as rose windows in the facade or large bays around the apse.

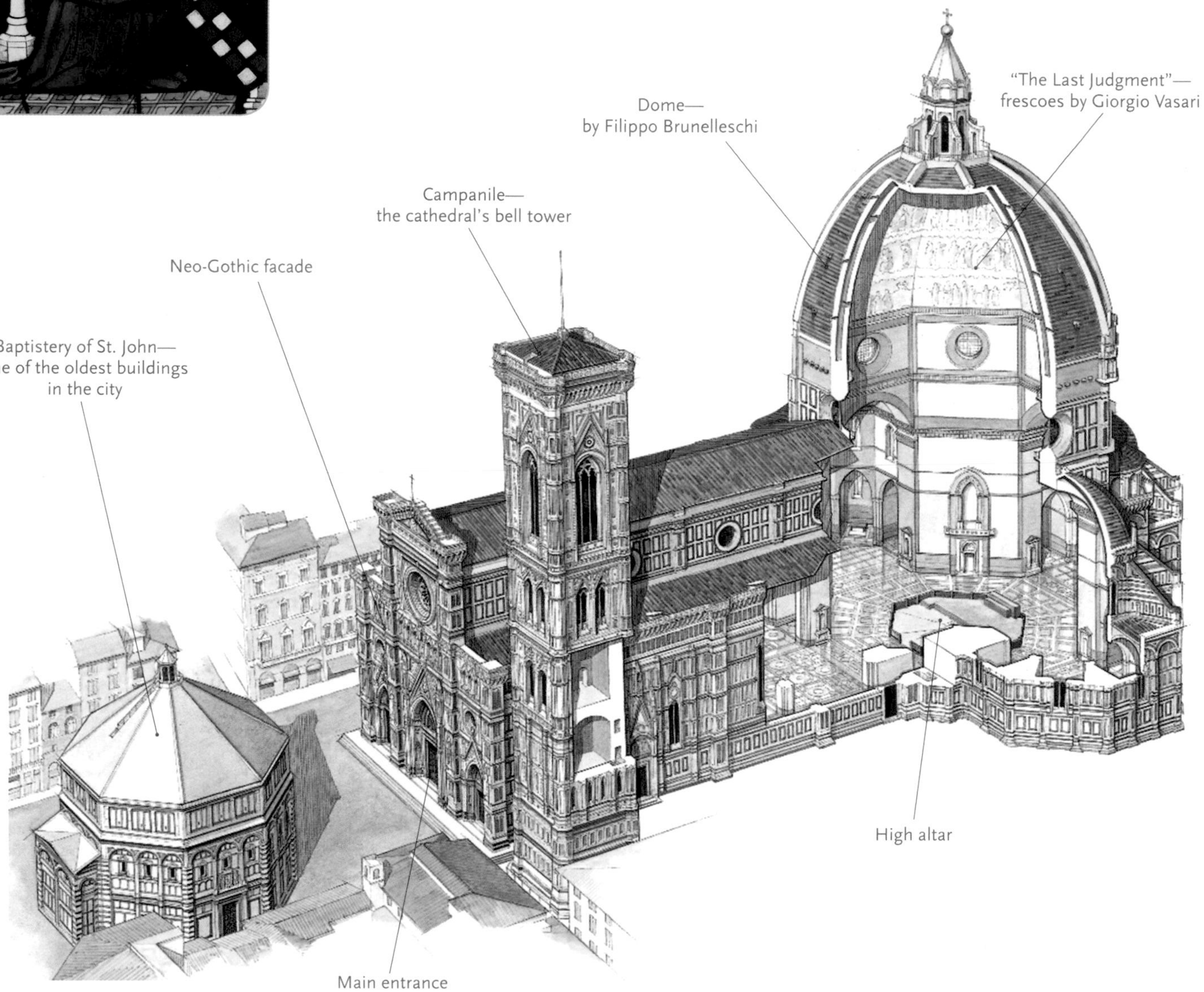

"The Last Judgment"—
frescoes by Giorgio Vasari

Dome—
by Filippo Brunelleschi

Campanile—
the cathedral's bell tower

Neo-Gothic facade

Baptistery of St. John—
one of the oldest buildings
in the city

High altar

Main entrance

1144
Imad ad-Din Zengi invades Edessa, ending the first Crusader state

1144
Pope Eugene III and Bernard of Clairvaux call for a Second Crusade

1146
Imad ad-Din Zengi is assassinated. Command of his armies passes to Salah-ad-Din

1147
Second Crusade is launched

Romanesque in Italy

From France, the new style spread to Britain, the Germanic lands, and the Italian states beyond the Alps. In Italy, and particularly in Tuscany, there were still many Roman ruins in existence. In 11th-century Florence, for example, an unknown architect built a Romanesque exterior for the city's octagonal baptistery, which exuded such a refined elegance that later generations, particularly during the Renaissance, were convinced it was built by Romans as a temple of Mars. The baptistery's use of alternating geometrical panels of white and green marble would become a leitmotif for Romanesque architecture throughout Tuscany, facilitated by the presence of several marble quarries in the region.

Roman precedent also exerted a strong influence on the builders of Florence's principal rival, the city of Pisa. Unlike in other cities, however, the Pisan architects chose to build their church not in the heart of the city but on a separate campus, complete with a basilica, a bell tower, a baptistery, and a *camposanto,* or cemetery. This cathedral was begun around 1063 and would become the most famous Romanesque church in Italy. Although its exterior is articulated with the same design of alternating marble panels pioneered in Florence, its main facade is made up of no fewer than four tiers of delicate columns placed over a row of seven pilaster-borne arches. Such a sumptuous arrangement was meant to advertise not only Pisa's growing prosperity, given its location at the mouth of the Arno River, but also its command of Roman architectural vernacular—to the extent that such was understood in the 11th century.

The nearby baptistery, begun in 1152, is a work of such exquisite proportions that to this day local guides are often prompted to sing a sequence of four separate notes. The sound resonates as it travels upward to form, near the domed summit, a perfect chord. Here, too, is a famous pulpit by Nicola Pisano (1220–1284), who in the 13th century would spearhead the so-called proto-Renaissance in Italian sculpture.

But the most celebrated feature of the Pisa sanctuary is undoubtedly its campanile, universally known as the Leaning Tower,

OPPOSITE ABOVE: *French abbot Bernard of Clairvaux is depicted in this stained-glass window from the Upper Rhine region, ca 1450. Bernard was the primary founder of the Cistercian order.*

OPPOSITE BELOW: *Known as the* **DUOMO**, *the basilica in Florence was begun in the 13th century, designed in the Gothic style by architect Arnolfo di Cambio. Europe's fourth largest cathedral, it was consecrated in 1436.*

HISTORY AND POLITICS

The Investiture Conflict

The emerging nation-states of Europe posed an obvious challenge to the traditional authority of the papacy in Rome. After Otto the Great (r. 936–973) unified the German feudal states into a kingdom, he claimed the title of Holy Roman Emperor previously bestowed upon the Frankish King Charlemagne in 800. The title would henceforth pass to various European rulers until the Napoleonic Wars of the early 19th century. But this raised a question: Who was the ultimate authority of Latin Christianity, the pope or the emperor? In the Byzantine Empire, it was the emperor who had appointed patriarchs. Therefore, Otto said, the Holy Roman Emperor should also stand above the Roman pontiff. Many Christians were sympathetic to that view, certainly given the string of corrupt popes who occupied the Holy See in the first part of the 11th century, when church appointments (or "investitures") were often sold to the highest bidder. At one point, in 1046, there were three popes competing for the throne. Only with Pope Leo IX (r. 1049–1054) did Rome initiate a genuine program of reform, which culminated in the papacy of Gregory VII (r. 1073–1085). To avoid any conflict, Gregory created the College of Cardinals as the body responsible for electing the pope, and firmly established the supremacy of the papacy over all of Europe's temporal rulers. When Holy Roman Emperor Henry IV refused to accept the pope's primacy, Gregory excommunicated him. The papal authority was accepted by all parties during the Concordat of Worms in 1122.

The reconciliation between Pope Alexander III and Emperor Frederick I is the subject of this fresco by Italian artist Spinello Aretino (ca 1350–1410).

1149 — **The new Church of the Holy Sepulcher is inaugurated**

1152 — **The baptistery of Pisa is built**

1154 — **Emperor Frederick Barbarossa invades Italy**

1160 — **The University of Paris is founded**

LIFE AND TIMES

Women Pilgrims to the Holy Land

Francisco de Zurbarán (1598–1664) painted this canvas of St. Jerome.

Unlike in ancient Judaism or Islam, pilgrimage had never been required of the Christian faithful, but that did not stop scores of European believers from undertaking the dangerous voyage to the Middle East. Many of these intrepid travelers were women. Among the first was a wealthy fourth-century noblewoman from France by the name of Aetheria or Egeria. Traveling from Egypt in the south to Edessa in the north, she recorded her impressions in a long letter called *Itinerarium Egeriae (The Travels of Egeria)*. She was soon followed by another noblewoman, a Roman lady named Paula, who sailed to Palestine in 382. Having settled in Bethlehem, she used her wealth to support Jerome's translation of the Bible from Greek into Latin. Many other pilgrims would follow, including the anonymous author of a travel guide to the Holy Land known as *The Breviary* of 530, until conditions of Christians in the Holy Land worsened.

designed as a series of superimposed marble colonnades of such delicacy that, when seen from a distance, the tower looks like it is carved from ivory. The Pisa sanctuary would influence the construction of many Romanesque churches throughout northern Italy, including the basilica of nearby Lucca.

Romanesque in Other Countries

Just before the advent of the Romanesque style, the builders in Hildesheim, in Germany, had reached back to the tradition of early Christian architecture to produce the great church of St. Michael, commissioned by Bishop Bernward in 1010. Often called a pre-Romanesque design, the church still retains the double transepts and multiple towers of earlier Carolingian and Ottonian styles. But it was the city of Cologne on the Rhine River that would truly become the great center of German Romanesque. Between the 11th and 13th centuries, no fewer than 12 churches would be built in the so-called Rhenish Romanesque style, including the Dominican Sankt Andreaskirche (St. Andrew's) begun in the early 12th century on the remains of an older Ottonian church dedicated to St. Matthew. Other major examples of monumental Romanesque are the cathedrals of Speyer, Worms, and Mainz.

In England, the Romanesque style was introduced by the Normans, which is why it is often referred to as "Norman architecture" in British literature. Its main features of small twin windows, round arches, and sturdy piers are virtually indistinguishable from contemporary buildings on the Continent. Key examples include Winchester Cathedral, begun in 1079, and the cathedrals of Ely (1083) and Durham (1093). In the heart

The Romanesque Baptistery of St. John in Florence, one of the oldest buildings in the city, probably dates from the 11th century. Its use of white and green marble would be imitated by Romanesque churches in Tuscany.

1170
Chrétien de Troyes writes the novella *Lancelot*

1170
Thomas Becket, Archbishop of Canterbury, is murdered on orders of King Henry II

1176
Salah-ad-Din reconquers Syria

1180
First appearance of glass windows in English homes

of London, a rare archetype of Romanesque architecture survives in the priory church of St. Bartholomew the Great, often overlooked by tourists. Founded in 1123 in Smithfield, it was meant to serve the needs of St. Bartholomew's Hospital nearby, the oldest still functioning hospital in Europe, built during the reign of Henry I (r. 1100–1135). Though originally conceived on a much larger scale, part of the church was demolished after the dissolution of the monasteries by Henry VIII in 1543, given its identity as an Augustinian priory. Its choir and transept crossing survived, however, and even escaped damage during World War II to become Britain's most pristine example of Romanesque architecture today. To raise funds for its upkeep, one of St. Bart's chapels was rented out in the 18th century to a printer, who around 1724 would employ a young American typesetter named Benjamin Franklin.

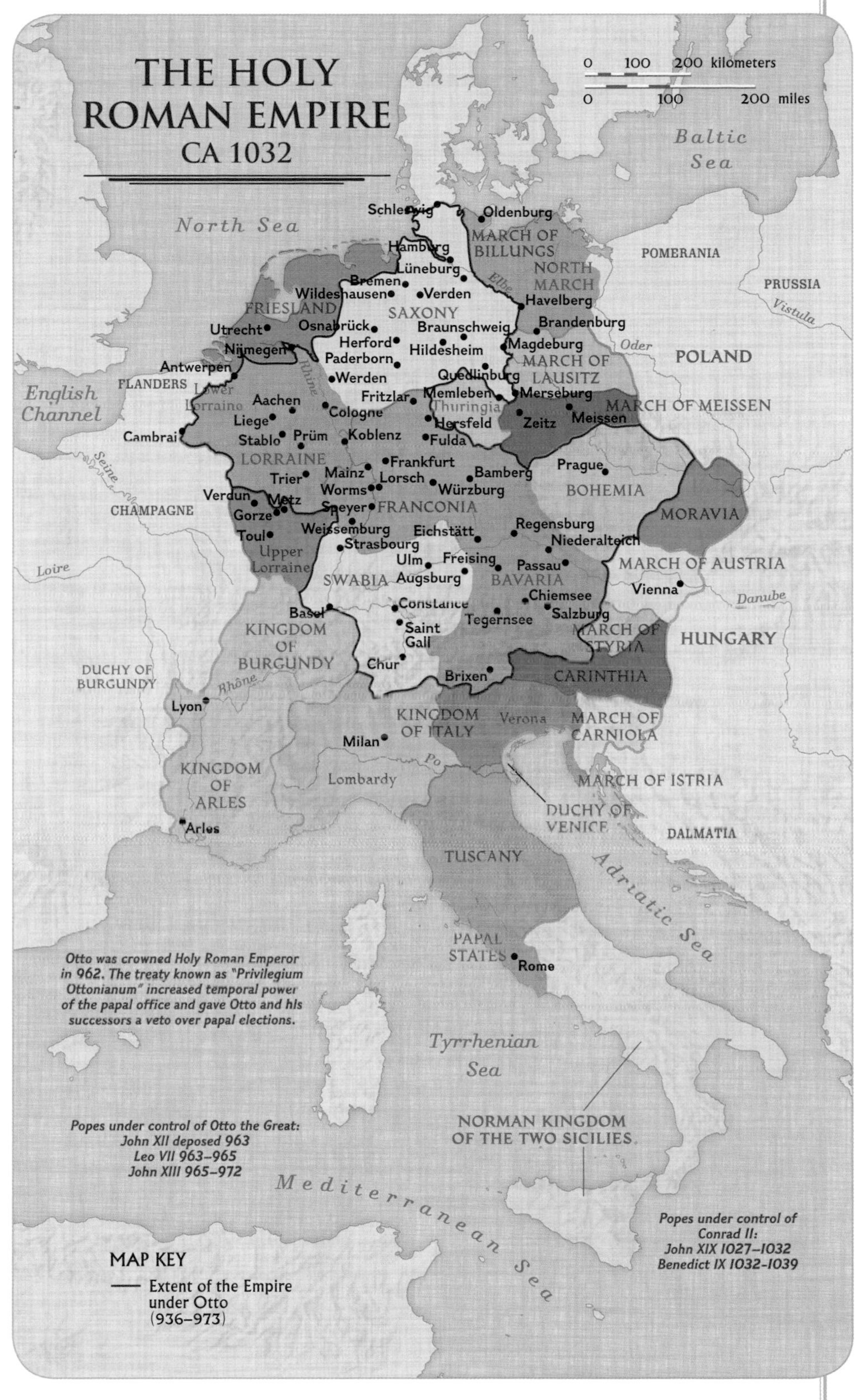

Romanesque Sculpture

After the disintegration of the Roman Empire, much of the Roman virtuosity in painting and sculpture disappeared, albeit with some exceptions. The art of the mosaic survived as the preferred decorative art in Byzantine churches, including those in Italy, like the Byzanto-Romanesque basilica of San Marco in Venice, which deliberately emulates Byzantine models. The mosaic cycle with scenes from the Old Testament in the narthex of San Marco is some of Italy's finest representative art from the Romanesque period.

After the suspension of the iconoclast laws of the eighth and ninth centuries, the art of painting was again revived in most Byzantine dominions, although its iconography was strictly confined to specific motifs and representational formulas, particularly

1185
First Carmelite monastery is built on Mount Carmel

1187
Salah-ad-Din defeats Crusader forces at the Battle of Hattin

1187
Salah-ad-Din besieges Jerusalem and captures the city

1189
King Henry II dies and is succeeded by Richard "The Lionheart"

A wide-angle view shows the central nave of Winchester Cathedral, which was begun in 1079. It is one of the largest cathedrals in England, with the longest nave and greatest overall length of any Romanesque church in Europe.

in the depiction of Christ, the Virgin Mary, and the saints. In the West, however, no such artistic tradition provided a link with the Roman past. The Carolingian and Ottonian revivals did provide an important creative stimulus, but much of this artistic endeavor was limited to the illumination of manuscripts and the applied arts, specifically the manufacturing of gold or silver reliquaries and liturgical implements. Little sculptural activity survived except for the production of crucifixes, usually in wood, or the creation of small miniatures in ivory. The art of carving in stone was all but forgotten.

All this changed almost overnight during the surge of Christian passion that swept Europe in the wake of the Crusades. The monumental churches that were now rising on the horizon of cities throughout Europe urgently needed sculptors. A popular subject was the Virgin Mary. In the Orthodox tradition, icons of Mary emphasized her role as the Theotokos, the God-bearer, a title established during the Council of Ephesus in 431. In the West,

1189
Third Crusade begins

1191
During the Third Crusade, Richard "The Lionheart" conquers Cyprus and Acre

1191
Second Era of the Maya civilization begins in Central America

1198
Pope Innocent III calls for a Fourth Crusade

however, her popularity was fueled by numerous apocryphal legends about her life and by the growing prominence of women in courtly circles. From the fourth century onward, the first churches were dedicated to the Virgin, including the Santa Maria Trastevere (340s) and the Santa Maria Maggiore (440).

Unbound by any concern for realism or classical ideals, the early sculptures of Mary and other saints have a naive and almost playful character. Their forms are shaped not so much by observation of the human body as by the demands of the architectural space they inhabit. That same dancelike, elastic fluidity is evident in the massive tympanum of Sainte-Marie-Madeleine in Vézelay. Its theme of the Mission of the Apostles, showing Christ in the center as he charges his disciples to bring the good news to the world, was bound to resonate in a time when many of France's able-bodied men were leaving on the long and perilous journey to free the Holy Land from Muslim rule. Each of the Apostles, clutching books of Scripture, freely gyrates around the figure of Christ as if they were figures on an illuminated page, rather than three-dimensional bodies obeying the laws of nature. Perhaps their energetic movements betray a nervous anxiety about their mission, for surrounding their tight semicircular space are lintels filled with devils and demons from an evil and pagan world, waiting to thwart their evangelizing efforts.

Anonymous artists created this mosaic of stories from the Book of Genesis in the narthex of the San Marco Basilica in Venice around 1200.

The New Monastic Orders

Art and architecture were not the only conduits by which the great spiritual revival of the early Middle Ages found expression. Whereas the Benedictines had largely dominated monastic life in Europe in the 11th century, a spate of new orders emerged in the 12th and 13th centuries—often as a reaction to the great wealth of Benedictine abbeys, such as Cluny. A more strict form of communal living was introduced by Bruno of Cologne in 1084 and named the Carthusian order, after the Chartreuse Mountains in the French Alps, where his first convent was located. Headed by a prior rather than an abbot, each Carthusian convent housed both monks and nuns in an atmosphere of great severity and abstention, allowing only one meal per day. Unlike the Benedictines, they devoted themselves to prayer, rather

> *God is not loved without a reward, although he should be loved without regard for one.*
>
> BERNARD OF CLAIRVAUX, *ON LOVING GOD*

PERIOD ARCHITECTURE

The Leaning Tower of Pisa

Begun in 1173, the bell tower of the Duomo of Pisa leans about 13 feet out of the perpendicular.

Begun in 1173, the Leaning Tower of Pisa is designed in the same style as the facade of the duomo, with a series of superimposed colonnades. Some 183 feet high, the tower actually began its tilt when it had only risen to about 30 feet and the underlying foundations gave way in the soft soil. Subsequent architects, including Giovanni di Simone, the designer of the *camposanto,* and the Gothic architect Tommaso da Pontedera, continued to build the tower in the hope that a stabilizing solution could be found, but the lean has continued. Despite modern attempts to correct it, today the 296-step tower, which weighs about 14,700 tons, leans about 13 feet out of the perpendicular. Recent efforts to drain the soft soil underneath have been successful in slowing the movement to about .040 inch a year.

1200
A collection of songs known as the *Carmina Burana* is composed

1203
Wolfram von Eschenbach composes the epic poem *Parsifal*

1204
Fourth Crusader army diverts to Constantinople and sacks the city

1204
Amsterdam is founded in the Low Countries

The Romanesque Period

1150–1250

A Romanesque plaque shows Christ, Mary, and John with angels.

A depiction of the crucified Christ from Limoges dates from ca 1220.

This reliquary plaque was made in Hildesheim around 1160.

than charitable works for the surrounding community. In the English-speaking world, such monasteries soon became known as "charterhouses"; the first one was built by King Henry II in Witham Friary, Somerset, as penance for the murder in 1170 of Thomas Becket, Archbishop of Canterbury.

Another contemplative order emerged at the beginning of the 13th century in the Holy Land. According to legend, its first convent was formed in 1185 by a French crusader named Berthold of Calabria on Mount Carmel, located near today's city of Haifa, as an act of penance for the violence perpetrated by Crusader knights. By 1214, the Carmelite order had been recognized by the patriarch of Jerusalem, with a mission to focus on acts of charity as well as individual and communal prayer, in imitation of the Virgin and the prophet Elijah. Thirty years later, the first Carmelite monasteries were founded in Kent, England, and in the south of France; by the end of the century, there were more than 150 Carmelite convents throughout Europe.

Perhaps the most influential new order from this era was the Cistercian order, first established in 1098 and also known as the Bernardine order, after its great protagonist, Bernard of Clairvaux. Named after the place of their founding, the French village of Cîteaux (named Cistercium in Latin), the order was established by a group of Benedictines in search of a cenobitic life that more faithfully followed the Rule of St. Benedict. The Cistercians soon distinguished themselves by their superior knowledge of agriculture, producing not only a great variety of crops but also excellent wines and ales. This is one reason why their settlements were avidly encouraged by local rulers and bishops throughout Europe. It has been estimated that by the second half of the 12th century, there were more than 330 Cistercian abbeys in Britain, France, Spain, Germany, Poland, Hungary, and Scandinavia, among others.

The intelligent creature
received the power of discernment
for this purpose,
that he might hate and shun evil,
and love and choose good,
and especially the greater good.

ANSELM OF CANTERBURY, *CUR DEUS HOMO*, CA 1095

The piety and social compassion shown by these new orders radiated into their surrounding regions, making the monasteries not only preeminent centers of Christian charity but also important sources of learning, medical care, social discourse, and scriptural research. This in turn fostered an educational revival. A new form of schooling known as "grammar schools" emerged, offering basic education in both reading and writing, as well as some rudimentary math. At the same time, a number of universities were established, beginning in Bologna, Italy (1088), and followed by Oxford (1096), Paris (1160), and Cambridge (1209), although such higher learning was still reserved for the children of urban elites. Nonetheless, these universities would lay the foundation for the great flowering of medieval scholarship in the century to follow. ■

OPPOSITE: *The great Romanesque monastery of Mont Saint-Michel on the northwestern coast of Normandy was begun in the 11th century. The abbey is protected as a French historic monument.*

1209 **The University of Cambridge is founded**

1212 **Children's Crusade begins**

1213 **Pope Innocent III calls for the Fifth Crusade, which begins later that year**

1217 **Henry III evicts French forces from England**

7
CHAPTER

THE MEDIEVAL CHURCH AT ITS ZENITH

1200-1400

Pope Innocent III ruled over the Church, one of abundant learning, renowned in discourse, and fervent in zeal.

THOMAS OF CELANO, 1228

As Europe entered the 13th century, the Catholic Church in the West reached its zenith. Never before had the Church held sway over almost every aspect of life, both sacred and secular, and it never would again. The power of Rome radiated from every monastery, church, and cathedral into medieval society, affecting every individual, from peasants to princes.

The High Middle Ages, the apogee of Catholic Christianity, also witnessed a decisive power shift from the Greek Church in the East to the Latin Church of the West. For the next five centuries, Europe would be decisive in the evolution of Christianity. Fittingly, the heyday of the Latin Church began with the Fourth Lateran Council of 1215, convoked by one of the greatest of medieval popes, Innocent III (r. 1198–1216). Innocent wanted to forge a Church in which the power of Latin Christianity radiated from every school, every monastery, and every church. He aimed to galvanize the clergy, who had in many places become lax and indolent. Innocent instigated a wholesale reform in the way clergy were educated, and in turn, were allowed to teach and preach to others. As a result, the role of the priests changed from being mere presiders over sacramental ceremony to pastors,

ABOVE: *A detail of a 13th-century Flemish tapestry shows a horse in a pleasure garden.*

OPPOSITE: *A view of the Umbrian town of Assisi, Italy—hometown of Francis, the founder of the Franciscan order.*

PRECEDING PAGES: *"St. Francis Receiving the Stigmata" was painted by Italian artist Niccolò Alunno (ca 1425–1502).*

actively serving the community of their parishes. Only the ablest teachers were to be appointed at cathedral schools, while bishops were held accountable for the inspirational quality of sermons preached in their dioceses. Abuses by the clergy, such as the exploitation of pilgrims attracted by saintly relics, or drunken or lewd behavior, were rigorously punished. Secular rulers did not escape the pope's zeal either; princes were urged to be vigilant for "blasphemies against Jesus Christ."

"The Taking of Constantinople" was painted by the Italian artist Palma Il Giovane (1548–1628).

OPPOSITE: *This view from the Gran Canal in Venice shows the Doge's Palace at right and the Campanile, or bell tower, at left.*

Such was Innocent's prestige that when the Lateran Council was announced, 71 patriarchs, more than 400 bishops, and more than 900 abbots agreed to attend, in addition to envoys from Holy Roman Emperor Frederick II, Byzantine Emperor Theodore I Laskaris, and the kings of France, England, Aragon, Hungary, Cyprus, and Jerusalem. Almost all of the pope's decrees were passed with little or no debate.

To further cement the growing power of the Holy See, Innocent sought to expand the Papal States, the realm governed by the pope as a secular ruler, beyond the original territory granted to the papacy in the eighth century. This included the Duchy of Rome (roughly analogous to today's province of Latium), as well as parts of Tuscany, Lombardy, and cities such as Ravenna. Innocent's aim was to increase the role of the papacy as a major political force on the Italian peninsula, which would have significant consequences during the Renaissance.

Fortunately, Innocent's grand design for revitalizing the Church coincided with a major economic revival throughout Europe, buoyed by expanding international commerce. As the new nation-states of France and Britain came into their own, the growing European stability encouraged trade contacts across the continent, from the Italian states in the south (particularly Florence and Pisa) to the cities of the Hanseatic League in the north, including Bremen, Hamburg, and Lübeck. At the same time, the decline of Constantinople in the wake of the city's sack in 1204 created a temporary vacuum in the trade with the Islamic Ottoman Empire, which the mercantile cities of Venice and Genoa rushed to fill. By the early 14th century, Venice had all but replaced the Byzantine rump state as the principal European conduit to trade with the Ottoman Empire. Vast wealth poured into the city, which would lay the financial basis for the role Venice was destined to play in the era of the Renaissance.

The rising prosperity also fueled a rapid growth of Europe's population, which had steadily declined after the fall of the Roman Empire. This population growth led to an

1200
The Bible is available in 22 languages

1200
The Cathedral of Notre Dame in Paris is completed

CA 1201
A major earthquake in the Levant kills more than a million people

1202
The Italian mathematician Leonardo Fibonacci introduces Arabic numerals in Europe

urgent quest for more inhabitable space. Across Europe, large tracts of forests and marshlands were cleared and drained to make room for new settlements, which in time would emerge as cities in their own right. This was particularly true in Germanic-speaking lands, where the growing scarcity of arable land prompted many people to cross the river Elbe and settle east of the traditional Frankish boundaries. All of these developments produced a degree of economic activity that, by some estimates, would not be surpassed until the 19th century.

Inevitably, these social movements were reflected in political changes as well. Following an ill-fated showdown with Pope Innocent III and the loss of Normandy after the Battle of Bouvines in 1214, King John of Britain was compelled to sign the Magna Carta, which greatly curtailed the virtually unchecked power of the English monarchy. Emperor Frederick II of the Hohenstaufen Dynasty was likewise forced to grant considerable autonomy to the various principalities under his sway.

The key engines of growth were the mercantile cities, rather than the Church or the temporal powers. It was a new middle class of merchants, craftsmen, artists, and other professionals who nurtured and sustained the European economy, and they demanded a say in the way they were governed. Some cities such as Florence and Cologne shook off the rule by local princes or bishops altogether, and instead appointed city councils made up of the leading mercantile families. In Germany,

SCRIPTURE AND FAITH

Dante's *Divine Comedy*

This 15th-century fresco in the Cathedral of Florence shows Dante holding his book The Divine Comedy.

La Divina Commedia, the great poem by Florentine poet Dante Alighieri (1265–1321), is often called the greatest literary work of the Middle Ages. Conceived as an allegorical journey through the Christian phases of the afterlife, it is also a commentary on both the social conditions and prevailing theological tenets of medieval Italy. The poem follows Dante as he travels through the three realms of the dead in the year 1300. The Roman poet Virgil takes him on a journey through the Inferno, or hell, populated by the souls of the damned (including people Dante knew personally), followed by a visit to Purgatorio, or purgatory, where those who committed any of the seven deadly sins are slowly cleansed through penance. Lastly, it is Dante's great (Platonic) love, the lady Beatrice, who takes him through Paradiso, or heaven, as a place of reward. Written in the hauntingly beautiful Tuscan vernacular, the poem had a major impact on the acceptance of Italian as a literary language.

1203
The University of Siena is founded

1204
Constantinople is sacked by militia of the Fourth Crusade

1204
The University of Vicenza is founded

1207
The German mystic Mechthild of Magdeburg is born

Devotional Objects

14TH CENTURY

This French gold chalice dates from 1325.

This 14th-century ciborium was made in Limoges.

The painting "St. Dominic Resurrects Napoleone Orsini" was rendered by Italian artist Benozzo Gozzoli (1420–ca 1497).

these became known as Imperial Free Cities, proud of the fact that they owed allegiance or tribute to no one, save the Emperor.

The New Orders of Poverty

The growing economy did not change the fact that the vast majority of the European population consisted of illiterate peasants, often living far from the social and spiritual safety net offered by the Church. It was precisely because of the needs of the rural peasantry that a new monastic movement was born, known as the friars of poverty. Unlike the monks of a previous era, these friars did not seek prayer and solitude behind monastery walls, but rather went out to engage with the ills and needs of the outside world. Rejecting the wealth and property often associated with traditional monasteries, these orders became known as mendicant orders, in which friars relied solely on alms and charity for their livelihood, as Jesus and the Apostles had once done.

The first of these orders was founded in 1215 by Dominic Guzman (1170–1221), a Spanish priest and diplomat who had traveled extensively through Europe before settling in Toulouse. Appalled by the ignorance and laxity of the clergy he met along the way, Dominic created a new monastic order dedicated to preaching the Gospel to the masses. This aim dovetailed perfectly with the pope's call for greater enlightenment of the Christian masses. Dominic's new monastic order was rapidly granted its papal patent under the name Ordo Praedicatorum (Order of Preachers), although it would soon become known as the Dominican order. A parallel order of Dominican nuns soon followed.

1209
The Franciscan order is recognized by the pope

1212
The Republic of Venice conquers Crete

1213
The Council of St. Albans, the precursor of the English Parliament, is founded

1214
King John of Britain is defeated at the Battle of Bouvines and loses Normandy

In the years to come, the Dominicans would provide basic education to thousands of the poor and illiterate, while popularizing simple prayer exercises such as the Rosary. By the same token, the Dominicans were vigilant for any form of heresy. Some scholars see the Dominican movement as a major factor in the emergence of the Inquisition, first established in Lombardy in 1231, some ten years after Dominic's death.

Another, even more influential order was established by the son of a rich silk merchant from Assisi, Tuscany, named Francesco di Bernardone (ca 1181–1226). After a youth of extravagant living, Francesco was

When I was in sin
it was bitter to look on lepers,
but the Lord brought me
among them, and
I showed mercy to them.

THE TESTAMENT
OF FRANCIS OF ASSISI, 1226

captured while serving as a soldier in a military campaign against Perugia, and spent a year as a prisoner of war. Released in 1203, he briefly resumed his halcyon lifestyle before experiencing a vision that compelled him to return to Assisi and embrace poverty. From that moment on, Francis devoted himself to ministering to the poor and the sick, even to victims of the dreaded disease leprosy, just as Jesus himself had done. Dressed in a rough garment, he would cheerfully move from one Umbrian village to the next, singing and glorifying God while admiring the beauty and perfection of Creation. His example was infectious. Scores of young men chose to join him, ready to subsist on whatever the local people were willing to give them.

In 1209, Francis successfully petitioned to have his new movement recognized by the pope, even though he was not an ordained priest and had no clerical education whatsoever. Astonishingly, Innocent III granted

HISTORY AND POLITICS

The Fourth Lateran Council

The Fourth Lateran Council, convoked by the activist Pope Innocent III in 1215 and attended by more than 400 bishops and patriarchs as well as more than 900 abbots and priors, was a milestone event in the evolution of the Latin Church. In all, the council approved some 70 canons or decrees. The first of these was the doctrine of transubstantiation, which had become a matter of controversy. The doctrine confirmed that during the consecration of the Eucharist, the substance of bread and wine is transformed, not into a mere symbol of Christ, but into Christ's actual body and blood—creating, in effect, a miracle akin to the miracles that Jesus had performed in his lifetime. The canon argued that the outward appearance of the bread and wine is not affected, since human senses are incapable of either perceiving or understanding the change. As a result, the mystery of substantiation made Mass a sacred and miraculous event. In the 16th century, the transubstantiation doctrine would be challenged by Martin Luther, who instead defined a "sacramental union" with the body and blood of Christ.

Another, more ominous development involved the last two canons adopted by the Council, which required Jews and Muslims living in Christian lands to "wear a special dress to enable them to be distinguished from Christians." The motive for this decision was to protect the Christian community from foreign influence. Nevertheless, the canon set in motion a process that would increasingly marginalize Jews in Europe, culminating in the creation of ghettos in the 16th century.

"Innocent III Approving the Franciscan Rule" is from a series of lunettes painted by Taddeo Gaddi (ca 1290–1366).

1214
Genghis Khan captures Zhongdu (Beijing)

1215
Pope Innocent III leads the Fourth Lateran Council

1215
Dominic Guzman founds the Dominican order

1218
Genghis Khan conquers Persia

his request, no doubt because the pope recognized the Franciscans as a powerful extension of his preaching program into the poorest regions of Italy. Officially founded one year later, the order adopted the humble name of Friars Minor, or Lesser Brothers. Francis's rule was simple: "To follow the teachings of our Lord Jesus Christ and to walk in his footsteps," later known as the Primitive Rule. This soon inspired a wealthy Assisi woman named Clare to create a similar order for women, known as the Poor Clares or Order of Poor Ladies. Later, another Franciscan order was established for laymen, known as the Third Order of Brothers and Sisters of Penance.

Scholasticism

The new emphasis on Church teaching and learning had a profound influence on the restoration of intellectual thought in Europe. As medieval universities grew and scholarly discourse spread, a new movement emerged that sought to reconcile the teachings of the Church with the great philosophers and scientists from Antiquity. Known as scholasticism, the movement used a process of dialectic discussion to see if the ancient authors could be validated through the tenets and revelations of the Christian faith.

In part, scholasticism was inspired by the rediscovery of the works of the great philosopher, author, and scientist Aristotle (384–322 B.C.E.), which had been preserved in monasteries throughout Europe, as well as the great Muslim libraries of Córdoba and Granada. Aristotle—the tutor of Alexander the Great—appealed to the medieval European mind because of the practical and tangible quality of his writings. His oeuvre was the basis of almost every aspect of medieval intellectual endeavor, from ethics to physics, from music to poetry, and from political theory to rhetoric and logic. There was only one problem: Aristotle was a pagan, who lived some three centuries before the birth of Christ. No matter how impressive his scholarly achievements, Aristotle's worldview did not allow for Christian revelation, which posed a significant challenge for scholastic thinkers of the period.

Accordingly, the academic revival produced a new type of scholar: the intellectual cleric, steeped in Church doctrine as well as the classics, exemplified by sages like Thomas Aquinas (1225–1274), William of Ockham (1287–1347), John Wycliffe (ca 1330–1384), and Thomas à Kempis (ca 1380–1471). Many of these scholars freely corresponded with one another, using Latin as their common language, thus creating a scholarly community that would lay the foundation for the great humanists of the Renaissance, including Marsilio Ficino, Thomas More, and Erasmus.

Of all 13th-century scholars, Thomas Aquinas was undoubtedly the most

> *You call him the dumb ox,*
> *but in his teaching*
> *he will one day produce*
> *such a bellowing that*
> *it will be heard*
> *throughout the world.*
>
> ALBERTUS MAGNUS ON HIS STUDENT, THOMAS AQUINAS

OPPOSITE: *Renowned Italian artist Giotto di Bondone (ca 1266–1337) painted "The Expulsion of the Devils from Arezzo" around 1299.*

SAINTS AND CLERICS

Francis of Assisi

"St. Francis of Assisi Preaching to the Birds" is a panel by Giotto di Bondone (ca 1266–1337).

Of all medieval saints, Francis of Assisi is undoubtedly the most popular. Though living in poverty, Francis reveled in the beauty of God's creation. When, early in his career, he was asked whom he wished to marry, he joyfully replied, "A more beautiful bride than you will ever see"—meaning Lady Poverty. One story relates how Christ appeared to Francis in a vision, telling him to "go and repair my house, which is falling into ruin." Eventually, this led Francis to create the order of Franciscans, dedicated to preaching and helping the poor. In 1219, he traveled to Damietta, Egypt, in an attempt to convert the Sultan of Egypt, then visited the Holy Land. To this day, the Franciscans manage many of the Christian sites in Israel. Upon his election to the papacy in 2013, Cardinal Jorge Bergoglio adopted the name of Francis I to signal his commitment to alleviating poverty, as Francis of Assisi had done before him.

1219 **Francis of Assisi travels to Damietta, Egypt**

1220 **Frederick II is crowned Emperor in Rome**

1220 **Chartres Cathedral is completed**

1220 **Henry III of England is crowned at Westminster**

"Thomas Aquinas and Heretics" was painted by Italian artist Andrea di Bonaiuto (active 1346–1379).

BELOW: *A detail of Aristotle and Plato is taken from the fresco "The School of Athens," by Raphael (1483–1520).*

influential. Thomas was born in 1225, the son of a leading local family in what is today the Lazio province of Italy. In 1239, he was enrolled at the University of Naples in preparation for a career as the abbot of a prominent monastery, such as Monte Cassino. Thomas, however, had other plans. Against the wishes of his family, he decided to join the newly founded Dominican order of friars. In 1245, he moved to Paris to continue his studies at the renowned University of Paris, which was rapidly becoming one of Europe's most influential centers of learning. Here, he fell under the spell of a Dominican scholar named Albertus Magnus (ca 1193–1280). Albertus was arguably the first important medieval scholar to discover the work of Aristotle, recognizing the immense relevance of Aristotle's empirical method to the medieval thirst for knowledge. But it was left up to Thomas to reconcile Aristotle's philosophy with the tenets of Christian revelation, by arguing that while much of what Aristotle wrote is true, it is not the whole truth. In this vein, Thomas was able to depict Aristotelian philosophy and Christian doctrine as complementary, rather than contradictory.

Between 1259 and 1268, as he taught at a variety of Dominican venues, Thomas produced a vast corpus of learned works. This included his famous *Summa Theologiae,* a comprehensive compendium that sought to summarize and explain Christian theology for the average clergyman. It is a token of Thomas's erudition that in the *Summa* he cited not

1220
Construction of Salisbury Cathedral begins

1225
The final version of the Magna Carta is issued

1227
Prince Bort is baptized in the Ukraine

1229
Frederick II signs a treaty with the Sultan of Egypt

only Christian sources, but also prominent Muslim and Jewish authors such as Avicenna, Averroës, Al-Ghazali, and Maimonides.

The *Summa* was still unfinished when Thomas experienced a vision in 1273. According to tradition, Thomas was praying before an image of the crucifixion when Christ suddenly spoke: "You have written well of me, Thomas. What reward would you have for your labor?" Thomas replied, "Nothing but you, Lord." The vision left Thomas so bereft that he refused to teach or write. When he was urged to take up the pen, he said, "I cannot, for all that I have written seems like straw to me." He died a few months later.

Thomas's greatest contribution to scholastic thought was his insistence that theology is a science, grounded in knowledge and observation like any other form of scientific endeavor, yet based on fundamental truths revealed by God. Although some of his works were condemned during his lifetime, the Church eventually recognized his oeuvre as foundational theological literature.

The Medieval Mystics

Scholasticism was not the only religious movement to emerge in the 13th century. Perhaps in a reaction to the intellectualization of theology, mystic currents sprang up all

"The Adoration of the Mystic Lamb" is a panel painted by Flemish artist Jan van Eyck (ca 1390–1441). The adoration of the mystic lamb was a medieval motif inspired by the Gospel of John.

1230
Leprosy is introduced to Europe, possibly via Crusader ships

1231
The Inquisition is established in Lombardy

1237
Frederick II defeats the League of Lombardy

1237
The Mongols invade Russia

Devotional Objects

1050–1350

This reliquary cross was created in Canterbury in the mid-11th century.

This host box from Limoges dates from the 14th century.

over Europe. Emphasizing the spontaneous transformation that religious fervor could bestow, mysticism became popular in many social classes, and particularly among women. Mechthild of Magdeburg (ca 1207–ca 1280) was a member of the German beguine movement (a lay organization devoted to charitable works) who began to experience a number of visions, which she faithfully described in her book *The Flowing Light of the Divine.* Her

> *He came in the form and clothing of a Man, as he was on the day when he gave us his Body for the first time; looking like a Human Being and a Man, wonderful, and beautiful, he came to me humbly.*
>
> HADEWIG OF BRABANT
> VISION SEVEN

writings elicited much opposition from the Church, not least because she was a woman, and a layperson at that. What's more, her book was written in the German vernacular rather than Latin, which earned her the scorn of the scholarly community. Ostracized and destitute, she was taken in by the nuns of a Cistercian monastery in Saxony, St. Mary's of Helfta, where she served as a model for a new generation of mystics.

Mechthild's life was closely paralleled by that of the 13th-century Dutch mystic Hadewig of Brabant, who lived in the duchy of Brabant, in today's southern Netherlands and northern Flanders. Hadewig, too, was a beguine who described her visions as an experience in which "my heart and my veins and all my limbs trembled and quivered with eager desire, and such madness and fear beset my mind that it seemed to me . . . that I must go mad." Writing in the vernacular of Middle Dutch, including her 1240 work, *The Book of Visions,* she soon gained a local following. Unlike Mechthild and most other women of her time, Hadewig was a highly educated woman who was fully conversant in contemporary theology and literature. Since few people outside the Low Countries could read Middle Dutch, her beautiful poems enjoyed only a limited following until her rediscovery in the 19th century. Today, Belgian critics consider her to be one of the most influential medieval authors to emerge from Flanders.

The Art of Illumination

The prodigious output of scholarly and sacred texts from 1200 onward inevitably revitalized the creation and publication of books. At this time, books were still copied by hand, which made them highly valuable artifacts—especially if they were illustrated with miniature paintings, known as "illuminations." Many such illuminated manuscripts were already circulating as early as the ninth century, during the Carolingian Renaissance. The unprecedented demand for scholarly publications as well as Bibles, Psalters, and other religious works, however, made the 13th century the apogee of the art of illumination.

Most of these illuminated books were created on calfskin vellum (from the Latin

OPPOSITE: *This is a detail of "The Adoration of the Magi," painted by Gentile da Fabriano (ca 1370–1427). The work, housed in the Uffizi Gallery in Florence, is considered his finest.*

1240
The Dutch mystic Hadewig of Brabant writes *The Book of Visions*

1240
The Mongols capture Moscow

1241
The Mongols invade Hungary and Poland, but then withdraw

1243
France and England agree to a five-year truce

vetulinum, literally "made from calf") or parchment made from the hides of goats and sheep. Originally, they were produced by skilled monks in monastic scriptoria (writing rooms), but by the 14th century, the manufacture had shifted to publishing shops in the leading cities. After the text had been written, leaving space for illustrations, the work would be passed to an artist who first drew the principal design in silverpoint. Colors would then be added, using a variety of pigments, which were ground and mixed especially for this purpose. Depictions of heaven or sacred figures would be highlighted with touches of gold, using either gold foil or specks of gold dust.

This detail of the arrest of Jesus is taken from the French illuminated manuscript the Très Riches Heures *of Jean, Duke of Berry.*

A famous example of such medieval illumination is the *Très Riches Heures,* a Book of Hours commissioned by Jean, the Duke of Berry, which contains 182 illuminations painted by the Limbourg brothers. Books of Hours were typical of the medieval passion for devotional sustenance. Conceived as breviaries, these books provided canonical prayers and reflections linked to the rhythm of everyday life—either by day, by month, or by season. While simple breviaries of this type were popular among a literate few, illuminated versions would become much sought-after works among the nobility, often commanding stupendous prices.

The International Style

Some historians have argued that the broad dissemination of illuminated manuscripts, often produced by renowned artists, was a major factor in the emergence of a new sacred art that is often referred to as the International Style. The high mobility of 13th-century artists between the rival courts of Europe accelerated the spread of the style as well. Consequently, for a brief time the International Style reigned supreme throughout Europe, from Bohemia and Italy to England and France. It introduced a new level of grace and elegance to European art, dispelling the awkward and distressed depiction of humanity in Romanesque art. Biblical characters and saints were now depicted with a greater interest in human anatomy, invariably clothed in rich and colorful garments designed to emphasize their sacred dignity. Perhaps in imitation of Roman sculpture, many such figures, in both painting and sculpture, assumed

1245
Pope Innocent IV strips Frederick II of the title of Holy Roman Emperor

1248
Work begins on Cologne Cathedral

1248
The Genoese capture the island of Rhodes

1250
The Saracens capture King Louis IX

a graceful, elongated curvature shaped by the drapery of their garments.

The movement probably originated in Bohemia and Italy, and from there was disseminated through the work of prominent artists such as the Italian painter Gentile da Fabriano; the Pisano family of Italian sculptors; the Dutch sculptor Claus Sluter; the German painter Conrad von Soest; and the Netherlandish painters known as the Luxembourg brothers. Polychrome wood carvings were particularly suited to this free-flowing style, as shown in countless altarpieces that have survived throughout Germany and eastern Europe.

Another medium that popularized the International Style was tapestry. The style's penchant for color and texture was superbly suited for tapestry, a form of decorative art that was much sought after not only for its aesthetic properties but also for its ability to help insulate the largely unheated homes and castles of the period. Thanks to the active patronage of the court of Burgundy, Arras and Tournai soon emerged as the dominant manufacturing centers of tapestry weaving, which exported their products throughout Europe.

Gothic Architecture

Undoubtedly, the medium in which the High Middle Ages found their greatest religious expression was the cathedral. Important changes in early 13th-century technology created a new idea of what sacred architecture should look like and what purpose it was meant to fulfill. Historians do not agree on the impulses that produced the Gothic style, but one important factor was surely the desire to open up the thick walls characteristic of Romanesque buildings to allow for the display of art in stained glass. In an age that prized preaching as the foremost activity of the clergy, and in which the vast

Italian sculptor Nicola Pisano (ca 1220–ca 1284) created this pulpit relief of the Adoration of the Magi in 1260.

LIFE AND TIMES

Medieval Pilgrimage

A night view shows the Cathedral of Santiago de Compostela in Spain.

During the 14th century, as a new religious fervor swept Europe, the custom of pilgrimage to sites devoted to prominent saints became highly popular. Some of these destinations included the shrine of St. James at the church of Santiago de Compostela in Spain; the reputed remains of the Three Kings in the cathedral of Cologne, Germany; the crown of thorns at Notre Dame in Paris; and the shrine of St. Thomas Becket in Canterbury Cathedral, England. Near the end of the 14th century, English author Geoffrey Chaucer wrote a collection of stories known as The Canterbury Tales, depicting a storytelling contest among pilgrims traveling to Canterbury Cathedral. The vivid and sometimes bawdy tales provide a fascinating portrait of English life in the High Middle Ages, often satirizing the role of clergy. Following Dante's example, Chaucer wrote in the vernacular, rather than Latin, thus popularizing the use of English as a literary language.

1251
King Mindaugas of Lithuania is baptized

1252
The Inquisition begins to use torture to extract confessions

1252
Florence begins to mint its own currency, the gold florin

1256
War erupts between Genoa and Venice

This detail is from the Très Riches Heures of Jean, Duke of Berry, *an illuminated manuscript created by the Limbourg brothers between 1412 and 1416.*

NOTRE DAME *is a historic Catholic cathedral that sits on the eastern half of the Île de la Cité in Paris. The 12th-century church is considered by many to be one of the finest examples of French Gothic architecture. It was one of the first buildings to use flying buttresses.*

majority of the faithful were illiterate, these great sheets became the people's Bible—key moments from the Old and New Testaments, illustrated in shimmering glass.

This did, however, demand a radically different approach to the mastery of load-bearing forces. The solution was to direct the weight of the vaulted roof into concentration points via the use of diagonal ribs, which themselves were supported by massive compound piers running the full height of the church. These piers, in turn, transferred the downward pressure of the vaults into exterior struts, known as flying buttresses, which became a dominant feature of Gothic cathedrals. Thus, whereas the Romanesque builder had sought to contain the weight of the building within, the Gothic builder moved it outside.

The result was an organic frame of thrust and counterthrust that freed the walls to serve as a membrane for any type of ornamentation, either in sculpture or in stained glass. At the same time, the structural needs of this rib-and-pier system shaped the top of each window into a pointed arch, which soon became the most recognizable element of the Gothic style.

Some of these features, such as the groined vault supported by ribs, were already

OPPOSITE: *A view of 12th-century Notre Dame from the south bank of the Seine River shows the cathedral's flying buttresses.*

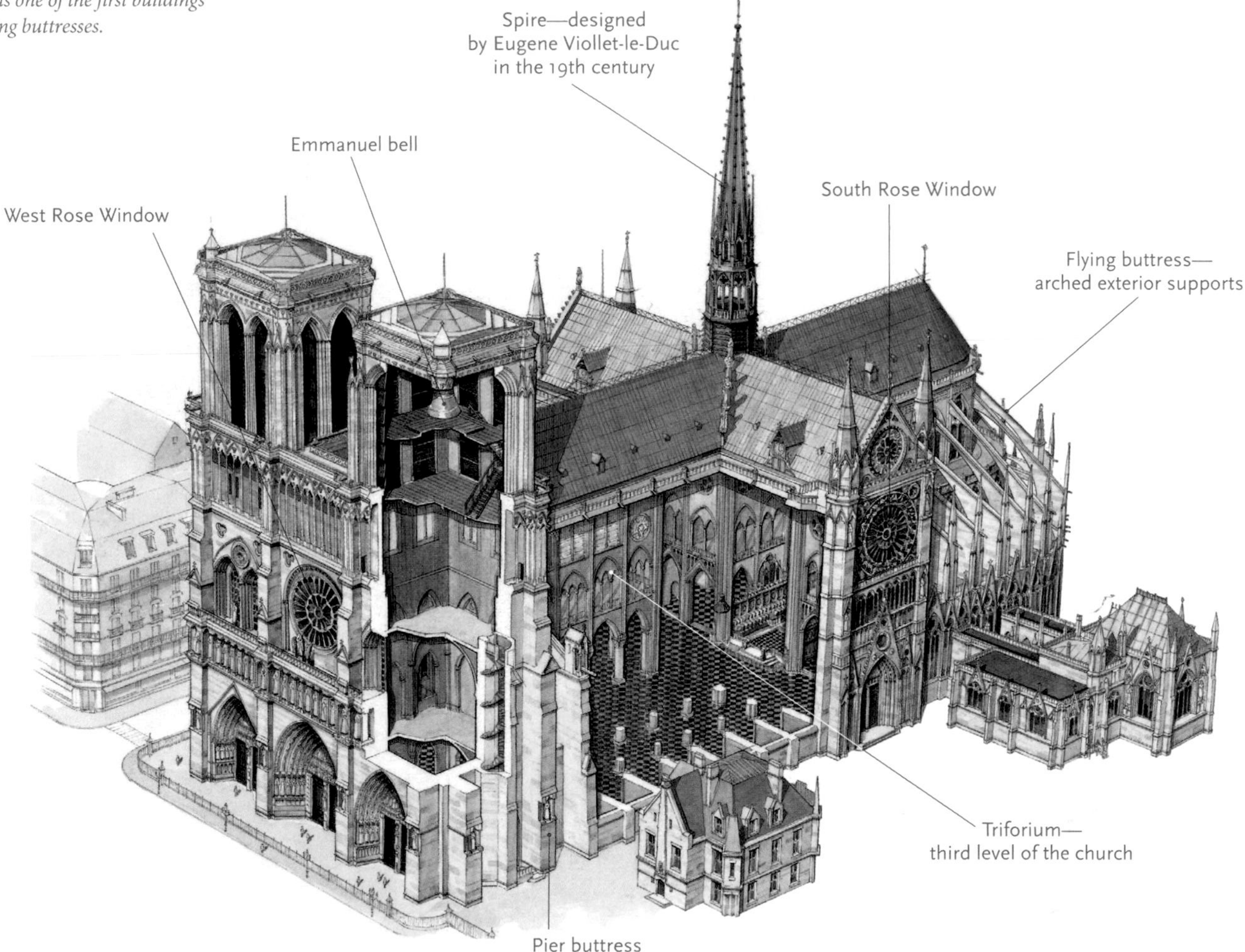

1258
The Mongols capture Baghdad and evict the caliphate

1259
Thomas Aquinas begins the *Summa Theologiae*

1259
Kublai Khan becomes Mongol ruler of China

1260
The first *Meistersinger* choral school is founded in Mainz, Germany

present in late Romanesque building, but it was not until the rebuilding of the choir of the Basilica of St.-Denis in Paris, completed by Abbot Suger in 1144, that these elements came together to produce a radically new concept in architecture. From there, the new Gothic style captured the imagination of builders throughout France. The Cathedral of Notre Dame in Paris, begun in 1163 and completed in 1200, was one of the first churches to be designed on Gothic principles from the ground up, closely followed by Chartres Cathedral (1194–1220) and Reims Cathedral (1225–1299). Chartres, in particular, is a striking example of what medieval worshippers saw when they entered a cathedral for the first time, for it is the only one that still retains its original stained-glass windows. For the illiterate faithful, stepping into this sacred space lit by dappled shafts of colored light, surrounded by bright scenes from the Old and New Testaments, must have been an overwhelming experience—truly a glimpse of the Heavenly Jerusalem, in the words of art historian Erwin Panofsky.

The invention of Gothic technology coincided with the rapid growth of urban wealth and the desire to express that wealth in magnificent monuments to God, often in competition with other cities. Thus, the period between 1190 and 1280, which historians refer to as High Gothic, saw an unprecedented outburst of building

The choir of the Basilica of St.-Denis in Paris, completed in 1144, is the first example of Gothic church architecture. It would ignite the development of churches using Gothic engineering principles throughout France.

1260
The Florentine Ghibellines defeat the papal Guelphs at Montaperti

1266
Kublai Khan asks the pope to send 100 Christian missionaries

1267
The Aztec settle in the Valley of Mexico

1270
French King Louis IX dies during the Eighth Crusade and is succeeded by Philip III

activity, not only in France but also in Germany, England, Italy, and Spain. As cathedrals topped by soaring spires rose to become the dominant feature on every skyline, they proudly declared the shift from the monastery to the city as the dominant center of Christian activity.

In time, as builders became more confident in the new technology, cathedral heights continued to rise as well. The proportion of the height of the nave to its width grew to 2:1 in many English cathedrals, and as much as 3:1 in Cologne Cathedral. The vault of the nave in Milan Cathedral would reach an astonishing height of 148 feet, while that of Beauvais Cathedral tops out at 157 feet, the highest vault of all Gothic structures in the world.

Soon, each region began to interpret the principles of Gothic building in their own terms, which led to a number of indigenous styles. In England, the late Gothic style produced such intricate forms as the depressed arch and other flamboyant motifs. In Germany, the *Hallenkirche* type became popular, by which the central nave and side aisles rose to equal height, creating a space of awesome visual power. In central Italy, builders adopted the pointed arch but never quite embraced the underlying rib-and-pier system. Most of them remained faithful to Romanesque principles, while relying more on mosaics, frescoes, and sculpture than on stained glass to inspire the congregation.

The Western Schism

Throughout the 13th century, the authority of the pope continued to rise vis-à-vis that of the emperor. The largely ceremonial title of Holy Roman Emperor, long held by the Hohenstaufen Dynasty of German emperors, was claimed in 1273 by a new family of growing power, known as the Habsburgs. In that year, Rudolf I of Habsburg was elected King of Germany, only to add the duchy of Austria to his domain several years later. Rudolf thereupon moved his capital to Austria, from where the Habsburgs would rule for more than six centuries, until 1918. During this time, Spain, Hungary, Flanders, and southern Italy would be added to the lands under Habsburg rule, so

PERIOD ART

The Gothic Arts

Europe would achieve its most homogenous cultural flowering in the so-called International Style, an aesthetic of grace in both portraiture and sculpture. Like Romanesque, the movement had its grounding in architecture, specifically the new Gothic style. Gothic was based on the discovery that the weight of the vaulted roof could be channeled through large piers to external flying buttresses, so that the walls—now freed from load-bearing duty—could be opened up with magnificent sheets of stained glass. The use of these massive piers, their ribs reaching high into the groined vaults, forced window spaces to become pointed—which subsequently became the signature "look" of Gothic architecture.

But Gothic was not limited to the visual arts. Music, too, was affected, since every cathedral or church now maintained a "chapel" of singers and musicians. The ars antiqua, an early polyphonic style based on the motet, was supplanted by the ars nova. Composers such as Frenchman Guillaume de Machaut (1300–1377) and Italian Francesco Landini (ca 1335–1397) probed for new, complex harmonies using a variety of rhythmic notation. The search for a more physical, more sensuous musical expression also affected entertainment at Europe's courts. Here, troubadours and music ensembles introduced forms of secular dance music such as the gavotte and pavane, which would become the basis for elements of the Baroque concerto in a later era. Italian composers also began to set poetic lyrics to catchy tunes, entirely devoid of any religious character, known as *frottolas;* in the 16th century, these would evolve into the songs called madrigals.

A group of troubadours appears in a 13th-century manuscript entitled Cantigas de Santa Maria.

1271
Marco Polo travels to China

1272
Henry III of England is succeeded by Edward I

1273
Rudolf I of Habsburg claims the title of Holy Roman Emperor

1274
Kublai Khan fails in his effort to capture Japan

that by 1700, the Habsburgs were the dominant power in Europe.

The papacy observed these developments with apprehension. Back in 1201, Pope Innocent III had declared that "it is the business of the pope to look after the interests of the Roman Empire, since the Empire derives its origin and its final authority from the papacy." That implied that the pontiff's authority was superior over that of the emperor, since it is the pope who "blesses him, crowns him, and invests him"—not the other way around. True enough, in 1245, Pope Innocent IV took the unusual step of stripping the defiant Frederick II (1194–1250) of his Holy Roman Emperor title after the latter refused to submit to Rome. The venerable title was only reinstated some 60 years later, on the far more pliable King Henry VII. When papal authority neared its apex at the end of the 13th century, Boniface VIII (r. 1295–1303) issued a papal bull, "Unam Sanctam," that sought to legitimize papal hegemony once and for all. The authority of the pope, the bull declared, was superior to *all* temporal powers, whether this involved princes, kings, or emperors. Only the pope had the power to invest kings—or declare them illegitimate, if the need indicated such.

Boniface may have overreached. The growing powers of France, England, and Germany, while pledging obedience to the pope in religious matters, were not inclined to subordinate their rule to the jurisdiction of the pontiff in Rome, particularly since

Just as the founder of the universe established two great lights in the firmament of heaven, the greater light to rule the day and the lesser light to rule the night, so too He set two great dignities in the firmament of the universal church… these are the papal authority and the royal power.

POPE INNOCENT III
LETTERS ON PAPAL POLICIES

LIFE AND TIMES

The First Public Hospitals

The massive casualties inflicted by the battles of the Crusades forced European physicians to significantly improve medical care, using some principles of medicine taught by Muslim and Byzantine physicians. This, combined with the growth of urban population centers, led to the development of the first public hospitals, which also drew on the experience of the Knights Hospitallers, who had built numerous hospitals in the Holy Land for pilgrims as well as for casualties of war. The Hospices of Beaune, France, one of the few medieval hospitals to have survived until the 20th century, offers an excellent impression of what these medical institutions looked like. Designed by the architect Jehan Wisecrère in the Flemish Gothic style and managed by the nuns of the Order of St.-Esprit, the hospital featured a large rectangular ward, appropriately named the Hall of the Poor, where patients were placed back-to-back in individual alcoves screened by curtains. The elderly, the sick, the disabled, as well as pregnant women were tended here without regard for their social station. A chapel featuring a polyptych of the Last Judgment by Flemish artist Rogier van der Weyden, located at the end of the hall, allowed patients to attend Mass without rising from their beds. More affluent patients were housed in a separate chamber, although their accommodations were largely the same. Similar public hospitals were built throughout Europe; by 1300, England alone had more than 200 facilities just for lepers. Many of these hospitals would be overwhelmed by the outbreak of the plague in the late 1340s.

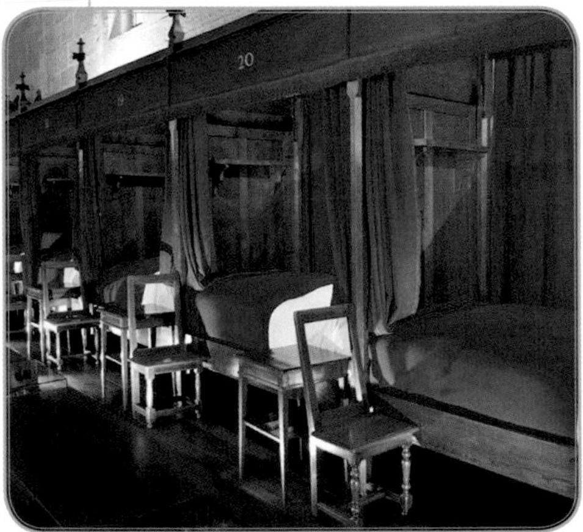

A view of the main ward of the Hospices of Beaune, France, a medieval hospital that continued to function until the 20th century

1278
The Santa Maria Novella is built in Florence

1280
Kublai Khan establishes the Yuan Dynasty in China

1283
The Teutonic order completes the conquest of Prussia

1284
Genoa defeats Pisa, precipitating its slow decline

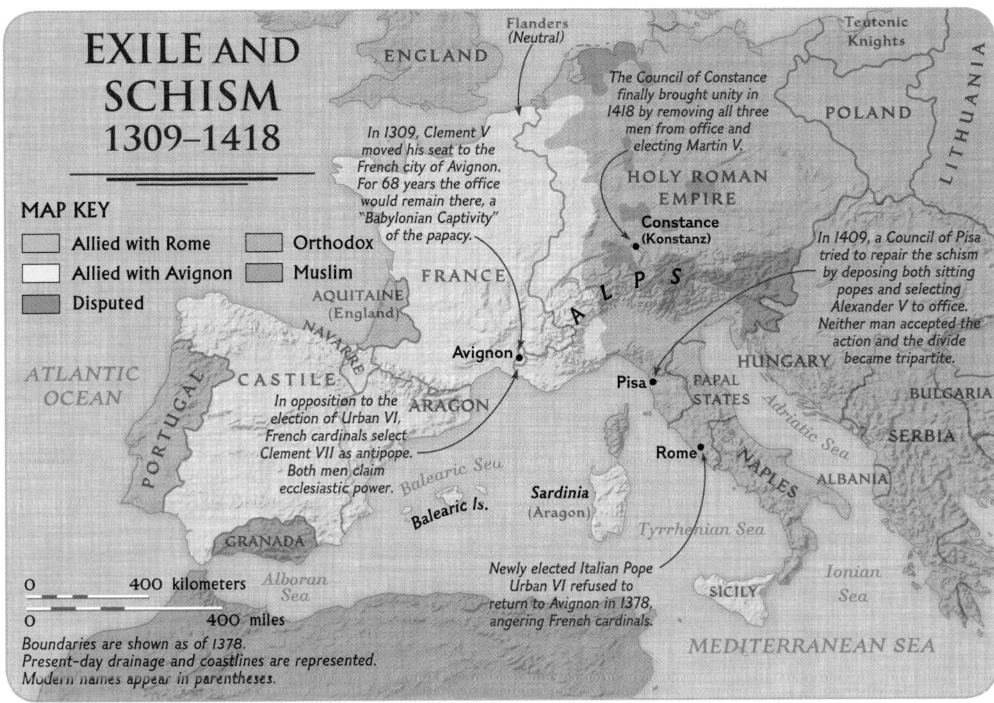
EXILE AND SCHISM
1309–1418
MAP KEY
Allied with Rome
Allied with Avignon
Disputed
Orthodox
Muslim
ENGLAND
Flanders (Neutral)
Teutonic Knights
The Council of Constance finally brought unity in 1418 by removing all three men from office and electing Martin V.
POLAND
LITHUANIA
In 1309, Clement V moved his seat to the French city of Avignon. For 68 years the office would remain there, a "Babylonian Captivity" of the papacy.
HOLY ROMAN EMPIRE
Constance (Konstanz)
In 1409, a Council of Pisa tried to repair the schism by deposing both sitting popes and selecting Alexander V to office. Neither man accepted the action and the divide became tripartite.
FRANCE
AQUITAINE (England)
ALPS
NAVARRE
Avignon
HUNGARY
ATLANTIC OCEAN
CASTILE
ARAGON
Pisa
PAPAL STATES
BULGARIA
PORTUGAL
In opposition to the election of Urban VI, French cardinals select Clement VII as antipope. Both men claim ecclesiastic power.
Adriatic Sea
SERBIA
Rome
NAPLES
ALBANIA
Balearic Sea
Balearic Is.
Sardinia (Aragon)
Tyrrhenian Sea
GRANADA
0 400 kilometers
0 400 miles
Alboran Sea
Newly elected Italian Pope Urban VI refused to return to Avignon in 1378, angering French cardinals.
SICILY
Ionian Sea
MEDITERRANEAN SEA
Boundaries are shown as of 1378.
Present-day drainage and coastlines are represented.
Modern names appear in parentheses.

such could have considerable financial consequences. The matter came to a head when King Philip IV of France (r. 1285–1314) clashed with Boniface over the removal of French religious figures from his government and the subsequent levying of taxes on all French clergy. After King Philip defiantly burned the papal bull in 1302, Boniface retaliated by excommunicating him. But then the pope died, unexpectedly, in 1303. A long and fractious conclave followed, in which (in a nod to King Philip) the archbishop of the French city of Bordeaux eventually emerged as the winner. This new Pope Clement V stunned Christendom, however, by refusing to move to Rome. Instead, he chose to settle in Avignon, in southern France. There the papal court remained for more than 70 years, presided over by six French popes who accomplished little—other than enjoying the superb climate and cuisine of Provence—in what some historians have called the "Babylonian Captivity of the Papacy." Only Gregory XI agreed to return to Rome in 1377, and only in response to the urgent pleas of the mystic Catherine of Siena. But the trials of the medieval papacy were far from over.

After a brief, one-year reign, Gregory died and the conclave appointed an Italian pope, Urban VI (r. 1378–1389). His perceived arrogance toward French cardinals riled the latter so much that they left Rome and elected a different pope, Clement VII, back in Avignon. By the time a special council was called to Pisa in 1409 to adjudicate the conflict, both popes had been succeeded by two new papal claimants, Boniface IX and Benedict XIII. The council responded by electing a third pope, Alexander V, and demanding that the other two pontiffs resign—which, not surprisingly, they refused to do. As a result, there were now *three* popes all claiming to be the legitimate heir of St. Peter. When Alexander died suddenly, he was succeeded by another

HISTORY AND POLITICS

The Papal Court in Avignon

The Palace of the Popes in Avignon, France, served as the pope's residence from 1309 to 1377.

In 1309, Pope Clement V chose the French city of Avignon as his official residence, spurning the Holy See in Rome. At the time, Avignon was still part of the independent kingdom of Arles, ruled by the House of Anjou based in Sicily. In 1348, Queen Joanna I sold the city to Pope Clement VI as a sovereign papal territory. In all, seven popes would rule from the city, living in a heavily fortified palace complex, built in the Gothic style during the 14th century. Inevitably, Avignon became a magnet for bankers, traders, poets, and artists. After Pope Gregory XI agreed to return to Rome, the policies of his successor, Urban VI, prompted French cardinals to establish an antipope, Clement VII, in Avignon, followed by the antipope Benedict XIII. Many in medieval Christendom viewed the outbreak of the plague in 1347 as divine punishment for the "captivity" of the Holy See in Avignon. Curiously, Avignon remained part of the Papal States until 1791, after the French Revolution.

1285
King Philip III of France is succeeded by Philip IV, "The Fair"

1285
An anonymous German poet writes the poem "Lohengrin"

1287
The Franciscan theologian William of Ockham is born

1291
The first bishop of Finland is appointed

antipope, John XXIII, who at one point in his life had been a mercenary; in fact, he'd only been ordained priest a day before his coronation. Clearly, the prestige and authority of the papacy had fallen to unprecedented depths.

The Western Schism was not resolved until the Council of Constance, which in 1415 prevailed on all three reigning popes to resign. Two did so voluntarily; only Benedict XIII refused to comply, and was subsequently excommunicated. A new pope, Martin V (r. 1417–1431) was elected, who resumed the legitimate line of the papacy (though some princes and archbishops continued to support Benedict XIII and his successor until 1429). When, in our modern day, Cardinal Angelo Roncalli was elected pope by the 1958 conclave, he pointedly took the name of John XXIII so as to affirm the illegitimacy of the antipope some 500 years earlier.

The Great Plague

Already tarnished by the Western Schism, the "long summer of the High Middle Ages," in David Bentley Hart's words, came to a cataclysmic end in 1347, when Europe was visited by the plague. This outbreak of the Black Death originated in Mongolia and was probably carried by Genoese merchant ships from the Crimea to southern Italy, from where it rapidly spread throughout the Mediterranean. By 1351, the pandemic had penetrated deep into Europe, reaching eastern Europe and even Russia; only isolated areas in Poland and the Low Countries were spared.

Medieval science was powerless to stop it. Some physicians believed the plague was carried by air from decaying corpses, aided by the humid conditions of summer; others believed that noxious fumes from sewers were at fault. Some civic authorities, such as the city of Pistoia, urged an evacuation of

"The Decameron" was painted by British artist John William Waterhouse (1849–1917) in 1916.

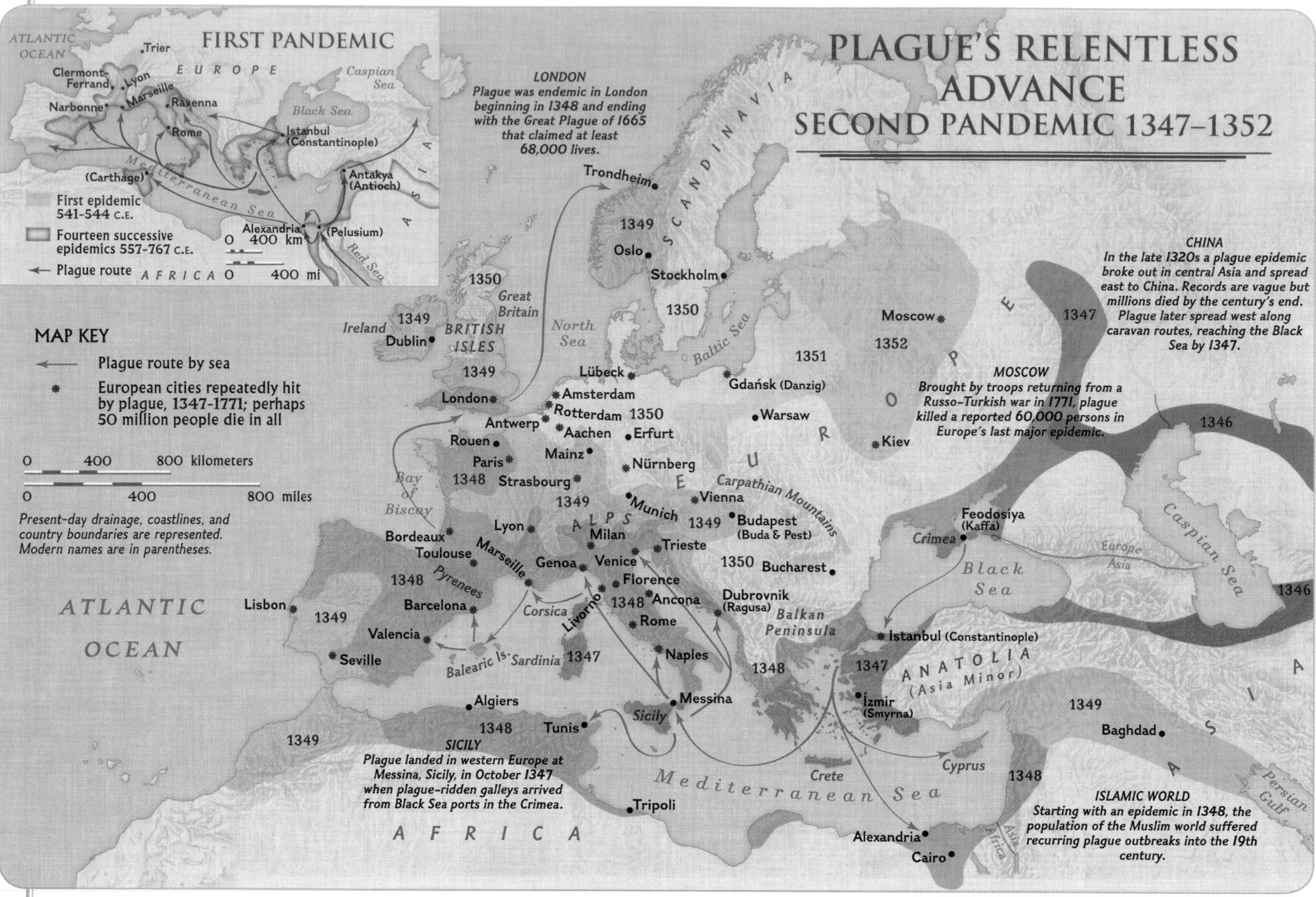

PLAGUE'S RELENTLESS ADVANCE
SECOND PANDEMIC 1347–1352
FIRST PANDEMIC
First epidemic 541-544 C.E.
Fourteen successive epidemics 557-767 C.E.
Plague route
MAP KEY
Plague route by sea
European cities repeatedly hit by plague, 1347-1771; perhaps 50 million people die in all
Present-day drainage, coastlines, and country boundaries are represented. Modern names are in parentheses.
LONDON
Plague was endemic in London beginning in 1348 and ending with the Great Plague of 1665 that claimed at least 68,000 lives.
CHINA
In the late 1320s a plague epidemic broke out in central Asia and spread east to China. Records are vague but millions died by the century's end. Plague later spread west along caravan routes, reaching the Black Sea by 1347.
MOSCOW
Brought by troops returning from a Russo-Turkish war in 1771, plague killed a reported 60,000 persons in Europe's last major epidemic.
SICILY
Plague landed in western Europe at Messina, Sicily, in October 1347 when plague-ridden galleys arrived from Black Sea ports in the Crimea.
ISLAMIC WORLD
Starting with an epidemic in 1348, the population of the Muslim world suffered recurring plague outbreaks into the 19th century.

OPPOSITE: *"St. Sebastian Interceding for the Plague Stricken" was painted by Josse Lieferinxe (active ca 1493–1508) in 1497.*

all healthy people from diseased neighborhoods. This sometimes worked, though not for reasons cited, for the plague was actually spread by black rats harboring infected fleas.

For most, this advice came too late. A society that had been so painstakingly built in the previous century was torn asunder as all social classes, from paupers to princes and bishops, were struck by the disease. As thousands died, the Christian order collapsed; thieves, rapists, and murderers roamed freely without any fear of retribution. Modern estimates vary wildly, but it is generally believed that some 25 to 30 percent of the European population was killed. Worldwide, the population was reduced from some 450 million in the 13th century to around 375 million in the 14th century.

The long period of the plague produced a fatalistic mood among many Europeans. The 1353 collection of novellas *The Decameron,* by Giovanni Boccaccio (1313–1375), relates how seven young women and three young men entertain each other with tales of love and death while sheltering in a villa outside Florence to escape the ravages of the Black Death. And yet, in the shadow of death that held Europe captive, the seeds of a great rebirth were about to be sown. ■

1294
The Franciscan missionary Giovanni di Monte Corvino arrives in China

1299
Reims Cathedral is completed

1300
Guillaume de Machaut, composer of ars nova, is born

1302
Pope Boniface VIII issues the bull "Unam Sanctam," asserting papal hegemony

8 CHAPTER

THE RENAISSANCE AND THE REFORMATION

1400-1550

Where the spirit does not work with the hands, there is no art.

LEONARDO DA VINCI

From 1400 onward, beginning in Italy, western Europe was swept by a new passion for classical models that in the 19th century would come to be known as the Renaissance. In due course, this revolutionized all fields of human endeavor, including the visual arts, architecture, science, and literature. But the new focus on humanist inquiry also unleashed long-simmering resentment at a Church that had become self-absorbed and beset by corruption, producing the Reformation in the process.

In 1401, the Florentine Guild of Cloth Merchants, known as the Arte di Calimala, announced a competition to design a new set of bronze doors for the Baptistery of St. John, an 11th-century building opposite Florence Cathedral. The idea to issue a competition was inspired by the fact that Florence had become a magnet for scores of talented artists and sculptors. The planned design envisioned a bronze door with ten sculpted panels. All competitors were asked to submit a model for one of these panels, depicting Abraham's sacrifice of Isaac. According to the story in Genesis, God decided to test Abraham by asking him to sacrifice his son Isaac as a "burnt offering." Deeply distraught, Abraham prepared to do as God had asked him, but at the last moment

ABOVE: *The famous "Mona Lisa," a portrait of Lisa del Giocondo, was painted by Leonardo da Vinci (1452–1519).*

OPPOSITE: *The well-known dome of the Cathedral of Florence was built between 1420 and 1436.*

PRECEDING PAGES: *"The Cestello Annunciation" was painted by Italian Renaissance artist Sandro Botticelli (1445–1510) in 1489.*

This section of the dome of the Cathedral of Florence shows the double shell structure designed by Filippo Brunelleschi (1377–1446).

an angel intervened, saying, "Now I know that you fear God" (Genesis 22:11-12). This moment, so charged with psychological drama, was now to be cast in gilded bronze.

Seven competitors submitted a design, but only the models of the winner and runner-up have survived. Both were young, aspiring goldsmiths: 24-year-old Filippo Brunelleschi and 23-year-old Lorenzo Ghiberti. Surprisingly, their designs were remarkably similar. Both sculptors openly modeled their saintly figures on pagan Roman art. Brunelleschi went as far as to include a copy of a Roman sculpture, "Boy with a Thorn," in his composition.

Classical sculpture had influenced Eastern and Western Christian art many times before, but never had pagan works been cited so brazenly, and without any regard for the obvious dissonance of using pagan models for sacred subject matter. Ghiberti's half-nude Isaac, for example, shone like a young Apollo. Even more remarkably, neither the Church authorities nor the wool guild objected. They rallied around the declared winner, Lorenzo Ghiberti, since the young artist had cast his design in one piece.

Most historians mark the Baptistery competition as the beginning of a movement that, many centuries later, would be named by the French historian Jules Michelet. In French, "Renaissance" means "revival" (or *Rinascità* in Italian). What Michelet tried to convey was that this new movement consciously tried to resurrect the great achievements of Antiquity in art, literature, architecture, and the sciences. But the Renaissance involved more than mere imitation of Greece and Rome. The thinkers of this era increasingly placed the human experience, rather than God and faith, at the center of man's existence. Whereas 13th-century scholasticism had sought to reconcile the intellectual fruits of Antiquity with Christian dogma, the humanists of the Renaissance believed that an uninhibited, empirical investigation of nature would not only validate ancient treatises but also reveal the boundless power and creativity of the divine.

"The Tribute Money" forms part of the fresco cycle of Italian painter Masaccio (1401–1428) in the Brancacci Chapel of the church of Santa Maria del Carmine in Florence.

1315 — **Outbreak of the Great Famine in Europe, which will last two years**

1321 — **The Dominican monk Jordanus arrives in India**

1321 — **Dante Alighieri completes his epic poem *Divina Commedia***

1323 — **Franciscan missionaries reach Sumatra**

The San Spirito in Florence, designed by Italian architect and engineer Filippo Brunelleschi (1377–1446), is one of the first churches in the Renaissance style.

It would be wrong to think that because the Renaissance empowered individuals to explore the world outside Church doctrine, they would somehow be less attached to Christian spirituality. In fact, the opposite is true. For many humanists, artists, and scientists, empirical exploration of the natural world meant they could experience the work of God in a more individual and *authentic* way. Artists like Botticelli would paint pagan subjects like the birth of Venus one day and be wholly devoted to a pious representation of the Nativity the next. Science and faith were not yet seen as two mutually exclusive domains, as they would be in a later age.

Nineteenth-century historians like Michelet liked to depict the Renaissance as a miraculous explosion of creativity after centuries of medieval ignorance, but this is a simplification. In many ways, the 15th-century Renaissance was a continuation of the intellectual reawakening of the 13th century, following its temporary disruption by the social and political upheavals of the 14th century, including the plague. The humanists of the 15th century—writers such as Leonardo Bruni and Marsilio

1329
Nicaea, site of the Nicene Council, falls to the Ottoman Turks

1330
The scholastic philosopher John Wycliffe is born

1347
Outbreak of the Black Plague, which will devastate Europe

1353
Boccaccio completes his novella collection *The Decameron*

Period Art

1400–1465

"David" is the work of Renaissance artist Donatello (ca 1386–1466).

This seated Madonna was created by Lorenzo Ghiberti (1378–1455).

Ficino—would see themselves as the direct descendants of Dante, Petrarch, and Boccaccio, just as the first great Renaissance artist, Masaccio, drew his inspiration from the 14th-century painter and architect Giotto di Bondone.

Indeed, it was in art that Florence would make its most significant impact on Western civilization. As Ghiberti set about to cast his great door in bronze—followed 20 years later by another set for the Baptistery, this time on the east doors, which Michelangelo would call the Gates of Paradise—Brunelleschi traveled to Rome to study Roman buildings. In some cases, these were still remarkably intact. Other architects had preceded him, but Brunelleschi's exploration was different in that his inquiry was rooted in science. By carefully measuring extant monuments, Brunelleschi discovered the sophisticated system of proportions by which the Romans were able to build monumental designs so effortlessly—the same system that had eluded the architects of intervening periods, including the Romanesque. Furthermore, in the process of sketching these proportions on paper, Brunelleschi made another important discovery. This was the law of linear perspective, which would transform the search for realism in Renaissance art.

Soon after his return to Florence, Brunelleschi's grasp of classical models was put to the test. For more than a century, the central crossing of the Florence Cathedral had not been covered by a dome, because medieval technology could not execute Arnolfo di Cambio's design for a cupola covering a space as wide as 295 feet. Using his detailed studies of the second-century Pantheon in Rome, Brunelleschi created an innovative design of two superimposed shells of light sandstone, one supporting the other. In 1446, the dome was completed, and the use of Roman architectural engineering fully validated.

But Brunelleschi did not end there. He wondered whether it would be possible to create an entire Christian basilica using the Roman—ergo, pagan—architectural vernac-

TOP: *"The Sacrifice of Isaac" was a competitive design submitted by Filippo Brunelleschi (1377–1446).*
BOTTOM: *"The Sacrifice of Isaac" was a competitive design submitted by Lorenzo Ghiberti (1378–1455).*

1368
The Ming Dynasty forbids Christianity in China, ending the Franciscan mission

1377
Pope Gregory XI agrees to return to Rome

1378
The election of the Italian Pope Urban VI prompts French cardinals to elect Clement VII

1379
Three claimants compete for the throne of St. Peter

ular. For an age that had grown accustomed to Gothic cathedrals as the highest expression of Christian faith, this was a daring proposition indeed. Despite tremendous challenges, the architect succeeded in producing a church in Florence entirely based on Roman design principles, known as San Lorenzo. Though completed well after Brunelleschi's death in the 1480s, the church is a stunning example of how the superb proportional system of Greco-Roman engineering could produce a basilica of great beauty and spiritual power. With San Lorenzo (as well as the Santo Spirito, completed in 1481), Brunelleschi had created an architectural language that would govern church design until well into the 19th century.

> *We likewise define that the holy Apostolic See, and the Roman Pontiff, hold the primacy throughout the entire world.*
>
> ECUMENICAL COUNCIL OF FLORENCE, 1439

Up to this point, the visual arts had been governed by strict stereotypes that harked back to Byzantine precedent. For example, to depict Mary's Annunciation, the artist had to choose from five distinct iconographical motifs. The Florentine Renaissance loosed these bonds by empowering poets, artists, and sculptors to depict human beings realistically, based on observation rather than Church doctrine (though, it should be said, still *inspired* by God). Thus, Masaccio (1401–1428) and his collaborator Masolino (1383–1447) revolutionized painting with their fresco cycle in the Brancacci Chapel in the Church of Santa Maria del Carmine, which uses Brunelleschi's new linear perspective to create a panorama of striking

PERIOD ART

The Sacred Art of Leonardo da Vinci

Few artists of the High Renaissance produced sacred art as meticulously as Leonardo da Vinci (1452–1519), a man who joined his pursuit of naturalism in art to a broad quest for scientific knowledge. Born in 1452 in the village of Vinci, the product of a fling between a young notary, Ser Piero, and a farmer's maid, Leonardo did not receive the formal education that his half brothers, the legitimate offspring of Ser Piero, would enjoy. But his father recognized Leonardo's skill in draftsmanship and apprenticed him to the studio of Andrea del Verrocchio, a leading Florentine painter. Here, Leonardo received a thorough training in Quattrocento style and technique, which is evident in his early paintings of the Madonna, a popular motif in Florence. Inexplicably, Lorenzo de Medici, the leading arts patron of Florence, never took to Leonardo, preferring young stars like Michelangelo. Leonardo left for the Duchy of Milan, where he would transform Renaissance portraiture with his groundbreaking experiments in manipulating light and shade. Here, too, he produced a masterpiece of Renaissance sacred art, the fresco "The Last Supper." After the fall of the Duke of Milan, however, Leonardo lost his footing. He undertook various projects in Florence, such as the fresco "The Battle of Anghiari," but never finished them. Nevertheless, his fame secured him a comfortable place at the papal court in Rome, and later at the court of King François I in Amboise, France. His last major work is "The Virgin and Child with St. Anne," a deeply emotional exploration of Mary's motherhood and suffering, left unfinished at his death in 1519.

"The Virgin and Child with St. Anne" is a late masterpiece by Leonardo da Vinci (1452–1519).

1380 The German theologian Thomas à Kempis, author of *The Imitation of Christ*, is born

1382 John Wycliffe translates the Latin Bible into English

1386 The artist Donatello is born

1389 A protest by Christians in Cairo leads to a fresh wave of persecutions

realism. The rendition of Jesus and his Apostles as fully realized human beings would exert a strong influence on Michelangelo's famous fresco cycle for the Sistine Chapel.

The great sculptor Donatello (1386–1466), a close friend of Brunelleschi, carved the first freestanding statue of the Renaissance with "St. George" (1437), followed by "David" (ca 1444), commonly regarded as the first nude sculpture conceived entirely in the round since Antiquity.

The Vatican did not try to suppress this new infatuation with pagan art and architecture; on the contrary, Pope Nicholas V (r. 1447–1455) encouraged the new monumentality in art made possible by classical models. Pope Julius II (r. 1503–1513) was an avid collector of Greek and Roman sculpture; under his pontificate and that of his successor, Leo X (r. 1513–1521), Rome would become a center of European art, based on the work of titans such as Raphael (1483–1520) and Michelangelo Buonarroti (1475–1564).

The Byzantine Exodus

The Florentine Renaissance was fostered to a considerable degree by a "brain drain" from the Byzantine Empire, which by now had entered its final phase. In the 15th century, Constantinople came under increasing threat from the Ottoman Empire to the south. Despite a temporary thaw during the reign of Emperor Manuel II Palaiologos (r. 1391–1425) and Sultan Mehmed I (r. 1413–1421), relations between the Byzantine and Ottoman domains rapidly deteriorated. In 1430, Thessalonica fell to the Ottoman forces. In a frantic effort to save his domain, Manuel II's successor, John VIII Palaiologos (r. 1425–1448) traveled to Italy in 1438 to attend the Council of Florence and enter negotiations for a reconciliation of the Greek and Latin Churches under the supremacy of the pope.

The council had originally been called to settle various matters related to the Great Western Schism. The Council of Constance of 1417, which had ended the Schism and declared one legitimate pope, had also decreed that Church councils would

Opposite: The Baptistery of St. John in Florence was the focus of a design competition in 1401.

HISTORY AND POLITICS

The Fall of Constantinople

After the sack of Constantinople by Crusaders in 1204, the Byzantine Empire had splintered into a number of Greek mini-states, including the states of Nicaea and Epirus, while the capital itself remained under Crusader control. The Nicaeans ousted the Latin conquerors in 1261, restoring Byzantine independence, but in the subsequent decades new threats arose from Serbia to the northwest and the Ottoman Turks to the southeast. The plague that devastated Europe also struck hard in Constantinople; by some estimates, more than half of the city's population died. Thus weakened, the Empire was powerless to stem the encroachment of its enemies. By 1453, the Byzantine realm had shrunk to a few square miles of land around the capital, protected by the Theodosian Walls. The new Ottoman Sultan, Mehmed II (1444–1481) wasted no time in exploiting the opportunity. While the last Byzantine Emperor, Constantine XI (1449–1453) sent urgent appeals for help to the West, the Turks besieged Constantinople. A vast Ottoman army of more than 50,000 soldiers faced a ragtag defensive force of some 7,000. At the last minute, a fleet of Venetian galleys arrived, bringing no more than 2,000 men. Mehmed II introduced the first long-distance mortar in history, a huge cannon cast by a Hungarian engineer named Orban. As the Ottomans closed in on May 29, 1453, Constantine XI threw off his imperial cloak and joined the defenders on the ramparts, where he died in battle. Thus, Constantinople fell, and the Byzantine Empire ceased to exist.

A 15th-century Turkish portrait shows Sultan Mehmed II, the conqueror of Constantinople.

1401
The competition for the Florence Baptistery panel doors is held

1415
Cosimo de Medici takes de facto control of the Florentine Republic

1417
The Council of Constance ends the Schism by declaring for one legitimate pope

1424
Masaccio and Masolino begin work on the Brancacci Chapel frescoes

This famous statue of David is an early masterpiece by Renaissance artist Michelangelo Buonarroti (1475–1564).

henceforth have supremacy over decisions by the pope—not an unreasonable decision, given the trauma of the recent conflict between popes and antipopes. But the aim of the Council of Florence (first convened in Ferrara) was to reverse that decision and restore the principle of pontifical supremacy, now that the papal line had stabilized. The presence of the Byzantine Emperor gave this idea legitimacy as well as a sense of urgency. Indeed, despite significant theological differences, a formal treaty of reunification between the Greek and Latin Churches was signed by Patriarch Joseph in 1439. But this historical agreement was short-lived. Patriarch Joseph died only two days later, and upon the embassy's return to Constantinople, the terms of the union found near-universal opposition among citizens and clergy. Thus, the treaty was never formally ratified—neither by Byzantium nor by any of the other Eastern Churches—and so the schism remained in place. Many believed, as one leader declared, that "it was better to be ruled by the sultan's turban than by the pope's tiara."

The failure of Emperor John's diplomacy was the signal for many Byzantine intellectuals that the end was near. One of Byzantium's foremost Neoplatonic scholars, Georgius Gemistus Pletho (1355–1454), who had mesmerized

1430
Thessalonica falls to Ottoman forces

1431
The Council of Basel tries to impose a series of reforms on the papacy

1433
The Neoplatonic scholar Marsilio Ficino is born

1437
Donatello carves "St. George," the first freestanding statue of the Renaissance

the Council of Florence with an erudite exposition on the "Differences Between Aristotle and Plato," refused to leave Florence after the conclusion of the council. In the years to come, he would inspire many Florentine humanists with his passion for Platonic thought. One of these was a priest named Marsilio Ficino (1433–1499), an eminent scholar of Antiquity who had translated all of Plato's works into Latin and was a friend of Cosimo de Medici (1389–1464), the de facto chancellor of Florence. Cosimo and Marsilio began a Neoplatonic circle, which was soon joined by another Byzantine émigré, John Argyropoulos, and would influence a generation of Renaissance humanists. In 1462, Cosimo established the Platonic Academy in Florence, led by Ficino, which guaranteed that Florence would remain the intellectual center of the early Renaissance throughout the remainder of the Quattrocento (the 15th century).

Unlike the *philosophes* of a later era, these early humanists embraced the tenets of classical philosophy (as well as the Jewish

"Celebration of Plato's Birthday at Lorenzo il Magnifico's Villa" is the work of 19th-century Italian artist Luigi Mussini (1813–1888). It was painted in the 1860s.

1439
The Byzantine patriarch, Joseph, agrees to reunification of the Greek and Latin Churches

1440
The reunification treaty is repudiated by Constantinople

1444
Donatello completes the bronze "David," the first freestanding nude since Antiquity

1446
The dome of the Florence Cathedral is completed

Devotional Objects

1400–1600

The "Doni Tondo" was painted by Michelangelo Buonarroti (1475–1564).

This ciborium reveals the transition between Gothic and Renaissance styles.

This 16th-century rosary belonged to Mary, Queen of Scots.

kabbalah and other Eastern wisdom sources) as an extension of their Christian universe, rather than its replacement. Like the scholastics of the 13th century, the Quattrocento humanists believed that all truth about the workings of nature and the condition of man ultimately stemmed from a divine source. What remained, therefore, was for humanists to harmonize these disparate worlds into a corpus of human knowledge.

Pletho and Argyropoulos were not the only émigrés to seek refuge on the Italian peninsula after the fall of Constantinople. Scores of musicians, poets, astronomers,

> *I listen to his precepts with incredible pleasure, because he is Greek, because he is an Athenian, and because he is Demetrius.*
>
> A STUDENT OF DEMETRIUS CHALCONDYLES, 1450

writers, architects, scientists, and artisans followed, making an incalculable contribution to the flowering of the Italian, and later European, Renaissance. Greek scholar Demetrius Chalcondyles (1423–1511) established a Greek-language school in Rome, restoring the use of Greek as a language of scholarship in Italy. He also published the first printed editions of Homer and Isocrates, while lecturing in Greek philosophy at the universities of Padua, Florence, and Milan. By the 16th century, the population of Greek refugees in Rome had grown so large that Pope Gregory XIII was persuaded to establish the Greek Pontifical College, open to all Eastern refugees who were prepared to embrace the Latin rites. The pope's aim went beyond pure charity. With the Greek college, he hoped to train a young, Greek-speaking cadre that one day could return to their native lands and actively proselytize among the Eastern Churches, with the hope of bringing about a reunion.

Venice, too, experienced a wave of Greek-speaking immigrants, not only in the lagoon city itself but also among its possessions in Crete and along the Dalmatian coast. Crete, in particular, would become a magnet for renowned Byzantine icon painters. It rapidly became a new artistic center of Greek Orthodox sacred art—a position that, some claim, it has held to this day.

The Crisis of the Renaissance Papacy

In 1431, the Council of Basel had tried to exploit the weakened state of the papacy to push through a number of reforms, aided by the fact that many bishops stayed away. The council's purpose was to curb the authority (and excesses) of the Holy See, to distribute power and funding among the dioceses and provincial councils, and to curtail papal patronage (including the granting of benefices, such as offices and estates). The practice of annates, the yielding of all first-year profits of a benefice to the papal treasury, was abolished. The process for electing the pope was modified, while the jurisdiction of the pontifical courts was sharply reduced.

These attempts to reform the Church from within were short-lived. In Rome, a small group of powerful Roman families—principally the Rovere, the Borgia, and the

OPPOSITE: *An interior view of St. Peter's Basilica in Rome, which was begun in 1506 and completed in 1626.*

1447 **The papacy of Pope Nicholas V begins**

1451 **Christopher Columbus is born**

1452 **Leonardo da Vinci is born as the illegitimate son of Ser Piero, a notary**

1456 **A hurricane ravages Tuscany**

S·PETRI GLORIAE SIXTVS·PP·V·
AEDIFICA

Medici—gained control of the College of Cardinals through threats and bribery. This all but guaranteed that the popes of the Renaissance were men bent on enriching and empowering their families, rather than on making urgent reforms in the governance of the Church. On the one hand, this meant that the arts flourished under their patronage. By 1513, with Michelangelo, Raphael, and Leonardo da Vinci working at the Vatican, Rome had eclipsed Florence as the reigning center of European art, and would retain this position well into the Baroque era, until the accession of Louis XIV to the French throne. But politically, the focus of the papacy changed as well. With little interest in theological matters but deeply immersed in the power politics of the Italian peninsula, the Renaissance popes injected themselves into territorial disputes while trying to expand the geographic reach of the Papal States. The fact that many powerful city-states of the Quattrocento—Ferrara, Milan, Florence, Perugia—were either in

An anonymous Spanish panel depicts the Borgia Pope Alexander VI, one of the Renaissance popes.

1462
Cosimo de Medici establishes the Platonic Academy in Florence

1464
Cosimo de Medici dies and is succeeded by his son Piero "The Gouty"

1466
Extensive flooding of the Arno causes great damage in Florence

1469
Piero de Medici dies and is succeeded by his son Lorenzo de Medici, "The Magnificent"

economic decline or under foreign occupation abetted this ambition.

The vast expenditures in the military and the arts required resources that the papacy did not have, dependent as it was on contributions from the faithful. In response, the popes turned to new financial instruments to fund their zest for aesthetic and military glory. Among the most notorious of these gambits, in addition to the outright sale of ecclesiastical offices, was the purveying of so-called indulgences. Traditionally, an indulgence was an instrument that, while not granting a Christian forgiveness of his sins, alleviated the penance that he would have to suffer either during his lifetime or during his stay in purgatory. According to Catholic doctrine, purgatory was the intermediate state between death and admission to heaven. In early Christianity, indulgences had been granted on the basis

OPPOSITE: An anonymous painting of Vatican Square shows the double colonnade designed by Gian Lorenzo Bernini (1598–1680) and completed in 1667.

Emperor Constantine laid the foundations for the first St. Peter's in the early fourth century. The church fell into disrepair and was torn down. In 1506, construction began on a new ST. PETER'S BASILICA *in Rome. It opened 120 years later, in 1626.*

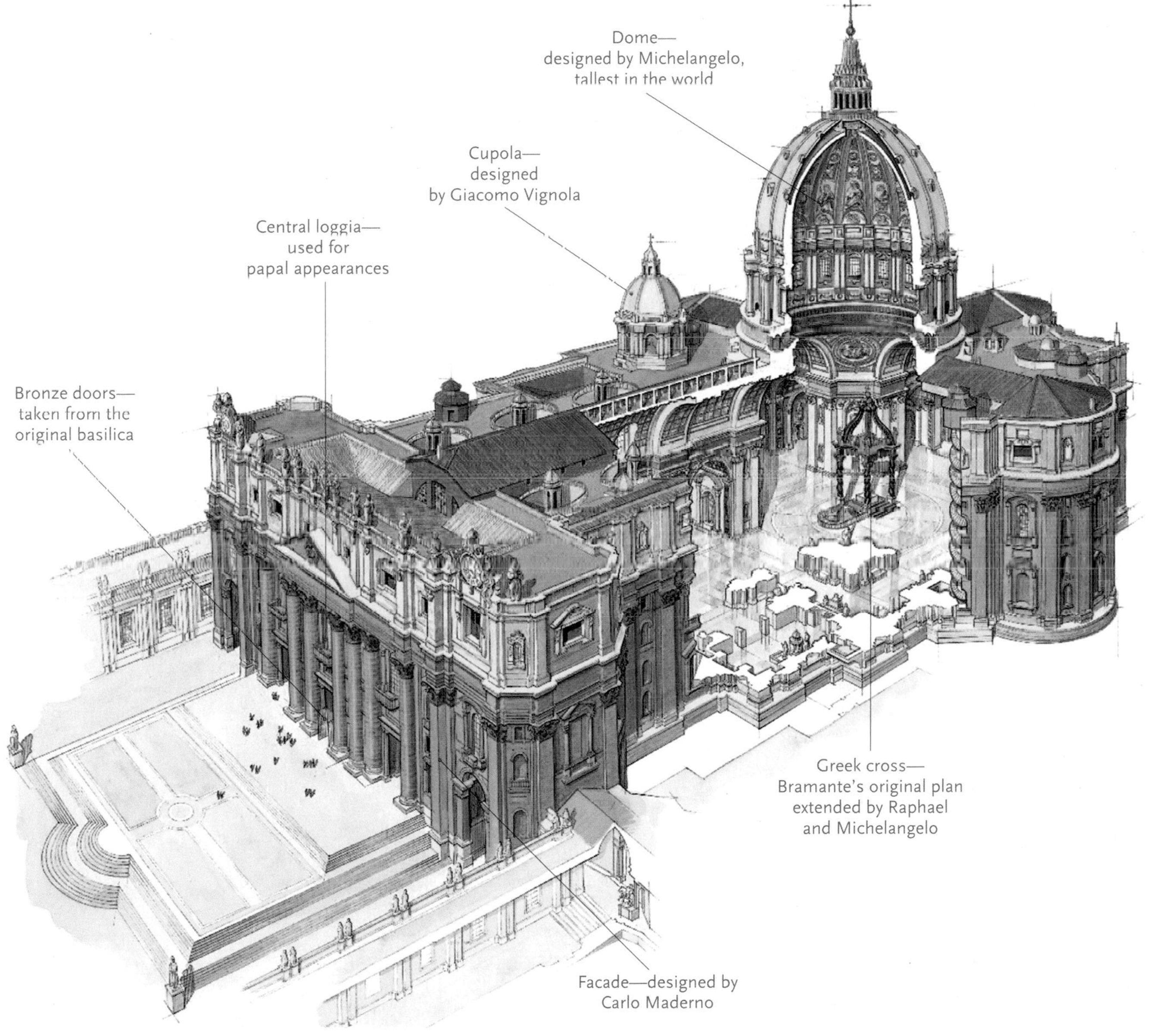

1469
Niccolò Machiavelli is born

1472
Dante's *Divina Commedia* is published

1472
Copernicus is born

1475
Michelangelo is born

Why does the pope, whose wealth today is greater than the wealth of the richest Crassus, build the basilica of Saint Peter with the money of poor believers?

MARTIN LUTHER, 1517

of extraordinary charitable works or a heroic defense of the faith. For example, martyrs destined to die in the arena were granted indulgences as a matter of course, as were Crusaders headed for battle.

During the Renaissance, the popes realized that the outright sale of such indulgences could become a very profitable source of income. The Borgia pope Alexander VI (r. 1492–1503) used the proceeds to finance his lavish support of the arts. It was during his reign that the architect Bramante (1444–1514), Raphael, Michelangelo, and other leading artists were invited to the Vatican. Pope Julius II continued to sell indulgences to raise funds to build the new St. Peter's Basilica. Pope Leo X, too, sent papal commissioners throughout Europe to find buyers. One of these vendors was a Dominican friar named Johann Tetzel, who in 1516 began to offer indulgences for sale in Germany. This infuriated a priest and theologian at the University of Wittenberg in Saxony, who was repelled by the idea that wealthy individuals could "buy off" their repentance (or that of their relatives) in purgatory. His name was Martin Luther (1483–1546).

The cycle of frescoes on the Sistine Chapel ceiling is a masterpiece by Renaissance artist Michelangelo Buonarroti (1475–1564). The chapel is in Vatican City's Apostolic Palace, the official residence of the pope.

QUAE SACRORUM SEDES
EMENDATORUM BELLI
DIRUTA FLAMMIS III.
EID. OCTOBR. CIϽIϽCCLX
MAXIMO NOS MOERO-
RE AFFECIT.
ANNI X. FINE PROS-
PERE PERACTO NUNC
PULCHRIOR SURREXIT
SOLI DEO CONSECRA-
TA VIII. EID. AUG.
CIϽIϽCCLXX.
FRIDERICVS · GVILELMVS · IV · REX · PORTAM
M · OCTOBR · D · XXXI · INDVLGENTIIS · ROMANIS
REFORMATIONIS · SACRORVM · PRAENVNTIAS
VALVAS · EX · AERE · FIERI · ATQVE · ILLAS · THESES
IN QVA MARTINVS LVTHERVS A DOM MDXVII
IMPVGNANDIS THESES AFFIXIT LXXXXV
INCENDIO VASTATAM REFECIT SIGNIS EXORNAVIT
INSCRIBI IVSSIT A DOM MDCCCLVII

The Ninety-Five Theses

On October 31, 1517, Luther sent the Bishop of Mainz a copy of his Ninety-Five Theses, which attacked indulgences as theologically invalid. The whole point of confession and penance, Luther argued, was that Christians could contemplate the error of their sinful behavior. Furthermore, only God had the power to remit sins—not the pope. To underscore his point, Luther nailed his Theses to the door of the castle church at Wittenberg. Unbeknownst to Luther, however, Bishop Albert of Mainz was deeply in debt and was hoping to receive a portion of the proceeds from Tetzel's fund-raising. He therefore ignored the letter.

Indulgences were not the only practice denounced by Luther. He also exposed the exploitation of gullible pilgrims who flocked to Saxony to see the largest concentration of relics in all of Europe. By one count, the region held more than 19,000 relics, including such items as "mother's milk" from the Virgin Mary and straw from the Bethlehem manger.

Initially, Luther had no intention of creating a new religious movement. Instead, he strenuously argued for reform, by urging the Church to return to the essential spiritual tenets espoused in the Gospels. But his Theses spread through Europe like wildfire, kindling a long-suppressed resentment against the willful abuses of the Catholic clergy and the papacy. Luther's vision tapped into other currents as well. The vast majority of believers were bewildered by the sudden Renaissance zeal to emulate pagan culture. As early as the 1380s, lay movements in the Low Countries and Germany had clamored for a return to simplicity and piety "in imitation of Christ," as Thomas à Kempis (1380–1471) proposed. In Prague, Jan Hus (1369–1415), too, accused the Church of abandoning the principles of the Bible. At Oxford, John Wycliffe (ca 1330–1384) had fulminated against the abuses of the papal court in Avignon and the worldly possessions of many of the English clergy. Elsewhere in Europe, humanism fanned

OPPOSITE: Martin Luther nailed his Ninety-Five Theses to the door of the Wittenberg Castle Church in 1517.

SAINTS AND CLERICS

Martin Luther

Martin Luther was born in Eisleben, Saxony, in 1483, the son of a leaseholder of various copper mines. Martin studied the usual medieval curriculum of rhetoric, grammar, and logic, and at age 19 entered the University of Erfurt, where he earned a master's degree in 1505. Martin reluctantly enrolled in law school while preferring to read the classics, including Aristotle. On July 2, 1505, he was struck by lightning while riding on horseback. Deeply frightened, he pledged to become a monk and entered an Augustinian monastery. But monastic life proved unsatisfying; despite long hours of fasting, confessions, and self-denial, he later said he "lost touch with Christ the Savior and Comforter." Ordained a priest, Martin was offered a position to teach theology at the newly founded University of Wittenberg in 1508. Five years later, upon earning his doctorate, he became professor of biblical exegesis, a position that he kept until his death. It was at Wittenberg that, based on his experience in the Augustinian monastery, he developed his doctrine of justification: that people can only receive God's grace through faith, rather than through religious ritual or charitable works. This would become a key tenet of Lutheranism.

In 1523, at age 41, Martin married a 26-year-old nun, Katharina von Bora, in protest against compulsory celibacy. She bore him six children. From 1526 onward, Martin was wholly devoted to building a new confessional church, including the development of a new Lutheran liturgy. He died after a prolonged illness in 1546 in the city of Eisleben, where he was born.

Lucas Cranach the Elder (1472–1553) painted this portrait of Martin Luther.

1478 — **During the Pazzi Conspiracy, Lorenzo's brother Giuliano is killed. Terrible retributions follow**

1481 — **Brunelleschi's San Spirito church is completed**

1481 — **Leonardo da Vinci paints his first masterpiece, "The Adoration of the Magi"**

1482 — **The monk Savonarola begins his fiery sermons in Florence**

"Luther Preaches Using His Bible Translation While Imprisoned in Wartenburg" is the work of Hugo Vogel (1855–1934).

a long-simmering resentment against the grip of the Church on public life.

Thus, Luther soon became the center of a group of reformers who wanted to move beyond the question of indulgences and other practices to tackle a host of other grievances, including the authority of the Church. The invention of the printing press in 1450 enabled these reformers to publish their views in pamphlets that were avidly read throughout the Continent.

The situation then escalated rapidly. In 1518, Luther was summoned to Rome to explain himself, but he refused to comply. Prince Frederick of Saxony took Luther under his protection, which gave Pope Leo X pause; he did not want a conflict with the German states. But when Luther refused to recant, the pope issued an encyclical in 1520 that declared Luther's Ninety-Five Theses to be a work of heresy. Luther responded by writing three treatises that would lay the foundation of the Lutheran Church. He argued that the saving grace of God's love could be received through faith and faith alone, rather than through good works, as the Catholic Church had preached. The true source of salvation, he preached, is the Gospel; only through the Gospel message could souls be saved. Therefore, only the three sacraments ordained by God in the Bible—baptism,

1483
Raphael is born

1483
Charles VIII is crowned King of France

1484
Sandro Botticelli paints "The Birth of Venus"

1492
Christopher Columbus sails on his voyage to the New World

We further order in this edict that all Jews and Jewesses of whatever age that reside in our domain and territories leave with their sons and daughters, servants and relatives large or small, of all ages.

ALHAMBRA DECREE, 1492

confession (or "reconciliation"), and the Eucharist—should be considered holy sacraments. The other Catholic sacraments, including marriage, confirmation, holy orders, and the anointing of the sick, were simply Christian practices, rather than instruments of divine grace. Furthermore, Luther called upon German princes to stop paying ecclesiastic tribute to Rome, to support an end to compulsory celibacy for clerics, and to become actively involved in creating an indigenous German Church.

The response was extraordinary. Many German kings and princes had long resented the dominant role of the Catholic Church in almost every aspect of life. Now, Luther's call gave them the opportunity to radically reorder the way the Church would operate in their domains. When, in 1526, the rulers of the 300-odd German states were given the choice to opt for either Catholicism or Lutheranism, a majority chose to create an indigenous Lutheran Church. This led to a war between German Protestant princes and the Holy Roman Emperor, Charles V, but the Augsburg Peace Treaty of 1555 affirmed their right to establish the religious character of their lands as they saw fit. Thus, Germany was cleft by a division between a largely Protestant north and a predominantly Catholic south that would not be healed until its political unification in the 19th century.

The Spread of the Reformation

From Germany, the reform movement spilled into the Low Countries, which were still under Spanish rule. Spanish King Charles V (r. 1519–1556) did not intervene when Lutheranism gained a massive following in Holland, but when his son Philip II (r. 1556–1598) used the Inquisition to enforce Catholic observance, the seven provinces in the north rose in revolt. After an 80-year war, these Dutch provinces gained their independence and chose the Dutch Reformed Church as the official denomination of the new republic. Southern Holland and the territory now known as Belgium, however, remained under Spanish rule and retained their Catholic character. Meanwhile, a theologian named Hans Tausen introduced Luther's views to Denmark, and from there Lutheranism would spread to Sweden and Norway in the subsequent centuries.

As the Reformation grew, other movements sprang up, including one inspired by French theologian John Calvin (1509–1564), who fled to Switzerland to organize the movement known as Calvinism. Calvin broke with Luther over a number of issues, including the celebration of the Eucharist (which in his view was meant to be symbolic) and the use of paintings and music in worship. Under his leadership, Geneva became the center of Calvinism.

In France, the Reformation emboldened King Charles VIII (r. 1483–1498) to invade Italy. He hoped to secure his claim on Naples and to be recognized as the new Holy Roman Emperor. While that gambit failed, a later successor, King Francis I (r. 1515–1547),

SAINTS AND CLERICS

Savonarola

This portrait of the monk Savonarola was painted by Fra Bartolommeo (1472–1517).

A devout Dominican friar, Girolamo Savonarola (1452–1498) was repelled by the sudden embrace of pagan motifs by early Renaissance artists and humanists as well as the excesses of the papacy. Shortly after his arrival in Florence in 1482, he launched a series of sermons that attacked the new "paganism" in the city, and predicted that if Florence—and much of Italy—did not return to traditional Christian obedience, the Church would suffer divine retribution. Florence rallied to his words; many priceless Renaissance paintings and books were burned in a "bonfire of the vanities." The friar also turned his wrath on the Medicis, the de facto rulers of Florence, which contributed to the ouster of Piero de Medici after the invasion by French King Charles VIII in 1494. Savonarola emerged as the new ruler of Florence, but his reign was brief. He was arrested on charges of heresy by officials of Pope Alexander VI and put to death.

1492
The Borgia pope Alexander VI begins his reign

1494
French King Charles VIII invades Italy and occupies Naples

1494
The Medici are ousted from Florence

1495
Leonardo da Vinci begins "The Last Supper" in Milan

HISTORY AND POLITICS

Thomas More

This portrait of Thomas More is by Hans Holbein (ca 1497–1543) in 1527.

Like his close friend Erasmus, English humanist and chancellor Thomas More (1478–1535) was not blind to the abuses within the Church, but he sought to correct them through gentle satire and erudite criticism, rather than radical calls for reform. The son of a judge, More served in the household of the Archbishop of Canterbury, John Morton, who sent him to Oxford University. Though tempted to become a monk, More stood for Parliament in 1504 and married a young woman named Jane Colt the following year. He gained Europe-wide renown for his book *Utopia* of 1516, which depicts an ideal society ruled by law, reason, and religion, and succeeded Cardinal Wolsey as Lord Chancellor in 1529. By then, his house in Chelsea had become a leading center of humanist learning. But More refused to support King Henry VIII in his quest of a papal annulment of his marriage to Queen Catherine. He was charged with treason in 1534 and beheaded the next year.

"Sixtus IV and Torquemada, Pope and Inquisitor" was painted by French artist Jean-Paul Laurens (1838–1921) in 1882.

was able to pressure Pope Leo X into accepting the French king as de facto head of the Church in France. By that time, Calvinism had made considerable inroads in France. When Francis suspended the persecution of Calvin's followers—known as Huguenots—the number of Calvinist churches grew rapidly. This would ultimately spark a bloody civil war in the second part of the 16th century, during the rule of King Henry of Navarre (1589–1610) and his consort, Marguerite de Valois (r. 1589–1599), as we will see in the next chapter.

Only Spain was able to resist the Reformation. With a large population of Muslims and Jews, Spain had traditionally been a tolerant nation. But this changed when the marriage of King Ferdinand II (r. 1479–1516) and Queen Isabella (r. 1474–1504) led to the merger of the kingdoms of Castile and Aragon in 1479. The royal couple was determined to transform the Iberian realm into a strong nation-state on the model of France and England, with Roman Catholicism as its unifying force. In 1492, they issued the notorious Alhambra Decree, which effectively forced non-Christians to either accept baptism or leave the country. Thousands of Jews and Muslims who had lived in Spain for generations were forced to flee. In that same year, Ferdinand and Isabella conquered Granada, the last Muslim holdout on the Iberian peninsula, and their dream of a religiously "pure" nation lay within their grasp.

1498
Charles VIII is succeeded by King Louis XII

1498
Savonarola is burned at the stake

1502
Piero Soderini is appointed *gonfaloniere* of the Florentine Republic for life

1503
The papacy of Pope Julius II begins

If God spares my life,
I will cause a boy that drives
a plough to know more
of Scripture than [the Pope] does.

WILLIAM TYNDALE, EDITOR OF THE FIRST ENGLISH BIBLE

To ensure that the *conversos*—Jews and Muslims who had agreed to be converted—remained true to the Christian faith, the Spanish Crown secured Pope Sixtus II's permission to activate the Inquisition in Castile. Until he was restrained by Pope Alexander VI, Grand Inquisitor and Dominican priest Tomás de Torquemada (1420–1498) is believed to have ordered the execution, usually by burning, of some 2,000 Spaniards accused of heresy.

The Reformation in England

In England, King Henry VIII (r. 1509–1547) had proudly worn his papal title, Fidei Defensor ("Defender of the Faith") while married to Queen Catherine, the daughter of King Ferdinand and Queen Isabella of Spain. But after nearly 20 years, when the Queen had still not borne him any surviving heirs save for a daughter, Mary, King Henry planned to set her aside in favor of a lady he had befriended at court named Anne Boleyn. Once it became clear that Pope Clement VII (r. 1523–1534) would not grant him an annulment, King Henry aligned himself with reformist circles in his realm, of which Anne Boleyn was a prominent member. In 1533, Henry and his chancellor, Thomas Cromwell, pushed through the Act of Succession, which declared his marriage to Catherine of Aragon unlawful and made the King the head of the newly formed Church of England, or Anglican Church. The clergy were ordered to pledge their loyalty to the King, rather than the pope.

Thus empowered, Henry was able to marry Anne Boleyn, but Cromwell, a fervent reformer, pushed for the wholesale suppression of English abbeys and monasteries. For hundreds of years, these abbeys had sustained much of the social and economic fabric of England. Shortly after

LIFE AND TIMES

The Printing Press

Until 1487, books were essentially bound, handwritten originals, copied laboriously from a source, as had been the case since before Antiquity. The first attempt to mechanize the book-copying process took place in China, where Bi Sheng experimented with various movable woodblock techniques during the Han Dynasty (206 B.C.E.–220 C.E.). But in Europe, the invention of the printing press is usually attributed to Johannes Gutenberg around 1450. Gutenberg was not a bookbinder, but a goldsmith who developed a special hand mold to rapidly produce movable metal type in a uniform style—a typeface, in short. The typeface itself was designed by Peter Schöffer, who created a type of 202 characters inspired by the German Gothic style of script. Other regions soon developed their own type styles; in 1470, Venetian typographers developed the "Roman"-type font.

The Renaissance printing presses revolutionized the distribution of new religious and political ideas, and broke the monopoly on knowledge among the titled and wealthy classes. One press could produce some 3,500 pages a day, not only for books but also for pamphlets that could be produced cheaply by the thousands. It has been estimated that by 1500, some 20 million printed books were in circulation. While the printing press was a key factor in the rapid spread of the Reformation throughout Europe, it also stimulated the acceptance of vernacular languages, replacing Latin as the international language of learning. For example, John Calvin's book *Institutes of the Christian Religion* (1536) was published in a French edition in 1541, which ensured its popularity throughout Europe.

This view shows a complete suite of 16th-century Flemish printing presses.

1506 **Bramante begins work on the new St. Peter's Basilica in Rome**

1508 **Michelangelo begins the ceiling frescoes for the Sistine Chapel**

1511 **Erasmus writes *The Praise of Folly***

1512 **The Medici seize power in Florence once again**

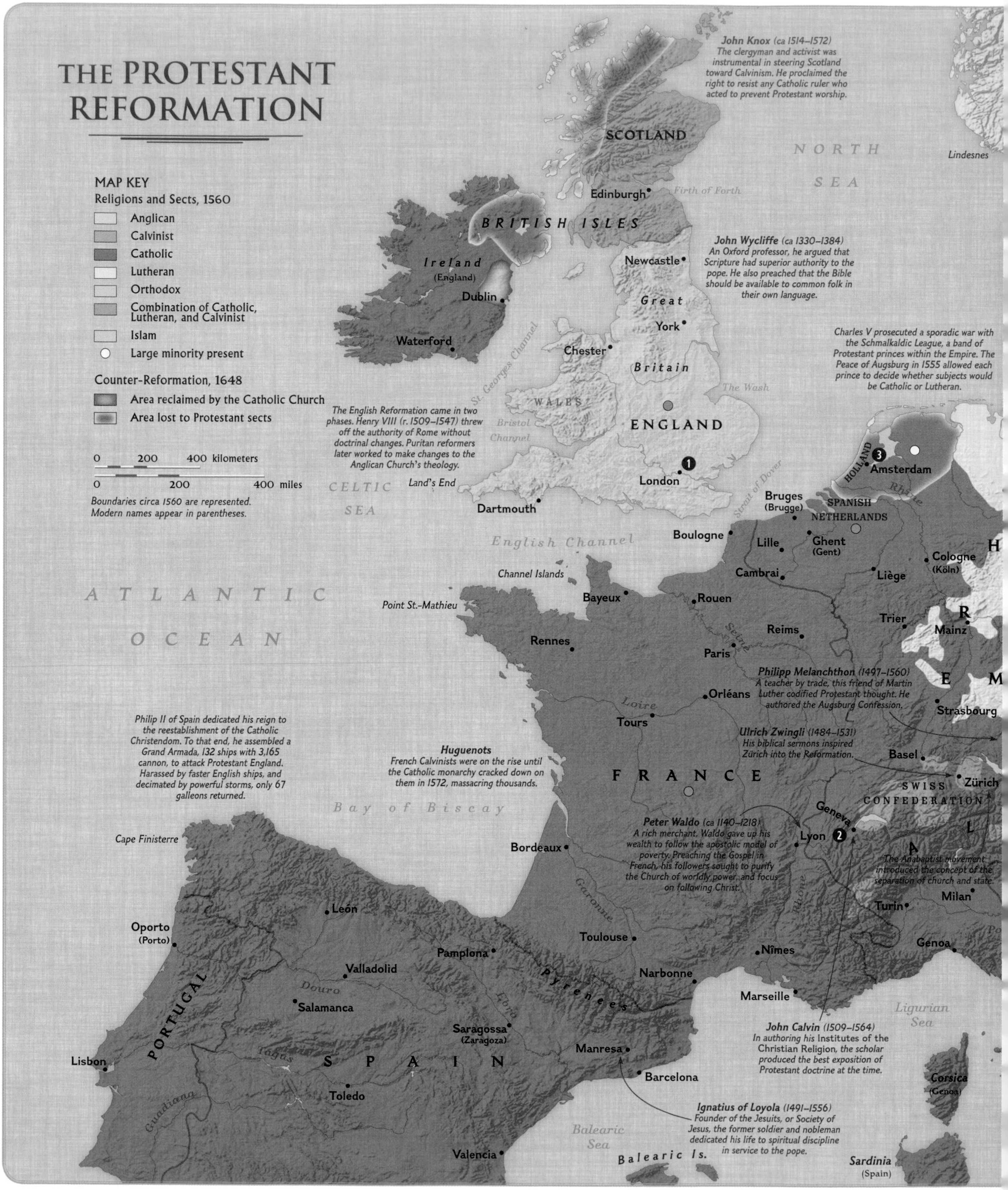
THE PROTESTANT REFORMATION
MAP KEY
Religions and Sects, 1560
Anglican
Calvinist
Catholic
Lutheran
Orthodox
Combination of Catholic, Lutheran, and Calvinist
Islam
Large minority present
Counter-Reformation, 1648
Area reclaimed by the Catholic Church
Area lost to Protestant sects
0 200 400 kilometers
0 200 400 miles
Boundaries circa 1560 are represented. Modern names appear in parentheses.
John Knox (ca 1514–1572)
The clergyman and activist was instrumental in steering Scotland toward Calvinism. He proclaimed the right to resist any Catholic ruler who acted to prevent Protestant worship.
John Wycliffe (ca 1330–1384)
An Oxford professor, he argued that Scripture had superior authority to the pope. He also preached that the Bible should be available to common folk in their own language.
Charles V prosecuted a sporadic war with the Schmalkaldic League, a band of Protestant princes within the Empire. The Peace of Augsburg in 1555 allowed each prince to decide whether subjects would be Catholic or Lutheran.
The English Reformation came in two phases. Henry VIII (r. 1509–1547) threw off the authority of Rome without doctrinal changes. Puritan reformers later worked to make changes to the Anglican Church's theology.
Philipp Melanchthon (1497–1560)
A teacher by trade, this friend of Martin Luther codified Protestant thought. He authored the Augsburg Confession.
Ulrich Zwingli (1484–1531)
His biblical sermons inspired Zürich into the Reformation.
Philip II of Spain dedicated his reign to the reestablishment of the Catholic Christendom. To that end, he assembled a Grand Armada, 132 ships with 3,165 cannon, to attack Protestant England. Harassed by faster English ships, and decimated by powerful storms, only 67 galleons returned.
Huguenots
French Calvinists were on the rise until the Catholic monarchy cracked down on them in 1572, massacring thousands.
Peter Waldo (ca 1140–1218)
A rich merchant, Waldo gave up his wealth to follow the apostolic model of poverty. Preaching the Gospel in French, his followers sought to purify the Church of worldly power, and focus on following Christ.
The Anabaptist movement introduced the concept of the separation of church and state.
John Calvin (1509–1564)
In authoring his Institutes of the Christian Religion, the scholar produced the best exposition of Protestant doctrine at the time.
Ignatius of Loyola (1491–1556)
Founder of the Jesuits, or Society of Jesus, the former soldier and nobleman dedicated his life to spiritual discipline in service to the pope.
SCOTLAND
NORTH SEA
Lindesnes
Edinburgh
Firth of Forth
BRITISH ISLES
Ireland (England)
Dublin
Waterford
Newcastle
Great Britain
York
Chester
WALES
ENGLAND
The Wash
St. Georges Channel
Bristol Channel
London
CELTIC SEA
Land's End
Dartmouth
Strait of Dover
HOLLAND
Amsterdam
Rhine
Bruges (Brugge)
SPANISH NETHERLANDS
Boulogne
Lille
Ghent (Gent)
Cologne (Köln)
Liège
Cambrai
English Channel
Channel Islands
ATLANTIC OCEAN
Point St.-Mathieu
Bayeux
Rouen
Trier
Mainz
Reims
Seine
Rennes
Paris
Orléans
Loire
Tours
Strasbourg
Basel
Zürich
SWISS CONFEDERATION
FRANCE
Geneva
Lyon
Bay of Biscay
Cape Finisterre
Bordeaux
Garonne
Rhône
Turin
Milan
Genoa
León
Oporto (Porto)
Pamplona
Toulouse
Nîmes
Valladolid
Narbonne
Pyrenees
Marseille
Ligurian Sea
Douro
Ebro
Salamanca
PORTUGAL
Saragossa (Zaragoza)
Manresa
Tagus
SPAIN
Lisbon
Barcelona
Toledo
Guadiana
Corsica (Genoa)
Balearic Sea
Balearic Is.
Valencia
Sardinia (Spain)

2 Geneva, Switzerland St. Pierre Cathedral was converted to the Swiss Reformed Church and used by John Calvin.

1 London, England Westminster Abbey received the status of cathedral to prevent its demolition.

3 Amsterdam, the Netherlands Catholic "Nieuwe Kerk" was rededicated to the Calvinist Dutch Reformed Church.

SCRIPTURE AND FAITH

Calvinist Doctrine

Catholic doctrine stipulated that people must choose between salvation or sin, because God gave them free will. Calvinism, by contrast, espoused the idea of predestination, whereby God decided who would receive salvation "without respect to their works." Only the "elect," John Calvin taught, would go to heaven, while all others would face damnation. Martin Luther also believed that the elect are predestined to salvation, but argued that all devout Christians were elect by virtue of their faith. Furthermore, Luther believed that the Church should be subordinate to the state, whereas Calvin argued that the Church should be separate from, and superior to, secular government. Local Calvinist congregations welcomed the involvement of laymen. This appealed to many in Europe who chafed under the autocratic rule of hereditary monarchies and the Catholic Church. Calvinism became the state religion in Scotland and Holland, and eventually moved to America in the form of Presbyterianism.

This portrait of John Calvin is by Ary Scheffer (1795–1858).

the Dissolution of the Lesser Monasteries Act was passed in 1536, scores of monks and nuns were forcefully evicted.

But Henry soon tired of Anne Boleyn. After she was executed on trumped-up charges of infidelity, the King once again warmed to the traditional Catholic rite, in part because his next consort, Jane Seymour, was believed to be a devout Catholic. In the coming decades, England would continue to oscillate between Reformist and Catholic sentiments, driven by Henry's whim. Nevertheless, the King's rule did see the publication of the first Bible in English in 1539, as well as the *Book of Common Prayer,* published during the reign of his son, Edward VI, in 1549. Over time, the Anglican Church would retain much of the original Catholic liturgy, albeit in a thoroughly English mold.

Other Protestant churches were founded by the Swiss preacher Ulrich Zwingli and the Scottish clergyman John Knox. The term "Protestantism" is rooted in the Latin *protestantem,* he who "publicly declares." What these Protestant movements shared with Luther and Calvin was a belief in the redemptive power of "*sola gratia, sola fide, sola scriptura*"—only grace, faith, and Scripture. This was a sharp break with Catholicism, which tied grace to good works and dispensed the teachings of Scripture only through clergy and the elaborate edifice of Catholic doctrine.

The king's majesty justly and rightfully is and ought to be supreme head of the Church of England.

THE ACT OF SUPREMACY

Protestantism did not come about without bloodshed. In German lands, thousands of peasants seized on Luther's tenets as justification to shake off serfdom. The German princes bloodily suppressed these protests. By some estimates, more than 100,000 peasants were massacred. One of their leaders, radical Protestant theologian Thomas Müntzer, was tortured and beheaded. In the years to come, the conflict between Catholic and Protestant communities would steadily tear apart the age-old social and political fabric of European Christendom in a series of devastating conflicts. ■

ABOVE: *Anne of Cleves was painted at her betrothal to Henry VIII in 1539 by Hans Holbein (ca 1497–1543).*

OPPOSITE: *This state portrait of King Henry VIII was painted by Hans Holbein (ca 1497–1543) in 1540.*

1513
The papacy of Medici Pope Leo X begins

1513
Michelangelo, Raphael, and Leonardo da Vinci are all working in Rome

1516
Johann Tetzel, a Dominican friar, offers indulgences for sale in Germany

1517
Martin Luther nails a copy of his Ninety-Five Theses on the castle church at Wittenberg

ANNO · ÆTATIS ·
· SVÆ · XLIX ·

9
CHAPTER

THE AGE OF DISCOVERY

1500-1650

Gold is a treasure, and he who possesses it can do all he wants while helping souls into paradise.

CHRISTOPHER COLUMBUS

From the early 16th century onward, European explorers pushed the boundaries of European Christianity into the far corners of the world, discovering new lands and civilizations in a way that would have a profound impact on the course of human history.

The reasons for the sudden zest for exploration were manifold. The fall of the Byzantine Empire to the Ottoman Turks forced European merchants to identify new sea routes to the east that bypassed Muslim territory. That quest, in turn, was necessitated by the rapid growth in the demand for spices from the East Indies, as Asia was called. Beginning in the late Middle Ages, spices had become increasingly important not only for medical, culinary, and cosmetic purposes, but also as a food preservative, a new need resulting from the rapid growth of the European population. By the 17th century, the quest for spices to vouchsafe food supplies had become such a priority that a fierce competition known as the Spice Race ensued among the European powers. The goal was to capture as many resource-rich territories in Southeast Asia as possible, in addition to strategic victualing stations along the way. This quest would eventually evolve into the creation of large colonial empires in the 19th century.

ABOVE: *Seventeenth-century explorers used astrolabes such as this as celestial navigation devices.*

OPPOSITE: *This view shows the scenic northern coast of the Ponta Delgada, Madeira.*

PRECEDING PAGES: *"The First Landing of Christopher Columbus" was painted by Dióscoro Teófilo Puebla Tolín (1831–1901) in 1862.*

Two other motives played a role. One was the avid search for gold and other precious metals to finance the growth of Europe's leading nation-states. It was the search for gold that would bring Spanish *conquistadores* to the shores of the Americas and lead Portuguese navigators to prowl the coasts of Africa. Such ambitions, however, were often concealed under the lofty goal of bringing the civilizing grace of Christianity to the remote regions of the Earth. When, upon his arrival in India in 1498, Portuguese explorer Vasco da Gama (ca 1460–1524) was queried about his intentions, his laconic response was "Christians and spices."

The Age of Discovery could not have come about without significant technological innovations rooted in the scientific curiosity of the Renaissance. Until the 1500s, most international trade was serviced by Venetian galleys capable of carrying as much as 250 tons of cargo. But these galleys were designed to sail in the coastal waters of the Mediterranean. They were not sufficiently seaworthy to cross the Atlantic, let alone the Pacific. Such blue-water vessels only emerged in 1450 in the form of the Portuguese caravel, a development usually credited to Prince Henry the Navigator (1394–1460), the third son of King John I of Portugal. Unlike Venetian galleys or other rigid single-mast ships, the caravel used two or three lateen sails so as to be able to tack into the prevailing westerly wind of the Atlantic. This gave Portuguese seamen

This anonymous portrait from ca 1524 is believed to depict Portuguese explorer Vasco da Gama.

OPPOSITE: *"Henry the Navigator, Prince of Portugal" is the work of the 15th-century artist Nuno Gonçalves.*

A detail of a terrestrial globe shows a Portuguese caravel, a highly maneuverable sailing ship, from around 1683.

1415
The Portuguese capture Ceuta on the northern African coast

1420s
The Portuguese establish settlements in the Azores

1450
Portuguese invent the caravel

1460
Portuguese explorer Vasco da Gama is born

a major technological advantage, notwithstanding the caravel's limited cargo capacity, and explains why Portugal would dominate the first phase of European exploration well into the 16th century. For navigation, the Portuguese experimented with astrolabes perfected by Muslim astronomers, which allowed seafarers to calculate their latitude based on the position of the stars.

Portugal's first attempts at long-distance seafaring were auspicious. After capturing Ceuta on the northern African coast in 1415, Portuguese ships began to explore the Atlantic coast of the African continent. The principal objective was to acquire slaves and spices, but explorers were lured by rumors of large gold mines as well. Henry the Navigator was also aware of legends that placed the remote Christian kingdom of Prester John deep in the heartland of Africa. By making contact with this ancient Christian community he hoped not only to expand the reach of Catholicism, but also to counter the growing Muslim domination of the continent.

By the 1420s, the Portuguese had established themselves on the Atlantic islands of Madeira and the Azores and began to move steadily southward. Senegal, Cape Verde, and what is today Sierra Leone were taken in the next few decades, which firmly established Portugal's reputation as a leader in long-distance navigation. In the wake of the fall of Constantinople, when Pope Nicholas V (r. 1447–1455) issued the papal bull "Romanus Pontifex," spurring Europe's monarchies to reverse Muslim conquests and find new territories to conquer, he granted Portugal dominion over all lands south of Cape Bojador, on the northern coast of what is now Western Sahara. His confidence was not misplaced. In 1488, Bartolomeu Dias succeeded in reaching the southern tip of the continent. He was followed by Vasco da Gama, who in 1499 rounded the cape and from there plotted a maritime course to India, stopping at ports in eastern Africa for provisioning. Goa, Malacca, and Hormuz all fell into Portuguese hands as key stations along the new sea route to the Indies.

In 1520, the Portuguese believed they had discovered the mystical land of Prester John when they made contact with members of the Ethiopian Church, one of the oldest forms of Eastern Christianity, who had thrived in Ethiopia despite being surrounded by Muslim territories. The vitality of the Ethiopian Church and the remarkable rock-hewn church buildings of Roha (today's Lalibela), built in the 12th century, left a great impression on the Portuguese. The Ethiopian Christians, led by Emperor Lebna Dengel, fervently hoped to conclude a treaty and bring Portuguese arms to bear against their increasingly hostile Muslim neighbors. But the Portuguese demurred when it became clear that the Ethiopians had no intention of

LIFE AND TIMES

The Legend of Prester John

This depiction of the legendary Prester John appears in a 16th-century chart of the Indian Ocean.

Among the many legends that circulated in medieval Europe was that of Prester (or Presbyter) John (or Johannes), a Christian patriarch and king who once ruled a Christian nation blessed with untold riches and inhabited by magical creatures. Some legends identified him as a descendant of one of the Three Magi who visited the infant Jesus in Bethlehem. In others, his kingdom was said to contain a fountain of youth and a mirror through which every region could be seen. Some legends placed his realm in India, possibly inspired by reports of Nestorian Christian communities there. Others said that his kingdom had once been based in central Asia before it was overwhelmed by Muslims, or by Mongol hordes. When the Portuguese made contact with Ethiopian Christians, they believed they had located the lost kingdom of Prester John at last. The legend continued well into the 17th century, as evidenced by Shakespeare's play *Much Ado About Nothing* (Act 2, Scene 1).

1477
Ptolemy's *Geographica* is republished in Rome

1481
Pope Sixtus IV builds the Sistine Chapel

1488
Bartolomeu Dias succeeds in reaching the Cape of Good Hope

1492
The last Muslim stronghold in Spain, Granada, falls to the Spanish monarchy

Navigational Objects

1650–1800

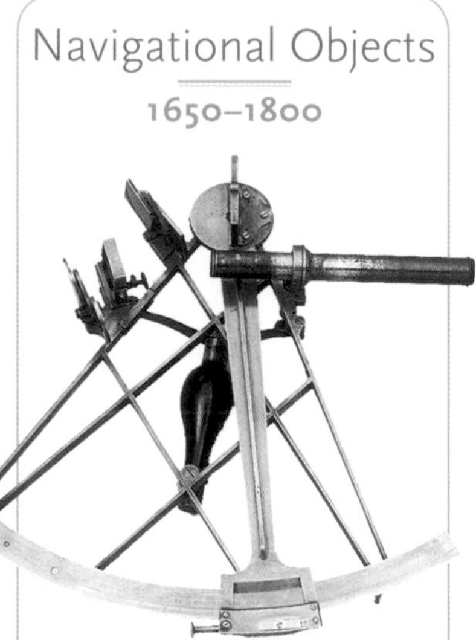

This sextant, used for calculating latitude, was built by George Adams in 1790.

Adam Heroldt built this armillary sphere of the Ptolemaic system in 1648.

abandoning their Eastern rites, still rooted in Monophysitism. When the charismatic Imam and warrior Ahmed al-Ghazi (r. 1529–1543) invaded Ethiopia and vowed to eradicate the Christian enclave, the Portuguese were slow to respond. Countless Ethiopian churches and monasteries, some hundreds of years old, were destroyed before the Portuguese finally joined the conflict and defeated al-Ghazi in 1543. Thus weakened, the Ethiopian community became the target of intense proselytizing efforts by Catholic Portuguese clergy. This prompted an outcry among Ethiopian monks, and all relations with the Portuguese were terminated.

A similar experience awaited Vasco da Gama upon his arrival in India. Here, too, an Eastern Christian movement had clung to its ancient traditions despite being isolated as a religious minority. As we saw, the "Church of Thomas" had been established here as early as the mid-second century C.E., albeit not by Thomas the Apostle himself but by Syriac missionaries who venerated Thomas as their patron saint. Adopted by the Nestorian Church of Persia, the Indian Church of Thomas had somehow weathered more than a millennium of political and religious upheavals, and still carved out an existence under the guidance of a patriarch based in Baghdad. Here too, after the initial excitement of meeting fellow Christians had passed, relations between the Portuguese and the natives soured after it transpired that

1492 Christopher Columbus lands in the New World

1494 The Treaty of Tordesillas divides the world between the Portuguese and the Spanish

1494 Pope Alexander VI issues a special indulgence for prayers made in front of images of Mary

1499 Vasco da Gama rounds the Cape of Good Hope

Indian Christians had no interest in converting to Catholicism. This would change in the decades to come, but for the time being, Portuguese efforts to convert new souls to the Latin rites were largely stymied.

The Spanish Conquest

Inevitably, Portugal's success in exploring Africa spurred Spain to undertake major naval expeditions as well, lest it be left behind in the rush for gold and Catholic souls. After the last Muslim stronghold of Granada had fallen in 1492, King Ferdinand and Queen Isabella were free to devote their resources to exploration. Whereas Portugal had traveled south, Spain opted to go west, across the vast Atlantic Ocean, in search of a new route to the East Indies.

The idea of finding a western route to the Indies amounted to a break with conventional Christian cosmology. Traditionally, European geography had been governed by the Genesis doctrine that the world was a flat surface underneath which lay purgatory and hell, and above which rose the canopy of heaven. The proportions of this cosmos were perfectly delineated in the Temple of Solomon: twice as long as it was wide. These dimensions were faithfully echoed in the construction of the Sistine Chapel, built by Pope Sixtus IV in 1481. Indeed, Michelangelo's fresco "The Last Judgment" in the chapel, completed in 1541, is a virtual map of this sacred cosmology, identifying the zones of heaven, earth, and hell, with Christ as the Supreme Judge at its center.

Michelangelo Buonarroti (1475–1564) painted the fresco of the Last Judgment in the Sistine Chapel between 1538 and 1541.

OPPOSITE: *A 12th-century Ethiopian church carved out of the ground is located in Roha, today's Lalibela.*

1500
Charles V, future King of the Spanish Habsburg Empire, is born

1503
Portuguese missionaries reach Ethiopia, but fail to make converts

1506
Francis Xavier, a co-founder of the Society of Jesus, is born

1513
Juan Ponce de Léon discovers Florida

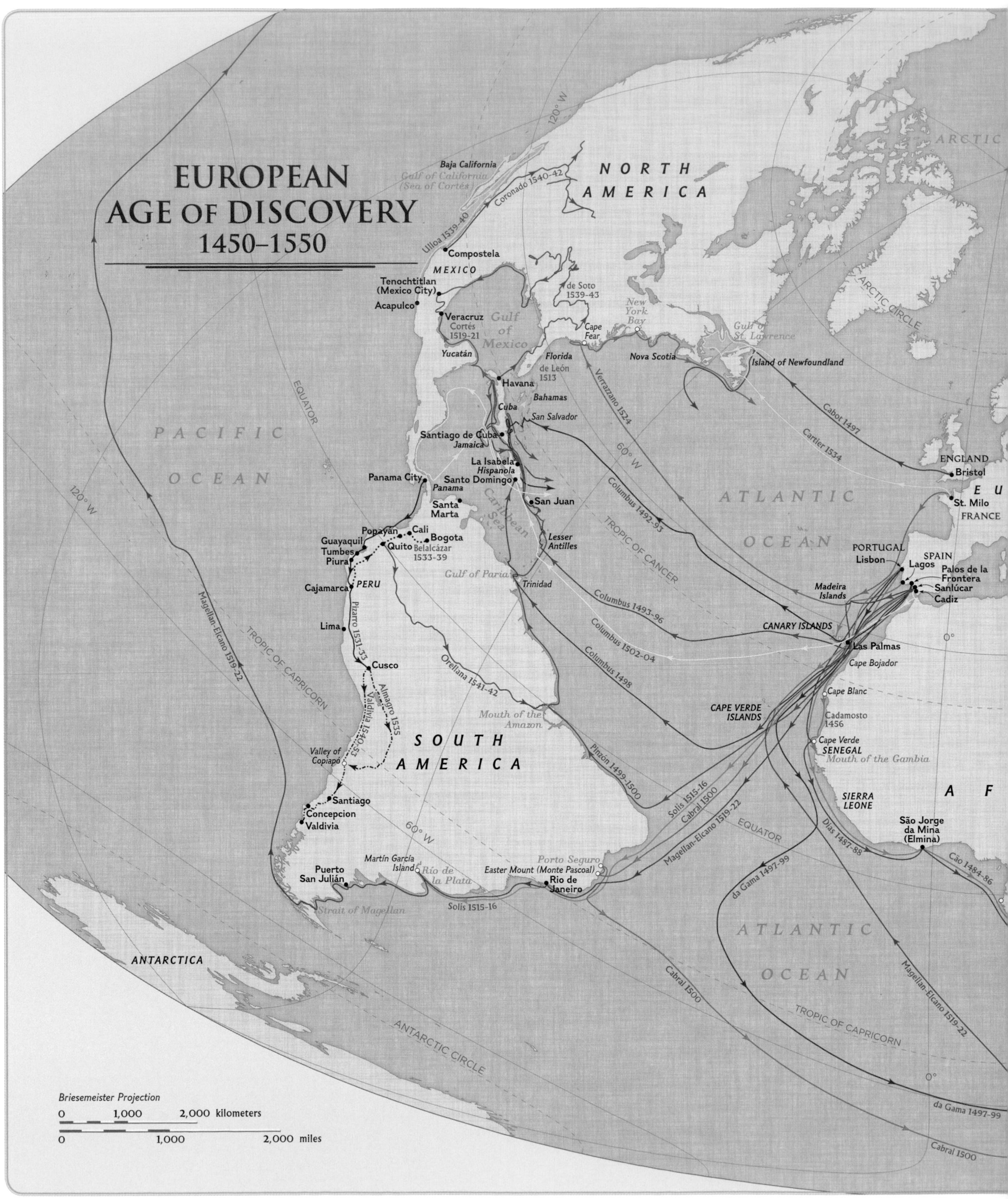

EUROPEAN
AGE OF DISCOVERY
1450–1550
NORTH AMERICA
SOUTH AMERICA
PACIFIC OCEAN
ATLANTIC OCEAN
ATLANTIC OCEAN
ANTARCTICA
Baja California
Gulf of California (Sea of Cortés)
Coronado 1540-42
Ulloa 1539-40
Compostela
MEXICO
Tenochtitlan (Mexico City)
Acapulco
Veracruz
Cortés 1519-21
Gulf of Mexico
Yucatán
de Soto 1539-43
New York Bay
Cape Fear
Gulf of St. Lawrence
Nova Scotia
Island of Newfoundland
Florida
de León 1513
Havana
Bahamas
Cuba
San Salvador
Santiago de Cuba
Jamaica
La Isabela
Hispanola
Santo Domingo
San Juan
Panama City
Panama
Santa Marta
Caribbean Sea
Lesser Antilles
Popayán
Cali
Bogota
Quito
Belalcázar 1533-39
Guayaquil
Tumbes
Piura
Cajamarca
PERU
Gulf of Paria
Trinidad
Lima
Pizarro 1531-33
Cusco
Orellana 1541-42
Almagro 1535
Valdivia 1540-51
Mouth of the Amazon
Valley of Copiapó
Santiago
Concepcion
Valdivia
Pinzón 1499-1500
Martín García Island
Río de la Plata
Puerto San Julián
Strait of Magellan
Solís 1515-16
Porto Seguro
Easter Mount (Monte Pascoal)
Rio de Janeiro
Magellan-Elcano 1519-22
EQUATOR
120° W
120° W
60° W
60° W
TROPIC OF CANCER
TROPIC OF CAPRICORN
ANTARCTIC CIRCLE
ARCTIC CIRCLE
ARCTIC
Verrazzano 1524
Cabot 1497
Cartier 1534
ENGLAND
Bristol
St. Milo
FRANCE
E U
Columbus 1492-93
Columbus 1493-96
Columbus 1502-04
Columbus 1498
PORTUGAL
Lisbon
SPAIN
Lagos
Palos de la Frontera
Sanlúcar
Cadiz
Madeira Islands
CANARY ISLANDS
Las Palmas
Cape Bojador
0°
Cape Blanc
CAPE VERDE ISLANDS
Cadamosto 1456
Cape Verde
SENEGAL
Mouth of the Gambia
Solís 1515-16
Cabral 1500
Magellan-Elcano 1519-22
SIERRA LEONE
A F
São Jorge da Mina (Elmina)
Dias 1487-88
Cão 1484-86
EQUATOR
da Gama 1497-99
Cabral 1500
Magellan-Elcano 1519-22
TROPIC OF CAPRICORN
0°
da Gama 1497-99
Cabral 1500
Briesemeister Projection
0 1,000 2,000 kilometers
0 1,000 2,000 miles

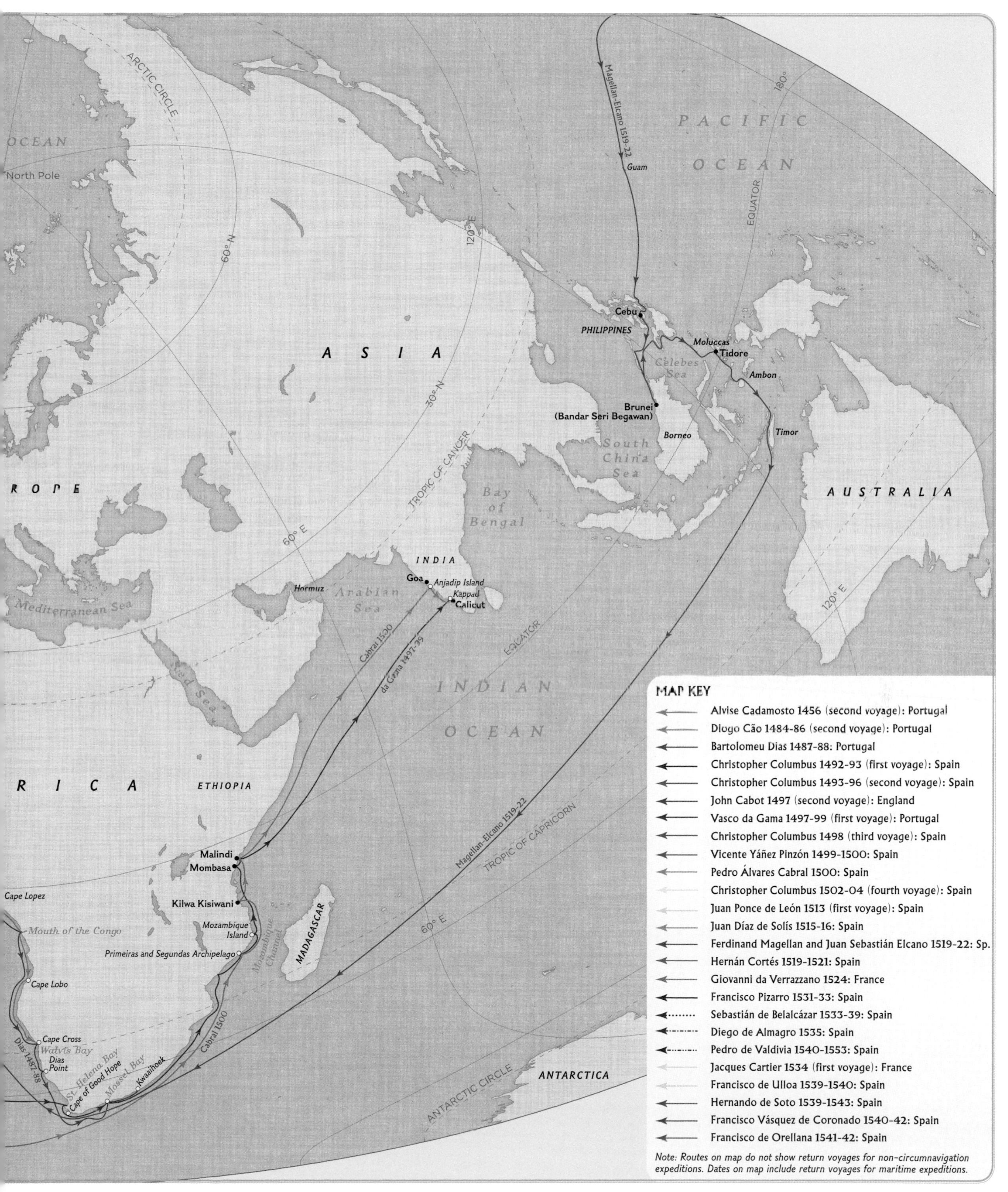

PACIFIC OCEAN
ASIA
AUSTRALIA
INDIAN OCEAN
ANTARCTICA
INDIA
ETHIOPIA
MADAGASCAR
PHILIPPINES
Magellan-Elcano 1519-22
Guam
Cebu
Moluccas
Tidore
Ambon
Brunei (Bandar Seri Begawan)
Borneo
Timor
Celebes Sea
South China Sea
Bay of Bengal
Arabian Sea
Mediterranean Sea
Red Sea
Hormuz
Goa
Anjadip Island
Kappad
Calicut
Cabral 1500
da Gama 1497-99
Malindi
Mombasa
Kilwa Kisiwani
Mozambique Island
Primeiras and Segundas Archipelago
Mozambique Channel
Cape Lopez
Mouth of the Congo
Cape Lobo
Cape Cross
Walvis Bay
Dias Point
Dias 1487-88
St. Helena Bay
Cape of Good Hope
Mossel Bay
Kwaaihoek
ARCTIC CIRCLE
TROPIC OF CANCER
EQUATOR
TROPIC OF CAPRICORN
ANTARCTIC CIRCLE
North Pole
OCEAN
ROPE
RICA
60° N
30° N
120° E
60° E
180°
MAP KEY
Alvise Cadamosto 1456 (second voyage): Portugal
Diogo Cão 1484-86 (second voyage): Portugal
Bartolomeu Dias 1487-88: Portugal
Christopher Columbus 1492-93 (first voyage): Spain
Christopher Columbus 1493-96 (second voyage): Spain
John Cabot 1497 (second voyage): England
Vasco da Gama 1497-99 (first voyage): Portugal
Christopher Columbus 1498 (third voyage): Spain
Vicente Yáñez Pinzón 1499-1500: Spain
Pedro Álvares Cabral 1500: Spain
Christopher Columbus 1502-04 (fourth voyage): Spain
Juan Ponce de León 1513 (first voyage): Spain
Juan Díaz de Solís 1515-16: Spain
Ferdinand Magellan and Juan Sebastián Elcano 1519-22: Sp.
Hernán Cortés 1519-1521: Spain
Giovanni da Verrazzano 1524: France
Francisco Pizarro 1531-33: Spain
Sebastián de Belalcázar 1533-39: Spain
Diego de Almagro 1535: Spain
Pedro de Valdivia 1540-1553: Spain
Jacques Cartier 1534 (first voyage): France
Francisco de Ulloa 1539-1540: Spain
Hernando de Soto 1539-1543: Spain
Francisco Vásquez de Coronado 1540-42: Spain
Francisco de Orellana 1541-42: Spain
Note: Routes on map do not show return voyages for non-circumnavigation expeditions. Dates on map include return voyages for maritime expeditions.

ABOVE: This portrait of Christopher Columbus was painted by Sebastiano del Piombo (ca 1485–1547).

RIGHT: This map of the known world is based on Geographica by the second-century geographer Ptolemy.

During the 13th-century scholastic period, however, a number of scholars had begun to argue that the world was a sphere, based in part on the work of Islamic astronomers. One of the most influential authors was Thomas Aquinas, who wrote in his *Summa Theologiae* that the Earth was round because of "the movement of heavy bodies toward the center." In the 15th century, the use of an orb to symbolize a king's temporal power on Earth became increasingly common. Lastly, during the Renaissance, a number of Roman geographical maps had surfaced, including Ptolemy's *Geographica,* which documented the world from the Atlantic Ocean to China in 180 degrees of longitude, and in 80 degrees of latitude from the Arctic to Africa.

Republished in 1477 in Rome, Ptolemy's cartography persuaded an Italian explorer named Christopher Columbus (1451–1506) that ships would not topple into an abyss at the end of Earth, and that the East Indies could be reached by sailing westward. He twice proposed this risky venture to the Portuguese King John II (r. 1481–1495), but the King's advisers argued against it. Portugal was on the verge of plotting a secret route to the Indies by going eastward around the Cape of Good Hope, and was not to be distracted by futile probes in the opposite direction. Columbus approached Ferdinand and Isabella of Spain, who were intrigued with his plan, if for no other reason than to try to beat the Portuguese to the Indies. Thus, on August 3, 1492, Columbus slipped the mooring lines of Palos de la Frontera, on the southwestern coast of Spain, to lead his flotilla into the great Atlantic unknown. Five weeks after a victualing stop in the Canary Islands, he made landfall on the Bahamas, believing he had reached the East Indies. Instead, he had discovered the New World.

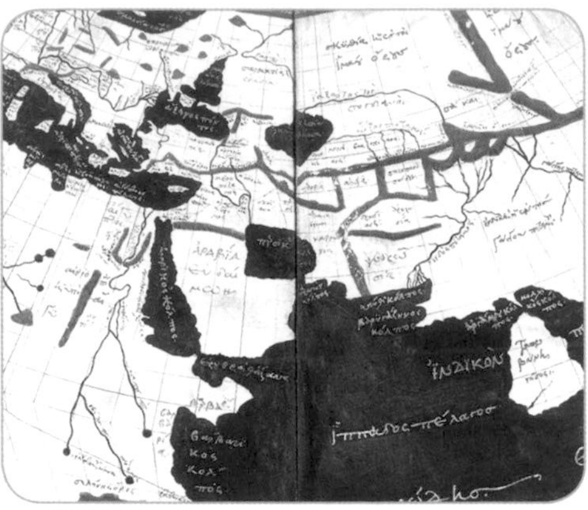

These two discoveries—the new Portuguese route to the east and Columbus's foray into the New World—convinced Pope Alexander VI that global exploration would become a strategic effort in advancing the Catholic cause. At the same time, he was aware that the competing ambitions of two major Catholic powers might lead to conflict. The pope therefore set an arbitrary dividing line, granting all new territory west of the Azores to Spain. Portugal strenuously objected. Subsequent negotiations produced the Treaty of Tordesillas of 1494, by which the two explorer nations carved up the world between themselves. Portugal gained control over Africa, Asia, and the eastern part of South America (analogous to today's Brazil), while Spain received all lands to the west of that line—much of which was still to be explored.

Spain wasted no time in seizing the land apportioned to it. In 1513, Juan Ponce de Léon sailed from today's Puerto Rico and discovered a landmass that he named Florida, given that it was Easter (or *Florida*) week. Six years later, conquistador Hernán Cortés reached the Yucatán Peninsula and

OPPOSITE: St. Andrew's Presbyterian Church in St. George's, Grenada, West Indies, was built in 1831 but suffered severe damage from Hurricane Ivan in 2004.

CA 1514
Scottish church reformer John Knox is born

1519
Hernán Cortés reaches the Yucatán Peninsula in Mexico

1520S
Ulrich Zwingli founds a reformist movement in Switzerland

1521
During the Diet of Worms, Martin Luther refuses to recant his Ninety-Five Theses

made contact with the Maya civilization. Soon, rumors reached Spain that precious metals could be found aplenty among the Aztec and Maya civilizations. This spurred a new wave of explorations with the full support of the new Spanish king, Holy Roman Emperor Charles V (1500–1558). In 1530, Francisco Pizarro landed in Peru with a force of a mere 200 men and succeeded in defeating the Inca forces. One by one, the indigenous civilizations of Central and South America were suppressed and replaced by colonial administrations.

Many—though not all—of these expeditions were accompanied by monks and priests, who at this stage were primarily Dominicans and Franciscans. Converting souls for Christendom was ostensibly one of the reasons why these expeditions were being financed by the Spanish Crown. Indeed, compared with the Portuguese experience in Africa, the Spanish were more successful with their proselytizing efforts in the Americas. While it is probably true that many natives agreed to be baptized for fear of retribution, others were genuinely moved by the humanity of Christianity, in sharp contrast to their indigenous traditions, which sometimes featured human sacrifice. When, in 1531, a Mexican peasant named Juan Diego claimed to have seen a vision of the Virgin Mary in Guadalupe, Mexicans converted by

[This city] is so beautiful and has such fine buildings that it would be remarkable even in Spain.

FRANCISCO PIZARRO
ON THE INCA CITY OF CUSCO

Anthony van Dyck (1599–1641) painted this portrait of Emperor Charles V in 1620.

1526
Charles V grants German princes the right to choose the church in their domain

1530
Order of the Regular Clerics of St. Paul, the Barnabites, is founded in Milan

1531
Juan Diego claims a vision of the Virgin Mary in Guadalupe

1532
Charles V agrees to a truce with reformists

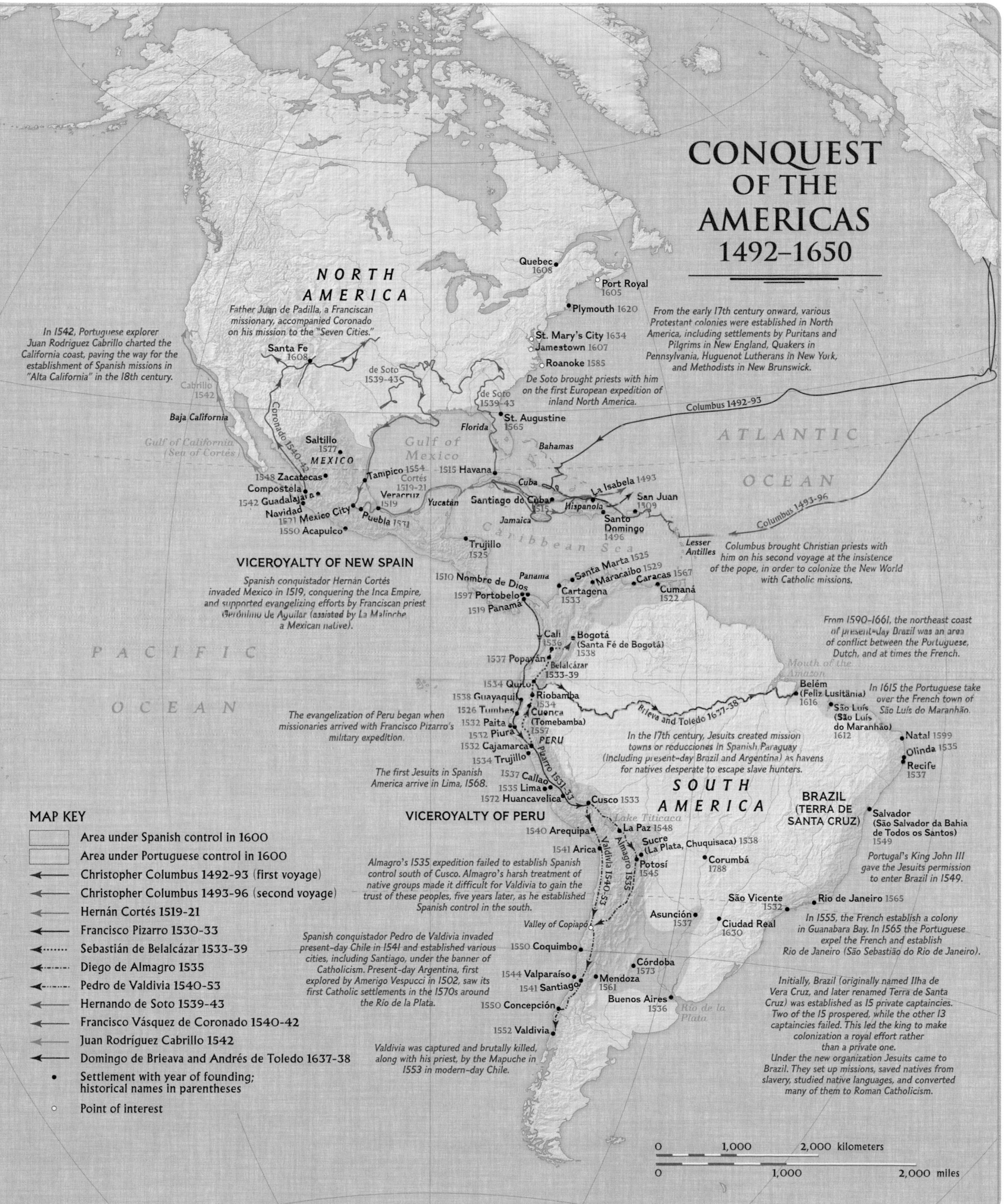

CONQUEST OF THE AMERICAS 1492–1650
NORTH AMERICA
Father Juan de Padilla, a Franciscan missionary, accompanied Coronado on his mission to the "Seven Cities."
In 1542, Portuguese explorer Juan Rodríguez Cabrillo charted the California coast, paving the way for the establishment of Spanish missions in "Alta California" in the 18th century.
Quebec 1608
Port Royal 1605
Plymouth 1620
St. Mary's City 1634
Jamestown 1607
Roanoke 1585
From the early 17th century onward, various Protestant colonies were established in North America, including settlements by Puritans and Pilgrims in New England, Quakers in Pennsylvania, Huguenot Lutherans in New York, and Methodists in New Brunswick.
De Soto brought priests with him on the first European expedition of inland North America.
Santa Fe 1608
de Soto 1539-43
Cabrillo 1542
Baja California
Coronado 1540-42
St. Augustine 1565
Florida
Columbus 1492-93
ATLANTIC OCEAN
Bahamas
Gulf of California (Sea of Cortés)
Saltillo 1577
MEXICO
Gulf of Mexico
1548 Zacatecas
Compostela
1542 Guadalajara
Navidad
Tampico 1554
Cortés 1519-21
1515 Havana
Cuba
La Isabela 1493
San Juan 1509
Veracruz 1519
Mexico City
Puebla 1531
1550 Acapulco
Yucatán
Santiago de Cuba 1515
Jamaica
Hispaniola
Santo Domingo 1496
Columbus 1493-96
Caribbean Sea
Trujillo 1525
Lesser Antilles
Columbus brought Christian priests with him on his second voyage at the insistence of the pope, in order to colonize the New World with Catholic missions.
VICEROYALTY OF NEW SPAIN
Spanish conquistador Hernán Cortés invaded Mexico in 1519, conquering the Inca Empire, and supported evangelizing efforts by Franciscan priest Gerónimo de Aguilar (assisted by La Malinche a Mexican native).
1510 Nombre de Dios
Panama
Santa Marta 1525
Maracaibo 1529
Caracas 1567
Cartagena 1533
Cumaná 1522
1597 Portobelo
1519 Panamá
From 1590-1661, the northeast coast of present-day Brazil was an area of conflict between the Portuguese, Dutch, and at times the French.
PACIFIC OCEAN
Cali 1536
Bogotá (Santa Fé de Bogotá) 1538
1537 Popayán
Belalcázar 1533-39
Mouth of the Amazon
1534 Quito
1538 Guayaquil
Riobamba 1534
Belém (Feliz Lusitânia) 1616
In 1615 the Portuguese take over the French town of São Luís do Maranhão.
1526 Tumbes
Cuenca (Tomebamba) 1557
Brieva and Toledo 1637-38
São Luís (São Luís do Maranhão) 1612
The evangelization of Peru began when missionaries arrived with Francisco Pizarro's military expedition.
1532 Paita
1532 Piura
PERU
1532 Cajamarca
1534 Trujillo
In the 17th century, Jesuits created mission towns or reducciones in Spanish Paraguay (including present-day Brazil and Argentina) as havens for natives desperate to escape slave hunters.
Natal 1599
Olinda 1535
Recife 1537
The first Jesuits in Spanish America arrive in Lima, 1568.
1537 Callao
1535 Lima
Pizarro 1531-33
1572 Huancavelica
Cusco 1533
SOUTH AMERICA
BRAZIL (TERRA DE SANTA CRUZ)
Salvador (São Salvador da Bahia de Todos os Santos) 1549
VICEROYALTY OF PERU
Lake Titicaca
1540 Arequipa
La Paz 1548
1541 Arica
Sucre (La Plata, Chuquisaca) 1538
Almagro 1535
Potosí 1545
Corumbá 1788
Valdivia 1540-53
Portugal's King John III gave the Jesuits permission to enter Brazil in 1549.
Almagro's 1535 expedition failed to establish Spanish control south of Cusco. Almagro's harsh treatment of native groups made it difficult for Valdivia to gain the trust of these peoples, five years later, as he established Spanish control in the south.
São Vicente 1532
Rio de Janeiro 1565
Asunción 1537
Ciudad Real 1630
Valley of Copiapó
In 1555, the French establish a colony in Guanabara Bay. In 1565 the Portuguese expel the French and establish Rio de Janeiro (São Sebastião do Rio de Janeiro).
Spanish conquistador Pedro de Valdivia invaded present-day Chile in 1541 and established various cities, including Santiago, under the banner of Catholicism. Present-day Argentina, first explored by Amerigo Vespucci in 1502, saw its first Catholic settlements in the 1570s around the Río de la Plata.
1550 Coquimbo
Córdoba 1573
1544 Valparaíso
Mendoza 1561
1541 Santiago
Buenos Aires 1536
Río de la Plata
1550 Concepción
1552 Valdivia
Initially, Brazil (originally named Ilha de Vera Cruz, and later renamed Terra de Santa Cruz) was established as 15 private captaincies. Two of the 15 prospered, while the other 13 captaincies failed. This led the king to make colonization a royal effort rather than a private one.
Under the new organization Jesuits came to Brazil. They set up missions, saved natives from slavery, studied native languages, and converted many of them to Roman Catholicism.
Valdivia was captured and brutally killed, along with his priest, by the Mapuche in 1553 in modern-day Chile.
MAP KEY
Area under Spanish control in 1600
Area under Portuguese control in 1600
Christopher Columbus 1492-93 (first voyage)
Christopher Columbus 1493-96 (second voyage)
Hernán Cortés 1519-21
Francisco Pizarro 1530-33
Sebastián de Belalcázar 1533-39
Diego de Almagro 1535
Pedro de Valdivia 1540-53
Hernando de Soto 1539-43
Francisco Vásquez de Coronado 1540-42
Juan Rodríguez Cabrillo 1542
Domingo de Brieava and Andrés de Toledo 1637-38
Settlement with year of founding; historical names in parentheses
Point of interest
0 1,000 2,000 kilometers
0 1,000 2,000 miles

An 18th-century Mexican painting depicts Indians being baptized by Dominicans. Beginning in the 16th century, Dominicans, Franciscans, and Jesuits developed missions throughout "New Spain."

the thousands; by the late 1530s, there were eight million Christians in Mexico.

Attempts at Reconciliation

The evangelizing success in the Americas and the flood of newfound wealth into Spanish, Portuguese, and Italian coffers galvanized a campaign that is often referred to as the Catholic Counter-Reformation, which would find its most uniform expression in the art and architecture of the period. For much of the early 16th century, many secular and spiritual leaders were still hoping that a European split along the lines of faith could be averted. For more than a thousand years, Europe had enjoyed a unique cultural and spiritual solidarity under the sign of the Latin cross; surely, such a remarkable unity should not be discarded lightly. Hope for reconciliation was further advanced by a perception in certain Catholic circles that the Lutherans and Calvinists were right on a number of issues. The papacy had become estranged from the urgent social

1534
The Act of Supremacy declares Henry VIII to be the supreme head of the Church of England

1535
Catholic soldiers retake the city of Münster

1536
John Calvin writes *Institutes of Christian Religion*

1541
Michelangelo completes his fresco "The Last Judgment"

Often we baptized in a single day 14,000 people, sometimes 10,000, sometimes 8,000.

PETER VAN GHENT, FRANCISCAN MISSIONARY IN MEXICO

and spiritual issues of the day. There *was* much corruption among the Catholic hierarchy, and many of the clergy had indeed strayed far from the precepts of the Gospels. Perhaps, then, the opposing parties could try to work out a compromise that would keep the Christian Church intact.

This was the thrust of a report by a special papal commission, which in 1536 minced no words in criticizing the laxity, ignorance, and abuse within the Church as many a Protestant had done. Five years later, an even more astonishing event took place. In the city of Ratisbon (today's Regensburg, Bavaria), six theologians—three Catholics and three Protestants—sat down for a colloquy at the request of Holy Roman Emperor Charles V with the aim of forestalling a permanent split of the Church. To accomplish such a reconciliation, the Emperor was willing to accept two key Protestant demands: that clergy would be allowed to marry, and that during the Eucharist the cup of wine should be shared by the congregation, not just the officiating clergy. That Charles considered himself authorized to rule on such pivotal issues of Catholic doctrine only underscores the tremendous influence that a Spanish emperor—and by extension, Spain—was able to wield in the middle of the 16th century.

Alas, the Ratisbon parlay failed because its tentative compromise was rejected by both Luther and the College of Cardinals. Its failure doomed the cause of the radical reform movement within Catholicism. If the Reformation could not be curbed by force of reason, henceforth it would be fought by the power of the sword.

The Council of Trent

Before an offensive on the Reformation could be contemplated, however, most Catholic

PERIOD ART

Lutheran Art

John Calvin banned all imagery and music from the church (other than unaccompanied congregational hymns), but most Lutheran churches did not. Lutheran congregations welcomed sacred art, not only because they had inherited many Catholic cathedrals but also because Lutheranism retained more elements of Catholic liturgy than Calvinism. For example, Lutheran churches retained the altar as a central element in worship to underscore the presence of Christ in the Eucharist, whereas many Calvinist churches removed the altar and grouped the congregation around the pulpit instead. Similarly, many converted Lutheran churches possessed large organs, which in the century to come would inspire such composers as Buxtehude, Telemann, and Bach. At the same time, German artists struggled to develop an authentic Lutheran art form that remained true to native and Lutheran traditions while absorbing the achievements of the Renaissance. Foremost among these were Albrecht Dürer (1471–1528), Matthias Grünewald (ca 1470–1528), and Lucas Cranach the Elder (1472–1553). Cranach was a court painter to the Elector Prince of Saxony, who enthusiastically embraced the Reformation. He was also a close friend of Martin Luther, painted his portrait, and stood as godfather to Luther's first child. Albrecht Dürer skillfully blended the German Gothic tradition with that of the Italian Renaissance to develop a unique style, popularized by his highly influential woodcuts. After 1520, Dürer was increasingly drawn to the writing of Martin Luther, which led to his painting "The Four Apostles" of 1526. The sober yet monumental portrayal underscored the paramount importance of St. Paul and the Gospels in the Lutheran faith.

"The Four Apostles" is the work of the German Renaissance artist Albrecht Dürer (1471–1528).

1541
The colloquy of Ratisbon seeks to reconcile Catholicism and Protestantism

1543
The Portuguese defeat the Islamic warrior Ahmed al-Ghazi in Ethiopia

1544
William I, founder of the Protestant royal house of Orange-Nassau, begins his reign

1545
The Council of Trent redefines Catholicism and launches the Counter-Reformation

This 18th-century Bolivian panel depicts the Virgin Mary surrounded by Indians.

OPPOSITE: *Nicolo Dorigati (active 1692–1748) painted this scene of the opening session of the Council of Trent in 1545.*

prelates realized that the Church first ought to put its house in order. Only a unified Church, convinced of its purpose and revitalized by theological clarity, would be in a position to stem the still-expanding wave of the Reformation. The result was the Council of Trent, which convened in 1545 and in many ways created the Catholic Church that has existed to this day.

Rather than addressing the issues of abuse that had compelled Luther to write his Ninety-Five Theses, as many reformers had hoped, much of the council's work was devoted to crafting a solid theological foundation. Meeting in 25 sessions between 1545 and 1563, its primary aim was to refute many of the doctrinal claims made by Lutherans and Calvinists in the preceding decades. Thus, the seven Catholic sacraments were formally declared to be valid instruments of grace. The Church, not the layman, remained the ultimate arbiter in the interpretation of Scripture. The transubstantiation (the change of bread and wine into the body and blood of Christ during the Eucharist) was affirmed, as was the idea that a moral life and good deeds, rather than faith alone, were needed to earn God's grace. Similarly, any idea of clergy being able to marry was firmly rejected; the state of celibacy was upheld.

To ensure the enforcement of these doctrinal tenets, a new Latin liturgy was adopted, which would become known as the Tridentine Mass. By and large, this new rite would remain in force from its publication in 1570 to the Second Vatican Council of 1962.

Following the Council of Trent, the Catholic Church went on the offensive. In 1588, Pope Sixtus V (r. 1585–1590) authorized the Inquisition to root out any form of "Protestant heresy" in Italian lands. In Poland, King Sigismund III abandoned his practice of religious tolerance and embarked on a policy of persecution, ostracizing all Protestants in his realm.

In France at this time, the Reformation had made impressive gains, particularly among the French nobility. By 1560, there were more than 2,000 Protestant churches on French soil. But tensions between French Protestants—predominantly Calvinists known as Huguenots—and Catholics continued to grow, as reflected in the conflicting ambitions of the Bourbons and the Guise factions within France's royal dynasty.

These tensions erupted in 1562 with the outbreak of the first of two French Wars of Religion. Ten years later, during the wedding of Marguerite de Valois (r. 1589–1599), the Catholic daughter of Catherine de Medici, to Protestant Prince Henry III of Navarre (r. 1589–1610), a group of attending Huguenot noblemen was assassinated, probably on orders of ruling King Charles IX (r. 1560–1574). The killings led to a wholesale slaughter of Huguenots by a Catholic mob in what became known as the St. Bartholomew's Day Massacre. More violence ensued until Henry of Navarre ascended the French throne in 1594 as King Henry IV. Though converted to Catholicism, Henry continued to have sympathy for the Huguenot cause and swore to protect its followers. In

> *To strive especially for the defense and propagation of the faith and for the progress of souls in Christian life and doctrine.*
>
> MISSION STATEMENT OF THE SOCIETY OF JESUS

1547
King Henry VIII of England dies and is succeeded by his son, Edward VI

1549
Thomas Cranmer's original Book of Common Prayer of the Church of England is published

1549
The first Jesuit missionaries reach Japan

1556
Archbishop Thomas Cranmer is branded a heretic by Queen Mary and burned at the stake

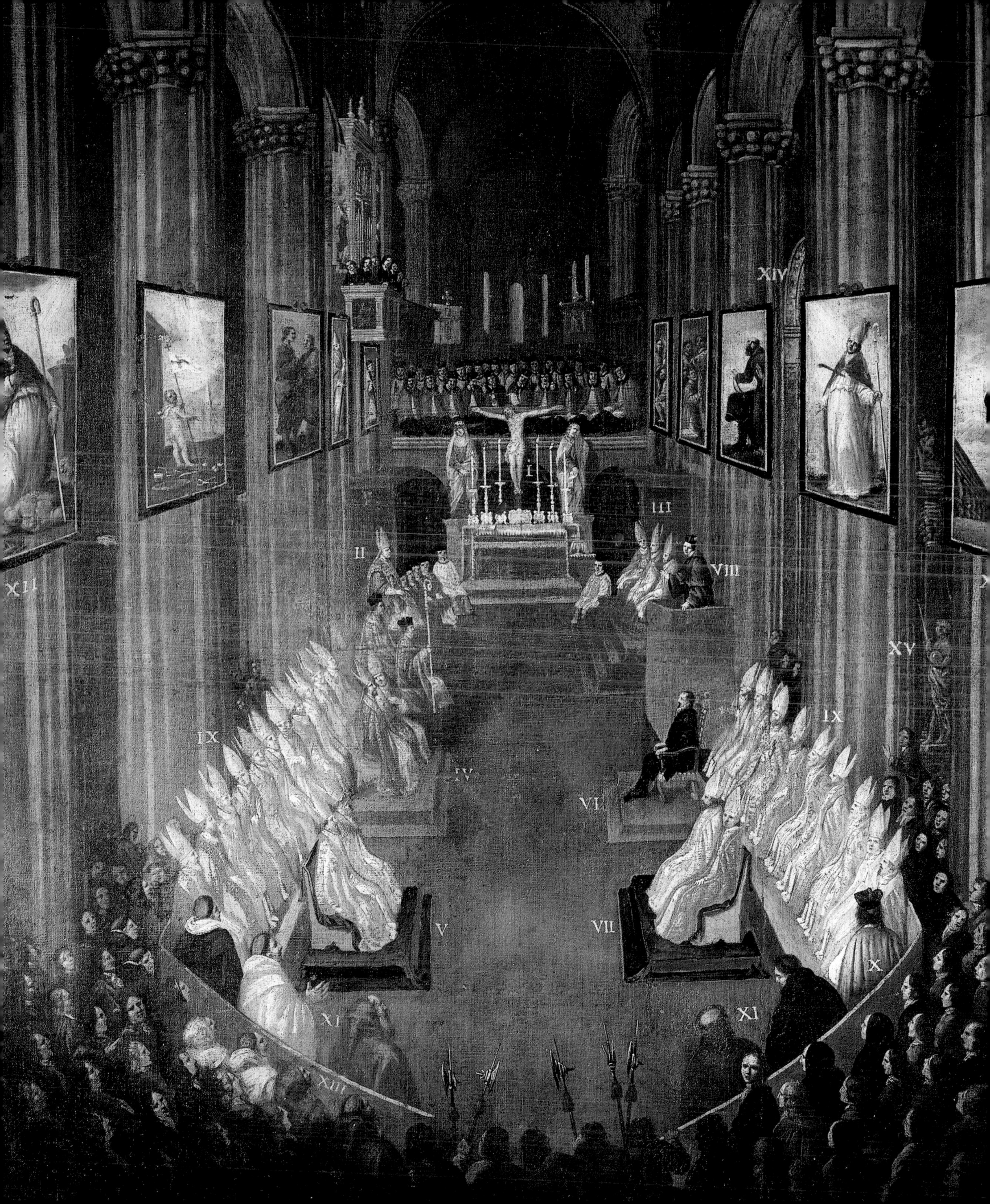

XIV
I
II
III
VIII
XII
XV
IX
IX
IV
VI
V
VII
X
XI
XI
XIII

"The St. Bartholomew's Day Massacre" is the work of the French artist François Dubois (1529–1584).

OPPOSITE: *"The Ecstasy of St. Teresa," designed and completed in white marble by Gian Lorenzo Bernini (1598–1680), is found in the Santa Maria della Vittoria, in Rome.*

1598, he issued the Edict of Nantes, rescinding the persecution of Protestantism and granting Huguenots a temporary relief from their trials.

The New Orders

To sustain the effort of combating Protestant movements, several new Catholic orders were created. One, known as the Theatines (named after Bishop Carafa of Theate, Abruzzi) focused on fostering discipline and spiritual renewal among the clergy and the laity. To do so they built a number of prayer rooms, or oratories, as well as hospitals and churches throughout Italy and Spain. Theatine monks were among the first to embark on the Spanish ships bound for Peru, India, and the East Indies.

Another order, the Barnabites—officially known as the Regular Clerics of St. Paul—focused on pastoral work, including preaching, ministering, and offering education to the young. Founded in Milan in 1530, this order, as its name suggests, was guided by the teachings of Paul. Much of its work was focused on encouraging a devotion to the Eucharist and the traditional doctrine of transubstantiation, rejecting Lutheran or Calvinist views on the sacrament. In addition to their vows of poverty, chastity, and obedience, Barnabite followers also took a fourth vow: to never accept any office or position of dignity, thus avoiding any temporal temptations.

The emphasis on piety led to the veneration of numerous mystics, including the Spanish Carmelite nun Teresa of Ávila (1515–1582) and Miguel de Molinos (1628–1697), who founded a movement focused on mystical contemplation known as Quietism. Elsewhere, particularly in Italy and northern Europe, the cult of

1559
John Knox begins the Protestant Reformation of Scotland

1560
The Inquisition is established in India by Thomas Christians

1561
Mary Stuart, Queen of Scots, returns to Scotland

1562
The First War of Religion in France begins

The pain was so great that I screamed aloud; but I also felt such infinite sweetness that I wished the pain would last forever.

TERESA OF ÁVILA, DESCRIBING HER RELIGIOUS ECSTASY

Mary became paramount. In 1494, Pope Alexander VI had declared that prayers made in front of images of Mary would result in special indulgence. This fueled a boom of depictions of Mary throughout Catholic Europe that would last well into the Baroque era.

But the order that would become inextricably identified with the Catholic Counter-Reformation was the Jesuits, or the Society of Jesus, founded in 1539 by Spanish theologian Ignatius of Loyola (ca 1491–1556). The Jesuits, known as "Soldiers of Christ," were unlike any other order. Fiercely devoted to obedience, both to the papacy and Catholic doctrine, one famous Jesuit expression was, "What I see as white, I will believe to be black if the hierarchical Church so wills it."

The aim of the Jesuits was to restore a true and fulfilling spirituality, one that allowed the faithful to surrender themselves to the contemplation of God. Loyola's *Spiritual Exercises,* a guidebook to meditation and prayer, was one path to achieve this; the other was a wholehearted surrender to imagery from the Gospels. Unlike the Calvinists, the Jesuits believed sacred art could transport the congregation into a pious trance, not unlike the stained-glass windows of an earlier era. The artists of the early Baroque, particularly Caravaggio (1571–1610), rose to the challenge by creating an unprecedented realism, often by virtue of dramatic light effects. Caravaggio's depictions of Jesus' arrest and his subsequent flagellation were so real that his contemporaries could truly imagine themselves being eyewitnesses to Christ's Passion.

The Jesuits saw themselves as elite soldiers on the front lines of the Counter-Reformation. They quickly identified education as a key opportunity to raise new generations beholden to Catholic doctrine. But their curriculum was not limited to religious indoctrination alone. Many Jesuit schools excelled in such Renaissance subjects as classical literature, languages, philosophy, rhetoric, science, and the arts. Indeed, many intellectuals of the coming Enlightenment would owe their educations to Jesuit schools. By the mid-17th century, Jesuits ran more than 500 schools and universities across Europe and, increasingly, in newly discovered territories as well.

SAINTS AND CLERICS

Ignatius of Loyola

Francisco de Zurbarán (1598–1664) painted this portrait of Ignatius of Loyola.

A Spanish knight and member of the Basque nobility, Ignatius of Loyola was devoted to a military career until he suffered a severe leg injury during the attempted Spanish conquest of the Navarre region in 1521. His long recovery led to a period of solitary meditation, in which he formulated his famous *Spiritual Exercises*—a four-week program designed to immerse a believer in the contemplation of the divine. Created for both laymen and clergy, the *Exercises* would form the foundation of the Jesuit campaign to imbue Catholicism with a renewed spirituality. He enrolled at the University of Alcalá, northeast of Madrid, and later continued his studies in theology in Paris. Here, he gathered a group of followers, including Francis Xavier (1506–1552) and Peter Faber (1506–1546), with whom he would become a potent force in the Catholic Counter-Reformation. Loyola was canonized by Pope Gregory XV in 1622 and is still venerated as the patron saint of soldiers.

1563
The Council of Trent is officially closed

1567
James VI ascends the throne of Scotland

1571
The artist Caravaggio is born

1572
During the St. Bartholomew's Day Massacre, thousands of French Huguenots are killed

By that time, the Jesuits were the vanguard of proselytizing efforts outside of Europe. Jesuit Francis Xavier (1506–1552), a co-founder of the Society of Jesus, undertook missions to Portuguese enclaves in India and even ventured as far as Japan and the Moluccas. Another Jesuit founder, Matteo Ricci (1552–1610), traveled to China on a Portuguese ship, mastered the Chinese alphabet, and developed the first map of the world in Chinese. In 1601, Ricci became an adviser to Chinese Emperor Wanli (r. 1572–1620). A half-century later, the Jesuit movement had grown to 25,000 members across the globe.

Thus, as the 16th century drew to a close, the Catholic Church refocused itself on three cardinal elements: Scripture, sacraments, and piety, in direct contrast to the Protestant emphasis on "only grace, faith, and Scripture." These tenets would guide Catholicism until the Second Vatican Council.

HISTORY AND POLITICS

The First Missions

While the official purpose of Spain's conquest of the New World was the conversion of native peoples to Catholicism, in reality the primary motive was the lust for gold and spices—since many still believed that Columbus had discovered a new route to the Indies, rather than the Americas. In the process, two advanced civilizations—the Maya and the Aztec—were demolished in less than 40 years after Columbus's original discovery. The Portuguese planted vast sugar plantations in their domains and raided the coasts of Brazil and the Caribbean to get the labor to work them. Thus, the Portuguese introduced the concept of hereditary slavery, soon to be joined by the British and French, who turned to Africa as the primary source of slaves. In the 17th century, however, Jesuit communities or "missions" began to spring up in Spanish Paraguay (which at the time included parts of Brazil and Argentina). Originally conceived by Francisco de Toledo, viceroy of Peru, as "concentration areas" to better govern the local population, many of these mission towns, or *reducciones,* became havens for natives desperate to escape the slave hunters. Some became townships with churches, schools, libraries, and local industries. Jesuit missions were also built among the natives of North America, including today's Ontario, Quebec, Michigan, and New York. In 1773, however, Pope Clement XIV (r. 1769–1774) ceded to intense Portuguese and Spanish pressure and disbanded the Society of Jesus, leading to the wholesale suppression of Jesuit activity in Latin America—an event that inspired the 1986 motion picture *The Mission*.

"The Slave Hunter" is the work of Jean-Baptiste Debret (1768–1848).

The Baroque

The new focus on emotional spirituality also affected church architecture of the late 16th and 17th centuries, producing a style that became known as the Baroque. Architects began to manipulate the traditional boundary between building and space, designing more sculptural churches. The idea is epitomized in the career of Gian Lorenzo Bernini (1598–1680), who was both a sculptor and an architect. Using every device at his disposal, including light effects and soaring domes filled with trompe l'oeil decoration, architects like Bernini created breathtaking illusions that could fill worshippers with religious ecstasy.

The new Baroque style swiftly swept through the Catholic south, producing such important works as St. Peter's (completed in 1626) and the visually stunning San Carlo alle Quattro Fontane (1638), but it didn't stop there. Its revolutionary approach to using the classical vernacular also resonated with the Protestant north, to the point that the Baroque soon lost its original association with the Counter-Reformation. One of the most dramatic examples is St. Paul's in London, a cathedral of the Church of England,

OPPOSITE: ST. PAUL'S IN LONDON, a cathedral of the Church of England, was designed by Christopher Wren (1632–1723) in 1669.

1583 The Jesuit Matteo Ricci reaches Beijing

1583 Astronomer Tycho Brahe proposes a heliocentric model of planetary orbits

1587 All Christian missionaries are expelled from Kyushu, Japan

1588 Pope Sixtus V institutes the Inquisition in Italy

designed by Christopher Wren in 1669. Though somewhat more restrained, the Baroque style was also adopted in Protestant Germany after the conclusion of the Thirty Years' War in 1648. The Russian Orthodox Church, too, embraced the Baroque in its monumental Peter and Paul Cathedral in St. Petersburg, designed by Swiss-Italian architect Domenico Trezzeni (ca 1670–1734). Meanwhile, the Jesuit Church of the Gesù in Rome, completed in 1584 and often described as the church with the first Baroque facade, would become the prototype for countless Jesuit churches in Latin America.

The Reformation in the North

At the dawn of the 17th century, it seemed that the religious conflict in Europe was stabilizing. Catholicism remained in firm control of southern and eastern Europe, including France and southern Germany as well as Poland, Hungary, and Bohemia, while the Reformation consolidated its position in the north, including the Scandinavian lands, northern Germany, Holland, and Scotland.

The cathedral church of the London Diocese was built after the Great Fire of London of 1666. The fifth church to be built on the site, it features a dome as wide as nave and aisles together.

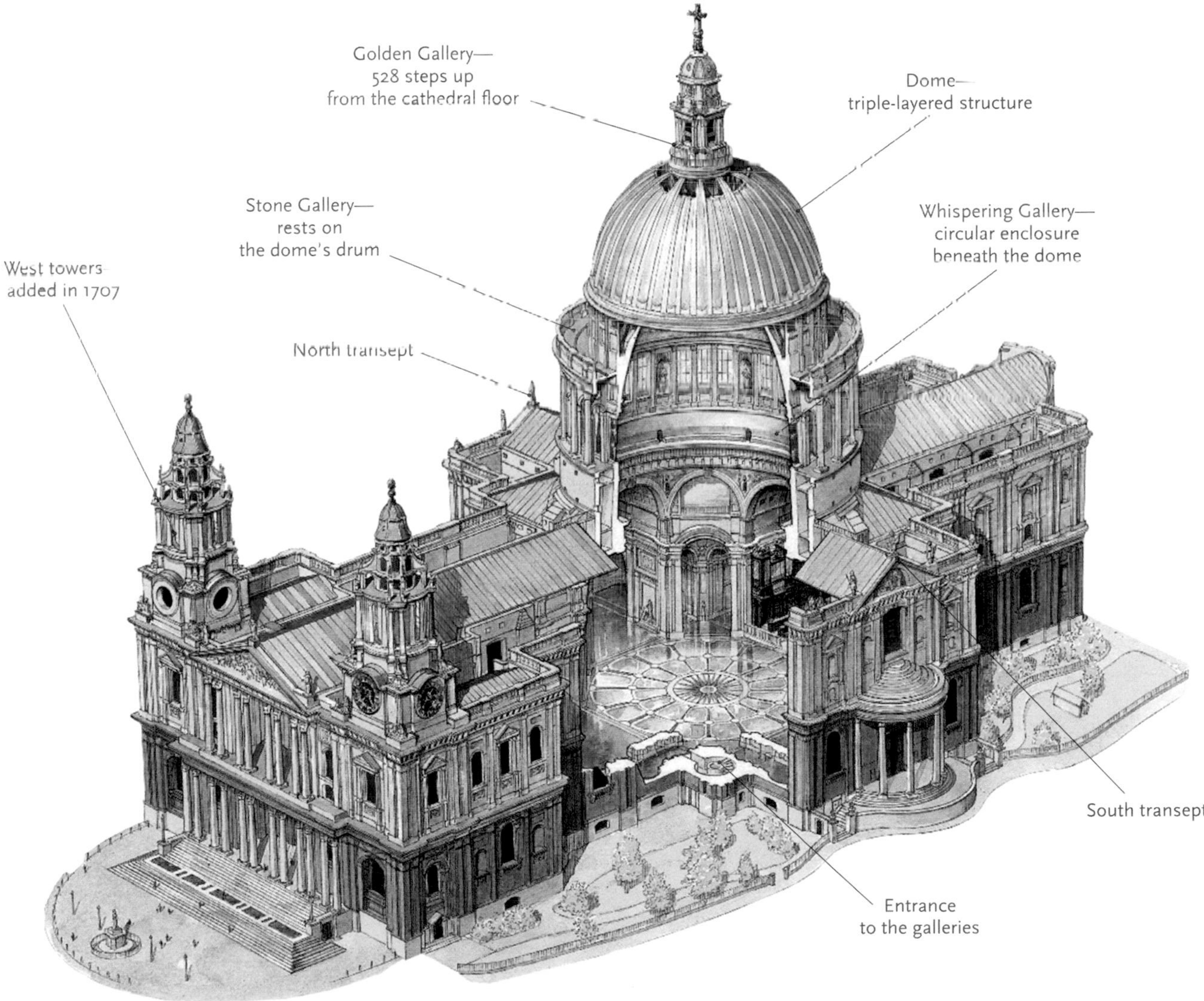

Golden Gallery—528 steps up from the cathedral floor

Dome—triple-layered structure

Stone Gallery—rests on the dome's drum

Whispering Gallery—circular enclosure beneath the dome

West towers added in 1707

North transept

South transept

Entrance to the galleries

1594 Henry of Navarre ascends the French throne as King Henry IV

1596 The Swedish Church formally adopts the Augsburg Confession to become Lutheran

1596 Dutch explorer Cornelis de Houtman reaches Java

1598 King Henry IV issues the Edict of Nantes, rescinding the persecution of Protestantism

Indeed, after England, it was in Scotland and Holland that Protestantism first succeeded in becoming the de facto state religion. In Scotland, a priest and notary named John Knox (ca 1514–1572) was deeply involved in attempts to reform the Catholic Church until political events, including the regency of Mary of Guise, forced his exile to Britain. Here, he played a key role in the still-ongoing English Reformation under Henry VIII's successor, King Edward VI (r. 1547–1553), until the

young king's untimely death led to the accession of the Catholic Mary Tudor. Knox moved to Geneva, where he fell under the spell of John Calvin. In 1559, he returned to Scotland to lead a Protestant Reformation along Calvinist lines, which was rapidly embraced by the Scottish nobility. In 1560, the Scottish Parliament adopted a Reformation Settlement, which established an uneasy coexistence between Calvinist doctrine and the existing system of church governance by bishops. But the accession of Mary Stuart, Queen of Scots, in 1561, inflamed tensions between Protestants and Catholics, and a bloody civil war ensued until James VI (r. 1567–1625) assumed the throne. Just four years into his reign, James confirmed the Reformation Settlement. The Kirk, or Reformed Church of Scotland—also known as the Presbyterian Church—became a reality.

Then, in 1603, an extraordinary event occurred. After English Queen Elizabeth I died without issue, James succeeded her as King James I of England, and the two realms

HISTORY AND POLITICS

The Thirty Years' War

The Thirty Years' War (1618–1648) was one of the most destructive conflicts ever fought on European soil. The immediate cause was the ongoing conflict between Protestant and Catholic states, despite hopes that the 1555 Peace of Augsburg would have laid those tensions to rest. In the years after the treaty, however, Calvinism continued its rapid growth in the north, alarming the Catholic states. Once hostilities broke out, political calculations ensured that the conflict dragged on. Charles V, the Holy Roman Emperor, was desperate to preserve the loyalty of numerous European principalities, while other European powers saw an opportunity to roll back the Emperor's grip on Europe. Holland was in open rebellion against Spain. Danish King Christian IV sided with Lower Saxony in an attack on imperial forces, soon joined by Swedish King Gustavus Adolphus. In 1635, prodded by his chief minister, Cardinal Richelieu, French King Louis XIII also launched an attack on Spanish troops in Germany and the Netherlands. The Portuguese exploited the moment to rise up against Spain as well. In the end, the Habsburg Empire was greatly diminished, with much of its realm splintered into more than 300 principalities.

Ernest Crofts (1847–1911) depicted the destruction of war in this canvas entitled "Wallenstein: A Scene of the Thirty Years' War."

The devastation wrought by the war was unprecedented. According to modern estimates, up to 40 percent of the population in German lands died. In some states, the male population was reduced by half, a result not only of military action but also of famine, disease, and malnutrition. After peace was finally concluded in 1648, many regions would take more than a century to recover.

1598
Dutch explorer Jan Huygen publishes an atlas of sea routes to the East Indies

1600
English traders form the East India Company

1601
Jesuit Matteo Ricci advises Chinese emperor Wanli

1602
The Dutch United East India Company, is formed, the first multinational corporation

(as well as Ireland) were joined together at last. Under his rule, Knox's efforts finally bore fruit when Presbyterianism was confirmed as the national faith of Scotland.

During all this time, the Seven United Provinces of Holland had continued their struggle against Spanish dominion. This so-called Eighty Years' War would not be settled until the Peace of Münster of 1648. Long before, however, Holland had entered a Golden Age, as its superior science and maritime technology turned it into one of the great powers of Europe. Much of this prosperity was due to the fall of Antwerp to Spanish forces in 1585, which caused an exodus of its Protestant population—including many skilled workers and merchants—to Amsterdam in the north. Despite its solid Calvinist foundation, the Dutch Republic opened its arms to religious refugees, regardless of their faith orientation. Thus, scores of Huguenots and even Jews from Spain and Portugal found a safe haven in Holland. Louise de Coligny, daughter of the prominent Huguenot leader Gaspard de Coligny, who had been killed during the St. Bartholomew's Day Massacre, even married the leader of the Dutch revolt against the Spanish, William I (r. 1544–1584), founder of the Dutch royal house of Orange-Nassau.

A man with God is always in the majority.

JOHN KNOX, FOUNDER OF PRESBYTERIANISM

Lutheranism rather than Calvinism swept the Scandinavian territories. In Denmark King Frederick I (r. 1523–1533) tried to keep tensions between Protestants and Catholics in check while closing a number of monasteries and actively abetting the growth of a national Danish Lutheran church. Swedish King Gustav I Vasa (r. 1523–1560) also broke away from Rome to establish an independent Church of Sweden, which formally adopted the Augsburg Confession in 1596 and became Lutheran. Finland and Norway developed Lutheran churches as well.

New Expeditions Overseas

In the midst of this religious upheaval, the age of discovery gained new impetus at the dawn of the 17th century, once again propelled by maritime science and technology. The sextant replaced the astrolabe as the principal instrument of navigation, while the Portuguese caravel was superseded by the three-masted, multidecked galleon. Based on the 15th-century carrack, the galleon was longer, with a raised forecastle and aftcastle, which gave it unprecedented stability in rough seas. Improvements in seaborne cannon turned the galleon into a formidable weapon: a broadside-cannoned, full-rigged sailing ship.

Though the galleon was originally developed by Portuguese shipwrights, Britain and Holland soon replaced Portugal as the principal shipyards of the 17th century. The Dutch improved on the galleon design to create the *fluyt,* a long-distance trading vessel that eliminated all armament in favor of maximum cargo space. This also cut down on the number of crew and cost about half as much to build.

With the fluyt, Holland rapidly pushed to the forefront of seafaring exploration. In 1596, a four-ship expedition led by Cornelis de Houtman dropped anchor on the shores of Java, thus beginning a nearly four-century occupation of the island group known today as Indonesia. Five years later, Willem Janszoon

OPPOSITE: *This portrait of King James I was painted by John de Critz the Elder (ca 1552–1642).*

This engraving of an astronomical sextant by Tycho Brahe (1546–1601) appeared in an atlas by the Amsterdam cartographer Joan Blaeu (1596–1673).

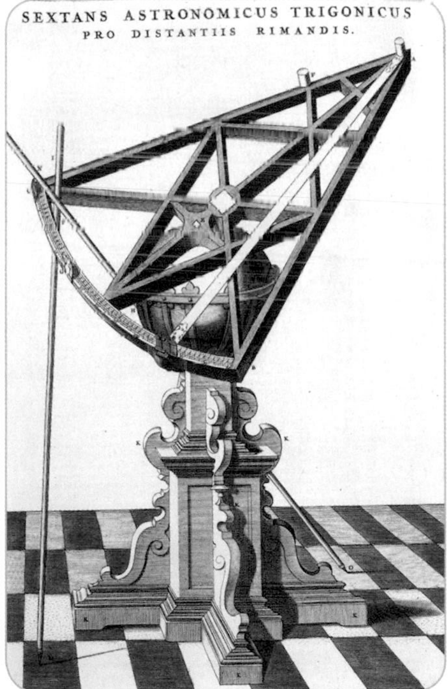

1603 — James VI of Scotland succeeds Elizabeth I of England as King James I

1608 — The English establish settlements in India

1609 — First Jesuit missions in South America

1609 — German astronomer Johannes Kepler's book ***Astronomia Nova*** is published

discovered a large landmass that became known as Terra Australis Incognita ("Unknown Land in the South"), today's Australia. In 1598, Dutch explorer Jan Huygen published a book detailing the principal sea routes to the East Indies, which in one fell swoop eliminated Portugal's competitive edge and unleashed a European race to the east. To fully exploit their gains, in 1602 Dutch traders formed the Vereenigde Oost-Indische Compagnie (VOC, the United East India Company), the first multinational corporation in history. For the next 200 years, the VOC would dominate European trade with Asia, dispatching 4,785 ships that carried 2.5 million tons of cargo, virtually monopolizing the trade in spices.

England, Holland's chief competitor, was alarmed by the string of Dutch successes. It had established its own East India Company in 1600 and soon thereafter embarked on several spectacularly successful expeditions. In 1608, British ships established their first foothold in India. By the end of the 17th century, England's Indian settlements had taken over from Portugal's as centers of trade, and England was moving to virtual control of the Indian subcontinent. In 1607, English entrepreneurs financed a three-ship expedition to the New World, leading to Britain's first permanent colony in America, in Jamestown, Virginia. A century later, James Cook sailed east to chart a course to Australia's west coast, naming it New South Wales. In 1787, a British convoy known as the First Fleet arrived with 751 convicts (including 188 women), thus converting their Australian territory into a large-scale penal colony.

Notwithstanding these commercial successes, however, evangelization efforts in the East Indies were less successful. On the Southeast Asian mainland, only the area analogous to today's Vietnam was receptive

The painting "Shipping in a Calm at Flushing," by Jan van de Capelle (1626–1679), depicts the naval might of 17th-century Holland.

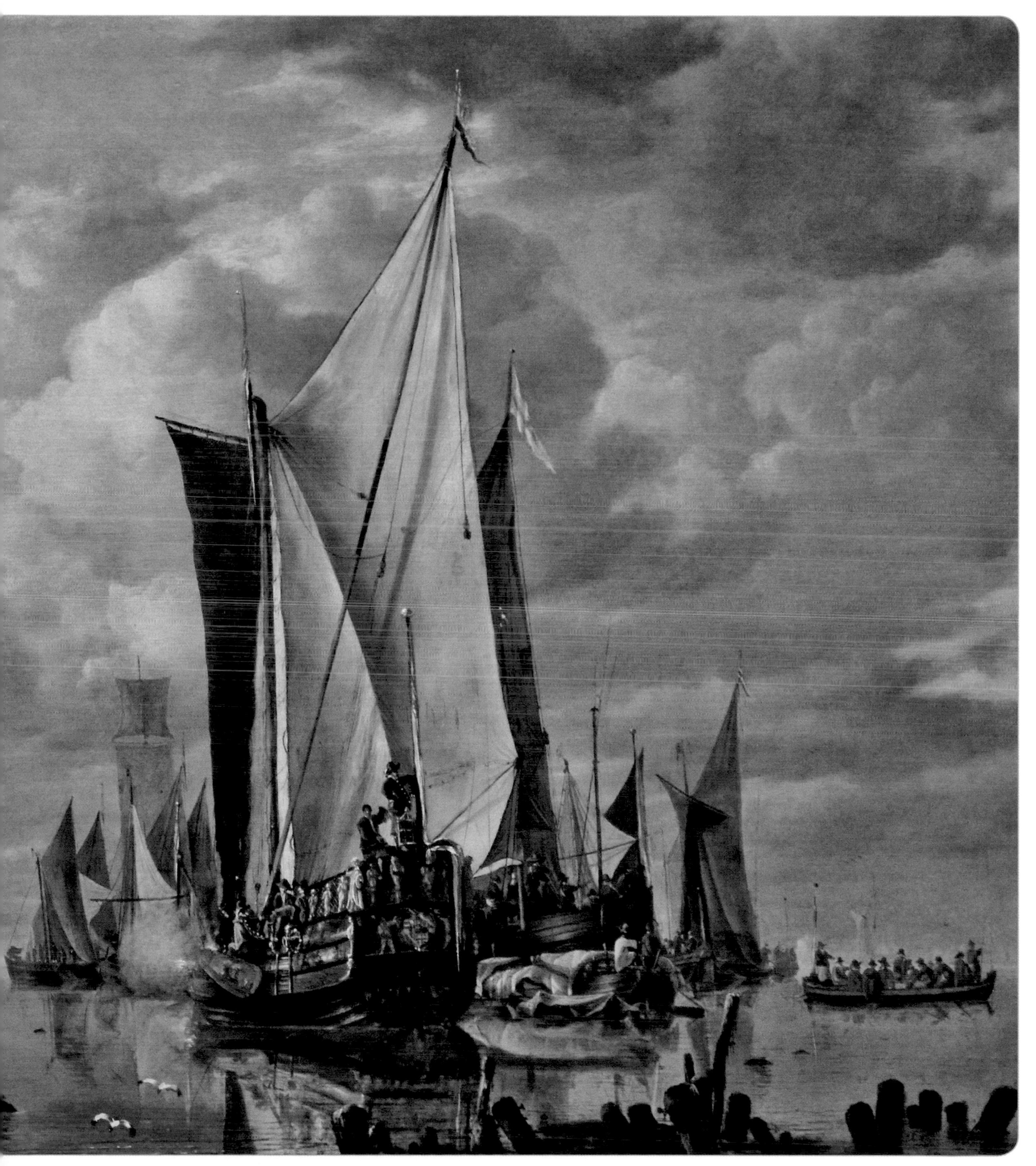

Period Objects

1750–1900

This East India Company vase was created by the 19th-century French School.

An 18th-century woman's dress carries the mark of the East India Company.

The Dutch VOC (United East India Company) maintained a large shipyard with warehouses in Amsterdam, as shown in this 1725 engraving by Dutch artist Joseph Mulder (1658–ca 1728).

to Christianity. The Philippines, by contrast, embraced Christianity wholeheartedly—a situation that continues to this day. Missionaries also made headway into Japan, but fears that a Western invasion was imminent prompted the local shoguns to suppress any further conversion activity.

The New World, by contrast, became a welcome haven for persecuted religious minorities in Europe. One of these was a group known as the Puritans, an English Protestant community along Calvinist lines that had much in common with Scottish Presbyterianism. During the reign of Elizabeth I (r. 1558–1603), England had become a formidable Protestant power. The Anglican Church, under the Queen's tutelage, became a true Protestant confession. Only during the interregnum of Oliver Cromwell, Lord Protector of England between 1646 and 1660, did the Puritan movement emerge as a leading religious and political force. Similar to the Scottish Presbyterians, the Puritans wanted to rid the Anglican Church of many lingering Catholic elements, such as the office of the bishop and ceremonial vestments, and refocus the faith on piety and simplicity. But the restoration of the English monarchy in 1662 put an abrupt end to their influence. Thousands of Puritans left Europe to settle in New England. Already, a Puritan colony had been established in Virginia as early as 1618, followed by a settlement in Salem, Massachusetts, in 1620. An offshoot of the Puritans, the so-called Pilgrims led by William Brewster (ca 1566–1644) established a colony in Plymouth that same year. Thus, the foundation was laid for a New World community that would prize political and religious freedom above all else.

But back in Europe, forces were gathering that would pose a new challenge to Protestantism and Catholicism alike. ■

OPPOSITE: *Artist George Henry Boughton (1833–1905) painted "The Landing of the Pilgrim Fathers."*

1612
A persecution of Christians in Japan begins

1618
Outbreak of the Thirty Years' War

1618
First Puritan colony of the New World is established in Virginia

1620
A Puritan colony is established in Salem, Massachusetts

10
CHAPTER

GALLIÆ CVSTODEM CHRISTVS PATRIÆ FATA

THE AGE OF ENLIGHTENMENT

1650-1800

I do not agree with what you say, but I'll defend to the death your right to say it.

VOLTAIRE

The destruction wrought by the Thirty Years' War would lead to the greatest crisis in Christianity since the Reformation. Europeans were deeply affected by the sheer violence of 17th-century religious conflicts. Particularly among intellectuals, the ravages of war prompted a deep skepticism about the lofty ideals of Christianity. If the purpose of the Christian faith was to foster love and compassion, how then could Christians engage in such wholesale slaughter? Or as the French philosopher Voltaire (1694–1778) put it, "Of all religions, the Christian should inspire the most tolerance. And yet, until now, Christians have been the most intolerant of men." Hence, these intellectuals believed, mankind should search for other principles to govern an ever more complex world.

Thus was born an age that became known as the Enlightenment, or more appropriately, the Age of Reason. The term tries to encapsulate various movements in the late 17th and 18th centuries that sought to create a new moral and ethical foundation for mankind, using humanist principles first developed in the Renaissance.

Led by a small but highly diverse group of intellectuals, ranging from Dutch philosopher Baruch Spinoza (1632–1677) and English physicist Isaac Newton (1643–1727) to German philosopher

ABOVE: *This medal commemorates the appearance of a bright comet in November 1618, noted by Galileo Galilei (1564–1642), among others.*

OPPOSITE: *The elegant but austere interior of St. Geneviève in Paris, renamed the Panthéon after the French Revolution, is an early example of French classicism. It was designed by Jacques-Germain Soufflot.*

PRECEDING PAGES: *"A Lecture on the Orrery" was painted in 1766 by British artist Joseph Wright of Derby (1734–1797).*

OPPOSITE: René Descartes is depicted with Queen Christina of Sweden in this painting by Pierre-Louis Dumesnil (1698–1781). Many 17th-century philosophers enjoyed celebrity status at Europe's courts.

Belgian artist Jean-Leon Huens (1921–1982) painted "Galileo Explaining Moon Topography to Skeptics."

Immanuel Kant (1724–1804) and French encyclopedist Denis Diderot (1713–1784), the Enlightenment was not a pan-European movement in the truest sense, since its advocacy was largely limited to intellectual and literary salons. Nevertheless, its influence on Europe's leaders and institutions was vast. In the growing American colonies, the principals of Enlightenment would strongly resonate with Benjamin Franklin (1706–1790) and Thomas Jefferson (1743–1826), and provide a major impetus for the American Revolution. In France, it would be influential in fostering the French Revolution.

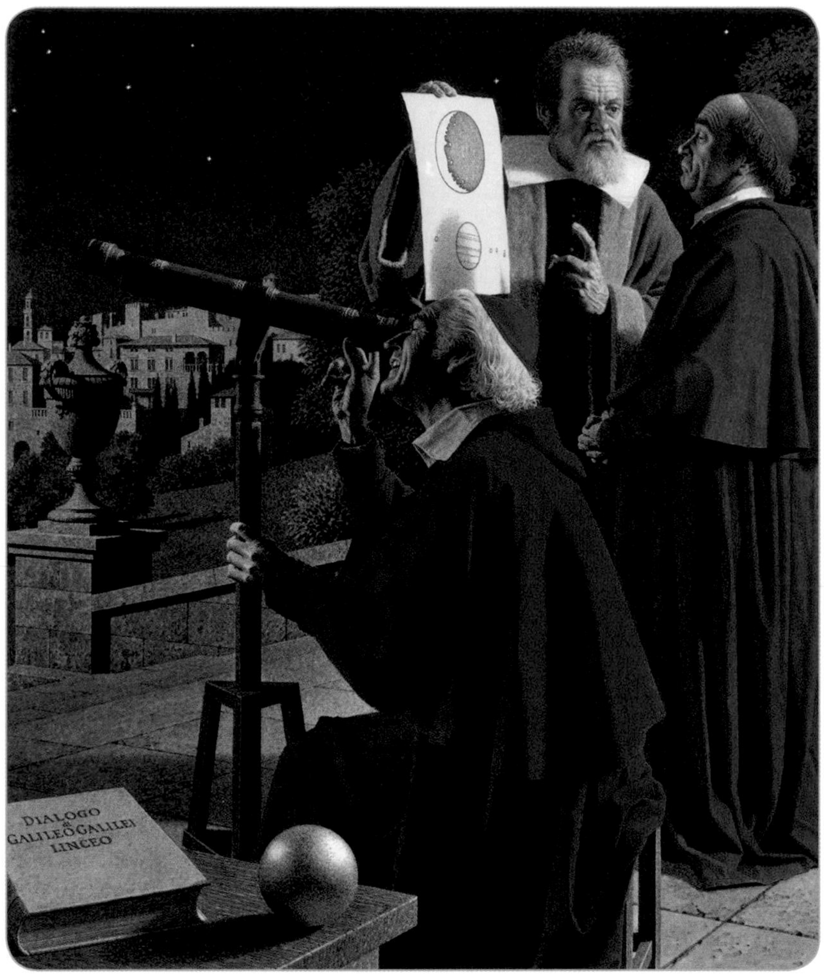

Several modern scholars have tried to identify a direct link between the Counter-Reformation and the Enlightenment. They believe that the anti-intellectual fervor of the triumphant Catholic Church challenged the scientific accomplishments of the Renaissance, thus leading to a reaction. An oft-quoted example is the famous trial of Italian physicist and astronomer Galileo Galilei (1564–1642), who, like Copernicus before him, had argued for a heliocentric model of the cosmos. In 1613, he was forced by the Church to recant. For many, this meant that the Catholic Church was an obstacle to science, too beholden to doctrine to tolerate independent research. On the other hand, Galileo had relied heavily on observations by Jesuit astronomers. Moreover, many of Europe's brightest minds, the cream of the Enlightenment, had been educated in Jesuit institutions.

Other authors have depicted the Age of Reason in strictly political terms, as a reaction against absolutism in all forms—emperor, king, or pope. Others again believe that the Enlightenment and its growing animus against the Church were to a large extent motivated by the great social and economic iniquities in European society. The horrific devastation of the Thirty Years' War, the terror of the Inquisition, the bloody suppression of Huguenots in France and Protestants elsewhere—all of these depredations had, in the end, served no purpose other than to confirm the power of Church and Crown. By some calculations, poverty, disease, and malnutrition in Europe were considerably worse in the 17th century than at any time during the High Middle Ages and the Renaissance. To some, it seemed that humankind was moving backward, rather than forward.

1623
French scientist and philosopher Blaise Pascal is born

1624
English philosopher Lord Herbert of Cherbury writes his treatise *On Truth*

1632
Dutch philosopher Baruch Spinoza is born

1632
English philosopher John Locke is born

Rationalism

As it progressed, the Enlightenment fostered several distinct movements. In France, René Descartes (1596–1650) argued that only reason, supported by scientific method and scholarly analysis, should be the basis for understanding universal truths and values. Instead of the pious submission advocated by the Catholic Church, or the strictures of faith propagated by Protestant movements, Descartes's rationalism suggested that deductive logic should be the only guiding beacon of human endeavor. For example, Descartes believed that God's existence could be inferred from man's rational understanding of a "supremely perfect being." A mathematician by training, Descartes was convinced that the new emphasis on scientific knowledge would make all preceding ideologies redundant. His book *Les Passions de l'Âme* (*Passions of the Soul,* 1649) warned its readers that its author would set forth his theories "as if no one had written on these matters before."

This idea of the Enlightenment as an intellectual tabula rasa on which mankind could entirely recalculate the purpose of its existence also animated other philosophers, but with other outcomes. The renowned Dutch philosopher Baruch Spinoza accepted rational thought as the key to understanding the human universe, but maintained that God

OPPOSITE: *Dutch philosopher Baruch Spinoza is portrayed in this canvas by an anonymous 17th-century artist.*

French artist Pierre-Denis Martin (1663–1742) depicts "Louis XIV and His Entourage" visiting the military infirmary known as the Hôpital des Invalides, which Louis founded.

1643
English scientist Isaac Newton is born

1648
The Treaty of Westphalia ends the Thirty Years' War

1649
French philosopher René Descartes publishes his book *Passions of the Soul*

1651
Thomas Hobbes publishes his influential book *Leviathan*

still stood at its center—though perhaps in an abstract sense. Both God and nature were closely intertwined, just as the mind and body were closely interrelated in man. Thus, Spinoza concluded, by trying to grapple with the fundamental truths about nature and human behavior, we could become not only more free, but also closer to God. This inspired him to undertake what may be the first instance of modern biblical criticism—the scholarly quest to discern the origins and meaning of biblical texts, outside of their presumed divine origin. For this he was expelled from his Portuguese Jewish community in Amsterdam, while his books wound up on the Catholic Index of forbidden books.

Deism

Similar attempts to reconcile rationalism with Christian ideas inspired a movement called Deism. Deism, based on the Latin word *deus* (God), held that rational thought, rather than divine revelation or mysticism, could prove the existence of God. English Deists such as Lord Herbert of Cherbury (1583–1648) and Matthew Tindal (1657–1733) believed that while God created the universe, he did not intervene in human affairs. Having given human beings the gift of reason and free will, God abstained from controlling human destiny but nevertheless expected men and women to live moral lives. This explained, in the Deist view, why there was so much violence, tragedy, and evil in the world despite God's innate goodness—and why it was up to mankind, guided by rational thought, to create order in the chaos. Tindal spoke of a "natural religion," which acknowledges the existence of God, but also imposes on human beings the "sense and practice of those duties which result from the knowledge of God." Such a natural religion, Tindal believed, was "universal" and not beholden to one particular revelation.

God designed all mankind to know what he wills them to know, believe, profess, and practice; and has given them no other means for this, but the use of reason.

MATTHEW TINDAL,
CHRISTIANITY AS OLD AS THE CREATION

Deism would gain a considerable following among intellectuals in the 18th century, including Thomas Jefferson and Benjamin Franklin. Thomas Jefferson, who would serve as the third president of the newly

Scientific Instruments
1640–1750

This wooden telescope from 1671 once belonged to Sir Isaac Newton.

J. G. Mitsdörffer developed this German solar microscope in 1751.

Blaise Pascal invented this detailed calculating machine in 1642.

1652
Russian Orthodox Patriarch Nikon changes Russian liturgy to the Greek model

1656–1657
Blaise Pascal publishes *Provincial Letters*

1657
English Deist theologian Matthew Tindal is born

1661
King Louis XIV of France establishes an absolutist monarchy

independent United States (r. 1801–1809) even produced a redacted edition of the Gospels, entitled *The Life and Morals of Jesus of Nazareth* (1820). The volume extolled Jesus as a great moral sage, but denied his divinity and excluded most miracles and other supernatural events.

HISTORY AND POLITICS

The Enlightenment and the American Revolution

Perhaps the most vivid application of Enlightenment ideals was the creation of a new republic, known as the United States of America, in the British colonies of the New World. Much of the growing disenchantment between the colonists and their mother country was caused by England's disastrous involvement in wars with France. Though England emerged triumphant in 1763, gaining French Canada in the process, its depleted treasury forced the Crown to raise taxes on the colonies. The settlers, a population of more than 1.5 million across 13 colonies, rose in protest. In 1770, a British platoon in Boston was pelted with snowballs and other objects. The soldiers opened fire in response, thus igniting the Revolutionary War. Years of hard fighting lay ahead, but in 1776, the newly formed American Continental Congress adopted a declaration of independence. It had been written by Thomas Jefferson, based on John Locke's theory that humans have certain inalienable rights, including the right to life, liberty, and property.

The newly formed republic of the United States was to be governed not by dynastic principles, but democratic ones, enshrined in a document known as the Constitution. Greatly influenced by Montesquieu's *De l'Esprit des Loix* (*The Spirit of Laws,* 1748), the Constitution separated the government into legislative, judicial, and executive branches, with the latter led by an elected president. Montesquieu's book also argued for an end to slavery, but it would take almost another century before this aspect of Enlightenment political theory would be written into American law as well.

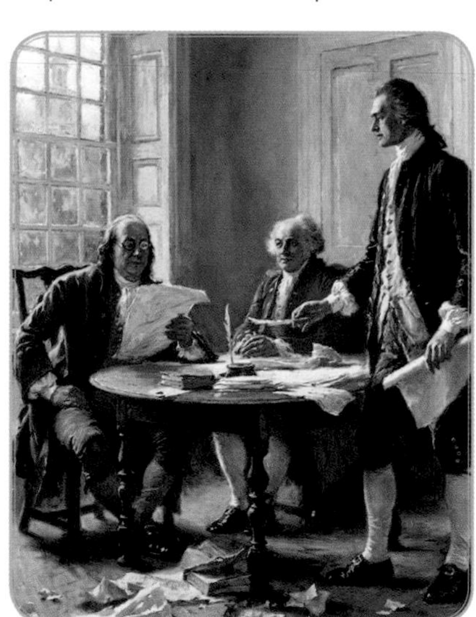

Eminent French artist Jean-Léon Gérôme (1824–1904) painted "Writing the Declaration of Independence in 1776."

Empiricism

A different school of thought was advanced by English philosophers who, in contrast to the rationalists, believed that the human senses, rather than deductive reasoning, should be the ultimate arbiter of truth. John Locke (1632–1704), often recognized as the principal exponent of empiricism, quoted Aristotle in arguing that a child at birth is a blank slate, and that all knowledge acquired through subsequent life is by virtue of sensory experiences. That process ultimately produces "that conscious thinking thing . . . which is sensible, or conscious of pleasure and pain, capable of happiness or misery, and so is concerned for itself, as far as that consciousness extends," he wrote. In a way, Locke formulated the basis of modern developmental psychology when he posited that much of what we are is the result of "little and almost insensible impressions on our tender infancies."

Sir Godfrey Kneller (1646–1723) painted this penetrating portrait of the British philosopher John Locke.

1682
Tsar Peter the Great ascends the throne of Russia

1685
Louis XIV revokes the Edict of Nantes, banning Protestantism from France

1686
The Church of Sweden issues a decree requiring all citizens to become literate

1687
Isaac Newton publishes *Mathematical Principles of Natural Philosophy*

Locke, too, was appalled by the violence of the religious wars of the past century, and believed the root of evil lay in the doctrinal differences between the various Christian movements. No man, Locke believed, could ever validate the truth claims of various confessions. As a result, he foreswore all Christian doctrine save for the Gospels themselves, and argued strongly that all nations should grant their citizens freedom in conscience and religion. Any attempt to impose religious conformity on an increasingly diverse population, he warned, was bound to provoke violence and social chaos, as indeed had happened in the preceding centuries.

Locke's appeal to sensory reason and tolerance had tremendous resonance in England and inspired other empiricists such as David Hume (1711–1776). Using rational arguments, Hume questioned the supernatural powers ascribed to Jesus and the Apostles. Another empiricist, Thomas Hobbes (1588–1679), used empirical principles to show that each individual possessed human rights. His highly influential book *Leviathan* (1651) posited that only a strong, hereditary monarchy could provide the necessary stability to avoid the crippling religious wars of years past.

Empiricism's most famous proponent, however, was the renowned physicist and mathematician Isaac Newton (1642–1727), whose groundbreaking discoveries in physics, including the laws of gravitation, seemed to prove Locke's theories. In his *Mathematical Principles of Natural Philosophy* (1687), Newton declared that faith in God should be grounded in the science of nature and the universe. Like the Deists, Newton believed in Jesus as the redeemer, but denied his divinity and the doctrine of the Trinity.

The French Enlightenment of the 18th Century

Locke, Newton, and other Deists would influence a second phase in the Enlightenment, which in the 18th century shifted its focus to France and Germany. The most influential German philosopher was undoubtedly Immanuel Kant (1724–1804), a professor of logic at the university of Königsberg. Blending both rationalism and empiricism, Kant argued in his *Kritik der reinen Vernunft* (*Critique of Pure Reason,* 1781) that knowledge can be grounded only on the rational

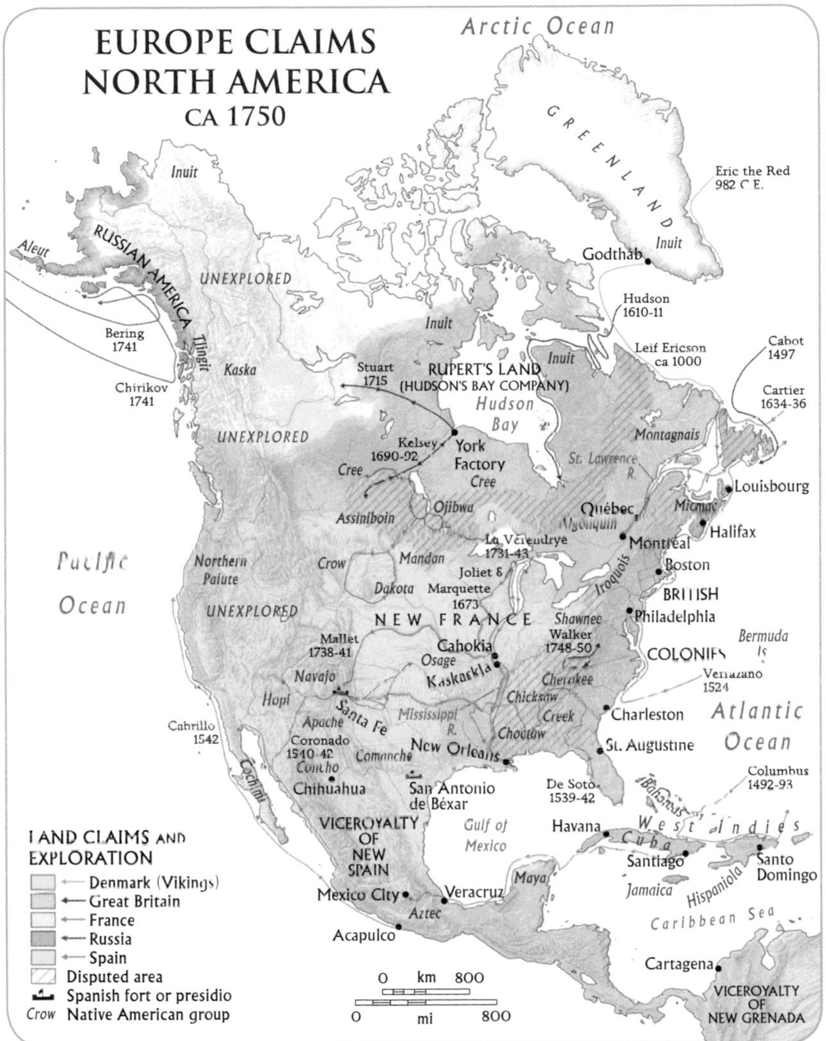

interpretation of natural phenomena. Thus, all supernatural phenomena attributed to God or Christ should be rejected. A moral life, Kant claimed, should be rooted in stern discipline and lived according to a universal system of ethics. Kant, however, discounted neither the existence of a divine being nor of immortality. Only the prospect of a judgment in the afterlife would convince people to live in mutual harmony with one another.

In France, the intellectual emphasis moved away from religion to the practical issues of the day, such as politics, the relations between nations, and the pursuit of science. If indeed science should be the basis of our rational existence, Denis Diderot believed, then human knowledge should be carefully collated and published for the edification of all mankind. Thus was born the *Encyclopédie* project, the first attempt since Pliny and Aristotle to create a categorical inventory of mankind's knowledge of the time. Co-written with Jean le Rond d'Alembert (1717–1783), the *Encyclopédie* combined science, philosophy, and physics with entries on more mundane subjects, such as French trades and engineering devices. After the first volume was published with great fanfare, a court verdict suspended the work when early drafts of the highly critical entries on religion were leaked. In 1752, the work resumed despite growing opposition among the French aristocracy, who saw its grip on French society threatened by the *encyclopédistes'* call for equality, intellectual liberty, and anticlericalism. Though only about 4,000 copies were sold, many historians believe that Diderot's *Encyclopédie* ultimately planted the seeds for the French Revolution.

Yet the Frenchman who would exert the greatest influence on contemporary political thought was François-Marie Arouet, better known as Voltaire. Part of Voltaire's appeal was the fact that he disseminated his ideas not only through philosophical tracts, as many of his fellow philosophes did, but also in the form of novels, poems, and plays, which gained broad popularity throughout Europe. Voltaire even wrote what is possibly the first example of science fiction, the novel *Micromégas* (1752), which features a visit by interstellar ambassadors eager to engage humans in philosophical debate. His smooth, accessible writing and sharp wit did not, however, disguise his almost polemical animus against the French "First Estate," the Catholic Church, which he denounced as feudal, dogmatic, and profoundly intolerant of social change. When, on November 1,

OPPOSITE: *Giovanni Battista Tiepolo (1696–1770), one of the last great Italian artists of the 18th century, painted "The Vision of St. Clemens" around 1735.*

French philosopher Voltaire is shown in his study in this French 18th-century illustration.

SCRIPTURE AND FAITH

Jean-Jacques Rousseau

Allan Ramsay (1713–1784) painted this portrait of Jean-Jacques Rousseau.

Geneva-born Jean-Jacques Rousseau (1712–1778) was one of the most influential Deist authors of his time. Raised a Calvinist, he journeyed to Paris in 1741 and soon moved in the circle of Diderot's encyclopedists. Upon his return to Geneva in 1754, he wrote the first of several important books, *Discourse on the Origin and Basis of Inequality Among Men,* which argued that property had imposed inequality and unhappiness on mankind, which heretofore had lived in pastoral bliss. Reflecting both empiricism and the growing evangelical sentiment of the time, his 1756 work *Émile, or On Education,* advocated that the ultimate religious experience was only to be found in a personal relationship with God, by virtue of man's conscience. His *Social Contract* of 1762 suggested that in a just society, only those religions should be tolerated that did not claim to have exclusive possession of divine revelation.

1711 English Empiricist philosopher David Hume is born

1712 German composer George Frideric Handel writes the *Messiah* oratorio

1713 French encyclopedist Denis Diderot is born

1715 Louis XIV dies and is succeeded by his great-grandson Louis XV

1755, a massive earthquake struck Lisbon, entombing thousands of worshippers during All Saints' Day Mass, Voltaire used the disaster as proof that the cosmos is devoid of a benevolent Father. How else could one explain this senseless devastation?

The Bourbon Dynasty

The shift among French philosophers from the lofty ideals of the 17th century to the more urgent issues of the day reflected the political changes in the country. In 1661, the Bourbon King Louis XIV (r. 1643–1715), the Sun King, had established an absolutist monarchy that by the end of the 17th century had gained total control of the French state—at the expense of the French nobility. Under Louis XIV's unprecedented 72-year rule, France emerged as the most powerful nation in Europe, eclipsing Spain and Holland after a series of crippling wars over territory and trade. By the dawn of the 18th century, France ruled continental Europe not only politically but also culturally. French, rather than Latin or Italian, became the lingua franca, the dominant language in European diplomacy as well as trade, music, literature, and art. This magnified the impact of the French philosophers, even though the Bourbons themselves were horrified by their liberal ideas.

Indeed, in 1685, Louis XIV shocked the world by revoking the Edict of Nantes, which in 1598 had grudgingly granted French Protestants a place in French society. Under the Sun King's reign, no dissent was to be tolerated. As a result of the revocation, Protestant parishes were disbanded, pastors exiled, and Protestant churches torn down. Some 200,000 Huguenots were forced to

Portuguese artist João Glama (1708–1792) painted this impression of the earthquake in Lisbon, which occurred on November 1, 1755—the church holiday of All Saints' Day.

flee the country and find haven elsewhere, including the Protestant north and the American colonies.

The Sun King's successor, Louis XV (r. 1715–1774), lacked his predecessor's strength. His reign would introduce the economic and political stagnation that ultimately led to the destruction of the French monarchy. Although his mistress, Madame de Pompadour, was in contact with French philosophers and tried to encourage social and political reforms (including the taxation of Catholic clergy), Louis lacked the character to stand up against the reactionary forces at his court. In 1726, the King signed a warrant for Voltaire's arrest and had him exiled to England, where the philosopher was introduced to the works of Isaac Newton. Voltaire was later allowed to return, though Louis XV banned him from Paris.

By that time, Voltaire's prestige and intellectual breadth had given him an entrée among Europe's crowned heads such as no other philosopher of the Enlightenment enjoyed. Many of these royals fashioned themselves as intellectuals themselves and eagerly basked in the glow of Voltaire's celebrity, while not always putting his ideas into practice. From 1736 onward, Voltaire corresponded regularly with King Frederick the Great of Prussia (r. 1740–1786), and following a visit to the King's court in Potsdam, was rewarded with an annual stipend of 20,000 francs. But when Voltaire challenged the president of the Berlin Academy of Science over some of his writings, King Frederick had him arrested.

Perhaps the greatest influence of Voltaire's writing, however, was felt not in Europe but in a nation that for centuries had isolated itself from European Christian civilization: the Empire of Russia.

The Russian Orthodox Church

With the encroachment of the Ottoman Empire on Christian territories in the East, the Russian Orthodox Church had emerged as the only viable successor to the Byzantine Empire and its Greek Christian rites. As we saw, the Byzantine emblem of the double-headed eagle, rooted in the *aquila,* the symbol of Roman military might, was adopted by Russian royalty in the mid-15th century. In 1547, the new Grand Prince of Moscow, Ivan IV Vasilyevich (r. 1547–1585), later known as Ivan the Terrible, reassumed the Byzantine title of Caesar or Tsar, ruling from Moscow.

The Russian Orthodox Church was also based in Moscow, so that temporal and spiritual power continuously jockeyed for influence over the faithful. After the patriarch of Moscow dared to speak up against Ivan's cruel tyranny, the Tsar had him arrested and killed. A later tsar, Alexei I, accused the reform-

OPPOSITE: *The unusual style of the Cathedral of Vasily the Blessed, or St. Basil's Cathedral, built on Red Square in Moscow in 1561, is meant to evoke flames rising into the sky.*

This view of the 1722 coronation of King Louis XV of France by Pierre-Denis Martin (1663–1742) depicts the Cathedral of Reims as it appeared in the 18th century.

1721 — Tsar Peter I abolishes the patriarchate of the Russian Orthodox Church

1721 — Johann Sebastian Bach writes the *Brandenburg* Concertos

1724 — German philosopher Immanuel Kant is born

1726 — Louis XV signs a warrant for Voltaire's arrest

Royal Artifacts

1650–1750

King Louis XV wore this crown of gilded silver during his coronation in 1722.

This golden snuffbox, adorned with diamonds, belonged to Louis XV.

Tsar Peter the Great presented this gold drinking cup to Frederick Augustus II.

minded Patriarch Nikon (1605–1681) of vying for the throne, and had him exiled to a remote monastery. Nikon's reforms, which sought to restore the Greek liturgy, led to a split in the Russian Orthodox Church between reformers and the so-called "Old Believers" who clung to traditional Russian rites.

Tensions between state and religion further increased when Tsar Peter I (r. 1682–1725) rose to power in 1682. Peter was determined to divorce Russia from its medieval past and turn it into a modern European nation. His famous "opening to the West" led to many important reforms in the fields of science, education, and religious observance. The Russian alphabet was simplified, the Russian calendar was replaced with the Western Julian calendar, and state investment poured into Russian industries. Taking a cue from Louis XIV, Peter abandoned the administrative system of local *uyezds* and concentrated the government in a new capital, St. Petersburg, from where it oversaw eight newly created provinces.

> *We must reduce our volume to the simple evangelists, select, even from them, the very words only of Jesus ... There will be found remaining the most sublime and benevolent code of morals which has ever been offered to man.*
>
> THOMAS JEFFERSON, "THE PHILOSOPHY OF JESUS OF NAZARETH"

In religious matters, too, the Tsar was influenced by European precedent. He was particularly intrigued by the idea of creating a national church under the auspices of the sovereign, rather than the pope or patriarch, as many princes in northern Europe had done. In 1721, the Tsar abolished the patriarchate and brought the Orthodox Church under state supervision, exercised by a synod of 12 clergymen appointed by Peter himself. To curb the powerful influence of Russian monks, the Tsar also forbade the construction of new monasteries and severely curtailed the influence of existing convents. Peter's successors continued this policy, so that by the end of the 18th century, some 560 out of 950 Russian monasteries had been closed.

Tsar Ivan IV, known as "The Terrible," appears as an intimidating figure in this 19th-century impression by Russian artist Victor Vasnetsov (1848–1926).

1727
Johann Sebastian Bach writes the oratorio *St. Matthew Passion*

1730
Matthew Tindal publishes the Deist book *Christianity as Old as the Creation*

1740
King Frederick the Great assumes the throne of Prussia

1743
Thomas Jefferson, the third president of the United States, is born

EXPANSION OF RUSSIA 1462–1796

Present-day Russia
Other present-day country boundaries
Grand principality of Moscow, 1462
Territory acquired by 1505 during reign of Ivan the Great
Territory acquired by 1598, year of death of Feodor I
Territory acquired by 1682, start of reign of Peter the Great
Territory acquired by Peter the Great and his successors by 1762
Territory acquired by Catherine the Great by 1796

Selected present-day country names shown in gray

Catherine the Great's "Toleration of All Faiths"

Though German by blood, Tsarina Catherine the Great (r. 1762–1796) inherited her predecessor's fascination with European thought. While still a princess married to the *tsarevich,* the future Peter III, Catherine was avidly reading the works of Voltaire and Montesquieu, as well as Diderot's formidable *Encyclopédie.* She was particularly impressed by their passionate advocacy of religious tolerance and freedom of thought. Having toppled her husband, Peter III, in a bloodless coup just one year after his ascension in 1761, Catherine tried to push through some religious reforms, albeit against staunch Orthodox opposition.

Catherine welcomed Jesuits after the suppression of their order in 1776, and that same year issued a decree known as the "Toleration of All Faiths." Muslims, long ostracized, were permitted to build mosques and allowed to undertake the hajj, the pilgrimage to Mecca, which had previously been denied. New Muslim townships were built with state support. Similarly, Jews were recognized as Russian citizens and permitted to worship and practice according to their faith, though they were subject to a special tax. Given the prominent role of Jews in trade, however, this led to growing tensions with Orthodox merchants. In 1785, Catherine was compelled to rescind the citizenship of Jews and declare them foreign residents instead.

Tsarina Catherine II of Russia, here shown in a portrait by Alexander Roslin (1718–1793), was much smitten with Voltaire and other French philosophers of the Enlightenment.

1748
French philosopher Montesquieu writes *The Spirit of Laws*

1748
The excavation of the Roman city of Pompeii begins

1751
Denis Diderot and Jean le Rond d'Alembert publish the first volume of the *Encyclopédie*

1752
Work on the *Encyclopédie* is temporarily disrupted because of a court injunction

Catherine II of Russia owned a copy of Denis Diderot's Encyclopédie and used it to develop a plan for a nationwide educational system in Russia.

OPPOSITE: *French mathematician Blaise Pascal is portrayed in this sculpture by the French sculptor Augustin Pajou (1730–1809) of 1785.*

The French Encyclopédie *was written by Denis Diderot with Jean le Rond d'Alembert between 1751 and 1757. The* Encyclopédie *was an attempt to catalog all of human knowledge.*

At the same time, Catherine continued to curb the secular power of the Orthodox Church. Church lands were appropriated, and only a small number of monasteries were allowed. No clergy served in any important government offices during Catherine's reign.

Even before her coronation, the Tsarina had initiated an ongoing correspondence with Voltaire. Under his guidance, she devoted her energies to reforming Russia's educational system, which (as elsewhere in Europe) was still in the hands of the Church. She drafted a major document, known as the "Bol'shoi Nakaz" ("Great Instruction"), which was to serve as the foundation for a nationwide educational system governed by enlightened ideals.

Then, in 1792, a mob toppled the French King Louis XVI (r. 1774–1792). Ironically, Louis XVI had been the first Bourbon king to attempt some reforms based on Enlightenment ideals. Despite fierce opposition from the French aristocracy, Louis had tried to abolish serfdom, lower the peasant tax, and adopt a greater tolerance toward Huguenot activity. In 1787, just two years before the Revolution, he signed the Edict of Versailles, which granted Calvinists, Lutherans, and Jews full legal status in the French kingdom. This was followed by a largely ceremonial "Declaration of the Rights of Man and

1752
Voltaire writes his novel *Micromégas*, the first work of science fiction

1754
Jean-Jacques Rousseau writes *Discourse on the Origin and Basis of Inequality Among Men*

1755
A massive earthquake hits Lisbon, destroying the city center

1756
Voltaire writes his "Poem on the Disaster of Lisbon"

Citizen" in 1789. Ostensibly in full accord with Enlightenment principles, it eliminated any form of persecution or discrimination on religious grounds within the French realm.

Alas, it was too little, too late. The King's disastrous economic policies, acerbated by France's previous involvement in the Seven Years' War (1756–1763), had plunged France into debt and led to a growing popular resentment against the privileges of the aristocracy. In 1792, after the outbreak of the French Revolution, the King and his wife, the Austrian-born Queen Marie Antoinette (r. 1774–1792), were arrested, and the following year they were both executed by guillotine.

Reason's last step is the realization that there are an infinite number of things that are beyond it.

BLAISE PASCAL, *PENSÉES*

The state-sanctioned murder of anointed royals sent shock waves through Europe. Almost overnight, the lofty ideals of the Enlightenment, admired by so many in the nobility and upper classes, turned into the nefarious seeds of insurrection. Instead of fostering a new system of international security, as many had hoped, the Age of Reason had destroyed one of Europe's mightiest dynasties.

The Reaction to the Enlightenment

Apart from the French Revolution, however, the impact of the Enlightenment on the European population at large was limited. The one aspect that did find broad support in most European nations was the philosophers' emphasis on the primacy of knowledge, and therefore education. As a result, school reforms were implemented that offered children much

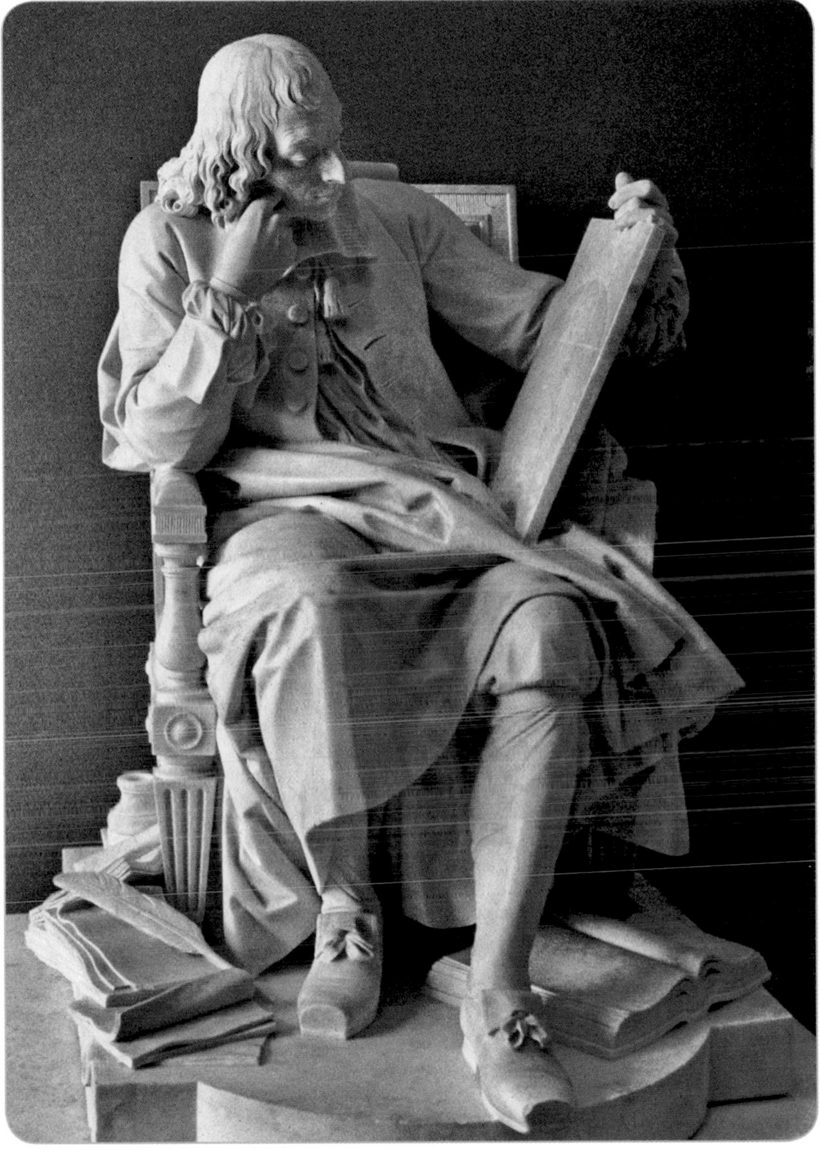

broader access to educational opportunities, regardless of their socioeconomic background. This, in turn, led to an increase in the European literacy rate, which prompted a greater need for books of all kinds, including devotional litera-

1756
Outbreak of the Seven Years' War

1758
Work begins on the Church of St. Geneviève in Paris, later known as the Panthéon

1762
Tsarina Catherine the Great assumes power in Russia in a bloodless coup

1762
Jean-Jacques Rousseau writes *The Social Contract*

ture. The publication of Bibles increased, particularly in French, Spanish, and Italian. The Church of Sweden (which included Finland, Latvia, and Estonia at the time) even issued a decree in 1686 requiring all male citizens to be able to read and write. This led to a nearly 100 percent literacy rate for males in Scandinavian lands by the early 19th century. Many women were still excluded from basic education, however. Elsewhere in Europe, literacy rates grew more slowly. As late as the mid-19th century, only some 55 percent of English women could read and sign their marriage certificate. This, however, was still a considerable improvement over the near total female illiteracy of the 17th century.

In some intellectual circles, the attempt to "rationalize" Christianity led to a reaction. The 17th-century scientist and mathematician Blaise Pascal (1623–1662) welcomed the growing role of physics and science in modern society, and is generally credited with the invention of the first mechanical calculator. After experiencing a vision in 1654, however, he turned against the anti-Christian sentiment of many of the early Enlightenment thinkers, and grew closer to the Jansenism movement advocated by his sister Jacqueline. The result was two important works, *Lettres provinciales* (*Provincial Letters,* 1656–1657) and *Pensées* (*Thoughts,* published after his death in 1670), in which he eloquently argued for the importance of the Christian faith in the human condition, and the idea that true vindication of God lies beyond man's grasp.

The Enlightenment also led to a number of initiatives in Protestantism. In some churches it fostered a renewed focus on spirituality beyond the scope of pure doctrine, in a quest for personal salvation through faith. One example is the movement called Arminianism, which arose amid the steadfastly Calvinist community of the Dutch Reformed Church. Initiated by a theologian named Jacobus Arminius (1560–1609), the movement rejected the Calvinist doctrine of predetermination, which states that each human being is predetermined to either receive

PERIOD ART

A New Focus in Art

The change from the triumphalist mood of the Counter-Reformation to a more intimate focus on personal spirituality also affected the artistic expression of the period. While in the art of Giovanni Battista Tiepolo (1696–1770) Italy experienced its last great burst of Baroque bravura, new developments were taking place in France and Holland. The Calvinist outlook of the Dutch Reformed Church banned any form of statuary or paintings from church buildings, giving their interiors an austere grandeur that fascinated painters such as Pieter de Hoogh (1629–1684) and Pieter Janszoon Saenredam (1597–1665). But such a ban did not apply to the domestic interiors of the growing merchant class, eager to spend their wealth—in patriotic fashion—on the work of local painters. Since Calvinist doctrine emphasized the importance of the Old Testament, themes from Hebrew Scripture enjoyed a broad revival among the "history painters" of the day, including Gerard van Honthorst (1592–1656) and Rembrandt van Rijn (1606–1669). Both artists had been influenced by the chiaroscuro light effects pioneered by Caravaggio. Rembrandt in particular created a style that enveloped its main characters in dark limbo, relieved only by a single source of light. In his treatment of Old Testament themes, Rembrandt often used Jewish subjects, having observed Amsterdam's Jewish community in great detail.

During the 18th century, the focus shifted once more, from Holland to France. With classicist artists such as Nicolas Poussin (1594–1665) and Jacques-Louis David (1748–1825), France succeeded Italy as the preeminent European center of art—a position that the nation would retain until well into the 20th century.

Dutch artist Rembrandt van Rijn (1606–1669) painted "The Sacrifice of Isaac" in 1636.

1763
Louis XV is forced to cede French holdings in North America to England and Spain

1770
British soldiers kill five American colonists in the Boston Massacre

1770
Paul-Henri Thiry writes his atheist tract *The System of Nature*

1773
The Society of Jesus (Jesuit order) is suppressed

Abraham van der Eyk (1684–1724) painted this "Allegory of the Theological Dispute Between the Arminians and Their Opponents" in 1718.

God's grace or not, regardless of the quality of his life. God's mercy was applicable to all, the Arminians argued, not just to the elect, provided they accepted Christ as their personal redeemer. That is why God gave man free will, so that each individual could resist sin on his own volition. Despite widespread condemnation in the Dutch Reformed Church, the Arminians (or *Remonstrants,* as they were also called) would have a powerful influence on Protestant thought in Holland and beyond.

In Germany, Lutheran theologian Philipp Jakob Spener (1635–1705) founded a movement called Pietism, which emphasized the nurturing of a deep and meaningful relationship with Christ. Spener advocated prayer and the reading of Scripture at home, not just during church assembly. This led to a high demand for Bibles in the German language, as well as devotional images used for private prayer, known as *Andachtsbilder.* Many of these ideas would return in the evangelicalism of the 19th century and later.

A similar reaction inspired John Wesley (1703–1791) to found the Methodist movement. Wesley was a graduate of Oxford University who became a priest in the Church of England in 1728. While at Oxford, he and his brother Charles had formed a study group known as the Holy Club. Because of their extreme devotion and methodical pursuit

1773
Catherine the Great issues the decree "Toleration of All Faiths"

1774
Louis XVI and his wife, Austrian Marie Antoinette, ascend the throne of France

1776
The American Continental Congress declares its independence from the British Crown

1776
Louis XVI supports the American Revolution with military assistance

of "biblical holiness," they became known as Methodists. In 1735, the Wesley brothers traveled to the British colony in Georgia to minister to the colonial settlers. Upon their return to Britain, Wesley continued to foster the Methodist movement within the Church of England, emphasizing charity and individual fulfillment. At the same time, Methodism spread rapidly in the American colonies, so that by 1779 nearly 10,000 followers existed along the eastern seaboard. A similar impulse gave rise to the Quakers, who likewise challenged the established Church of England.

The new yearning for individual piety also affected the Orthodox Churches. In 1793, the Eastern Orthodox monk Paisius Velichkovsky (1722–1794) collected a group of inspirational texts written between the 4th and 15th centuries, and published them in Church Slavonic under the title *Philokalia (Love of the Beautiful)*. The *Philokalia* was rapidly translated and, using the new mechanized printing presses, distributed throughout the Eastern realm, particularly Russia. The beauty and humble piety expressed in these texts kindled a deep spirituality into Eastern Orthodoxy, harkening back to the purity of early Christianity.

English artist William Hamilton (1751–1801) painted this portrait of John Wesley, co-founder of the Methodist Church.

PERIOD MUSIC

Sacred Music of the Baroque

The growing use of communal hymns, combined with the desire for devotional music of greater emotional force, led to an era of sacred music known as the High Baroque. In both Protestant and Catholic lands, this produced a group of highly influential composers whose works continue to be performed to this day. Among other forms, the oratorio—a musical drama inspired by Scripture—gained great popularity, particularly during Lent when opera performances were forbidden. An example is the famous *Messiah*, by German composer George Frideric Handel (1685–1759), written after his move to England in 1712. In Italy, the priest and virtuoso violinist Antonio Vivaldi (1678–1741) became a leading composer of concertos, cantatas, and sacred vocal music while teaching at the Ospedale della Pietà orphanage and music school in Venice. But the greatest Baroque composer of sacred music was undoubtedly Johann Sebastian Bach (1685–1750). While serving as *kapellmeister* (musical director) in various positions at Mühlhausen, Köthen, and Leipzig, Bach produced a vast corpus of concertos (including the well-known *Brandenburg* Concertos of 1721), as well as religious cantatas and oratorios. During his time at the St. Thomas Church in Leipzig, for example, Bach composed a new cantata each Sunday and feast day according to Lutheran liturgy—producing a total of 300 such choral works, of which only 200 survive. His most famous sacred work is the *Matthäus-Passion* (*St. Matthew Passion*), an oratorio written in 1727 for solo voices, double choir, and double orchestra, which was rediscovered by Felix Mendelssohn in 1829. Today, it is revered as a masterpiece of devotional music.

Johann Sebastian Bach composed the St. Matthew Passion *(BWV 244) around 1727.*

1780
Native workers in Spanish-owned mines of Peru stage a revolt

1781
Immanuel Kant writes his book *Critique of Pure Reason*

1783
The American Revolutionary War ends with recognition of America's independence

1785
Catherine the Great rescinds part of the "Toleration of All Faiths" decree

The New Classicism

The 18th-century emphasis on reason did not fail to have a deep impact on church architecture as well. By midcentury, the Baroque had reached its final stage in a style known as Rococo. Rationalist thought, much admired by the architects of the time, rejected the theatrical excesses of Rococo in favor of a new emphasis on order, rigor, and spiritual tranquility. This inspired a return to the austere elegance of Roman architecture, first revisited during the Renaissance. As early as the 1720s, English architects of elegant country homes had begun to experiment with the designs of the Italian Renaissance architect Andrea Palladio, which emphasized the elegance of simplicity. This was followed in 1748 by the discovery of the Roman city of Pompeii, which had lain buried under ash since the eruption of Mount Vesuvius in 79 C.E.

An interior view of the St. Geneviève church in Paris, now known as the Panthéon, shows the dome with the fresco "The Apotheosis of Saint Geneviève," by Antoine Gros (1771–1835).

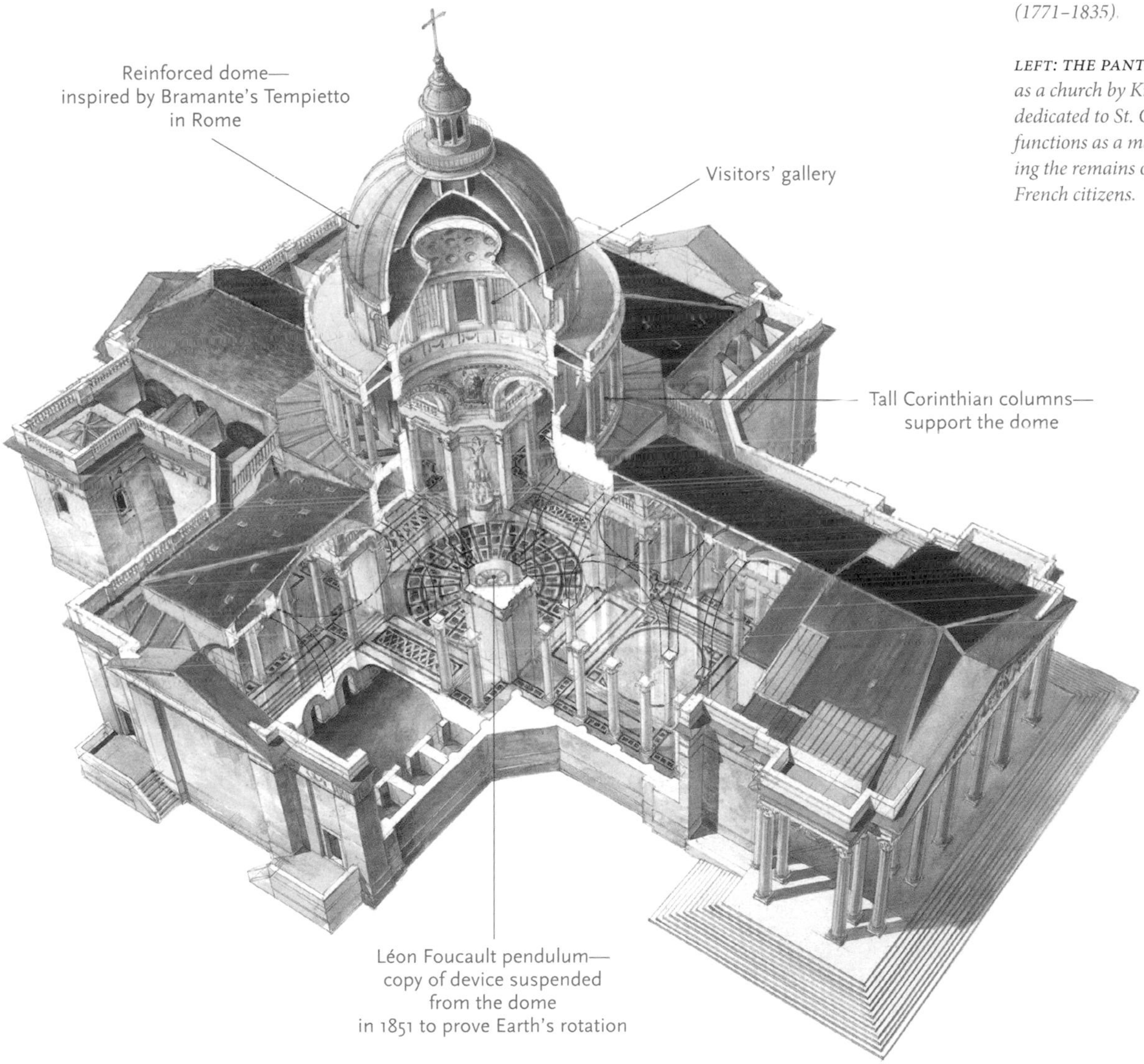

LEFT: THE PANTHÉON was built as a church by King Louis XV and dedicated to St. Geneviève. It now functions as a mausoleum containing the remains of distinguished French citizens.

Reinforced dome—
inspired by Bramante's Tempietto
in Rome

Visitors' gallery

Tall Corinthian columns—
support the dome

Léon Foucault pendulum—
copy of device suspended
from the dome
in 1851 to prove Earth's rotation

1787
Louis XVI signs the Edict of Versailles, granting religious freedom

1789
The French Revolution begins

1789
The "Declaration of the Rights of Man and Citizen" is signed in France

1791
Mulattoes in French-controlled Haiti rise in rebellion

HISTORY AND POLITICS

The Other Revolutions

During the Haitian revolution of 1791, cities and plantations were torched.

The American and French Revolutions were not the only rebellions that shook the 18th century. In 1780, native workers who had been conscripted to work in Spanish-owned mines in Peru rose in revolt. Led by Jesuit-trained José Gabriel Condorcanqui (ca 1742–1781), who claimed to be a direct descendant of the last Inca ruler, Túpac Amaru, the poorly armed rebels attacked the city of Cuzco but were no match for Spanish reinforcements rushed to the scene. Condorcanqui was captured, tortured, and killed, but the rebellion continued and even spread to neighboring Bolivia. Not until 1782 was the native revolution of Peru defeated, though it would inspire the Latin American revolutions in the century to come. Similarly, mulattoes in French-controlled Haiti rose in rebellion in 1791, after being denied the right to vote. Sugar and coffee plantations throughout the island were destroyed and their French owners massacred. A rebel leader, Toussaint L'Ouverture, joined forces with the Spanish and in 1801 declared Haiti's independence.

The extraordinarily detailed fragments of Pompeian architecture, discovered by Spanish engineer Rocque Joaquin de Alcubierre (1702–1780), caused a sensation in architectural circles. They prompted an urgent desire to resurrect classical building methods with an almost archaeological fidelity. The result was a style called Classicism, which by and large would dictate European architecture until the advent of Modernism in the early 20th century.

The first major church to be built in the new Classicist style was the Church of St. Geneviève in Paris, renamed the Panthéon after the French Revolution. The church was commissioned by King Louis XV to fulfill a pledge made during his illness in 1744. A relatively young architect named Jacques-Germain Soufflot (1713–1780) was charged with the task. Soufflot rejected the Baroque paradigm that was still popular during Louis XV's reign. Instead, he devised a church based on a Greek cross, in which the nave was organized with three successive crossings, each surmounted by a dome. The elevations were kept remarkably smooth and austere, relieved only by the soaring Corinthian pilasters supporting the domed ceiling. To enhance the monumentality of this design, Soufflot increased the church's dimensions beyond anything built in Paris at that time, with a length of 360 feet and a height of 272 feet. As Soufflot wrote, he tried to "combine the classic orders with the lightness" of Gothic cathedrals.

Classicism—or Neoclassicism, as it is sometimes called—quickly spread through Europe and its overseas colonies. In the newly independent United States, it found an ardent supporter in Benjamin Latrobe (1764–1820), a British architect who, following his move to America in 1796, almost single-handedly developed the Federal style in the republic's new capital of Washington, D.C. In 1805, Latrobe designed the first classical church on American soil: the Catholic Cathedral of Baltimore, Maryland, in which the influence of Soufflot's St. Geneviève is tangible.

I went to America,
to convert the Indians;
but oh! who shall convert me?
What is He that will deliver me
from this evil heart of mischief?
I have a fair summer religion.

JOHN WESLEY,
FOUNDER OF THE METHODIST CHURCH

Napoleon Bonaparte

The ultimate consequence of the Age of Reason for the world is that it produced the French Revolution, and by extension a man called Napoleon Bonaparte. In the early 19th century, this would lead to one of the greatest conflicts in European history: the Napoleonic Wars, an even more bloody episode than the Thirty Years' War. At the conclusion of this conflict, many vestiges of the Catholic Church in areas under Napoleon's control, including Spain, France, Italy, and the Low Countries, would be forever extinguished. Thus, out of the ashes of Waterloo rose a new Europe: a modern Europe that, buoyed by the Industrial Revolution, would extend its influence far across the globe. ■

OPPOSITE: *French artist Jean Huber (1721–1786) painted the bucolic "Voltaire Conversing with the Peasants in Ferney," underscoring the popular appeal of this French philosopher.*

1792
French King Louis XVI is toppled from his throne

1793
Orthodox monk Paisius Velichkovsky publishes the *Philokalia*

1793
Louis XVI and Marie Antoinette are executed by guillotine, to the outrage of Europe

1794
Russian Orthodox missionaries arrive in Alaska

11
CHAPTER

> *Prayer does not change God, but it changes him who prays.*
>
> SØREN KIERKEGAARD

THE AGE OF COLONIALISM

1800-1900

In the 19th century, Christendom went through another major transformation that brought profound social, economic, and political changes to the six inhabited continents. Many of these changes were propelled by technological change. At the beginning of the century, during the Napoleonic era, most people lived much as they had during the Renaissance, or even the Roman Empire. The horse was the primary mode of transportation. The principal source of illumination was the wax candle. Most of Europe's cities were plunged in darkness during the night—as indeed had been the case since the Roman era. Information was transmitted by handwritten mail, with transit times measured in the distance a horse could travel in a day—usually between 15 and 20 miles. Seaborne traffic was dependent on favorable winds.

By the end of the 19th century, all of these axioms of human activity had been revolutionized by a string of technological advances. Major cities were now lit at night by gaslight, led by Paris, which had installed the first gas lamps as early as 1820. For the first time in history, rail networks and the steam-driven locomotive made long-distance travel affordable for millions,

ABOVE: *"First Communion" by French sculptor René de Saint-Marceaux (1845–1915) expresses the increased popular piety of late 19th-century France.*

OPPOSITE: *The Victoria Memorial in Calcutta, built between 1906 and 1921, is enveloped in ground fog on a cold winter morning.*

PRECEDING PAGES: *Swiss artist Arnold Böcklin (1827–1901) created a sensation in 1880 with his Symbolist impression of "Die Toteninsel" ("The Island of the Dead"), inspired by the English Cemetery in Florence.*

Period Objects

1800–1900

Henry Fox Talbot's camera of 1835 is one of the oldest surviving cameras.

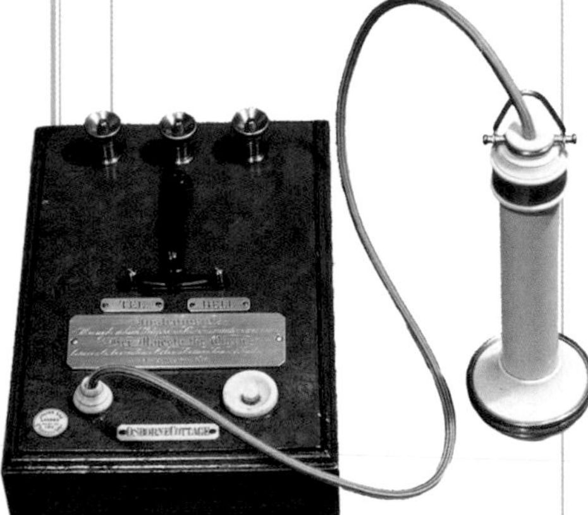

This Bell telephone of 1877 was used by Queen Victoria at Osborne House.

Charles Darwin used this sextant during his voyage on H.M.S. Beagle.

allowing them to escape the confines of their village or township, if only for the weekend. At the same time, the steam-driven turbine transformed seagoing traffic. As early as 1807, the *North River Steamboat* carried passengers from New York City to Albany, a distance of 150 miles, in the then astonishingly short time of 32 hours. In 1838, the British paddle steamer *Great Western* made its first Atlantic crossing. By the latter part of the century, ocean liners offered passage between continents on a regular schedule, having changed a hazardous sea voyage into a comfortable and even luxurious experience.

Similarly, human communication was transformed by the steam-powered rotary printing press and the telegraph. It usually took eight to ten days for a letter to pass from London to Washington, D.C.—the time it took for a ship to cross the Atlantic. In 1858, a message was transmitted in a matter of minutes, when Queen Victoria sent a telegram to President James Buchanan using the just-completed transatlantic telegraph cable.

These and other technological changes, which together are referred to as the Industrial Revolution, had a profound social and political impact. Mechanization, made possible by steam power, obliterated the centuries-old apprentice model, in which productivity was measured by what human hands could accomplish. As machines became more prevalent and efficient, manufacturing increased tenfold, then a hundredfold. All this required labor—industrial labor, trained to perform the same mechanical tasks over and over again, often for as much as ten or twelve hours per day.

Before the 1830s, Europe's societies were overwhelmingly agrarian, with most farmers—or peasants—practicing subsistence agriculture, raising a diverse spectrum of crops to feed their families. The high demand for industrial

This 19th-century transatlantic ship, depicted by French marine painter Louis le Breton (1818–1866), uses a steam-driven paddle wheel. The steam-driven turbine revolutionized long-distance travel.

1799
Napoleon Bonaparte assumes power in France as First Consul

1801
Napoleon Bonaparte negotiates a concordat with the Vatican

1802
Gia Long unifies Vietnam and establishes the Nguyen Dynasty

1804
Napoleon Bonaparte crowns himself Emperor of the French

An unknown 19th-century artist captured the bleakness of English industrial towns in the middle of the 19th century in "Nantyglo Ironworks" (1829).

labor pulled thousands of these farmhands to the cities, transforming places like Birmingham and Manchester into major metropolitan centers. The impact on food production was mitigated, however, by equally rapid improvements in agricultural technology, such as the development of the iron plow, the seed drill, and the threshing machine. Steam power also enabled vast infrastructure projects, including the digging of major canals and the construction of road and railway networks.

Thus, despite the hardship of working in mills or factories (including the egregious exploitation of child labor), the Industrial Revolution did cause standards of living to rise after a long decline in the 18th century. Workers' wages rose, albeit slowly, while food costs dropped because of improvements in production and transportation. By the second half of the 19th century, the endemic famine and malnutrition that had been the scourge of Europe had all been eradicated.

On the downside, the concentration of industrial labor in urban areas led to shantytowns with unsanitary conditions, where disease was often rampant. Though child mortality remained stubbornly high well into the 1870s, Europe's population continued

1805
Lord Nelson defeats Napoleon at the Battle of Trafalgar

1807
The Peninsular War begins

1807
A steamboat carries passengers from New York City to Albany in 32 hours

1807
German philosopher Georg Hegel publishes *The Phenomenology of the Spirit*

OPPOSITE: *German artist Franz Xaver Winterhalter (1805–1873) painted this portrait of a youthful Queen Victoria in 1842, just five years into her reign.*

The Breakers, a grand mansion in Newport, Rhode Island, built by American architect Richard Morris Hunt (1827–1895) for Cornelius Vanderbilt III, captures the opulence of the American Gilded Age.

to grow at an alarming rate. In England, the population doubled between 1801 and 1850, and doubled again between 1850 and 1901. Though the Industrial Revolution was relatively slow in coming in France and Germany, by the 1870s, their population structures had been radically changed as well. As several historians have noted, were it not for the Industrial Revolution, this population growth would have strained available food supplies in Europe to the breaking point. Mechanization had become an existential necessity.

The Victorian Age

While the gulf between haves and have-nots—the nobility and the new industrial barons on the one hand, and the agrarian and industrial poor on the other—remained as wide as ever, a new social class made its appearance. Vastly improved educational opportunities—a consequence of the Age of Reason—produced a new middle class of professionals, such as doctors and lawyers, as well as entrepreneurs, shopkeepers, and artisans. The growth of the middle class led to a new emphasis on civic services and urban beautification. In Paris, the prefect Baron Haussmann forcefully destroyed entire neighborhoods to create the wide boulevards bordered by elegant apartment blocks that we so admire today. Instead of the cathedral, the nuclei of urban life now became the railway station, the hotel, the theater, and the opera house.

1807 British missionary Robert Morrison begins a Mandarin translation of the Bible

1808 Jesuit priest Miguel Hidalgo y Costilla launches the Mexican War of Independence

1810–1820 Francisco Goya documents the horrors of the Peninsular War in the series "The Disasters of War"

1810 The Second Great Awakening emerges in New England

Overall, the 19th century was an era of irrepressible optimism. With Britain now emerging as the dominant global power, the century has often been equated with the improbably long reign of Queen Victoria (r. 1837–1901).

We are not interested in the possibilities of defeat. They do not exist.

QUEEN VICTORIA

The later decades of the Victorian age were an unprecedented period of peace, growth, and prosperity, which would become known in France as the Belle Époque and in the United States as the Gilded Age. Contemporary observers saw the era as the culmination of all that had passed before, not only in a political and economic sense, but also culturally and morally. Victorians believed they stood at the pinnacle of human progress. With the never-ending stream of technological innovations—in electricity, in chemistry, in engineering—there were no limits to what mankind could achieve. All this was bound to have an impact on how people saw their relationship with God, and their perceived mission to carry the "civilizing force" of Christianity into the far corners of the globe.

The Napoleonic Era

Before these tremendous changes could come to pass, a series of conflicts struck Europe (and indeed, the New World) that are collectively known as the Napoleonic Wars. Born in 1769, in Ajaccio, the capital of Corsica, Napoleon Bonaparte (r. 1799–1815) was active as a second lieutenant in an artillery regiment during the French Revolution. His efforts in suppressing clashes between revolutionaries, royalists, and Corsican nationalists eventually came to the attention of Robespierre, a prominent leader of the French Revolution. In 1795, Napoleon further distinguished himself by defending the revolutionary government in Paris against a royalist uprising. He subsequently rose through the military ranks, and in 1796 launched a daring invasion of northern Italy, evicting Austria from the region. Radicals in the republican government known as the Directoire urged him to continue south, seize Rome, and depose the pope. Napoleon demurred, knowing that such an act would earn him the enmity of Catholic Europe.

For the next few years, the young officer consolidated his power until he staged a coup d'état in 1799. Worn out by the constant chaos of the Directoire, the French people welcomed his autocratic regime with open arms.

PERIOD ART

Romanticism

"Two Men Contemplating the Moon" was painted by Romantic artist Caspar David Friedrich (1774–1840).

The Industrial Revolution led to a reaction in creative circles, producing several movements known as romanticism. Instead of science and reason, these artists, writers, and composers emphasized emotion as the main source of the aesthetic experience. In painting, this produced the hauntingly beautiful art of Caspar David Friedrich (1774–1840), Eugène Delacroix (1798–1863), and Arnold Böcklin (1827–1901). Böcklin's painting "Die Toteninsel" ("Island of the Dead," 1880) caused a sensation. It inspired scores of prints, books, and even symphonic poems. Music, too, experienced a romantic phase, exemplified by composers such as Felix Mendelssohn (1809–1847), Johannes Brahms (1833–1897), and Gustav Mahler (1860–1911). Brahms's *Ein Deutsches Requiem (A German Requiem,* 1868), based on the Lutheran Bible in German, is one of the outstanding sacred works of the epoch. Among others, it inspired French composer Gabriel Fauré (1845–1924) to compose a requiem in French (1890), which today ranks among the most popular works in religious music.

1811 **Simón Bolívar proclaims the independence of Venezuela**

1812 **Napoleon Bonaparte invades Russia**

1813 **Napoleon is defeated at the Battle of Leipzig**

1814 **Holland cedes southern Africa to the British Empire**

HISTORY AND POLITICS

Liberation Movements in Latin America

Rafael Salas (1824–1906) painted this portrait of revolutionary Simón Bolívar.

This century saw a series of revolutionary movements in Latin America. In 1808, a Jesuit-trained priest, Miguel Hidalgo y Costilla (1753–1811), launched the Mexican War of Independence. After Napoleon's defeat, royalist elements in Mexico, fearing for their aristocratic privileges, declared their independence from Spain. Other revolutionary movements led to the foundation of today's Costa Rica, Honduras, Nicaragua, Guatemala, and El Salvador.

In South America, the torch of freedom was lit by Simón Bolívar (1783–1830) in 1811. His struggle would result in the freedom of today's Colombia, Ecuador, Panama, and Venezuela. Meanwhile, revolutionary José de San Martín (1778–1850) was fighting to liberate the southwest of the continent. In 1821, he officially declared Peruvian independence.

Brazil gained its independence in a bloodless coup by Pedro I (r. 1822–1831), the regent who had been appointed by his father, Portuguese King João VI (r. 1816–1826).

Having built up a vast army, the Grande Armée, Napoleon embarked on a series of conquests that completely upstaged the European order of the past two centuries. He defeated the forces of Prussia, Austria, and Russia, entered a peace treaty with Britain, and engineered his own elevation to Emperor by Pope Pius VII in 1804. But the British soon broke their peace treaty to form a series of anti-Napoleonic coalitions with, among others, Russia and Austria. In retaliation, Napoleon planned to invade the British Isles, but these plans came to naught when the French fleet was destroyed at the Battle of Trafalgar in 1805. A disastrous invasion of Russia in 1812 led to the death of more than half a million French troops and the evisceration of the Grande Armée.

During this period, Napoleon did manage to implement a number of reforms in the countries under his sway, inspired by the principles of the French Revolution. A number of institutes of higher learning were created, thus restoring, to some degree, the proud tradition of European academia that had been eradicated by the suppression of Jesuit learning in 1767. In France and elsewhere, a uniform tax code was adopted that no longer excluded the nobility, the clergy, and other privileged classes. Another important contribution was the Napoleonic Code, a uniform civil code that granted unfettered freedom of religion. In 1801, Napoleon also negotiated a concordat with the Vatican, which duly restored the Roman Catholic Church as the principal religious institution of France. But the agreement fell short of confirming Catholicism as France's official state religion in order to protect the religious freedom of Huguenots, Jews, and other religious groups. What's more, members of the French clergy were obligated to swear an oath of allegiance to the state, which henceforth was responsible for their salaries.

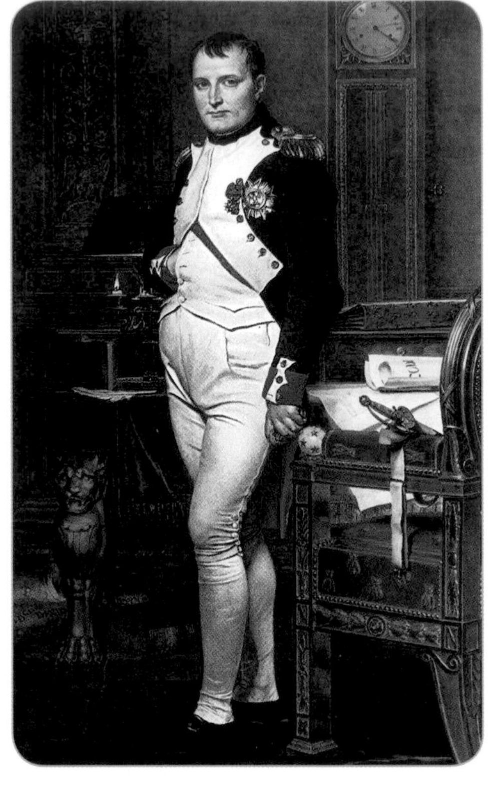

The Napoleonic era left a number of important legacies. In Napoleon's vicious treatment of noncombatants, particularly in Spain, where the horror of the Peninsular War was captured in Francisco Goya's print series "Los Desastres de la Guerra" ("The Disasters of War," 1810–1820), the Napoleonic Wars presaged the mass civilian casualties of wars to come. The Napoleonic Code, on the other hand, gave Europe its first uniform judicial grounding. The Code would remain in force long after Napoleon's defeat at the Battle of Waterloo in 1815, and parts of it are still on

ABOVE: *Renowned French artist Jacques-Louis David (1748–1825) painted "The Emperor Napoleon in His Study at the Tuileries" in 1812, at the height of Napoleon's career.*

OPPOSITE: *"The Battle of Waterloo" by William Holmes Sullivan (1836–1908) captures the intensity of early 19th-century combat at close quarters.*

1815
Napoleon suffers his final defeat at the Battle of Waterloo

1815
The eruption of the Sumbawa volcano kills more than 50,000 people

1819
Sir Stamford Raffles acquires the port of Singapore from the local Malay governor

1820
The first American missionaries arrive in Hawaii

Gustave Moreau

the books to this day. By the same token, however, Napoleon's subjugation of national Church institutions continued the marginalization of Christianity in Europe, which would accelerate as Europe's industrialization grew and prosperity increased.

Lastly, Napoleon's fall also marked the ascendancy of the Prussian House of Hohenzollern in Germany. Prussian armies had been decisive in defeating Napoleon at Waterloo. From this time forward, the Hohenzollern monarchy emerged as the dominant power of continental Europe, propelled by a sense of Protestant manifest destiny. In rattling its

Skillful conquerors do not get entangled with priests. They contain them and use them.

NAPOLEON BONAPARTE

saber and flexing its militarist muscle, the Hohenzollern Crown saw itself as the new leader of an old European struggle: a *Kulturkampf*, or "cultural struggle," between nationalist Protestantism and the crumbling power of international Catholicism.

Berlin, the capital of the Prussian kingdom, did not fail to make good on this vision. In mid-century, Prussia initiated two wars, one against Catholic Austria and another—a far more fateful conflict—in 1870 against imperial France, ruled by the ineffectual Napoleon III (r. 1852–1870). Prussian arms proved victorious in both, and France was humiliated to the core. In the Hall of Mirrors at Versailles, the former symbol of French absolutist hegemony, German Hohenzollern King Wilhelm I (r. 1861–1888) was declared emperor of a new Deutsches Reich, or German Empire, that combined 27 German kingdoms and principalities into a vast nation-state. Thus were sown the seeds of German militarism of the 20th century.

OPPOSITE: *The 1876 painting "Pietà," by French artist Gustave Moreau (1826–1898), is one of the best-known works of the 19th-century Symbolist movement.*

Intellectual Currents of the 19th Century

As the 19th century progressed, both Catholicism and Protestantism came under assault by a number of new intellectual movements. In 1859, British naturalist Charles Darwin (1809–1882) published his book *On the Origin of Species*, based in part on his observation of the extraordinary life-forms of the Galápagos Islands. Darwin concluded that life on Earth was the product of an evolutionary process of natural selection. Although he did not address the evolution of human beings specifically (though he would do so in 1871 in a book entitled *The Descent of Man*), the implications were clear. The suggestion that the Creation story in the Book of Genesis is an allegorical rather than a literal account had already been debated at length by 18th-century philosophers. Darwin, however, argued that the process of natural selection had been largely arbitrary, without the intervention of a benign deity. It was simply a matter of the survival of the fittest.

Darwin's theories seemed to be closely aligned with the ideas of a German philosopher named Georg Wilhelm Friedrich Hegel (1770–1831). Hegel, too, believed that history followed a particular model, which he called the dialectic principle. Echoing what would become an important theme in Victorian

SCRIPTURE AND FAITH

Doré Bible

Gustave Doré (1832–1883) painted "The Angel of Tobias" in 1865.

With the invention of the rotary printing press in 1843, combined with steadily improving literacy rates on the Continent, newspapers, magazines, and books began to supplant oral transmission as the principal conduit for information in Victorian society. The invention of the steel engraving process made it possible to equip mass-produced books with images of often astonishing detail. One of the most popular books to be illustrated in this manner was the edition of the Bible by French artist Gustave Doré (1832–1883). Published in 1866 in France, and subsequently in an English translation by the British house of Cassell and Co., the Doré Bible enjoyed a huge popularity across Europe. The artist's vivid reconstruction of biblical scenes, rendered with great virtuosity, would influence Bible illustrations until well into the 20th century. Doré went on to illustrate works by Dante, Milton, Shakespeare, and Balzac.

1821
José de San Martín proclaims Peru as an independent state

1822
The Society for the Propagation of the Faith is founded in Lyon, France

1835
The Anglican church of St. Andrew's is built in Singapore

1837
Queen Victoria assumes the throne at age 18

An encounter with exotic animals, such as these giant tortoises, on the Galápagos Islands was instrumental in Charles Darwin's formulation of his evolutionary theory described in On the Origin of Species *of 1859.*

political thought, he posited that humanity was on a constant course of ascendancy, propelled by the dynamic of certain theses being challenged by antitheses, thereby producing a higher, more advanced synthesis. Unlike Kant, Hegel believed that there was no limit to what the human mind could imagine or achieve. In his book *Die Phänomenologie des Geistes* (*The Phenomenology of the Spirit,* 1807), Hegel even said that eventually human consciousness would attain the full knowledge and understanding of the universe and the "Absolute Spirit"—divinity itself. But Hegel, who had attended a theological seminary, did not reject the role of God in man's existence. In a book published after his death, he wrote, "God is not an abstraction, but a concrete God . . . he is the process of differentiating, namely, love and Spirit."

Such notions were vehemently rejected by a Danish Lutheran-trained philosopher named Søren Kierkegaard (1813–1855). Instead of lofty visions of Hegelian idealism or Victorian optimism, Kierkegaard saw the world in pessimistic terms, viewed through the prism of an individual who is faced with the senseless tragedy and injustice of modern times. "Revelation is marked by mystery, eternal happiness by suffering," he wrote; "the certitude of faith [is marked] by uncertainty." Kierkegaard recognized the essential ethical values of Christianity but failed to see this reflected in the organized religion of his time, particularly the Lutheran Church of Denmark, which he criticized remorselessly. What was needed instead, he argued in his book *Kjerlighedens Gjerninger* (*Works of Love,* 1847), was a renewed emphasis on the early Christian ideal of *agapè,* the Greek word for charitable love.

It is not important for God to have visible evidence so that he can see if his cause has been victorious or not; he sees in secret just as well.

SØREN KIERKEGAARD, *WORKS OF LOVE*

1838
The British paddle steamer *Great Western* makes its first Atlantic crossing

1839
The first of several Opium Wars breaks out between China and the British Empire

1839
Louis Daguerre develops the first viable form of photography

1841
Henry Fox Talbot announces his silver-iodide calotype process, creating modern photography

Kierkegaard's philosophy was not for the masses. His sometimes impenetrable writings, combined with the limited footprint of the Danish language, restricted his influence to a narrow circle until he was recognized as an important forerunner of 20th-century existentialism.

The inevitable consequence of both Hegelian and Darwinian models was an evolutionary reassessment of the individual himself. Twenty-eight years after the publication of *The Descent of Man*, an Austrian professor of neuropathology named Sigmund Freud (1856–1939) wrote a book called *Die Traumdeutung* (*The Interpretation of Dreams*, 1899). Having researched the human unconscious, aided by hypnosis, Freud found that man's essential being was not his soul, as Christianity believed, but his sense of self, his psyche. In Freud's view, a person's individual character was shaped not by the desire for moral rectitude or salvation, but by desires rooted in childhood development. The moral strictures imposed by religion and Victorian norms, said Freud, had repressed many of these latent desires. This carried the risk of damaging the health of the psyche and producing aggression, neurotic behavior, or even crime. Like the Darwinians, Freud rejected the traditional monotheistic view of God as a benign creator, and instead equated the yearning for religion with a child's need for a powerful father figure. Whereas religion was once necessary to restrain humanity's violent impulse, he said, it had now been made redundant by science and reason. In a later work, *Obsessive Actions and Religious Practices* (1907), Freud went as far as to claim that intense faith could assume the symptomatic behavior of neurotic obsession.

Though many of Freud's theories would be modified or rejected by his followers in the decades to come, there is no question that his identification of the psyche as the primary motive for human behavior would become the foundation for a discipline of tremendous consequence in the modern age, known as psychology.

The most damaging attack on Christianity, however, was delivered by the theory that society was driven not by a search for greater moral and intellectual fulfillment, as the Victorians believed, but by an intense class struggle between the poor and the elites over control of a nation's wealth or "capital." First espoused in a pamphlet called *The Communist Manifesto* (1848), co-authored by two German political theorists, Friedrich Engels (1820–1895) and Karl Marx (1818–1883), this idea of a historical class conflict was fully developed in a later book by Marx called *Das Kapital* (*Capital*, 1867). According to Marx, who grew up in a privileged family in Trier, all of history was essentially determined by a clash between those who controlled resources and production, and the dispossessed, whose sole function was to serve as labor. This phenomenon,

LEFT: *British portrait painter George Richmond (1809–1896) painted this watercolor of a youthful Charles Darwin in the late 1830s.*

Photographer Max Halberstadt (1882–1940) took this photograph of Sigmund Freud, inscribed by Freud with the legend "Prof. Sigm. Freud with kind regards, 1921."

1843
The rotary printing press is invented, spawning the modern newspaper

1845
Baptist churches in the American South break away from the North over the issue of slavery

1847
Danish philosopher Søren Kierkegaard writes *Works of Love*

1847
French forces attack Danang in Vietnam

for which he coined the term "capitalism," was bound to run its course, said Marx. Its internal contradictions would eventually lead to self-destruction and the emergence of a new social order, which he called socialism. In this new utopia, all resources and wealth would be shared, all class distinctions would be eradicated, and all power would be distributed.

PERIOD ARCHITECTURE

Revival Church Architecture

The Victorian penchant for delineating history as a sequence of periods produced a desire to dress new churches in decorative styles of the past. The Industrial Revolution, which allowed the mechanical manufacture of virtually anything, abetted this movement. The result was a series of neo-isms, designed to express the unique "character" of the congregation or its civic setting. Neo-Gothic architecture, for example, was deemed appropriate for cathedrals, whereas more intimate parish churches were often conceived in the traits of Neo-Romanesque or Neo-Byzantine. Neo-Romanesque would particularly flourish in the American East and Midwest, and exert a strong influence on the Chicago School, including Henry Richardson, Louis Sullivan, and ultimately, Frank Lloyd Wright. In Cologne, Germany, the Neo-Gothic movement stimulated a desire to finish the city's cathedral, first begun in 1248, but left abandoned in the 16th century. A fund-raising campaign raised $1 billion (in today's currency) to finish the massive building in 1880. In France, the architect Eugène Viollet-le-Duc used his "scientific" knowledge of medieval styles to restore and "improve" churches such as Sainte-Marie-Madeleine in Vézelay and Notre Dame in Paris, doing considerable damage in the process.

In the latter part of the century, a new style emerged: a blending of previous European styles, including Renaissance, Baroque, and classical elements. Known as beaux arts, after the school in Paris that became the preeminent center of architecture, it exerted a strong influence on European church design.

A shot of Cologne Cathedral reveals the huge Neo-Gothic spires, the second tallest in Europe, completed in 1880.

For many who had become disenchanted with organized religion, notwithstanding the lofty social goals espoused in the Gospels, Marxism proved to be a heady tonic. Here was not only an ideology, but also a political program, a call to action that could truly create a society where all were equal, where possessions would be shared, and where no one would go hungry. As some historians have pointed out, throughout the Middle Ages the Church had stood on the side of the poor. But by the second half of the 19th century, many Christian churches had moved resolutely to the opposite side, choosing the side of the established order. With some exceptions, the church organizations in England and France

Modern bourgeois society, springing from the wreck of feudal society, has not abolished class antagonisms. It has but substituted new classes, new conditions of oppression.

FRIEDRICH ENGELS AND KARL MARX, *THE COMMUNIST MANIFESTO*

made only token efforts to ameliorate the truly appalling conditions among industrial workers, particularly in London. An inspection in the 1860s of some of the thousands of tenements in that city, for example, revealed that as many as ten people lived in one room.

In France, the lingering divisions produced by the revolutionary era also alienated many from the French Catholic Church, which remained a staunch supporter of the restored Bourbon monarchy (1814–1848).

1848
Friedrich Engels and Karl Marx publish *The Communist Manifesto*

1853
Baron Haussmann begins a radical redevelopment of Paris

1853
The Crimean War begins, foreshadowing industrial warfare

1858
Queen Victoria sends the first transatlantic telegraph via undersea cable

Fear of political reform and liberalization was likewise the reason why the Vatican continued to resist the peaceful unification of Italy, delaying Italy's emergence as a modern European nation until 1871.

In 1848, when many European capitals were struck by a wave of popular protest, most Catholic bishops firmly supported the established powers and the political repression that followed. Throughout this turbulent period, the Catholic Church increasingly found itself on the wrong side of history.

Among laborers, this led to much disenchantment with organized Christianity. As the historian Diarmaid MacCulloch has noted, by 1869, church attendance among Berlin's working class had dropped to one percent. Their allegiance had shifted to the other ideological spectrum, to socialism as embodied in the German Social Democratic Party, the first major socialist organization in Europe. Though the true impact of Marxism would not be felt until the 20th century, it is not without reason that many historians have called Marx one of the most influential figures in modern history.

The Great Awakenings

Even as Christianity saw itself marginalized in Europe by ideology and the modern state, it experienced a surge of renewal in the United States. Some authors suggest that the so-called Second Great Awakening (after the initial awakening in the mid-18th century) was motivated in part by the wholesale destruction of churches and church property during the American Revolution. Over the next few decades, the population spread rapidly across the Appalachians, where there were few churches. On top of that, many Methodist and other English clergy had elected to go back to England following the Declaration of Independence, leaving people without pastors to officiate. These developments forced the population, particularly in rural areas, to meet in tents or camps, using a largely improvised combination of prayer, preaching, and hymns. Freed from much of the doctrinal debate that characterized European Christianity, the simple joy of communal singing and prayer instilled in these congregations a unique sense of emotional

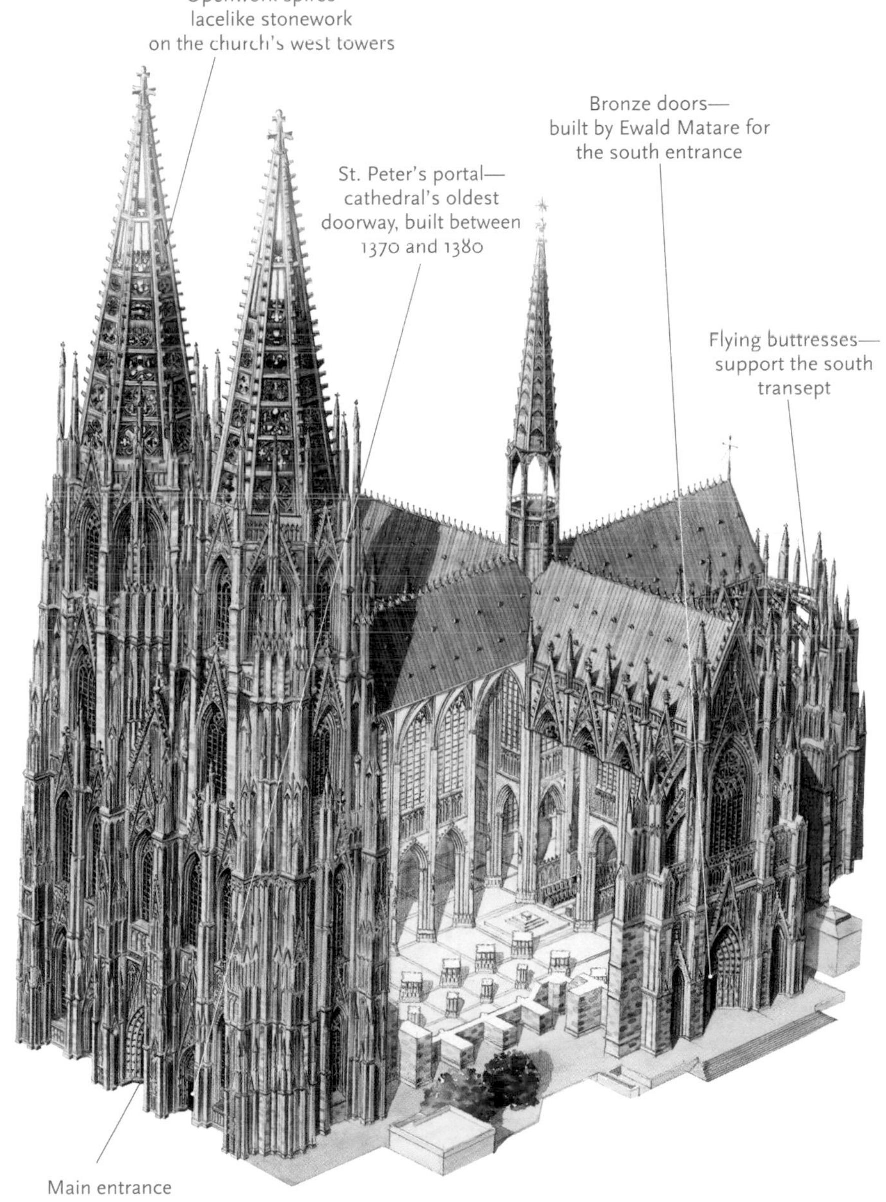

Work on the vast **COLOGNE CATHEDRAL**, *begun in 1248, was halted in 1473 and only resumed in 1842, using 19th-century Neo-Gothic principles and methods.*

1859
Charles Darwin publishes *On the Origin of Species*

1860
Abraham Lincoln is elected 16th president of the United States

1861
Wilhelm I assumes the throne of the kingdom of Prussia

1861
Seven states in the American South form the Confederate States of America

Reform the world by example, and you will act generously and wisely.

JEREMY BENTHAM, ADVOCATE OF THE BENEVOLENT EMPIRE

intensity. As such, the revival movement was—perhaps unconsciously—an agglomeration of Pietist, Presbyterian, and Puritan ideas, but it was highly effective. Like the frontiersmen of decades past, these worshippers felt as if they stood on the cusp of a new discovery, a spiritual experience on distinctly American terms. The traveling preacher, moving from one town to the next, became a common sight. It has been estimated that near the end of the 18th century, Methodist congregations alone were served by more than 80 traveling preachers.

By 1810, the Second Great Awakening was gaining momentum in New England, where it galvanized preachers such as Lyman Beecher (1775–1863), a co-founder of the American Temperance Society, and Charles Finney (1792–1875), who has been called the father of modern revivalism. As we saw, Presbyterianism was one of the oldest religious movements in America, first introduced to the New World by the Ulster-Scots clergyman Francis Makemie (1658–1708) in 1683. Beecher, Finney, and other Presbyterians were united in the vision that America's destiny lay in becoming a Christian nation of impeccable moral, social, and spiritual standards—a "Benevolent Empire," as some coined it.

A Methodist preacher is exhorting a crowd on his improvised stage in this 1839 watercolor, painted during the Second Great Awakening in the United States.

In the 1820s, a native of Vermont named Joseph Smith (1805–1844) experienced a number of visions that reportedly led him to discover various documents, including a record of ancient prophets who lived in America. Translated in English, this became the Book of Mormon, the foundational literature of the Church of Jesus Christ of Latter-Day Saints. In 1831, Smith moved west with his followers, later establishing communities in Ohio, Missouri, and Illinois. After his violent death in 1844, the Mormon Church continued to grow through the remainder of the 19th century, particularly in its new base in Utah, despite tensions between Mormons and other Americans.

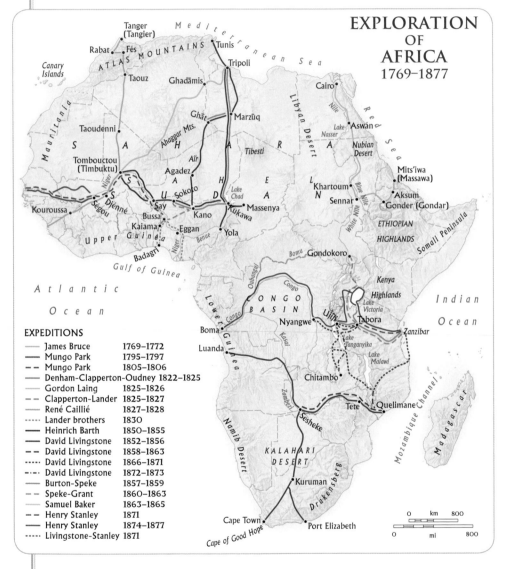

EXPLORATION OF AFRICA 1769–1877

EXPEDITIONS

James Bruce	1769–1772
Mungo Park	1795–1797
Mungo Park	1805–1806
Denham-Clapperton-Oudney	1822–1825
Gordon Laing	1825–1826
Clapperton-Lander	1825–1827
René Caillié	1827–1828
Lander brothers	1830
Heinrich Barth	1850–1855
David Livingstone	1852–1856
David Livingstone	1858–1863
David Livingstone	1866–1871
David Livingstone	1872–1873
Burton-Speke	1857–1859
Speke-Grant	1860–1863
Samuel Baker	1863–1865
Henry Stanley	1871
Henry Stanley	1874–1877
Livingstone-Stanley	1871

So energetic was the mood of the Great Awakening that it inspired many new social movements. Thousands of volunteers joined in campaigns to help the poor, to proselytize, to promote women's rights, or to curb excesses such as alcohol abuse, which was growing rapidly. One particular target was the "sin" of human slavery. During his tenure as the second president of Oberlin College, for example, Finney actively engaged students and faculty in working the Underground Railroad, a clandestine network of safe houses designed to spirit slaves from southern plantations to havens in the North. Some estimates suggest that as many as 100,000 slaves reached safety using various channels of the Underground Railroad.

The Great Awakening also transformed the emerging denominations of the South. The Baptist confession, originally founded by John Smyth in 1609 as a movement emphasizing adult baptism and personal responsibility for moral purity, was brought to the New World by Roger Williams 30 years later. Amid the revivalist mood of the early 19th century, numerous Baptist churches were founded in the South. Thousands of converts were made among the slave population, with the grudging permission of slave owners. But many southern Baptist churches refused to denounce slavery as their northern counterparts did, and in 1845 broke away from the North by forming the Southern Baptist Convention. Similarly, Presbyterianism experienced a split between Old School Presbyterians, largely favored in the South, and the more liberal wing known as New School Presbyterians in the North.

1861
The Confederate attack on Fort Sumter ignites the American Civil War

1861
Charles Dickens writes *Great Expectations*

1862
Prussia launches the "Culture Struggle" against Catholic Europe by invading Austria

1862
Abraham Lincoln issues the Emancipation Proclamation, ending slavery in the U.S.

"The Hour of Emancipation, 1863," painted by American artist William Tolman Carlton (1816–1888), captures the anticipation and joy among African Americans following the Emancipation Proclamation by President Abraham Lincoln.

The Methodist Church experienced a split as well. Its community, too, was profoundly affected by slavery. John Wesley, co-founder of the Methodist faith, had declared its opposition to slavery from the start. In 1794, a freed slave and Methodist preacher, Richard Allen, founded the African Methodist Episcopal Church in Philadelphia. By the end of the 18th century, both white and black Methodists attended Sunday schools on a regular basis.

Still, the issue of slavery continued to fester in North-South relations. Even though Abraham Lincoln (r. 1861–1865), a Republican politician, was not a declared abolitionist, his views on slavery were well known. His election in 1860 as the 16th president of the United States set in motion the events that led to the Civil War, the bloodiest conflict ever fought on American soil. Keen to avoid an irrevocable split of the nation, Lincoln temporized on the slavery issue until 1862, when he issued the Emancipation Proclamation that would legally liberate all slaves in the rebellious states. At the time, there were around four million slaves in American servitude.

With the defeat of the Confederacy in 1865, the northern and southern denominations worked to heal the rifts, which in some cases took many years. Although the Southern Baptist Convention did not reunite with its northern counterpart, it did issue an apology to African Americans in 1995 "for condoning and/or perpetuating individual and systemic racism in our lifetime."

SCRIPTURE AND FAITH

The Quakers

Edward Hicks (1780–1849) painted "Penn's Treaty With the Indians" around 1840.

Among the many religions whose adherents moved to America in search of freedom, the Quakers fill a special place. George Fox (1624–1691) founded the religion in the 17th century as a search for authentic spirituality. Quakers distinguished themselves by their avoidance of worldly concerns, favoring plain dress, plain speech, and separate education for their children. The earliest Quakers did not fare well in Massachusetts, but a more favorable climate was found in the Rhode Island Providence Plantation, where the Baptist Roger Williams (1603–1683) espoused freedom of religion and separation of church and state. The colony of Pennsylvania—William Penn's "Holy Experiment"—was the most receptive. Penn (1644–1718), himself a Quaker, set down an example of religious tolerance and concern for social justice that would come to characterize Quakerism in America. By the early 19th century, virtually all Quakers were united in their opposition to slavery. Nevertheless, theological differences led to a split that would not be mended for nearly a century. In the process, modern Quakerism became the diverse confession of today.

1863
Alexei Khomyakov's *The Church Is One* is published

1864
Cheyenne and Arapaho Indians are massacred at Sand Creek, Colorado

1865
The Confederate States of America is defeated, ending the Civil War

1865
Joseph Lister develops antiseptic surgery

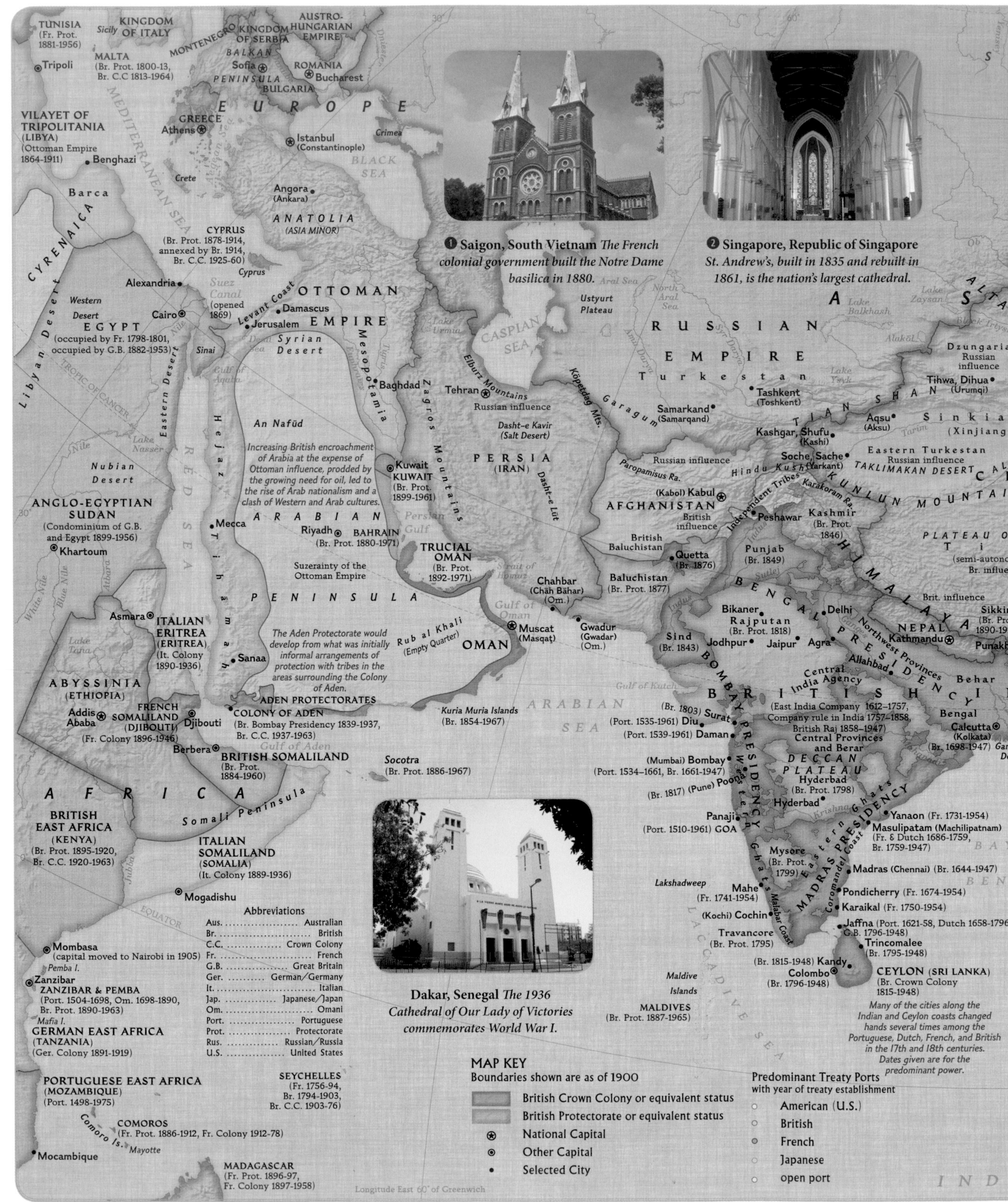

TUNISIA (Fr. Prot. 1881-1956)
KINGDOM OF ITALY
Sicily
MALTA (Br. Prot. 1800-13, Br. C.C 1813-1964)
MONTENEGRO
KINGDOM OF SERBIA
AUSTRO-HUNGARIAN EMPIRE
BALKAN PENINSULA
Sofia
ROMANIA
Bucharest
BULGARIA
Tripoli
EUROPE
GREECE
Athens
Istanbul (Constantinople)
Crimea
BLACK SEA
VILAYET OF TRIPOLITANIA (LIBYA) (Ottoman Empire 1864-1911)
Benghazi
MEDITERRANEAN SEA
Crete
Angora (Ankara)
ANATOLIA (ASIA MINOR)
Barca
CYRENAICA
CYPRUS (Br. Prot. 1878-1914, annexed by Br. 1914, Br. C.C. 1925-60)
Cyprus
Alexandria
Suez Canal (opened 1869)
Levant Coast
OTTOMAN EMPIRE
Damascus
Jerusalem
Western Desert
Cairo
EGYPT (occupied by Fr. 1798-1801, occupied by G.B. 1882-1953)
Libyan Desert
Sinai
Syrian Desert
Mesopotamia
Baghdad
TROPIC OF CANCER
Eastern Desert
Lake Nasser
Nile
Hejaz
An Nafūd
Increasing British encroachment of Arabia at the expense of Ottoman influence, prodded by the growing need for oil, led to the rise of Arab nationalism and a clash of Western and Arab cultures.
Nubian Desert
RED SEA
Kuwait
KUWAIT (Br. Prot. 1899-1961)
ANGLO-EGYPTIAN SUDAN (Condominium of G.B. and Egypt 1899-1956)
Khartoum
Mecca
ARABIAN PENINSULA
Riyadh
BAHRAIN (Br. Prot. 1880-1971)
Persian Gulf
TRUCIAL OMAN (Br. Prot. 1892-1971)
Suzerainty of the Ottoman Empire
Tihāmah
Asmara
ITALIAN ERITREA (ERITREA) (It. Colony 1890-1936)
The Aden Protectorate would develop from what was initially informal arrangements of protection with tribes in the areas surrounding the Colony of Aden.
Rub al Khali (Empty Quarter)
OMAN
Muscat (Masqaṭ)
Gulf of Oman
Sanaa
ABYSSINIA (ETHIOPIA)
ADEN PROTECTORATES
COLONY OF ADEN (Br. Bombay Presidency 1839-1937, Br. C.C. 1937-1963)
Addis Ababa
FRENCH SOMALILAND (DJIBOUTI) (Fr. Colony 1896-1946)
Djibouti
Gulf of Aden
Berbera
BRITISH SOMALILAND (Br. Prot. 1884-1960)
Socotra (Br. Prot. 1886-1967)
Kuria Muria Islands (Br. 1854-1967)
AFRICA
Somali Peninsula
BRITISH EAST AFRICA (KENYA) (Br. Prot. 1895-1920, Br. C.C. 1920-1963)
ITALIAN SOMALILAND (SOMALIA) (It. Colony 1889-1936)
Mogadishu
EQUATOR
Mombasa (capital moved to Nairobi in 1905)
Pemba I.
Zanzibar
ZANZIBAR & PEMBA (Port. 1504-1698, Om. 1698-1890, Br. Prot. 1890-1963)
Mafia I.
GERMAN EAST AFRICA (TANZANIA) (Ger. Colony 1891-1919)
PORTUGUESE EAST AFRICA (MOZAMBIQUE) (Port. 1498-1975)
SEYCHELLES (Fr. 1756-94, Br. 1794-1903, Br. C.C. 1903-76)
COMOROS (Fr. Prot. 1886-1912, Fr. Colony 1912-78)
Comoro Is.
Mayotte
Mocambique
MADAGASCAR (Fr. Prot. 1896-97, Fr. Colony 1897-1958)
Longitude East 60° of Greenwich
Abbreviations
Aus. ... Australian
Br. ... British
C.C. ... Crown Colony
Fr. ... French
G.B. ... Great Britain
Ger. ... German/Germany
It. ... Italian
Jap. ... Japanese/Japan
Om. ... Omani
Port. ... Portuguese
Prot. ... Protectorate
Rus. ... Russian/Russia
U.S. ... United States
Aral Sea
Ustyurt Plateau
CASPIAN SEA
Elburz Mountains
Tehran
Russian influence
Zagros Mountains
Dasht-e Kavir (Salt Desert)
PERSIA (IRAN)
Dasht-e Lūt
Köpetdag Mts.
Garagum
RUSSIAN EMPIRE
Turkestan
Lake Balkhash
Tashkent (Toshkent)
Samarkand (Samarqand)
Dzungaria Russian influence
Tihwa, Dihua (Urumqi)
TIAN SHAN
Aqsu (Aksu)
Sinkiang (Xinjiang)
Kashgar, Shufu (Kashi)
Soche, Sache (Yarkant)
Eastern Turkestan Russian influence
TAKLIMAKAN DESERT
Paropamisus Ra.
Russian influence
Hindu Kush
Karakoram Ra.
KUNLUN MOUNTAINS
(Kabol) Kabul
AFGHANISTAN
British influence
Independent Tribes
Peshawar
Kashmir (Br. Prot. 1846)
PLATEAU OF TIBET (semi-autonomous Br. influence)
British Baluchistan
Quetta (Br. 1876)
Punjab (Br. 1849)
Chahbar (Chāh Bahār) (Om.)
Baluchistan (Br. Prot. 1877)
HIMALAYA
BENGAL PRESIDENCY
Gwadur (Gwadar) (Om.)
Bikaner
Rajputan (Br. Prot. 1818)
Delhi
Brit. influence
Sikkim (Br. Prot. 1890-1918)
NEPAL
Kathmandu
Punakha
Sind (Br. 1843)
Jodhpur
Jaipur
Agra
Northwest Provinces
Allahabad
Behar
BOMBAY PRESIDENCY
Central India Agency
BRITISH INDIA (East India Company 1612–1757, Company rule in India 1757–1858, British Raj 1858–1947)
Bengal
Calcutta (Kolkata) (Br. 1698-1947)
Ganges Delta
Gulf of Kutch
ARABIAN SEA
(Br. 1803) Surat
(Port. 1535-1961) Diu
(Port. 1539-1961) Daman
Central Provinces and Berar
(Mumbai) Bombay (Port. 1534–1661, Br. 1661-1947)
DECCAN PLATEAU
Hyderbad (Br. Prot. 1798)
(Br. 1817) (Pune) Poona
Hyderbad
Western Ghats
Eastern Ghats
Panaji (Port. 1510-1961) GOA
Yanaon (Fr. 1731-1954)
Masulipatam (Machilipatnam) (Fr. & Dutch 1686-1759, Br. 1759-1947)
MADRAS PRESIDENCY
Mysore (Br. Prot. 1799)
Madras (Chennai) (Br. 1644-1947)
Lakshadweep
Mahe (Fr. 1741-1954)
Pondicherry (Fr. 1674-1954)
Karaikal (Fr. 1750-1954)
Coromandel Coast
(Kochi) Cochin
Malabar Coast
Jaffna (Port. 1621-58, Dutch 1658-1796, G.B. 1796-1948)
Travancore (Br. Prot. 1795)
Trincomalee (Br. 1795-1948)
(Br. 1815-1948) Kandy
Colombo (Br. 1796-1948)
CEYLON (SRI LANKA) (Br. Crown Colony 1815-1948)
Maldive Islands
MALDIVES (Br. Prot. 1887-1965)
LACCADIVE SEA
Many of the cities along the Indian and Ceylon coasts changed hands several times among the Portuguese, Dutch, French, and British in the 17th and 18th centuries. Dates given are for the predominant power.
MAP KEY
Boundaries shown are as of 1900
British Crown Colony or equivalent status
British Protectorate or equivalent status
National Capital
Other Capital
Selected City
Predominant Treaty Ports with year of treaty establishment
American (U.S.)
British
French
Japanese
open port

1 Saigon, South Vietnam *The French colonial government built the Notre Dame basilica in 1880.*

2 Singapore, Republic of Singapore *St. Andrew's, built in 1835 and rebuilt in 1861, is the nation's largest cathedral.*

Dakar, Senegal *The 1936 Cathedral of Our Lady of Victories commemorates World War I.*

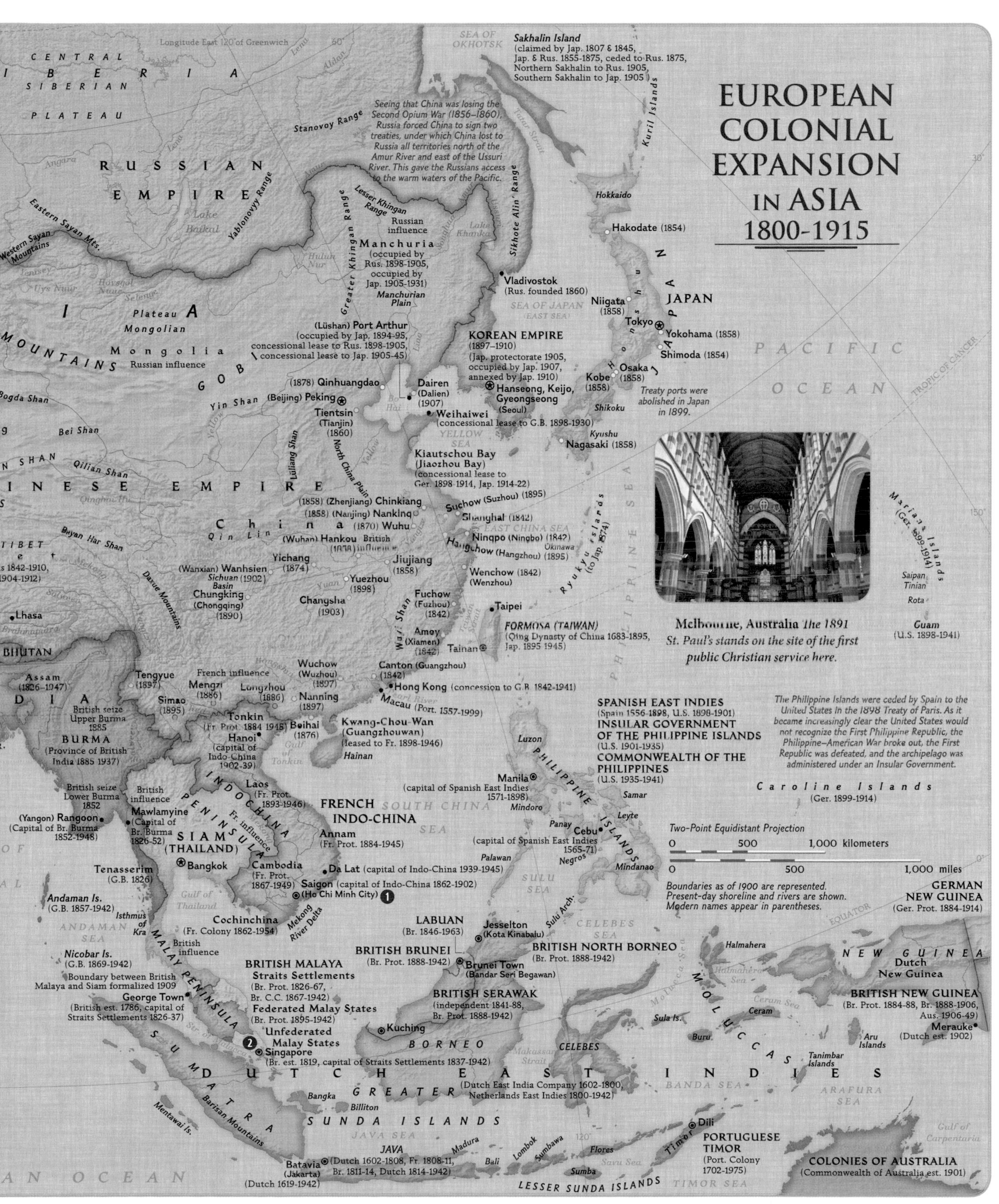

Melbourne, Australia The 1891 St. Paul's stands on the site of the first public Christian service here.

Colonial Expansion

Elsewhere in the world, the European powers continued to aggressively expand their spheres of influence. In the 17th and 18th centuries, the primary lure of Asia had been spices and tea. Now, with industrialization growing apace, the demand shifted to rubber, tin, and oil, in addition to sugar, coffee, and cocoa. The development of the steamship, combined with substantial improvements in cannon and musketry, enabled the European powers to vastly extend their colonial control.

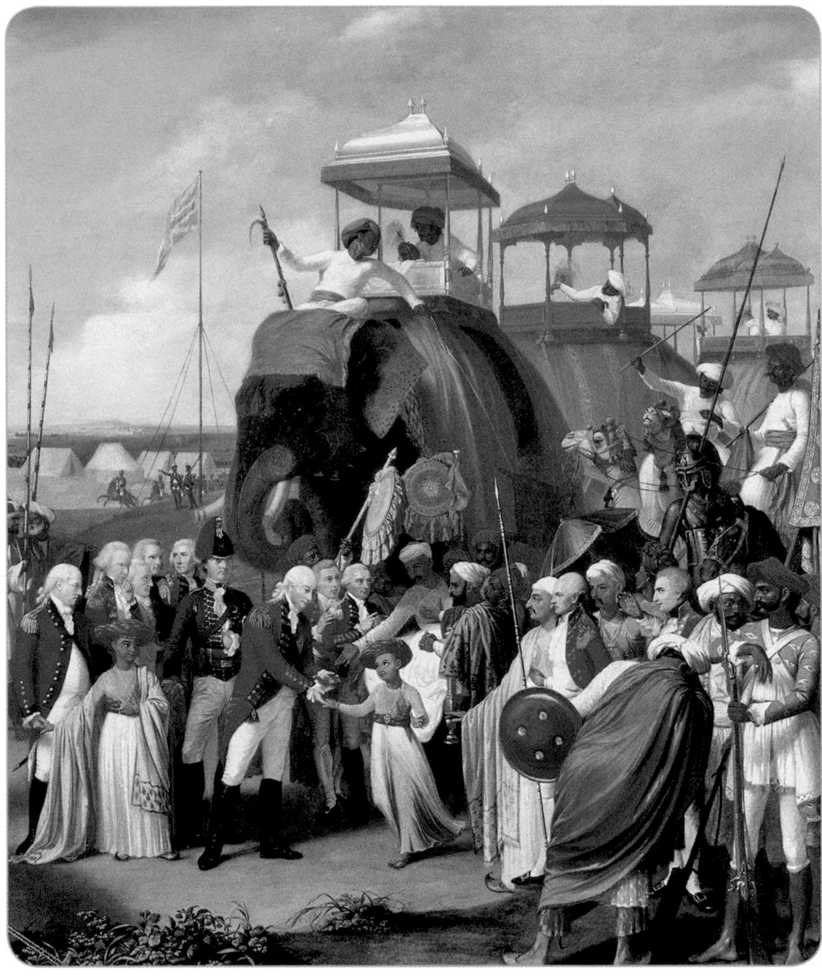

Once again, England took the lead, using India as its base. In 1819, British statesman Sir Stamford Raffles (1781–1826) struck a deal with a Malay governor to acquire the old Portuguese trading port of "Singapura." Raffles shrewdly declared Singapore a tax-free port, drawing trading ships from all around the region at the expense of Dutch ports in the East Indies. Singapore's population exploded from 340 to 10,000 in just five years. By the end of the 19th century, Singapore was the leading transit point for tin (needed for the newly invented canning process) and rubber, the demand for which was soaring following the development of the automobile. But the port's principal source of revenue was another commodity altogether: opium, which accounted for 50 percent of Singapore's revenues.

Few, if any, attempts were made by British colonials to convert the natives under their sway to Anglicanism. As early as 1835, a church dedicated to St. Andrew was built in Singapore, close to the administrative district, but for the purpose of serving British colonials. The Dutch, too, were content to leave local faith traditions in place. Protestant Holland had captured Cape Town in 1652, but ceded much of its control of southern Africa to Britain in 1814. The Dutch then concentrated on the Dutch East Indies and surrounding territories. The first church to rise in Java was the Blenduk Church, built in 1753 in the late Baroque style then still in fashion. Located in the port city of Semarang, it was primarily built to serve colonial adherents of the Dutch Reformed Church, complete with rattan seats on a white-and-black-tiled floor. The expatriate Catholic community was graciously permitted to use the edifice until they could build their own church.

The situation was quite different in French Indochina. Despite the political turmoil of

1865
The Ku Klux Klan is founded

1866
Gustave Doré's illustrated edition of the Bible is published

1867
Karl Marx publishes *Capital*

1867
The United States acquires Alaska from Russia

the early 19th century, successive French governments realized France needed to catch up in the colonial race with its European rivals. French troops occupied Algeria in 1830, followed by the conquest of other African colonies, in which more than 150,000 French soldiers and untold numbers of native warriors died. France also set its sights on Vietnam, newly unified by the Nguyen Emperor Gia Long in 1802 with French support.

Since the foundation of the Society of Foreign Missions of Paris in 1658, hundreds of French missionaries had roamed through Southeast Asia in search of souls to save. Their missions now provided the French government with the perfect pretext to intervene militarily. In 1847, French forces attacked Danang in retaliation for the presumed persecution of French missionaries by Emperor Tu Duc. Fourteen years later, Napoleon III occupied Saigon. By 1883, Vietnam had become a French protectorate.

In 1887, the French Third Republic (1870–1940) consolidated its Asian holdings, including Cambodia, into a federation known as French Indochina. In 1893, Laos was added as well. The British, meanwhile, seized Burma to act as a buffer between French and British spheres of influence.

A similar race for colonial possessions took place in Africa. King Leopold of Belgium established the Congo as his private preserve in 1876. Britain took control of Egypt in 1882. Two years later, the Conference of Western Powers carved Africa up into British, French, and German spheres.

The French set out to create beautiful, French-style administrative centers in places

OPPOSITE: *"The Reception of the Mysorean Hostage Princes by Lieutenant General Lord Cornwallis," by Robert Home (1752 1834), depicts the conclusion of one of Britain's wars with Indian rulers—in this case Tipu Sultan, ruler of Mysore.*

A late 19th-century photograph shows French archbishop Philippe-Prosper Augouard, founder of the diocese of Brazzaville, accompanied by a fellow cleric and Congolese attendants, after the area north of the Congo River was colonized by the French in 1880.

1868
Johannes Brahms composes *A German Requiem*

1869
Pope Pius IX convokes the First Vatican Council

1870
Outbreak of the Franco-Prussian War

1871
The forces of Emperor Napoleon III of France are defeated by Prussia

like Saigon and Hanoi. Gustave Eiffel, the engineer who designed the Eiffel Tower for the International Exposition in 1889, was prevailed upon to build Saigon's lovely post office in 1886. In the countryside, however, the French ran large rubber, cocoa, and coffee plantations using local labor as virtual serfs. The same was true for the Calvinist Dutch, who used Java, the largest island of the Dutch East Indies, to produce a third of the world's rubber and a fifth of its coffee and oil, while keeping most of its population in poverty.

In Indochina the French actively nurtured the growth of a native Catholic population. Between 1877 and 1880, a stupendous Neo-Romanesque cathedral was built in the heart of Saigon, using red bricks from Marseille and stained glass blown in Chartres. Of all of the legacies of the French colonial era, this one has endured: Today, with some 5.6 million adherents, Vietnam has the fifth largest Catholic population in Asia, organized in 26 dioceses.

The title of this print, "The White Fathers of Cardinal Lavigerie in Africa," refers to a priestly missionary order named after its members' white cassocks. Their efforts against the African slave trade were so successful they won the pope's support.

OPPOSITE: *Vincent van Gogh (1853–1890) formulated the principles of modern expressionist art with "The Good Samaritan" of 1890, inspired by an original painting by Eugène Delacroix (1798–1863).*

> *Expect great things from God; and attempt great things for God!*
>
> WILLIAM CAREY, THE DEATHLESS SERMON

The territory that beckoned the colonial powers above all was imperial China. In the early 19th century, the British had begun to trade with Chinese warlords and smugglers, paying for Chinese goods with opium cultivated in India. The opium supply stoked a growing dependency among the Chinese peasantry. In addition, China suffered a major peasant revolt known as the Taiping Rebellion between 1850 and 1864, prompted by widespread famine. Scores of towns and villages were utterly destroyed. Thus, China was exhausted and unable to stem the influx of European traders eager to exploit its local resources.

Missionary Outreach in the Colonies

Notwithstanding the policies of their national governments, missionaries from numerous church organizations fanned out through the European colonies in order to improve the lives of indigenous people. These missionaries built the first schools and hospitals in many regions. Most churches considered overseas missionary work a moral duty, with the aim of bringing both Christian salvation and the "civilizing" force of European culture to undeveloped regions. In Britain, for example, William Carey (1761–1834) organized the English Baptist Missionary Society for deployment in the Raj (India), while the London Missionary Society targeted its efforts on Africa, Asia, and the Middle East. In 1807, British missionary Robert Morrison traveled to China and produced the first Bible in Mandarin. In France, the Paris Foreign Missions Society focused on Southeast Asia; one of its missionaries, Augustin Schoeffler (1822–1851), would later be canonized as a saint.

As a result of their efforts, by the beginning of the 20th century there were some 1.4 million Catholics and more than half a million Protestants in China alone. The American evangelical movements harbored as much zeal for missionary work as their European counterparts. In the years to come, American missionaries would fan out to Asia, Latin America, and Africa, thus laying the foundation for the "American century." ■

1871 The Italian peninsula is unified in a kingdom for the first time in its history

1871 Charles Darwin publishes *The Descent of Man*

1871 King Wilhelm I proclaims the German Reich in the Hall of Mirrors at Versailles

1875 Hudson Taylor begins an evangelizing mission in China

12 CHAPTER

THE MODERN WORLD

1900-Today

If through necessity or fear . . .
the workman must accept
harder conditions . . .
he is made the victim of force
and injustice.

POPE LEO XIII, "RERUM NOVARUM"

The comforting Victorian concept of history as an unwavering ascent of Christian civilization was utterly destroyed by the barbarity of World War I, the first war to be conducted on an industrial scale. It left the world bereft of many of its cherished beliefs, and adrift in a search of a new purpose for mankind.

The century had opened on a wave of optimism. In 1900, Paris was once again host to a major world exhibition, the Exposition Universelle, in which every major nation on Earth proudly showcased its great achievements. More than 50 million people visited the fairgrounds to admire such novelties as the diesel engine, motion pictures, escalators, gramophones, and, more ominously, a recoilless cannon forged by the Krupp works in Germany.

In the United States, the dawn of the modern age saw an unprecedented rise in immigration, particularly from eastern and southern Europe. In 1907, a peak year, more than 1.2 million immigrants entered the country, often prodded by religious, racial, or political persecution at home. As a result, America's religious map changed. Catholics had already become the country's largest single denomination in 1850, but by 1890 their population had

ABOVE: *David Jagger (1891–1958) painted this moving portrait of a Jewish refugee set adrift by the upheaval of the 20th century.*

OPPOSITE: *A colorized photo captures the exuberance of national pavilions at the 1900 Paris Exposition. The pavilions were built in plaster along the Seine River.*

PRECEDING PAGES: *"The Sacrament of the Last Supper," by Spanish Catalan surrealist artist Salvador Dalí (1904–1989), completed in 1955, is one of the most popular religious paintings of the 20th century.*

tripled, largely as a result of immigration from Europe. This led to tensions, particularly in the South, with the formation of groups like the Ku Klux Klan, which actively promoted discrimination against Catholics, Jews, and African Americans.

Abroad, the general prosperity of the age fueled a growing missionary outreach to the West's colonial possessions. By 1900, there were some 100 translations of the Bible in circulation, with another 300 translation projects under way. Some 45,000 nuns were working in missions overseas. Catholic missionaries were permitted to enter Japan, where they were astonished to find remnants of Japanese Christianity dating back to the 17th century. Before the outbreak of World War I, there were more than 2,000 Catholic priests working in China, 800 of them ethnic Chinese. Protestant missionaries were focusing on converting souls in British-ruled India and in Africa.

Inevitably, missionaries from different confessions who worked in the same area came in contact with one another. Unified by often appalling conditions and a yearning for home, these missionaries found that their doctrinal differences began to melt away. Many Protestant and Catholic men and women worked together in fighting poverty,

In this photo taken shortly before his death in 1965, humanitarian, biblical scholar, and physician Albert Schweitzer talks with Peace Corps volunteers in Gabon, West Africa.

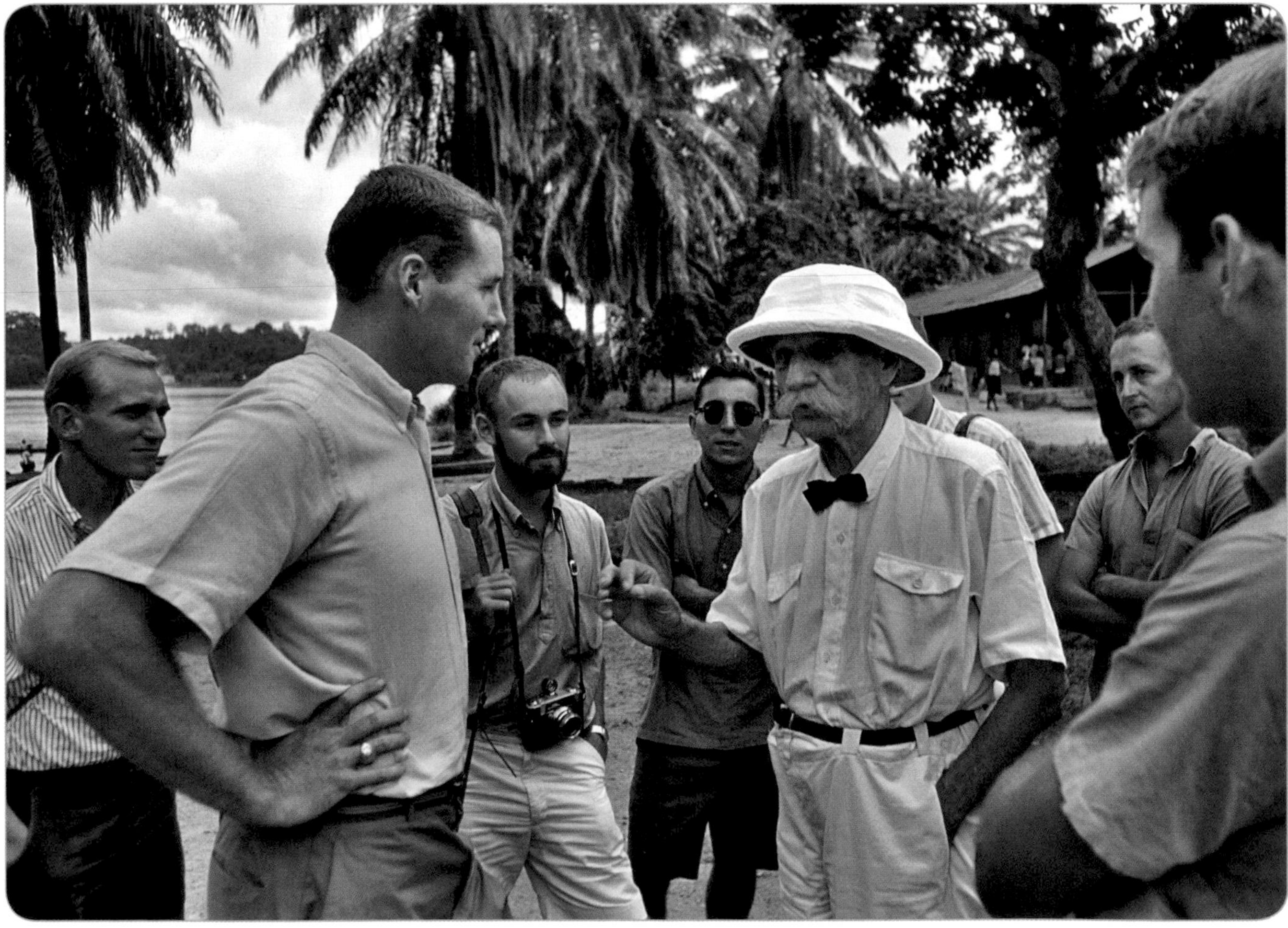

1890
Gabriel Fauré composes his *Requiem*

1893
The World's Columbian Exposition is in Chicago, introducing beaux arts architecture to the U.S.

1896
The first modern Olympic Games are held in Athens, Greece

1899
Sigmund Freud publishes *The Interpretation of Dreams*

malnutrition, and disease. Thus, it could be said that the ecumenical spirit of the 20th century was truly born in overseas missions. In 1910, the first World Missionary Conference was held in Edinburgh, which by 1921 spawned the International Missionary Council. The primary objective of the council was to provide a common link between the various missionary associations, with the goal of jointly developing solutions to problems such as slavery, disease, and opium addiction.

The Age of Piety

The late 19th century also saw a sharp upswing in popular piety, particularly in southern countries such as Spain, Italy, and France. Some historians have interpreted the new piety as a reaction against the monotony and bleakness of the industrial age, particularly among the uneducated labor class. In France, the new emphasis on piety was a reaction to the anticlerical stance of the Third Republic, formed after France's humiliating defeat by Prussia in 1871. The confiscation of the Papal States by the newly unified kingdom of Italy in 1870 stirred much sympathy for the papacy, which now saw its sovereign territory reduced to the tiny area of the Vatican. In response to the sharp growth in religious fervor, Pope Pius IX (r. 1846–1878), the longest-reigning pope in history, created more than 200 new bishoprics.

In 1891, Pius's successor, Pope Leo XIII (r. 1878–1903), decided to tackle the twin modern threats of materialism and Marxist communism. The result was the encyclical "Rerum Novarum" ("Of New Things"), better known as "Rights and Duties of Capital and Labor," which would guide papal policy through the early 20th century. In it, the Church denounced—belatedly—the "misery and wretchedness pressing so unjustly on the majority of the working class," and strongly lobbied for the right of workers to join unions. "Rerum Novarum" pierced the darkness of Catholic social complacency that had reigned for much of the 19th century.

Many Christians, however, looked elsewhere to cope with the changes of the modern age. Theologians such as the Catholic Alfred Firmin Loisy (1857–1940) and the Protestant Albert Schweitzer (1875–1965) fomented a movement called Biblical Modernism that searched for the spirit, rather than the letter, of the Bible. By approaching Scripture from a rational perspective, using the tools of textual criticism, these "modernists" sought to separate the supernatural accounts of miracles and early Christian dogma from the authentic words of Jesus. A renowned philosopher, physician, and organist, Schweitzer wrote *Geschichte der Leben-Jesu-Forschung* (1906), published in English in 1910 as *The Quest of the Historical Jesus.* The book is often cited as a key inspiration for the historical Jesus movement, a prominent discipline in New Testament studies today. Such liberal currents were, however, harshly denounced by the Church, notably in a 1907 encyclical by Pope Pius X (r. 1903–1914).

> *Jesus is a figure designed by rationalism, endowed with life by liberalism, and clothed by modern theology in a historical garb.*
>
> ALBERT SCHWEITZER, *THE QUEST OF THE HISTORICAL JESUS*

CLERICS AND SAINTS

Women and Nursing

An acute shortage of Red Cross volunteers and equipment prompted posters such as this one.

Since the early Middle Ages, nursing and hospital care had been closely associated with religious orders. In the 19th century, the modern concept of nursing evolved, based on the pioneering work of Florence Nightingale and Marianne Cope. Many religious orders, including the Sisters of Mercy, the Sisters of Charity, and the Sisters of St. Mary, devoted their ministry exclusively to nursing. Protestant churches developed a similar ministry through the deaconess movement, which originated in Germany in the 1830s and soon spread throughout Europe, including Great Britain. In the United States, the Methodist Church built a number of hospices and hospitals as early as the 1850s. The massive casualties of World War I led to an acute crisis in nursing care and to a massive drive on all sides to recruit laywomen to assist in the treatment of wounded soldiers.

1900 — **Boxer Rebellion leads to mass murder of Chinese Christians and Western missionaries in China**

1900 — **The International Exposition in Paris opens**

1906 — **Albert Schweitzer writes *The Quest of the Historical Jesus***

1907 — **An unprecedented 1.2 million immigrants, mostly Catholics, enter the United States**

Devotional Sculptures
1920–1960

This Pietà, by Will Lammert (1892–1957), commemorates the German Ravensbrück concentration camp.

Paul Landowski (1875–1961) sculpted the Christ the Redeemer statue, which stands on a mountain overlooking Rio de Janeiro, Brazil.

The Outbreak of World War I

In the summer of 1914, most people in France, Britain, and Belgium had never heard of Franz Ferdinand, heir to the Habsburg throne of Austria-Hungary. In 1867, the ancient Habsburg Empire had morphed into a large, multinational realm anchored on the "merger" of two major entities: the Austrian Empire and the Hungarian kingdom. Led by Emperor Franz Joseph I (r. 1848–1916) in Vienna, one of the longest-reigning monarchs in history, the so-called "dual monarchy" ruled over a vast swath of Europe in which 12 different languages were spoken. This unwieldy state was slowly torn apart by ethnic tensions between Slovaks, Croats, Serbs, and other ethnicities. Though Catholics formed the majority, the realm also numbered 3 million Orthodox Christians, 2.6 million Calvinists, 1.3 million Lutherans, and 2 million Jews.

This powder keg of ethnic tensions exploded when on June 28, 1914, Archduke Franz Ferdinand and his morganatic wife, Sophie, were assassinated by Serbian-trained terrorists in Sarajevo. Kaiser Wilhelm II of Germany, brimming with indignation, demanded that Austria exact revenge against Serbia, lest her passivity be mistaken for weakness. By the time Austria finally issued an ultimatum to Serbia, the Russian Tsar, the traditional protector of the Slavs of Serbia, had also begun to rattle his sword. This, in turn, forced France to join the fray, for France and Russia had recently concluded a joint defensive pact. This was the great tragedy of early 20th-century Europe: Its kingdoms were locked in the grip of treaty obligations that were supposed to secure the peace, yet only served to thrust the continent into war.

Many modern authors, however, believe that a major European war was inevitable.

1907
Pope Pius X denounces liberal movements in modern Christianity

1908
Britain launches its all-metal dreadnought, igniting a naval arms race

1910
The first World Missionary Conference is held in Edinburgh

1914
Archduke Franz Ferdinand of Austria-Hungary is assassinated in Sarajevo

Armed to the teeth by the Industrial Revolution, and with competing nationalistic and imperialist aims, the European powers were bound to come to blows. But nobody anticipated that the war would devolve into carnage on such a vast scale. Between 1914 and 1917, a thousand men would die on a daily basis in the Ypres sector alone. On the opening day of the Passchendaele Offensive of 1917, the British suffered more than a hundred thousand casualties. By that time, such numbers were commonplace.

No Christian confession of any kind was prepared to cope with the impact of this massive institutionalized slaughter. Ideas of transnational religious solidarity were abandoned as nationalist passions rose on both sides of the conflict. The only redemptive aspect of the war was that in the trenches, differences between Protestant and Catholic victims and caretakers dissolved. Nuns, chaplains, and pastors, aided by heroic members of the Red Cross, tended to the needs of the wounded without any regard for their religious affiliation.

The war took a dramatic new turn in 1917 when the German foreign secretary, Arthur Zimmerman, sent a secret telegram to the Mexican government. The missive promised to restore territories lost to the United States, such as Texas, Arizona, and New Mexico, if Mexico would join the war on the side of

OPPOSITE: *Emperor Franz Joseph I of Austria-Hungary meets with church leaders in Budapest in this color lithograph by Gyula Benczúr (1844–1920).*

An anonymous war photographer captured this image of an Anglican Church service for British infantry about to be sent into battle during World War I.

1914
As World War I breaks out, Germany launches an invasion of Russia and France

1917
After the Zimmerman Affair, the United States enters World War I on the side of the Allies

1918
In November, an armistice is agreed to, ending World War I

1918
Kaiser Wilhelm II of Germany abdicates and leaves for exile in Holland

imperial Germany. The telegram was intercepted by British intelligence and promptly forwarded to Washington, where it caused an uproar. On April 2, 1917, a deeply vexed President Woodrow Wilson (1913–1921) asked Congress to declare war on Germany and Austria. Though it would take more than a year before a new American expeditionary force could be formed, trained, and shipped to Europe, the American entry was ultimately decisive. By October 1918, a million American soldiers were in action on the Western Front. At that time, Germany saw the writing on the wall. Its civilian government rushed to negotiate an armistice, not only under pressure from an Allied offensive, but also because strikes were spreading throughout the cities of Germany. On November 9, Kaiser Wilhelm II, the man who called himself the "All-Highest," abdicated the German throne. He fled on a train to Holland, where he was given asylum. Two days later, at the 11th hour on the 11th day of the 11th month of 1918, the armistice went into effect, and the "Great War" came to an end. More than 8 million soldiers had died, with countless more maimed or missing.

During World War I, many Allied medical stations were established in rural churches in Flanders or northern France.

The Impact of the Great War

The Great War left deep scars on European Christianity. In virtually every belligerent country, the national church had rallied to the colors in a surge of nationalism, rather than appealing to a sense of Christian solidarity. The impact of World War I was deeply felt in the battle zones, particularly in the Catholic nations of France, Belgium, Italy, and Austria-Hungary and the Orthodox states of Serbia and Russia. Here, many church structures were utterly destroyed. Some modern scholars have argued that Rome's erstwhile political influence was forever swept away. But Protestant churches suffered as well. In Germany, the national Lutheran Church *(die Evangelische Kirche),* which had long been associated with the Hohenzollern Dynasty, suffered widespread disaffection when the German Kaiser abdicated and the monarchy came to an end.

Of the four European empires that went to war in the name of God and country, three ceased to exist: the Orthodox Russian Empire, the Protestant German Empire, and the Catholic Austro-Hungarian Empire.

OPPOSITE: *Francis Luis Mora (1874–1940), an American painter of Hispanic descent, depicts a Thanksgiving service in Notre Dame Cathedral in Paris after the signing of the Armistice in 1918.*

1919 Ottoman Turkey initiates systematic persecution of Christian Armenians

1919 The terms of the Treaty of Versailles impose crippling reparation payments on Germany

1920 The United States prohibits the sale of alcohol

1921 The ecumenical International Missionary Council is formed

RIGHT: "Three Women Grieving for a Lost One" forms part of a moving 1918 triptych entitled "Remembering the Dead," by French artist André Devambez (1867–1944).

BELOW: A color photograph depicts the Syriac Orthodox patriarch Ignatius Elias III and his followers in 1922 in Jerusalem, then located in the British Mandate of Palestine.

The Russian Empire collapsed in the wake of the Russian Revolution of 1917 and the subsequent Bolshevik coup led by Vladimir Lenin (r. 1917–1924) that created the Soviet Union. Only the British Empire remained in existence, but its economic and political foundations were severely battered by the human and financial tolls of the war. Almost immediately after the cessation of hostilities in November 1918, the issue of Home Rule in Ireland rose again, with the Protestant north (or Ulster) pitted against the largely Catholic Irish south.

Elsewhere, the violence continued. In Ottoman Turkey, more than a million Armenian Christians were massacred. With Ottoman rule tottering, Greece invaded Asia Minor but was pushed back by the Turkish army under Mustafa Kemal. Tremendous destruction was visited on the people of Asia Minor, and priceless monuments were destroyed. Kemal, better known as Atatürk (r. 1923–1938), would go on to topple the Ottoman Sultan and establish the modern republic of Turkey. In eastern Turkey, large numbers of Syriac Christians fled to Iraq and Syria, which had become a French protectorate. There they slowly built new Christian enclaves in several cities, including Aleppo, which would suffer widespread destruction after the outbreak of the Syrian insurrection in 2011.

The Treaty of Versailles, signed in 1919, was supposed to guarantee the peace, but instead it ensured that another world war would be inevitable. Crushing terms were imposed on the new German republic, including the loss of 25,000 square miles of territory and billions of dollars in reparations.

1921
Adolf Hitler takes control of the National Socialist (Nazi) Party of Germany

1923
Adolf Hitler stages an attempted putsch in Munich, prompting his arrest

1929
The Wall Street crash leads to the Great Depression throughout the world

1929
Pope Pius XI and the dictator of Italy, Benito Mussolini, sign the Lateran Treaty

As another consequence of the war, the United States now emerged as the world's leading superpower. U.S. forces had suffered 320,000 casualties, compared with the 6.2 million men lost by France and the 7.2 million men killed, maimed, or missing in Germany. What's more, both France and Britain were now heavily indebted to America because of their war expenditures.

The Interbellum

The interbellum, the decades between the two World Wars, was a period of intense reflection for many Christian denominations in Europe as well as the United States. Vowing to avoid any conflagration in the future, Pope Pius XI (r. 1922–1939) became an active European diplomat, denouncing economic exploitation in his encyclical "Quadragesimo Anno" ("In the 40th Year," 1931), while striking concordats with the government of Poland and, less salutarily, with Mussolini's Italy and Hitler's Germany.

In the United States, religious movements coalesced around two competing ideas: a liberal current, espousing greater freedom in religious self-determination, and a fundamentalist trend, advocating a firm adherence

1932
The Association of Baptist Churches is formed in the United States

1933
Franklin Delano Roosevelt becomes the 32nd president of the United States

1933
Adolf Hitler is elected chancellor of Germany

1933
Eugenio Pacelli (the future Pope Pius XII) negotiates a "Concordat" with the Hitler regime

"The Signing of Peace in the Hall of Mirrors," by Sir William Orpen (1878–1931), commemorates the Treaty of Versailles, negotiated in the same Hall of Mirrors where Kaiser Wilhelm I had proclaimed the unified German Reich in 1871.

to orthodox Protestant conservatism. To bolster their theological positions, American churches began to organize themselves in associations. The Association of Baptist Churches was founded in 1932. In 1939, the Methodist Episcopal community joined with the Methodist Protestant community to heal its 19th-century split and become the Methodist Church. Seven years later, the Church of the United Brethren in Christ and the Evangelical Church came together to form the Evangelical United Brethren Church.

In this same period, Protestant missionaries began to make significant inroads in Asia, particularly in Japanese-occupied Korea, where there were soon flourishing Presbyterian and Methodist communities. For many Koreans, Christianity served as an important deterrent against Japanese efforts to impose the Japanese Shinto religion as well as Japanese language and customs. By 1934, there were nearly 170,000 Protestants in Korea, a number which would grow to some 8.6 million by the end of the 20th century.

At the same time, all of the former belligerents of World War I experienced a profound social and cultural transformation. During the war, tens of thousands of women

1933
The German Reichstag passes the Enabling Act, granting Adolf Hitler dictatorial powers

1934
The German Protestant Church splits

1935
Workers complete the Nativity facade of the Sagrada Família church in Barcelona

1936
Hitler remilitarizes the Ruhr region, but none of the European powers move to stop him

In the furrow of peace ... others sowed the tares of suspicion, discord, hatred, calumny, a secret and open fundamental hostility to Christ and His Church.

POPE PIUS XI, "MIT BRENNENDER SORGE"

had been recruited to work in factories, as drivers, as conductors, and in a host of other jobs previously occupied by men. While many women gladly returned to their traditional role of homemakers, many did not, and demanded to retain the careers they had carved out for themselves. On both sides of the Atlantic, this led to an economic downturn when millions of soldiers were released to civilian life and unemployment rose.

These social changes had profound repercussions in America. Women lobbied successfully for the right to vote, while Prohibition—making the sale of alcoholic beverages illegal—was formally adopted in 1920. With wages continuing to drop, the gap between rich and poor became ever greater. In the 1920s, the wealthy one percent of the population saw their income increase by a factor of eight, while the income of the average worker only increased one percent per year. Much of the new wealth was invested in the stock market, to the point that stock prices climbed to unsustainable levels.

The Great Depression

On October 29, 1929, the New York Stock Exchange suffered a devastating collapse. As a result, industrial production dropped 46 percent in the United States, 23 percent in Great Britain, and 41 percent in Germany. Unemployment in Germany grew by more than 230 percent, while in America it soared by 600 percent. But in Germany, the effects were more severe. The country was still struggling to rebuild its economy while trying to meet its crippling reparation payments.

By the time Franklin D. Roosevelt (r. 1933–1945) succeeded Herbert Hoover as president, the overall U.S. economy had shrunk by an astonishing 31 percent. In response, President Roosevelt offered a "New Deal," whereby national wealth and income would be more equitably shared. Vast public works, such as the Tennessee Valley Authority and other projects funded by the Works Progress Administration, created nearly nine million jobs for Americans.

The German Republic, governed by a constitutional assembly based in Weimar, did not have the resources to mount such

ABOVE: *One of the signature achievements of President Franklin Delano Roosevelt prior to World War II was a program of legislative reforms known as the New Deal.*

LEFT: *This World War I poster was part of a nationwide British program to recruit women for service in a variety of functions.*

1937
Pope Pius XI issues the pastoral letter "With Burning Concern"

1937
Dietrich Bonhoeffer writes *The Cost of Discipleship*

1938
Hitler arranges the Anschluss, or merger of Austria with the German Reich

1939
The Methodist Episcopal joins with the Methodist Protestant community

massive public works. The only thing that Weimar politicians could offer were words of encouragement, and the promise that things would get better. This created an opportunity for an Austrian ideologue and postcard illustrator named Adolf Hitler (r. 1933–1945).

Dorothea Lange (1895–1965) captured the hopelessness of the Depression in this famous photograph of Florence Thompson, a 32-year-old migrant mother trying to make a living as a crop picker in California.

In 1921, Hitler had become the leader of the NSDAP, the National Socialist German Workers Party. Two years later, he tried unsuccessfully to stage a coup against the Weimar Republic. Hitler was arrested and put in a (rather comfortable) prison, where he wrote his manifesto *Mein Kampf* (*My Struggle,* 1924).

The book set out what would become the principal platform of the future Nazi regime. The cause of Germany's ills, said Hitler, was the outrageous terms of the Treaty of Versailles, compounded by Jewish control of the nation's levers of power and the acute threat of a Communist takeover. The combustible mix of anti-Semitism (which had always lain just below the surface in 19th-century Europe), fear of Communism, and German nationalist sentiment propelled Hitler to power in 1933.

Church Response to Hitler

Many German clergy, both Protestant and Catholic, could not resist being drawn to Hitler's vision of a prosperous state, based on the rule of law and order. Throughout the 1920s, left-wing and right-wing strikes and clashes had crippled Germany's cities. Moreover, the Vatican had always identified Communist atheism as its greatest existential threat. Given that Hitler was widely seen as the most powerful bulwark against Communism, many Catholic priests supported the Nazis' rise to power. Their sentiments were confirmed when the papal Cardinal Secretary of State, Eugenio Pacelli (the future Pope Pius XII), negotiated a special "Concordat" with the Hitler regime that secured full religious freedom for German Catholics. In return, Hitler obtained the Vatican's consent to the dissolution of Catholic labor unions and parties in Germany.

The Concordat was a reflection of a similar treaty that had been negotiated between the pope and the totalitarian ruler of Italy,

OPPOSITE: *Following the conclusion of the Lateran Treaty between Italian dictator Benito Mussolini and the Vatican, Mussolini ordered a large avenue to be built—Via della Conciliazione ("Road of Reconciliation")—to reconnect Vatican City with the heart of Rome.*

1939
Pope Pius XI dies and is succeeded by Pope Pius XII

1939
The *St. Louis,* carrying 937 German Jews, is denied entry by the U.S. and Canada

1939
Hitler attacks Poland, leading to the outbreak of World War II

1941
Imperial Japanese forces bomb the American fleet at Pearl Harbor, Hawaii

CLERICS AND SAINTS

Dietrich Bonhoeffer

Dietrich Bonhoeffer is shown during his 1939 sojourn in London.

One of the most prominent dissenters during the Nazi era was Lutheran pastor Dietrich Bonhoeffer, who founded the Confessional Church together with Martin Niemöller. Bonhoeffer studied theology in Berlin and later at Union Theological Seminary in New York. Bonhoeffer strongly opposed the Nazi rise to power, and was one of the first German pastors to denounce the persecution of Jews. He served as chaplain to a Lutheran congregation in London, but returned to Germany in 1935 to continue his opposition to Nazism. From 1941 onward, Bonhoeffer became involved with various plots against Hitler led by the Abwehr, German military intelligence. Among his best-known works is *Nachfolge (The Cost of Discipleship)*, inspired by the Sermon on the Mount and written in 1937. He was arrested in 1943 and executed just two weeks before the Allies liberated the concentration camp where he was held.

Benito Mussolini (r. 1925–1943), in 1929. The so-called Lateran Treaty granted the Vatican the status of a sovereign state, and Catholicism was recognized as Italy's state religion. Three years later, Mussolini went out of his way to publicly reconcile with Pope Pius XI. To many, this suggested that institutional Christianity, and certainly Catholicism, could find a way to coexist with a Fascist dictatorship.

Protestant clergy were intrigued as well. The close link between the German state and German Protestantism had never been completely abandoned, and the Church remained quite powerful: In 1933, more than 45 million Germans declared an affiliation with a Protestant denomination. "The idea of a strong authority and a close bond between throne and altar, of the kind that existed in the empire between 1871 and 1918," the historian Wolfgang Benz explains, "was in keeping with Protestant tradition." What's more, some liberal Protestant theology had always harbored an undercurrent of anti-Semitism. A key example is the work of the German theologian Gerhard Kittel (1888–1948), author of *Theologisches Wörterbuch zum Neuen Testament (Theological Dictionary of the New Testament)*. After the Allied victory, Kittel was arrested and ordered to stand trial for his virulent attacks on Judaism, but he died before the proceedings could take place.

By 1934, the German Protestant Church had split into the Deutsche Christen ("German Christian") movement, which openly sympathized with the Nazi regime, and the Bekennende Kirche ("Confessional Church"), which remained loyal to democratic principles and the rule of law. After Hitler rose to power, the German Christians won some 75 percent of German presbyteries, thus gaining full control of the National

Ein Volk, ein Reich, ein Führer!

Synod that would soon became an extension of Nazi religious policy.

It is therefore not surprising that when Hitler proposed the *Ermächtigungsgesetz* (Enabling Act), which would give him full dictatorial powers without interference from the German Reichstag (parliament), the crucial "yes" vote was cast by the center block of Christian parties. As the Nazi terror deepened and the persecution of Jews escalated, it was left up to dissidents such as Martin Niemöller (1892–1984), Karl Barth (1886–1968), and Dietrich Bonhoeffer (1906–1945) to lead the Protestant opposition.

The Catholic Church in Germany experienced a similar split. Many clung to the increasingly elusive protection of the Concordat while others, both clergy and laymen, were repelled by the brutal repression of Jews and other minorities. Even Pope Pius XI could no longer remain silent when the Nazi oppression went into high gear in

1937. Deeply committed to social justice, the pope issued the encyclical "Mit Brennender Sorge" ("With Burning Concern"), which denounced the Nazi harassment of the Catholic Church and the excesses of its racial laws. Written as a pastoral letter in German, it was smuggled into the country and read simultaneously from Catholic pulpits on Palm Sunday of 1937. Unfortunately, Pope Pius XI died in February 1939, just seven months before the outbreak of World War II.

The Nazi Holocaust

As the world was convulsed by the aggressive conquests of the Axis forces—Germany, Italy, and Japan—the Nazi regime implemented the Final Solution, which condemned approximately six million Jews to the gas chambers in death camps throughout the Third Reich. Scores of dissident priests, pastors, and Christian laymen as well as political opponents were killed as well. Much has been written in recent years about what the Allies knew about the Holocaust, and whether they could have acted sooner to prevent or mitigate it. Some historians cite the case of the *St. Louis*, an ocean liner with 937 German Jewish refugees on board, which was denied entry by Cuba, the United States, and Canada in 1939,

OPPOSITE: A propaganda lithograph of German dictator Adolf Hitler is inscribed "One People, One Country, One Leader!"

This haunting photograph of children in a Nazi extermination camp was taken in 1945.

1946
Despite free elections promised by Soviet leader Joseph Stalin, an "Iron Curtain" descends

1955
Martin Luther King and Ralph Abernathy initiate the Montgomery bus boycott

1956
Soviet leader Nikita Khrushchev launches a new oppression of the Russian Orthodox Church

1957
The Southern Christian Leadership Conference, a platform for civil rights activism, is formed

on the eve of World War II. Others, however, have argued that until the first death camps were liberated by the Russians in late 1944, the sheer magnitude of this evil was simply inconceivable in the minds of Western leaders. As President Roosevelt put it, the best way to end the Holocaust was to defeat Nazi Germany as swiftly as possible.

Indeed, after an almost uninterrupted string of victories, the German army was finally checked at the Battle of Stalingrad, the gateway to the oil fields of the Caucasus, in early 1943. After the successful Allied invasion of Normandy in June 1944, most German generals knew that the war was lost, but their oath of loyalty to Hitler kept many of them committed to fanatical resistance, right up to the moment that the Soviet armies entered Berlin. On May 7, 1945, Hitler committed suicide.

The War in the Pacific

Since its invasion of China in 1931, the militarist regime of imperial Japan had been plotting to capture the oil-rich islands of the East Indies, given that Japan itself had no natural resources to speak of. In an effort to contain Japanese militarism, President Roosevelt placed an embargo on exports of oil and scrap metal to Japan in July of 1941. In response, a Japanese fleet of aircraft carriers launched a surprise attack on the U.S. Navy base at Pearl Harbor, Hawaii, on December 7. Fortunately, the U.S. carrier fleet was at sea, and thus spared destruction. Using these precious carriers, the U.S. struck back at the Battle of Midway in 1942. From that point on, U.S. forces steadily rolled back Japanese conquests in the Pacific, though at a horrific cost in casualties.

> *Here one can truly speak and hear about sin and grace and the love of God . . . the Black Christ is preached with rapturous passion and vision.*
>
> DIETRICH BONHOEFFER
> ON THE ABYSSINIAN BAPTIST CHURCH IN HARLEM

1962
Pope John XXIII convenes the Second Vatican Council

1963
John F. Kennedy, the first Catholic U.S. president, is assassinated in Dallas

1963
Martin Luther King delivers his "I Have a Dream" speech

1968
Frank Borman electrifies the world by reading from Genesis while circling the moon

In 1945, a clergy member says prayers for fallen American soldiers during a battle on the island of Ie-shima.

Meanwhile, the Japanese shut down all Western missions in their newly conquered territories, imprisoning thousands of Christian nuns and missionaries. In China alone, some 1,000 Protestant missionaries and their families were interned, most of whom wound up in a notorious camp in Weihsien, Shandong Province. Many prisoners, including children, died as a result of maltreatment. Surprisingly, indigenous Protestant or Catholic churches were largely left unmolested as long as they abstained from any political activity. As a result, untold numbers of downed airmen and Allied soldiers were rescued by Asian church organizations, keeping them hidden from the Japanese. Some historians have argued that the experience also allowed native churches in Southeast Asia to develop an independent authenticity and vitality, released from the paternal supervision of the West.

After the successful liberation of the Philippines, when much of the Japanese Navy lay at the bottom of the sea, the Japanese unleashed one last and desperate weapon: waves of *kamikaze* suicide pilots, trained to fly their planes straight into American ships. Fearful that in the face of such suicidal tactics, an invasion of the Japanese homeland could claim up to half a million American lives, President Harry Truman (who had succeeded President Roosevelt upon his death in April 1945) made the controversial decision to drop an atomic bomb on the Japanese city of Hiroshima. Three days later, another atomic bomb devastated the city of Nagasaki, and Japan capitulated at last.

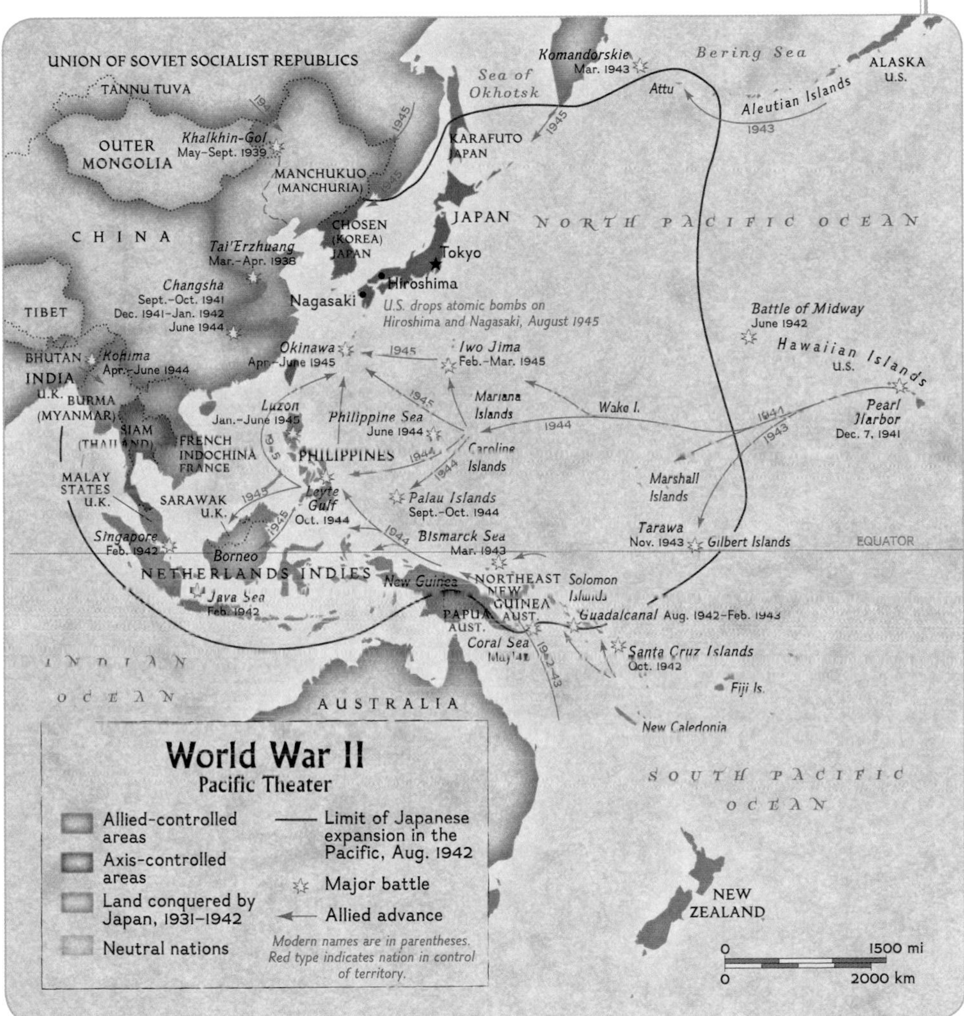

1968
The Chinese Missions Overseas is formed in Taiwan to send missionaries into China

1971
***A Theology of Liberation* by Peruvian priest Gustavo Gutiérrez is published**

1973
Evangelical minister Billy Graham attracts more than four million people in Korea

1978
Israel and Egypt sign the Camp David peace accords

VNA FIDES

European Christianity After World War II

World War II was the largest and deadliest war ever fought on the planet. Historians estimate that more than 100 million uniformed men and women fought in 30 countries, while somewhere between 50 and 80 million people, civilian and military, died in the conflagration. The war eradicated what remained of the religious infrastructure in Germany. Countless church treasures across Europe were destroyed as well. In all, World War II dealt a blow to European Christianity from which it would only slowly and painfully recover. Some scholars believe that the deep roots of Christendom on the Continent were destroyed forever.

What is needed at the present time is a new enthusiasm, a new joy and serenity of mind in the unreserved acceptance by all of the entire Christian faith.

POPE JOHN XXIII AT THE OPENING OF THE SECOND VATICAN COUNCIL

Indeed, the remainder of the 20th century saw a continuing exodus from organized religion throughout Europe. At the outbreak of the war, Soviet dictator Joseph Stalin (r. 1922–1953) had granted the Russian Orthodox Church, long oppressed in Soviet Russia, a measure of freedom, provided it rallied the Russian masses to the "Great Patriotic War" against Nazism. Seminaries, churches, and monasteries were reopened, but the respite was temporary. At the height of the Cold War between the U.S.S.R. and the United States, Nikita Khrushchev (r. 1953–1964) launched a renewed attack on the Russian Orthodox Church, shuttering two-thirds of all churches. Large numbers of priests and nuns were arrested on trumped-up charges.

In Europe, where churches had been full during the years of Nazi occupation, an

OPPOSITE: *The Second Vatican Council, opened by Pope John XXIII on October 11, 1962, brought together nearly 3,000 bishops as part of a program to introduce modern reforms to the Catholic Church.*

SCRIPTURE AND FAITH

The Evangelical Movement

Since World War II, the evangelical movement has become one of the most vibrant and fast-growing movements in Christianity. Some historians believe that in the United States, the evangelical movement grew as an alternative to the growing split between liberal and fundamentalist movements in mainstream confessions. According to the historian David Bebbington, evangelicalism is based on four key tenets: the life transforming experience of being "born again" in Christ; a close personal identification with the Gospel; belief in the redemptive power of Christ's death and resurrection; and a dedication to social initiative. As we saw, the evangelical movement has its roots in the ideas of many 18th-century preachers, including John Wesley, who believed that the Catholic and Anglican traditions had buried the pure power of Christian salvation under the weight of ecclesiastical doctrine. But the most influential figure in postwar evangelicalism was undoubtedly Billy Graham (born 1918). A native of Charlotte, North Carolina, and an ordained Southern Baptist minister, Graham launched his first "crusade" in 1949 in Los Angeles. Delivering sermons in tents erected in parking lots, Graham inveighed people to "accept Jesus Christ as their personal savior." At one event in 1953, he cut the ropes separating whites from blacks in his audience, and from 1954 on insisted on integrated seating at all appearances in the South. The impact of his teachings, broadcast on the emerging medium of television and countless other media outlets, was incalculable. Some believe that during his 400 crusades in 185 countries, he touched the lives of more than 2 billion people.

Billy Graham's 1972 Campus Crusade for Christ was the first to blend sermons with rock bands and singers such as Johnny Cash.

1978 Anglican archbishop Desmond Tutu leads the South African Council of Churches

1979 Pope John Paul II's visit to Poland energizes the liberation movement Solidarity

1989 The Berlin Wall falls

1991 The Union of Soviet Socialist Republics (U.S.S.R.) is disbanded

PERIOD ARCHITECTURE

La Sagrada Família

The interior nave of the Sagrada Família resembles a forest of trees.

One of the most imaginative examples of modern church design is the Sagrada Família (Holy Family) by Catalan architect Antoni Gaudí (1852–1926). A devout Catholic, Gaudí began work on the Sagrada Família in 1883, blending Gothic motifs with elements of art nouveau. In addition, he adapted many organic forms seen in nature, such as the hyperbolic paraboloid and the helicoid. Gaudí created a model that he suspended from the ceiling, upside down, to see how the laws of gravity resolved the principal engineering issues. He became so absorbed in the construction that he moved his bed into the crypt of the church. In 1926, he was hit by a tram while crossing a nearby street. Nobody recognized him, so he was taken to a paupers' hospital, where he died two days later. Construction continued in fits and starts. The Nativity facade was completed in 1935, on the eve of the Spanish Civil War. After the war, progress was slow. The Passion facade was not completed until the late 1980s. In November 2010, Pope Benedict XVI consecrated the partially completed church, in anticipation of its full completion by 2026.

exodus was in full swing. By the end of the century, only one in six Europeans would still attend religious services on a regular basis. The charismatic Pope John XXIII (r. 1958–1963) sought to stem this development by reconnecting Catholicism with the postwar era. In October 1962, he convened the historic Second Vatican Council, which brought together nearly 3,000 bishops from all parts of the globe. The pope pushed through a number of reforms, including a greater role for the laity and a renewed ecumenical outreach to other Christian faiths. As a result, Mass is now said in the vernacular of

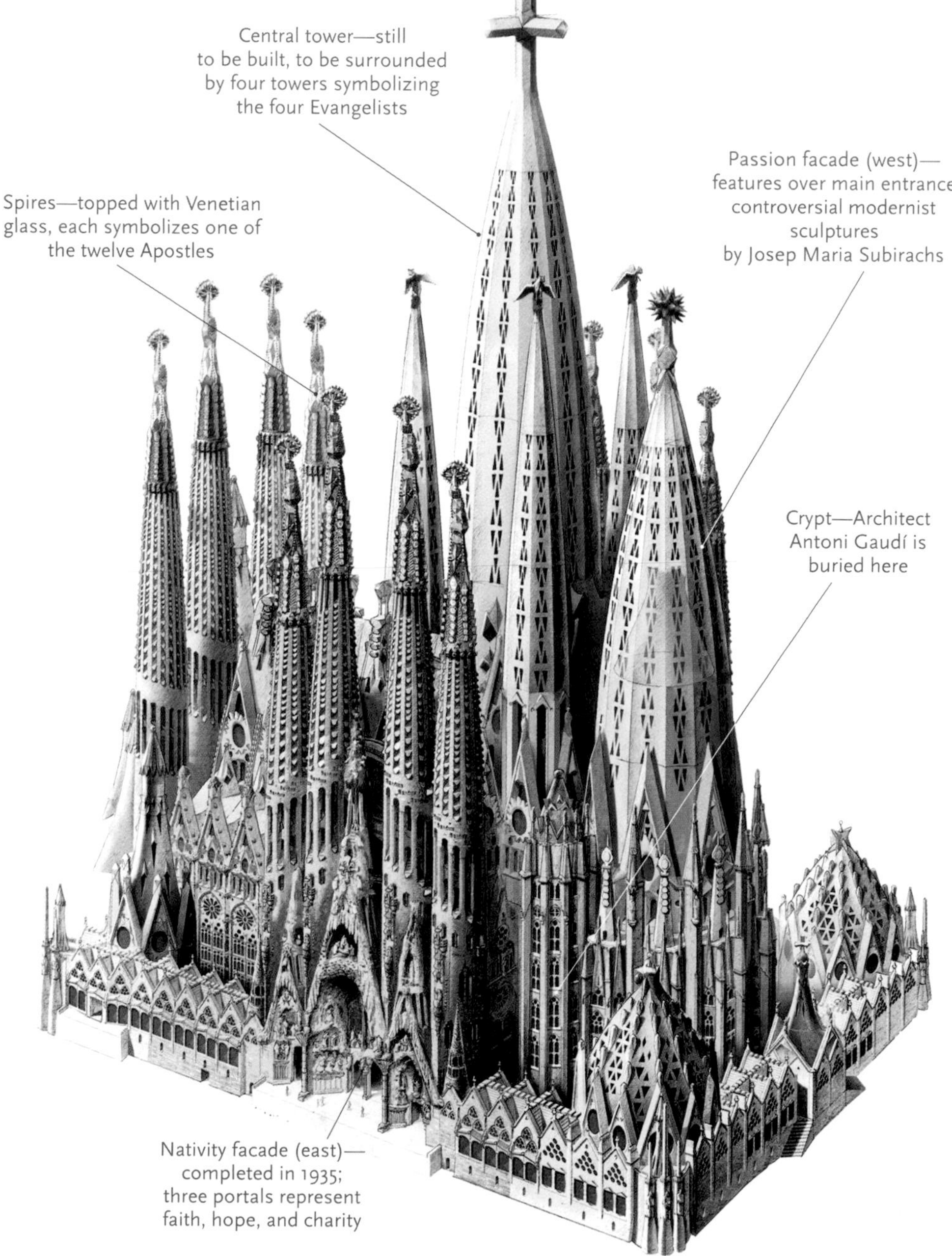

1991
The Russian Orthodox Church is restored and resumes worship

1994
Nelson Mandela is elected South Africa's first black president

1994
Israel's Yitzhak Rabin and Jordan's King Hussein I sign the Israeli-Jordanian Peace Treaty

1994
Desmond Tutu exhorts postapartheid South Africa to tolerate diversity

the region, rather than in Latin, and modern sacred music and art have once again assumed an important place in Catholic liturgy.

The Church in Latin America and Asia

Other important developments were taking place in the Americas. In 1968, Latin American bishops made poverty and social justice the primary aim of their pastoral work. Inspired by the writings of Brazilian philosopher Paulo Freire (1921–1997), the bishops pledged to help the poor secure equal access to housing, food, education, and medical care. Eventually, this inspired a movement

Our Lord wants me to be a free nun covered with the poverty of the cross.

MOTHER TERESA

called liberation theology; the term was coined by the Peruvian priest Gustavo Gutiérrez (b. 1928) in his book *Teología de la liberación* (*A Theology of Liberation,* 1971).

The movement soon ran afoul of more conservative elements in the Catholic Church. Priests espousing liberation theology were condemned for being overly sympathetic to Marxist ideology—an accusation that was not far off the mark. Many priests had moved from pastoral work into political activism, particularly in autocratic countries such as El Salvador.

A social revolution of quite a different kind was quietly being forged in India by a humble nun of Albanian origin, who would gain worldwide renown as Mother Teresa (1910–1997). Born in Skopje (in today's Macedonia) as Agnes Bojaxhiu, she joined the Sisters of Loreto as a missionary at age 18 and, upon taking her vows in India, chose the name of Sister Teresa. In 1946, the young nun experienced a "call with a call," as she termed it, to leave the convent and live among the poor of Calcutta. After receiving basic medical training, she plunged into the slums and eventually established the Missionaries of Charity. By 1997, the order had grown to more than 4,000 sisters running charity centers, orphanages, and AIDS hospices

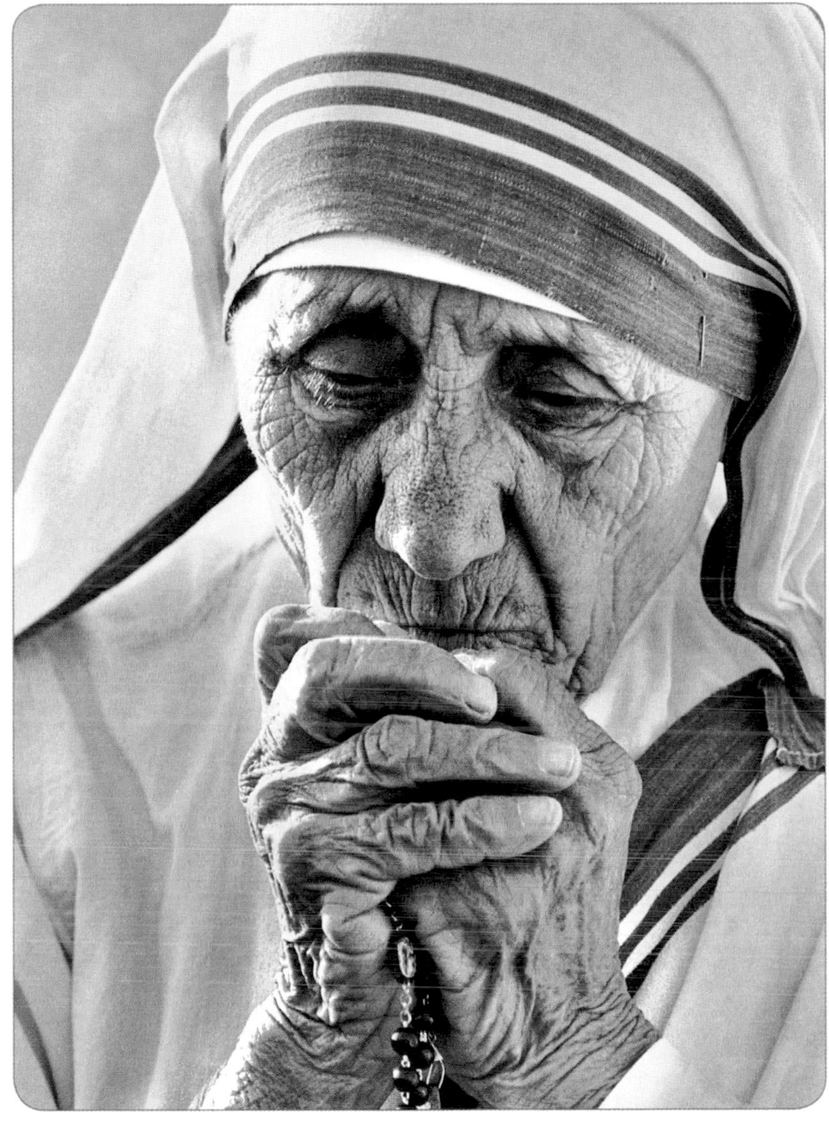

No 20th-century figure so exemplifies the idea of Christian compassion as Mother Teresa, who devoted her career to helping the poor in Calcutta and around the world.

OPPOSITE: *The* SAGRADA FAMÍLIA *was consecrated by Pope Benedict XVI in 2010, and is expected to be fully completed by 2026.*

2001 — Al Qaeda terrorists use airliners to destroy the World Trade Center in New York

2001 — U.S. and Allied forces invade Afghanistan to oust the Taliban and destroy al Qaeda

2003 — U.S. forces invade Iraq to oust the government of Saddam Hussein

2004 — Four Southern Baptist ministers are killed in the aftermath of the invasion of Iraq

around the world, caring for not only the poor and homeless but also victims of floods, epidemics, and political upheaval.

Christianity in Eastern Europe

Upon his election in 1978, few could have foreseen the impact Pope John Paul II (r. 1978–2005) would have on world events. The first non-Italian pope since the Dutch Adrian VI (r. 1522–1523), John Paul firmly aligned himself with liberalization movements in Eastern Europe. During a visit to his native Poland in 1979, where the Catholic Church served as the principal opposition to Communist rule, he elicited a huge turnout—by some estimates, a third of the nation's population. The pope threw his support behind a local union leader named Lech Walesa. One year later, Walesa negotiated the Gdansk Agreement, which became the first step toward a free and democratic Poland and the fall of the Soviet bloc. Though conservative in outlook, the pope actively abetted the Christian opposition in other Soviet bloc countries, and made major strides in improving relations with the Eastern Orthodox and Anglican Churches, as well as Judaism and Islam.

In Russia, the Russian Orthodox Church only began its long program of restoration after the disintegration of the Soviet Union in 1991. One year later, the vast Cathedral of Our Lady of Kazan in St. Petersburg, which had been cynically converted into a Marxist "Museum of the History of Religion and Atheism," was once again opened for church services.

In East Germany, a Communist nation under Soviet control, the Lutheran Church had largely flourished underground. It was instrumental in the fall of the Berlin Wall in 1989 and the subsequent liberation of Eastern Europe. Today, however, the Lutheran Church in the former DDR suffers from the same decline in attendance that churches experience elsewhere in Europe. Materialism, fostered by modern consumer culture, is often cited as the principal cause of the decline, but political factors and the painful memory of the two World Wars are undoubtedly factors as well. ■

The massive Cathedral of Our Lady of Kazan in St. Petersburg was used by the Soviet regime as the Museum of the History of Religion and Atheism. Now it is once again used for Russian Orthodox liturgy.

HISTORY AND POLITICS

The Civil Rights Movement

The civil rights movement of the 1960s coincided with a growing emphasis on social justice in religious movements throughout the world. Equal rights were traditionally an important issue for several American denominations, including the Episcopal and Methodist Churches, but the civil rights movement became closely associated with a Baptist minister named Martin Luther King, Jr. (1929–1968). The son of a minister, King studied at Crozer Theological Seminary and received his doctoral degree from Boston University in 1955. At the age of 25, he became pastor of the Dexter Avenue Baptist Church in Montgomery, Alabama. In his sermons he often emphasized the need for social compassion and love, inspired by Jesus' Sermon on the Mount and the writings of Mahatma Gandhi. In 1959, he traveled to India with the financial aid of a group of Quakers. As he noted in a radio address, the experience deepened his conviction that "the method of nonviolent resistance is the most potent weapon available to oppressed people in their struggle for justice and human dignity." He joined the Montgomery bus boycott, organized in response to the arrest of Rosa Parks, an African-American woman who refused to give up her seat to a white person. In 1957, King helped form the Southern Christian Leadership Conference, which became a major force in civil rights activism. He gained national prominence with his "I Have a Dream" speech during the 1963 March on Washington. In 1964, the same year Congress enacted the Civil Rights Act, prohibiting discrimination based on race, color, religion, sex, or national origin, King received the Nobel Peace Prize. Tragically, he was assassinated in 1968.

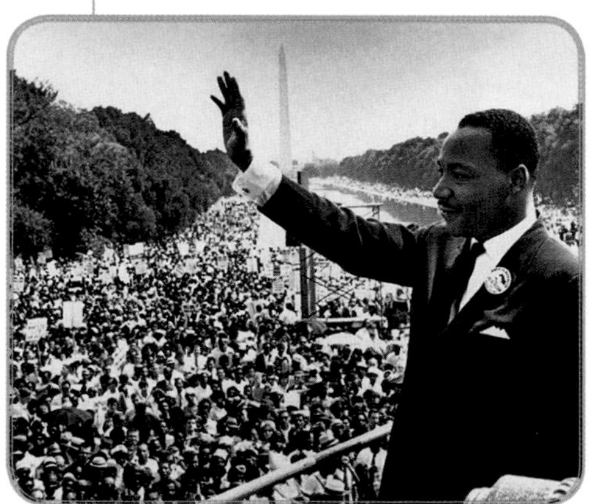

The Reverend Martin Luther King, Jr., waves at participants in the 1963 civil rights march from the Lincoln Memorial.

2007 — **The first Bible in Kriol, an Australian indigenous language, is completed**

2012 — **Severe fighting during the Syrian civil war destroys large parts of Muslim and Christian Aleppo**

2013 — **Pope Benedict XVI resigns, the first pope to do so in nearly 600 years**

2013 — **Pope Francis I is elected pontiff and vows to dedicate his papacy to fighting poverty**

МУЗЕЙ ИСТОРИИ РЕЛИГИИ И АТЕИЗМА

Epilogue

CHRISTIANITY IN THE 21ST CENTURY

How can it be that it's not news when an elderly homeless person dies of exposure, but it is news when the stock market loses two points?

POPE FRANCIS I

As the second decade of the 21st century unfolds, Christianity once again faces an era of profound change. The world is being transformed in almost every field of human endeavor. Words, pictures, and sounds can now boomerang across the globe in seconds, rousing or inflaming thousands. Human beings have been given the means to instantly connect with people anywhere on the planet, but the impact of this incredible power has yet to unfold.

Perhaps the greatest challenges facing Christianity in this era of globalization are the urgent social questions of our modern world. How can Christian ideals of selfless love and compassion be reconciled with a modern consumer culture that celebrates individual satisfaction? How can women achieve equality with men at all levels of society, including worship? How relevant are teachings on contraception, when the world population is expected to reach 10 billion in the next 30 years, and one-fourth of the globe suffers from hunger? Can Scripture guide us in the protection of scarce resources such as clean air, potable water, and sustainable energy?

One thing is clear: The growth centers of Christian life are no longer found in its traditional base, the continent of Europe, but in the territories of its former colonial possessions. Today, a majority (55 percent) of the world's Anglicans live in sub-Saharan Africa.

OPPOSITE: *Sunday morning services at the New Life Church of Colorado Springs, a leading Evangelical mega-church with up to 14,000 members that uses a range of modern media technologies*

Let the King
Of Glory enter in
Title: Prepare The Way Author: Jared Anderson CCLI# 397437 Copyright: 2004
Vertical Worship Songs

In Nigeria, there are now more than twice as many Protestants as in Germany, the birthplace of the Protestant Reformation. And whereas Catholicism in Europe has only grown one percent since the fall of the Soviet bloc in 1989, it is up 5 percent in North America, 6 percent in South America, 12 percent in Asia, and an impressive 22 percent in Africa.

Modern Protestantism

According to Pew Research, Protestants account for roughly half (51.3 percent) of the adult population and nearly two out of three (65 percent) Christians in the United States. American Protestantism now encompasses more than a dozen major denominational families, including Baptists, Methodists, Lutherans, and Episcopalians—all with unique beliefs, practices, and histories between them.

A key example is the Episcopal Church of the United States, which grew independent of the Church of England almost from the beginning. By 1966, Church membership was at an all-time high, reaching 3.5 million. At that time, the civil rights movement and the turmoil of the Vietnam War oriented the Church toward a more liberal course. In 1976, its General Convention approved the ordination of women priests. Three years later, the Church adopted a fully revised version of the Anglican Book of Common Prayer, modernizing the text but forging deep divisions in its community.

The Church consecrated its first female bishop, Barbara Harris, in 1989, and in 2006

The Soweto Gospel Choir, composed of singers drawn from different churches around Soweto, South Africa, is a vivid example of the vibrancy of the Christian faith on the African continent.

Katharine Jefferts Schori became the first woman presiding bishop of the Episcopal Church. Currently, there are nearly 4,000 female priests and bishops in the Church. Women represent more than 40 percent of all ordinations to the priesthood.

Similarly, in 1979, the Church adopted a resolution that banned a candidate's sexual preference as a factor in the consideration for ordination or office. In 2003, Gene Robinson became the first openly gay priest to be ordained as bishop. In 2012, the Church authorized "a provisional rite of blessing for same-gender relationships."

These and other controversial topics have led to schisms within the Episcopal Church as well as tensions within the international Anglican Communion, particularly with the more conservative Anglican Church in Africa. However, the autonomy of all national churches is a key feature of the Anglican Communion.

Social issues are roiling many other Protestant communities, including the Methodist Church. According to the World Council of Churches, membership in the Methodist Church now exceeds 10 million members worldwide, with more than 54,000 pastors presiding over about 42,000 congregations. In the United States, they form the second largest group of American Protestants, making up about 12 percent of the total U.S. Protestant population. While the United Methodist Church welcomes all ethnic and social groups, including the gay community, it holds that marriage should be between a man and woman. Similarly, women may be ordained as members of the clergy, but not if they are openly practicing a nonheterosexual lifestyle.

Of all Protestant denominations, the modern Baptist community is perhaps the most diverse. In the United States, it includes groups such as the Southern Baptist Convention, the American Baptist Churches USA, and the National Baptist Convention. Around 40 percent of all Baptists are part of the evangelical tradition, while some 60 percent consider themselves part of the historically African-American Protestant tradition.

The Baptist movement has generally hewn to a conservative stance on social issues. The Southern Baptist Convention, for example, does not welcome women as pastors. In 2006, the American Baptist Churches USA was split over the question of whether gay or lesbian members should be admitted.

By contrast, the Presbyterian Church (USA) voted in 2014 to redefine marriage as a union "of two people," allowing its ministers to perform same-sex marriages where they are legal. Similar resolutions have been adopted by the Quakers and the United Church of Christ.

Almost all Protestant denominations have suffered some erosion of membership in the United States. For example, 8.3 percent of people who were raised Baptist no longer worship regularly. Since its heyday in the 1960s, membership in the Episcopal Church is now down to 1.9 million. And while the Presbyterian Church numbered 3.1 million members in the 1980s, membership dropped to 1.8 million in 2012.

This erosion is compensated to some degree by growing numbers in other parts of the world. For example, while Lutheranism has not seen any growth in North America, Europe, or Latin America, its communities in Asia and Africa continue to expand. And with 80 million members in 160 churches, Anglicans form the third largest Christian communion in the world, after the Roman Catholic Church and the Eastern Orthodox Church.

Modern Catholicism

According to a recent Pew Research report, Catholicism in the United States has grown due to the rapid increase of the Latino community, which today makes up around 18 percent of the total U.S. population. By 2050, that number is expected to grow to 30 percent. A recent *Time* study showed, however, that even

CHRISTIANITY TODAY

❶ **Los Angeles, United States** *Postmodernist Cathedral of Our Lady of the Angels was dedicated in 2002.*

❷ **Brasília, Brazil** *Designed by Oscar Niemeyer, the soaring glass cathedral was finished in 1970.*

❸ **Abuja, Nigeria** *Africa's largest Christian population is in this country, home of this Christian Ecumenical Center.*

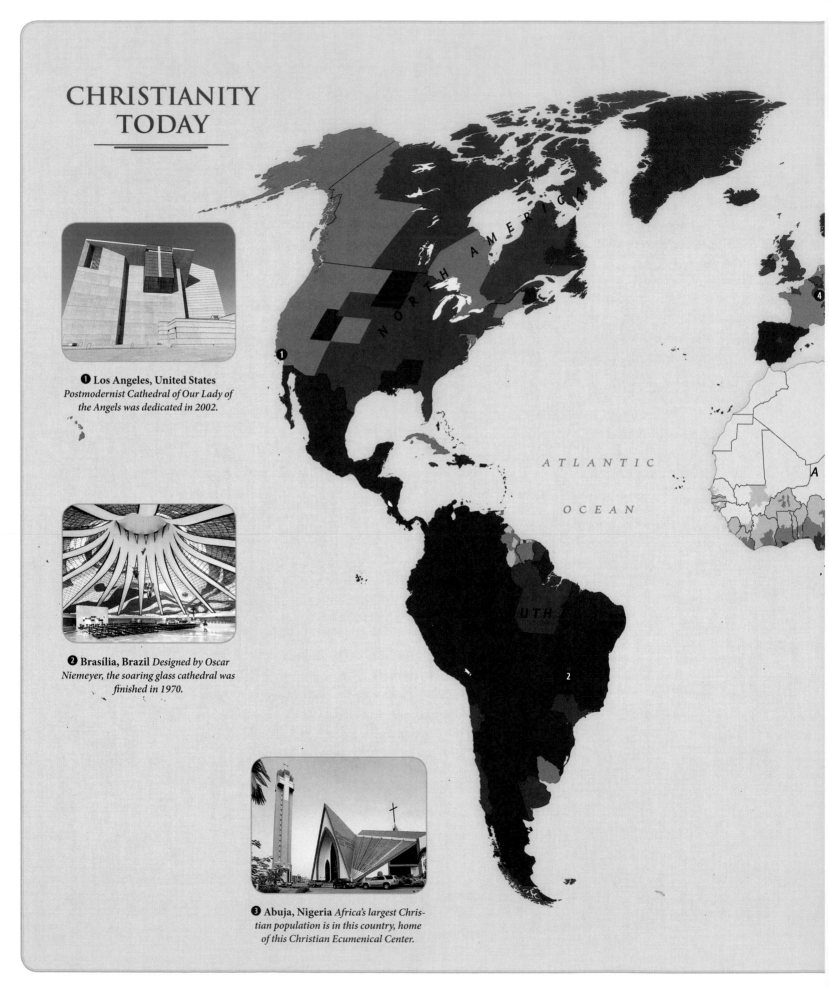

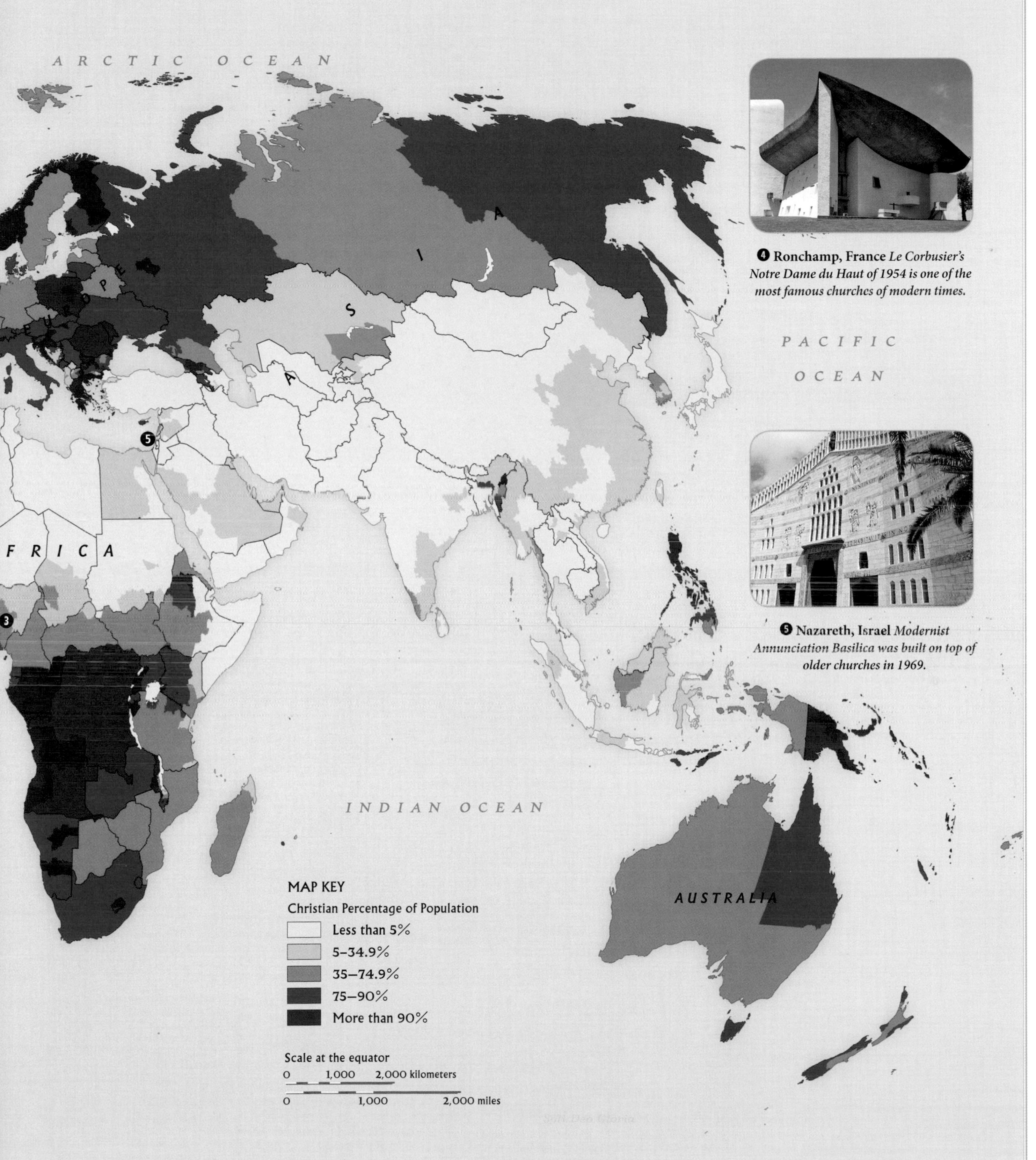

❹ **Ronchamp, France** *Le Corbusier's Notre Dame du Haut of 1954 is one of the most famous churches of modern times.*

❺ **Nazareth, Israel** *Modernist Annunciation Basilica was built on top of older churches in 1969.*

though Latinos added between 25 and 30 million Catholics to the American population, the overall percentage of Catholics in the U.S. remained constant at 25 percent. The corollary is that without the growth of the Latino community, Catholicism in the United States might have suffered a considerable loss.

Many Catholics in the West report a sense that Rome is out of touch with the modern world, particularly with regard to topics such as birth control, celibacy, and the ordination of women priests. Others feel that instead of being preoccupied with human sexuality, the Church should focus more on issues that lie at the core of the Gospels, such as poverty, social injustice, and the unequal distribution of wealth. The abuse crisis—with hundreds of Catholic priests around the world accused of molesting minors under their care—has further shaken the Catholic Church. Several Vatican observers believe that the global abuse scandal was a major factor in Pope Benedict XVI's decision in 2013 to resign—the first pope to do so in nearly 600 years.

There is no question, however, that Benedict's successor, Pope Francis I, has injected a new sense of vigor and purpose in the Catholic Church. Deliberately assuming a humble lifestyle in imitation of his great model, Francis of Assisi, the new pope refused to move into the lavish papal apartments just vacated by his predecessor. Ironically, it is this humble demeanor that has magnified the pontiff's celebrity, even though he has not made any fundamental changes in Church doctrine. That may change when the Synod of Bishops plans to convene for an extraordinary session in the near future. In the meantime, the pope has resolutely focused Rome's primary mission on the plight of the poor.

Evangelicalism

One of the most vibrant movements in Christianity today is undoubtedly Evangelicalism. As we saw before, the evangelical movement is not constrained to a single church or denomination, but is manifest across multiple Protestant groups around the world. Central to the evangelical experience is the sense of individual conversion, of being "born again" in the full grace of God's salvation. But even within this definition, several different movements are at work. One is fundamentalism, which rejects all historical criticism of Scripture and believes the Bible to be "inerrant." Another is Pentecostalism, first sparked by the Azusa Street Revival in Los Angeles. Its adherents believe in the active presence of the Holy Spirit as manifested in prophecy, in speaking in tongues, and in divine healing. What these evangelical movements have in common is a willingness to break with established tradition so as to find a more authentic experience of being a Christian.

Many others, however, wonder whether the Bible is still relevant in an age of stupendous scientific and technological advancement. And yet, if there is anything that the history of Christianity has shown us, it is that time and again, inspired thinkers such as Thomas Aquinas and Erasmus were able to reconcile Christian ideals with the changing priorities of their age. "Scientists have to acknowledge that science does not have all the answers," the renowned physicist Ian Barbour once wrote, "and theologians have to recognize the changing historical contexts of theological reflection."

Throughout its 2,000-year history, Christianity has shown a remarkable resilience in adapting to the needs and pressures of the time. And so, the question of what it means to be a follower of Christ continues to be a relevant and urgent one in the 21st century. ■

OPPOSITE: *With his humble lifestyle, telegenic personality, and a fierce commitment to alleviating poverty, Pope Francis I has injected a new sense of purpose into the Roman Catholic Church.*

FURTHER READING

Christianity: General History

Armstrong, Karen. *A History of God.* New York: Ballantine Books, 1993.
Collins, Michael, and Matthew Price. *The Story of Christianity.* New York: DK Publishing, 1999.
González, Justo L. *The Story of Christianity,* Vols. 1, 2, and 3. New York: HarperCollins, 2010.
Hart, David Bentley. *The Story of Christianity.* New York: Metro Books, 2007.
Hillerbrand, Hans J. *A New History of Christianity.* Nashville: Abingdon Press, 2012.
MacCulloch, Diarmaid. *Christianity: The First Three Thousand Years.* New York: Penguin, 2009.
Mullin, Robert Bruce. *A Short World History of Christianity.* Louisville, Ky.: Westminster John Knox Press, 2008.

The Life of Jesus

Borg, Marcus J. *Jesus: Uncovering the Life, Teachings, and Relevance of a Religious Revolutionary.* San Francisco: HarperSanFrancisco, 2006.
Charlesworth, James H. (ed.). *Jesus' Jewishness: Exploring the Place of Jesus in Early Judaism.* New York: Crossroad, 1991.
Chilton, Bruce. *Rabbi Jesus.* New York: Doubleday, 2000.
Crossan, John Dominic. *Jesus: A Revolutionary Biography.* New York: HarperCollins, 1994.
Crossan, John Dominic, and Jonathan L. Reed. *Excavating Jesus: Beneath the Stones, Behind the Texts.* New York: HarperCollins, 2001.
Ehrman, Bart. *Jesus: Apocalyptic Prophet of the New Millennium.* New York: Oxford University Press, 1999.
Evans, Craig. *Jesus and His World: The Archaeological Evidence.* Louisville, Ky.: Westminster John Knox Press, 2012.
Fredriksen, Paula. *Jesus of Nazareth, King of the Jews.* New York: Alfred A. Knopf, 1999.
Horsley, Richard A. *Jesus and Empire: The Kingdom of God and the New World Disorder.* Minneapolis: Fortress Press, 2003.
Levine, Amy-Jill (ed.). *Historical Jesus in Context.* Princeton, N.J.: Princeton University Press, 2006.
McCane, Byron R. *Roll Back the Stone: Death and Burial in the World of Jesus.* Harrisburg, Pa: Trinity Press International, 2003.
Meier, John P. *A Marginal Jew: Rethinking the Historical Jesus,* Vols. 1, 2, and 3. New York: Doubleday, 1994.
Porter, J. R. *Jesus Christ: The Jesus of History, the Christ of Faith.* New York: Barnes and Noble, 1999.
Reed, Jonathan L. *The HarperCollins Visual Guide to the New Testament.* New York: HarperCollins, 2007.
Sanders, E. P. *Jesus and Judaism.* Philadelphia: Fortress, 1985.
Senior, Donald. *Jesus: A Gospel Portrait.* Mahwah, N.J.: Paulist Press, 1992.
Stemberger, Günter. *Jewish Contemporaries of Jesus: Pharisees, Sadducees, Essenes.* Minneapolis: Fortress, 1995.

Early Christianity

Ehrman, Bart D. *Lost Christianities: The Battles for Scripture and the Faiths We Never Knew.* Oxford, UK: Oxford University Press, 2003.
Elsner, Jas. *Imperial Rome and Christian Triumph.* New York: Oxford University Press, 1998.
Grant, Robert M. *Augustus to Constantine: The Emergence of Christianity in the Roman World.* New York: Harper & Row, 1970.
Humphrey, Hugh M. *From Q to "Secret" Mark: A Composition History of the Earliest Narrative Theology.* London: T & T Clark, 2006.
Jeffers, James S. *The Greco-Roman World of the New Testament Era: Exploring the Background of Early Christianity.* Downers Grove, Ill.: InterVarsity Press, 1999.
Kee, Howard Clark. *The Beginnings of Christianity: An Introduction to the New Testament.* London: T & T Clark, 2005.
Mack, Burton L. *The Lost Gospel: The Book of Q and Christian Origins.* San Francisco: HarperSanFrancisco, 1993.
Neusner, Jacob. *Judaism When Christianity Began: A Survey of Belief and Practice.* Louisville, Ky.: Westminster John Knox Press, 2002.
Pagels, Elaine. *Beyond Belief: The Secret Gospel of Thomas.* New York: Random House, 2003.
Pagels, Elaine. *The Gnostic Gospels.* New York: Random House, 1979.
Porter, Stanley (ed.). *Paul and His Theology.* Pauline Studies, Vol. 3. Leiden, Netherlands: Brill, 2006.

Christianity in the Middle Ages

Bredero, Adriaan H. *Christendom and Christianity in the Middle Ages.* Grand Rapids, Mich.: Eerdmans Publishing, 1994.
Grant, Edward. *God and Reason in the Middle Ages.* Cambridge, UK: Cambridge University Press, 2001.
Hannam, James, *The Genesis of Science: How the Christian Middle Ages Launched the Scientific Revolution.* Washington, D.C.: Regnery Publishing, 2014.
Jenkins, Philip. *The Lost History of Christianity.* New York: HarperCollins, 2008.
Le Beau, Bryan, and Menachem Mor (eds.). *Pilgrims and Travelers to the Holy Land.* Omaha: Creighton University Press, 1996.
Logan, Donald. *A History of the Church in the Middle Ages.* Oxford, UK: Taylor & Francis, 2012.
Wright, Thomas. *Early Travels in Palestine.* New York: Ktav Publishing, 1968.

Christianity in the Modern Era

Bays, Daniel H. *A New History of Christianity in China.* Oxford, UK: John Wiley & Sons, 2012.
Bebbington, David W. *Evangelicalism in Modern Britain: A History from the 1730s to the 1980s.* London: Routledge, 1993.
Benz, Wolfgang. *A Concise History of the Third Reich.* Oakland: University of California Press, 2006.
Bergen, Doris L. *Twisted Cross: The German Christian Movement in the Third Reich.* Chapel Hill: University of North Carolina Press, 1996.
Blumhofer, Edith L. *Restoring the Faith: The Assemblies of God, Pentecostalism, and American Culture.* Urbana and Chicago: University of Illinois Press, 1993.
Hockenos, Matthew D. *A Church Divided: German Protestants Confront the Nazi Past.* Bloomington: Indiana University Press, 2004.
Marsden, George M. *Fundamentalism and American Culture.* Oxford, UK: Oxford University Press, 2006.
McGoldrick, James E., Richard C. Reed, and Thomas H. Spence. *Presbyterian and Reformed Churches: A Global History.* Grand Rapids, Mich.: Reformation Heritage Books, 2012.
Noll, Mark A. *The Rise of Evangelicalism: The Age of Edwards, Whitefield and the Wesleys.* Downers Grove, Ill.: InterVarsity Press, 2003.
Pew Research Center, Pew Forum on Religion & Public Life. *U.S. Religious Landscape Survey: Religious Affiliation: Diverse and Dynamic.* 2008.
Robert, Dana. *Christian Mission: How Christianity Became a World Religion.* Hoboken, N.J.: Wiley-Blackwell, 2009.
Roozen, David A., and James R. Nieman. *Church, Identity, and Change: Theology and Denominational Structures in Unsettled Times.* Grand Rapids, Mich.: Eerdmans Publishing Company, 2005.
Stein, Leo. *Hitler Came for Niemöller: The Nazi War Against Religion.* Gretna, La.: Pelican Publishing Company, 2003.
Webber, Christopher L. *Welcome to the Episcopal Church: An Introduction to Its History, Faith, and Worship.* Harrisburg, Pa.: Morehouse Publishing, 1999.
Woods, Thomas. *How the Catholic Church Built Western Civilization.* Washington, D.C.: Regnery Publishing, 2005.

ABOUT THE AUTHOR

Dr. Jean-Pierre Isbouts is a humanities scholar and graduate professor in the doctoral programs at Fielding Graduate University in Santa Barbara, California. Dr. Isbouts has published widely on the origins of Judaism, Christianity, and Islam, including the best sellers *The Biblical World,* published by the National Geographic Society in 2007, and *In the Footsteps of Jesus,* published by the National Geographic Society in 2012. His other books include *Young Jesus: Restoring the "Lost Years" of a Social Activist and Religious Dissident* (Sterling, 2008); *From Moses to Muhammad: The Shared Origins of Judaism, Christianity and Islam* (Pantheon Press, 2010); and *Who's Who in the Bible,* published by the National Geographic Society in 2013. An award-winning filmmaker, Dr. Isbouts has also produced a number of programs, including *Charlton Heston's Voyage Through the Bible* (GoodTimes, 1998), *The Quest for Peace* (Hallmark, 2003), and *Young Jesus* (PBS, 2008). His website is www.jpisbouts.org.

BOARD OF ADVISERS

Bart D. Ehrman is the James A. Gray Distinguished Professor of Religious Studies at the University of North Carolina at Chapel Hill. He is the author or editor of 29 books on the New Testament and early Christianity, 4 of which have been on the *New York Times* Best Sellers list. His books have been translated into 27 languages.

Steven Feldman works with early-career scholars in helping them transform dissertations into publishable academic books. Previously, he served as web editor and director of educational programs for the Biblical Archaeology Society and managing editor of both *Biblical Archaeology Review* and *Bible Review,* published by the Society.

Robert Bruce Mullin is the SPRL Professor of History and World Mission at the General Theological Seminary of the Episcopal Church in New York. He is the author of seven books, including *A Short World History of Christianity,* which will go into a second revised edition in late 2014.

ACKNOWLEDGMENTS

The Story of Christianity is the fulfillment of a lifelong dream. Both as an archaeologist and a historian, I have long been astonished by the persistence of Christianity's imprint on human history. This book is an attempt to document Christian civilization in all of its varied forms—my only wish is that somehow, we could add sacred music to the mix. Perhaps a future electronic edition?

Once again, I must thank Lisa Thomas, senior editor at National Geographic's Book Division, for collaborating on the concept for this book, and for her strong and unerring support throughout. In the same breath I must express my deep gratitude to my wonderful editor, Barbara Payne, on this, our third book, together. Many thanks also to the superb team at National Geographic, including Cinda Rose for her beautiful and sensitive layouts, Matt Propert for his excellent photo research, Carl Mehler for his wonderful maps, and Greg Villepique for his copyedit.

Special thanks are due to the panel of distinguished scholars who reviewed the manuscript, specifically Bart D. Ehrman, James A. Gray Distinguished Professor of Religious Studies at the University of North Carolina at Chapel Hill; Robert Bruce Mullin, SPRL Professor of History and World Mission at the General Theological Seminary of the Episcopal Church in New York; and my dear friend Steven Feldman, previously the director of educational programs for the Biblical Archaeology Society and managing editor of *Biblical Archaeology Review* and *Bible Review.*

In addition, I have profited from the research of many other scholars, notably the recent published work of David Bebbington, Michael Collins, Justo González, David Bentley Hart, Hans Hillerbrand, Diarmaid MacCulloch, Jacob Neusner, Elaine Pagels, and Matthew Price. I also wish to thank my pastor, Monsignor Lloyd Torgerson of St. Monica's Church in Santa Monica, California, for his spiritual guidance. Needless to say, any errors in the narrative are mine alone.

I must especially thank my doctoral students at Fielding Graduate University who assisted me in my research, particularly with regard to modern movements in Protestant confessions, including Adam Baldowski, Colleen Cleveland, Ericka Goerling, Ann Ritter, Lisa Swain, and Larry Taylor. I also owe a debt of gratitude to those who read the manuscript and offered many helpful comments, including Marian Galanis, Bianca Martino, and Nick Isbouts.

Thanks are due to my agent, Peter Miller, and his staff at Global Lion Intellectual Property Management. And finally, I must express my deepest gratitude to my wonderful wife, Cathie, who continues to be my muse and my indefatigable companion during our many journeys through the Middle East.

Jean-Pierre Isbouts

ILLUSTRATIONS CREDITS

All photographs by Pantheon Studios, Inc., unless otherwise noted:

Front Cover, curaphotography/123RF;
Back Cover (LE), Holy Family With St. John (Doni Tondo), 1504–1505 (oil on panel) (see also 156576), Buonarroti, Michelangelo (1475–1564)/Galleria degli Uffizi, Florence, Italy/The Bridgeman Art Library; (CTR), © Thierry Seni/Hemis/Corbis; (RT), Alfredo Dagli Orti/The Art Archive at Art Resource, NY; Author photo, Fielding Graduate University

2-3, Kenneth Garrett/National Geographic Creative; 4, Matt Propert/National Geographic Creative; 6, Grant V. Faint/Getty Images; 7, Frank Chmura/Getty Images; 13, St. Michael (tempera on panel), Byzantine, (14th century)/Byzantine Museum, Athens, Greece/The Bridgeman Art Library; 16, Gary Cralle/The Image Bank/Getty Images; 18 (LO), Michael Melford/National Geographic Creative; 20, Leen Ritmeyer/Ritmeyer Archaeological Design; 24, Samuel H. Kress Collection/Photograph © Board of Trustees, National Gallery of Art, Washington; 25, Sites & Photos/Art Resource, NY; 26-27, The Eucharist (fresco), Paleo-Christian, (second century)/Catacombs of Priscilla, Rome, Italy/The Bridgeman Art Library; 30, The Pharisees Question Jesus, illustration for *The Life of Christ*, ca 1886–1896 (gouache on paperboard), Tissot, James Jacques Joseph (1836–1902)/Brooklyn Museum of Art, New York, U.S.A./The Bridgeman Art Library; 32, Jesus Cures the Woman Who Bleeds, Scenes From the Life of Christ (mosaic), Byzantine School, (sixth century)/Sant'Apollinare Nuovo, Ravenna, Italy/Giraudon/The Bridgeman Art Library; 33, Jesus Walks on Water and Saves Peter, eighth panel of the North Doors of the Baptistery of San Giovanni, 1403–1424 (bronze), Ghiberti, Lorenzo (1378–1455)/Baptistery, Florence, Italy/The Bridgeman Art Library; 36 (UP), Wikimedia Commons; 36 (LO), Alfredo Dagli Orti/The Art Archive at Art Resource, NY; 38, The Entry of Christ Into Jerusalem, from a series of scenes of the New Testament (fresco), Barna da Siena (fl. 1350–1355)/Collegiata, San Gimignano, Italy/The Bridgeman Art Library; 39 (LE), Duby Tal/Albatross/Alamy; 39 (RT), Jim Richardson/National Geographic Creative; 40 (LE), Pantheon Studios, Inc./Courtesy of the Classical Numismatic Group, Inc.; 40 (RT), Cinda Rose; 41, "The Taking of Christ" (oil on canvas), Caravaggio, Michelangelo (1571–1610) (follower of)/Private Collection/© Lawrence Steigrad Fine Arts, New York/The Bridgeman Art Library; 43, Wikimedia Commons; 44, Ossuary of the High Priest Joseph Caiaphas, North Talpiot, Jerusalem (stone)/The Israel Museum, Jerusalem, Israel/Israel Antiquities Authority/The Bridgeman Art Library; 45, Deposition from the Cross, detail of the Virgin Mary, 1436 (tempera & gold on panel), Angelico, Fra (Guido di Pietro) (ca 1387–1455)/Museo di San Marco dell'Angelico, Florence, Italy/The Bridgeman Art Library; 46-47, "The Disciples Peter and John Running to the Sepulchre on the Morning of the Resurrection," ca 1898 (oil on canvas), Burnand, Eugene (1850–1921)/Musée d'Orsay, Paris, France/Giraudon/The Bridgeman Art Library; 48, Michael Melford/National Geographic Creative; 50 (UPRT), James L. Stanfield/National Geographic Creative; 52 (LE), Moses and the Tablets of the Law, La Hire or La Hyre, Laurent de (1606–1656)/Private Collection/Photo © Bonhams, London, UK/The Bridgeman Art Library; 52 (RT), © National Gallery, London/Art Resource, NY; 53, Gianni Dagli Orti/The Art Archive at Art Resource, NY; 54, The Martyrdom of St. Stephen by Juan de Juanes/Photo © Tarker/The Bridgeman Art Library; 55 (LE), Wikipedia; 55 (RT), Gianni Dagli Orti/The Art Archive at Art Resource, NY; 56 (LE), © Dea/Veneranda Biblioteca Ambrosiana/Art Resource, NY; 56 (RT), St. Peter and St. Paul (fresco), Italian School, (15th century)/Chiesa di Santa Maria Maddalena, Gressan, Italy/Seat Archive/Alinari Archives/The Bridgeman Art Library; 57, Marco Lachmann-Anke/Alamy; 60, Scala/White Images/Art Resource, NY; 62-63, "The Fire of Rome, 18 July 64 AD" (oil on canvas), Robert, Hubert (1733–1808)/Musée des Beaux-Arts André Malraux, Le Havre, France/Giraudon/The Bridgeman Art Library; 65, © The British Library Board; 66, Cameraphoto Arte, Venice/Art Resource, NY; 67 (UP), "Triumph of Faith—Christian Martyrs in the Time of Nero, 65 AD" (oil on canvas), Thirion, Eugène Romain (1839–1910)/Private Collection/Photo © Bonhams, London, UK/The Bridgeman Art Library; 71, Wikimedia Commons; 72, Aureus (obverse) of Diocletian (A.D. 284–A.D. 305) cuirassed, wearing a laurel wreath (gold) Inscription: IMP C C VAL DIOCLETIANVS P F AVG, Roman, (fourth century A.D.)/

Private Collection/The Bridgeman Art Library; 73, Heritage Images/Getty Images; 75, The Milvian Bridge, Rome (photo)/De Agostini Picture Library/The Bridgeman Art Library; 76, The Dream of Constantine, from The Legend of the True Cross cycle, completed 1464 (fresco), Francesca, Piero della, (ca 1415–1492)/San Francesco, Arezzo, Italy/The Bridgeman Art Library; 77, The Battle of the Milvian Bridge, in the Room of Constantine, Raphael Rooms, ca 1520–1524 (fresco), Romano, Giulio (1492–1546)/Vatican Museums and Galleries, Vatican City/© Stefano Baldini/The Bridgeman Art Library; 78-79, Moses With the Tablets of the Law, sixth century (fresco)/Monastery of St. Catherine, Mount Sinai, Egypt/Index/The Bridgeman Art Library; 80, Viacheslav Lopatin/Shutterstock; 81, The inner compartment of the reliquary of the True Cross, one of the richest and most elaborate ensembles of Byzantine enamels to have survived the sack of Constantinople in 1204/Werner Forman Archive/The Bridgeman Art Library; 83, Christopher Chan/Getty Images; 84 (LE), St. Helena with the True Cross, 1525 (oil on panel), Cranach, Lucas, the Elder (1472–1553)/Cincinnati Art Museum, OH, U.S.A./Bequest of Mary M. Emery/The Bridgeman Art Library; 84 (RT), Scala/Art Resource, NY; 85, Algol2/Bigstock.com; 88, Matt Moyer/National Geographic Creative; 90 (LE), Tino Soriano/National Geographic Creative; 90 (RT), Keenpress/National Geographic Creative; 92 (UP), Pilgrim flask (clay), Byzantine/Ashmolean Museum, University of Oxford, UK/The Bridgeman Art Library; 92 (LO), Liturgical vessel (pyxis) with Christ and the Virgin, seventh century A.D. (silver with gilding), Byzantine School (seventh century)/Museum of Fine Arts, Boston, Massachusetts, U.S.A./The Bridgeman Art Library; 93, George Steinmetz/National Geographic Creative; 94 (LE), Interior view of the Oratory, ca A.D. 430 (photo), Paleo-Christian, (fifth century)/Oratorio di Galla Placidia, Ravenna, Italy/Giraudon/The Bridgeman Art Library; 94 (RT), Triumph of St. Thomas Aquinas, detail of figure below the throne, from the Spanish Chapel, ca 1365 (fresco), Andrea di Bonaiuto (Andrea da Firenze) (fl. 1343–1377)/Santa Maria Novella, Florence, Italy/The Bridgeman Art Library, 96, www.BibleLandPictures.com/Alamy; 97 (LE), Werner Forman/Art Resource, NY; 97 (UPRT), Medallion (obverse) of Constantius II (317–361), minted at Antioch, Syria (gold), Roman, (fourth century A.D.)/Hermitage, St. Petersburg, Russia/The Bridgeman Art Library; 97 (CTR RT), Necklace, ca sixth–seventh century (gold & emeralds), Byzantine/Private Collection/Photo © Christie's Images/The Bridgeman Art Library; 97 (LORT), Brooch in the form of a Greek cross (gold & precious stones), Byzantine School, (sixth century)/Museo Nazionale del Bargello, Florence, Italy/Giraudon/The Bridgeman Art Library; 100, Three Cappadocian Fathers: St. Gregory of Nazianzus, St. John Chrysostom, and St. Basil the Great, by an anonymous artist from the Byzantine school, 17th century/De Agostini Picture Library/Gianni Dagli Orti/The Bridgeman Art Library; 101, George Steinmetz/National Geographic Creative; 103, Unloading grain from the ship *Isis Giminiana*, from Ostia, second–third century (fresco), Roman/Vatican Museums and Galleries, Vatican City/Ancient Art and Architecture Collection Ltd/The Bridgeman Art Library; 104, Rabouan Jean-Baptiste/Hemis/Corbis; 105, Emperor Justinian I and his retinue of officials, guards, and clergy, ca A.D. 547 (mosaic), Byzantine School (sixth century)/San Vitale, Ravenna, Italy/Giraudon/The Bridgeman Art Library; 106-107, bpk, Berlin/Alte Pinakothek, Bayerische Staatsgemäldesammlungen, Munich/Art Resource, NY; 108, Riccardo Spila/SOPA/Corbis; 109, Cameo depicting a triumphant emperor trampling barbarians, from Kusadek (sardonyx), Roman (fourth century A.D.)/Narodni Muzej, Belgrade, Serbia/Giraudon/The Bridgeman Art Library; 110 (UPLE), Buckle, 500s (bronze & garnets), Ostrogothic (sixth century)/Cleveland Museum of Art, OH, U.S.A./Purchase from the J. H. Wade Fund/The Bridgeman Art Library; 110 (CTRLE), Two eagle-shaped fibulae, discovered in a cemetery in the province of Badajoz, Spain, sixth century (gilt bronze, garnets, & rock crystal), Visigothic (sixth century A.D.)/© Walters Art Museum, Baltimore, U.S.A./The Bridgeman Art Library; 110 (LOLE), The shrine of St. Patrick's Bell, from Armagh, Ireland, ca 1100 (bronze with silver & gold filigree, crystal, & glass) (see also 344383), Celtic, (12th century)/National Museum of Ireland, Dublin, Ireland/The Bridgeman Art Library; 110 (RT), Forum Ancient Coins; 111, Wikimedia Commons; 112, St. John Chrysostom, by Emmanuel Lambardos, Icon, 17th century/De Agostini Picture Library/Gianni Dagli Orti/The Bridgeman Art Library; 113, St. Benedict (fresco), Starnina, Gherardo (ca 1354–1409/13)/Santa Maria del Carmine, Florence, Italy/Photo © Boltin Picture Library/The Bridgeman Art Library; 116 (LE), St. Augustine and St. Monica (oil on canvas), Assereto, Giovacchino (1600–49)/Minneapolis Institute of Arts, MN, U.S.A./The John R. Van Derlip Fund/The Bridgeman Art Library; 116 (RT), Chris Hill/National Geographic Creative; 117, Album/Art Resource, NY; 118, Attila (ca 406–453) and His Army Marching on Paris (fresco), Delaunay, Jules Elie (1828–1891)/Pantheon, Paris, France/Giraudon/The Bridgeman Art Library; 119 (LE), The Baptism of Clovis I (465–511) in 496 B.C., from the right transept (mural), Blanc, Joseph Paul (1846–1904)/Pantheon, Paris, France/Giraudon/The Bridgeman Art Library; 120, Ms 241 f.1 Historiated initial "A" depicting St. Gregory, from the Antiphonal for the consecration of the Abbey Church of Vauclair, 1257 (vellum), French School, (13th century)/Bibliothèque Municipale, Laon, France/Giraudon/The Bridgeman Art Library; 121, Bettmann/Corbis; 122, The Walters Art Museum, Baltimore, U.S.A.; 123, Mohammed (ca 570–ca 632) and the Archangel Gabriel, from the "Siyer-i Nebi" (gouache on paper), Turkish School, (16th century)/Topkapi Palace Museum, Istanbul, Turkey/Bildarchiv Steffens/The Bridgeman Art Library; 124 (LE), Annie Griffiths/National Geographic Creative; 124 (RT), bpk, Berlin/Uffizi, Florence, Italy/Alfredo Dagli Orti/Art Resource, NY; 126-127, The Victory of Heraclius and the Execution of Chosroes, A.D. 628, from the True Cross Cycle, completed 1464 (fresco), Francesca, Piero della, (ca 1415–1492)/San Francesco, Arezzo, Italy/The Bridgeman Art Library; 128 (UPLE), Album/Art Resource, NY; 128 (CTRLE), Votive cross in gold and precious stones. Goldsmith's art, Visigothic civilization/De Agostini Picture Library/Gianni Dagli Orti/The Bridgeman Art Library; 128 (LOLE), sixth-century shield umbo depicting battle scenes, from Nocera Umbra, Italy, Longobard civilization/De Agostini Picture Library/A. de Gregorio/The Bridgeman Art Library; 128 (RT), Gianni Dagli Orti/The Art Archive at Art Resource, NY; 129, Marco Lachmann-Anke/Alamy; 130, Erich Lessing/Art Resource, NY; 131, Charlemagne (747–814) crowned King of Italy in 774 (oil on canvas), French School (19th century)/Château de Versailles, France/Index/The Bridgeman Art Library; 132-133, CCI/The Art Archive at Art Resource, NY; 134, Walter Bibikow/age fotostock, 135, The Vladimir Madonna and Child, Russian icon, Moscow School (tempera on panel), Rublev, Andrei (ca 1370–1430) (circle of)/State Russian Museum, St. Petersburg, Russia/The Bridgeman Art Library; 136, Dmytro Lepetiuk/National Geographic Your Shot; 137 (LE), Tsar Symeon I of Bulgaria defeating the Byzantine army, led by Procopius Crenites and Curtacius the Armenian in Macedonia, Fol. 108r from Chapter VII of the *Madrid Skylitzes* (vellum), Byzantine School (12th century)/Biblioteca Nacional, Madrid, Spain/Photo © Tarker/The Bridgeman Art Library; 137 (RT), Erich Lessing/Art Resource, NY; 138-139, Gerd Ludwig/National Geographic Creative; 140, ushi/Shutterstock; 141, Gerd Ludwig/National Geographic Creative; 142, Maltings Partnership, Derby, England; 143 (LE), St. Sergius of Radonezh (ca 1314–1392) overseeing the construction of a cell and church at Zagorsk (vellum), Rublev, Andrei (ca 1370–1430)/Private Collection/RIA Novosti/The Bridgeman Art Library; 143 (UPRT), © The Trustees of the British Museum. All right reserved; 143 (CTRRT), © The Trustees of the British Museum. All right reserved; 143 (LORT), © The Trustees of the British Museum. All right reserved; 144, The Holy Trinity, 1420s (tempera on panel) (for copy see 40956), Rublev, Andrei (ca 1370–1430)/Tretyakov Gallery, Moscow, Russia/The Bridgeman Art Library; 145, Gavin Hellier/JAI/Corbis; 146 (LE), Gianni Dagli Orti/The Art Archive at Art Resource, NY; 146 (RT), Gerd Ludwig/National Geographic Creative; 147 (UP), Ms Pers.113 f.49 Genghis Khan (ca 1162–1227) in battle, from a book by Rashid-al-Din (1247–1318) (gouache), Persian School (14th century)/Bibliothèque Nationale, Paris, France/The Bridgeman Art Library; 147 (LO), Nestorian subject, perhaps Palm Sunday, mural painting from Cristano Qoco Temple, Xinjiang, China, Chinese Civilization, Tang dynasty, late ninth century/De Agostini Picture Library/The Bridgeman Art Library; 148, Hulagu Khan on the throne, miniature from a Persian manuscript, manuscript 1113 folio 113, Persia/De Agostini Picture Library/The Bridgeman Art Library; 149, Chuck Wightman; 150 (LE), Pantheon Studios, Inc./Courtesy Matrakçı Nasuh; 150 (CTR), Pantheon Studios, Inc./Courtesy Nvvchar; 150 (RT), Eddie Gerald/Alamy; 151 (LE), AarStudio/iStockphoto; 151 (RT), Babak Tafreshi/National Geographic Creative; 152 (LO), © The Trustees of the British Museum/Art Resource, NY; 153, Tino Soriano/National Geographic Creative; 154 (CTRLE), Dish depicting King Yazdgerd III (632–651) hunting (gilded silver), Sasanian School (seventh century)/Bibliothèque Nationale, Paris, France/Flammarion/The Bridgeman Art Library; 154 (LOLE), © The Trustees of the British Museum/Art Resource, NY; 154 (RT), Khosrow II stealing the True Cross, scene from the Stories of the Cross, 1410, by Cenni di Francesco di ser Cenni (active 1369–1415), fresco, Chapel of the Holy Cross, Church of St. Francis, Volterra, Tuscany, Italy, 15th century/De Agostini Picture Library/A. de Gregorio/The Bridgeman Art Library; 156, Battle of Siffin/British Library, London, UK/© British Library Board. All Rights Reserved/The Bridgeman Art Library; 157, "The Crusaders' entry Into Constantinople, 12th April 1204," 1840 (oil on canvas), Delacroix, Ferdinand Victor Eugène (1798–1863)/Louvre, Paris, France/Giraudon/The Bridgeman Art Library; 158, Icon (tempera on panel), Rublev, Andrei (ca 1370–1430)/Tretyakov Gallery, Moscow, Russia/The Bridgeman Art Library; 159, DEA L. ROMANO/age fotostock; 160-161, "The Battle of Montgisard, 25th November 1177," ca 1842 (oil on canvas), Larivière, Charles-Philippe (1798–1876)/Château de Versailles, France/Giraudon/The Bridgeman Art Library; 162, Werner Forman/Art Resource, NY; 164 (UPLE), Gianni Dagli Orti/The Art Archive at Art Resource, NY; 164 (RT), Ms Fr. 6465 fol.202 Entry of Louis VII (ca 1120–1180) King of France and Conrad III (1093–1152) King of Germany into Constantinople during the Crusades, 1147–1149 (vellum) (see also 38992), Fouquet, Jean (ca 1420–1480)/Bibliothèque Nationale, Paris, France/The Bridgeman Art Library; 166-167, "Godfrey of Bouillon (ca 1060–1100) Depositing the Trophies of Askalon in the Holy Sepulchre Church, August 1099," 1839 (oil on canvas), Granet, François-Marius (1775–1849)/Château de Versailles, France/Giraudon/The Bridgeman Art Library; 168, Wikimedia Commons; 169, Ruel Nicholas; 170, Richard I the Lionheart (1157–1199) King of England, 1841 (oil on canvas), Blondel, Merry Joseph (1781–1853)/Château de Versailles, France/Giraudon/The Bridgeman Art Library; 171 (LE), Gianni Dagli Orti/The Art Archive at Art Resource, NY; 171 (CTR RT), Gianni Dagli Orti/The Art Archive at Art Resource, NY; 172, The History of Pope Alexander III (1105–1181): The Entrance of the Pope and Emperor Frederick Barbarossa (ca 1123–1190) into Rome, 1407 (fresco) (detail), Spinello or Spinelli, Aretino Luca (ca 1340–1410)/Palazzo Pubblico, Siena, Italy/The Bridgeman Art Library; 173, Wikimedia Commons; 176, Tino Soriano/National Geographic Creative; 179, Alfredo Dagli Orti/The Art Archive at Art Resource, NY; 180 (LO), Maltings Partnership, Derby, England; 181, Pope and Emperor, ca 1408–1410 (fresco), Spinello or Spinelli, Aretino Luca (ca 1340–1410)/Palazzo Pubblico, Siena, Italy/The Bridgeman Art Library; 182 (LE), Anonymous Artist, Francisco de Zurbarán, Samuel H. Kress Collection, Photograph © Board of Trustees, National Gallery of Art, Washington, DC; 184, Ivan Vdovin/Getty Images; 185 (RT), Gianluca Colla/National Geographic Creative; 187, JoseIgnacioSoto/iStockphoto; 188-189, Scala/Art Resource, NY; 190, Uliana Bazar; 192, "The Taking of Constantinople" (oil on canvas), Palma Il Giovane (Jacopo Negretti) (1548–1628)/Palazzo Ducale, Venice, Italy/The Bridgeman Art Library; 193 (RT), David Lees/Corbis; 194 (UPLE), Chalice, French, ca 1325 (silver gilt)/Victoria & Albert Museum, London, UK/The Bridgeman Art Library; 194 (LOLE), Ciborium, from Limoges (copper plated with gold and enamel), French School, (14th century)/Germanisches Nationalmuseum, Nuremberg (Nürnberg), Germany/The Bridgeman Art Library; 194 (RT), St. Dominic resurrects Napoleone Orsini, 1461–1462, by Benozzo Gozzoli (1420–ca 1497), tempera on wood, 25 x 35 cm/De Agostini Picture Library/M. Carrieri/The Bridgeman Art Library; 195, Innocent III (1160–1216) approving the Franciscan Rule, from the cycle of paintings "Stories of St. Francis of Assisi," by Taddeo Gaddi (active 1362–1385)/De Agostini Picture Library/G. Nimatallah/The Bridgeman Art Library; 196, The Expulsion of the Devils

From Arezzo, 1297-99 (fresco), Giotto di Bondone (ca 1266–1337)/San Francesco, Upper Church, Assisi, Italy/Giraudon/The Bridgeman Art Library; 197, St. Francis of Assisi preaching to the birds (oil on panel), Giotto di Bondone (ca 1266–1337)/Louvre, Paris, France/The Bridgeman Art Library; 198 (LE), Aristotle and Plato: detail from the School of Athens in the Stanza della Segnatura, 1510–1511 (fresco) (detail of 472), Raphael (Raffaello Sanzio of Urbino) (1483–1520)/Vatican Museums and Galleries, Vatican City/The Bridgeman Art Library; 198 (RT), Scala/Art Resource, NY; 199, The Adoration of the Mystic Lamb, from the Ghent Altarpiece, lower half of central panel, 1432 (oil on panel) (see 472324), Eyck, Hubert (ca 1370–1426) & Jan van (1390–1441)/St. Bavo Cathedral, Ghent, Belgium/© Lukas—Art in Flanders VZW/The Bridgeman Art Library; 200 (UP), V&A Images, London/Art Resource, NY; 200 (LO), Host Box, from Limoges, ca 1300 (copper, gilt, & enamel), French School, (14th century)/Germanisches Nationalmuseum, Nuremberg (Nürnberg), Germany/The Bridgeman Art Library; 201, Adoration of the Magi, or Strozzi Altarpiece by Fabriano da Gentile (1370–ca 1427), tempera on wood, 203 x 282 cm, detail, 1423/De Agostini Picture Library/G. Nimatallah/The Bridgeman Art Library; 203 (LE), Relief depicting the Adoration of the Magi from the pulpit, 1260 (stone), Pisano, Nicola (ca 1220–1284)/Baptistery, Pisa, Italy/The Bridgeman Art Library; 203 (RT), Raul Touzon/National Geographic Creative; 204 (LO), Maltings Partnership, Derby, England; 205, Perig/Shutterstock; 207, 102-0002738 T.I.I. Cantiga 34, illustration from *Cantigas de Santa Maria,* made under the direction of Alfonso X ("The Wise") King of Castille and Leon (1221–1284) (vellum) (see also 68647), Spanish School, (13th century)/Biblioteca Monasterio del Escorial, Madrid, Spain/Index/The Bridgeman Art Library; 209, Radius Images/Getty Images; 210-211, "The Decameron," 1916 (oil on canvas), Waterhouse, John William (1849–1917)/© Lady Lever Art Gallery, National Museums Liverpool/The Bridgeman Art Library; 213, St. Sebastian Interceding for the Plague Stricken, 1497–1499 (oil on panel), Lieferinxe, Josse (Master of St. Sebastian) (fl. 1493–1508)/© Walters Art Museum, Baltimore, U.S.A./The Bridgeman Art Library; 214-215, Annunciation (tempera on panel), Botticelli, Sandro (1444/5–1510)/Galleria degli Uffizi, Florence, Italy/The Bridgeman Art Library; 216, Exterior view of the Dome, ca 1420–1436 (photo), Brunelleschi, Filippo (1377–1446)/Duomo, Florence, Italy/Ken Welsh/The Bridgeman Art Library; 218 (UP), Plan, Section, and Elevation of Florence Cathedral, from *Fragments d'Architecture du Moyen Age et de la Renaissance,* engraved by Jules Adolphe Chauvet (b. 1828) (litho), Duquesne, Eugene (fl. 19th century) (after)/Private Collection/The Stapleton Collection/The Bridgeman Art Library; 218 (LO), The Tribute Money, from the Brancacci Chapel, ca 1426 (fresco), Masaccio, Tommaso (1401–1428)/Santa Maria del Carmine, Florence, Italy/The Bridgeman Art Library; 219, Nave and choir of Santo Spirito, Florence, designed by Filippo Brunelleschi (1377–1446) (photo)/Santo Spirito, Florence, Italy/The Bridgeman Art Library; 220 (UPLE), David, ca 1440 (bronze), Donatello, (ca 1386–1466)/Museo Nazionale del Bargello, Florence, Italy/The Bridgeman Art Library; 220 (LOLE), Seated Madonna, painted terra-cotta sculpture by Lorenzo Ghiberti (1370/78–1455)/Museum of Fine Arts, Budapest, Hungary/The Bridgeman Art; 220 (UPRT), The Sacrifice of Isaac, bronze competition relief for the Baptistery Doors, Florence, 1401 (bronze), Brunelleschi, Filippo (1377–1446)/Museo Nazionale del Bargello, Florence, Italy/The Bridgeman Art Library; 220 (LORT), The Sacrifice of Isaac, bronze competition relief for the Baptistery Doors, Florence, 1401 (bronze), Ghiberti, Lorenzo (1378–1455)/Museo Nazionale del Bargello, Florence, Italy/The Bridgeman Art Library; 222, Matt Propert/National Geographic Creative; 223, Portrait of Sultan Mehmet II (1432–1481) (w/c on paper), Turkish School (15th century)/Topkapi Palace Museum, Istanbul, Turkey/Giraudon/The Bridgeman Art Library; 224, David, 1501–1504 (marble), Buonarroti, Michelangelo (1475–1564)/Galleria dell'Accademia, Florence, Italy/The Bridgeman Art Library; 225, Erich Lessing/Art Resource, NY; 226 (UP), Holy Family With St. John (Doni Tondo), 1504–1505 (oil on panel) (see also 156576), Buonarroti, Michelangelo (1475–1564)/Galleria degli Uffizi, Florence, Italy/The Bridgeman Art Library; 226 (CTR), Silver and silver-gilt ciborium, transitional style, late Gothic and early Renaissance, ca 1530; crucifix, 17th century/Thomas Lumley Antiques, London, UK/The Bridgeman Art Library; 226 (LO), Rosary belonging to Mary Queen of Scots, 1587 (gold & pearl) (see also 279121), English School (16th century)/His Grace the Duke of Norfolk, Arundel Castle/The Bridgeman Art Library; 227, Design Pics Inc./National Geographic Creative; 228 (UP), Alinari/Art Resource, NY; 228 (LO), Scala/Art Resource, NY; 229, Maltings Partnership, Derby, England; 232, Pantheon Studios, Inc./Courtesy AlterVista; 233, Martin Luther, 1529 (oil on canvas), Cranach, Lucas, the Elder (1472–1553)/Schlossmuseum, Schloss Friedenstein, Gotha, Germany/Bildarchiv Foto Marburg/The Bridgeman Art Library; 234, "Luther Preaches Using His Bible Translation While Imprisoned at Wartburg," 1882 (oil on canvas), Vogel, Hugo (1855–1934)/Hamburger Kunsthalle, Hamburg, Germany/The Bridgeman Art Library; 235, Portrait of Savonarola (panel), Bartolommeo, Fra (Baccio della Porta) (1472–1517)/Museo di San Marco dell'Angelico, Florence, Italy/The Bridgeman Art Library; 236 (RT), © RMN-Grand Palais/Art Resource, NY; 240 (LE), Portrait of Jean Calvin, 1858 (oil on canvas), Scheffer, Ary (1795–1858)/Musée de la Vie Romantique, Paris, France/Roger-Viollet, Paris/Bridgeman Images; 240 (RT), Wikimedia Commons; 241, Portrait of Henry VIII (1491–1547) aged 49, 1540 (oil on panel), Holbein the Younger, Hans (1497/8–1543)/Palazzo Barberini, Rome, Italy/The Bridgeman Art Library; 242-243, "The First Landing of Christopher Columbus (1450–1506) in America," 1862 (oil on canvas), Puebla Tolin, Dioscoro Teofilo (1832–1901)/Ayuntamiento de Coruna, Spain/The Bridgeman Art Library; 244, Hubertus Kanus/Photo Researchers/Getty Images; 245, Astrolabe (metal), French School (17th century)/Musée National de la Renaissance, Ecouen, France/Giraudon/The Bridgeman Art Library; 246 (LE), Portrait presumed to be of Vasco da Gama (1469–1524) ca 1524, Portuguese School, (16th century)/National Museum of Ancient Art, Lisbon, Portugal/The Bridgeman Art Library; 246 (RT), F.41v A Caravel, detail from *Cosmographie Universelle,* 1555 (w/c on paper), Le Testu, Guillaume (ca 1509–1573)/Min. Defense—Service Historique de l'Armée de Terre, France/Giraudon/The Bridgeman Art Library; 247 (LE), Scala/White Images/Art Resource, NY; 247 (RT), Add 5415A f.15v Prester John, detail from a portolan chart of the Indian Ocean, ca 1558 (detail of 67657), Homem, Diego (16th century)/British Library, London, UK/© British Library Board. All Rights Reserved/The Bridgeman Art Library; 248 (UPLE), Sextant (brass, wood, & glass), Adams, George (1750–1795)/Private Collection/The Bridgeman Art Library; 248 (LOLE), Armillary sphere made on the Ptolemaic system, Rome, 1648 (brass) (see also 259557), Heroldt, Adam (fl. 1648)/Science Museum, London, UK/The Bridgeman Art Library; 248 (RT), George Steinmetz/National Geographic Creative; 249, Sistine Chapel: The Last Judgment, 1538–1541 (fresco) (pre-restoration), Buonarroti, Michelangelo (1475–1564)/Vatican Museums and Galleries, Vatican City/The Bridgeman Art Library; 252 (LE), Christopher Columbus (oil on panel), Piombo, Sebastiano del (S. Luciani) (ca 1485-1547)/Metropolitan Museum of Art, New York, U.S.A./Peter Newark Pictures/The Bridgeman Art Library; 253, Matt Propert/National Geographic Creative; 254, "Emperor Charles V (1500–1558) on Horseback," 1620 (oil on canvas), Dyck, Sir Anthony van (1599–1641)/Galleria degli Uffizi, Florence, Italy/The Bridgeman Art Library; 256, First Baptism of the Indians by the Dominicans (oil on canvas), Mexican School (18th century)/Museo Nacional de Historia, Castillo de Chapultepec, Mexico/Giraudon/The Bridgeman Art Library; 258, The Virgin Mary with Indian donors, 1752 (oil on wood panel), Bolivian School, (18th century)/Brooklyn Museum of Art, New York, U.S.A./Museum Expedition 1941, Frank L. Babbott Fund/The Bridgeman Art Library; 259, Opening session of Council of Trent in 1545 by Nicolo Dorigati (active 1692–1748), 1711, Italy, 16th century/De Agostini Picture Library/A. Dagli Orti/The Bridgeman Art Library; 260, St. Bartholomew's Day Massacre, ca 1572–1584 (oil on panel), Dubois, François (1529–1584)/Musée Cantonal des Beaux-Arts de Lausanne, Switzerland/De Agostini Picture Library/G. Dagli Orti/The Bridgeman Art Library; 261 (LE), Ecstasy of St. Teresa (marble), Bernini, Gian Lorenzo (1598–1680)/Santa Maria della Vittoria, Rome, Italy/The Bridgeman Art Library; 261 (RT), St. Ignatius Loyola (oil on canvas), Zurbaran, Francisco de (1598–1664)/Private Collection/The Bridgeman Art Library; 262, "The Slave Hunter" (oil on canvas), Debret, Jean-Baptiste (1768–1848)/Museu de Arte, São Paulo, Brazil/Giraudon/Bridgeman Images; 263 (UP), Cedric Weber/Shutterstock; 263, Maltings Partnership, Derby, England; 264 (LE), "Wallenstein: A Scene of the Thirty Years' War" (oil on canvas), Crofts, Ernest (1847–1911)/Leeds Museums and Galleries (Leeds Art Gallery) UK/The Bridgeman Art Library; 264 (RT), James I, half-length portrait, Critz, John de, the Elder (ca 1552–1642)/Roy Miles Fine Paintings/The Bridgeman Art Library; 265, Astronomical sextant of Tycho Brahe (1546–1601) from an atlas by Joan Blaeu (1596–1673) Amsterdam, 1665 (colored engraving), Dutch School (17th century)/Private Collection/Archives Charmet/The Bridgeman Art Library; 268 (UPLE), Vase, East India Company (ceramic), French School (19th century)/Musée des Arts Décoratifs, Bordeaux, France/Giraudon/The Bridgeman Art Library; 268 (LOLE), Woman's dress, stamped with East India Company mark, ca 1785–1790 (cotton), English School (18th century)/© Cheltenham Art Gallery & Museums, Gloucestershire, UK/The Bridgeman Art Library; 268 (RT), East India Company Shipyard and Warehouse in Amsterdam, 1725 (engraving), Mulder, Joseph (1658–ca 1728)/Bibliothèque des Arts Décoratifs, Paris, France/The Bridgeman Art Library; 269, "The Landing of the Pilgrim Fathers," 1620 (oil on canvas), Boughton, George Henry (1833–1905)/Sheffield Galleries and Museums Trust, UK/Photo © Museums Sheffield/The Bridgeman Art Library; 270-271, "The Orrery," ca 1766 (oil on canvas), Wright of Derby, Joseph (1734–1797)/Derby Museum and Art Gallery, UK/The Bridgeman Art Library; 273, Obverse of medal commemorating the brilliant comet of November 1618. This comet prompted many pamphlets, including Galileo Galilei's (1564–1642) polemical masterpiece *"Il Saggiatore"* ("The Assayer"). (Rome, 1623)/Universal History Archive/UIG/The Bridgeman Art Library; 274, Galileo explaining moon topography to skeptics (color litho), Huens, Jean-Léon (1921–1982)/National Geographic Creative/The Bridgeman Art Library; 275, Christina of Sweden (1626–1689) and her Court: detail of the Queen and René Descartes (1596–1650) at the Table (oil on canvas) (see 28038), Dumesnil, Pierre-Louis the Younger (1698–1781)/Château de Versailles, France/The Bridgeman Art Library; 276, Louis XIV (1638–1715) and his entourage visiting Les Invalides, 26th August 1706 (oil on canvas), Martin, Pierre-Denis (1663–1742)/Musée de la Ville de Paris, Musée Carnavalet, Paris, France/The Bridgeman Art Library; 277 (LE), Benedict Spinoza (1632–1677) (oil on canvas), Dutch School, (17th century)/Herzog August Bibliothek, Wolfenbüttel, Germany/The Bridgeman Art Library; 277 (UPRT), Telescope belonging to Sir Isaac Newton (1642–1727) 1671, English School/Royal Society, London, UK/The Bridgeman Art Library; 277 (CTRRT), Solar Microscope, Berlin 1751 (brass, wood, & glass), Mitsdoerffer, J. G. (fl. 1751)/Deutsches Historisches Museum, Berlin, Germany/© DHM/The Bridgeman Art Library; 277 (LORT), Calculating machine invented by Blaise Pascal (1623–1662) in 1642 (wood & metal), French School (17th century)/CNAM, Conservatoire National des Arts et Métiers, Paris/Archives Charmet/The Bridgeman Art Library; 278 (LE), "Writing the Declaration of Independence in 1776" (oil on canvas), Ferris, Jean Leon Gerome (1863–1930)/Virginia Historical Society, Richmond, VA, U.S.A./The Bridgeman Art Library; 278 (RT), Portrait of John Locke (1632–1704) (see also 1419), Kneller, Sir Godfrey (1646–1723) (after)/Private Collection/Photo © Philip Mould Ltd, London/The Bridgeman Art Library; 281 (LE), "Voltaire (1694–1778) in His Study" (oil on canvas), French School, (18th century)/Musée de la Ville de Paris, Musée Carnavalet, Paris, France/Giraudon/The Bridgeman Art Library; 281 (RT), Jean-Jacques Rousseau (1712–1778) (oil on canvas), Ramsay, Allan (1713–1784)/Château de Coppet, Paris, France/Giraudon/The Bridgeman Art Library; 282-283, "Earthquake in Lisbon," painting by Joao Glama (1708–1792), 1755, Portugal, 18th century/De Agostini Picture Library/Gianni Dagli Orti/The Bridgeman Art Library; 284, Keren Su/Getty Images; 285, "The procession of King Louis XV (1710–1774) after his coronation, 26th October 1722," 1724 (oil on canvas), Martin, Pierre-Denis (1663–1742)/Château de Versailles, France/The Bridgeman Art Library; 286 (UPLE), The Crown of Louis XV, 1722 (gilded silver, replacement stones, & pearls), French School (18th century)/Louvre, Paris, France/Peter Willi/The Bridgeman Art Library; 286 (CTRLE), © RMN-Grand Palais/Art Resource,

NY; 286 (LOLE), bpk, Berlin/Grünes Gewölbe, Staatliche Kunstsammlungen, Dresden, Germany/Art Resource, NY; 286 (RT), Tsar Ivan IV Vasilyevich "the Terrible" (1530–1584) 1897 (oil on canvas) (detail of 89327), Vasnetsov, Victor Mikhailovich (1848–1926)/Tretyakov Gallery, Moscow, Russia/The Bridgeman Art Library; 287, Portrait of Catherine II (1729–1796) of Russia (oil on canvas), Roslin, Alexander (1718–1793) (after)/Museum of Art, Serpukhov, Russia/Giraudon/The Bridgeman Art Library; 288 (LE), Portrait bust of Catherine II (the Great) (1729–1796), 1770s (marble), Collot, Marie-Anne (1748–1821)/Hermitage, St. Petersburg, Russia/The Bridgeman Art Library; 288 (RT), L'Encyclopédie by Denis Diderot, Jean-Baptiste Le Rond d'Alembert, 1751–1757, Private Collection/De Agostini Picture Library/The Bridgeman Art Library; 289, Blaise Pascal (1623–1662)/Photo © Tarker/The Bridgeman Art Library; 291, Wikimedia Commons; 293 (UP), Scott S. Warren/National Geographic Creative; 293 (LO), Jean-Benoît Héron/Pantheon Studios, Inc.; 294, Burning of the Town of Cap-Français, Saint-Domingue (Haiti), 1795 (color engraving), French School, (18th century)/Private Collection/Archives Charmet/The Bridgeman Art Library; 295, "Voltaire Conversing With the Peasants in Ferney" (oil on panel), Huber, Jean (1721–1786) (attr. to)/Musée des Beaux-Arts, Nantes, France/Giraudon/The Bridgeman Art Library; 298, Steve Raymer/National Geographic Creative; 300 (UPLE), Mousetrap camera, ca 1835 (wood), English School (19th century)/NMPFT, Bradford, West Yorkshire/The Bridgeman Art Library; 300 (CTRLE), Bell telephone used by Queen Victoria at Osborne House, Isle of Wight, 1877–1878 (mixed media), English School (19th century)/Science Museum, London, UK/The Bridgeman Art Library; 300 (LOLE), T675 Charles Darwin's sextant, from his five-year voyage on H.M.S. *Beagle*, made by Newman, 1831–1836/© Royal Geographical Society, London, UK/The Bridgeman Art Library; 301, Nantyglo Ironworks, ca 1829 (w/c on paper), English School (19th century)/National Museum Wales/The Bridgeman Art Library; 302, Nathan Benn/Corbis; 303 (LE), Queen Victoria (1837–1901) 1842 (oil on canvas), Winterhalter, Franz Xaver (1805–1873)/Château de Versailles, France/Giraudon/The Bridgeman Art Library; 303 (RT), "Two Men Contemplating the Moon," ca 1819–1820 (oil on canvas), Friedrich, Caspar David (1774–1840)/Galerie Neue Meister, Dresden, Germany/© Staatliche Kunstsammlungen Dresden/The Bridgeman Art Library; 304 (LE), Portrait of Simón Bolívar (1783–1830), Venezuelan general, patriot, and revolutionary, by Rafael Salas (1824–1906), South America, 19th century/De Agostini Picture Library/M. Seemuller/The Bridgeman Art Library; 305, Battle of Waterloo, 18th June 1815, 1898 (color litho), Sullivan, William Holmes (1836–1908)/Private Collection/The Bridgeman Art Library; 307, "The Angel of Tobias," ca 1865 (oil on canvas), Doré, Gustave (1832–1883)/Musée Unterlinden, Colmar, France/The Bridgeman Art Library; 308, Frans Lanting/National Geographic Creative; 309 (RT), A signed photograph of Sigmund Freud, ca 1921 (sepia photo), Halberstadt, Max (1882–1940)/Private Collection/Photo © Christie's Images/The Bridgeman Art Library; 310, jan kranendonk/Shutterstock; 311, Maltings Partnership, Derby, England; 312-313, The Peabody Essex Museum; 315 (LE), "The Hour of Emancipation," 1863 (oil on canvas), Carlton, William Tolman (1816–1888)/Private Collection/Photo © Christie's Images/The Bridgeman Art Library; 315 (RT), "Penn's Treaty With the Indians," ca 1830–1840 (oil on canvas), Hicks, Edward (1780–1849)/Museum of Fine Arts, Houston, TX, U.S.A./Bayou Bend Collection/Gift of Alice C. Simkins in memory of Alice N. Hanszen/The Bridgeman Art Library; 318, "The Reception of the Mysorean Hostage Princes by Lieutenant General Lord Cornwallis (1738-1805)," ca 1793 (oil on canvas), Home, Robert (1752–1834)/National Army Museum, London/The Bridgeman Art Library; 319, Archbishop Augouard (1852–1921) leaving with another brother for an excursion, 1912, from *Monseigneur Augouard*, published in Paris in 1924 (b/w photo), French photographer (20th century)/Private Collection/Archives Charmet/The Bridgeman Art Library; 320, The White Fathers of Cardinal Lavigerie in Africa, cover of a schoolbook, engraved by L. Geisler, ca 1880–1890 (color litho), Daacher, C. (19th century)/Private Collection/Archives Charmet/The Bridgeman Art Library; 322-323, The Art Archive at Art Resource, NY; 324, Chris Hellier/Corbis; 325, Jewish Refugee, Vienna (oil on canvas), Jagger, David (1891–1958)/Nottingham City Museums and Galleries (Nottingham Castle)/The Bridgeman Art Library; 326, James P. Blair/National Geographic Creative; 328 (UPLE), bpk, Berlin/Nationalgalerie, Staatliche Museen/Art Resource, NY; 328 (LOLE), iladm/Shutterstock; 328 (RT), Emperor Franz Joseph I (1830–1916) and Empress Elizabeth (1837–1898) in Budapest, 8th July 1896 (color litho), Benczur, Gyula (or Julius de) (1844–1920)/Private Collection/Archives Charmet/The Bridgeman Art Library; 329, Open-air church service before battle, World War I (colored photo), English photographer, (20th century)/Private Collection/© Look and Learn/Elgar Collection/The Bridgeman Art Library; 330, HIP/Art Resource, NY; 331, Service in Notre Dame, giving thanks for victory after the Great International War, 1918 (oil on canvas), Mora, Francis Luis (1874–1940)/Private Collection/Photo © Christie's Images/The Bridgeman Art Library; 332 (LE), His Beatitude Ignatius Elias III and his followers, Jerusalem, Israel, 1927 (autochrome), Williams, Maynard Owen (1888–1963)/National Geographic Creative/The Bridgeman Art Library; 332 (RT), Three Women Grieving for a Lost One, central panel of the triptych "Remembering the Dead," ca 1918 (oil), Devambez, André (1867–1944)/Musée Antoine Lecuyer, Saint-Quentin, France/Giraudon/The Bridgeman Art Library; 334, "The Signing of Peace in the Hall of Mirrors, Versailles, 28th June 1919," 1919 (oil on canvas), Orpen, Sir William (1878–1931)/Imperial War Museum, London, UK/The Bridgeman Art Library; 335 (LE), God Speed the Plough and the Woman Who Drives It, First World War poster, American (color litho), English School (20th century)/Private Collection/Photo © Barbara Singer/The Bridgeman Art Library; 335 (RT), Oscar White/Corbis; 336, Destitute pea pickers in California. Mother of seven children. Age 32. Nipomo, California, 1936 (b/w photo), Lange, Dorothea (1895–1965)/Private Collection/Universal History Archive/UIG/The Bridgeman Art Library; 337, James L. Stanfield/National Geographic Creative; 338 (LE), bpk, Berlin/Rotraut Forberg/ Art Resource, NY; 338 (RT), One People, One Country, One Leader! ca 1940 (lithograph)/Private Collection/The Bridgeman Art Library; 339, Children in a Nazi extermination camp in Eastern Europe ca 1945/Universal History Archive/UIG/The Bridgeman Art Library; 341, Hulton-Deutsch Collection/Corbis; 342, Album/Art Resource, NY; 343, JP Laffont/Sygma/Corbis; 344 (RT), Maltings Partnership, Derby, England; 345, Bettmann/Corbis; 346, Hulton-Deutsch Collection/Corbis; 347, Dick Durrance II/National Geographic Creative; 349, Johann Rousselot/laif/Redux; 350, Brett Schewitz; 352 (UP), ZoonarJunie Pham/age fotostock; 352 (CTR), Atlantide Phototravel/Corbis; 352 (LO), Friedrich Stark/Alamy; 355, AP Photo/Gregorio Borgia.

INDEX

Boldface indicates illustrations.

D

E

F

G

K

L

M

N

THE STORY OF CHRISTIANITY

Jean-Pierre Isbouts

Published by the National Geographic Society

Gary E. Knell, *President and Chief Executive Officer*
John M. Fahey, *Chairman of the Board*
Declan Moore, *Executive Vice President; President, Publishing and Travel*
Melina Gerosa Bellows, *Executive Vice President; Publisher and Chief Creative Officer, Books, Kids, and Family*

Prepared by the Book Division

Hector Sierra, *Senior Vice President and General Manager*
Janet Goldstein, *Senior Vice President and Editorial Director*
Jonathan Halling, *Creative Director*
Marianne Koszorus, *Design Director*
Lisa Thomas, *Senior Editor*
R. Gary Colbert, *Production Director*
Jennifer A. Thornton, *Director of Managing Editorial*
Susan S. Blair, *Director of Photography*
Meredith C. Wilcox, *Director, Administration and Rights Clearance*

Staff for This Book

Barbara Payne, *Editor*
Sanáa Akkach, *Art Director*
Matthew Propert, *Illustrations Editor*
Cinda Rose, *Designer*
Carl Mehler, *Director of Maps*
Matthew W. Chwastyk, *Manager, Map Research and Production*
Michael McNey, Gregory Ugiansky, Mapping Specialists, and XNR Productions, *Map Research and Production*
Marshall Kiker, *Associate Managing Editor*
Judith Klein, *Production Editor*
Lisa A. Walker, *Production Manager*
Galen Young, *Rights Clearance Specialist*
Katie Olsen, Ruth Ann Thompson, *Production Design Assistants*

Production Services

Phillip L. Schlosser, *Senior Vice President*
Chris Brown, *Vice President, NG Book Manufacturing*
Nicole Elliott, *Director of Production*
George Bounelis, *Senior Production Manager*
Rachel Faulise, *Manager*
Robert L. Barr, *Manager*
Neal Edwards, *Imaging*

The National Geographic Society is one of the world's largest nonprofit scientific and educational organizations. Its mission is to inspire people to care about the planet. Founded in 1888, the Society is member supported and offers a community for members to get closer to explorers, connect with other members, and help make a difference. The Society reaches more than 450 million people worldwide each month through *National Geographic* and other magazines; National Geographic Channel; television documentaries; music; radio; films; books; DVDs; maps; exhibitions; live events; school publishing programs; interactive media; and merchandise. National Geographic has funded more than 10,000 scientific research, conservation, and exploration projects and supports an education program promoting geographic literacy. For more information, visit www.nationalgeographic.com.

For more information, please call 1-800-NGS LINE (647-5463) or write to the following address:

National Geographic Society
1145 17th Street N.W.
Washington, D.C. 20036-4688 U.S.A.

For information about special discounts for bulk purchases, please contact National Geographic Books Special Sales: ngspecsales@ngs.org

For rights or permissions inquiries, please contact National Geographic Books Subsidiary Rights: ngbookrights@ngs.org

Library of Congress Cataloging-in-Publication Data

Isbouts, Jean-Pierre.
The story of Christianity : a chronicle of Christian civilization from ancient Rome to today / Jean-Pierre Isbouts. -- 1st [edition].
pages cm
Includes bibliographical references and index.
ISBN 978-1-4262-1387-8 (hardcover : alk. paper) -- ISBN 978-1-4262-1447-9 (hardcover (deluxe) : alk. paper)
1. Church history. I. Title.
BR145.3.I83 2014
270--dc23
2014017247

Printed in the United States of America

14/RRDW-CML/1